INDO-PERSIAN TRAVELS IN THE AGE OF DISCOVERIES, 1400–1800

MUZAFFAR ALAM and SANJAY SUBRAHMANYAM

CAMBRIDGE
UNIVERSITY PRESS

CAMBRIDGE UNIVERSITY PRESS
Cambridge, New York, Melbourne, Madrid, Cape Town, Singapore,
São Paulo, Delhi, Dubai, Tokyo

Cambridge University Press
The Edinburgh Building, Cambridge CB2 8RU, UK

Published in the United States of America by Cambridge University Press, New York

www.cambridge.org
Information on this title: www.cambridge.org/9780521129558

First published 2007
This digitally printed version 2009

A catalogue record for this publication is available from the British Library

ISBN 978-0-521-78041-4 Hardback
ISBN 978-0-521-12955-8 Paperback

For John F. Richards

Contents

List of illustrations — *page* viii
List of maps — x
Preface — xi
A note on transliteration — xv
A note on calendars — xvi

1 Introduction: the travel-account from Beijing to the Bosphorus — 1
2 From Timur to the Bahmanis: fifteenth-century views — 45
3 Courtly encounters — 93
4 An ocean of wonders — 130
5 When Hell is other people — 175
6 A western mirror — 243
7 The long road to Rum — 296
8 On early modern travel — 332

Bibliography — 364
Index — 384

Illustrations

1 Babur crossing the Son river, *Bābur Nāma*, Persian text, late sixteenth century, National Museum, New Delhi, No. 50.336. *page* 22

2 Representation of the Ka'aba in Mecca with details of the holy sites surrounding it, *Rauẓa-i Khair ul-Bashar*, National Museum, New Delhi, No. 55.56/1. 39

3 Map (*ṣūrat*) of the country (*dayār*) of Sind and parts of Hind from Ibn Khurdadbih, *Ṣuwar al-aqālīm wa masālik-i mamālik*, ms copied in 831 H. (1427–8), National Museum, New Delhi, No. 56.96/4. 56

4 Scene from the *Ā'īna-yi Sikandarī*, *Khamsa* of Amir Khusrau of Delhi, ms copied on 18 Zi-Hijja 901 H (28 August 1496), National Museum, New Delhi, No. 52.81. 63

5 Single caparisoned elephant, *Fīl-nāma*, National Museum, New Delhi, No. 78218. 77

6 Pierpont Morgan Library, New York, M. 525, fos. 83v–84, *Livro de Lisuarte de Abreu*, combat between Portuguese and Ottoman fleets. Caption reads: "This was the first encounter that Dom Fernando had with the galleys at Cape Mocadam in the year 1555". 98

7 Darab in a boat on a Greek island, encounters Mehrasp, a Parsi adventurer, *Dārāb-nāma*, National Museum, New Delhi, No. L53.2/9. 110

8 Los Angeles County Museum of Art, M. 75.4.28 Emperor Jahangir triumphing over Poverty, *c.* 1622, attributed to Abu'l Hasan. 124

9 Death of a rich and greedy merchant, who had wanted to enslave Tamrusia, widowed queen of Amman, *Dārāb-nāma*, National Museum, New Delhi, No. L53.2/9. 141

10 Los Angeles County Museum of Art, M. 78.9.14, portrait of Mirza Rustam Safavi, *c.* 1640, attributed to Hashim. 206

11 Scene with monstrous creatures, *'Ajā'ib al-Makhlūqāt*, National Museum, New Delhi, No. 57.26/2. 213

12 Map (*ṣūrat*) of 'Iraq-i 'Arab, from Ibn Khurdadbih *Ṣuwar al-aqālīm wa masālik-i mamālik*, National Museum, New Delhi, No. 56.96/4. 218

13 Title page of the abridged English translation of the *Bayān-i Wāqiʿ* (1788). 253
14 The bazaar of Mina in Mecca, showing the three noted sites from where the *ḥājīs* throw stones at Satan, *Futūḥ al-ḥaramain* by Jami, National Museum, New Delhi, No. 61.89. 279
15 Tipu Sultan in combat, *Tūzak-i Āṣafiya*, No. 59.138, National Museum, New Delhi, folio 321. 315
16 Los Angeles County Museum of Art, M. 83.105.2, portrait of Ibrahim ʿAdil Shah II, *c.* 1675. 350
17 Portrait of Tavernier in "Oriental costume", engraving by Johann Hainzelmann, Paris (1679), based on a portrait by Largillière. 354

Maps

1	Nikitin's travels to India.	*page* 84
2	Seydi 'Ali Re'is's itinerary.	102
3	Major trade routes in Mughal India.	203
4	Map of Nadir Shah's campaigns.	257
5	The route of the envoys to Istanbul.	320

Preface

This book has been very long in the making, so long that at times we despaired of ever completing it. Its origins date back largely to a set of leisurely and pleasurable conversations between the authors in Dakshinapuram, on the campus of Jawaharlal Nehru University in New Delhi, in the early 1990s. We had met first in 1985 in Yogyakarta, and then renewed our acquaintance in Delhi in early 1989. Many cups of *chāi* and *vāi* were drunk in those days, as we became not merely collaborators but close friends. While discussing the possibilities of ploughing new furrows in the field of Mughal studies, the question of the Persian language travel-account came up. We embarked on our study of them soon after, partly encouraged by our friend (the late) Denys Lombard, who solicited a text from us that eventually appeared in a collection on Asian travel-accounts edited by his wife Claudine Salmon (entitled *Récits de voyage des Asiatiques*). Our initial interests were in travellers from Central Asia and Iran who came to India, and it was hence for obvious reasons that we began with an analysis of the text of Mahmud Wali Balkhi, that had been edited by Riazul Islam. However, we soon began to cast our net wider. After having read through the text of Mutribi Samarqandi, we turned our attention to writings having to do with "internal" travels in South Asia, such as those of Anand Ram "Mukhlis" and Abu'l Faiz "Faizi". However, a discussion of these latter accounts could not eventually be included in this book, and will appear in a companion volume concerned with travels within Mughal India.

The corpus continued to grow with the passage of years, and our joint work proceeded in fits and starts, mostly in Delhi, but also in other places such as Leiden, Paris and eventually Chicago, Oxford and Los Angeles. Several distractions came our way, in the form of individual as well as collective projects, that unfortunately took precedence over this one. Our own travels too became an obstacle to this book on travels. Others who were working at the same time on similar materials, notably Simon Digby, continued to publish their own essays drawing upon similar texts to ours. In at least one instance, that of Mutribi, a translation and commentary in English appeared, by Richard C. Foltz. We, for our part, continued to publish isolated essays, but hesitated to turn the whole into a monograph until we were encouraged to do so by the enthusiasm shown by a number of seminar audiences, both in India and elsewhere, to whom these materials were presented. The renewed interest shown in the European travel-account of the early modern period seemed to us to justify a whole book, rather than a set of scattered essays, on the world of the Indo-Persian travel text. Cambridge University Press accepted this project with alacrity, and has since shown much patience with us.

Many colleagues and friends have shown us great kindness along the way. Papers drawing on these materials have been presented in Bamberg, Cambridge, Chicago, Heidelberg, London, Los Angeles, New Delhi, Oxford, and many other places, whether in conferences or as lecture presentations. Amongst our friends and colleagues, Simon Digby, Suraiya Faroqhi, Bert Fragner, Robert McChesney and Christine Noelle-Karimi shared with us some of their extensive knowledge of these materials. Juan Cole was particularly helpful in regard to contacts between Iran and Mughal India, a subject that has long interested him. Kathryn Babayan pointed us in the direction of valuable texts and editions, time and again; to her, we are particularly grateful. Michael Fisher shared some of his thoughts as the project was nearing a close. Our colleagues in Ottoman studies, Cornell Fleischer and Cemal Kafadar, were of the greatest help in thinking through the conceptual difficulties posed by these texts. The late Jean Aubin and Denys Lombard were present to aid us in early stages of this project, and we fondly remember their help and advice. Jos Gommans and Dirk Kolff were helpful in arranging a stay for us in Leiden.

Regarding libraries and archives, some merit special mention. The National Museum in New Delhi – and in particular Dr Naseem Akhtar – generously allowed us to dip into its vast collections for purposes of illustrating this text. The staff of the Asiatic Society of Bengal, the British Library, the Bodleian Library in Oxford, the Government Oriental Manuscripts Library and Research Institute in Hyderabad, the Regenstein Library in Chicago, and other institutions were always of great help.

The generosity, humour and hospitality of Rizwana Khatun also made this book possible, since she has indulged our lengthy conversations on this and other subjects from the days in Dakshinapuram onwards. Innumerable others have heard one section of this book or another, and we can hardly begin to list the audiences and individuals who have helped us clarify a point or seek out an additional reference. Still, we must thank a loyal set of audiences in the Oriental Institute in Oxford, who sat through an extensive set of lectures on this subject in 2004; and amongst the best of listeners there, we thank John D. Gurney above all, but also Imre Bangha and Fariba Adelkhah. Caroline Ford gave generous advice and forceful encouragement as the project drew to a close, and more or less obliged us to clear our desks.

This is a book about travel-narratives, and it is also a book that carries an engagement with narrative production within it. Our declared intention from the outset was not to take apart our narratives into bite-sized chunks and rearrange them thematically or otherwise, in keeping with our own idiosyncratic tastes. Rather, we wished to follow our travellers and listen to them, and also take the manner in which they organised their materials seriously. Where we have taken obvious liberties is in terms of choosing which accounts to classify and analyse with others, that is to say in how we have gone about the division of chapters. Yet here too, we hope that our choices will not appear entirely devoid of reason or plausibility.

The book consists of eight slightly unequal chapters. After a survey of some other neighbouring travel literatures, from Beijing to the Bosphorus, we plunge in the first chapter directly into an unusual seventeenth-century account in verse of a female pilgrim to the *ḥajj*. Having given the reader a foretaste of things to come, Chapter 2 then looks to a few accounts from the fifteenth century, notably those of 'Abdur Razzaq Samarqandi, and the Russian traveller Afanasii Nikitin. These set the stage, as it were, for the core of the book which is concerned with the India of the Mughals and its external relations.

The three chapters that follow explore different aspects of the view of India as seen by visitors from Central Asia, the Ottoman domains and Iran. One of these looks to "courtly encounters", in the form of the sixteenth-century account of the Ottoman admiral Seydi 'Ali Re'is, comparing it to the texts of Mutribi Samarqandi from the 1620s, and the Iranian embassy to Thailand in the late seventeenth century. The next chapter focuses in large measure on the combination of travels and wonders, with a central emphasis on the voyage from the late 1620s of Mahmud Wali Balkhi. Chapter 5 then considers a series of disgruntled travellers, who made their way from Safavid Iran to Mughal India, and found that what they encountered was not to their taste. These travellers, for whom travel itself was a form of hell, thus represent one end of a spectrum, as opposed to others who are seemingly all-too-happy to encounter and absorb the "wonders" they see en route. Chapter 6 then reverses this view to a large extent by examining the account of a traveller from Mughal India, Khwaja 'Abdul Karim Shahristani, who found his way westwards, to Iran, the Hijaz and the Ottoman empire. Chapter 7 continues the westward exploration by looking at travellers from India to the Ottoman empire, and comparing their vision with those of the travellers examined earlier whose itineraries took them in the opposite direction. Finally, the concluding chapter seeks to return to a comparative perspective, by considering the difference between the body of texts surveyed and analysed in this work, and the far more common, as well as far more celebrated, European travel-accounts of the early modern period.

Writing this book has been an unusual exercise, not least of all because it has proceeded in fits and starts over so many years. We should not leave the reader with the impression that this has been a joyless task, or one in which we have not taken pleasure. Indeed, we hope that some of our own enjoyment in reading these texts comes through these pages, and that we have not produced a text that serves – as the sour Swiss writer Béat Louis de Muralt put it in the eighteenth century – only to persuade our readers not to travel.

Chicago and Los Angeles

A note on transliteration

The Persian and Indian terms not in common use in the English language have been italicised, and their plurals have been indicated usually by adding the letter *s*. However, we have chosen not to add diacritical marks in the text for proper nouns, such as the names of persons and places. We have, however, used the spiritus asper (ʻ) and spiritus lentis (ʼ) for the *ʻain* and *hamza* respectively. In order to transliterate words and phrases in Persian, we have used a modified version of the system in F. Steingass's *Comprehensive Persian–English dictionary*, while avoiding the excessive use of apostrophes. We have therefore preferred to diverge from his usage with regard to combined words, as can be seen in forms such as "Niẕām-ud-Dīn" rather than "Niẕāmu'd-Dīn", or "Quṭb-ul-Mulk" in place of "Quṭbu'l-Mulk". In regard to Turkish, we have followed standard modern conventions in that language. In regard to Chinese, we have normally followed the Pinyin system of transliteration.

A note on calendars

Since many of the texts that are discussed use the lunar Hijri calendar, we have tried, to the extent possible, to give both the original dates and the equivalents in terms of the Common Era (CE). In the interests of clarity, it may be pointed out that the following broad equivalents apply: 800 H. is 1397–8 CE; 900 H. is 1494–5 CE ; 1000 H. is 1591–2 CE; 1100 H. is 1688–9 CE; 1200 H. is 1785–6 CE. Further, the succession of months is as follows.

1. Muharram
2. Safar
3. Rabi‘ I
4. Rabi‘ II
5. Jumada I
6. Jumada II
7. Rajab
8. Sha‘ban
9. Ramazan
10. Shawwal
11. Zi-Qa‘da
12. Zi-Hijja

"Kh." stands for "Khurshidi", and "Sh." for "Shamsi" (calendars used in Iran).

CHAPTER 1

Introduction: the travel-account from Beijing to the Bosphorus

Travel is the patron of man,
it is the court where status is gained;
travel is treasure, and the master of skill.
If a tree were able to move,
it would not be the victim of the saw and the axe.
. . .
Hell in this world is the same as travel.
That's why Travel (*safar* سفر) looks like Hell (*saqar* سقر) in writing.
Muhammad Mufid Mustaufi Yazdi (*c.* 1670)[1]

A CONSPECTUS

A thousand years ago, a great Muslim intellectual and polymath, native of the Central Asian region of Khwarizm, embarked on a study of distant and exotic matters, namely matters Indian. A contemporary and sometime correspondent of the celebrated Avicenna (Ibn Sina), this intellectual was no armchair scholar but came to derive his knowledge of India from first-hand experience and travel, related in large measure to his association with Sultan Mahmud of Ghazna (*c.* 971–1030), who raided northern India on several occasions. As he wrote in the opening passages of his own work, "No one will deny that in questions of historic authenticity hearsay does not equal eyewitness; for in the latter the eye of the observer apprehends the substance of that which is observed, both in the time when and in the place where it exists, whilst hearsay has its peculiar drawbacks." These drawbacks included the fact that lies were frequently told and transmitted, whether from self-interest and the desire for profit,

[1] For both verses, making opposite claims, see Mirza Muhammad Mufid Mustaufa ibn Najm-ud-Din Mahmud Bafiqi Yazdi, *Jāmi'i Mufīdī: Persian text of XI century A.H. on history of Yazd, by Muḥammad Mufid Mustowfi Bafiqi*, ed. Iraj Afshar, 3 vols. (Tehran, 1960–3), Vol. III; and the discussion in Chapter 5 below.

or from ignorance, or even from habitual mendacity. Still, our Khwarizmi intellectual was equally aware that to be an eyewitness was not all: "for the object of eye-witness can only be actual momentary existence, whilst hearsay comprehends alike the present, the past and the future".[2] Happy the writer then who not only has been there, and seen what he described, but also has access to the textual traditions of the places he wishes to write about. Happy then the man who can call himself Abu Raihan Muhammad ibn Ahmad al-Biruni (973–1048), author, amongst a variety of other texts, of the work we have cited from above: the *Kitāb fī Taḥqīq mā lil-Hind*.

Were one to eavesdrop on most discussions regarding al-Biruni, however, one could very easily conclude that the man was an outlandish exception, a freak phenomenon in an Indo-Persian (or, in his case, Indo-Perso-Arabic) world where few others cared to reflect on travel and first-person experience. We are often reminded that his work on India (unlike his other works on mathematics and astronomy) was little read for nearly two centuries after it was written, until it was cited by the Persian historian Rashid-ud-Din (d. 1318). In the period that we shall study here too, al-Biruni seems hardly to be a writer whose name is on the lips of every writer and intellectual, although almost all those whom we shall consider in the following pages were fluent readers of Arabic. The fate of the *Kitāb al-Hind* thus seems to lead paradoxically to the ineluctable conclusion of an Oriental lack of enterprise and curiosity, confirming the clichés that so many leading scholars of Islam have long sustained.[3] One al-Biruni can hardly be thought to be representative of anything besides his own extraordinary genius.

To whom does the medieval and early modern travel-account really belong then? The reader uneasily astride the twentieth and twenty-first centuries may be forgiven the presumption that such accounts are above all products of the Western pen, setting down what has been seen by the roving Western eye.[4] The search through bookstores and even libraries

[2] Edward C. Sachau, *Alberuni's India: an account of the religion, philosophy, literature, geography, chronology, astronomy, customs, laws and astrology of India about A.D. 1030*, 2 vols. (London, 1910); for the text, see Abu Raihan Muhammad ibn Ahmad al-Biruni, *Kitāb fī Taḥqīq mā lil-Hind min maqūlah maqbūlah fī al-'aql aw marẕulah* (Hyderabad, 1958).

[3] See Bernard Lewis, *The Muslim Discovery of Europe* (New York, 1982).

[4] This is certainly the broad impression one has from the massive and recent Jennifer Speake, ed., *Literature of travel and exploration: an encyclopaedia*, 3 vols. (London, 2003), where almost none of the travellers discussed in the present volume find a place. See also Peter Hulme and Tim Youngs, eds., *The Cambridge companion to travel writing* (Cambridge, 2002), which again embodies a rather similar Europe- (and even Anglo-)centred view.

of today confirms this primarily Occidental leaning of the popular travel-account, and is crystallised in the typical photograph of the author–traveller that accompanies the text: usually a man, dressed in rugged outdoor clothes, he stands squinting against the harsh sun of a distant (and often either tropical or mountainous) land where he finds himself.[5] In view of the association, moreover, of travel and anthropology that has become very nearly a cliché since Claude Lévi-Strauss penned his *Tristes tropiques* (first published in 1955), the Occidental vocation of even the erudite travel-account is neatly confirmed by author after author.[6] Less academically, one can equally run the gamut from Frédéric Sauser (1887–1961), better known by his *nom de plume* of Blaise Cendrars, whose celebrated and suggestively titled book, *Bourlinguer* (with its implicit image of an errant sailing ship), sums up the genre with elegance and multi-layered irony, to the hyper-Occidental V. S. Naipaul, each casting his picaresque or jaundiced eye on people and places in various incarnations of both Occident and Orient.[7]

The purpose of this book is resolutely to argue otherwise. However, this is only one of its purposes, for if the empirical demonstration of the falsity of the idea summarised above were all that interested us, the job could be done rather quickly. It would be sufficient, for example, to list the rather copious production of travel-literature in non-Western languages and have done with it, with the mass of materials in Chinese alone being enough to clinch the argument. Yet the problem remains of what this literature meant in different historical and societal contexts, of both its location in a broader canon, and its significance in social and historical processes, going beyond the mere fact of its existence as a sort of exotic curiosity, a subsidiary entry in a universal encyclopaedia under the heading of, say, "Travel-Accounts (Other)".

Our concern here is with a specific historical period, namely that extending from the fifteenth to the eighteenth centuries, and with a geographical area, that which we shall term as inhabited by "Indo-Persian culture". Like all cultural zones, this one too is nebulous, far clearer at

[5] See, by way of a random example, Robert D. Kaplan, *The ends of the earth: from Togo to Turkmenistan, from Iran to Cambodia – a journey to the frontiers of anarchy* (New York, 1996), described by the *New York Times Book Review* on the blurb as "travel writing from hell".

[6] Claude Lévi-Strauss, *Tristes tropiques* (Paris, 1955); the standard English translation also appears as *Tristes Tropiques*, tr. John and Doreen Weightman (Harmondsworth, 1976). However, see also, for a general consideration, Clifford Geertz, *Works and lives: the anthropologist as author* (Stanford, 1988).

[7] Blaise Cendrars, *Bourlinguer* (Paris, 1974); the text was completed in 1947. Naipaul's acerbic travelogues include *An area of darkness* (London, 1964) and *Among the believers: an Islamic journey* (London, 1981).

its centre than at its edges. It includes the Indo-Gangetic region of what was termed "Hindustan" in the centuries after the formation of the Sultanate of Delhi in the early thirteenth century, drifts northward in part in the direction of Central Asia, and we shall even find ourselves from time to time in the core of Iran, or as far west as the Ottoman heartland and the Arabian peninsula.[8] Our central argument concerns the relationship between the definition of this cultural region, and the genre of travel-writing, which we shall submit were intimately related. How, and through what mechanisms, we cannot specify in this introductory chapter, for such an exercise demands rather more patience on the reader's part. It requires the reader, in sum, to accompany us on several voyages, with a series of travellers from the middle years of the fifteenth century through to the end of the eighteenth century, and to such fabulous, far-away places as Burhanpur, Khwarizm and Mashhad.

The figure of the Oriental traveller conjures up in the modern imagination the world of Sindbad the Sailor from the *Arabian Nights*, a reference that is probably, on balance, more important to a modern Western or westernised audience than to the authors of our period, or indeed to their readers. Immortalised in turn for the English-language reader by that other inveterate traveller and sometime translator, "the careless but fascinating" Sir Richard Burton, the voyages of Sindbad were compared by Burton to Daniel Defoe's Captain Singleton, but he did equally note that the compiler of the travels had drawn on a number of earlier empirical travel or geographical accounts, including al-Idrisi, Ibn al-Wardi, and also Qazwini's *'Ajā'ib al-Makhlūqāt*.[9] Recent analysts have analysed the role, in much medieval travel literature the world over, of the equivalent of *'ajā'ib*, which Roy Mottahedeh translates as "marvels, wonders and astonishing things", and which he also compares to the Latin *mirabilia*.[10] Despite this, however, the name of Sindbad, and his numerous and usually disastrous voyages, are often thought to represent the perverse triumph of "travel fiction" over "travel fact", and he may thus be opposed easily enough to the quintessential Western traveller, with his empirically

[8] A recent collection that attempts to explore various aspects of the history of this zone is Muzaffar Alam, Françoise N. Delvoye and Marc Gaborieau, eds., *The making of Indo-Persian culture: Indian and French studies* (New Delhi, 2000).

[9] Roy P. Mottahedeh, "'Ajā'ib in The Thousand and One Nights", in Richard G. Hovannisian, Georges Sabagh and Fedwa Malti-Douglas, eds., *The Thousand and One Nights in Arabic literature and society* (Cambridge, 1996), pp. 29–39. The characterisation of Burton is borrowed from Mottahedeh.

[10] Mottahedeh also notes that *'ajā'ib* is often found together with *gharīb* ("strange") and its equivalents, which then yokes it definitively to travel.

grounded character.[11] For the figure of the Western traveller is nowhere better represented than by the thirteenth-century Venetian, Marco Polo (1254–1324), who in himself constitutes something of an industry, ever since his *Description of the World*, written by an amanuensis Rustichello of Pisa, saw light, at the end of the thirteenth century.[12] Even in the late twentieth century, every few years seemed to produce yet another monograph on this visitor to the court of Qubilai Khan in China, and even those writings that are ostensibly aimed at debunking his travels (transforming him, as it were, into a version of the mendacious Sir John Mandeville) eventually wind up confirming by devious means the centrality of this figure.[13] The closest "Oriental" counterpart that has been found to Polo is in fact a personage from the far west of the Islamic world, namely the fourteenth-century *'ālim* and traveller from the Maghreb, Ibn Battuta (1304–77), whose travels between the 1320s and the 1340s quite closely parallel those of the illustrious Venetian.[14] Both begin in the western Mediterranean, both contain important sections on India (though Ibn Battuta's is far more significant in its details of the interior of Hindustan under the Sultans), and both eventually attain the Far East, where Polo's text is eventually far more plentiful in its details than that of Ibn Battuta, whose stay was considerably shorter and largely limited to the coastal regions.

It seems perfectly just, then, to see Marco Polo's account as a sort of template, onto which later travellers to Asia are fitted, and which becomes a standard against which even earlier accounts (like those of William of Rubruck, or John of Plano Carpini) are retrospectively measured.[15] In this

11 Thus, see the very ambiguous evocation of the story of Sindbad and the roc at the very outset of Stephen Greenblatt, *Marvelous possessions: the wonder of the New World* (Chicago, 1991).

12 See for example, H. Watanabe, *Marco Polo bibliography, 1477–1983* (Tokyo, 1986), to which must be added the numerous items from the latter half of the 1980s and the 1990s. The standard translation is Ronald Latham, *Marco Polo: the travels* (Harmondsworth, 1958). The most recent major contribution to Polo-graphy is John Larner, *Marco Polo and the discovery of the world* (London, 1999).

13 See the recent controversy around Frances Wood, *Did Marco Polo go to China?* (London, 1995). The recent book by David Selbourne, *The city of light* (London, 1997), purporting to recount a translated version of the travels of one Jacob d'Ancona from 1270 to 1273 (without providing readers either with a text, or with indications of the manuscript's provenance), seems no more than an attempt to invent a suitable "Jewish Marco Polo".

14 R. E. Dunn, *The adventures of Ibn Battuta, a Muslim Traveler of the fourteenth century* (Berkeley, 1986); Ibn Battuta, *Voyages d'Ibn Battūta*, tr. C. Defremery and B. R. Sanguinetti, revised by Stéphane Yerasimos, 3 vols. (Paris, 1997).

15 See Christopher Dawson, *Mission to Asia* (Toronto, 1980), originally published in 1955 as *The Mongol mission*. Thus, we read (p. xxiii) that William of Rubruck's narrative is "even more direct and convincing than that of Marco Polo in his own time".

view of matters, it is easy enough to treat Ibn Battuta as the Arab version of Marco Polo, and this very fate has equally been reserved for the celebrated seventeenth-century traveller Evliya Çelebi (lately termed "The Turkish Marco Polo"), on whom more below. Having thus "explained" these other travellers, as more or less successful adherents to a school of travel-writing to which they did not, for the most part, really subscribe, we can then do away with the necessity of analysing them in any detail, beyond pillaging them, that is, for one or the other fact. Thus, the relative silence in terms of monographs on Ibn Battuta's *Riḥla*, compared to the profusion on Marco Polo, tells its own tale, both about academic prejudices, and about modern-day readers' tastes.[16]

The travel-accounts we are concerned with also come from a neglected tradition. Some have been edited, a few translated, and selections from some others are available to the specialist reader. Yet they have attracted all too little attention as a corpus, and this is also the case with what one might have expected to be a far better-known corpus, namely the body of Ottoman travel-writings. For the Ottomans possess a number of advantages in comparison with the Indo-Persian world, notably that both proximity and history render the Ottomans almost "European" in the eyes of the early modern historiography. However, a look at the case of the most celebrated of the Ottoman travellers, Evliya Çelebi, is somewhat chastening. Born in Istanbul in 1611, we are aware that Evliya was a well-educated man, who was not merely well versed in Qur'anic studies (which he mastered with a certain Mehmed Efendi), but that he had also studied calligraphy, poetry, Arabic grammar, and even music under the patronage of the palace, where he was trained to be a functionary. From the age of about twenty-nine years, his voyages begin, with a first visit in 1640–1 to the eastern littoral of the Black Sea. Subsequent years see him in the

[16] Ibn Battuta's account should ideally be read in the context of a far larger corpus of Arabic travel-accounts, which includes Ibn Fadlan, *Voyage chez les Bulgares de la Volga (il y a mille ans)*, tr. Marius Canard (Paris, 1988), and which is discussed for the classical period in Houari Touati, *Islam et voyage au Moyen Age: histoire et anthropologie d'une pratique lettrée* (Paris, 2000). The corpus continues with the embassy-account to Istanbul of Abu'l Hasan 'Ali al-Tamgruti (1589–90) and the Hajj account of Abu Salim 'Abdullah al-'Ayyashi from the seventeenth century. For the former, see Henri de Castries, *Relation d'une ambassade marocaine en Turquie, 1589–1591* (Paris, 1929), and for the latter, Abderrahmane El-Moudden, "The ambivalence of *rihla*: community integration and self-definition in Moroccan travel-accounts, 1300–1800", in Dale F. Eickelman and James Piscatori, eds., *Muslim travellers: pilgrimage, migration, and the religious imagination* (Berkeley, 1990), pp. 76–9. Also see the valuable recent collection by Nabil Matar, *In the land of the Christians: Arabic travel-writing in the seventeenth century* (New York and London, 2003), which includes the accounts of Ahmad bin Qasim (1611–13), Ilyas Hanna al-Mawsuli (1668–83) and Muhammad bin 'Abd al-Wahhab al-Ghassani (1690–1).

Caucasus, Crete, as well as Damascus, Palestine and Syria; then, from the 1650s, the elevation of his patron Melek Ahmed Pasha to the post of Grand Vizier enabled him to prosecute a series of further voyages to the Lake Van region, Bosnia, Albania and Kosovo. The last phase of his travels then takes him to Mecca, which he visited in 1671 as a pilgrim, and the Greek islands, as well as Sudan and Ethiopia, that he was able to visit while resident in Egypt in the closing years of his life. Evliya died, it would seem, in late 1684 or early 1685, leaving his master-work, *Seyahatnāme*, incomplete on his death. Yet, even the unfinished monument is daunting enough. We have before us ten volumes of travels, interspersed with other reflections, to be sure, but taking us from the city of Istanbul and its environs (described in the first volume) to Egypt and regions to its south in Africa, that occupy the tenth tome.

Yet the attention devoted to this monument has been somewhat modest, when all is said and done. In the 1830s, Joseph von Hammer-Purgstall published the first excerpts in translation, while a partial edition of the first volume appeared some years thereafter. Since that date, besides a serviceable if philologically unsatisfactory edition of the ten volumes of the text (published in Istanbul, by various hands, between 1896–7 and 1938), a number of partial translations and studies have appeared, notably a very valuable glossary of the *Seyahatnāme* by Robert Dankoff, and a translation, with a commentary and introduction, of the sections concerning Diyarbekir, by Martin van Bruinessen and Hendrik Boeschoten.[17] Yet, as a recent historian remarks, "Evliya Çelebi is known to historians as an observer of public buildings, such as mosques, *medreses* and city walls, as a valuable source on languages and dialects and, much too rarely, as an artist of narration."[18] Again, Cemal Kafadar has noted how Evliya's "gargantuan work seems to have gone largely unnoticed in Ottoman belles-lettres" until the late nineteenth century, despite its indubitable status as "the most monumental example of the first person narrative", perhaps in the seventeenth-century world as a whole.[19] How can this relative neglect be explained?

[17] Robert Dankoff, *An Evliya Çelebi glossary: unusual, dialectal and foreign words in the Seyahatnāme* (Cambridge, Mass., 1991); Martin van Bruinessen and Hendrik Boeschoten, *Evliya Çelebi in Diyarbekir: the relevant section of the Seyahatname edited with translation, commentary and introduction* (Leiden, 1988).

[18] Suraiya Faroqhi, "Red Sea trade and communications as observed by Evliya Çelebi (1671–72)", in Faroqhi, *Making a living in the Ottoman lands, 1480 to 1820* (Istanbul, 1995), p. 231.

[19] Cemal Kafadar, "Self and others: the diary of a dervish in seventeenth-century Istanbul and first-person narratives in Ottoman literature", *Studia Islamica*, 69, 1989, p. 126.

Several elements of a response suggest themselves. To begin with, the very size of the text itself is somewhat discouraging, as it does not lend itself to the retrospective imposition of the sort of accessible plot that is available for Marco Polo, or even Hernán Cortés. If well-defined plot there is, it must resemble Proust or Musil in its complexity, rather than the watered-down versions of the *Odyssey* to which readers of the travel-account were doubtless accustomed by the nineteenth century.[20] Second, we must take into account the conviction that existed by the eighteenth century in Europe that such late examples of non-European literature offered little by way either of edification or of instruction to the reader, who was better off with the ancient texts of the East, rather than reading writers who were often disconcertingly lacking in the properly exotic, such as it was construed in that epoch. Such specimens of the Indo-Persian travel-account that found rapid approval, and hence were quickly translated, were thus precisely those that compared the Indo-Persian world with Europe, and found the former wanting in crucial respects. Thus, the vogue for the accounts of European travellers to these exotic parts corresponded, quite logically, with a relative neglect of the literature produced in those very parts, unless they came (as did texts in Sanskrit collected during the late eighteenth century) overlaid with a thick veneer of antiquity. A third reason why a text such as that of Evliya Çelebi might have found it difficult to attract a large readership in Europe was the vexed issue of its truth value, in view of the difficulties in regulating the passage between one truth-régime and another in the period. The supernatural intervenes numerous times in his text, which is also full of religious and Qur'anic references. If the text could not be read, as was the *Thousand and One Nights*, for its sheer entertainment, and if it did not meet the increasingly stringent conditions under which "real" scientific and ethnographic knowledge was meant to be produced under the supervision of the academies in Europe, it was difficult to comprehend what one might do with such a literary outpouring.

On the other hand, this view of neglect must undoubtedly be nuanced by taking into account the great celebrity of the personage of Evliya in the Turcophone lands, so widespread that he has been compared to the legendary Mulla (or Khwaja) Nasruddin. As a recent translator of some excerpts of his work into French remarks:

[20] Cf. Mary W. Helms, *Ulysses' sail: an ethnographic odyssey of power, knowledge, and geographical distance* (Princeton, 1988).

Discovered in the beginning of the nineteenth century, the "Book of Voyages" continues to attract the attention of researchers, but also that of the man on the street. In Turkey, Evliya is in effect a personage as famous and sympathetic as Nasreddin Hodja, a legendary personage of the thirteenth century, known for his humour. "I have (or you have) become a voyager like Evliya" (*Seyyah oldum/ oldun Evliyā gibi*) is an expression that is often utilised to designate someone who voyages a lot. No historian, no ethnographer, no folklorist who is writing an historical monograph on a town, a region, or a profession, can afford to ignore the work of Evliya Tchelebi.[21]

The lot of Evliya's work can be usefully compared with three other texts that are from the same broad period. The first, the *Mirāt-ül-memālik* ("Mirror of Kingdoms") of Seydi 'Ali Re'is, has been the object of some erudite attention in Europe since the nineteenth-century translation by the Hungarian savant, Arminius Vambéry, and is also relatively well known in Turkey. It relates the travels of its author, an Ottoman admiral of the 1550s, to India and Central Asia, after a shipwreck while fighting against the Portuguese in the western Indian Ocean.[22] Another text, that of Mehmed Achik bin Ömer, entitled *Menāzir-ül-'avālim* ("Visions of the Universe"), recounting the author's travels between 1575 and 1600, still awaits a complete edition and detailed study, and thus marks one end, as it were, of the spectrum between fame and obscurity. A third author enjoyed far greater, if posthumous, success, and this was not so much by penning travel-accounts as by putting together compendia. The author in question is Katib Çelebi (or Haji Khalifa) (1609–57), among whose works on Ottoman naval battles was one which included a substantial résumé of the work of Seydi 'Ali Re'is, which was one of the earliest books that was actually printed in Turkish, by the press of Ibrahim Müteferrika in Istanbul in 1729. This work was translated into English in the 1830s, but another of his works, the encyclopaedic *Cihān-numā*, also printed by the same Istanbul press in 1732, was translated earlier still into European languages, something of an irony in view of its own heavy dependence on European sources.[23]

21 Faruk Bilici, "Introduction", in Evliyā Tchélébi, *La Guerre des Turcs: récits de batailles extraits du Livre de voyage*, tr. F. Bilici (Paris, 2000), p. 22.

22 See Arminius Vambéry, ed. and tr., *The travels and adventures of the Turkish admiral Sidi Ali Reis in India, Afghanistan, Central Asia and Persia* (London, 1899; reprint, Lahore, 1975). For a recent, and far more satisfactory, French translation, see Seyyidi [Seydi] 'Ali Re'is, *Le miroir des pays: une anabase ottomane à travers l'Inde et l'Asie centrale*, tr. Jean-Louis Bacqué-Grammont (Paris, 1999); and for a modern Turkish text, Seydi 'Ali Reis, *Mir'ātü'l-Memālik*, ed. Mehmet Kiremit (Ankara, 1999).

23 Katib Çelebi, *Gihan Numa, Geographia orientalis*, tr. M. Norberg, 2 vols. (Londini Gothorum, 1818).

Other texts have had to await the twentieth century before attracting any attention beyond that of diligent archivists and cataloguers of manuscripts. Thus, we have the account of a certain Osman Agha ibn Ahmed Temeshvarlï, who was imprisoned in Hungary and Austria for eleven years from 1688 to 1699, and who appears to have written his memoirs (which are thus above all an account of captivity, but sharing significant aspects with the travel-account) in the early 1720s.[24] First published in a German translation in the 1950s, the text has subsequently been edited, and other translations in European languages have also appeared. Better recognised, and belonging also to a particular sub-genre, are the accounts of Ottoman ambassadors to foreign courts, of which a number of well-known examples exist, in particular from the eighteenth century.[25] Evliya Çelebi's account of his visit to Vienna in 1665 is at times counted as one of the earliest amongst these; a significant example, which at times served as a model for other later writers, is the embassy-account of Yirmisekiz Çelebi Mehmed Efendi to the court of the young Louis XV in 1720–1.[26] In the same line of accounts, one may equally number the reports from Revolutionary and Napoleonic France of Morali Seyyid 'Ali Efendi and Seyyid 'Abdürrahim Muhibb Efendi, the first dating from the years 1797 to 1802, and the second from 1806 to 1811.[27]

Taking one thing with another, then, we observe that the early modern travel-account was certainly known and practised in the Ottoman lands, even if the dimensions of the corpus are admittedly more limited than those of the corpuses in Spanish, Portuguese, French, Dutch or English, which were veritably exploding in the sixteenth and especially the seventeenth centuries. Further, unlike the latter cases, the history of these accounts is not intimately linked to that of the printing-press, since few of the Ottoman texts came to be printed until the nineteenth century. The question of the readership of these texts is hence bound up with the sphere of the circulation of manuscripts, something that brings them closer to the Indo-Persian texts that we shall be examining at length below, none of which was printed until the era of the early lithographs of the nineteenth

[24] Osman Agha de Temechvar, *Prisonnier des Infidèles: un soldat dans l'Empire des Habsbourg*, tr. Frédéric Hitzel (Paris, 1998).

[25] Some thirty such accounts are to be found listed in Faik Reşit Unat, *Osmanlï Sefirleri ve Sefaretnāmeleri* (Ankara, 1968); they concern embassies to Vienna, Berlin, St Petersburg, Paris, Madrid, Morocco, Iran, the Mughal court and Bukhara.

[26] For his account, see Julien-Claude Galland, *Le Paradis des infidèles: un ambassadeur ottoman en France sous la Régence*, ed. Gilles Veinstein (Paris, 1981).

[27] Morali Seyyid 'Ali Efendi and Seyyid 'Abdürrahim Muhibb Efendi, *Deux Ottomans à Paris sous le Directoire et l'Empire: relations d'ambassade*, tr. Stéphane Yerasimos (Paris, 1998).

century. In the absence of printing, the conditions of the production and circulation of these texts are rather more difficult to pin down than are those of printed texts, the study of which has made notable advances in recent decades. Yet, the careful pursuit of intertextual clues can sometimes yield significant results, as can a study of the dispersion of the manuscripts themselves. These are themes that will be touched upon from time to time in the pages that follow, in more specific contexts.

Passing from the western extremity of Asia towards South Asia, and the Far East, we notice an extremely uneven distribution of travel-literature, in both time and space. Outside of the narrow Indo-Persian sphere – that is to say, the central object of the present work – the South Asian subcontinent itself is rather dismaying in its lack of travel-accounts. The great classical and post-classical literatures in Sanskrit, Tamil, Pali and the Prakrits can between them hardly conjure up an example worthy of the name, beyond the highly stylised imaginary voyage, in which a territory is traversed and described by a flying messenger, often a bird or a cloud, traversing the distance between two separated lovers. We also periodically encounter other flying vehicles or beings (such as the semi-divine beings called *gandharvas*), whose travels at times permit them, or at any rate the authors of the texts in question, to attempt a sort of rapid survey of the landscapes that are thus overflown. Classicists may find the roots of such imaginary voyages in the epic texts themselves, with the *Rāmāyaṇa* alone providing a certain number of short but interesting examples.

Remarkably, even the rise to prominence of the regional vernacular literatures in South Asia, from the early centuries of the second millenium of the Common Era, does not significantly alter this situation.[28] Rather like a neighbouring literature, that in Malay, the South Asian vernacular languages of the sixteenth, seventeenth and eighteenth centuries are singularly poor in respect of travel-accounts, with the sole genre that sometimes approximates the type being the hagiography, in which the travels of a saint such as Chaitanya (in the late fifteenth and early sixteenth centuries) are described by a later author. Among major south Indian languages such as Telugu, therefore, it is necessary to await the end of the eighteenth, or the beginning of the nineteenth century, for the first travel-accounts written in the first person to emerge. Similarly, in Bengali, one of the earliest travel-narratives that is available to us is the *Tīrthamaṅgal*

[28] It would seem that some stylised Jaina travel-texts may be found in medieval western India (Gujarat and Rajasthan), but they have as yet been largely untapped by scholars (private communication from Mukund Lath, University of Jaipur).

of Bijoyram Sen, that has been recently presented as a "description in verse of a pilgrimage undertaken by the author's patron Krishnachandra Ghoshal, brother of Joynarayan Ghoshal, a powerful political figure of mid-eighteenth-century Bengal".[29] Of some interest is the fact that this text (though not a first-person travel-narrative) bore extensive signs of the influence on it of Indo-Persian culture, in terms of its vocabulary but also perhaps in the very choice of form.

In marked contrast to this curiously barren South Asian vernacular landscape is the very richest of the corpuses in Asia, namely that in Chinese. Students of ancient Indian history have long used as staple fare a certain number of these Chinese texts (usually in late nineteenth- or early twentieth-century English translation), such as that of Faxian (Fa-hsien, *c.* 334–420), entitled *A Record of Buddhist Kingdoms*, set down in about 416 CE.[30] This account, like many others of its genre, was authored by a Buddhist monk who sojourned in first western China, and then Central Asia, India and Sri Lanka. The text has been associated with a series of new literary developments that characterise the so-called "Six Dynasties period" (222–589 CE) in China, and has recently been described as being part of the rise to prominence of "works of historiographical travel writing [that] shared a common style: objective, third-person narrative; emphasis on factuality; and production based on the compilation and processing of a variety of information including other texts".[31] Some two centuries later, under the early Tang dynasty, the account of the Buddhist monk from Henan, Xuanzang (or Hsüan-tsang), entitled *A Record of the Western Region*, also of travels to western China, Central Asia, and India, between 629 and 645 CE, appears to continue the same tradition.[32]

Despite this remarkable, and precocious, development in terms not only of travel-literature, but of travel-description linked with xenology, analysts of Chinese travel-accounts have been somewhat reticent to draw certain conclusions that are in fact striking to the eye of the South Asianist. To be sure, it is possible to some extent to circumscribe these

[29] Kumkum Chatterjee, "Discovering India: travel, history and identity in late nineteenth- and early twentieth-century India", in Daud Ali, ed., *Invoking the past: the uses of history in South Asia* (Delhi, 1999), p. 198.

[30] James Legge, tr., *A record of Buddhistic kingdoms: being an account by the Chinese Monk Fa-hien of his travels in India and Ceylon (A.D. 399–414) in search of the Buddhist Books of Discipline* (Oxford, 1886).

[31] Richard E. Strassberg, *Inscribed landscapes: travel writing from imperial China* (Berkeley, 1994), p. 33.

[32] Samuel Beal, tr., *Si-yu-ki: Buddhist records of the Western world translated from the Chinese of Hiuen Tsiang (A.D. 629)* (London, 1884).

Buddhist travel-texts within a specific context, which would also embrace the rare early Japanese travel-account such as the description of his voyage to China by the monk Ennin (794–864).[33] Such a comparison may, however, conceal as much as it reveals. For, while the Japanese travel-literature that follows during the medieval period (that is, up until the middle of the fifteenth century) largely consists of a rather repetitive series of accounts by Buddhist monks – which have (it has recently been tactfully noted) "a rather limited documentary interest", being mostly concerned with reflections on the human condition provoked by a state of separation – the Chinese corpus is seemingly far larger and far more diverse.[34] In the Japanese accounts, the itineraries taken by the traveller, which are usually within Japan itself, are often shrouded in mystery, as indeed is the precise identity of their authors (beyond the fact that they are Buddhist monks). Besides reflecting on the problem of "sufferings from attachment" (the Japanese Buddhist term, *bonnō*), they also seem to gravitate somewhat predictably around a series of topoi, of which the most significant is the meeting between the monk and the woman of pleasure (*yūjo*), which naturally raises the text to a metaphorical and trans-historical level.

The Chinese case stands quite apart, for both its literary construction, and its notably empirical orientation. It would appear that some chronological separation is possible within this rather long tradition. To begin with, we have the journeys of the Buddhist monks surveyed briefly above, including journeys to India and Sri Lanka, all of which may be dated to the years from the third to the seventh centuries. The period from the middle of the eighth century on then sees the emergence into prominence of the so-called "lyric travel-account" (*yu ji*), with a dominant emphasis on certain types of aesthetic and moral imperatives, albeit within the framework of a first-person narrative. A subsequent phase, from the eleventh and early twelfth centuries, then permits the consolidation of the travel-account, with the new and flourishing genre of the travel-diary (*ri ji*) being a remarkable innovation of this epoch, even if an early example of the travel-diary may already be found with Li Ao (772–836), who documents in his *Diary of My Coming to the South* his journey to a place

33 Edwin Reischauer, *Ennin's diary: the record of a pilgrimage to China in search of the law*, 2 vols. (New York, 1955).

34 Jacqueline Pigeot, "Le voyage comme expérience de la condition humaine au Japon (XIIe–XVe siècle)", in Claudine Salmon, ed., *Récits de voyage des Asiatiques: genres, mentalités, conception de l'espace* (Paris, 1996), p. 31. See also Donald Keene, *Travelers of a hundred ages: the Japanese as revealed through 1,000 years of diaries* (New York, 1999).

where he was exiled, possibly on account of his own outspoken views. The years after 1100 thus see a profusion of such accounts, selections from about twenty-five of which have been published in a remarkable recent anthology by Richard Strassberg (besides another twenty-five-odd earlier accounts).[35]

The reader of these accounts is struck by their persistent attention to nature and to landscapes, which are constantly evoked as if the main concern of the greater part of these accounts was simply to conjure up scenic beauty. Thus, an account by Wang Shizhen (1526–90), a particularly distinguished writer of the later sixteenth century, evokes a visit to the celebrated Daoist site of Zhang's Cave, in Jiangsu. Having first described the approach to the spot by boat, on bright green water, with mountains on either side, lofty trees and fields with their harvest "like yellow clouds", the author then moves on to speak of how he and his companions moored their boat, while an increasingly heavy rain began to fall on them. Eventually, the author (himself injured in one foot) and his companions (who are clearly and quite painstakingly identified) were obliged to take sedan chairs to accomplish their voyage. The account continues:

> Mr. Chang [Zhang], who had traveled there before, said I should enter through the rear of the cavern, not through the front . . . So I determined to enter from the rear. With numerous torches brought along to lead the way, we squeezed our bodies through an opening and descended into it, one by one, like a line of fish. As we gradually descended, it became more and more slippery; furthermore, the slanting steps could not accommodate our feet. The foot in the back had to wait for the one in front to be firmly planted before moving, and we were forced to hold on to each other's shoulders to steady ourselves . . . I could barely see the person in front of me, for he appeared like a bird in the fog. Moreover, whatever I heard sounded like someone speaking in a jar. When a torch was lit, I cried out in surprise: a myriad giant stalactites all hung suspended, like mountains high and low, shaped like bronze vessels, forming an intricate design, crystalline and gleaming – it was beyond description.[36]

Later, Wang would compare the stalactites and stalagmites that he saw to dragons, some submerged and hornless, others leaping and horned, or to lions, crouching elephants, and even "foreign Buddhist monks".

[35] Strassberg's *Inscribed landscapes* contains texts ranging chronologically from Ma Ti-po and Wang Xizhi (or Wang Hsi-chih, *c.* 303–61), to Gong Zizhen (or Kung Tzu-chen, 1792–1841), and can usefully be complemented by an earlier volume, almost exclusively devoted to Chinese travels "abroad", i.e., Jeannette Mirsky, ed., *The great Chinese travelers* (Chicago, 1964).

[36] Cf. Strassberg, *Inscribed landscapes*, p. 301, extract from Wang Shih-Chen, *The mountain-dweller of Yen-chou's writings.*

Throughout, we note the lyricism of the account, but equally the marks of a striking precision, and of the careful control over both the tone and the content of the description.

Such texts as these are further enhanced in their effect by the tradition of engraving the text (or a part thereof) at the very sites that inspired their composition. Comparable, perhaps, to the graffiti tradition at the medieval site of Sigiriya in Sri Lanka, these inscribed texts were at times then reproduced by means of rubbings, and also themselves became centres of interest for local visitors. Yet, the relative importance of this powerful aestheticising tradition, where humans and social relations are consciously made to appear virtually absent, and other dispositions in the travel-acount remains unclear in this context. A recent extended essay by Strassberg, that introduces the corpus he translates, takes a somewhat affirmative stance in declaring:

> [The] travel writing of Imperial China may seem far removed from the historical and intellectual foundations of the West, as remote in its forms and concerns as the land itself. The writers, like their original audience, were mostly degree-holding literati, usually officials and poets as well, whose public lives revolved around climbing up, slipping down, seeking entrée to, or rejecting entirely the ladder of bureaucratic success. In a country without a strong maritime or colonial tradition, their itineraries were primarily internal. Theoretically, they scorned the pursuit of commercial profit and also showed little interest in foreign countries and non-Chinese ethnic groups . . . The literary forms of Chinese travel writing evolved out of a matrix where narrative was dominated by the impersonal style of official, historical biography, and subjective autobiographical impulses were largely subsumed within lyric poetry.[37]

This is contrasted to a Western tradition of travel-writing that begins by representing "exotic, marginal worlds as fearful zones", but then, over the "Age of Exploration", eventually transforms the genre itself, and also moves its object from a fearsome, savage domain of primarily "repressed anxieties" to "a means of facilitating the desires of writers and readers for a more liberated, autonomous existence". In other words, travel-writing may be related in the Western context to the idea of self-fashioning, both of the individual traveller and of the collectivity of home society from which he originates; in contrast, the Chinese case is seen as one where the place of travel literature is quite different from the above, less humanistic, less ethnographic, and above all less transformative.

[37] Strassberg, "Introduction: the rise of Chinese travel writing", in *Inscribed landscapes*, pp. 3–4.

This contrast can quickly be overemphasized, as even a little attention to the translated corpus introduced by the statement cited above can demonstrate. The simplest mode of counter-argument would be to take the marginal writers from amongst those writing travel-accounts in Chinese, such as Yelu Qucai (or Yeh-lü Ch'u-ts'ai, 1189–1243) and Sa Dula (also known as Sa Tianxi, *c.* 1300–80), the first ethnically of Khitan origin and quite closely associated with Chinggis Khan, and the latter himself a Muslim, and also of Central Asian origin. Thus, Sa Dula, in his account of a visit to Dragon Gate (Longmen), an important complex of Buddhist caves and temples in Henan, adopts a rather different tone from the one that we have cited above. Of the statues, he notes that all of them "were damaged long ago. They have been defaced by people. Some have heads broken off, some have lost their bodies; their noses, ears, hands, and feet are missing, either partially or completely." These temples and sculptures, so he assures us, were commissioned in the past by sovereigns and princes, but even their inscriptions have now been scraped off. Why has this happened, asks Sa Dula, before proceeding to some rather unexpected conclusions. For this takes him first to the story of Sakyamuni (Buddha), a sage from a "Western Region", who had given up the royal life for one of frugality. But these temples and caves are then a travesty of his thought, for they are clearly a waste of people's wealth and energy, writes Sa Dula. Buddhists, for him, are then treading "a dim and murky path", the ultimate proof of which is the fact that their temples have been destroyed rather than "standing in imposing grandeur".[38]

This rather trenchant view of Buddhism thus stands apart from the generalisation presented above, both in terms of its blunt tone, and its use of particular forms of empirical reason as applied to social phenomena. Sa Dula appears here very nearly as a crude Darwinist: the religion that cannot survive is hardly fit to do so. In contrast, the earlier account of Yelu, *Record of a Journey to the West* (1228), is very nearly a classic piece of xenology, providing a concise description of the Altai range, Khotan, Otrar, Bukhara and Samarqand, the last of which comes in for particular praise. More puzzling is an account of the city of "Black India" (*Heise Yindu*), which the writer claims to have visited after a sojourn at Balkh. The account runs:

> The people of this kingdom also have a written language, but it differs in alphabet and sound from that used in the Buddhist kingdoms. There are many

[38] Strassberg, *Inscribed landscapes*, pp. 266–8.

Buddhist statues throughout this kingdom. The people do not butcher cows or goats but do drink their milk. According to their custom, when the husbands die first, the wives are cremated together with them. I inquired about the location of the Buddhist kingdoms, and they indicated that they lay to the southeast. After investigation, I concluded that this kingdom is not northern India proper; the habitants are a border people on the north of India. The local inhabitants have never seen snow. There are two harvests of wheat every year. At the height of the summer, they set out pewter vessels in the sand and are immediately able to solder them. When the dung of horses falls to the ground, it begins to boil. The moonlight shines down on people like the summer sun in the Central Plains of China.[39]

This last piece of hyperbole aside, the impression is of an area to the south-east of Afghanistan, perhaps western Sind. References are equally made in the text to the production of sugarcane, as well as to a "great river as broad as the Yellow River" that flows to the south-east, with a "swirling current [that] is swift and dangerous", before entering the Southern Ocean, again prompting comparisons with the Indus.

That this sort of description does not stand alone is suggested by a recent analysis of the accounts of the envoys sent by the northern Song dynasty to the Liao, located to their north-east beyond the Great Wall, from which at least eight distinct texts have come down to modern-day scholars. The first of these is by Song Tuan (1008), and the last in the series is authored by Shen Gua (1075). These texts deal with issues of frontier geography, but eventually go far beyond matters of measuring itineraries, and the distance between stages. For what eventually emerges, over three-quarters of a century and more of contact, is a complex view combining a sort of strategic geography with an image of the society of the "Other" (that is, the Liao), its nature and the roots of its difference from Chinese society, which are at times simplistic, but at others remarkably sophisticated. It appears that the setting down of these texts, generically termed *yulu* by the first half of the eleventh century, was done following a set of instructions which declared (in the words of the *Qingyuan tiao fa shilei*, a normative text of the late twelfth century): "Each emissary who returns from a barbarian country shall give an account, of both the banquets and the formal presents, as well as of what he has seen and heard up to and including the customs, and what is produced in those lands."

In concrete terms, the results of this initiative were quite considerable. As a recent study by Christian Lamouroux analyses the matter, after a first

[39] Strassberg, *Inscribed landscapes*, pp. 231–2.

chronological stage with a relatively great preoccupation with "filling up" the unknown space, as it were, with topographical points of orientation, one moves in the next moment to a description of the places as they were seen, the rivers and mountains that circumscribed them, the length of the town walls (if such existed), and eventually to ethnographic detail.[40] Mixed marriages, and table-manners, are amongst the elements that seem to receive particular attention. Thus, the description of the southern and central capitals of the Liao, by Lu Zhen in 1009, provides us great details of the physical layout of these, which were obviously of keen strategic interest to his readers. The names of each of the doors to the city is given, as are those of the weapons carried by the soldiers. However, it is clear that these accounts do not attempt any particular precision when describing the intervening countryside between the fortified centres; some of them pay little attention to it, while others choose an aestheticising rather than an objectivist mode in this latter context.

The emergence of the ethnographic aspect is also of some interest in this sequence, and we may take by way of example the following early passage from Wang Zeng (emissary in 1012), where the "barbarian lands" are described as follows:

> The inhabitants live in grass-huts and houses made of planks; they occupy themselves in farming and planting; however, they have no mulberries. All their planting is done along the length, and at the top of mud-banks, for they take precautions against the obstructions produced by the sand that the wind brings. In the mountains, large pine trees are very abundant. At the bottom of gorges, the greater part [of the people] are occupied in making charcoal; at times one sees them raising and grazing cows, horses and camels; they also have a good number of sheep with black fleece, and pigs. Still others have carts and tents that they take with them when they go in search of water and grazing, and in order to hunt with the bow and the net. They only eat boiled grain and sweet cakes.[41]

Here, the emphasis seems very largely on the differences between the material life of the "barbarians" as a whole, and that of the Chinese: the absence of mulberries is naturally a telling point. However, later writers like Shen Gua (in 1075) take far greater care to distinguish, for example, between the Xi and the Bohai, rather than lumping all the "barbarians" into a single category. It is noted that there are linguistic differences

[40] Christian Lamouroux, "De l'étrangeté à la différence: les récits des émissaires Song en pays Liao (XIe s.)", in Salmon, ed., *Récits de voyage des Asiatiques*, pp. 101–26.

[41] Edouard Chavannes, "Voyageurs chinois chez les Khitan et les Joutchen", *Journal Asiatique*, 9, 9, 1897, pp. 428–9, cited in Lamouroux, "De l'étrangeté à la différence", p. 115.

between them, and further that the Xi are more inclined to be woodworkers and artisans. This empirical accumulation of detail, and the imposition of finer gradations than the rather summary categories that existed at the start of the embassies, nevertheless leaves open the issue of how such "ethnographic information" was really digested, and whether it was capable of shifting the basic matrix of perception. The late account of Su Che (dating to 1089) is telling here, for, although he notes that the northern barbarians have "a nature similar to that of wild beasts", he does nevertheless temper this by noting that "the reasons on account of which they protect their families and near and dear ones, take care of themselves, raise their cattle, bring up their children, love their land to the point of defending their chiefs, do not differ from those of the Chinese". Here then is a piquant moment, when the "barbarian" practically acquires the same attributes as the Chinese themselves; it is a moment which can be compared to other weaker versions of the same trend, where the Liao state appears as a somewhat inferior copy of the Chinese empire. Thus, as Lamouroux perceptively puts the matter, the trend seems to be to move from a fairly radical brand of otherness to a more tempered gradation, where the Liao are themselves sorted out internally, and ranked, as it were, on a loose scale of comparison with the Chinese.

The analysis of these texts is thus salutary for our purposes, since it brings out a point that we shall be at pains to develop over the course of our own analysis of various texts. This is the delicate interplay between the accumulation of empirical information, and the formation and transformation of the categories of perception themselves. If at times the weight of information seemingly breaks the bonds, so to speak, of the matrix, at other moments it is the larger schema (which may be literary and generic convention, or a larger set of cultural rigidities) that wins the day, and the fine-tuned observation of the traveller is simply unable to find an adequate reception. Nevertheless, it is of capital importance to pay attention to this delicate interplay between empirical content, the tone and style of the account, and its broader structural characteristics, rather than subsuming the former aspects under the latter. Were we to do so, we would not only do injustice to the texts, but render them that much the poorer for the reader.

Before entering the texts themselves, a brief reflection may be in order on hermeneutic strategies, to explain the "linear" readings followed here. The growing distrust for narrative in the post-Second World War academic context has led to the proliferation of transversal modes of reading texts: in these, one usually first defines some (reasonably arbitrary) heads of analysis, next one takes the text apart into bite-sized fragments, then one reconfigures the "constituent units" of the text with the heads of analysis in mind.[42] We shall distance ourselves here from such a procedure, which seems to us to be an arbitrary formal abuse of the text, and instead consciously *follow* its grain rather than go against it. Thus, rather than talk to the text, in order to highlight some preconceived notions, we shall attempt here to listen to the text, its shifts in tone, rhythm and conception. We could, if we wished, justify ourselves with reference to such general formulae as "the return of the narrative", but it is in fact not clear to us that narrative ever really went away; the point is not to impose on the primary narrative of the text another, abruptly orthogonal and omniscient, modern authorial narrative.

AN ECCENTRIC EXAMPLE

The travel-narratives that we are concerned with are, for the most part, first-person accounts, though we shall make the rare exception to that category. As such, the travel-texts, sometimes known in Persian as *safar nāmas*, are not susceptible of neat demarcation within the larger corpus of first-person accounts, a fact that we have already noted above with the case of the so-called "captivity accounts" of Ottomans in Europe. This said, there is still some point in attempting to define some rules of thumb in order to delimit the travel-account within the larger enveloping corpus. Now, first-person accounts in Persian from India and Iran are to be found in fairly large numbers in the sixteenth and seventeenth centuries, from the autobiographies of Babur, Shah Tahmasp and Jahangir (the first of which was known in Mughal India not only in its original Turkish, but in its late sixteenth-century Persian translation by 'Abdur-Rahim Khan-i Khanan, the *Wāqi'āt-i Bāburī*), to the memoirs of Jauhar Aftabchi, Bayazid Bayat and Gulbadan Begam.[43] Indeed, given Babur's peripatetic life, there is surely very good reason indeed to want to read the *Bābur Nāma* as a travel-account of sorts.[44]

[42] Monographs that follow this strategy are legion; an example is Helms, *Ulysses' sail*; but also see Mary Louise Pratt, *Imperial eyes: travel writing and transculturation* (London, 1992).

[43] We have cited these texts at length elsewhere in this work, except Shah Tahmasp Safavi, *Tazkira-i Shāh Ṭahmāsp*, ed. D. C. Phillott (Calcutta, 1912), which is discussed in detail by Kathryn Babayan, *Mystics, monarchs and messiahs: cultural landscapes of early modern Iran* (Cambridge, Mass., 2002), pp. 295–348.

[44] Zahir-ud-Din Muhammad Babur, *Bāburnāma: Chaghatay Turkish text with Abdul-Rahim Khankhanan's Persian translation*, ed. Wheeler M. Thackston, 3 vols. (Cambridge, Mass., 1993). The same is true in an even greater measure of the account of Babur's descendant of the tenth

If we nevertheless abstain from this temptation here, it is for two reasons. First, because in some cases (the *Bābur Nāma*, for example) these texts are too well known even to an English-language readership for the exercise to be particularly rewarding to the reader; second, and more important on balance, because of an awareness that in many of these cases, we would do violence to *other* aspects of the texts, by forcing them into the mould of a travel-account. In sum, what distinguishes our texts from others is not necessarily that they explicitly term themselves travel-accounts, with the word *safar*, *riḥla* or their equivalent in their titles. Rather, it is the dominance of travel as an organising notion in the narrative, whether or not this explicit identification has been made by way of nomenclature; this conceptual presence is often accompanied by an explicit, and even philosophical, reflection on the meaning of travel.[45] Again, it is necessary to be cautious in this respect, for we are aware that travel as a metaphor plays a key role in Persian literature from at least the time of Farid-ud-Din 'Attar (d. 1221), whose celebrated *Manṯiq-uṯ-Ṯair* is a sort of parable, wherein travel takes the place of a form of religious or spiritual quest. In the case of the greater part of our texts, we shall, however, find the sense of this relationship reversed, as what is metaphorical elsewhere comes to be oddly literalised.

The exercise that we are engaged in is one that would, in other more self-confident times, have been termed a reflection on the "history of mentalities". Recent historiography has, however, warned us to beware of this overly facile term, which covers a multitude of sins, and which can become distressingly vague in its application.[46] In our own defence, it must be stated that the collective entity that we are concerned with, which produced the texts which are under analysis here, was a relatively

generation, Mirza 'Ali Bakht Bahadur Muhammad Zahir-ud-Din Azfari, writing in the early nineteenth century; cf. *Wāqi'āt-i Azfarī*, ed. Syed Hamza Hussain Omari, gen. ed., T. Chandrasekharan (Madras, 1957), as also the analysis in Muzaffar Alam and Sanjay Subrahmanyam, "Power in prison: a Mughal prince in Shahjahanabad, ca. 1800", in Véronique Bouillier and Catherine Servan-Schreiber, eds., *De l'Arabie à l'Himalaya: chemins croisés, en hommage à Marc Gaborieau* (Paris, 2004), pp. 303–34.

45 A crucial early example in Persian is the travel-account of the Isma'ili poet Nasir-i Khusrau (1004–88), for which see *Nāṣir-i Khusraw's Book of travels (Safarnāmah): a parallel Persian–English text*, ed. and tr. Wheeler M. Thackston (Costa Mesa, 2001); and Charles Schefer, tr., *Sefer nameh: relation du voyage de Nassiri Khosrau en Syrie, en Palestine, en Egypte, en Arabie et en Perse, pendant les années de l'hégire 437–444 (1035–1042)* (Paris, 1881).

46 See G. E. R. Lloyd, *Demystifying mentalities* (Cambridge, 1990). Admittedly, Lloyd's purposes are far narrower than his title suggests, as his final resolution of matters around the notion of "modes of reasoning" brings out. Where this leaves the issue of sensibilities, for example, is entirely uncertain.

Figure 1. Babur crossing the Son river, *Bābur Nāma*, Persian text, late sixteenth century, National Museum, New Delhi, No. 50.336.

homogenous one, even if geographically dispersed across Iran, Central Asia, northern India (Hindustan) and even the Deccan. This is a group that corresponds in some general sense to what would be termed "the literati" in an imperial Chinese context, or, somewhat more optimistically, a "Republic of Letters" in the context of eighteenth-century Europe. The group in question for our purposes was a Persophone one, but not necessarily monolingual. If some of our authors are divided between Persian and Turkish, or Persian, Arabic and Turkish, still others (in the case of northern India) also partake of the vernaculars of that region, sometimes subsumed under the general notion of Hindawi.

The formation of this sphere of exchange, or ecumene as it has recently been termed by C. A. Bayly, is sufficiently complex to merit a study of its own, but some prefatory remarks may be in order here.[47] We are aware, though, that Persian began its career in northern India even before the foundation of the Sultanate of Delhi, under the Ghaznavids in the Punjab.[48] Thus, by the fifteenth century, when we begin our account, Persian had already had an extensive career in India, as a language linked to state-building, but also to religious and intellectual ferment. The language was used not only by migrants from Iran or Central Asia, as well as by local converts to Islam, but also increasingly by Hindus, who seem to have had growing access to it from the fourteenth and fifteenth centuries. A symbolic moment of great importance in this respect is the reign of Sikandar Lodi (1489–1517), when access to the *madrasas* is opened up in a significant fashion to Hindus, belonging, it would appear, largely to such groups as the Kayasthas and Khattris, but also probably including some of the scribal Brahmin castes.[49]

Entering this world implied access to a shared language and cultural vocabulary, but it also brought with it a literary canon that was transmitted, with the inevitable mutations wrought by time, from generation to generation. This structure of intellectual and literary references is a key aspect of the texts that we shall be examining, and it defined a world whose limits were seen largely in "secular" terms, if one might use such a term as early as the period in question. Thus, beyond the references to the Qur'an, or to the traditions of the Prophet (*ḥadīs̤*), with which these

[47] C. A. Bayly, *Empire and information: intelligence gathering and social communication in India, 1780–1870* (Cambridge, 1996), pp. 180–211.

[48] Sunil Sharma, *Persian poetry at the Indian frontier: Mas'ūd Sa'd Salmān of Lahore* (New Delhi, 2000).

[49] For a discussion, see Muzaffar Alam, "The culture and politics of Persian in precolonial Hindustan", in Sheldon Pollock, ed., *Literary cultures in history: reconstructions from South Asia* (Berkeley, 2003), pp. 131–98.

texts are also interspersed, one finds a set of poets of reference: inevitably, Sa'di, Nizami, Maulana Rum, 'Attar, Anwari, and a number of others find a place here.

The world we are concerned with is, we have noted, largely one of the circulation of manuscripts, and of orality: print does not make an appearance here until the late eighteenth or early nineteenth centuries. It is also a predominantly masculine world, for, although women surely partook of Persian literature, they represent a minority voice that is often hard to identify. An examination of the biographical dictionaries of poets reveals very few female names, and this is equally true of writers in prose. Indeed, Persian is something of an exception in this respect, for the Indian vernaculars of the period do have their fair share of female authors, in particular among those who compose devotional or erotic verse. In contrast, the occasional figure of the courtesan, or the erudite princess (such as Gulbadan, or in the seventeenth century, Jahanara and Zaib-un-Nisa), aside, women are a regrettably minor presence in Persian literature of the fifteenth to the eighteenth centuries.

If this is true of literature in general, it is even more true of the travel-account, which seems as a rule to have particularly privileged the male voice. Yet there are a few exceptions, and we may commence our journey into the world of the Persian travel-account with one such, even if it is geographically somewhat peripheral to our concerns. The account in question is the work of an anonymous Iranian woman, probably from the late seventeenth century, that is, the last decades of Safavid rule.[50] We know that she was a resident of Isfahan (though originally from a suburb of Qazwin called Daulatabad), and that she was the widow of a certain Mirza Khalil, who had apparently been a *raqam-nawīs* ("secretary") (or *munshī* ("scribe")) in the financial department of the Diwan-i A'la. Little other information is forthcoming concerning this highly unusual author, but, from a passage where she writes of the town of Urdubad (near the Ars river) with a certain affection, it has been suggested that this place may have been her birth-place, and thus perhaps her maternal grandparents' home. The author still had relatives there, besides a particularly close friend who had lived with her in Isfahan. Another

[50] Anonymous, "Safar Nāma-i Manẓūm-i ḥajj", ed. Rasul Ja'fariyan, in *Mīrāṣ-i Islāmī Irān* ("The heritage of Islamic Iran") (1373–4 Sh. / 1994–5), vol. IX pp. 337–91. The editor's introduction occupies pp. 337–46, and the text follows. The edition is based entirely on Tehran University Library, Mss. No. 2591 (though the editor has identified another manuscript that may be of the same text, in Baku, entitled, "Manāzil bain Iṣfahān-o-Makka"). The text has also been published separately as *Safar Nāma-i Manẓūm-i Ḥajj*, ed. Rasul Ja'fariyan (Qom, 1374 Sh. / 1995).

place that seems to call for particular attention is Kharwaniq in Ahr province, where the youthful governor (*ḥākim*) would appear to have been a relative. It may be noted that, in order to undertake the travel, the author has to leave her children behind in Isfahan, a fact for which she periodically expresses regret in her account.

If the author is unusual, so too is the text, which is written in the verse (*maṣnawī*) form, and comprises 1,200 verses.[51] Of these, a few verses do tell us about the author's life, as has been noted above, and the circumstances leading up to the voyage. It would seem that even after being widowed, she continued to live in Isfahan and had a fair number of relatives there, but that she did not get along with them, and hence thought to travel. Since she was going to travel, she decided that going to Mecca to perform the *ḥajj* was the best idea, and possibly a way of getting around the objections of interfering relatives.[52] The explicit idea was of consoling herself after her husband's recent death, but we may also remark that she must have belonged to a privileged family in order even to think of this. There are some other hints in the text itself in this direction: thus, during the voyage itself, she complains that at times one finds oneself in a dark pit, but at others in a "glittering house" (*ā'īna-k̲h̲āna*). It is also clear that the author was a woman of some education, and her style is quite explicitly influenced by that of the great poet Nizami Ganjawi, whom she both cites and mentions in her text.

We may briefly consider the itinerary described in the text, following the introductory section devoted to travel plans (*āhang-i safar*), and a brief visit to the tomb of the author's husband outside Isfahan. The main stages of the first part of the voyage are Kashan, Qom, Sawah and Qazwin, that is heading due north-west of Isfahan in the direction of the Caspian Sea. The town of Qazwin itself occupies a significant place in the description (for reasons we have noted above), and the traveller proceeds thereafter to Miyana, Tabriz and Urdubad, before making for Nakhjawan and Erevan in Armenia. The next section then brings us to the author's entry into the Ottoman domains, where she descends as far south as the

[51] For an earlier instance of a verse-text, see Muhyi Lari (*c.* 1510), *Futūḥ al-Ḥaramain*, ed. Rasul Ja'fariyan (Qom, 1373 Kh. / 1994); another edition is Muhyi Lari, *Futūḥ al-ḥaramain: Shā'ir-i sadah-i nuhum wa āg̲h̲āz-i sadah-i dahum*, ed. 'Ali Muhaddis (Tehran, 1366 Kh. / 1987). Much earlier, in the sixth century, we also find some verses (*qaṣīdas*) of Khaqani on the *ḥajj*, Medina, etc.

[52] It would have been highly unusual for a woman from India in the same period (or even later) to make the *ḥajj* in this fashion, on her own initiative, and still more so to leave an account. Cf. Barbara D. Metcalf, "The pilgrimage remembered: South Asian accounts of the *ḥajj*", in Eickelman and Piscatori, eds., *Muslim travellers*, pp. 85–107 (the title is somewhat misleading, as the essay deals solely with texts from the colonial period onwards).

Euphrates, the course of which she follows westward to Aleppo (Halab). We now follow the voyage through Damascus, to the Hijaz, with the *ḥajj* caravan making first for Medina, then Baqi, and at last to Mecca. After a period spent in the area, at 'Arafat and Mina, as well as Mecca and Medina, the text ends while the author is on her way back to Aleppo. We may note that the latter part of the journey, in the Ottoman domains, was clearly done as part of a *ḥajj* caravan, while it would seem that the earlier travels in Iran were accomplished in a small group, perhaps simply the author accompanied by a few servants, and companions.

To partake somewhat of the flavour of the text, we translate some of the initial verses, in which the author sets the context for her eventual departure for the *ḥajj*. Thus, the text begins as follows:

> When the deceitful, turning sky slashed my liver,
> snatching off my friend, my life's breath,
> restful sleep was outlawed from my bed,
> and no other salve came to my mind but travel.
> I had neither sleep at night, nor peace by day,
> until I readied myself for circling the Ka'aba.
> I girded my waist, and stretched out my arms,
> taking a brave step in that direction.
> Not one of my family was by my side,
> like Majnun, I headed into the desert.
> Of what use is human friendship?
> God's companionship is enough for the helpless.
> Seeing my family's faithlessness,
> I left Isfahan as swift as the wind.

The first section takes her then to her husband's grave, where she meditates a while, and recalls the luxury of her past life in Isfahan. This done, the journey begins in earnest, and the husband receives little further attention, with the first sections of the travel-account proper being rather functional in character. The distances traversed are given in terms of leagues (*farsang* or *farsakh*), first to the pleasant town of Mominabad, and then along a route interspersed with mountains and streams, as the author makes for Kashan. Four relatively uneventful days are spent here, and the traveller then departs for Sansan, where she attempts to take rest at a somewhat uncomfortable inn (*ribāṭ*), after having spent some time on a bumpy road. For the first time, we find the thought that the journey might turn out not to be as much of a pleasure as had been anticipated. The next stop is then Qasimabad, where the inn is somewhat better, and it is here that we find an oblique mention of travelling companions (*rafiqān*). The travellers now arrive at the great religious centre of Qom, where they make it a point to render homage to the tomb of Ma'suma, the sister of Imam 'Ali Raza, before resuming the journey by night, in order to be able to attain Sawah. Here, we gather that the travellers are on camel-back, and it is by this means of transport that they eventually arrive, weary of the road, at the town of Sawah.

However, a disappointment is in store for them: Sawah is like a veritable desert (*kharābabād*), like Destiny turned upside down, the town being largely abandoned, with the metaphorical owl hooting over it, as it were. It is with a great sense of relief that they move on from there, to Khushka, a place by a winding river. Here, the party rests at an inn by the river, and then again sets out at night. This pattern of night travel seems to be on account of the heat of the day, though this fact is never made explicit. Despite this stratagem, our traveller is frankly miserable, and confesses that she broke down and cried from time to time, as her bones began to ache from all the travel. The moonlit nights were but a small consolation, until they reached Arasang, a pleasing place, with plane trees lining the route for two leagues along the way. The road is no longer bumpy, indeed it is so flat it might have been the familiar *maidān* of Isfahan, surrounded by gardens and streams.

Yet, once more, it was necessary to leave Paradise for Hell, as it were, as the next stage was again rather rough. After some leagues of misery, the traveller arrived at last in sight of the town of Qazwin. The air (*hawā*) in Qazwin was not known to be particularly fine, she notes, as the weather kept changing between hot and cold, and though it was warm when they entered the town, it became quite chilly the next morning. Here, the party stayed for all of twelve days, and quite enjoyed themselves despite the critical remarks. They strolled on the streets with regular trees on both sides, and it was as if in those twelve days, they had a taste of all the four seasons. The party then decided to leave the place and go to Daulatabad for a brief stay. This was a spot located some three leagues from Qazwin proper. Here, on camping, the author evokes a sense of past times, remembering her own father and grandfather, and rendering a brief description of the town, where the girls all look like dolls with red cheeks, and were most welcoming to the author. After staying there four days, with every sense of enjoyment, the time came to move on. One league outside the town, she met up with a youth, who had been sent out to accompany her. He was called Darvesh, and is described as being wise and well-mannered. He asked her to come and stay in his house, at a place called Khurramabad, which had earlier been deserted, but was now repopulated, in part on the efforts of this very youth. He was extremely hospitable, and gave her all sorts of comforts; indeed, he was as a veritable slave to her, to the point that she became quite flustered. This welcome was even beyond what she had got from her own relatives in Isfahan, she declares. The implicit notion is that the wealthy widow is being cunningly courted, perhaps on account of instructions sent out by well-meaning friends and relatives. However, this is to no avail, and she presently takes leave, departing at night. As for the pleasant young man, he accompanied her for two way-stations, and she praises him, saying that his mother should be lauded too for having brought him up so well. Could such hospitality be found elsewhere in Iran?

The party having rested awhile at a village, they once again made their way, this time through the desert (*ṣaḥrā*), until they reached the Dasht-i Minu, around which area the landscape became verdant once more. The route was like this for six leagues at a stretch; and the breeze was paradisaical, with the perfume of amber. This is a part of the route where the traveller will do well to dawdle a little, our author writes, so pleasant is it. So, proceeding relatively slowly, they arrived at Khurram Darra, a populous village (*deh*), with plenty of water, where they made camp. As sunset came, and darkness spread over the sky, they set out once more, having saddled up (literally, having "tied the camel-litter" (*maḥmil*)).

Though our traveller advanced, she assures her readers that her heart stayed behind, as it were, in the places they had just traversed. The next place they passed was Sultaniyya, where she decided not to stay, as it was in her view an accursed town. Instead they made for Zanjan, where the party camped for a day and rested. Everyone was tired, both our traveller and her companions. There is a suggestion that there were some mischief-makers in the place, and that this posed a problem. So, they moved on quickly, even though the route that they followed was not of the best. They advanced by five leagues, and we note that they are still in the so-called Dasht-i Minu. Another potential suitor arrives to pursue the prosperous widow but to no avail, as the party moves on to Koh-i Qaplantu. They knew this was a hard route, and our traveller confesses her trepidation at this prospect, for this was the beginning of mountainous country (*kuhistān*). The mountains were very steep, and it seemed at times that the camel was flying in the sky, while, at other times, he bent so low, it seemed he was eating grass. At times, one could hear the angels (*malak*) reading their prayers (with their prayer-beads), and at other times one could count the golden scales on the backs of fish. This section was of four leagues' duration, and presently, with God's aid, they managed to see the town of Miyana in front of them. On descending from the mountains, they found it was extremely hot, while the people in that area (*wādī*) were also not of pleasant countenance.

Our traveller has also fallen ill by now, though this is only hinted at indirectly at this stage in the text. Despite being feverish, she must bear up with more leagues of rough route, though she confesses that her body was aching, and she was feeling quite heartsick and despondent. The others in the party try to encourage her, telling her that the destination is not far. So, passing through slightly better country, somewhat fuller of greenery, they reach sight of the settlement of 'Abbas Neki around sunrise. Here, the party camps by the side of a field, and the traveller is still feverish, which causes her body and lips to burn. In fact, on this front, things were getting worse and worse, but in spite of this they travelled all night long. Then, at long last, the medicines she was taking began to have an effect. As the fever was leaving her bones, they moved on, with the idea that the town of Tabriz was some seven leagues distant. That night, the traveller was unable to sleep, and the route was also particularly bumpy. By the time she reached Tabriz, she also began to think of reaching Urdubad. After six days in the town, she leaves and advances five leagues to a town called Sar.

We may pause briefly to take stock of the first part of the text, where a number of the author's literary habits have been laid bare. It is worth noting that, despite the ostensibly religious character of the journey (the destination is, after all, the Hijaz), the text in its first sections is fairly worldly in its orientation. With the exception of the visit to the shrine in Qom, no particular religious exertions are to be noted, with the author obviously preferring to restrict herself, on the one hand, to a description of places, landscapes and the sentiments they evoke, and, on the other hand, to concentrating on a personal itinerary of encounters and illnesses. Some literary devices are also on repetitive display. Thus, the sun seems always to turn saffron (*za'frān*) as evening falls, and the sky inevitably takes on clothes of purple. On more than one occasion, the author herself leaves a town like a sharp wind (*ṣarṣar*). We may also note that nature is compared to artifice, rather than the other way around: thus, wayside flowers are said to be as pretty as if a master of embroidery had done *chikan*-work there. In comparison to male authors, wine-metaphors are rare, and one of the relatively uncommon references to the Saqi (wine-bearer), whose hand is reddened as if with red tulips (*lāla*), occurs in the section near Tabriz.

The voyage continues then, with a brief stay at Sar, a pleasant hamlet, full of gardens, and waters flowing through its canals. Now they travel more by day rather than exclusively by night. They stay once more at the house of a local notable (*dihqān*), who again is a distinguished and hospitable man, treated locally like a prince. The night passes quickly enough, and the traveller (on a fast she-camel) and her companions leap ahead like leopards into the mountains. This enjoyable, if rough, journey came to a halt at a place where a male relative of hers lived, and he welcomed her with great hospitality and several good things to eat; a restful night was spent, and they departed at dawn. This time they went into further mountain ranges; and this passage too was full of flowers, and the sound of nightingales, as well as the sight of streams. Two leagues were traversed, and they thought that it was time to take rest, both for themselves and also for the good of the camel (*shutur*), which is here allowed to take voice (by way of poetic licence) and suggest it is quite weary. So, the party dismounts near a half-ruined village, which is unnamed.

It seems the weather is better here than in the earlier phase and there is more greenery. A new phase begins though, which is again in a desert area. There are no flowers, or greenery, or even grass to be seen in the approach to Kharwaniq. Here, they meet the young and competent *ḥākim* (or local governor), again related to the author, and termed a veritable Aristotle in his understanding. This youthful notable, another suitor by all accounts, takes care of her for four days in the best style. He would salute her every morning, and ask her to state what her requests were so that he could serve her like a slave (*g̱hulām*). He wanted her to stay for a week, but on the fifth day she left, while he sent his own servants to accompany her on the way. Four leagues from the spot, she reached Uri, a pleasant place with its gardens and water flowing. This is a populated hamlet with all sorts of goods, and she stayed there as a guest of a local notable; but, alas, she gets the fever once more that evening. Nevertheless, the next morning she sets out. At one league from the place, they reached the banks of the Ars river, and crossed it; some lines are devoted to the snake-like river, and the play of the waters. She crossed the river in a boat (*sanbak*), and is presently at the town of Urdubad, to which she has been looking forward for some time now.

Here, our author is given a particularly warm welcome, and many people, both young and old, come to see her, and accompany her litter like waves on the Red Sea. Presently, she reaches the quarter where a friend from Isfahan lived. This woman was closer to her than a sister, it is stated, but, unfortunately, they were separated from each other by a distance of forty way-stations (*manzil*), so that they were both in a constant state of separation (*hijrat*). It would seem they had spent two decades apart, but, at last, the dark night of separation had been transformed into the dawn of meeting with the beloved.[53] Our traveller spends all of twenty days here, "in the lane of that valued heart-burning friend" (*ba kū-'i ān garāmī yār-i dil soz*). The characteristic diction of Persian poetry of the epoch aside, the particular expressions of affection used for this friend (termed at one place the author's "sweet life", *jān-i shīrīn*) seem to lend credibility to a distinct suggestion of homo-eroticism in this section.[54] The author laments that Fortune did not allow her to enjoy herself to the full, as she was ill a good part of the time in Urdubad; she could hence not keep company (*ham-ṣuḥbat*) with her friend for more than a mere instant (*yak zamān*). Her other relatives and friends in that place were also extremely hospitable, and the place and its water and air were wonderful; it was at the edges of the mountains, in a valley of pleasant climate. The author declares she is ashamed that she was unable to be worthy of her friend's hospitality, as she was so ill. First, there were the pains of separation, then those of illness. When the time came to leave, both friends hung their heads in grief. When she left, the friend shed tears of blood, and her skirt was coloured by this. She wept so, that it was as if she were in mourning, and others too wept at this spectacle of grief. The friend neither ate nor drank water all day long, as tears kept flowing like rain. When evening came, the sun itself went to hide its face in the river.

At length, our author managed to tear herself away and advanced to Faizabad, where she did not rest but instead looked at the gardens; even here, she continued to think of the painful separation from her friend. The gardens seemed insipid and uninteresting, as she kept weeping. Evening came, and she advanced from that place, consoling herself with the thought that she was going to the House of God. So, she pushed ahead with her camel and went towards a spot near Ardabil, but here too she continued to miss her friend. There was a great storm here at night, which made travel rather difficult. At last, the party managed to get beyond the stormy phase, and the camel was urged towards Nahram.

53 "Safar Nāma-i Manẓūm-i ḥajj", p. 360.

54 This theme is dealt with more extensively in an essay by Kathryn Babayan, "'In spirit we ate of each other's sorrow': female companionship in seventeenth-century Safavi Iran", in Kathryn Babayan and Afsaneh Najmabadi, eds., *Middle Eastern and sexuality studies: translations across temporal and geographical zones of desire* (Ann Arbor, forthcoming).

Again, the habit in this phase was to spend the night in places, and to start the journey in the morning, rather than the other way around.

In this fashion, they eventually reached Nakhjawan, a place with an unpleasant climate, in our author's view. When she drank water there it was like blood, and she fell ill immediately, a recurring theme, as we have seen by now. For eight days, she nursed this illness on the spot. She was also told that there were many bandits (*rahzan*), and was advised not to travel alone. The advice was instead that she should wait to get together some other people, in order to travel more safely. This was not a happy solution, and she hence prayed to God: "You have called me to Your House, now help me to reach there. Cure me, I am in a helpless state, far away from my family and friends." In response to this prayer (*du'ā*), and two tears that wet her skirt (*dāman*), the request was answered. The next day, friends brought news that a caravan (*qāfila*) had arrived there. She was also told that the 'Ajam Aqasi, the Amir-ul-Hujjaj (or head of the *ḥajj* caravan) from Iran, was himself on his way there. This was very pleasing news indeed, and she presently got together with the caravan, in order to head towards Qarabaghlar. There were horses everywhere, and they advanced like the waves of the ocean for four leagues. After this, everyone unloaded their camels at Shalil. Here, they rested till late afternoon and then advanced as swift as birds.

They were travelling once more by night, and the caravan appeared beautiful in the moonlight. In the valley of Injaq, which they passed through, they were, however, greatly beset by gnats, mosquitoes and flies (*pashsha*), as they advanced eight leagues to Erevan. However, this too turned out to be a place where the climate did not suit the author, and the water was so bad in character that it drove her quite mad, and finished off her last remaining strength. She began to doubt whether she would ever return to Isfahan, as she could scarcely eat in this condition. Twenty days were spent like this, in a state of exhaustion and depression. For the first time since the beginning of the voyage, an explicitly exotic social spectacle is noted, as churches (*kalīsa*) come in sight, and they spend one night in a town of the Christians, called Shirwan.

ENTERING THE OTTOMAN DOMAINS

These are still Safavid territories though, and they remain within the jurisdiction of the Shah until they arrive at, first, Qurkh and then Kirmanlar. Here, the travellers heave a sigh of sadness. Everyone was a fierce lion in his own land, they reflect, but now they would be subject to humiliations at the hands of the dreaded Ottomans ("Rumis" or Romans). So, in anticipation of this, they sleep an unhappy sleep, realising that, from this point on, the name of Haidar (which is to say 'Ali) will become hard to mention, as they are in the land of fanatic Sunnis.[55] Advancing five leagues, a river is crossed, and, another seven leagues later, they arrive at a high and formidable hillside fort called Aqni'a Qarshash, which is the first manifest sign of Ottoman power (*nishān-i Rūm*) in the area, where the Rumis swarm like ants. They stay for two days at this fort, and then advance another three leagues, eventually reaching Qara Hamza.

After a brief stay at an inn, the caravan advances as far as Qarchai, which is once more swarming with Ottoman soldiers who begin to demand taxes (*'ushūr*) from the goods (*ajnās*) of the travellers. After four days, they go on from there by six leagues to a place called Chuban Garapasi in the same valley, having now entered an open plain (*bayābān*), en route to the town of Erzurum. Here, from fear of the Ottomans, no one unloads their goods. Instead, that very night, they set out again, till they come to a place called Baba Khatun in the morning, ten leagues from Erzurum, and then decide to keep going from there. At two leagues distance, they are accosted once more by Rumi soldiers who want taxes and tribute (*kh̲arāj-o-bāj*) amounting to ninety *tomāns*. The 'Ajam Aqasi enters into an argument with them, and the faces on both sides become flushed. Swords leave their scabbards, arrows begin to fly, and some gunshots are fired. The people of the Iranian party are as brave as lions, the author assures us, in this engagement that takes place on a bridge, so that some blood is spilt in this process.

The men in the party advance to the front, but, when the Rumis see this, they also advance to loot the caravan which has been abandoned by the men. However, the Iranian Hajis then come back to defend the caravan on their horses. Some elephants too fall into the water. At length, the Rumis flee like dogs, and, giving thanks to God, the Iranian party advances. Moving rapidly and taking short rests, they make their way to Erzincan, and, a league beyond, the Iranian Hajis are able to see the Euphrates from the foot of the mountain. They make camp by the banks of that river, and sleep. The next morning, they think of advancing, for no one feels safe in this area, and they are determined to get out of there as soon as possible. However, they are in mountainous country, which makes rapid movement difficult. The party seems to be mixed in terms of

[55] "Safar Nāma-i Manẓūm-i ḥajj", p. 365.

its mounts, for some are still on camels while others are on horseback. Five days are spent in these mountains, and they are at the upper part of the Euphrates, which roars by as if it is a python with its mouth open. If one's foot were to slip, the river would swallow one up instantly, the author assures us. At one place, the foot of the author's camel slips, and they begin to slide down. Somehow, God saves her, and gives her a new lease of life, for a brave man from amongst the Hajis, a saviour like the Prophet Khizr, grabs hold of the camel and stops it from sliding further.

Making their way through winding roads and semi-deserted villages and copper mines, the poor Hajis advance slowly, with a good number of horses and camels dying in this area. It is thus to their great relief that they reach the town of Agin, thanking God for his mercy. This is a fine place on the banks of the Euphrates that gives out a cool breeze. The water is like glass and there are lovely gardens all around. Unfortunately the people there are all born out of wedlock (*ḥarāmī*), whether dignitaries or common-folk, notes our author, whose hostility towards the Ottomans is unremitting. In view of the fact that they are surrounded thus by robbers, the caravan decides once more to leave as quickly as they can. It is a very hard day's journey that follows. On the one hand, there is the awful sight of Rumis in a crowd, and, on the other hand, they fear for their lives and goods. It is as if the Day of Judgment (*qiyāmat*) is at hand. The land is sweet, but it is as if they have poison in their mouths; the Hajis also are being robbed left and right, to the extent that they have only sighs left in their wallets. So, she warns the reader in verse, do not take the route to Agin, for you may lose your goods, your life, and even your faith (*dīn*, rhyming with "Agin"). It would have been much better to go via Mosul, she feels retrospectively, and thus avoid this unsavoury route.

At last, it seems, things are on the mend, as they make their way from the Ottoman heartland and its miseries. They are not far from Aleppo now, and the town appears in the distance, like a nostalgic reflection (*shabīh*) of Isfahan. The shops, *maidān* and bazaar are in fact all like the Safavid capital, declares our relieved author. All sorts of strength-giving fruits are available there; the figs in particular are as sweet as sugar, and highly recommended, while the water-melons too are as red as rubies, delicate, sweet and full of water. The town-dwellers are kinder than even your own sisters and mothers, in notable contrast to the dreaded Rumis (though we are still in Ottoman territory). As Aleppo (Halab) is Isfahan's twin, tears begin to flow from her eyes as she remembers her own homeland (*waṭan*). She lets out a heart-burning sigh, enough to burn up the whole world, recalls her children and relatives at home, and weeps like a flute (*ney*). May she now be saved from further sufferings! Her body is tired, she is sick of the saddle, and she cannot take any more, she declares. For how much longer must she tolerate this separation? She begs the breeze to carry a message to Isfahan to this effect. She is melting like a candle in this separation (*hijr*), in order to receive the gift of circumambulating the Ka'aba from God. Then, she departs from Paradise-like (*jannat-sarisht*) Aleppo after six days, during the course of which they buy provisions for their further journey. They have been joined by another *qāfila*, also from Iran, making up a huge and noisy crowd.

Once more, in this phase, the tendency is to depart in the middle of the night in the usual noisy fashion, placing their saddles on their camels. The shifting pattern is interesting. First, as we have noted, while in Iran, they travel by night, beginning at nightfall; then by day in the mountains, setting out at dawn; and now, in the phase beyond Aleppo, they start in the middle of the night (*nima-'i shab*). The first phase is broadly to Tabriz, the second from Tabriz to Aleppo, and the third from Aleppo on. The caravans are heading now for the heartland of Sham (Syria), and here they change their pattern, in order to leave at nightfall. Travelling all night long, they camp briefly in the morning by an orange grove (*nāranj-o-turanjistān*), at the gates of Syria. The Iranian pilgrims declare that they are downcast (a pun on the word Sham, meaning both "Syria" and "evening"), for this is the place where the Umayyads (the descendants of Abu Sufyan) had been at the time when Husain (the King of the Martyrs, or *shāh-i shahīdān*) had been brutally killed. They must have carried his head through here, reflects our author, and the buildings must have bowed their own heads as he passed. The traveller's own eyes are filled with tears at this imagined "memory".

Our author, nevertheless, is greatly enamoured of the place. For this place is not just Sham, it is Paradise-on-Earth, no less. There are fountains everywhere, washing her heart of all rancour. Rather than expand on this, she focuses on the water and bread there. The water is like elixir here, so sweet and fragrant that it gives you new life, while the bread (*nān*) here is as white as snow (*barf*), or a piece of the moon, and made as if milk would drip from it. As for the fruits there, what can one say of the grapes, which are beyond all praise? Then there is another delicious fruit (*kuyaj*), as well as roses, all beyond compare. After two days, the Iranian caravan meets up with the Ottoman Amir ul-Hajj, and his army. His party is compared to the Darya-i Muhit (or "Circumscribing Ocean") in relation to the two other caravan-seas.[56] They advance together as far as Damascus. Here, the Iranians, cursing, wailing and crying, pass through the valley of this evil place (*kharābastān*), but curiously do not stop long at Damascus, the place of the accursed Al-i Sufiyan (Umayyads). Six leagues beyond Damascus, they reach the army camp (*lashkargāh*) of the Pasha, where an even larger army waits. There was also a huge crowd of pilgrims and attendants now, and, after staying five days, on the sixth day they advance with the Pasha. At first, they pass through plains full of flowers. There are 130 companies (*bairāq*) of 30 soldiers each, most armed with guns, and 300 others on camel-back. The caravan is thus with a full escort now, and there are also 40 singers and musicians accompanying them; there are also camels carrying money from the Ottoman treasury. This is all a most impressive sight and our author spends some verses describing it.

The desert part of the voyage now finally begins, the area being filled, it is noted, with evil people (*shaiṭān*) all along the way. In this desert, for the first two leagues, are the sinners of the past who have been transformed into rocks. This is the land of those who have disobeyed the prophets Lut (Lot), Salih and Hud (Heber), and been destroyed as a consequence. No grass is to be seen, only thorns, and one could notice birds, but no animals save some rabbits, lizards and the odd scorpion. Travellers passed through there with their heads bowed. One oasis follows another in the account, as the caravan continues, usually by night, and very occasionally by day when the distance between two oases justifies it. The text contains few details here, save that they are accompanied by the Pasha and other important people. Eventually, they reach ʻAqaba, a difficult part of the route, and from there go on to Mudawwara, a distance of some ten leagues. With their brightly coloured flags, it is noted, the caravan transforms the desert into a garden, while the caravan on the move with the Pasha is termed an impressive sight, like Solomon's Throne, the *Takht-i Sulaimān*. Passing the night at the Qilʻa-i Haidar (which the author prefers in this sectarian version to its other name, Khaibar), the Pasha orders the caravan to move on to Muʻazzam, where the tents are spread once more. Sixteen further leagues take them to Maghash al-Ruzz and then to Madiyan-i Salih, at a distance of twenty leagues. In passing the latter spot, those in the caravan empty their guns

[56] See, in this context, Suraiya Faroqhi, *Pilgrims and sultans: the hajj under the Ottomans 1517–1683* (London, 1994), pp. 58–73 (on the Damascus caravan), 134–9 (on Iranian pilgrims). The route described here is quite unorthodox from the viewpoint of Faroqhi's map of "Pilgrimage routes to Mecca and Medina" (facing p. 1).

(*top-o-tufang*) in the air, according to the custom.[57] Occasionally the quality of the fruit or other produce strikes our author, but the only other matter worth remarking is the desert sunset, for which a verse from Nizami is cited: "As if the 'Anqa bird had swallowed the ruby grain".[58]

The picturesque thus takes over in the narrative. The music accompanying them is like the music produced by David, and they now appear to be relaxed in their movements, after the vexations of the earlier part of the desert journey. When night falls, there are hundreds of lamps and candles to be seen, and the people in the caravan are now in a state of expectation, impatient to kiss the threshold of the Prophet. Advancing by torchlight at night, when dawn breaks and the sun rises, they see the date-groves at a distance. This is the sign that they have come to the vicinity of Medina, which is soon visible from behind the hills. This is a great moment of joy, when the author speaks to her heart about her faith. For this is the shrine of their master, the Prophet of the Prophets. Here sleeps the leader, who will deliver them in the life hereafter, the Chosen One, the King of the Pious. Illiterate by title (*'ummī*), the Friend of God, he is the Matchless Prophet. A good number of such devotional verses follow, all in praise of the Prophet apart from others that praise his daughter Fatima.

Our author now moves to a description of the shrines of the Jannat ul-Baqi. Here are the graves of the Chahar Mas'um, the Four Innocents who were mistreated by the world; they will recommend the author and her community in the hereafter. The first is Hasan, the favourite of the Prophet, and the source of pleasure for his mother Fatima Zehra and his father Haidar; the second is 'Ali ibn Husain; the third is Imam Baqir, king of certain knowledge (*'ilm ul-yaqīn*), the Fifth Imam; and the fourth grave is that of the True Master, Imam Ja'far Sadiq. She begins to weep at this significant Shi'i site, the place where even Gabriel spreads his wings and stops awhile. But here she is astonished and disappointed to see little material decoration, save the divine light that pervaded the land. All four graves are in the same enclosure, and covered with some old sack-cloth (*kuhna būriya*). This prompts the following verse from our traveller's pen:

> That place, twin to the garden of Paradise,
> does not even have a candle burning here.
> O breeze, go back to Isfahan,

[57] "Safar Nāma-i Manẓūm-i ḥajj", p. 380; also see Khwaja 'Abdul Karim, *Bayān-Wāqi': a biography of Nādir Shāh Afshār and the travels of the author*, ed. K. B. Nasim (Lahore, 1970), discussed in Chapter 6 below.

[58] "Safar Nāma-i Manẓūm-i ḥajj", p. 381.

and give the news to the Sultan of Iran.
O just king! Where are you?
Why are you indifferent to this Paradise-like place?
Come and see how the Prophet's family is treated.
Each of them is like an illumined star,
but all of them are in one *sarāy*,
with a wooden enclosure, and covered with sack.
O slave of Haidar's descendants,
send carpets becoming of their stature.
Decorate this heavenly garden with golden candles,
shining like the brilliant sun.[59]

Thus, she demands, let the eyes of their rivals (*raqīb*) open, on seeing all this; the Safavids and Ottomans are treated here, in an interesting metaphor, as rival lovers.

Now, the Pasha had decided to stay in Medina two days, and the second afternoon the Iranians too have to leave the place, weeping, for their heart is not yet full, nor have they kissed the Prophet's threshold enough. Once more, they enter the desert, and three leagues from there, take off their shoes and don the *iḥrām-i ḥaram*, the special garb of the Hajji, at the Masjid-i Shajra, the mosque for the Shi'is. From now on, our traveller states, there would be no more music, as each pilgrim would say "Labbaik" (I am present). The party thus advances by stages until they reach the Wadi-i Fatima. Their habit in this part of the journey is to spend a part of the night at a spot and then move on. At last, they think, with their eyes lighting up, the separation from the Beloved is coming to an end, as they advance towards the Ka'aba. All their pains and sorrows are set aside. On the fifth (implicitly, of the month of Zi-Hijja), the Ka'aba appears before them like the moon. Here, in low-lying gravelly land, they pitch their tents, and here too our author remembers and integrates verses from Nizami into her text:

How fortunate are they who, after a wait,
attain their desires at last.

Our author declares that she is so happy that she almost goes into a faint. She can neither open her mouth nor even express her happiness. It is nearly as if she has no strength left to go around the Ka'aba. Some time later, she feels somewhat better but still no words will come out. At length, with a great effort, she performs a prostration (*sijda*) before God

[59] "Safar Nāma-i Manẓūm-i ḥajj", p. 383.

Figure 2. Representation of the Ka'aba in Mecca with details of the holy sites surrounding it, *Rauẓa-i Khair ul-Bashar*, National Museum, New Delhi, No. 55.56/1.

and asks him for help, demanding that, on the Day of Judgment, she should not be in the company of Christians (*naṣārā*).[60] Then, crossing the Bab-us-Salam Gate with the sense that she has become indifferent to all things worldly, but that her heart is still full of fear (*khauf*) for the sins she has committed, tears come welling out of her eyes. What can she tell of the place where she finds herself? In her state of exaltation, the Ka'aba appears like a tall youth (*naujawān*) standing in front of her, like a cypress tree, wearing a fragrant cover like a saddle-cloth, and an embroidered sash on his waist (these being the Qur'anic verses on the Ka'aba cover). She says to her heart: "Do you know where you have come? You are in the harem of God [*ḥarīm-i kibriyā*]." Her heart replies: "Are you awake or dreaming?" "No, she is awake", she replies. So saying, she begins to carry her sins into what she terms the "Lane of Yazdan" – Yazdan being the Persian, pre-Islamic god, carried over here to mean Allah – as she begins to circumambulate the Ka'aba. After walking round it seven times, the burden of her sins is lessened. Then, she left for Safa, where, similarly, she dusts her skirt off metaphorically, and gets rid of some of her sins. But the path is all too short for the multitude of her sins, even though she takes it seven times. She then performs her ablutions with Zamzam water, and drinks some of it. This rids her of much of her sorrow, pain and ills.

Now, she ties on her new garb for the *ḥajj* proper at 'Arafat. This is to happen the next day, and, during the intervening night, she stops at Mina and rests there. Then in the mid-morning (*chāsht*), she reaches 'Arafat. Despite the fact that, as a mere clod of clay, she cannot perform a worthy pilgrimage, she persists. In the afternoon, she goes on to Mush'ir. By the time she reaches there, night has fallen. Here, she puts out her prayer tent, and chooses a bunch of pebbles to be thrown to kill the Devil (*shaiṭān*). All night long, she prays to God, to forgive her for her sins. Much repentance is expressed over the course of several verses. When morning comes, she goes out of the valley of Mush'ir and reaches the Jamra-i 'Uqba where she threw the stones. Then, in Mina, she settles her camp, buys a camel, and then sacrifices it on 'Id (that is, the tenth day of Zi-Hijja). She also cuts some of the hair in the front of her head, according to the custom. Then, she returns to the Ka'aba and goes around it again seven times. Only then does she have the sense of receiving the "letter of freedom from the hell-fire" (*khaṭṭ-i āzādī az dozakh*), that is, to the effect that her sins are washed off. Our relieved traveller now goes

[60] The significance of this rather obscure request is unclear to us.

back to Safa, in order to thank God. The rituals of the *ḥajj* have now been completed, but she nevertheless goes a second time to Mina. She tries to clear her heart of any residual impure thoughts, once more going through the ritual of stoning the three pillars. This ritual is repeated on a third occasion too.

Now, at last, our author turns to recounting the festivities at Mina organised by the Ottomans. These are so formidable that the planet Venus (Zehra) herself would have been prepared to dance there. There are illuminations for two leagues distance, and fireworks, and all sorts of other such celebrations, organised by people from Syria. Noise and drums (*naqqāra*) are constantly to be heard everywhere, while cannons are also being fired from time to time. It is as if the heavenly cock were crowing mightily. This goes on till dawn, and the next evening the Egyptians and the people of the Sharif are in charge of the celebrations. This goes on for three days in Mina. On the third day, she leaves for the Bait ul-Haram, and then settles her camp nearby. After a couple more days passed in prayer, this period comes to an end.

Seven days after the 'Id-i Qurban, the caravan and the Amir ul-Hajj prepare to depart. Each bone in her body gives a sigh at this, so regretful is she. Her heart, already wounded from earlier separations, now feels this would be another separation. On the other hand, she has to go to Medina. So, with tears in her eyes, she metaphorically tears her garment. One more prayer is addressed to God asking for His Mercy. A farewell has to be said, nonetheless. It had taken her seven months to arrive there, passing through mountains and deserts, taking great risks. At times, her camel had almost fallen to its death, and at others she had taken a rock for a bed. So, regretfully, she leaves Mecca, climbing her camel's saddle. Even the saddle seems like a coffin to her. However, whether she wanted to or not, the Amir ul-Hujjaj was going to take her along.

With this pain of separation in her breast, she reaches Medina. Once more, she goes to the Prophet's shrine, and the desire to visit this holy place consoles her somewhat. On the fifth day, the Pasha orders them to leave from here. They enter the desert, once more as swift as the wind. Her heart is now full of a still further separation, that from Medina. She once more reproaches the turning sky (*gardūn-i ghaddār*) for his mischief, but notes in passing that the Pasha too is in a great hurry. The return is so rapid that there is very little rest to be had. The party make it back post-haste to the doors of Syria, with practically no time to eat or take rest. Having entered the town of Darwaza-i Sham, they take rest there, with the author remarking:

How good it would be,
not to have to go to the Ka'aba;
or having gone there,
how good if one did not have to return.
The way back from there seemed to turn
my being into dust.
An axe seemed to cut
my feathery life-line in half.

On reaching Syria, the tired pilgrims decide to rest for twelve days. Then, they tie up their goods and turn in the direction of Aleppo, and from there to 'Urfa. And here our text abruptly ends.

REFLECTIONS

The text of the widow of Mirza Khalil, which is unfortunately our only identification for the author of our travel-narrative, is both characteristic and atypical in the tradition that we shall survey in the chapters that follow. As we have remarked above, it is certainly rare as a text, insofar as female authors scarcely exist otherwise amongst our corpus. We have followed the text closely by way of example (and always at the risk of trying the reader's patience), in order to make plain a methodological point already set out somewhat summarily above. It is, of course, clear that one could treat this text principally as a source of information, in order to demonstrate, for instance, the particular troubles faced by the Iranians in performing the *ḥajj* in the late seventeenth century, and we can also glean numerous useful details on how precisely the *ḥajj* was performed in the period.[61] The fact that the graves of the Shi'i Imams in Medina were apparently neglected at this time, and covered with ordinary sack-cloth or a split reed-mat, eliciting a poetic protest from the author, is significant from the point of view of sectarian history.

Of particular significance is the unremitting hostility shown to the Ottomans in the text, which may be contrasted to the treatment of others (such as the inhabitants of Aleppo), who lived under Ottoman domination but were not themselves considered to be "Rumis". The fact that

[61] See Ahmad Miskin, *Ḥajj Nāma*, excerpts of which are published as an appendix to Muhyi Lari, *Futūḥ al-ḥaramain*, ed. Ja'fariyan; and, more generally, for Iranian accounts of the *ḥajj* (largely from the period of the Qajar dynasty), see Rasul Ja'fariyan, ed., *Ba Sū-i Umm-ul-Qurā* (Qom, n. d.), containing the texts of Hajji 'Ali Isfahani, Muhammad 'Ali Mirza ibn Fath 'Ali Shah, Mirza Muhammad Muhandis and the editor. Compare Bert G. Fragner, *Persischen Memoirenliteratur als Quelle zu neueren Geschichte Irans* (Wiesbaden, 1979).

Iranian (and Shi'i) pilgrims were generally persecuted was widely believed at this time, as we see from the following verse by the poet Husain Abiwardi.

> Each member of that impure group,
> every year martyrs Hajis for no reason.
> The Ka'aba, mourning the massacre of these innocents,
> turns its cloth ever to black.
> On account of these martyrs from 'Ajam,
> the waters of Zamzam hide underground in shame.[62]

However, our purpose in choosing this text to begin our exposition is somewhat different. For the text in question is particularly unusual in being a text written in verse, and thus bound to formal requirements from which prose texts were, at least to an extent, liberated. How could such a text have been composed? We must imagine that the author kept notes of her travels, and from these composed a text at the end of the voyage, at a moment when the exigencies of literary convention could more easily be met. The question then poses itself as to the nature of the text, as memory (and thus retrospective in character) as opposed to contemporary, on-the-spot portraiture on the hoof (as it were), and reflecting the shifting moods of the moment.

Our position is that, paradoxically, though most of the texts that we shall consider (like their counterparts in a Chinese, Ottoman or Spanish context) were composed or revised substantially at the end of the cycle of voyage, yet they, at least usually, contain something of a fragrance of the shifting moment, and have not been rendered uniform or even overly coherent by the retrospective pen. Ostensibly an account of the pilgrimage of a pious Shi'i woman from late Safavid Iran to Mecca and Medina, our text is in the final analysis much more. The closing sections, especially after the departure from Aleppo, fulfil the requirements of the *ḥajj*-account admirably, and we get the perfect mix of devotional subjectivity and local colour for the armchair voyager, notably in the description of the *ḥajj* caravan, and the celebrations at Mina. The dominant mood is, however, devout, even if sectarian, within the confines of what is demanded of a pilgrim.

[62] "Safar Nāma-i Manẓūm-i ḥajj", pp. 344–5. See also Rasul Ja'fariyan, "Ḥujjāj-i Shi'i dar daura-i Ṣafawī", in Ja'fariyan, *'Ilal-i bar uftādan-i Ṣafawiyān: Mukāfāt nāma, bi ẓamīma-i chand risāla wa maqāla dar bāra-i Fitna-i Afghān wa masā'il-i siyasī-farhangī-i daura-i Ṣafawī* (Tehran, 1372 Sh. / 1993).

In relation to this, however, the earlier sections pose something of a problem, if coherence is our principal objective. Far lighter in tone, they seem to address another vein in the listener or reader, and bring forth the portrayal of a middle-aged widow, still vigorous enough for arduous travel, and still young enough to be courted (albeit unsucessfully), but of a sufficient independence of spirit not only to undertake a voyage such as this, but then to set it down by way of a literary composition. Our author dislikes Sunnis and Ottomans, and expresses this in no uncertain terms, but this is only to be expected. The travails of the voyage, the difficulties of mountainous terrain, the illnesses that travel must bring, all these are deftly woven into the verse, giving the reader a notion of the author as thinking, feeling and suffering subject. However, the text in its first sections, that take us as far as the borders of Armenia, attempts far more, and in a manner that is rather different from what follows. This is all the more reason then to follow these texts as they progress rather than cut them up into the pieces of a jigsaw puzzle, to be recomposed at the modern-day reader's fancy. Incoherence – or, if one prefers, inconsistency – is a virtue that needs its advocates too. This lesson is one that we shall attempt to follow into the texts that occupy us in the following chapter, which is concerned for the most part with texts from the fifteenth century. Later chapters will then take us, in a roughly chronological fashion, through the sixteenth, seventeenth and eighteenth centuries, to the eve of the period when British colonialism gradually began to transform Persian into a provincial language.

CHAPTER 2

From Timur to the Bahmanis: fifteenth-century views

> Through Fate's command, and the order of Divine Destiny,
> which cannot be contemplated by human reflection,
> I was assigned to Hind, but how can I describe,
> how perplexed I was in that dark region?
>
> 'Abdur Razzaq Samarqandi, *Maṯla' us-Sa'dain*

INTRODUCTION

The first set of travel-narratives dealing with South Asia that we are concerned with derive from the fifteenth century, a period when a series of kingdoms, themselves formed in the crucible of Indo-Persian culture, had each been in existence for a century or more. These embrace such kingdoms as the Sultanates of Delhi, Gujarat, or the Deccan (the last ruled over by the Bahmani dynasty), but we must also include amongst their number the so-called Vijayanagara empire that had flourished in the southern Deccan from the middle years of the fourteenth century onwards, and is often erroneously classed as a "Hindu" empire. The early history of such kingdoms is usually traced back to the beginning of the thirteenth century, when the so-called "Slave Dynasty" of rulers (themselves of largely Central Asian Turkish origin) came to establish their power in the Indo-Gangetic plain, after a century and a half of periodic incursions into the region, from centres in Afghanistan such as Ghazna and Ghur. This simple chronology can be nuanced with reference to the presence of the Ghaznavid state in Punjab from earlier on, which had produced and patronised some of the important early poets and litterateurs in Persian in South Asia.[1] Further, it is now clear that Delhi had to

[1] Sunil Sharma, *Persian poetry at the Indian frontier.*

struggle for a good part of the thirteenth century to establish its paramountcy over rival centres such as Multan and Bayana in northern India.

Be that as it may, it is clear that the southward and eastward expansion of the Delhi Sultanate in the late thirteenth and early fourteenth centuries defines a new set of departures for the career of Indo-Persian culture.[2] This must naturally be seen in the context of a larger crisis that gripped the states of the Islamic world, which was triggered off by the celebrated Mongol attempts to build an empire of continental dimensions in the thirteenth century. Since the Sultanate of Delhi was amongst the few states that was able successfully to ward off Mongol military pressure, it was natural enough that South Asia (and particularly Hindustan) would emerge as a powerful pole of attraction for divines, poets, and others, who had been displaced from both Transoxania and Iran itself.[3] In the latter case, we are aware that after the fall of Baghdad to the Mongols (in 1258), a form of compromise was struck within a generation. The Mongols converted to Islam, founding the Il-Khanid dynasty in Iran, while Persian men-of-letters and administrators learnt to serve the new power, even in a situation of considerable uncertainty for themselves.[4] Nevertheless, this shift in circumstances, allied with the foundation of a number of new political centres in South Asia, facilitated the migration of Persophone literati and intellectuals eastwards. It is of this process, from the fourteenth century, that Jean Aubin has written: "Although theologians, jurists and traders from Arab countries were very much present, this military and spiritual undertaking on the part of Persian Islam transformed the Indo-Muslim civilization into a civilization of Persian culture."[5]

A gradual transformation is thus visible in the Indo-Gangetic plain in the transition between the Khaljis and the Tughluqs, which occupies the second quarter of the fourteenth century. Ibn Battuta, present in North India in these years, presents us a view of a court-culture wherein Turkic elements still had a significant role to play, but this grew less evident as the years wore on. The agents of change were numerous, but in

[2] For an excellent panoramic view of developments, see Simon Digby, "Before Timur came: provincialization of the Delhi Sultanate through the fourteenth century", *Journal of the Economic and Social History of the Orient*, 47, 3, 2004, pp. 298–356.

[3] See the useful discussion in Peter Jackson, *The Delhi Sultanate: a political and military history* (Cambridge, 1999).

[4] Jean Aubin, *Émirs mongols et vizirs persans dans les remous de l'acculturation* (Paris, 1995).

[5] Jean Aubin, "Merchants in the Red Sea and the Persian Gulf at the turn of the fifteenth and sixteenth centuries", in Denys Lombard and Jean Aubin, eds., *Asian merchants and businessmen in the Indian Ocean and the China Sea* (Delhi, 2000), p. 80.

addition to the impulses that came from court-society, we must also take into account the part played by the Sufi orders, that came to be present along the length of the Indo-Gangetic plain, but also in the Deccan, where the Bahmani Sultanate declared its independence from Delhi in the middle decades of the fourteenth century, under Sultan 'Ala-ud-Din Hasan Bahman Shah (r. 1347–58). There has been some debate in recent years on the precise nature of the Sufi intervention in this Islamic "frontier-region", and the relative importance in it of violent and quietist elements.[6] This matter is not of direct concern for us here; rather, what appears significant is the role of Sufis as vectors of a new Indo-Persian cultural ferment, in part carried from northern India into the Deccan, and partly the result of the fact that the Bahmani Sultanate enjoyed direct maritime connections with the Persian Gulf ports throughout its existence. The Persian connection is nowhere better illustrated than by the case of the installation in Bidar (one of the Bahmani capitals) of the Ni'matullahi order, founded by Shah Ni'matullah Wali Kermani (d. 1430–1).[7]

We must hence imagine a South Asian world, by the mid fourteenth century, in which it was possible for a member of the Persian-speaking élite to travel from centre to centre, finding patrons and audiences in places as far-flung as the Sultanate of Ma'bar (centred at Madurai, and soon after to be conquered by Vijayanagara), Honawar (on the Kanara coast), Gujarat, Gulbarga, Bengal, Bihar, the Gangetic *doāb* (the fertile area between two rivers), and the Punjab. Ibn Battuta himself, though an Arabic-speaker with an imperfect understanding of Persian, availed himself of many of the same circuits in his travels in the 1330s and 1340s. Not only this: as Persian grew in significance as a language of communication, even the court-centres that were outside the direct influence of the Sultanate of Delhi testify to its use, at least for some limited purposes. Such was clearly the case with the Kakatiya kingdom based at Warrangal (before its conquest by the Sultans of Delhi in the early fourteenth century), and this remained equally true of Vijayanagara in later years, as we shall see below.[8]

[6] Carl W. Ernst, *Eternal garden: mysticism, history and politics at a South Asian Sufi center* (Albany, N. Y., 1992), pp. 97–105.

[7] Jean Aubin, "De Kûhbanân à Bidar: la famille Ni'matullâhi", *Studia Iranica*, 20, 1991, pp. 233–61.

[8] On this point, see Velcheru Narayana Rao and David Shulman, *A lover's guide to Warangal: the 'Krīḍâbhirāmamu' by Vinukoṇḍa Vallabharāya* (New Delhi, 2002).

FLEEING TIMUR

We have already noted above that the Sultans of Delhi were remarkably successful in holding off Mongol incursions into their territories in the thirteenth and early fourteenth centuries, during the heyday of Chinggis Khan and his successors. By so doing, they set themselves apart from their contemporaries in both Central Asia and Iran, and indeed in some parts of West Asia. They did not have the same measure of success though in dealing with another great conqueror from the north, namely Amir Timur Gurgan (1336–1405), who captured and sacked Delhi after a rapid and bloody campaign, in December 1398. It has been suggested that this expedition was largely motivated by Timur's desire to firm up the position of his grandson, Pir Muhammad-i Jahangir, to whom he had granted the "domain of Mahmud of Ghazna", which is to say the upper valley of the Indus. In a "Victory Bulletin" (*fatḥ nāma-yi Dehlī*), issued from Khulm in late March 1399, and drafted by Khwaja Ahmad Simnani, Timur made his own official position clear:

> In the year that we decided to leave on a campaign and in a holy war to the land of infidels (*dayār-i-kufr*) in certain regions of Hindustan, we were told that since Sultan Firoz Shah had passed from this life to the hereafter, some of the slaves that he had purchased against gold had refused to hand over Delhi and the lands of Islam to his descendants, and that they had taken to tyranny and oppression; they had made rapine and pillage their rallying signs . . . closed the doors to the passage of merchants, and taken brigandage to its height.[9]

The reference is thus to the death of Sultan Firoz Shah Tughluq at Delhi (used here as a pretext), but there is also a significant series of mentions of what have been termed "the fundamental preoccupations of Tamerlane [Timur]: illegitimacy, anarchy, brigandage, impediments to commercial circulation".

It is this invasion that provides the context for the first of the travel-accounts that we shall briefly deal with in this chapter. The account in question is a hagiographical text, dealing with the life of a Sufi saint, Sayyid Muhammad al-Husaini (often termed Gesudaraz ("Long Tresses")), and written by one of his close disciples, Shah Muhammad 'Ali Samani, who compiled it partly from extant materials shortly after the

[9] Jean Aubin, "Comment Tamerlan prenait les villes", *Studia Islamica*, 19, 1963, p. 90. For this campaign and its context, also see Beatrice Forbes Manz, *The rise and rule of Tamerlane* (Cambridge, 1989), esp. pp. 71–73.

saint's death.[10] The text in question, the *Siyar-i Muḥammadī*, is thus not technically a first-person account unlike the bulk of those that we shall deal with in the pages that follow. However, it is still sufficiently close to the spirit of the travel-account to justify its inclusion here, as a rather particular sort of travel-text. It should be noted that the travel portion is inserted in a far larger work that is in turn divided into nine chapters, the first one containing the genealogies (both spiritual and literal) of the saint, and a brief biography of his life before his arrival in Gulbarga, in the Deccan. Subsequent chapters deal respectively with his accomplishments, his lifestyle, his teachings, his treatises, his sons, his spiritual successors (or *k̲h̲alīfas*), a description of some of his friends, and a selection of his letters.

The saint had an unusually long life, and his official lifespan is of just over a hundred years, from 1321 to 1422. Born in Delhi, he had apparently migrated once to the Deccan as a young man with his father, when the Sultan Muhammad Shah Tughluq transferred his capital briefly to Daulatabad. He returned to Delhi, however, and was taken under the wing of one of the leading Sufis of the Chishti order, Shaikh Nasir-ud-Din Chiragh-i-Dehli (d. 1356). However, it is reported by Shah Muhammad 'Ali Samani, when he was eighty years of age (by the lunar calendar), which is to say in the year AH 801, on 7 Rabi' II (17 December 1398), because of the disturbance (*ḥādis̤a*) caused by the Mughal (Timur) in Delhi, he left that town through the Bhilsa gate; Shah Muhammad adds significantly that "the writer of these lines was with him".[11] In this sense too, we are in the presence of a first-person account, even if the author is somewhat self-effacing.

The precise date of the departure is rather important. We are aware that Timur had already received a number of notables (*maliks*), as well as Sayyids and *'ulamā'* before entering the city of Delhi, and had probably reassured them that they would be well-treated. The Central Asian conqueror had the reputation for being selective in his use of terror, and Muslim divines and holy men were normally not targeted by his troops. However, it is certain that news of the enormous massacre perpetrated on 3 Rabi' II 801 H (that is, 13 December 1398), by his troops, must also have

10 Shah Muhammad 'Ali Samani, *Siyar-i Muḥammadī* (compiled AH 831), ed., with an Urdu translation, by Sayyid Shah Nazir Ahmad Qadiri Sikandarpuri (Gulbarga, 1399 H / 1979). Also see Digby, "Before Timur came", pp. 325–30, and Richard M. Eaton, *The new Cambridge history of India*, vol. I.8: *A social history of the Deccan, 1300–1761: eight Indian lives* (Cambridge, 2005).

11 *Siyar*, Persian text, p. 26; Urdu translation, p. 32.

come to the ears of the inhabitants of Delhi. In this bloodbath, which took place at Loni on the banks of the Yamuna, several tens of thousands of prisoners (*asīr*) were killed as a matter of precaution before Timur's troops entered the city. Though some of Sayyid Muhammad al-Husaini's contemporaries do not seem to have taken alarm at this sign and preferred to stay on in Delhi (this was the case for Shaikh Ahmad Maghribi, cited by Aubin), he, like some others, clearly thought he had best put some distance between himself and the site of these atrocious events. Three days after Sayyid Muhammad left Delhi, on 20 December 1398, Maulana Nasir-ud-Din 'Umar read the *khuṭba* in the city in the conqueror's name, while a week later, on 26 December, the celebrated general massacres (*qatl-i 'āmm*) began, leaving several thousand dead over the next few days.

Our travellers were safe from all this, however. For Sayyid Muhammad and his party had meanwhile reached Bahadurpur, where a certain Malik Muhammad Khan Afghan and Maulana Baha-ud-Din, two of the saint's disciples, received him, and made some houses available for his use inside the *qaṣba*. Maulana Baha-ud-Din was in addition authorised by the saint to mediate with other potential disciples on his behalf. Sayyid Muhammad presently decided to leave the *qaṣba* on 18 Rabi' II, and sent a message on to one Maulana 'Ala-ud-Din in Gwaliyar, whom he had trained earlier in Delhi for a period of ten years. The letter is recounted in detail in the text, and is significantly called a *farmān* ("royal order"). It runs as follows:

> O my spiritual son, Maulana 'Ala-ud-Din Gwaliyari! Accept and read these greetings from Muhammad al-Husaini. Misfortunes have caused us to leave Delhi, and they are of indescribable and immeasurable dimensions. It is our intention to come to Gwaliyar. Bring Farid Khan with you, and receive me en route. Tell Sharaf Aflah too of my imminent arrival in that city. He too may come and meet me at the edge of the town. *Subḥān Allāh-il-'Aẓīm.* What a wonder of God that we are obliged by misfortune to come and seek help from you, rather than grant you favours. What God wills he does. He may turn the belly into the back, and the back into the belly. Do not delay. There is no time even to take breath for even while on my way, I may be caught up with.

Having sent this letter, it is reported, Sayyid Muhammad (still accompanied by the text's author) left Bahadurpur on 20 Rabi' II for Gwaliyar. Twenty *kos* short of Gwaliyar, it is noted that he reached an open wilderness (*bayābān*), where a large number of Hindus were gathered. These Hindus were about to plunder their caravan, and those in the caravan were full of fear and had begun to cry out. At this moment, an armed party became visible, coming from Gwaliyar. The people of the caravan initially feared that these were reinforcements to the plunderers.

But when the armed party from Gwaliyar saw the saint, they got off their horses and bowed to him. Only then were those in his party reassured. These included his family and sons, his friends like Sayyid Abu'l Ma'ali, Maulana Muhammad Mu'allim, Maulana Shaikhu, Sayyid Taj-ud-Din, Maulana Muhammad Basat Tarash and others, who realised that the armed men had in fact been sent by Maulana 'Ala-ud-Din. For their part, the ill-disposed Hindus dispersed quietly, and conflict was thus avoided. The saint's precautions, and his extensive network, thus proved crucial in the affair. The solitary or unprotected traveller was obviously not welcome on the roads in these times of "calamity".

Thus, on 22 Rabi' II, Sayyid Muhammad at last reached Gwaliyar, was lodged in Maulana 'Ala-ud-Din's house, and a particular ritual (*kandūrī fātiḥa*) was performed to celebrate his arrival. The next day, Maulana 'Ala-ud-Din presented the Sufi Shaikh a list with his own name, those of his sons, and other members of his household, and announced that they were all henceforth his slaves. All the slave-girls and boys in the household, as well as the horses, cows and oxen, all the provisions, and all he had in cash and kind (including books) were entirely offered to him. The Shaikh took some cash, some provisions and books, and then blessed the Maulana and embraced him (implicitly returning the rest). The son of the Maulana, Abu'l Fath, who had already been a disciple of Gesudaraz some two years before, was also present on this occasion, and thus witnessed this significant exchange.

Some two months seem to have been spent comfortably by the party in Gwaliyar. It was thus only on 17 Jumada II, that Sayyid Muhammad left there for the town of Bhander. On the same day, before leaving, it is noted that he conferred *k͟hilāfat* (a form of spiritual succession) on Maulana 'Ala-ud-Din, and a description follows of the writing of the formal document, or *miṣāl-i k͟hilāfat.* A certain Maulana Hamid-ud-Din, who had been *muftī* of Delhi, and who was now in the party (as a disciple of Gesudaraz), wrote the text. It turned out that Maulana 'Ala-ud-Din was the first official *k͟halīfa* of the saint, a fact that was commented on by Maulana Hamid-ud-Din. When this remark was made, Sayyid Muhammad replied that it was not he who conferred *k͟hilāfat* of his own will; rather, he had been told (by God) that he had to do so. Had it been in his own authority, he declared somewhat disingenuously, he would have given it first to his own sons.

While at Bhander, the son of a certain Maulana Zu'l-qarnain, who was a great savant (*dānishmand*), and also a disciple of Nasir-ud-Din Mahmud Awadhi (that is, Chiragh-i-Dehli), and a large number of

Afghans and clansmen decided to become Gesudaraz's disciples. It is noted that Muzaffar Khan, *ẕābiṯa* ("governor") of the place, also came to meet him. From Bhander, the party then went on to Iraj (or Irja). Again, when Sayyid Muhammad arrived there, a large number of nobles, men and women, *'ulamā'* and *mashā'ikh*, came to receive him. A number of names are given: Sayyid Ikram, Sayyid Mahan, Maulana Amir-ud-Din, Qazi Burhan-ud-Din, Sayyid Ahsan, Shaikh Khwandmir and Sulaiman Khan of Iraj came there, and asked to become disciples. It is specified that this Shaikh Khwandmir was the son of the *Shaikh-ul-Islām* of Iraj, and came accompanied by his brothers too. Still accumulating disciples and honours, the saint now moved on from Iraj to Chhatra, where again he gathered many disciples: Qazi Ishaq, Muhammad Rukn (the *muftī* of the place) and his brothers, Qazi Sulaiman and his brothers, the chief *qāẓī* of the place (Qazi Minhaj Mudarris), and the sons of the *ḥākim* ("governor") of the town, together with many other clans (*khail*) of residents (*qaṣbā-tiyān*). Thus, what begins as a mournful journey of exile begins to resemble a triumphal procession, with all the trappings one associates with the latter.

The itinerary itself is significant, as Sayyid Muhammad obviously chooses to pass through all the significant urban centres that are within his range, rather than taking the shortest possible route. His next stop is thus Chanderi;[12] and here too, he gathers disciples whose names are mentioned in a list. Among these is Shaikh Nasir-ud-Din, son of Khwaja Ya'qub of Chanderi, who hosts him in his own house. The son of the *muftī* of Chanderi, who was known as Qazi-i Khwajagi ("The Great") on account of his science and wisdom, also becomes his disciple. An anecdote typical of such Sufi narratives of initiation finds a small place here. It is reported that Shaikh Nasir-ud-Din asked for some teaching and guidance about mystic litanies (*talqīn-i ẕikr*), and Gesudaraz replied that it was his practice to bestow such teaching only on those who brought wood-logs for him from the jungle. But since Nasir-ud-Din was a Shaikh, and the son of a Shaikh, as well as the holder of a high position, and could not be asked to do this, he should hence continue as he was. So saying, the saint left the town, and passing through Miyandhar went on to Baroda. He reached Baroda on the night of 'Id-ul-Fitr, and camped by a large tank (*ḥauẓ*). Here, Adam Khan and his sons arranged for hospitality to be provided to him, news of his imminent arrival having preceded him. After

[12] *Siyar*, Persian text, p. 31; Urdu translation, p. 39.

a few days, it is noted that Zafar Khan and Nisar Khan offered to pay his expenses for the rest of his journey. Still continuing his meanderings, this time in a westerly direction, it is noted that in the month of Zi-Qa'da, Gesudaraz graced Khambayat by his presence; here Zafar Khan came to welcome him six *kos* outside the town, and presented him goods as offerings (*futūḥ* and *kandūrī*). Another anecdote emerges from the author's pen to mark the occasion. It is stated that on their meeting, Gesudaraz addressed Zafar Khan and asked him bluntly: "Is there anyone with you now who can dare speak of your shortcomings, and warn you of their consequences?" Qazi Sulaiman, a close confidant of Zafar Khan replied: "What about Khawand Khan, who never violates any injunction of the *sharī'a*?" Gesudaraz said that if there was only one such, then Zafar Khan was regrettably surrounded by a bunch of flatterers. All those around hung their heads in shame at this cutting remark. The implicit idea is clear enough, for it falls on the saint and mystic to cut through worldly hypocrisy, and reveal the truth of the political system.

It is noted that Gesudaraz stayed on some time in Gujarat. During this time, people from Khambayat and other places came and asked to become his disciples. A list of names is again given, including those of a few who were already his disciples. Gesudaraz now proposed to return at length to Baroda, and began to plan a journey through Miyan Sultanpur, to arrive at Daulatabad, where we have noted he had already been in his youth. In Daulatabad, he thus paid homage to the grave of his own father Sayyid Yusuf. In nearby Fathbad or Deogir, the *muqṭa'dār*, 'Azd-ul-mulk, came and made offerings on behalf of Firuz Shah Bahmani, described as the Badshah of Gulbarga. It is reported that Sultan Firuz had heard of the imminent arrival of Sayyid Muhammad, and hence instructed his *muqṭa'dār* to do the necessary. In response to this kindness, Gesudaraz left there for Dar-ul-mulk Ahsanabad – that is to say, the city of Gulbarga itself. Here, it is noted that Sultan Firuz met him outside the town with an armed party, and ceremonially kissed his feet (*pābos kard*). He insisted that Sayyid Muhammad should adopt Gulbarga as his residence. On this, the Sufi meditated a while, and then replied, "I wish I could accept your request. But it seems you have only a few years left of your life. If I live in Gulbarga, and you are no longer there, how shall I get relief and comfort?" The Sultan then said, "If I have only a few years left, request God to lengthen my life." Sayyid Muhammad assured him that he would do so that very night. The Sultan should return the next day for his decision. When the Sultan came again the next day to kiss his feet, and sat before him, he repeated his request once more. This time, the Sayyid said,

"I prayed for your long life, and the Divine Response was that He had increased your life. So long as I remain alive, you will too." The hagiographer comments that it came to pass more or less in that way. The two died within a few days of each other: first the Sultan died, and then the Sufi.

The Sultan now went back to the city and the saint joined him there a few days later. It is stated here that Sayyid Muhammad Gesudaraz lived for 105 years, 4 months and 12 days (by lunar reckoning), and that he died on a Monday, in the morning between the *'ishrāq* and *chāsht* prayers, on 16 Zi-Qa'da 825 (1 November 1422). The author adds piously: "May I too, on the Day of Judgement, be raised with him and his ancestors. Sayyid Muhammad had wanted that his dead body should be washed by Maulana Baha-ud-Din and Maulana Siraj-ud-Din. And so it was done." An appropriate chronogram is given for the date of his death: *Makhdūm-i dīn-o-duniyā shud* ("He became Master of Faith and the World"), yielding the desired date of 825 Hijri.[13]

Economical to the point of being laconic, the text of Gesudaraz's travels nevertheless contains a number of significant features that it may be useful to bring out here. Descriptions of the landscape and the countryside are virtually absent in the text, which is organised above all as an itinerary between urban centres. The dominant trend here is to stress the human network that seems to support the Sufi's travels from place to place, as he moves, so to speak, from one red carpet to another, and from one actual or potential disciple's household to that of another. Space is thus organised through the holy man's aura, stretching out from Delhi (his normal place of residence), to the Deccan, some thousand kilometres distant; the engagement with temporal power is another conspicuous feature of the narrative, as we see a list of governors, princes and rulers engaging with Sayyid Muhammad as he makes his way over a political landscape that is apparently fragmented, but also remarkably united in its vocabulary and assumptions. Had Sayyid Muhammad been the emissary of some powerful monarch, he would hardly have met with better treatment, and it is thus logically to the narrative of one such emissary that we shall now turn.

THE RELUCTANT AMBASSADOR

Our second narrative is also linked to the history of Timur, though it is somewhat more distant in time from the life of the Great Emir. The text

[13] *Siyar*, Persian text, p. 36; Urdu translation, p. 44.

in question is authored by a certain Kamal-ud-Din ʻAbdur Razzaq ibn Ishaq Samarqandi, whom we shall refer to hereafter simply as ʻAbdur Razzaq.[14] This author, voyager and savant was born in Herat in 1413, thus eight years after the death of Timur, and at a time when that city had emerged as the chief political centre of the region of Khorasan, under Timur's son Mirza Shahrukh. Like his father, ʻAbdur Razzaq too entered the service of this powerful Timurid ruler, and had been in his employ for four years (from 1437 on), when he was engaged on a mission to the port of Calicut in south-western India. It is the account of this voyage, which lasted from January 1442 to January 1445, that will concern us here. It is to be found inserted, though, in a far larger text that he authored, entitled *Maṯlaʻ us-Saʻdain wa Majmaʻ ul-Baḥrain* ("The Rising of the Auspicious Twin-Stars, and the Confluence of the Oceans"), which is an elaborate history of Timur and his family, running from about 1304 to 1470 (that is from the time of Abu Saʻid Bahadur Khan's birth, to about a decade before ʻAbdur Razzaq's own death, which occurred in 1482). ʻAbdur Razzaq, it may thus be noted, survived his master Shahrukh by nearly four decades, and also served later Timurid princes such as Abu Saʻid Mirza.[15]

The sending of ʻAbdur Razzaq to India is undoubtedly linked to Mirza Shahrukh's own desires to create a larger web of semi-formal and suzerain relations, going beyond the domains of Khorasan, Sistan and Mazandaran that he had initially inherited, and then Transoxania, whose control he had wrested from his nephew, Khalil Sultan. Of the various states that emerged from the fragmentation of Timur's super-state after 1405, it is clear that Shahrukh's possessed the greatest stability, and his successful containment of a series of rebellions in the years from 1405 to 1408 were a sign of this, as were the institutional means that were deployed to this end (namely the strategic use of *suyurghāl* land-grants).

[14] For the Persian text, see ʻAbdur Razzaq ibn Ishaq Samarqandi, *Maṯlaʻ us-Saʻdain wa Majmaʻ ul-Baḥrain*, vol. II, parts II and III, ed. Muhammad Shafiʻ, 2nd edn (Lahore, 1365–8 H / 1946–9), pp. 764–71, 775–91, 796–830, 842–51. For the most recent translation (which we have emended from time to time), see Wheeler M. Thackston, "Kamaluddin Abdul-Razzaq Samarqandi: mission to Calicut and Vijayanagar" in *A century of princes: sources on Timurid history and art* (Cambridge, Mass., 1989), pp. 299–321. This replaces the earlier translation in R. H. Major, *India in the fifteenth century: being a collection of narratives of voyages to India* (London, 1857), pp. 1–49, based in turn on E. M. Quatremère, "Notice de l'ouvrage persan qui a pour titre: Matla-assaadein ou majma-albahrein, et qui contient l'histoire des deux sultans Schahrokh et Abou-Said", in *Notice et extraits des manuscrits de la Bibliothèque du Roi et autres bibliothèques*, vol. XIV, part I (Paris, 1843).

[15] C. P. Haase, "ʻAbd-al-Razzāq Samarqandī, Kamāl-al-Dīn bin Jalāl-al-Dīn Eshāq", in Ehsan Yarshater, ed., *Encyclopaedia iranica*, vol. I, Part I (New York, 1982), pp. 158–60.

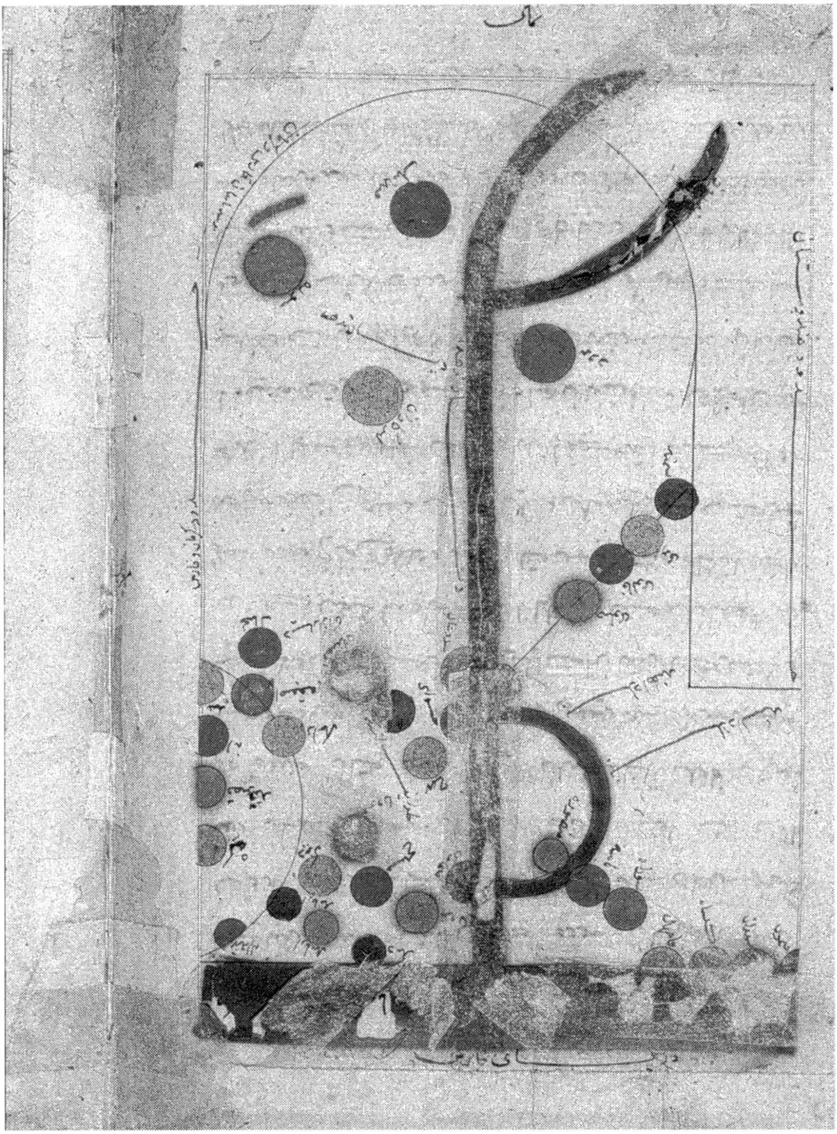

Figure 3. Map (*ṣūrat*) of the country (*dayār*) of Sind and parts of Hind from Ibn Khurdadbih, *Ṣuwar al-aqālīm wa masālik-i mamālik*, ms copied in 831 H. (1427–8), National Museum, New Delhi, No. 56.96/4.

By the late 1430s, Shahrukh had successfully consolidated his power, and he could look southwards again.

It is in this context that the "invitation" from the Samudri Raja of Calicut (Kozhikode), in the south-western Indian region of Kerala, providentially came to the court of Herat. The port, one of the most important in the east–west trade of the Indian Ocean, had emerged into prominence after the decline of the earlier centre of Kollam (or Quilon), and served two functions. First, Calicut gave access to the rich pepper-growing lands located somewhat to the interior on the slopes of the western Ghats, and pepper was a much-prized commodity in the trade of this epoch. Second, Calicut was also a major entrepôt in terms of long-distance maritime trade, a rich centre that had already been visited by Ibn Battuta a century earlier, and which gave shelter to a variety of merchant communities, including those from 'Iraq, the Persian Gulf, the Red Sea, and Egypt. Though ruled over by a non-Muslim (*kāfir*) king, the port still was regarded by Muslim merchants as a particularly safe haven, and they also considered the relationship between political power and their commerce as symbiotic. As a Muslim chronicler from the region, Zain-ud-Din Ma'bari, was to write in the 1570s:

> The most powerful sovereigns [of Malabar] are the Tiruvadi, the king of Kulam [Kollam], Kumhari [Comorin], and the land between these two points, while to the east thereof extend many kingdoms; the Kulatiri, prince of Hili [Eli], Maravi [Madayi], Jarapatan, Kannanur, Edakkad, Darmapatan, et cetera; however, more powerful than them, and possessed of greater fame, is al-Samiri [Samudri], whose domain extends between these two kingdoms. He is a great sovereign thanks to the favour (*barakat*) of the Din al-Islam, and of his love for the Muslims, and the liberal manner in which he treats them, above all the foreigners (*al-ghurabā'*).[16]

This port, then, celebrated for its reception of strangers, was the destination of our Timurid ambassador, but some travails had to be endured before he found himself there. His travel-narrative, probably written some two decades after the actual voyage, is remarkable for its vividness and precision, and the beginnings of the section on travel at least are characterised by clarity of expression, and are set down in an elegant literary Persian, with not too much hyperbole (as is characteristic of most Timurid texts of the period, which are relatively understated in style).[17]

[16] Zain ud-Din Ma'bari, *Tuḥfat al-mujāhidīn fī ba'ẓ-i aḥwāl al-Burtukāliyyīn*, ed. and tr. David Lopes, *História dos Portugueses no Malavar por Zinadím* (Lisbon, 1899), text, p. 27; translation, p. 25.

[17] See the important study by John E. Woods, "The rise of Tîmûrid historiography", *Journal of Near Eastern Studies*, 46, 1987, pp. 81–108.

As the narrative progresses though, when enthusiasm seizes 'Abdur Razzaq (as when talking of his numerous illnesses), we shall see that his poetic spirit takes flight. Throughout the text, a fairly large number of verses and hemistichs are interwoven, usually taken rather deftly from the great masters of medieval Persian poetry, including those from India.

'Abdur Razzaq promises his readers a narrative that will enter into "the minutest details . . . [with] all sorts of marvellous facts and wonderful matters worthy of notice" from the three years of his travels. He begins then by invoking the Qu'ran (10: 22), as is often the case in our texts, with an appropriate verse linked precisely to travel: "It is He who hath given you conveniences for travelling by land and by sea." The omniscience of God is equally invoked thereafter, as also the fact that the fates of all humans "are in the grasp of fate and the clutches of destiny", an occasion for 'Abdur Razzaq then to cite a verse from the celebrated poet, Anwari (a particular favourite of several of the authors that we shall have occasion to study in the pages that follow). The verse in question runs, rather gloomily:

> If everything in the fate of beings were not predetermined,
> How then does Man's state go against his own will?
> Truly, for better or worse, Destiny has every man's reins in its hands,
> for no matter what one does, one still finds that things end in error.[18]

The reason for this tone shall presently become clear, for the first part of the journey turns out to be rather miserable, not least of all on account of what our author terms "the terrors of a sea-voyage". But prior to that, there is also a rather more general reflection on the journey in its entirety, in the form of a verse that has often intrigued analysts. This runs as follows:

> Through Fate's command, and the order of Divine Destiny,
> which cannot be contemplated by human reflection,
> I was assigned to Hind, but how can I describe,
> how perplexed I was in that dark region?

This reads like a rather damning indictment of India, as a veritable "dark region" (*iqlīm-i ẓalmānī*), which cannot be calculated to win the reader's

[18] Our translation differs here somewhat from that of Thackston, *A century of princes*, p. 299. Thackston also does not cite the names of the poets drawn upon, which are however furnished by the text's editor, Muhammad Shafi' (on p. 765). This popular verse is equally cited by a later author, Asad Beg Qazwini, but with the two following lines added; see. Muzaffar Alam and Sanjay Subrahmanyam, "Witnessing transition: views on the end of the Akbari dispensation", in K. N. Panikkar, Terence J. Byres and Utsa Patnaik, eds., *The making of history: essays presented to Irfan Habib* (New Delhi, 2000), pp. 104–40.

sympathy for that land. However, another rather more metaphorical reading is possible, which would link this phrase to the Qur'anic description of the *baḥr-ul-ẓulmāt*, thus rendering it a reflection on the intervening sea-voyage rather than on India itself. In any event, even if this is 'Abdur Razzaq's initial diagnosis, we shall see that other parts of the text tend to nuance it to a fair extent.

Our envoy seems to have set out from Herat then, in January 1442 (the month of Ramazan 845), with horses, supplies and generous financial support from Mirza Shahrukh, the "Felicitous *Khāqān*" of the text. Heading due south for the Persian Gulf, he passed through the deserted regions of Makran and Sistan, before arriving after eighteen days' travel in the town of Kerman. Here, he notes the recent return from India of a certain Amir Burhan-ud-Din, a descendant of Shah Ni'matullah Wali (mentioned above), who had presumably been in the Deccan. The end of the month of fasting was spent there, and the envoy and his party (the composition of which remains vague at this stage) made their way eventually to the port of Hurmuz. This centre was not under direct Timurid control, being ruled by the Turan Shahs, but the shadow of Mirza Shahrukh still made itself felt.[19] The ruler promptly arranged a ship to ferry the party from the mainland to his island state; but, once there, 'Abdur Razzaq had to spend some time awaiting another vessel, which gives him occasion to describe Hurmuz, albeit in a rather formulaic manner. So, we read:

> Hurmuz, which they call Jarun, is a port in the midst of the sea, with no equal on the face of the earth. Merchants from the seven climes, Egypt, Syria, Anatolia, Azerbaijan, Arabian and Persian 'Iraq, Fars, Khorasan, Transoxania, Turkestan, the Qipchaq steppe, the Qalmaq regions, and all the lands of the east, China, Machin, and Khan Baliq, all come to that port, and seafaring men from Machin, Java, Bengal, Ceylon, the cities of the Land below the Winds (*zīr-i bād*), Tenasserim, Soqotra, Siam (*shahr-i nav*), and the Maldive Islands, to the realm of Malibar, Abyssinia and Zanj, the ports of Vijayanagara, Gulbarga, Gujarat, and Cambay, the coast of the Arabian peninsula to Aden, Jiddah and Yanbu', bring to that town precious and rare commodities.

After this extensive list, we are insistently told once more that goods and people from the world over can be found there, and further that the trade

[19] On Hurmuz, see the classic essay by Jean Aubin, "Les princes d'Ormuz du XIIIe au XVe siècle", *Journal asiatique*, 241, 1, 1953, pp. 77–138; as also the first sections of Aubin, "Le royaume d'Ormuz au début du XVIe siècle", in *Le latin et l'astrolabe*, Vol. II: *Recherches sur le Portugal de la Renaissance, son expansion en Asie et les relations internationales* (Paris, 2000), pp. 287–376.

is taxed a tenth (*'ushr*), save gold and silver, on which no duties are paid. It is equally noted that "adherents of various religions, even infidels, are many in the city, but they deal equitably with all". This to the point that the town is known as the Abode of Peace (*dār al-aman*), while it is equally noted that the people there are "as flattering as Persians, and as profound as Indians" (*tamālluq-i 'Irāqiyān wa ta'ammuq-i Hindiyān*), a rather kinder view of Indians than the one we have noted above.[20]

But things eventually do not turn out all that well at Hurmuz. To begin with, the party is delayed unnecessarily by the rulers (*ḥukkām*) of the place, until the sailing season is rather advanced. Eventually, at the very end of the season (also the worst time from the point of view of piracy), the party is given two ships. 'Abdur Razzaq's first maritime experiences are not happy: "When the smell of the ship (*bū-i kashtī*) reached my nostrils and I experienced the terror of the sea", he writes, "I lost consciousness to such an extent that for three days I was dead to the world, save for the rising and falling of my breath." Besides, the merchants on his ship (which was soon separated from the other), who had some experience of the voyage, complained loudly that the best season for sailing was past. They hence disembarked at considerable financial loss (*tabāhī*) in Masqat, while the rest of the embassy managed to continue as far as Quryat. Here, they were definitively stranded by unfavourable winds, and 'Abdur Razzaq now grew truly despondent at the untoward turn. As he himself writes: "My mind (*khāṭir*) turned dark and my brain was perplexed." His condition is worsened by a chance encounter with a merchant returning from India to Herat, who puts him in mind of his place of origin. This is the occasion to recall a celebrated verse from the great poet, Hafiz:

> When I begin to weep at the time of the travellers' evening prayer,
> I relate my tale with the cries and wails of the stranger.
> Recalling friend and home, I cry so hard,
> that I would root out the custom of travel from the world.
> I am from the land of the beloved, not of the rival.[21]
> O Guards! Take me back to my comrades.[22]

This is a recurrent theme that we shall find in these accounts, namely the railing against travel, which is seen at such moments as a wholly unnecessary and unfortunate activity. The rather pathetic evocation of "the

[20] 'Abdur Razzaq, *Maṭla' us-Sa'dain*, text, p. 769. 'Iraq here means 'Iraq-i 'Ajam, that is to say Persia.

[21] A variant reading has *gharīb* ("stranger") for *raqīb* ("rival").

[22] *Maṭla' us-Sa'dain*, text, pp. 770–1. We differ again from Thackston's translation, p. 301.

travellers' evening prayer (*namāz-i shām-i gharībān*)" is brought out even further by the powerful line declaring that the poet would gladly "root out the custom of travel from the world (*az jahān rāh-o-rasm-i safar bar andāzam*)". These are themes that we will find taken to their high point of development by a particularly reluctant traveller of the seventeenth century, Muhammad Mufid of Yazd.

The account continues with the altogether unhappy episode of the embassy's stay at Quryat through the hot season, running through the months from May to September 1442. But in the text of the *Maṯla' us-Sa'dain* itself, the travel account is interrupted, as 'Abdur Razzaq passes for a time to events that do not concern him personally, namely the great political events of the year 846 Hijri, including "the expedition of Mirza Sultan Muhammad bin Mirza Baysungar towards 'Iraq".[23] These having been dealt with presently, he then returns to his own travails, which continue through the month of Muharram (which largely coincided with May, in 846 H), a period when the heat in the desert region where he was reached such a height that "rubies would have burned in the mines, and marrow in the bone". This occasions the composition by 'Abdur Razzaq of some rather mediocre poetry, eventually leading to a discussion of his health and that of his companions (who are mentioned explicitly here for the first time). It turns out that our envoy is accompanied by his elder brother, Maulana 'Afif-ud-Din 'Abdul Wahhab, who was, however, not destined to go as far as India. As his brother, 'Abdur Razzaq himself, and their other companions had fallen seriously ill from the heat, they decided to move on to Qalhat, and thence to a place called Sur (or Basur), reputed to have a better climate.

At Qalhat, things worsened though, and it is here – speaking of his own health – that 'Abdur Razzaq's prose takes on a certain pompous weight, as he recalls despondently how he prepared himself for the onset of death. Yet, eventually, it is 'Abdul Wahhab who is carried away, and buried at a shrine near Qalhat. Oddly enough, the recollection of his brother's death summons up in our author not a religious reflection, but a secular verse in Arabic, from a pre-Islamic poet 'Amr bin Ma'dikarb, regretting how "eventually one is abandoned by one's brother, by the life of one's father, [by all] except the twin-star Farqadan". Realising that no good would come from remaining there, at length 'Abdur Razzaq decides to "set forth

[23] These events occupy pp. 771–75 of the edited text of the *Maṯla' us-Sa'dain.*

in any ship bound for India". Comparing himself ruefully to Moses, cast into the waters of the Nile, he embarks on the sea-voyage.

But once on the waters, the account resumes a decidedly more cheerful tone. The sea air rather suits our voyager, his illness begins to clear up, and the ship makes rapid progress towards the coast of India. On cue, he recalls verses from the great poet of Indian Persian, Amir Khusrau Dehlawi (1253–1325), citing abundantly from the latter's great *maṣnawī* (epic narrative poem), *Qirān-us-Sa'dain* (composed in 1287), to describe the ship through a series of rather elaborate similes.[24] The ship thus appears, amongst other guises, as "an Indian-born slave-girl (*jārya-i hindī nazhād*) whose language is soft and sweet", besides being compared to "an overawing cloud like a sea-bird in flight; a straightened bow that is still perfectly curved like the revolving, ever-moving, dome of the sky; and [with] a mast firm and stable as the Pole star". In the end, then, the much dreaded sea-voyage itself turns out to be rather an anti-climax after the long and disastrous period on shore, and at the end of a rapid eighteen-day crossing, the vessel drops anchor safely at the port of Calicut (Kalikot, in the text), the destination of our envoy. It is to the ruler (*wālī*) of this place that 'Abdur Razzaq carries a series of presents from Shahrukh, including a horse, a pelisse, headgear and ceremonial robes. This, then, is the moment when he explains to his readers how the embassy came to be sent out from Herat at all.[25]

It turns out that Shahrukh had, some years earlier, sent some envoys to the Sultanate of Bengal, at this time under the rule of Nasir-ud-Din Mahmud Ilyas Shah (r. 1433–59). These envoys had, on their return sea-voyage, "been stranded in Calicut with emissaries from Bengal", and on this occasion had been received by the Samudri Raja, on whom they had impressed the great power of the Timurid monarch, who (it is claimed) was at this time called upon to regulate outstanding disputes between the Sultanates of Bengal and Jaunpur. At any rate, the Samudri Raja seems to have been sufficiently impressed to send an embassy of his own to Herat, in which the chief envoy was a Persian-speaking Muslim. In 'Abdur Razzaq's version, this envoy was sent "to say that in his port [Calicut] in the Friday prayer and the holiday prayer, the *khuṭba* of Islam was

[24] On Amir Khusrau, see Mohammad Wahid Mirza, *The life and works of Amir Khusrau* (Delhi, 1935), and more recently Zoe Ansari, ed., *Life, times and works of Amīr Khusrau Dehlavi* (New Delhi, 1975).

[25] On 'Abdur Razzaq at Calicut, see also Richard M. Eaton, "Multiple lenses: differing perspectives of fifteenth-century Calicut", in Laurie J. Sears, ed., *Autonomous histories, particular truths: essays in honor of John Smail* (Madison, Wisc., 1993), pp. 71–86.

Figure 4. Scene from the *Ā'īna-yi Sikandarī*, *Khamsa* of Amir Khusrau of Delhi, ms copied on 18 Zi-Hijja 901 H (28 August 1496), National Museum, New Delhi, No. 52.81.

recited, and if His Majesty [Shahrukh] would allow it, they would recite the *khuṭba* in his royal name". The envoy seems to have gone even further than this, and delicately suggested to Shahrukh that if only he were to send an appropriate ambassador to Calicut, the Samudri might convert to Islam. Or rather, as ʿAbdur Razzaq himself elegantly puts matters, "the lock of darkness and error would be loosed from his dark heart, and the brightness of the light of faith would enter through the window of his mind". This proposition seemed reasonable to Shahrukh; as for why ʿAbdur Razzaq was chosen, this seems to have been on account of rivalries in the court, for he hints darkly that some of the *amīrs* plotted against him, "thinking that I might not return from the voyage".

This circumstantial explanation makes it clear that ʿAbdur Razzaq was a somewhat reluctant envoy, and this reluctance was turned into outright distaste when he found that the conversion of the Samudri Raja (whom he dismissively titles the *wālī* of Calicut) was pretty much a chimera. The port itself made a favourable impression on him, and he describes it in terms that are very similar to his description of Hurmuz.

Calicut is a safe port (*amanābād*), equal to Hurmuz in its mercantile population from every land and region, and the availability of rareties of all sorts from Daryabar, especially the Land below the Winds, Abyssinia, and Zanj. From time to time, ships come from God's House [*Baitallāh*], and other towns in the Hijaz, and stop for a while in this port. It is a city of infidels, and therefore is in the Abode of War (*dār-ul-ḥarb*). However, there is a Muslim population resident, with two congregational mosques, and on Fridays they pray with peace of mind. They have a religiously observant *qāẓī*, and most of them are Shafiʿi by sect.

The main difference, of course, is that Hurmuz is a city within the proper sphere of Islam, with a population of infidels, whereas in Calicut the roles are reversed. In each of the two cases, mutual tolerance is described as the rule, and the "security and justice" in Calicut are praised by him unstintingly. Goods can be left on the street, it would seem, without fear of thieves, on account of the watchmen of the state (*amīnān-i dīwān*). As for duties, at one-fortieth (and that too, only on sales), they are even lower than at Hurmuz; and the unhappy custom of seizing the contents of ships that stray into the port is unknown here, even if it is practised elsewhere (as by the pirates, *dūzdān*, of Sangisar, into whose hands the other ship of the Timurid party had fallen meanwhile).[26] All these then are the laudable aspects of Calicut, so far as our envoy is concerned.

[26] This group, though robbed, was eventually set free, and rejoined ʿAbdur Razzaq at Calicut. "Sangisar" in this account is Sanghameswar, on the Indian west coast.

Against that, the people of the port and its environs do not quite meet his standards. A verse that finds a place in his text shortly into his description of India is telling in this respect, concerning what he terms "a people the likes of whom I had never imagined". Of them he writes:

> A strange nation, neither men nor demons,
> meeting whom would drive one mad.
> Had I seen their likes [even] in a dream,
> it would have shaken my heart for years.
> Moon-like faces please me,
> not any ill-proportioned black thing.

These *hindū'ān* or *hindawiyān* (the manuscripts vary on this) simply cannot meet with his approval, for a variety of reasons. There are, to begin with, colour prejudices that seem to run through the descriptions of "naked blacks with loin-cloths tied from their navels to their knees, in one hand an Indian dagger (*katāra*) like a drop of water, and in the other a leather shield as large as a cloud". Worse is the absence of proper hierarchy as expressed through appropriate dress-codes, which would form a part of civilized society as 'Abdur Razzaq would understand it; in Calicut, on the contrary, "both king and beggar look alike", and the only ones who are able to distinguish themselves are the Muslims, who "wear fine clothing in the Arab fashion".[27] This view is confirmed when he is given an audience by the king (here, *pādishāh*), three days after his arrival, and finds him to be "as naked as the others". Though the court of the ruler (at last termed the Samiri) is crowded with several thousands of men, including the chief Muslim of Calicut (*kalāntar-i Musalmānān*), the lack of etiquette displeases 'Abdur Razzaq once more. The letter from Shahrukh is read out, but makes no great impression; the horse, robes and other gifts are also handed over, but the envoy notes that "the Samiri did not pay full respect, and I returned to my quarters from the assembly". Clearly, the expectations of the Timurid court were that the envoy would be treated better bearing in mind that Shahrukh had received emissaries and messages from "the rulers of the inhabited quarter of the globe, east and west, land and sea" (as the text tells us somewhat earlier), in view of the fact that his court was the *Qibla* and Ka'aba on which they all depended. One cannot but suspect that the inflated claims imposed by the Timurid inheritance rather exacerbated matters here.

[27] This question is also commented on by Phillip B. Wagoner, "'Sultan among Hindu kings': dress, titles and the Islamicization of Hindu culture at Vijayanagara", *Journal of Asian Studies*, 55, 4, 1996, pp. 851–80.

The stay at Calicut seems to have lasted some four months, from November 1442 to early April 1443. These were unhappy times for 'Abdur Razzaq, a fact that he makes no effort to conceal in his account, for he refers to this period as a time when "we were afflicted by having to stay in that infelicitous place". To be sure, he has some positive things to say about Calicut as a port; in addition to the remarks that we have already noted, he writes, for example, that the people of the area are "brave seafarers", that the port is plentifully supplied with goods, and that piracy is unknown there. But, against this, the disappointment at being unable to make any headway in the matter of the conversion of the Samudri (as had been so broadly hinted at by the envoy to Herat), clearly colours his vision of the infidels of the town. Thus, one passage runs: "Everything is to be found in the port, and the only crime is to kill cows and eat beef. If anyone kills a cow and is found out, that person is immediately put to death. They venerate cows to such an extent that they rub the ashes of its dung on their forehead. God's curses upon them (*Alaihim la'n Allah ta'āla*)". The violence of the last Arabic phrase is still something of an exception though, rather than reflective of a more general, and explicit, disapprobation concerning all manner of exotic social arrangements. There is another moment when 'Abdur Razzaq chooses the ethnographic mode, that is in his description of succession and polyandry in Calicut, an early version of what was to become a topos in sixteenth-century European accounts in regard to the Nayars of Kerala.[28] Here, the tone of disdain is far more discreet than in the passage cited above, and indeed the vocabulary is remarkably restrained. Thus, with respect to the Samudri, he writes:

> When he dies, his sister's son takes his place and [the throne] is not given to son, brother or other relative. No one becomes king by force. The infidels are of many sorts, Brahmins, yogis (*jogiyān*), and others. Although they all share the same polytheism and idolatry, every group (*qaum*) has a different system. There is one group whose women have multiple husbands, each of whom has a specific task to perform. They divide the day and night, and each one goes to her quarters at a specified time. So long as one is there, no other can go in. The Samiri is of this group (*qaum*).

There is a sense, still, of mounting frustration as time passes, and the embassy is left sitting on its hands, as it were. A resolution is thus sought,

[28] Joan-Pau Rubiés, *Travel and ethnology in the Renaissance: South India through European eyes, 1250–1625* (Cambridge, 2000), pp. 215–19.

and it emerges from the mystic sphere, in the form of a dream, in which Shahrukh appears to ʿAbdur Razzaq one night. Stroking the envoy's face, he tells him not to be distressed, and ʿAbdur Razzaq (who wakes and informs his companions of the dream) is quite reassured by this.[29] Indeed, a happy resolution is at once at hand, for that very day, an unexpected envoy arrives from the ruler of Vijayanagara (*pādishāh-i Bījānagar*), described as "a vast kingdom and magnificent realm", asking the Samudri to send the Timurid envoy on to his court.

MANAGING THE WINDFALL

It is to be emphasised then, that the visit to Vijayanagara was not on the cards when ʿAbdur Razzaq left Herat, and indeed it is not at all clear whether the Timurid court at that time knew of the existence of the Vijayanagara (or Karnataka) kingdom, that had been founded in the middle of the fourteenth century, at roughly the same time as the Bahmani Sultanate of the Deccan. It is certain that the traders and rulers of Hurmuz, in the Persian Gulf, were aware of the commercial importance of Vijayanagara, but this is no guarantee that the kingdom had entered into standard Timurid xenology by 1440. At any rate, what is clear is that before the arrival of the envoy from Vijayanagara at Calicut, the kingdom is never before mentioned in ʿAbdur Razzaq's text. He thus begins by providing a brief account of Vijayanagara, as he perceived it from Calicut.

The ruler of this kingdom, it was claimed by his envoys, "possessed 300 ports, each as large as Calicut, and . . . it took two or three months to traverse his realm by land". Clearly, this polity is quite a different affair from Calicut, which has obviously been something of a let-down for ʿAbdur Razzaq. Even though its ruler does not possess jurisdiction (*ḥukm*) over Calicut, it is clear to the Timurid envoy that the Samudri is "still in great awe of him". It is thus with a sense of relief and expectation that he departs Calicut, taking a ship from the harbour of Pantalayini northward to Mangalore, which defines the limit of Vijayanagara rule on the Kanara coast. After a brief rest of two or three days at that port, he then begins his journey inland, which takes him through a series of temples (*but-k͟hānas*),

29 See later instances of such dream interventions in Chapters 4 and 5 below; and for a general reflection, see Sara Sviri, "Dreaming analyzed and recorded: dreams in the world of medieval Islam", in David Shulman and Guy G. Stroumsa, eds., *Dream cultures: explorations in the comparative history of dreaming* (New York, 1999), pp. 252–73.

as well as pleasant gardens and other spots of natural beauty, before reaching the city of Vijayanagara itself towards the end of April 1443 (also the end of the month of Zi-Hijja 846 H), that is almost exactly a month from the date of his departure from Calicut.

This passage from the coast to the inland political centre obviously left 'Abdur Razzaq greatly impressed, and even his criticism of local religious observances is limited to one or two passing remarks. For the rest, two complementary, and positive, aspects of the country are stressed: first, the flourishing state of nature and of rural life; and second, the brilliant craftsmanship produced by talented human hands in the area. Thus, even the idol-houses (*but-k̲h̲āna*) are treated in very large measure using a secular vocabulary, which downplays their religious function, and instead emphasises their role quite simply as buildings. It is the same tone that other writers of the period take while describing pre-Islamic (say, Sasanian) structures in lands that have been converted to Islam.

A first example of this occurs within a few days of 'Abdur Razzaq's arrival in Mangalore, and before he crosses the Western Ghats, the chain of mountains that divide the coastal strip from the interior plateau. He writes:

> Within three leagues (*farsang*) of Mangalore, I saw an idol-house the likes of which is not to be found in all the world. It was a square, approximately ten yards (*gaz*) a side, five yards in height, all [covered] with cast bronze, with four porticos. In the entrance portico was a statue in the likeness of a human being (*ba ṣūrat-i ādamī*), full stature, made of gold. It had two red rubies for eyes, so cunningly made that you would say it could see. What craft and artisanship!

Later, having traversed the Ghats, he arrives at Belur, where again he is much impressed by the "idol-house . . . so tall that it can be seen from several leagues away", adding that "no description of that building could do it justice". The building, and in particular an interior platform with "a conical dome of dark blue stone with various designs carved", inspire the following verse.

> What can I say of that dome,
> delicate as a copy of Paradise brought to the world ?
> The curve of its high arch like a new moon,
> so tall it rubbed up against the celestial sphere.

The stone carvings are compared to those of the Franks and Chinese (*firangī* and *k̲h̲aṭā'ī*), again metaphors that stress the interesting association of craftsmanship and exotic origin but that also play with the idea that infidel hands can still craft such wonders. To be sure, 'Abdur Razzaq wants his readers to recall that this is still a place of the unbelievers (*bedīn*), and also mentions the music and dances that are performed in the course of this unacceptable worship (*'ibādat-i ghair maqbūla*), but the dominant tone is of wonder (*'ajā'ib*), where all is "beyond description", with decorations that are "of extreme delicacy". These idol-houses are portrayed as great centres of riches (and here, we enter more familiar territory): they have votive offerings brought from far and wide, the population of the whole village "receives a treatment [a kind of subsidy]" from them, and, in the case of Belur, it is even compared to a sort of infidel Ka'aba.

The reader's appetite has presumably been whetted, after the disappointing times at Calicut, but 'Abdur Razzaq now chooses, for reasons of chronological discipline, to interrupt his narrative, and to digress for the space of a chapter on an "account of the sending of an ambassador (*īlchī*) to Egypt (Misr) and other matters".[30] Returning then to his travels, he reminds his readers that he is now in Vijayanagara, "a city of enormous magnitude and population, with a king of perfect rule and hegemony (*dar kamāl-i salṭanat wa jahānbānī*), whose kingdom stretched from the borders of Ceylon [Sarandip], to the province of Gulbarga, and from the borders of Bengal to the region of Malibar, more than a thousand leagues". This is an impressive statement, which at one and the same time brings out the huge size of the enterprise, places it in a more familiar geographical context, and gives it a highly positive flavour. This is further stressed when the account assures us that "most of his [the king's] regions were flourishing", which recalls the earlier passage from Mangalore to Belur, where the traveller and his companions "passed by flourishing towns and villages every day". The measures of the ruler's power are two: one is commercial in nature, namely the vast number of ports he controls (in stark contrast, one may add, to Shahrukh); and the other is military, and is stated in terms of elephants (a thousand, "with bodies like mountains and miens like demons"), and also in terms of his soldiers who number over a million. 'Abdur Razzaq then goes on to assure the reader that, in Hindustan, there is no ruler (*rāy*) more independent (*khwudrāi*) than this king, and expresses his conviction that the stories of the *Kalīla-o-Dimna*

[30] *Maṭla' us-Sa'dain*, text, pp. 791–6.

(the Perso-Arabic version of the Panchatantra fables from India) result from the collective wisdom of the Brahmins of this very kingdom.[31]

An ingenious method is now employed to aid the reader to obtain the true measure of the city that 'Abdur Razzaq is about to describe in detail. This is to superimpose the imagined city of Vijayanagara on that of Herat, far more familiar to his readers.[32] By this means, the three outermost walls of the fortifications of Vijayanagara are placed atop Herat, and since the first two exceed the Timurid capital in size, the description must spill over into the countryside of Khorasan. It is with the third level of fortifications that 'Abdur Razzaq claims to achieve some form of loose fit, as we see from the following passage.

The third wall would reach from the shrine of Imam Fakhr-ud-Din Razi [in Herat], to the dome of Muhammad Sultanshah. The fourth would extend from the Injil Bridge to the Kard Bridge; the fifth from the gate of the Bagh-i Zaghan to the Ab-i Chakan Bridge; the sixth from the Malik Gate to the Firozabad Gate; and the seventh, the innermost, is ten times the size of the *chārsū* in Herat, and that is the court (*dargāh*) of the king [in Vijayanagara].

All this is not calculated to flatter Timurid pretensions, even if we know that parts of this description draw on purely conventional imagery (for instance, it is not clear that Vijayanagara city really had seven concentric walls, this being a typical stylised description). Equally, the bald claim at the outset of this section that "the city of Bijanagar [is one] whose inhabitants have no equals in the world", was bound to attract the reader's attention, since it comes framed in a passage that is not otherwise marked by much hyperbole.

This topographical comparison yields quickly enough though to a section whose tone is markedly different, being written in elaborate and hyperbolic rhymed prose. The occasion for this is the description of the bazaars of the town, which (it is noted) lie for the most part between the third and the seventh walls (counting from the outside in), with the centre being defined by the king's palace (*sarāi-i rāy*), where the tallest building is the *aiwān-i sulṭān*, or king's portico. The shift in tone may be remarked if one takes up, by way of example, the following passage:

31 'Abdur Razzaq is presumably referring to the Persian version, prepared in the twelfth century by Abu'l Ma'ali Nasrullah, at the Ghaznavid court, though he probably also knew the Arabic text of Ibn al-Muqaffa'.

32 On Herat in the period, see Maria Szuppe, *Entre Timourides, Uzbeks et Safavides: questions d'histoire politique et sociale de Hérat dans la première moitié du XVIe siècle* (Paris, 1992).

The bazaars are extremely broad and long. Flower sellers have tall platforms in front of the stalls, and on both sides they sell flowers. In that city, there are aromatic flowers continually in bloom, and as necessary as they deem food to be, they cannot bear to be without flowers. The practitioners of every craft have stalls adjacent to one another. The jewellers sell pearls, diamonds, rubies and emeralds openly in the bazaar, pearls (*marwārīd*) of good water, and royal pearls which even the divers in the Ocean of Wisdom have not seen the equal of, and which seem to be made from the jewels of the heart that are provided by He who is a Jewel in the Sky. These pearls are such that the field of the moon of the fourteenth day caught fire simply by gazing on them.[33]

After this purple passage on pearls, other stones such as rubies and diamonds are all praised in turn in the most high-flown way. Having completed this literary *tour de force* to his satisfaction, 'Abdur Razzaq moves on to a far more prosaic description of the palace and its immediate environs, the seat of royal power in the city. The Persian aesthetic sense of the epoch is pleased here, for we are told that "in that pleasant open space [at the centre], and royal court, is much flowing water and nice streams". The account then proceeds to concentrate on a series of organising institutional themes, namely the nature of public administration and justice, the working of the treasury, and then a long and particularly elaborate disquisition on the subject of elephants, which are seen as both the main military support and the specificity of this kingdom. These descriptions precede an account of the king himself (Deva Raya II, whose name is only later mentioned), and of certain royal customs, and then a series of anecdotes from hearsay and eyewitness accounts.

These descriptions seem intended to demonstrate that in Vijayanagara, a series of institutions exist that correspond to those from the world that the Timurids were rather more familiar with, namely that extending from China via Central Asia, to Iran and the Mediterranean. Vijayanagara is thus presented as far more akin to this world than is, say, Calicut; at any rate, 'Abdur Razzaq does not deem it necessary to describe the functioning of the Samudri's kingdom as he does that of the Vijayanagara ruler. The first aspect that attracts his attention is the office of the *dannāyak*, who is associated with the revenue-administration (*dīwān-kh̲āna*), the place where he works being a pillared hall that is compared to the classic *chihil sutūn* "the forty-pillared hall" of Sasanid times. Here, one finds a number of scribes (*nawīsindagān*) who keep records, either on Indian coconut-palm leaf (*ba barg-i jauz-i hindī*), or, when the record is meant to be

[33] Thackston, *A century of princes*, p. 308 (*Maṯla' us-Sa'dain*, text, pp. 799–800).

permanent and reliable (*daftar-i mu'tabar*), with white colour on black stock. The same *dannāyak* receives petitioners in a style that would be familiar to readers from the Persian world: they offer a gift, and, after prostration, state their case. However, what transpires here is distinguished from what 'Abdur Razzaq is familiar with in his own environment, for the *dannāyak* (who sits alone) simply delivers a judgment in keeping with the rules or customs (*bā qā'ida*) of the kingdom, while no one else is permitted to speak or intervene. The power of this *dannāyak* is thus considerable, and it is mentioned that he is a eunuch (*khwājasarā*), who goes about in some pomp, accompanied by eulogists, and protected by parasols (*chatr*).

A second passage then turns to another institution, namely the treasury (*ẕarrāb khāna*). Five sorts of coins are mentioned, the *varāha*, the *partāb* (worth half of the first), the most common of all called the *fanam*, a silver coin called the *tār*, and a copper coin, the *chītal*. The military-fiscal system is then rapidly set out, with a certain emphasis on its centralisation (which is in fact belied by other evidence): "It is the rule in this kingdom that cash (*zar*) from all the territories is brought in to the treasury (*ẕarrāb khāna*) at a stipulated period. If the *dīwān* wishes to give cash to anyone, he writes [a note] on the *ẕarrāb khāna*. The soldiers (*sipāhiyān*) collect their pay (*marsūm*) every four months. Nobody is assigned anything on any province (*wilāyat*)."[34] A third set of discursive passages then moves on to the elephant stables (*fīl-khāna*), which are described as being next to the *dīwān-khāna*. It is here that 'Abdur Razzaq can give some play to a form of exoticism, which he has denied himself in the previous passages, preferring there to stress the close parallels between Vijayanagara and the kingdoms of the Perso-Islamic world. Great attention is devoted to the food (*kichrī*) that is fed to the elephants, the manner in which they are chained, and how they are captured and tamed by the elephant-keepers (*fīl-bān*). Special mention is made too of a particular white elephant (with lentil-sized albino spots) that the king reputedly possesses, and which is "taken every morning into the *rāy*'s presence, for he considers the sight of it a favourable omen". Elephants, it seems, are central to royal life in Hindustan; the kings all hunt them and trade in them; wrong-doers (*gunāhgārān*) are cast beneath their feet as a punishment.

Elephants provide an exotic touch then, as do betel-leaves in a later passage. 'Abdur Razzaq also notes that (in implicit contrast to the

[34] *Maṭla' us-Sa'dain*, text, p. 802; and Thackston, *A century of princes*, p. 309. We prefer to translate *ẕarrāb khāna* by "treasury" rather than "mint".

Timurid domains) Vijayanagara has much by way of what he terms *kharābāt* – a category which would include taverns, gaming-houses, and also brothels – the tax on which yields some 12,000 *fanams* a day, which is paid out to the guards (*'asasān*) in the city, whose headquarters (*shaḥnā-gāh*) is opposite the treasury. The place where the prostitutes (*qahbagān*) ply their trade is of particular interest to him, and is described as having the form of a street 20 twenty yards wide, and 300 yards long, located behind the treasury.

Along both sides [of the road] are chambers and platforms. In front of the chambers, in place of plinths, are raised stone platforms, beautiful but small. Along both sides of the road are pictures of lions, leopards, tigers and other animals, depicted with such verisimilitude that one would think they were alive. Following [the hour of] the afternoon prayer, chairs and seats are placed at the doors of the chambers, which are as clean as can be, and there the prostitutes sit. Each of them is richly arrayed with pearls and jewels, and elegant clothes on their bodies. They are very young in age, and perfect in beauty. And before them stand one or two slave-girls (*jārya*), praising pleasure, with the doors of joy open, and the instruments of music (*asbāb-i ṭarab*) ready and laid out. Whoever comes there and wishes to do so, enjoys himself. The people there (*ahl-i kharābāt*) take care of the guests' belongings, and if anything is lost, they compensate them.

The modern-day reader may draw his or her own conclusions on how the still-youthful 'Abdur Razzaq, who was about thirty at the time of his stay in Vijayanagara, came to accumulate such details, as the contemporary reader of the account must have done as well. As if to compensate for these overly revealing details, 'Abdur Razzaq moves quickly on to his dealings with the king, and ostentatiously makes it a point on the next occasion that he refers to the city, to term it "a great city, and abode of darkness (*shahr-i mu'aẓẓam wa manzil-i ẓalāl*)".[35] Nevertheless, the king himself makes an extremely favourable impression on the envoy, who notes besides that (and unlike the mediocre treatment he had received in Calicut), in Vijayanagara he was "assigned extremely fine quarters, the equivalent of which in Herat would be located over the Malik Gate, the main thoroughfare". Summoned a few days after his arrival (in the month of Muharram) to the court, he went with a gift of five horses, and robes in silk and satin, to be received once more in a pillared hall reminiscent of classical Iran (the recurrent topos of the *chihil sutūn*). The king here, as in Calicut, is surrounded by a throng, but the contrast is otherwise striking: "He wore a tunic (*qabā*) of Zaituni [Chinese] satiny silk, and a necklace of

[35] Thackston, *A century of princes*, p. 310; *Maṭla' us-Sa'dain*, text, p. 807.

lustrous pearls, the worth of which the jeweller of the mind could scarcely appraise. He was of dark complexion (*sabza rang*), slim, tallish in height, and very young. On his cheeks were the dark traces of down, but nothing on his chin. His face was chiselled (*bag̲h̲āyat maṭbū'*)." The envoy is brought before him, bows, and is invited to take a seat. He presents his letter of credentials, which are then handed over to an official. The king says, through a Persian-speaking interpreter (*kalīma-chi*), doubtless the same who was used to deal with the Deccan rulers, that he is pleased to receive an emissary from the great *pādishāh*. The conversation is short, for it is hot and uncomfortable (it is the month of May). There is time only for the envoy to receive a ceremonial gift of camphor (*kāfūr-i jaudāna*), 500 *fanams* in cash, and a bunch of betel-leaf (*tambūl*) (besides a Chinese fan, that the king presents him on an impulse, from his own hand). Nevertheless, he retires to his quarters with a sense of satisfaction. A considerable daily ration of meat has also been granted to the Timurid party (two sheep and four pairs of fowl), besides rice, oil, sugar, and a cash-allowance, as if to confirm their status.

Thereafter, 'Abdur Razzaq reports that he was invited to the court twice a week, usually at the end of the day, and was asked about Shahrukh by the Vijayanagara ruler. Food was never offered to him, and the king is even said to have remarked once: "Your kings invite emissaries to banquets, [but] since you and I do not eat each other's food, let this package of gold be the emissary's banquet." The same gifts are given him on each occasion, and he seems particularly to have been struck by the betel-leaves, that he describes in some detail as similar to an orange-leaf but longer, noting that, although they were in use in Hindustan, the Arab lands, and even Hurmuz, they were apparently largely unknown in Herat. This leads him to give details of how the leaf is eaten, with betel-nut and quick-lime, and at times a bit of camphor added on. As for the effects, they are many and invariably positive. "The cheeks glow, and a pleasant sensation, like that of wine, is produced. It assuages hunger [but] also makes one who is already satiated desirous of food. It eliminates unpleasant odours from the mouth, and makes the teeth strong." Not only this, the betel-leaf is also associated by him with virility, and used to explain how the king of Vijayanagara has as many wives and concubines (*qumma*) as he does, who are perhaps 700 in number, and whom he nevertheless manages to keep in strict check. This is associated with the common formula of royal power as expressed through sexual conquest: "Throughout his realm, wherever there is a beautiful girl, he persuades the girl's mother and father and has her brought with much celebration to his harem." Moreover, in order to shore up his view of the quasi-magical power of the betel-leaf, 'Abdur Razzaq has recourse to a particularly clever device, namely Persian poetry from India, which has the ability to domesticate the unfamiliar. And once more, as on his sea-voyage, his poet of choice is the prestigious Amir Khusrau, whose *Qirān-us-Sa'dain* is deftly cited:

> A chew of betel bound into a hundred leaves,
> came to hand like a hundred-petaled flower.
> Rare leaf, like a flower in a garden,
> Hindustan's most beautiful delicacy,
> sharp as a rearing stallion's ear,
> sharp in both shape and taste,
> its sharpness a tool to cut roots,
> as the Prophet's words tell us.
> Full of veins with no trace of blood,
> yet from its veins blood races out,
> wondrous plant, for placed in the mouth,
> blood comes from its body like a living thing.[36]

The full citation is a long one, twice as long as the passage we have cited here, and it is by no means the last time that 'Abdur Razzaq will cite this poet as a handy bridge between his own readers and an unfamiliar Indian reality.

Still, it would seem that, even if royal virility is assured, royal power in Vijayanagara is somewhat insecure. This is illustrated by 'Abdur Razzaq through a long anecdote gleaned from hearsay (and possibly apocryphal), concerning an assassination attempt on the king by his brother some months earlier, when the Timurid envoy himself was still at Calicut. It is claimed that the brother in question had hired two murderers with daggers, to get rid of not merely the king but most of the grandees (*umarā'*) and ministers. Since, so it is claimed, "it is customary among the infidels not to eat in each other's presence", the matter was rendered all that much easier, for the targets were invited to a banquet, led off separately to eat, and then killed. Only the king, who had some sort of intuition, refused to go (a verse from Nizami, about a duck and a hawk, is cited for this intuition). His brother was hence obliged to stab him openly in the throne room, but the former survived the wound. Recovering his force, he hence summoned guards (*jāndār*) to his aid, and cried out: "I am alive and well. Seize this bastard (*ḥarāmzāda*)." The crowd then summarily

[36] Amir Khusrau, *Qirān-us-Sa'dain* (Aligarh, 1918), p. 185. For a more recent edition, see Amir Khusraw Dehlawi, *Qirān-us-Sa'dain*, ed. Ahmad Hasan Dani (Islamabad, 1976).

killed the brother, who had meanwhile gone out to the palace balcony to announce that he was now king. There then followed a ruthless counter-offensive, in which all those "suspected of having a hand in the affair were brought down . . ., killed, their skins stripped, their bodies burned, and their families reduced to annihilation". Among the fortunate survivors was the *dannāyak*, who was temporarily absent in Ceylon, but who was summoned back post-haste. 'Abdur Razzaq does not present a clear judgment on the affair, though one gathers that he feels the retaliation went beyond the necessary bounds. Yet, it is for him an impressive display of royal power.

The account returns, after this brief digression into the realm of hearsay, to the usual mode of the eyewitness account. The next item to occupy 'Abdur Razzaq's attention is the great festival (which he terms *mahnāvamī*, for *mahānavamī*) that he terms an "imperial festival" of the infidels (*kuffār*). On this occasion, he notes, a gathering takes place of the leaders and chiefs from across the kingdom, who arrive with the key symbol of power, namely elephants that are "boiling like the sea and thundering like clouds". This festival is placed by him at the full moon of the month of Rajab that year (that is, November 1443, arguably rather too late in the year). The centre-piece of this event for him is undoubtedly the elephants, but one also finds a repeated emphasis on the existence of human and animal figures in local traditions of representation, on the sides of the pavilions (*chahārṭāq*) for example. 'Abdur Razzaq claims to have had a place of honour in order to view the festivities; there were nine arches in a particular pillared hall (once more, the *chihil sutūn*), with the king at the fifth arch, and the Timurid envoy at the seventh. The elephants are described at some length ("the wise Brahmins and demonaic elephants" being an interesting pairing), but the words are not 'Abdur Razzaq's own. Rather, once more he has extensive recourse to Amir Khusrau's *Qirān-us-Sa'dain*, even if he changes the verse order of the poet on occasion, and drops a few verses here or there. Thus, for example:

> The elephants' bodies bent the earth,
> and created quakes the world over.
> All that monstrous ivory made
> the face of the world into a chess-board.

Similarly, while describing the women singers (*muṭribān wa qawwālān*) who took part in the festival, "with beautiful garments and enchanting countenances like fresh roses", he returns once more to the *Qirān* for verses to supplement his own invention. Equally described in some detail

Figure 5. Single caparisoned elephant, *Fīl-nāma*, National Museum, New Delhi, No. 78218.

are the acrobats (*bāzigarān*) and their tricks with elephants, and music. It is noted that all this is inserted in a formal ceremony, wherein "each group that sings or performs before the king is rewarded with gold and garments (*jāmā*)", with the festival going on in the king's presence for three whole days.

After the festival is over, 'Abdur Razzaq resumes his periodic visits to the royal presence, where he is once again asked about Shahrukh, as well as for description of "the *amīrs*, the army, the number of horses, and a description of cities of the realm like Samarqand, Herat and Shiraz". These discussions inevitably take place through an interpreter (*tarjumān*), and there is also talk of a return embassy which will be sent with gifts of elephants and eunuch slaves. However, a series of clouds is on the horizon, the first in the form of a group (*jamā'at*) of merchants from Hurmuz, who begin to spread rumours casting doubts on 'Abdur Razzaq's credentials as a Timurid envoy. Added to this is news of an impending invasion by the Bahmani Sultan, termed "the king of Gulbarga, Sultan 'Ala-ud-Din Ahmad Shah", who had apparently decided that the internal dissensions at Vijayanagara (following the assassination attempt) provided him a splendid opportunity to demand a sum of money as tribute. The conflict is posed in explicitly religious terms, with the Bahmani Sultan claiming that he wishes to free Vijayanagara of "infidel rule (*qā'ida-i kufr*)", and Deva Raya for his part responding as follows (in 'Abdur Razzaq's rather fanciful words): "Whatever he [the Sultan] can take of my kingdom, he will consider booty (*ghanīmat*) and give to his Sayyids and *'ulamā'*, just as I will give whatever I can seize of his kingdom to the thread-wearers (*zunnārdār*) and Brahmins."

Now, this conflict worsened 'Abdur Razzaq's situation considerably, for it required the *dannāyak* ("the *wazīr* who paid kind attention to me") to depart to the war-front, and in his absence a certain Hanamba (perhaps Hanumantha), termed a "thread-wearer", emerged into prominence. He is termed "a short-statured, evil man, a vile, penny-pinching wretch possessing all bad qualities and devoid of any redeeming features". He apparently was influenced by the view of the Hurmuzis who cast doubts on 'Abdur Razzaq, and hence promptly stopped his daily allowance; the rumour began to take shape that the envoy was in fact a mere charlatan, a merchant (*saudāgar*) who had deviously got hold of a Timurid letter of credentials. But all was not lost, even in what 'Abdur Razzaq now bitterly terms an abode of infidelity (*kufristān*). Thus:

In this weariness, a few times I met the king on the way. He drew back the reins of favour (*'inān-i 'ināyat bāz kashīd*), and asked about my condition. Still, in truth, he possessed excellence of character.

If all this is justice, so be it.

But, fortunately, a happier ending was on the cards. For the return of the *dannāyak* from the front saw matters take a turn for the better. The deputy was chastised and the allowance resumed, and an additional cash-grant given. It was also decided to send two men from Khorasan (Khwaja Mas'ud and Khwaja Muhammad) as return envoys to Shahrukh, with gifts and goods. A last interview with Deva Raya was granted, where he apparently hinted that he had had doubts about the authenticity of 'Abdur Razzaq. This is a rather curious passage, in which he puts direct speech into the Vijayanagara ruler's mouth, using the prefatory phrase "he might as well have said (*zabān-i hāl mi guft*)", in order to make explicit what was apparently never said. There also follows the transcript of a brief letter addressed by Deva Raya to Shahrukh, as follows:

It was our intention that with these royal gifts and presents to the Hazrat-i Khilafat, an alliance (*tawassul*) might be sought. But one group here has claimed that 'Abdur Razzaq is not from amongst your servants (*mulāzimān*). In the description of your qualities, it is written that you have royal traits and imperial glories, combined with the purity of the prophets and the qualities of the saints. So it is stamped on the tongues of the great and the small, and the speech of each news-bearer, and in the writing-pen of each scribe (*muḥarrir*).

A verse now follows, praising Shahrukh and comparing him metaphorically with the prophets of old; whether this was in fact in the original letter, or an addition of ʻAbdur Razzaq is less than clear. But even this verse could not conceal the lukewarm quality of the farewell, which eventually made the mission into rather less than a glorious success. The tone is thus bitter, as the envoy packs his bags to leave "that terrible place of infidelity and error" (*ān wahshatābād-i kufr-o-ẓalāl*). The departure from Vijayanagara is on 5 December 1443, and the Kanara port of Bakanur is reached some eighteen days later. Here, the events are mixed; ʻAbdur Razzaq is blessed by meeting an old saint, Amir Sayyid ʻAla-ud-Din Mashhadi, who is allegedly over 120 years of age, but one of the return envoys, Khwaja Masʻud, dies there. This summons up the following verse:

> Only this wicked temple knows
> on which brick we shall lay down our heads.

The fasting month of Ramazan is spent in that port, from where the party (now numbering some twenty persons) makes for Honawar, where a ship awaits them. The party is still destined to remain on shore for a while, eventually boarding their vessel only on 15 March 1444. But ʻAbdur Razzaq now has recourse to divination (*fāl*), and is consoled by the signs, for the Qur'anic verse that emerges is: "Fear not; thou hast escaped from unjust people." As he writes, "suddenly, I had every expectation of deliverance and redemption".

This view turns out to be rather too optimistic though. At first, the voyage goes smoothly, and the travellers in the party exchange tales and stories. But some days out to sea, a great storm arises, and the ship's master and pilot (*muʻallim* and *mallāḥ*) are left incapable of mastering their vessel. The passengers (*musāfirān*) begin to cast their goods into the water to lighten the ship, as "the planks which had been joined together in an unbroken line (*khaṭṭ-i musalsal*), flew apart like cut-out letters". Several verses, largely in Persian, and a few in Arabic, intersperse this description, including the following citation from the Iranian poet, Salman Savaji (regarding a ship tossed in a storm):

> Sometimes lifted so high that the horseshoe
> of the new moon rubs the horses' legs.

Sometimes sunk so low that Corah's [buried] treasure
rises over the steeds' stirrups.[37]

Or again, the following verse from Hafiz, which 'Abdur Razzaq claims he repeated to himself time and again, in the face of the storm:

The dark night, the fearsome waves,
and the awesome whirlpool;
How can those who bear no burden,
and live on the shore,
imagine our condition?

The storm seems to have gone on for a time, while the travellers cursed their ill-luck and prayed to God by turns. 'Abdur Razzaq himself notes that he deplored how the Age (*zamāna-i g͟haddār*) seemed to have decreed that he would never finish the work of the state (*maṣlīḥat-i mulkī*) on which he had been sent, or even thank and repay his patron (*mun'im*), namely Mirza Shahrukh. Then, all of a sudden, the tempest ceased, in time for the travellers to celebrate the feast of 'Id al-Azha on board. The calm sea now permitted them to sight Mount Qalhat, and early in the month of Muharram (some thirty-five days after setting out from Honawar), they were nearly ashore.

A brief gap follows once more in the travel narrative, which turns to relating events not directly concerned with the voyage, namely "the events of the year 848 [and] the weakness and malady of the Khaqan-i Sa'id", followed by an account of the despatch of Shaikh Nur-ud-Din Muhammad al-Murshidi and Maulana Shams-ud-Din Muhammad Abhari in an embassy to Egypt, and finally a chapter "on the *wilāyat* of Balkh and the death of Amir Firuzshah, and the succession of Amir Sultanshah Barlas".[38] We then return to the last leg of the voyage, with 'Abdur Razzaq resuming his narrative from the time his ship is about to drop anchor in Masqat. Here, after repairs, the ship sets forth, and Amir Khusrau is cited one last time *in extenso*. Again, the heat of the Persian Gulf strikes our traveller, for once more 'Abdur Razzaq finds himself there in the months of May and June. A painful voyage takes the ship limping from Masqat to Khurfaghan, and then to Hurmuz, where they arrived to receive the depressing news that Shahrukh was ill. Besides, on account of the great heat, they cannot travel through the desert and must wait seventy days in Hurmuz, before resuming the journey through Awghan and Tarzak.

[37] *Kulliyāt-i Salmān Sāvajī*, ed. 'Abbas 'Ali Wafa'i (Tehran, 1382 Sh. / 2004).
[38] *Maṭla' us-Sa'dain*, text, pp. 831–42.

Yet, there is a sense in the narrative that 'Abdur Razzaq's safe return is meant to be, and another event seems to confirm the predestination of the *fāl* at Honawar. For, the very day of 'Abdur Razzaq's arrival in Hurmuz, a holy man in the city of Herat, the Shaikh-ul-Islam Baha-ud-Din Shaikh Umar, meets 'Abdur Razzaq's brother, Sharif-ud-Din 'Abdul Qahhar, purely by chance, and miraculously informs him that his brother has returned to Hurmuz. Thus, gathering strength against the heat (and the fact that he has fallen ill once more), 'Abdur Razzaq continues his voyage on a litter (*maḥaffa-i rawān*) through Farfhan and Sirjan. Eventually, he joins the retinue of a great Shaikh, and returns in his company to Herat via Kerman (where an unpleasant encounter with the local *dārogha* is recounted).[39] The entry into Herat is accomplished in January 1445, thus exactly three years from the time of 'Abdur Razzaq's departure; it is marked in the text with a suitable citation from Hafiz, on the subject of separation and union.

The very day after his return, 'Abdur Razzaq was received at the Timurid court with the emissaries from Vijayanagara, Khwaja Muhammad and Khwaja Jamal-ud-Din (Khwaja Mas'ud having died *en route*, as noted above). Here, he was invited to sit down, and asked to recount what he had seen of "the rulers of those realms, and my adventures on the sea and in the ship". This is the crowning moment for 'Abdur Razzaq after all he has endured. He is greatly praised by the ruler, "both in my presence and in my absence". He is frequently summoned to the court, when Shahrukh is in need of distraction, and asked to recount the "novelties of the kingdoms of the infidels (*gharā'ib-i mamlikat-i kuffār*)". As for the Vijayanagara emissaries, they are properly entertained (and received twice a week at court), after they have presented their gifts of rubies and Indian aromatics (*aqāqīl-i Hindī*); they are eventually sent back after three months with horses, cash and other gifts.

Now, of these emissaries, only one represents Deva Raya, the other (Jamal-ud-Din) in fact being an envoy of a certain Fath Khan, described as a member "of the family (*nasl*) of Sultan Firoz Shah, king of Delhi", who was resident in exile at the court of Vijayanagara. He had reputedly sent a petition (*'arẓdāsht*) that ran as follows:

When the victorious train of His Highness the Sahib-Qiran [Timur, Master of the Conjunction] came to the land of Hindustan, there was none among our

[39] The *dārogha* is reported to have remarked sarcastically, "What a good trade (*khush sauda-ist*)! Giving fifty thousand dinars and getting back ten thousand dinars", referring to the cost of the mission, which he saw as excessive.

renowned Sultans then alive to make obeisance and render fealty to him. In their ignorance, Mallu [Khan] and Sarang [Khan] created a disturbance and effaced the foundation of the dynasty. This humble one has suffered much misfortune in exile (*dayār-i ghurbat*) for a long time now but hopes that the servants of the royal threshold will summon me to the court so that perhaps through His Majesty's good fortune, I may be restored to my native land (*waṭan-i māluf*).

In response to this and the other letters he received, Shahrukh is reported to have sent a reply to Deva Raya, which was eventually sent back with a new envoy of his own, a certain Maulana Nasrullah Junabidhi. This letter is summarised as follows:

It has reached our ears that Fath Khan, one of the descendants (*farzandān*) of Sultan Firozshah, has taken refuge in your court. Now, if you can, restore him to the land of his ancestors (*pidarān*); otherwise, send him to our court that we may equip him with soldiers of the world, and God's destiny willing, return him to the land of his fathers and forefathers, and seat him on the throne of the Sultanate.

Not only this, in vengeance for the manner in which the merchants of Hurmuz had vilified 'Abdur Razzaq at the Vijayanagara court, it is reported that an edict (*nishān*) was sent, summoning the *wazīr* of Hurmuz, Khwaja Muhammad Baghdadi, to Herat, to account personally for what had transpired. Finally, on the intervention of the ruler of Hurmuz and that court, a compromise was reached: 'Abdur Razzaq was presented with five Abyssinian slaves, and a good number of bolts of cloth, to compensate him for the malice he had suffered. The travel-account can now conclude, all outstanding matters having been tied up. And so 'Abdur Razzaq writes:

It is hoped that the intelligent readers (*arbāb-ul-albāb*), 'May they be happy and achieve excellence' [Qur'anic verse], would not look with an overly critical eye at the account of the voyage to Hindustan (*dāstān-i safar-i Hindustān*) even if it has dragged on too long. These details that I have given, and that have been accumulated, result from the dictum, 'Those who receive orders are helpless.'

I do not speak, even if it is I who speak.

COMPARATIVE NOTES

A quarter-century after 'Abdur Razzaq's visit, another visitor to the Deccan left a fairly detailed account of his travels to the region. This was Afanasii Nikitin, a native of Tver' in Russia, whose "Voyage beyond the Three Seas" (*Khozhdenie za tri moria*) has been known to Anglophone readers from at least the middle of the nineteenth century, and had been published in Russian as part of the so-called "L'vov Chronicle" as early as 1792.[40] A significant body of twentieth-century literature has formed in Western languages over the years on Nikitin and his text.[41] This travel-account has a relatively significant place on account of its precocity in Russian literature, for although pilgrimage accounts are known from the Kievian period, non-religious or "secular" travel-accounts only begin to appear in numbers somewhat later.[42] Nikitin left his native town in 1466, as part of a group of merchants whose intention it was to trade with the lands of the Caspian Sea littoral, and to go as far as Shirwan. Unfortunately for him, the group was attacked on the Volga, and Nikitin himself robbed and taken prisoner. On his eventual release, our merchant made his way, first, with a Russian ambassadorial party to Derbend, and then via Iran to Hurmuz, where he remained for some time, until April 1469. By this time, Nikitin had been isolated from his erstwhile companions, and it was hence as a solitary traveller that he made his way from Hurmuz to the Deccan, where he remained in the domains of the Bahmani Sultanate until January 1472. He then undertook a return voyage that was no more tranquil than the outward one, and, having reached Crimea via Hurmuz, Lar, Isfahan and Tabriz, eventually appears to have died somewhere near Smolensk in December 1472. The travel-account might have disappeared with its author, but it appears that the text was then transmitted by other merchants to the deacon Vasilii Mamyrev, secretary to the Prince of Muscovy.

[40] For a translation into French which we have largely relied on (accompanied by the Russian text and extensive notes), see Jean-Yves Le Guillou, *Le voyage au-delà des trois mers d'Afanasij Nikitin (1466–1472)* (Quebec, 1978); also see another translation by Charles Malamoud, "Le voyage au-delà des trois mers d'Athanase Nikitine", *L'Ethnographie*, 76, 81–2, 1980, pp. 85–134. For an earlier German translation, see Karl H. Meyer, *Die Fahrt des Athanasius Nikitin über die drei Meere: Reise eines russischen Kaufmannes nach Ostindien, 1466–1472* (Leipzig, 1920). We have preferred not to use the English translation published in Moscow in 1960, which has been heavily (and justly) criticised by Lowell R. Tillett, "Afanasy Nikitin as a cultural ambassador to India: a bowdlerized Soviet translation of his journal", *Russian Review*, 25, 2, 1966, pp. 160–9.

[41] See, for example, Walther Kirchner, "The voyage of Athanasius Nikitin to India, 1466–1472", *American Slavic and East European Review*, 5, 1946, pp. 46–54; A. S. Morris, "The journey beyond three seas", *Geographical Journal*, 133, 4, Dec. 1967, pp. 502–8; Gail Lenhoff, "Beyond Three Seas: Afanasij Nikitin's journey from orthodoxy to apostasy", *Eastern European Quarterly*, 13, 4, 1979, pp. 432–47; also the classic and much-discussed interpretation of N. S. Trubetskoi, "Afanasij Nikitin's journey beyond the Three Seas as a work of literature", in Ladislav Matejka and Krystyna Pomorska, eds., *Readings in Russian poetics: formalist and structuralist views* (Cambridge, Mass., 1971), pp. 199–219 (the essay first appeared in 1926).

[42] See Gail Lenhoff, *The making of the medieval Russian journey* (Ann Arbor, 1978).

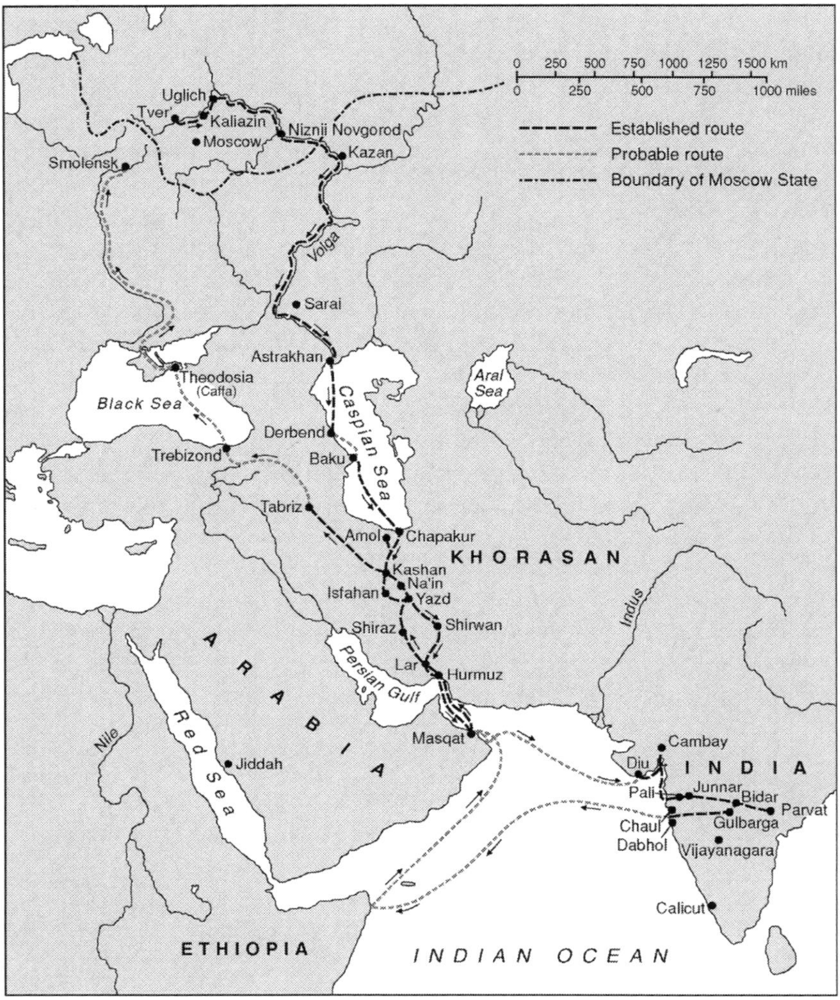

Map 1. Nikitin's travels to India.

Nikitin had clearly travelled before, to Georgia, Crimea, Wallachia and other lands; the idea of travelling some distance was hence not unfamiliar to him, although he does tell his reader mournfully that "he who travels a lot in numerous foreign lands falls into a multitude of sins and cannot keep the Christian faith". It seems clear that he possessed a fair command of Persian, and he also appears to have had some notions of Arabic and

Turkish, all of which are combined with the Russian of his basic narrative to form a sort of "sabir" (to employ the expression of one of his modern translators into French) or pidgin. Further, at times during his voyage, Nikitin appears to have presented himself as a Muslim merchant, calling himself Khwaja Yusuf Khorasani, by his own account. This confusion of identities, when added to the shifting linguistic registers within the text proper, lends the account a character that is clearly different from that of 'Abdur Razzaq, whose own identity remains stable and relatively confident throughout his Indian sojourn, and who does not seem to have been at all preoccupied (as Nikitin was) by the possibility that he might have to convert to another religion. The Russian text is written in a curiously religious tone, something that emerges from the very outset. Thus:

> By the prayer of our most holy fathers, o Lord Jesus Christ, have pity on me, your servant, on me the sinner Afanasii son of Nikita. I, sinner, have recounted my voyage beyond the three seas: the first is the sea of Derbent, the *dorija* of Khwalis; the second is the Indian sea, the *dorija* of Hindustan; the third is the Black Sea, the *dorija* of Istanbul.[43]

We may now follow him on his passage down the Volga to Astrakhan, then along the western shore of the Caspian Sea (the "sea of Derbent" in his terms). Crossing the Iranian plateau via Kashan and Yazd, our Russian traveller finds his way via the southern town of Lar to Hurmuz ("where there is a burning sun, that can burn up a man"), from where he makes his way to Cambay (Khambayat) in 1469. After travelling from Gujarat to the Deccan, where he spends somewhat less than three years, Nikitin eventually embarks on a ship from the western port of Dabhol, to make his way via a complex maritime route via the African east coast to Masqat and then Hurmuz. In 1472, he recommences his overland travels, and this time passes through Isfahan and Tabriz on his way to the Black Sea. He crosses this sea too – the third of the "three seas" of the title – and eventually follows the Dnieper to Kiev and Smolensk. The manuscript ends in this last phase of the voyage, somewhat short of Kiev; the last paragraph begins with a prayer to "God the Protector" (*Allāh Parwardigār*), and is almost entirely a curious amalgam of Arabic and Persian invocations to Allah. This rather enigmatic end will call for further comment in our analysis of the text.

Nikitin's text, though rich, is quite economical in expression, making up barely fifteen pages in its printed Russian version. The greater part of it

[43] Le Guillou, *Le voyage*, p. 23. We set aside the recent claim that he travelled from 1468 to 1475.

is taken up by the Indian sojourn, and the voyage to and from India is dealt with in a relatively summary fashion. Let us follow Nikitin then from the time of his arrival in the Bahmani port of Chaul, where he has made his way from Cambay.

Here, it is the Indian country. The people go about naked here; the women do not cover their heads, their breasts are bare, their hair is made into a single plait. All of them have large bellies; they bring children forth into the world each year; there are plenty of children there! Both men and women are wholly black. Wherever I went, a crowd followed me; they were astonished to see a white man.[44]

This lack of etiquette and proper dress is not simply the case with the common people, for Nikitin (like ʻAbdur Razzaq in Calicut) is astonished that even the princes and princesses of the Konkan coast have no more than a cloth around their heads – or, with the women, on the shoulders – and another around their waist. But matters take on a different (and, on the face of it, somewhat more reassuringly civilised) turn as one enters the interior, and attains towns such as Junnar, the principal seat of a certain Asad Khan, a Bahmani notable. Here, for the first time, we encounter a reference to the formidable personage of a certain *malik ut-tujjār*, who is presented as a superior authority, obeyed by men like Asad Khan. This great lord commands as many as 200,000 armed followers, and – in Nikitin's bald account – is much given to combat with the Kafirs (*Kafarŭ*) further south in Vijayanagara, though with rather mixed success. For "the ruler (*Sultan Kadamŭ*) of India" who "resides in a mountain in Vijayanagara" is himself very powerful, and his city is protected by three moats and a river that must be forded, besides a thick jungle. To face this formidable foe, the Malik's army too comprises many horses and elephants, and warriors drawn from lands to the north and the west, such as men from Khorasan, Arabs, Turkomans, and also others from "the land of Jagatai" (meaning natives of Central Asia). A somewhat longer description of the *malik ut-tujjār* may be found later in the text, closer to the moment when Nikitin begins to think of returning home to Russia.

Five hundred men dine with the *malik ut-tujjār* each day. Three Viziers also dine with him, and with each of them are 50 men, and 100 other lords who are bound to the *malik ut-tujjār* by oath. He has 2,000 horses in his stables, of which a thousand are kept saddled and ready day and night; he also has a hundred

[44] Le Guillou, *Le voyage*, pp. 25–6.

elephants in his stables. Each night, a hundred men in armour guard his court, as well as twenty trumpeters, twenty drummers, and men who are assigned in pairs to beat a great drum.[45]

The reference is to a well-known personage of the epoch, the Bahmani *wazīr* Khwaja Mahmud Gawan Gilani, who held extensive power through a good part of the reign of Muhammad Shah Bahmani (r. 1463–82).[46] This then is the first register of four in Nikitin's account, a political one. His concern is to describe the polity of the Bahmanis and its magnificence, although this powerful state is one where a huge gap exists between "the peasants who are poor, and the lords [who are] very powerful with a great apparatus". Carried about on their silver palankeens, surrounded by horsemen, musicians, elephants, dancers and the like, these great lords are in Nikitin's view mostly foreigners, and – so he states – for the most part from Khorasan. The Sultan himself resides in Bidar, "their great city", and "the throne of Muslim Hindustan", where Nikitin spent some four months after his initial sojourn at Junnar. The Sultan's palace is described in conventional terms: it has 7 gates, and at each gate one finds 100 guards and 100 *kāfir* scribes, who take note of those who enter and leave. The palace itself "is truly marvellous, with a good deal of sculptures in gold; the stones are sculpted and gilded in a truly wonderful fashion, and there are many vases everywhere".[47] This is a highly militarised society, where each night the city is patrolled by guards (*kotwāls*) on horseback, and in armour, each carrying a torch; besides, the great lords such as the *malik ut-tujjār*, Asad Khan, Nizam-ul-Mulk, and Farhad Khan, all have extensive armed retinues that they take to war.

A second register concerns the commercial possibilities in India and the neighbouring countries. Here, Nikitin remains quite sceptical. It appears to him that everything in India is dreadfully expensive. Early in his stay, he denounces those who had misled him into trying his luck in India, instead of returning to Russia from Iran:

These infidel dogs had led me astray; they had told me that there were goods of all sorts in quantity, but there is nothing for our land. The goods are free from duties only if one takes them to Muslim lands. But if one carries them by water, some of them do not pay taxes. But these people do not allow us to pass without

[45] Le Guillou, *Le voyage*, p. 38.

[46] For this personage, see H. K. Sherwani, *Maḥmūd Gāwān, the great Bahmani wazir* (Allahabad, 1942).

[47] Le Guillou, *Le voyage*, p. 30.

extracting some taxes from us. There are many duties and pirates on the sea. They rob all the *kāfirs*, but not the Christians or the Muslims.[48]

Arriving at Bidar, the commercial prospects do not seem too good to him either. There was the problem of Nikitin's own limited resources, for he had a single colt with him that he wished to sell, and few other goods – the rest having been robbed from him on the way. This may explain the markedly sour tone of his remarks on Bidar: "For the Russian land, there are no goods here. They are all black, all rogues, all the women are whores; there is charlatanism everywhere, theft and lies, and servants kill their masters with poison." Yet, the commercial instincts of the merchant do surface periodically in the account, notably in a passage where he describes the ports and lands that he has heard of or frequented, beginning with Hurmuz, and proceeding via Calicut and Ceylon, to the unidentified "Shabait" (perhaps Thailand) and Pegu. Still, it would appear that the Russian merchant who read Nikitin's account would not have been particularly motivated to travel to India; the commercial odds seem distinctly stacked against any successful venture.

This is further aggravated by the curious character of another set of passages in the text, these being within a distinctly religious register. We have already noted that religious references colour the text from the very outset, and there is also a particular religious anguish that appears from time to time – when Nikitin begins to fear that his too-close proximity to Muslims has taken him away willy-nilly from his Orthodox faith. Islam is present everywhere in his account, from the early moment when Nikitin's party is misled by false rumours on the Volga by three "infidel Tartars". On entering Iran, our Russian merchant appears to have begun a rapid apprenticeship on matters of the Muslim faith, though he does claim somewhat erroneously that the martyrdom of Husain took place at Rayy rather than in Karbala. Still, as far as Hurmuz, Nikitin seems to have scrupulously observed the Christian festivals, and he notes that, in the Persian Gulf port, "I celebrated my first Easter." Then, for a time, as we have seen, Nikitin appears to have chosen to present himself in the guise of a Muslim Khorasani merchant, by the name Khwaja Yusuf, though he never makes it clear when this transformation occurred. This disguise was successful for a short period, but soon after his arrival in Junnar, the Bahmani governor there, Asad Khan, saw through him.

[48] Le Guillou, *Le voyage*, pp. 27–8.

And there, at Junnar, the Khan took away my colt. He had found out that I was not Muslim but rather Russian. He said to me: "I'll return your colt to you and give you a thousand gold pieces, but accept our faith, the faith of Muhammad (*makhmet-deni*). But if you do not accept our faith, that of Muhammad, I will take away the colt and I will charge you a poll-tax of a thousand gold pieces". And he gave me four days' time, until the Day of the Lord, during the Assumption fast. But the Lord God had pity on me on this His holy day; He did not keep me – poor sinner – from His grace, and He did not wish that I should perish in Junnar with these infidels. On the eve of the day of Our Saviour, Khwaja Muhammad from Khorasan arrived. I pleaded with him to intercede on my behalf. He went to the town and met the Khan; he arranged it so that I did not have to convert, and brought back my colt. Such was the miracle of the Lord on the day of the Saviour! So, my brother Christians from Russia, those of you who want to go to the lands of India, you may as well abandon your faith in Russia, and after having called on Muhammad, you may then go to the land of Hindustan.[49]

Subsequently, Nikitin seems to have resumed his disguise as a Muslim, though he also shed it periodically – as we shall see below. At a later moment in his account, he claims that he was taunted by Muslims, who claimed that though he said he was not a Muslim, "you do not know about Christianity". This matter was further aggravated by the fact that, during the time he spent in the Deccan, Nikitin appears gradually to have lost track of the Orthodox calendar, and to have aligned himself instead to the Muslim lunar calendar. By the fifth year of his travels, he writes, "I did not know the date of the Christian Easter – the Resurrection of Christ – and I fasted with the Muslims during their fast, and I ceased to fast when they ceased", which is to say at the 'Id al-Kabir. This dilemma, of a believing Christian who "spent four Easters in Muslim lands, and did not abandon the Christian faith", is one then that strongly marks the account.

But Nikitin's religious gaze cannot be reduced to the straightforward tension between Muslims and Christians. Judaism appears briefly in his account, when he mentions Jews in connection with the mysterious land of "Shabait"; but the larger category that interests him when writing in his religious register is the *kāfirs* of India. The framework of understanding obviously draws on the vocabulary and terms of his Muslim informants, yet Nikitin attempts to bring something original to the matter. While living in Bidar, he informs us, he made the acquaintance of a number of *kāfirs*, and explained to them that "I was not Muslim, that I was *Isa-diniei*, a Christian, that my name was Afanasii and my Muslim name was Khwaja

[49] Le Guillou, *Le voyage*, p. 27.

Yusuf Khorasani. They then ceased to conceal anything from me: neither on matters of eating, nor of trade, nor of prayer, nor even other things. They even ceased to conceal their women." This great spirit of bonhomie, entirely the result of Nikitin's revelation that he was not Muslim, apparently led his interlocutors to explain various matters of religion to him, and even to take him on a pilgrimage to a great religious centre that he simply terms "Parvat", describing it as "their Jerusalem or their Mecca".[50] These peoples are, in his view, divided into "eighty-four religions", but they still share a number of characteristics. One is their devotion to idols, or *but*, which reside in "idol-houses" (*but-kh̲āna*). Here, Nikitin is fully located within the Persian vocabulary concerning idol-worship in India, and he describes these "idols" in some detail – in particular one "that is sculpted in stone, is very large, with a tail that extends outwards, with an arm that is raised high and outstretched like Justinian, the emperor of Constantinople, and in his left hand he has a lance; he wears nothing, save on his behind which is covered with a piece of cloth, and his visage is monkey-like". These same discussions lead him to conclude that "some of them eat mutton, chicken, fish and eggs, but members of none of these faiths eat beef".

This takes us to the fourth and final register of Nikitin's account, namely the broadly ethnographic one. Some of this is directed at the *kāfirs*, their manner of praying ("facing the east, in the Russian manner"), their eating habits ("their food is bad"), and so on, but we also get a persistent attention directed at the virtue (or lack thereof) of women, almost from the outset. Thus, we learn that "in the land of India, foreigners stay in inns. Women make food there for the foreigners. They make the beds and sleep with the foreigners. If you wish to have intimate relations with one or the other of them, you give her two *jitals*; if you don't want to have such relations, you give her just one; for she is a woman, a friend, and intimate relations cost almost nothing; for they like white men." Or again, somewhat later in the text: "In India, it is thought that women have little value. If you want to know one, it is two *jitals*; and if you want to throw your money away, give her six. Such is their custom. Slaves, both men and women, are very cheap; four *fanams* for a lovely girl, and five for a lovely black one." Similar themes are found in a later passage regarding Pegu, which Nikitin had not actually visited. He writes that in Pegu,

[50] Commentators have so far been unable to identify "Parvat", but the literal meaning of the term (which is to say "mountain") suggests a possible identification with Tirumalai-Tirupati.

The women sleep during the day with their husbands; at night, they go off to foreigners and sleep with them. They even give them [the foreigners] money, and bring sweetmeats along, besides sweet wine. They feed foreigners and give them drink because they like them. They like foreigners, white men, because their own men are very black. If a woman conceives a child with a foreigner, her husband gives him a present; if the child is born white, the foreigner then has to pay a tax of eighteen *tangas*, and if it is born black, he pays nothing. Whatever he has eaten and drunk is given to him free.[51]

Here, we see a number of characteristic features: Nikitin's preoccupation with blackness (that of others) and whiteness (his own); his constant assertion of how desirable he himself is seen as; and a view of India as a sort of sexual paradise, which is somewhat at odds with the rather tortured vision of himself that he presents in other parts of the text.

Thus, despite the occasional glimpses we get of a possible life of pleasure, the thrust of Nikitin's text is rather discouraging. Travel to India, it would seem, involves much trouble. From a commercial point of view, the advantages are few and the travails many: "To live in Hindustan means spending all one's means, for in that place everything is dear. I, a single man, spent two-and-a-half *altins* a day on my board, and I drank neither wine nor mead." While some of the kingdoms are grand, much of the power appears to be in the hands of the Muslims, who cannot from Nikitin's perspective be seen as a positive force. This may be the reason for his interest in, and scarcely concealed admiration for, Vijayanagara (which he never actually visited), since he sees this kingdom as resisting the great power of the Bahmani Sultan and his Malik-ut-Tujjar. Most serious of all is the problem of religious disorientation. Nikitin assures us time and again that, though a sinner, he is still a believing and practising Christian, and it is this practice that he finds difficult to sustain as he travels. On arriving in the western Indian port of Dabhol, he writes of how he "an impious servant of the Most High God, Creator of the sky and the earth, thought of the Christian faith, of the baptism of Christ, of the fasts established by the Holy Fathers, of the commandments of the apostles, and I thought of returning to Russia". Yet, his return voyage proved problematic too, including an unplanned visit to East Africa. By the time of his return to the Crimea, we find our merchant from Tver' quite unable to distinguish between the words for God that were in use in the lands he had visited, and those that he should have employed in his own native context. The text ends then,

[51] Le Guillou, *Le voyage*, p. 34.

enigmatically, with declarations that include the terms Khuda, Allah-o-Akbar, al-Rahman al-Rahim. We can only think of the puzzlement of his first readers in Muscovy. Is this what travelling in India did to a man, even an experienced merchant?

Nikitin was certainly not the only Russian merchant to travel to India in the years from 1400 to 1800, though he remains by far the most celebrated. Still, we cannot be certain that later travellers to Iran, such as Fedot Afanasiyev Kotov, who visited and described Iran in about 1623–4, during the latter years of the reign of Shah ʿAbbas I, knew of his account. Kotov did not make the journey as far as India, and had to content himself and his readers therefore with a brief description of the Indians or "Multanis" that he came to know in Isfahan. He noted that their dead were cremated, that they were given to wearing white clothing, and also remarked that "they are not robust and their faces are bloodless and lean and dark".[52] This Russian merchant and traveller did, however, leave a detailed description in his 'statement' (*statya*) of Shiʿi religious practices in Iran, including an extended reflection on Muharram festivities. This interest in Iran is explicable in view of the growing commercial relations between Russia and Safavid Iran, when compared with the halting diplomatic dealings and trade that had characterised the time of Nikitin; it is no coincidence that Kotov's text is described as "in the nature of a report rather than a personal journal or literary work". The very personal account by the fifteenth-century merchant from Tver' is hence rendered all the more curious and significant by the fact that it was the product of a historical accident, just as the visit to Vijayanagara of ʿAbdur Razzaq Samarqandi simply occurred because the Timurid ambassador was in a sense disappointed by what he saw and experienced in Calicut. The "accidental traveller" is thus a character that we neglect at our own cost, even as the "reluctant traveller" seems more often the rule than the exception in later times. But it is not such characters that will occupy us in the chapter that follows, but instead accounts by deliberate, official or semi-official travellers, writing "statements" like Kotov, for a more-or-less assured readership.

[52] P. M. Kemp, tr., *Russian travellers to India and Persia (1624–1798): Kotov, Yefremov, Danibegov* (Delhi, 1959), pp. 36–7.

CHAPTER 3

Courtly encounters

The True God made the world and ennobled it,
and Adam made it most noble of all.
O my heart! Seek out the True God! Become a traveller!
Enter the sea of the knowledge of God! Become a mariner!

Seydi ʿAli Reʾis, *Mirʾāt al-mamālik*

INTRODUCTION

Three-quarters of a century have passed since the time of that unhappy traveller Nikitin. Much has happened in that time, whether at the level of the social, the economic or the political. By the third quarter of the sixteenth century, South Asia, once the domain of a set of quite compact regional states, is increasingly coming under the sway of a single, vast, truly imperial polity – that of the Mughals.[1] We know a good deal about the Mughals, for they have left us with very rich sources, ranging from elaborate chronicles and administrative orders (*farmāns, sanads* ("royal and princely orders") and the like) to court-poetry, and including a set of quite diverse narrative sources that span a significant social spectrum. With the Mughals, as with the earlier Sultanates, one can find Sufi collective biographies (*tazkiras*) and the "table-talk" (*malfūẓāt*) of saints, but one can also find materials in both Persian and the vernacular languages that capture the fine grain of individual experience far better than is the case for the earlier centuries. Little work has been done for the totality of the corpus of first-person accounts in the Mughal domains, but there are some texts that have deservedly received much attention, including that classic autobiographical text the *Bābur Nāma*, to which we have referred briefly above, and the *Humāyūn Nāma*, authored by Babur's own

[1] The best general account of the Mughals remains John F. Richards, *The New Cambridge History of India*, vol. I. 5: *The Mughal empire*, (Cambridge, 1993).

daughter Gulbadan Begam, and the *Ardhakathānak*, the autobiography in verse of a Jain merchant called Banarasidas.[2]

The travels that we shall consider in this chapter and the following one are of a somewhat different nature from these classic texts. Chronologically arranged, they span over a century and a half, from the 1550s to the late 1680s. We begin with a brief consideration of the reluctant travels in India of the Ottoman admiral Seydi 'Ali Re'is, then move on to the visit by the savant Mutribi Samarqandi to the court of the Mughal emperor Jahangir in the 1620s. The following chapter then takes us into an extended consideration of the travels of Mahmud bin Amir Wali Balkhi to Mughal India in the late 1620s, and we close with a reflection on the issue of "wonders and marvels" by comparing his text with that of Muhammad Rabi', secretary of the Safavid embassy to the court of Thailand in the 1680s. These travels all have one feature in common: the travellers are moving initially from west to east (or perhaps more accurately from north-west to south-east) in an Asian context. They thus voyage from what were considered in the epoch to be the central lands of Islam to areas such as India or Southeast Asia, where followers of various other forms of belief were to be found, not least of all Hindus (*hunūd*), other idol-worshippers (*but-parastān*) and infidels (*kuffār*). It is hence obviously of some interest to trace the longer-term movements in attitudes, and ask ourselves how and in what measure these writers differ from 'Abdur Razzaq Samarqandi, whose travels of the 1440s have occupied us in an earlier chapter; another potentially interesting comparison, which we shall however not pursue here, would be with the envoy sent from the Nizamshahi kingdom of Ahmadnagar to the Safavids in the mid sixteenth century, who thus moved in the opposite direction.[3] His text, which does contain some elements of the travel-account in it, must nevertheless be considered to be principally a chronicle, since its seven parts cover much of the history of the Timurids and Safavids, as well as smaller dynasties in India. Texts that come framed in a context of

[2] Mukund Lath, *Ardhakathānaka, half a tale: a study in the interrelationship between autobiography and history* (Jaipur, 1981); Jauhar Aftabchi, *Tazkirāt ul-Wāqi'āt*, trs. into Urdu by S. Moinul Haq (Karachi, 1955); Gulbadan Begam, *Humāyūn Nāma*, ed. and tr. Annette S. Beveridge (reprint, Lahore, 1974).

[3] Only two sections of the very elaborate text by this author have been published so far; see Khwurshah ibn Qubad al-Husaini, *Tārīkh-i Quṭbī, nīz musammā bih Tārīkh-i Īlchī-i Niẓām Shāh: Maqālah-i panjum, tārīkh-i Āl-i Tīmūr az Tīmūr tā Akbar*, ed. Sayyid Mujahid Zaydi (New Delhi, 1965); and Khwurshah ibn Qubad al-Husaini, *Tārīkh-i īlchī-i Niẓām Shāh: Tārīkh-i Ṣafawīyah az āghāz tā sāl-i 972 Hijrī Qamarī*, ed. Muhammad Riza Nasiri and Koichi Haneda (Tehran, 2000).

diplomacy could thus differ quite substantially in their final form, as we shall see below.

AN ADMIRAL ASHORE

The first of our travellers, Seydi 'Ali Re'is, is somewhat exceptional in that he visited India without actually wishing to do so. He was thus not a reluctant traveller as such, but one who was surprised by his own itinerary, thus becoming very nearly a metaphorical embodiment of the unfortunate voyager, as we see from the Turkish expression: "He has encountered the misfortunes of Seydi 'Ali" (*bashïna Seydī 'Alī hālleri geldi*).[4] The travel-text he authored is entitled *The mirror of kingdoms* (*Mir'ātü'l-Memālik*) but we are aware that he toyed for a time with giving it the rather more gloomy title of the *Book of torments*. This rather pessimistic title would in fact not have done proper justice to his travels either, which, though interspersed with misfortunes, were not exactly dominated by them in reality.

How could an Ottoman admiral find himself in the Mughal domains in the mid 1550s, even against his own will?[5] The answer does not in fact lie in the contacts that the first Mughal emperor Babur had with the Ottoman world. Rather, events transpired as a result of the networks of the Indian Ocean world into which the Portuguese had irrupted in the late 1490s, creating a state (the *Estado da Índia*) based in equal measure on trade and plunder.[6] By 1506, the Mamluk Sultanate of Egypt had been persuaded to send a maritime expedition to counter this new threat, and even if this expedition (led by Amir Husain Mushrif al-Kurdi) was not successful, it served as a precedent for the Ottomans once they entered the Red Sea in 1516–17. Thus, in 1525, the governor of Jiddah, Selman Re'is, submitted a report to the Ottoman Sultan, presenting him with the idea

4 Seyyidi [Seydi] 'Ali Re'is, *Le miroir des pays*, p. 15. For a modern Turkish edition of the text, which we draw upon together with the French translation, see Seydi 'Ali Re'is, *Mir'ātü'l-Memālik*, ed. Mehmet Kiremit. For a Persian translation, see Seydi 'Ali Re'is (Sayyidi 'Ali Katibi), *Mir'āt al-mamālik: Safar Nāma ba Khalīj-i Fārs, Hind, Māwarannahr wa Irān*, tr. Mahmud Tafazzuli and 'Ali Ganjali (Tehran, Sh. 1355 / 1976).

5 The most recent reflection on Seydi 'Ali's work is Palmira Brummett, "What Sidi Ali saw: the Ottomans and the Portuguese in India", *Portuguese Studies Review*, 9, 1–2, 2001, pp. 232–53. This seems to be based in large measure on Vambéry, ed. and tr., *The travels and adventures of the Turkish admiral*, though an edition of the text is periodically cited. However, our point of view will, from time to time, differ from that of the author of this interesting essay.

6 For an important exploration of Ottoman–Portuguese rivalry in the period, see Giancarlo L. Casale, "The Ottoman age of exploration: spices, maps and conquest in the sixteenth-century Indian Ocean", Ph.D. dissertation, Harvard University, Cambridge, Mass., 2004.

that the moment was ripe to seize control of the trade into the Red Sea by gaining control of a certain number of strategic ports in the western Indian Ocean.[7] It would seem that this report did not immediately attract royal attention. However, in the 1530s, the spice trade through the Red Sea briefly touched a new low, and there were even shortages of pepper in the palace. Rumours began to abound that the Ottomans were constructing a fleet in Suez, with the intention of deploying it in the western Indian Ocean. In 1538, this fleet finally emerged into open waters under the command of the Governor of Egypt, Süleyman Pasha, and proceeded to lay siege to Diu, which had at that time recently fallen under Portuguese control. Though unsuccessful in India, Süleyman did manage to seize Aden, and in 1547 and 1552 the Ottomans made further progress by taking Ta'izz and Sana'a.[8] In 1541, the Portuguese for their part responded to this attack by mounting an attack of their own on the Ottoman port of Suez.

Meanwhile, from the early 1540s, the Ottoman ruler Süleyman "the Lawgiver" was beginning negotiations with Dom João III for the passage of Muslim ships, and for establishing the line Shihr–Aden–Zeila as a frontier between the spheres of influence of the Portuguese and Ottoman fleets. During the same period, in 1534, the Ottomans had taken Baghdad, and eventually, in 1546, Basra too became an Ottoman province. In 1543, Ayaz Pasha, governor of Basra, made efforts to shore up the defences of his port, and also occupied Al-Hasa on the western shore of the Persian Gulf. In 1552, the Ottomans then proceeded to occupy Katif, and tried to break the blockade placed on them by the Portuguese at Hurmuz. In this context, the celebrated Ottoman admiral and intellectual Piri Re'is was sent out in 1552 from Suez with a fleet of thirty vessels. He first took Masqat, which was held at that time by the Portuguese, besieged Hurmuz (with no success), and, having plundered Qishm, eventually brought his fleet into Basra. But Piri Re'is was thereafter unable to bring his fleet out of the Gulf, being frustrated by superior Portuguese maritime power. He eventually came back to Suez with a single ship, and was executed for

[7] See Michel Lesure, "Un document ottoman de 1525 sur l'Inde portugaise et les pays de la Mer Rouge", *Mare Luso-Indicum*, 3, 1976, pp. 137–60.

[8] For the general context, see Salih Özbaran, *The Ottoman response to European expansion: studies on Ottoman–Portuguese relations in the Indian Ocean and Ottoman administration in the Arab lands during the sixteenth century* (Istanbul, 1994); and for a more specific study, Dejanirah Couto, "No rasto de Hādim Suleimão Pacha: alguns aspectos do comércio do Mar Vermelho nos anos de 1538–1540", in Artur Teodoro de Matos and Luís Filipe F. Reis Thomaz, eds., *A carreira da Índia e as rotas dos estreitos: actas do VIII Seminário Internacional de História Indo-Portuguesa* (Angra do Heroísmo, 1998), pp. 483–508.

his pains. A further Ottoman rescue attempt for the surviving fleet of seventeen vessels under Murad Re'is also failed. This was the context then for the sending of Seydi 'Ali Re'is to the Persian Gulf in late 1553, and his absence from the Ottoman heartland until the middle of 1557.

It has been remarked that in 1555, at the time that Seydi 'Ali was off on his expedition, Sultan Süleyman had ordered Özdemiroghlu 'Osman Pasha to organize the province of Habesh (Abyssinia), and to consolidate the Ottoman positions in Suakin and Massawa. Shortly thereafter, in 1559, the Ottoman governor of Al-Hasa attacked Bahrein, but the Portuguese then counter-attacked, and the Ottomans had to retreat, so that a stalemate was eventually reached. The Ottomans were left with Al-Hasa and Katif at the head of the Gulf, as well as Basra, while the Portuguese for their part could not be dislodged from Hurmuz. In these circumstances, negotiations were resorted to. The governor of Basra sent an envoy to Hurmuz to discuss the resumption of trade; and in 1564, the Sultan wrote to Portugal, demanding safe passage on land and sea for traders between their two spheres of domination. A recent authoritative history of the Ottoman empire thus notes that "to the Sultan, these events on the fringes of the southern ocean probably seemed unimportant next to his major concerns with Iran, Hungary and the Mediterranean, and it was Hungary and the Mediterranean that were to dominate his final years".[9] Be that as it may, for Seydi 'Ali the time that he himself spent on "the fringes of the southern ocean" was of sufficient importance for him to write a detailed account of what came to pass in those years.

We may briefly rehearse the main steps of his itinerary. Seydi 'Ali had been designated admiral by the Grand Vizier Rüstem Pasha in late November 1553, when the Sultan was in his winter quarters at Aleppo, preparing for a further campaign against the Safavids. Descending the Tigris via Mosul and Baghdad, the admiral arrived in Basra in February 1554, where he was welcomed by the governor Mustafa Pasha. After several frustrating months in Basra and its environs, he eventually set sail with fifteen vessels in mid July 1554, and after little over a month of incident-free navigation, suddenly encountered a Portuguese fleet of some twenty-five ships.[10] This engagement passed off without great loss, but the same was not true of the next combat off Masqat in early September. Here, the

[9] Colin Imber, *The Ottoman empire, 1300–1650: the structure of power* (Basingstoke, 2002), p. 59.

[10] This was the fleet commanded by Dom Fernando de Meneses. For a Portuguese account of the same engagement, see Diogo do Couto, *Da Ásia, década sexta, parte segunda* (reprint, Lisbon, 1974), pp. 538–48.

Figure 6. Pierpont Morgan Library, New York, M. 525, fos. 83v–84, *Livro de Lisuarte de Abreu*, combat between Portuguese and Ottoman fleets. Caption reads: "This was the first encounter that Dom Fernando had with the galleys at Cape Mocadam in the year 1555".

Figure 6. (*cont.*)

Ottoman fleet suffered major losses, and a severe storm that followed also blew them as far to the east as Gwadar in Baluchistan. Reduced to the command of a mere nine vessels, Seydi ʿAli now attempted to make his way back to Ras al-Hadd, when an even more frightening tempest carried him beyond Diu to the coast of Gujarat, where he made landfall at Daman (which at this time was yet to fall into Portuguese hands).[11] From the point of his arrival in Gujarat, Seydi 'Ali was an admiral without a fleet, who thus made his way first via Surat (which he left in late November) to Ahmadabad, and then westward to Sind via Patan and Parkar to the domains of the Arghuns and Tarkhans, two clans that disputed the control of the lower Indus valley. After some months spent there, the Ottoman party decided to head north, to the parts that the returning Mughal emperor Humayun was gradually bringing under his control.

Seydi 'Ali's itinerary thus took him first to Multan and then Lahore, but the Mughal governor there refused to let them take the route via Kabul, insisting instead that he and his party present themselves to Humayun at Delhi. This takes us to the best-known part of the account, namely the encounter between the Mughal emperor and the Ottoman admiral, who arrived in Delhi in late October 1555. Here he remained for three months, witnessing the circumstances of the death of Humayun and the succession of Akbar in early 1556. Eventually, in February 1556, Seydi 'Ali and his much-diminished party were able to leave Delhi, pass through Lahore, and then make their way via Kabul to Badakhshan, and from there to Samarqand, where they arrived on 10 June 1556. The intention was to pass via Bukhara and Khiva to the north of the Caspian Sea, and thus return to the Ottoman domains without entering into contact with the Safavids. This plan could not, however, be put into effect on account of the problematic conditions in the region. First, Seydi 'Ali was wounded in the course of a chaotic skirmish between Sayyid Burhan (at that time the Khan of Bukhara), and Khwarizm Shah Sultan. Then the difficult steppe area of the Dasht-i Qipchaq had to be traversed. Besides, unbeknownst to Seydi 'Ali, by early autumn 1556 Astrakhan had fallen to Ivan the Terrible, and it hence eventually seemed far more prudent to negotiate with the Safavids, a known evil, rather than with an unknown one. Thus, by early November 1556, at the start of the month of Muharram, Seydi 'Ali Re'is found himself in Mashhad, treading the difficult ground of Sunni–Shi'i theological disputes with Safavid princes Ibrahim Mirza and Sulaiman Mirza. Still, the peace that had

[11] The Portuguese chronicler Couto claims that Seydi 'Ali chose to go "to Cambaya, because he could not return to Constantinople, since the Turk was certain to cut off his head", a reference to the earlier fate of Piri Re'is; Couto, *Da Ásia, década sexta, parte segunda*, pp. 486–7 (for the death of Piri Re'is), 546–7 (for Seydi 'Ali).

been signed between Ottomans and Safavids at Amasya in late May 1555 had changed the situation considerably from that in late 1553. Thus, after a short and difficult sojourn at Mashhad, the Ottoman party found its way then to Rayy and Qazwin, where Shah Tahmasp and his court were to be found. After a suitable reception by the Iranian sovereign, and an exchange of courtesies and literary compositions (again somewhat marred by the habitual theological disputes), Seydi ʿAli was at last able to depart for Baghdad, and from there – mounting the Tigris as he had descended it three years before – made his way via Ankara to Istanbul, where he arrived at last in May 1557. The text itself seems to have been drafted in its final version in the middle of the month of Safar 965 H (corresponding to early December 1557). The admiral needed, without doubt, to justify to the Sultan and his court what must have, on the face of it, appeared to be a rather disastrous expedition. He clearly succeeded in fair measure, for, unlike Piri Re'is, we know of no adverse consequences that he suffered. On the contrary, he seems to have been well received and well treated until his death in Istanbul a few years later, in January 1563.

How did Seydi ʿAli Re'is manage to spin the dross of disaster into the gold of success? To understand this, we must look briefly at least to what we know from other sources concerning this personage. Born in about 1498, he came from a family with a naval tradition in the Black Sea area, and both his grandfather and father, Hüsein Re'is, had occupied positions in the arsenal at Istanbul. Seydi ʿAli himself participated as a young man in the conquest of Rhodes in 1522, and by the late 1530s he was a commander of some importance in the Ottoman operations at Preveze against Andrea Doria.[12] Subsequently, he also held a post as the chief of the arsenal of Istanbul, as well as in the Ottoman Mediterranean fleet. In these years, he seems to have found the time to pen other texts on geography, navigation and astronomy, notably the *Mir'āt-i Kā'ināt* ("Mirror of the Universe"), *Hülāsatü'l-hey'e* ("The Essence of Astronomy") and the *Kitābü'l-muḥiṭ fī ʿilmi'l eflāk ve'l-ebḥār* ("Comprehensive Book in the Sciences of the Heavens and the Seas").[13] Besides, he was a reasonably accomplished composer of chronograms and of improvised

[12] Couto for his part identifies Seydi ʿAli as "a corsair who was called Alecheluby, who had been treasurer in Cairo, a very rich man and well considered by the Baxás"; Couto, *Da Ásia, década sexta, parte segunda*, p. 537.

[13] See William Brice, Colin Imber and Richard Lorch, *The Dā'ire-yī Mu'addel of Seydī ʿAlī Re'īs* (Manchester, 1976).

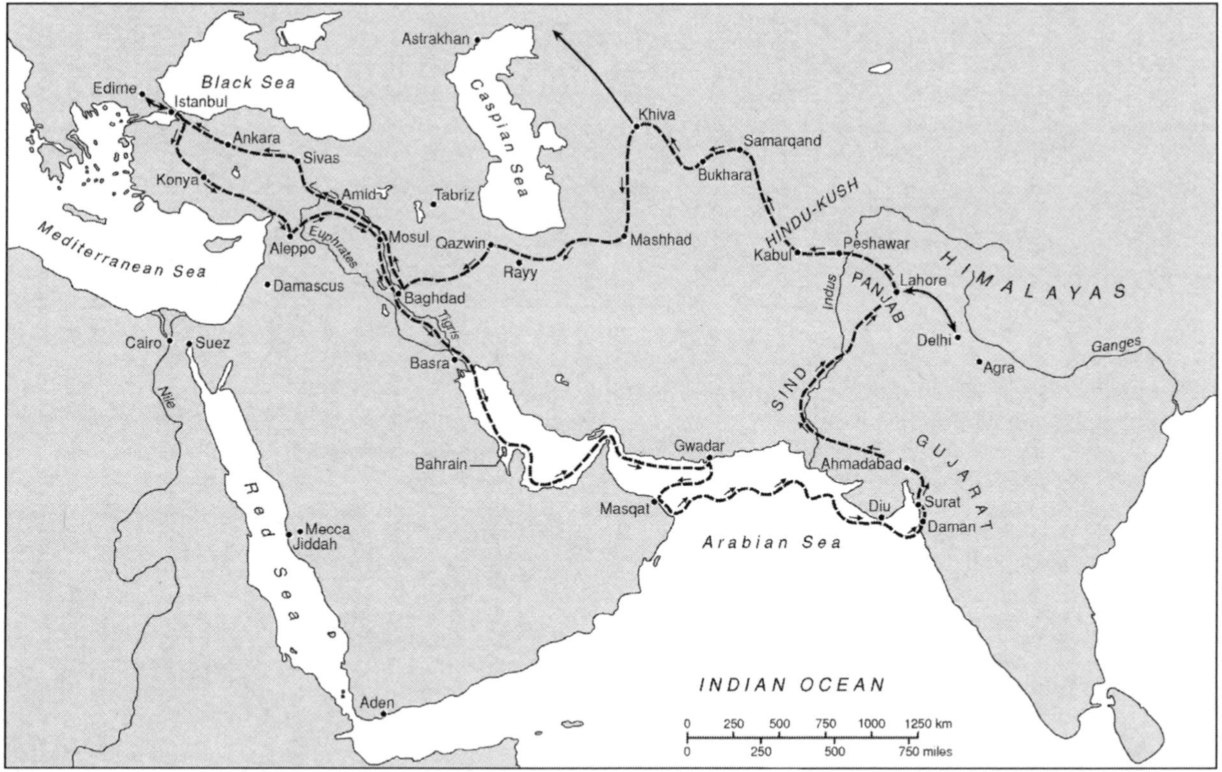

Map 2. Seydi ʻAli Re'is's itinerary.

verse, in addition to having a command of poets in Turkish and Persian, including such masters as Nizami, Hafiz, Sa'di, and Amir Khusrau. With the skills of an accomplished courtier, the admiral thus was able to recover from adverse circumstances, presenting himself in court after court as the envoy-at-large of his master, the Ottoman Sultan. We shall have occasion to see this in the paragraphs that follow.

We may enter the text then some way into its progress, when the ragged remnants of the Ottoman fleet find themselves in November 1554 off the coast of Gujarat, after the engagements and storms that have been mentioned above. They have already passed "before Somnath, and finally had arrived at Diu. But since Diu was in the hands of the *kāfirs* [Portuguese] this place only made us fearful. This day, we did not raise the sails again, but continued on. Progressively the wind grew stronger, and we could not control the rudders of the ships."[14] From here on, things grew worse and worse. The mariners, despite their best efforts, were unable to control their vessels, and were barely able to keep themselves on their feet. The wind and the noise of the storm grew to such a point that it seemed to be "a day of the end of the world (*qiyāmat*)". Thus it was at last that they sighted land, "in the country of Gujarat, in Hindustan (*diyār-i Hindūstān'da vilāyet-i Gücerāt*), but we did not know where". But the troubles of the fleet were not quite over. The ships were now dragged into a whirlpool (*çatlaq*), and despite the fact that the anchors were thrown out, it seemed the ships might soon sink. Seydi 'Ali and the others began to prepare for their end:

> We broke open the chains of the oarsmen, and everybody became naked, some getting ready barrels, others planks, and everyone took the occasion to pardon one another. As for this humble author, he too became naked. I freed the slaves I possessed and I vowed to spend a hundred *florī* [if I were saved] for the poor in Mecca – may God honour the place!

But the worst did not really come to pass. Instead, somewhat later in the day, they could spy the port of Daman through the storm, and see some other ships that lay closer inland.

Seydi 'Ali and his men remained in this situation, at anchor off Daman, for all of five days of incessant rain. Three of the other ships went down meanwhile, but the admiral's vessel resisted still.[15] Thus, at the end of five days "the favour of the True God manifested itself", the wind dropped,

[14] Seyyidi [Seydi] 'Ali Re'is, *Le miroir des pays*, p. 59; Seydi Ali Re'is, *Mir'ātü'l-Memālik* (Turkish text), p. 86.

[15] In Couto's version, of a total of nine galleys with which Seydi 'Ali made his escape, seven arrived in Surat, one in Daman, and one in a port called "Danú"; *Da Ásia, década sexta, parte segunda*, pp. 547–8.

and the sea became calm once more. The cannon and some other valuable materials were quickly unloaded from the ships and taken into the fortress of Daman, where they were put in the charge of the governor (*ḥākim*) there, a certain Malik Asad, described as "one of the *amīrs* of Sultan Ahmad, the emperor of Gujarat". It is significant that the title *pādishāh* is accorded here by Seydi 'Ali even to a relatively modest regional ruler. While in Daman, Seydi 'Ali began to make the first of his diplomatic contacts, this one with certain captains of ships from the Kerala port of Calicut. The admiral claims that these men came and explained to him that their own ruler accepted the overlordship of the Ottoman Sultan, and that they continued the fight against the Portuguese day and night, to which Seydi 'Ali responded with a letter addressed to the Samudri Raja (*Pādishāh Sāmirī*) stating the following: "If God wills, you are assured that the august fleet (*donanma-yi hümāyūn*) will arrive soon from Egypt, and deliver this land from the hands of the *kāfirs*. For your part, you should continue to act in a valiant fashion." The Ottoman party led by him was, however, at that time in no position to aid others, or even defend themselves. Thus, on hearing rumours of the imminent arrival of a Portuguese fleet in Daman, they were obliged to make at once for Surat (which was better defended than Daman), and Seydi 'Ali notes that several members of his party deserted him to join the service of Malik Asad. After further minor adventures, the Ottomans found themselves at last in Surat, "three months exactly after having left the port of Basra".

This is a moment for the admiral to take stock of the situation in India, concerning which he has so far said very little in his text. Thus, we learn from him that in Surat, he and his companions were welcomed by "people of Islam" (*ehl-i Islām*), and were told by them that "what we pray for is that, God willing, the land of Gujarat (*vilāyet-i Gücerāt*) will soon be reunited with the Ottoman domains (*memālik-i 'Oṣmāniyye*), and that on account of this the ports of India will be delivered from the hands of the *kāfirs*, who are as lowly as the dust".[16] It turned out that, in the recent past, the Gujarat kingdom had been riven by dissensions. One of the great *k͟hāns*, a certain Nasir-ul-Mulk, had thus rebelled against the ruler Ahmad Shah, and attempted to become sovereign himself by seeking an alliance with the Portuguese governor (the loan-word *g͟huvernadora* is in fact used), "the chief of the *kuffār* who are to be found in Goa". He had offered the Portuguese a series of ports, and so it was that, soon after the

[16] Our understanding differs from that of Brummett, "What Sidi Ali Saw", p. 238, who believes that the Muslims asked to be delivered "from the hands of the vile Indian infidels".

arrival of Seydi 'Ali and his party, a great Portuguese fleet also arrived in the area.[17] The Ottoman party thus found itself drawn into the conflict, preparing to combat the alliance of the Portuguese and Nasir-ul-Mulk. Seydi 'Ali claims that various attempts were made to assassinate him, whether by ambush in his tent or through poison. A Portuguese envoy (*elçi*) also tried to persuade the governor of Surat, Khudawand Khan, to hand the Ottoman admiral over to them, allegedly declaring: "We are not at war with you. It is the Admiral of Egypt (*Mïsr Kapudanï*) that we want", further evidence that the Portuguese were well aware of the prestigious character of the commander who had landed by chance on Indian shores. However, he survived all these attempts, and meanwhile Sultan Ahmad Shah for his part managed to reconsolidate his own position, defeating a series of rivals in first Bharuch and then Ahmadabad. With the eventual death of Nasir-ul-Mulk, it seemed that Seydi 'Ali and his men were in a rather better situation than when they found themselves initially off Daman.

It is also clear that a very large number of men had meanwhile deserted the admiral, preferring to take up service (*naukarī*) instead in Gujarat. This was to the point that it became evident that there were not enough crewmen left to sail the surviving Ottoman vessels back to the Red Sea, and they had to be handed over to the commander of the fort of Surat, with the idea that he would pay a proper price for them.[18] Accompanied by a mere fifty men, including Mustafa Agha, head of the janissaries of Egypt, and 'Ali Agha, head of the musketeers, Seydi 'Ali hence was now obliged to seek another route home, namely by heading over land to the capital of the Gujarat Sultanate. This decision was quickly made, and on 1 Muharram 962 H (26 November 1554), the party left Surat for Ahmadabad, passing through Bharuch and Champaner. This is one of the few occasions when Seydi 'Ali takes some trouble to describe what he saw en route. On an earlier occasion, he has briefly mentioned the existence of a tree that resembles the date-palm, and which yields a "marvellous wine (*'aceb sharāb*)", so that "at the foot of each tree, there

[17] This was the fleet headed by the new *capitão-mor do mar da Índia*, Fernão Martins Freire. For a Portuguese view of the matter, which does not, however, mention Nasir-ul-Mulk by name, see Diogo do Couto, *Da Ásia, década sétima, parte primeira* (reprint, Lisbon, 1974), pp. 38–45. Elsewhere in the same text (p. 187), Couto does, however, mention that the Portuguese had some "secret dealings with certain captains of Cambay" in regard to Daman.

[18] Couto claims that Khudawand Khan (whom he terms "Caracem", or Qara Hasan) eventually agreed to have each of the galleys broken up in six parts to ensure they would not be used further; see *Da Ásia, década sétima, parte primeira*, pp. 43–4.

is a tavern (*mey-kh̲āne*) where the people (*kh̲alq*) enjoy themselves all the time".[19] However, during the journey northward in Gujarat, he delivers a longer description, which it may be worth citing at length:

On the road, strange trees were to be seen. For example, there was one species where the top of each one rose up as high as the sky, and on which there were some astonishing bats, which from one wing to the other were fourteen spans in width. Bats of this type were to be seen on each tree in an uncountable number. The roots of these trees fall back down from above, and when they come back to earth, cross each other and thus make up new trees. In this way, for example, from one tree, ten or twenty excellent trees, or even more, are formed. In this country, the name of the said tree is *tūbī*, and several thousand men can shelter under their shade. All along the route, there are largely only oleanders to be seen. In the country of Gujarat, parrots are to be found in infinite number. These places are also a good climate for monkeys. In all the places where we halted each day, some thousands of monkeys awaited us. The greater part of them carried their offspring in their hands. Each of them made strange gestures, as in the anecdote of Jihan Shah which proclaims that amongst the monkeys, none of them is in command. In the evening, they return to their homes.[20]

Within a brief time, Seydi 'Ali and his party arrived at the court of Ahmadabad, only to find themselves again in the presence of a Portuguese envoy, who once more demanded of Sultan Ahmad and his *wazīr* 'Imad-ul-Mulk that Seydi 'Ali be handed over to them.[21] On this occasion, the following response on the part of 'Imad-ul-Mulk is reported: "We need the *Pādishāh-i Rūm*. If our ships cannot go to his ports, our situation will take a turn for the worse. Further, he is the emperor of Islam (*Islām pādishāh*). Is it proper then to ask us to hand over his admiral?"[22] After an exchange of words, in which the Portuguese envoy taunted the Ottomans that "even a bird could not fly from the ports of India" without their permission, Seydi 'Ali and his group were left somewhat disoriented. To

19 Seydi Ali Reis, *Mir'âtü'l-Memâlik*, p. 93.

20 Seyyidi [Seydi] 'Ali Re'is, *Le miroir des pays*, p. 68; Seydi Ali Re'is, *Mir'âtü'l-Memâlik*, p. 95. Neither we nor the translators and editors of the text have been able to identify the anecdote of Jihan Shah. The editor Kiremit (p. 215) suggests that it refers to Jihan Shah Qara-qoyunlu, the Iranian ruler.

21 This envoy may have been a certain Diogo Pereira, for whom see Jorge Manuel dos Santos Alves, *Um porto entre dois impérios: estudos sobre Macau e as relações luso-chinesas* (Macau, 1999), pp. 68–82. For another Portuguese envoy sent to Ahmadabad, probably in 1555, namely a certain Tristão de Paiva, see *Da Ásia, década sétima, parte primeira*, pp. 186–97. The "Madre Maluco" of the Portuguese text is 'Imad-ul-mulk.

22 The passage that follows (Seydi 'Ali Re'is, *Mir'âtü'l-Memâlik*, p. 96) in fact has Seydi 'Ali replying to the Portuguese envoy. Brummett, 'What Sidi Ali Saw', p. 243, argues, on the contrary, that he "zealously replied to Imad ül-mülk".

be sure, the option was available of returning home by land rather than by water, but the manner of doing so was unclear. Seizing the occasion, Ahmad Shah seems to have offered the Ottoman admiral a sizeable revenue-assignment in the area of Bharuch. But he refused, fortified – so it would seem – by a subsequent dream in which Hazrat ʿAli appeared to him, and gave him a sign of Divine Favour.

Still, it remained to be seen how the party could continue without further threat from the Portuguese or indeed from other potential enemies, such as hostile Rajputs. In this context, Seydi ʿAli produces one of the rare "ethnographic" observations we find in his text with regard to India, and it concerns a group that he calls the *bāt*, in fact referring to the *bhāṭs*.[23] Of them, he writes the following.

> There is a category (*tāyife*) of people called the *bāt* amongst the *bāmīn* [Brahmans] – who are people who are knowledgeable (*ʿālim*) in the extreme – of the *kāfir bāniyān* who live in those lands there. They take on the responsibility of conducting merchants and voyagers (*ticārī ve sāyir*) safe and sound when they go from one kingdom (*vilāyet*) to another. In exchange, they are given a certain salary. In this way, if on the road, *kāfir* Rajputs – which is to say *hindū* horsemen – arrive with the intention of sacking and pillaging the caravan, the said *bāts* unsheath their daggers, press them to their breasts and say: "If you cause damage to the caravan whilst we are its guarantors, we will kill ourselves." Then, out of respect for them, the Rajputs do not attack them or interfere, and one can pass that place safe and sound. If the Rajputs cause even an iota of damage, the said *bāts* are in fact obliged to kill themselves. If they do not do so, no one would have any confidence in this category of people any more, and this principle (*qāʿide*) would no longer work. If by chance damage is caused to a caravan and if the *bāts* kill themselves, according to their vain beliefs, grave consequences ensue for the Rajputs and they merit being put to death. As a result, the Rajput chiefs (*bigleri*) who are in the land then conduct a general massacre (*qatl-i ʿāmm*) in regard of all the male and female Rajputs whom they find there, along with their dependents. Therefore, in Ahmadabad, the Muslims sent us two *bāts* to whom a salary was given.[24]

Thus protected, the Ottoman party made its way westwards, arriving after a voyage of some eight days (probably on camel-back) in the city of Patan. Here, attempts were made to embroil them in a dispute between two rival parties, Sher Khan and Musa Khan on the one hand, and Baluch

[23] On the *bhāṭs* or *chāran*, see Reginald E. Enthoven, *The tribes and castes of Bombay*, vol. 1 (reprint, Delhi, 1975), pp. 123–31. The colonial ethnographer notes that they numbered about 32,000 in the 1901 census, and adds: "Not a century ago the faith placed in the word of a Bhát was perhaps the only means of obtaining the requisite feeling of security necessary to conduct business of any kind" (p. 130).

[24] Seyyidi [Seydi] ʿAli Re'is, *Le miroir des pays*, pp. 70–1; Seydi ʿAli Re'is, *Mir'ātü'l-Memālik* (text), p. 97.

Khan, ruler of neighbouring Radhanpur, on the other. But Seydi 'Ali refused to take sides, instead justifying his need to return quickly to the Ottoman territories on the grounds that he had a direct order (*fermān-i sherīfī*) from his ruler to that effect. One of his own poems marks the occasion, and runs as follows, each verse ending with the word *seferin* ("travel").

> He who makes the voyage to Patan in Hind,
> may he choose a stormy voyage of his own accord.
> By dint of crying, my eyes have become valleys of tears,
> my eyes say: "We've made the voyage from Yemen."
> With the flow of my tears, the skirt of my robe is stainless,
> as if I'd made the voyage from Aden.
> My heart is full of blood like a sack full of musk,
> so why should I make the journey to Khotan?
> O God! Let it be your will
> that your servant "Katibi" travel to his own land again.

But the admiral's native land (*vaṭan*) was still a long way off. A month after the departure from Ahmadabad, by the beginning of the month of Rabi I (25 January 1555), the Ottoman party had arrived at last in Parkar, after having encountered further troubles with Rajputs (whom Seydi 'Ali always makes it a point to denominate as "*Rashput kāfiri*") and other local rulers. The *bāts* were allowed to return to Ahmadabad, and the party then plodded on for fifteen further days through the "sandy plain of the desert" until the "frontier of Sind" (*ser-ḥadd-i Sind*) was crossed at Vank. Almost as soon as the Ottomans entered Sind, they found themselves embroiled once more in a dispute, on this occasion between Shah Hasan Mirza, described as the Sind Padishah, and his rival Mirza 'Isa Tarkhan, ruler of Thatta. The latter, it turned out, had decided of late to have the *k̲h̲uṭba* read out and the ceremonial drums (*naqqāra*) sounded in the name of the returning Mughal ruler, Humayun, who after a period of exile in Iran was now once more staking his claim to rule northern India. Shah Hasan wanted a stop put to this, and, in order to enlist the support of the Ottoman party, offered Seydi 'Ali the governorship of Lahori Bandar, as well as robes of honour for his entourage. There appear to be two principal reasons for the welcome that was given the Ottoman party here, as much as in the Gujarat court. First, there was the enormous prestige which the Ottomans clearly enjoyed in these lands, especially after their successful campaigns in Egypt, the Hijaz and most recently 'Iraq. A second reason was a more pragmatic one, for it was clearly believed that Ottoman subjects were particularly proficient in the use of firearms. So, Seydi ʿAli came to be placed in charge of a battery that was aimed at forcing Mirza ʿIsa to surrender. However, the cannonade against Thatta proved ineffective, and Seydi ʿAli also implies that the fighting was not conducted very seriously, since the two parties – the Arghuns and Tarkhans – were in fact closely connected with each other. He even claims that Shah Hasan told him: "Do not attack the Muslims, and make sure that there are no balls in your muskets, for all of us are one people! The greater part of our brothers and our children are over there [in Thatta]."[25] Clearly, all-out war was not an option, and so the end result was a compromise between the two parties, which Seydi ʿAli claims to have mediated. Mirza ʿIsa ceased to use Humayun's name in the Friday prayer, and also sent back Shah Hasan's wife, Haji Begam, who had been in his custody. This had a rather unexpected effect. Ten days after her arrival, Shah Hasan was found dead, and many suspected that she had poisoned him. Seydi ʿAli cites a misogynist Turkish verse by Hamdi, with approval, on the occasion:

> If you're a man, don't believe woman, my brother!
> Women have even misled the prophets.

This circumstance led to the succession of the deceased monarch's brother, Sultan Mahmud, with whom the relations of the Ottomans were far more tense. Seydi ʿAli and his party now came to gain possession of some boats, and embarked on the Indus, eventually arriving at Nasirpur. Everywhere, different armed bands seemed to be engaged in pillage, at times Rajputs, at others, Chaghatays. Eventually, an interview was arranged with Mirza ʿIsa, who advised them to sail upriver. Several weeks seem to have been passed in this way, sailing up and down the river, sighting fearsome crocodiles, and uncertain of which route to take. Eventually, it was decided to abandon the boats, and, using horses, camels and mules, instead take the land route to Sultanpur, Ucch and Multan, in order to make contact with the Mughal court. Seydi ʿAli intended to bring good news to Humayun: namely that both Mirza ʿIsa and Sultan Mahmud had decided to have the *khuṭba* read in his name. At first a desert route was tried between Sultanpur and Ucch, but this proved too hard, on account of the unhealthy water, and the "ants as large as sparrows"; in the end, a route through the jungle was taken, with the party being escorted by ten musketeers in the vanguard and ten others at the rear.

[25] Seydi ʿAli Reʾis, *Mirʾātüʾl-Memālik*, p. 100.

Figure 7. Darab in a boat on a Greek island, encounters Mehrasp, a Parsi adventurer, *Dārāb-nāma*, National Museum, New Delhi, No. L53.2/9.

Thus, by the middle of the month of Ramazan (early August 1555), the Ottoman party found itself in Multan, and was able to go in pilgrimage to the tombs of Shaikh Baha-ud-Din Zakariya, Shaikh Rukn-ud-Din and Shaikh Sadr-ud-Din.

AT THE MUGHAL COURT

The real purpose was after all to make contact with the Mughal court, and in pursuit of this ambition the Ottoman party made its way from Multan to Lahore, arriving in the latter city in late August. It was known that the westward route via Qandahar had been rendered problematic on account of disputes and rebellions amongst the Uzbeks. Seydi 'Ali for his part had made sure, even before arriving in the Mughal domains, that he had appeared, at least to an extent, as a Mughal partisan, especially in his last dealings with the Arghuns and Tarkhans. To be sure, his initial acts on behalf of Shah Hasan might have been interpreted otherwise, but he implies that in the reconciliation between Mirza 'Isa and Sultan Mahmud, he had had a positive role to play by suggesting that both accept the suzerainty of the Mughals. Nevertheless, Seydi 'Ali continues to insist that his visit to Delhi was not of his own volition, but because of the insistence of the governor of Lahore, a certain Mirza Shah. Here then is how the Ottoman admiral presents his welcome at the Mughal court:

> When we arrived in the capital of Hind (*pāy-i takht-i Hind*) – which is to say the city of Delhi – at the end of the month of Zi-Qa'da [mid October 1555], Humayun Padishah was informed. As a mark of honour and respect to the Fortunate [Ottoman] Emperor, he sent the Khan-i-Khanan as well as other Khans and Sultans, and 400 elephants and several thousand men to meet us. He sent this humble servant a horse, 2 robes of honour (*khil'at*), and a gift of money. The Khan-i-Khanan offered us a sublime feast, and since, in the country of Hind, councils are held at night in most cases, I was taken in the evening, with all sorts of courtesies and marks of respect, to the august council of the emperor.[26]

Seydi 'Ali was obviously rather well prepared for this meeting. He had taken along certain presents, which he naturally insists were poor in nature, but, more importantly, he had composed a chronogram to celebrate the Mughal reconquest of Hindustan. This verse ran as follows.

> A Shah of the rank of Jem, and of august fortune,
> that is, of the Indian clime, who, like fire itself,
> put the Afghans to flight and took Delhi!
> The rebels submitted.
> For this conquest, the following chronogram was said:
> "This is the rise of August Fortune."

The chronogram's flattering content essentially derived from the pun that linked the Mughal ruler's own name, Humayun, with the "august fortune" that appears twice in the verse, first as *hümāyūn bakht*, and then, in the chronogram line: *tālī'-i devlet-i hümāyūnesh*. Not content with this, Seydi 'Ali then proceeded to recite two other *ghazal* compositions of his own in Turkish, which appear to have appealed so much to Humayun that he offered him a large revenue-assignment (the word *cāy-gīr* or *jāgīr* appears here in one of its early uses), and also suggested that he remain at least a year at the Mughal court.[27] Seydi 'Ali demurred, insisting that he had "gone to sea on the orders of the Fortunate Emperor to attack the *kāfirs*", and that he had only come to India by accident, on account of

[26] Seyyidi [Seydi] 'Ali Re'is, *Le miroir des pays*, p. 80: Seydi 'Ali Re'is, *Mir'ātü'l-Memālik* (text), p. 107.

[27] Contrast Iqtidar Alam Khan, "The Mughal assignment system during Akbar's early years, 1556–1575", in Irfan Habib, ed., *Medieval India 1: Researches in the History of India, 1200–1750* (Delhi, 1992), p. 66: "The term *jāgīr*, commonly used in seventeenth-century papers to describe the revenue-assignment, does not occur in any work compiled before Akbar."

tempests and storms (*tūfān*). His real purpose, he averred, was to ensure that Gujarat was once more delivered from these Portuguese unbelievers. However, Humayun insisted he stay at least until the end of the winter rains (*birishkāl*), when the roads would be safer. He also is reported to have declared that he needed the Ottoman admiral's skills: "Show me how one uses astronomical tables and the perpetual calendar for solar and lunar eclipses, as well as the astrolabe, teach me the treatise on the equinoctial circle. If you manage to do all this in three months, you will be given leave to depart." As it happens, this is not an improbable scenario, for we are aware that Humayun had long had a fascination with astronomy and astrology.[28] In any event, Seydi 'Ali now went to work in earnest, resting neither by day nor by night, in his own version. At length, all the skills that Humayun demanded had been taught to him, and Seydi 'Ali had also composed another flattering chronogram – this one on the occasion of the conquest of Agra.

Still, the Ottoman admiral draws out his narrative of these few months at the Mughal court, reproducing two rather tedious letters that he received from Sind at this time, from Sultan Mahmud and his *wazīr*. For, clearly, this is the high point of his narrative, that which he can best use in order to demonstrate to the Ottoman ruler that, from the jaws of disaster, he was still capable of extracting a passable diplomatic triumph. He insists, for example, that his poetic triumphs were such that Humayun had begun to call him the "second Mir 'Ali Sher Nawa'i", in honour of the great eastern Turkish poet from late fifteenth-century Herat. This notion of a diplomatic triumph is surely the central point of the next anecdote, which has arguably become the best-known part of Seydi 'Ali's account. By the time of the anecdote, Seydi 'Ali notes, he and Humayun had become virtually inseparable, whether by day or by night. He then continues:

One day the Padishah asked this humble servant: "Which is greater, the Vilayet-i Rum or that of Hindustan?" This servant responded: "O Padishah! When one says Rum, if one means Rum proper, that is the Vilayet-i Sivas, then Hindustan is larger than it. But if one means those lands that have submitted to the Padishah-i Rum, then Hind is not even a tenth of it." The Padishah said, for his part: "What one means is the whole", and I responded: "O Padishah! What is

[28] For instance, see Khwandamir, *Qānūn-i Humāyūnī, also known as Humāyūn Nāma: a work on the rules and ordinances established by the emperor Humayun and on some buildings erected by his orders*, ed. M. Hidayat Hosain (Calcutta, 1940). Humayun's proximity to the Shattari Sufi order may also have a bearing on the matter.

evident to the spirit of this humble servant is the fact that certainly the Padishah-i Rum is the equal of Alexander who ruled over the world, and was master of the seven climes. Now the life and the duration of the reign of Alexander are known from the chronicles. To this extent, to admit that Alexander passed through the seven climes in totality and that he reigned over them is, if one employs reason, an impossible thing. For the length of the inhabited quarter of the world is 180 degrees, and at the equator, its width is 66 degrees. According to books on astronomy, its surface is 4,000 times 1,668,600 *parasangs*. Therefore, he could not have traversed the totality of this or ruled over it. Surely, like the Padishah-i Rum, he must have possessed a part of each clime, and it is for this reason that it is said that he reigned over the seven climes".[29]

Seydi 'Ali was deploying his astronomical skills here then to make a rather devious political point, namely to elevate the Ottoman Sultan over other rulers in the world on the basis of a geographical logic. In this version, Humayun fell in with his line of reasoning:

The Padishah [Humayun] asked me then: "Does the Padishah-i Rum have a part (*hisse*) in each of the seven climes?" One responded: "There is first Yemen which is in the first clime; sacred Mecca which is in the second; Egypt which is in the third; Aleppo which is in the fourth; the capital of the kingdom, well-guarded Constantinople, which is in the fifth; Küfe, which is in the sixth; Buda and Pecs which are in the seventh. In each of these lands, there are to be found *beylerbeys* and *qāẓīs* who rule and govern in his name."

However, the admiral was not content to let the matter go at that, and wished to make an even taller claim, inflating the universal pretensions of Sultan Süleyman even further. In order to do so, he launches into a rather involved anecdote involving the recognition even in China of the Ottomans. He thus added:

Besides, God knows that I have heard it said by merchants called Khwaja Bakhshi and Qara Hasan, who are in the port of Surat in the land of Gujarat, that in the land of China (*vilāyet-i Chīn*), when Muslim merchants wish to offer prayers on the occasion of the Feast of the Sacrifice (*bayram*), each community (*her ṭāyife*) had wanted to pronounce the *khuṭba* in the name of its own Padishah. Then the merchants of Rum went to the sovereign of China (*khāqān-i Chīn*) and represented the following to him: "Our Padishah is the Padishah of Mecca, Medina and the direction of the prayer (*qibla*)." Even though he was a *kāfir*, the monarch showed evidence of his justice (*inṣāf*) and said: "Pronounce the *khuṭba* then in the name of the Padishah of Mecca and Medina." The merchants from Rum gave the preacher (*khaṭīb*) a robe of honour, mounted him on an elephant, and paraded him through the city. Thereafter, the prayer was heard and the *khuṭba*

[29] Seyyidi [Seydi] 'Ali Re'is, *Le miroir des pays*, pp. 86–7; Seydi 'Ali Re'is, *Mir'ātü'l-Memālik*, pp. 115–16.

was read in the land of China in the name of the Padishah-i Rum. To whom else has such a thing ever happened?

This was reportedly the clinching argument, leading Humayun to say to the assembled nobles in his court: "It is true that on Earth, the Fortunate [Ottoman] Sovereign (*khūndigār*) alone has the right to be called Padishah, he and no other." The improbability of such a statement is of course manifest, and is a part of Seydi 'Ali's high rhetoric. The fact that the Qara Hasan in question was himself an Ottoman subject (and perhaps the nephew of Khwaja Safar-us-Salmani) naturally renders this testimony all the more dubious. Let us lay aside the details of these anecdotes for a time. It may now be worthwhile to consider at least briefly some of the key aspects of Seydi 'Ali's construction of India, before turning to a last set of passages in which he treats his own intervention in Mughal politics at the death of Humayun.

Recent studies of Ottoman policy with regard to India and the Indian Ocean suggest an alternation in political dominance between those at the Sublime Porte who were inclined to favour a relatively aggressive policy, and others who preferred a circumscribed vision of the Ottoman participation in affairs to the south-east.[30] In particular, it has been argued that the period of dominance of Rüstem Pasha (Grand Vizier from 1544 to 1553, and 1555 to 1561, and Sultan Süleyman's son-in-law) in the latter half of the 1540s and 1550s marked a low point in Ottoman interest in Indian Ocean adventurism, when compared to the earlier phase of Ibrahim Pasha, as well as a later period when the dominant personality was that of Sokollu Mehmed Pasha. In this view then, though Seydi 'Ali's writings were eventually recovered and made use of by Sokollu Mehmed, their ideological slant is nevertheless the somewhat modest one of Rüstem Pasha, where Ottoman claims over India are kept to a relatively limited level.

This is certainly helpful in understanding Seydi 'Ali, the surface of whose rhetoric can at times leave one with the opposite impression. Thus, on his return to the Ottoman domains, he reports a conversation at Amid with the celebrated commander and governor Iskender Pasha, at the end of which he reflects on how his mind continued to be preoccupied with the "desire for reunion with the Vilayet-i Rum expressed by the port of Hurmuz and the kingdom of Gujarat".[31] This is balanced overall by a

[30] Casale, "The Ottoman Age of Exploration", pp. 133–6.

[31] Also see Brummett, "What Sidi Ali Saw", p. 245. For earlier relations between Hurmuz and the Ottomans, see Dejanirah Couto, "Trois documents sur une demande de secours ormouzi à la Porte ottomane", *Anais de História de Além-Mar*, 3, 2002, pp. 469–93.

tone of "Rumi patriotism", in which we find reflections to the effect that "on the surface of the earth, there is not even one land (*vilāyet*) comparable to Rum, nor one other Padishah who is equal to the [Ottoman] Padishah, Refuge of the World", accompanied by Seydi 'Ali's own verse that runs:

> Compared to the Padishah-i Rum,
> those who are kings (*shāh*), in reality
> resemble veiled (*ḥacebde*) Padishahs.

Or again, we have the response given by Seydi 'Ali to a question posed to him by Shah Tahmasp in Qazwin: "Amongst the lands that you have seen in traversing the world, in which one did you find the city that most pleased you?" To this, the admiral apparently responded with a verse declaring:

> Though I've traversed and visited,
> every city in the world (*dünyā*),
> there is none that could compare
> to Istanbul and Galata.[32]

Yet, this strong dose of patriotism comes to us mitigated by a wider vision. We have already seen that, in the account of the voyage to India, the enormous prestige that the Ottoman name enjoyed is stressed time and again. Everywhere in the world that Seydi 'Ali visits, from Daman to Delhi, the mere mention of Sultan Süleyman's name seems to open all doors. There is also the clear suggestion that the association of the Ottomans with firearms also played no small role in the desire of various groups to seek alliances with the small body of armed men that Seydi 'Ali led. However, the dominant topos in the whole narrative is a different one. For Seydi 'Ali presents a situation where, in place after place, he encounters disputes that he has to resolve. Rather than the voyager who must solve riddles or conundrums, a figure also known from classical times, Seydi 'Ali presents himself as a solver of disputes, as someone who can render Solomonic (or perhaps Süleymanic) justice in place after place. Even on the rare occasions, such as in Sind, where he is drawn to take

[32] Seyyidi [Seydi] 'Ali Re'is, *Le miroir des pays*, p. 127; Seydi 'Ali Re'is, *Mir'ātü'l-Memālik*, p. 158. In an earlier conversation at Samarqand with a certain Baraq Khan, Seydi 'Ali had replied to a similar question by quoting the poet Nejati: "The heart prefers its usual carpet to Paradise / Each one prefers his native town to Baghdad" (*Le miroir des pays*, p. 101; *Mir'ātü'l-Memālik*, p. 131). On Nejati, also see Walter G. Andrews, Najaat Black and Mehmet Kalpakli, ed. and tr. *Ottoman lyric poetry: an anthology* (Austin, 1997), pp. 36–44.

sides, in the dispute between the Arghuns and Tarkhans, his role is presented as that of the mediator, who resolves the conflict and brings both under the common umbrella of Mughal sovereignty. This self-presentation as mediator, and judge, is paired with his sense of himself as the purveyor of the *mot juste* and the chronogram, thus a man whose literary talents and vast *savoir-faire* go together with a sense of balancing the disputed affairs of the world.

The last set of materials that concern his stay in Delhi brings this out clearly enough. Having completed his task of instructing Humayun in the astronomical texts that he desired to know, Seydi 'Ali notes that it nevertheless required some effort for him to obtain formal permission to depart from Delhi. Eventually, through the intercession of a young courtier and keeper of the seals (*mühr-dār*) Shahin Beg, he was able to do so, and on the presentation of two further odes (*g̲h̲azal*) to Humayun, the Mughal emperor gave him leave (*ruk̲h̲ṣat*), along with a present of a horse and a robe of honour. At this point, Fate intervened. On a Friday, at the hour of the evening prayer, Humayun was hurrying down the stairs when he fell, and was grievously – and even mortally – injured. Confusion reigned at the court, since the heir, Jalal-ud-Din Muhammad Akbar, was not present, and the Khan-i-Khanan too was absent for a time. Seydi 'Ali thus claims that, as usual, it was he who had to intervene to set matters right, as the courtiers went about wringing their hands and saying "What will happen to us?" The admiral thus pointed to an Ottoman precedent, stating that when Sultan Selim had died, the Grand Vizier, Piri Mehmed Pasha, had ensured that word did not get out of this until Süleyman was able to return to the court and mount the throne.[33] He thus advised that, in this case too, a ruse should be used in order to conceal the emperor's death for a certain time, while Akbar returned to the capital. So, he writes:

Amongst those close to the Padishah [Humayun], there was a person called Munla Bi-kesi who had a certain resemblance to him, but who was somewhat smaller. Finally, on Tuesday, he was installed on the throne that had been placed under an arch that overlooked the river, he was dressed up in the emperor's clothes, his face and eye were covered in bandages, Khushhal Beg stayed close to him and the Mir Munshi directly in front. All the Sultans, Mirzas, the subjects and the common people arrived, saw the emperor from the bank of the river and

[33] Compare Gilles Veinstein, "Un secret d'état: la mort de Soliman le Magnifique", *L'Histoire*, 211, June 1997, pp. 66–71, and Veinstein, "La mort de Mehmed II (1481)", in Nicolas Vatin and Gilles Veinstein, eds., *Les Ottomans et la mort: permanences et mutations* (Leiden, 1996), pp. 187–206.

made prayers for him. Joyful music was played, the physician was given a robe of honour, and it was asserted that the Padishah was in good health.[34]

On Akbar's eventual return, this imposture could finally be dispensed with, and the death of Humayun was at last announced to the public at large. By then, however, Seydi 'Ali had already left for Lahore via Sonepat, Karnal and Thanesar, having announced all along the way that Humayun was still in good health. He would then make his way in mid February 1556 back from Lahore to Mankot for a brief interview with the newly crowned Akbar and Bairam Khan, before returning to Lahore, and then travelling on to Kabul, and eventually into Central Asia.

We could notionally follow Seydi 'Ali through his long sojourn into Central Asia and then Iran, and finally back into the Ottoman domains. Rather than do so, we would prefer to limit ourselves here to some further remarks concerning his stay in India. It must be noted first of all that the visit of the Ottoman admiral did leave some documentary traces in the subcontinent besides his own memoirs. The references to his presence in Gujarat in the Portuguese chronicles of the period have already been mentioned above; but Seydi 'Ali also features briefly in a letter written from the Mughal court to Sultan Süleyman. This letter, begun when Humayun was still alive, and completed after the accession of Akbar, was obviously carried back personally by Seydi 'Ali himself, and was apparently drafted by a certain Khwaja Mahmud Lari. After elaborate addresses of several lines to the recipient, the letter goes on to state the following.

Praise and gratitude to Allah that, with infallible keys, the doors of Divine Victories have opened, and the throne of the *salṭanat* and *k̲h̲ilāfat* of the lands of Hind and Sind has been firmly reestablished with the grace of Divine Resources, and through the noble benefit of your Solomon-like magnificence. Although I have not been in communication and correspondence with your glorious *k̲h̲ilāfat*, yet by the constant support of noble precepts (*ak̲h̲lāq*), and the evident signs of gracious favours and the virtue of the affection of that leader of the kings of the world [i.e. Süleyman], I have always been blessed with a desire for alliance and friendship [with you].

Even if a hundred deserts intervene
between the Ka'aba and the heart,
still a window of the harem
opens into its enclosure.

[34] Seyyidi [Seydi] 'Ali Re'is, *Le miroir des pays*, pp. 90–1; for the original text, see Seydi 'Ali Re'is, *Mir'ātü'l-Memālik*, pp. 120–1.

[Thus] a desire has ever remained hidden and stored in my heart to open the doors of correspondence [with you]. This [desire] could not however be realised; the desired beloved that I had hoped for has not shown her face from behind the curtain of the bridal chamber.

In the meanwhile, the high-statured and illustrious Sayyid 'Ali Qapudan, who is amongst your most devoted and noble servants, and who had been deputed to serve with his contingent in the army in Egypt, was divinely constrained to come over to the *wilāyat* of Gujarat. When he heard of my victory, he arrived in Delhi, the Heaven-like capital of the [reconquered] countries, and gave me auspicious news of the prevalence of prosperous conditions [in your country] and the dignity of your illustrious and august person. It was learnt that the honoured servant [Sayyid 'Ali] was here without the permission of that Essence of Kingship [i.e. Süleyman], and I hence did not trouble him to stay on here. He thus left in your direction so that he might strengthen the chains of union and love [between us], and be a mediator of the special ties making up our bond.

For this reason I send you this letter and impinge on your blessed time, stringing rubies from the mines of love together with the precious pearls of my dedicated sincerity, in keeping with the custom of devoted lovers and special friends. It is hoped and desired that the domain of our compact may be opened with the keys of sincerity from that direction as well. May the doors of correspondence remain open forever, and the foundation of the tall edifice of our union be strengthened in such a manner that it continues to be protected from any possibility of damage or fissure.[35]

This flowery letter, together with the memoirs themselves, must have been part of the argument that Seydi 'Ali carried back to show how effectively he had comported himself in very difficult circumstances. The reputation of the admiral appears to have been sealed even before he returned – having been given up for dead – to Istanbul, for he reports that Iskender Pasha told him (on hearing parts of his account): "We too have a certain knowledge of the parts of the world (*eṭrāf-i 'ālem*), but in truth, what you have recounted surpasses it a thousand times."[36] Yet this new knowledge was not ethnographic in character, nor was it meant to

[35] The text of the letter may be found in 'Abdul Husain Nawa'i, *Shāh Ṭahmāsb Ṣafawī: Majmu'ah-i asnād wa mukātabāt-i tārīkhī hamrāh ba yāddāsht-hā-yi tafṣīlī* (Tehran, 1971), pp. 306–8. An older translation may be found in Joseph de [von] Hammer, "Memoir on the diplomatic relations between the courts of Delhi and Constantinople in the sixteenth and seventeenth centuries", *Transactions of the Royal Asiatic Society*, 2, 1830, pp. 476–7. It is generally agreed to be genuine, unlike a far more controversial letter in Turkish from Humayun to Süleyman of October 1548, reproduced in Ibrahim Hakki, "Hint Türk Hükümdari Hümayun Şahin Ḳanuniye gönderdiği bir mektup", *Yedigün*, 8, 202, 1937, pp. 7–9. For a full discussion of these documents, see also Riazul Islam, *A calendar of documents on Indo-Persian relations, (1500–1750)*, vol. II (Karachi, 1982), pp. 295–301; also Naimur Rehman Farooqi, *Mughal–Ottoman relations: a study of the political and diplomatic relations between Mughal India and the Ottoman empire* (Delhi, 1989), pp. 15–17.

[36] Seydi 'Ali Re'is, *Mir'ātü'l-Memālik*, p. 163.

be so. It was instead a "mirror of kingdoms", and hence above all an attempt to capture the changing political circumstances in India and Central Asia. Seydi 'Ali, we have seen, is a very indifferent ethnographer for the most part, and even on leaving Delhi throws in a mere handful of passages to sum up his Indian experience. Some of these address the peculiarities of certain animals in India, such as certain bizarre types of antelopes and buffaloes, and a single passage returns to the question of the "Hindus". Here, Seydi 'Ali writes:

> We saw the marvels and wonders (*'acāyibin ve gharāyibin*) of Hind. Amongst all the wonders, one is that the people of Gujarat call the *kefer* unbelievers *bāniyān*, and those of Hindustan call them *hindū*. They are not People of the Book (*kitābī*). They believe in the eternity of the world. When one of them dies, one puts the body back in the clothes that he wore when he was alive, and then burns it on the banks of a river. If it is a man, and if he leaves behind a wife, and she cannot have children, they do not burn her. But if she can remarry, they burn her, willy-nilly. If the woman burns of her own will, her relatives rejoice and play string instruments. If a certain number of Muslims (*ehl-i Islām*) get together, and take her away from the hands of her family when they want to burn her, she becomes their property, and no one can claim her back. For this reason, when someone is ready to be burned, they [the Hindus] recruit some of the Padishah's men so that the [Muslim] population (*khalq*) does not stop them.[37]

This is a curious variant of an altogether common topos, that of the *sati* or "virtuous wife", which is to be found as much in European travel-accounts as in non-European ones. The emphasis here is on the practice as one that was, above all, abhorrent to the Muslim population of India; yet, at the same time, we are informed that the Mughal rulers supported and even defended it to an extent. The image carried back by Seydi 'Ali, then, was not of a wholly Muslim India, but of an India where the non-Muslim population is scarcely worthy of attention, save as a curiosity or as a nuisance (as with the Rajputs encountered in Gujarat and Sind). Nevertheless, it is clear that power in India is held above all by the Muslims, and that most of them are overawed by the might and majesty of the Ottomans. It is an image that would have held little relevance for Ottoman policy-makers by the 1580s, when the Mughals had seized Gujarat and had begun to see themselves in as grandiose terms as the Ottomans. In these middle decades of the sixteenth century, it still provided a vision of an Indian Ocean world where the struggle was globally one between the Portuguese and the Ottomans, with all other parties being only of local importance.

[37] Seyyidi [Seydi] 'Ali Re'is, *Le miroir des pays*, pp. 92–3; Seydi 'Ali Re'is, *Mir'ātü'l-Memālik*, p. 123.

It is in this first incarnation that the work served to save Seydi 'Ali's own skin, besides becoming (as noted above) a part of the repertoire of texts used by Sokollu Mehmed Pasha to think through Ottoman relations with the kingdoms of India. It was only decades later, in the seventeenth century, that the work would achieve notoriety, thanks to its partial inclusion in Katib Çelebi's compendium on naval campaigns of the Ottomans, *Tuhfetü'l-kibār fi Esfāri'l-biḥār.*[38] By this time, its political immediacy and significance had been lost, and it must have appeared to its readers to be above all a book of adventures, of one man's struggle against heavy odds to return to his beloved homeland.

MUTRIBI'S MARVELS

The Mughal court, for its part, seems not to have retained a clear memory of Seydi 'Ali Re'is's visit. In 1608, when a certain Central Asian named Aqam Haji appeared in Jahangir's court in Agra, claiming to be an envoy of the Ottoman Sultan Ahmed I (r. 1603–17), he was turned away. Jahangir himself wrote in his memoirs: "He had with him a letter of doubtful origin (*kitābat-i majhūl*). In view of his circumstances and his proceedings, none of the servants of the court believed in his being an ambassador." More to the point, he added: "From the time of Timur, no one ever came on behalf of the Qaisar [of Rum] as an envoy or otherwise. How could one then believe that this Transoxanian was the envoy of the Ottoman Sultan?"[39] In this section, we shall turn to a consideration of another example, namely of a Central Asian who was rather better received than Aqam Haji. This was the poet, Mutribi al-Asamm al-Samarqandi, who visited Jahangir's court in the late 1620s.[40] By some definitions, Mutribi's *khāṭirāt* might not be considered travel-literature at all, since there is no real itinerary, no sense of movement in space and time together, and the text is in fact essentially a memoir of conversations and discussions.[41] Nevertheless, it captures two central features of travel

[38] See Katib Çelebi, *Tuhfetü'l-kibar fi Esfāri'l-biḥār*, ed. Orhan Şaik Gökyay (Istanbul, 1973); also James Mitchell, *The history of the maritime wars of the Turks, translated from the Turkish of Haji Khalifeh* (London, 1831).

[39] Riazul Islam, *Calendar*, vol. II, pp. 310–11, citing Nur-ud-Din Muhammad Jahangir, *Tūzuk-i Jahāngīrī*, ed. Syud Ahmud Khan (Aligarh, 1864), pp. 68–9.

[40] Mutribi Samarqandi, *Khāṭirāt-i-Muṭribī Samarqandī (being the memoirs of Muṭribī's sessions with Emperor Jahāngīr)*, ed. 'Abdul Ghani Mirzoyef (Karachi, 1977). A recent translation, somewhat unsatisfactory, is by Richard C. Foltz, *Conversations with Emperor Jahangir by "Mutribi" al-Asamm of Samarqand* (Costa Mesa, 1998).

[41] Surinder Singh, "The Indian memoirs of Mutribi Samarqandi", *Proceedings of the Indian History Congress, 55th Session, Aligarh, 1994* (Delhi, 1995), pp. 345–54. Also Richard C. Foltz, "Two

texts rather neatly: the incessant comparisons between two cultures (here Central Asia, and Mughal North India), and the insistence on the aspect of wonders (*'ajā'ib*) in at least a part of the text.

The text is situated in a period in Mughal history in which – unlike the case of Seydi 'Ali – other source-materials are by no means in short supply. The monarch Nur-ud-Din Muhammad Jahangir (r. 1605–28) is, after all, himself the author of a highly accomplished autobiographical work in Persian, the *Tūzak-i Jahāngīrī*.[42] In this work, Jahangir shows off his vast culture and curiosity, concerning both nature and artefacts; nothing, from melons, to elephants, to the themes favoured by *dhrupad* poet–composers, seems to escape his probing pen. The court-chronicles of the reign, such as that of Mu'tamad Khan, the *Iqbālnāma-i Jahāngīrī*, supplement this "internal" perspective, of kingship seen from the inside out, and we may add a number of other personal memoirs (and travel-accounts) that date from this reign, and which shed light on a variety of political and cultural institutions at work in this epoch of the Mughal meridian. We may list among these 'Abdul Latif Gujarati's travel-text from 1607–10, Asad Beg's account of his vicissitudes, both in the Deccan and at Jahangir's court, and Mirza Nathan's well-known chronicle-cum-memoir from the early seventeenth century.[43] The text that we shall deal with below is, however, rather different in its character from all of these.

Mutribi begins his work with a brief introduction, which sets the stage for the account of the twenty-four conversations between him and Jahangir. Here, after praising God and the Prophet, the author reflects on the nature of faith, which he divides into two aspects: Thanksgiving and Patience. The text, he notes, illustrates the first of these notions, and is one of thanksgiving to Allah, for having allowed the author the privilege, for a time, of the company of one of the greatest rulers of the age (a string of epithets follows), namely Jahangir. The meetings appear to have taken

seventeenth-century Central Asian travellers to Mughal India", *Journal of the Royal Asiatic Society of Great Britain and Ireland*, Series 3, 6, 3 (1996), pp. 367–77.

42 Alexander Rogers and Henry Beveridge, tr. and ed., *The Tūzuk-i-Jahāngīrī or memoirs of Jahāngīr*, 2 vols. (London, 1909–14).

43 See N. D. Ahuja, "Abd al-Latīf al 'Abbāsī and his account of Punjab", *Islamic Culture*, 41, 2, 1967, pp. 93–8. Also 'Ala-ud-Din Isfahani, called Mirza Nathan, *Bahāristān-i-Ghaybī: a history of the Mughal wars in Assam, Cooch Behar, Bengal, Bihar and Orissa . . .*, tr. M. I. Borah, 2 vols. (Gauhati, 1936). This text is often read together with another interesting (somewhat later) memoir of Mughal dealings with their eastern frontier, namely Shihab-ud-Din Talish's *Fathiyya-i 'Ibriyya* (*c.* 1670), for which see Ahmad bin Muhammad Wali Shihab-ud-Din Talish, *Tarikh-i Asham, récit de l'expédition de Mir-Djumlah au pays d'Assam*, translated from the earlier Hindustani translation of Mir Husaini, by Théodore Pavie (Paris, 1845); and Jadunath Sarkar, *Studies in Aurangzib's reign* (Hyderabad, 1989), pp. 114–48.

place in Lahore, through the mediation of a certain Khwaja Fakhr-ud-Din Husain, son of Maulana Khwaja Khan Diwan. They began on Wednesday, 19 Rabi' I AH 1036 in the afternoon, thus rather late in Jahangir's reign, in December 1626; the text itself was written down from Thursday, 9 Jumada II of the same year (late February 1627), when the recollections were still fresh in Mutribi's mind.

The meetings are described using the term *wāqi'a* – "happenings". Thus, in the very first meeting, Jahangir asks Mutribi why, after spending a month in Lahore, he had only now come to the court. Mutribi answers that he was finishing a text in honour of Jahangir (the *Nuskha-yi Zība-yi Jahāngīr*), and had only now found a chronogram to close it.[44] On being presented with the text, Jahangir is pleased, and asks Mutribi whether he would rather stay in the Mughal court, or go back to his homeland, or whether he wanted to make the *ḥajj* pilgrimage to Mecca and Medina. Mutribi, ever the courtier, says that he is at the ruler's disposal. Jahangir then tells him he has four gifts for him, but that he would give them one after the other. They were, money for his expenses, a *khil'at* (ceremonial and honorific robe) to wear, a horse and saddle, and a slave to serve him. Which of these did he want first? Mutribi replies in poetry on the importance of money (*zar*), and is at once given a platter full of money, amounting to 1,000 Rupees. In addition, he is given Rs 500 on the part of the consort, Nur Jahan. Mutribi immodestly compares himself to Hafiz Shirazi before Timur, on the conquest of Shiraz by the latter, and recounts an elaborate anecdote on the meeting between the two. Timur too had given Hafiz money and a *khil'at*, though not a horse and a saddle.

The stage has now been set for the subsequent meetings and conversations, which will have a more explicitly comparative and reflective nature for the most part. In the second meeting, the ruler's brother-in-law Asaf Khan or Khwaja Abu'l Hasan, the *dīwān*, Khawass Khan, Bahadur Khan of Mawarannahr, and several other *amīrs* were present. Jahangir now enquired on the state of the burial-place of his illustrious ancestor, Timur, in Samarqand, and Mutribi replied that details were to be found in his own text, the *Nuskha-yi Zība*. The emperor wished to know precise details of the colour of the gravestone, and, asking for a square black stone to be brought, asked Mutribi to compare it in his mind's eye with the

44 For this text, see Mutribi Samarqandi, *Nuskha-yi Zība-yi Jahāngīr*, ed. Isma'il Bikjanuf and Sayyid 'Ali Mawjani (Qom, 1377 Sh. / 1998). Also see the earlier text by the same author: Mutribi Samarqandi, *Tazkirat ush-Shu'rā'*, ed. Asghar Janfida and 'Ali Rafi'i 'Ala Marwdashti (Tehran, 1377 Sh. / 1998).

gravestone. Mutribi replied that there some differences, since the stone before him was duller than the other.[45] (At this point in the text, Mutribi gives details of the construction of Timur's burial-place, by way of an aside.) He was then given another *khil'at*, a Kashmiri shawl, a turban and other gifts; his son Muhammad 'Ali, too, was given expensive brocade clothes. The horse and the saddle were saved up for the next day.

We have now understood that Mutribi represents a window into Central Asia for Jahangir, as a sort of authentic eyewitness (*bayān*) to affairs in Transoxania, and we can now move on to the aspect of wonders. The next day, some European merchants (*tujjār-i firang*) who were present, gave tributes (*peshkash-hā*) to Jahangir. A small booklet (*kitābcha*), four fingers long, was in the emperor's hand; it had twelve folios, and the paper was a brownish colour. The book was in a small locked box, and, calling Mutribi, Jahangir asked him to guess which book it was. The former confessed ignorance, and the emperor opened the box and gave it to him with a stick, and explained that one could write on the paper with it, but also rub the writing off. Mutribi was astonished, and by way of demonstration Jahangir wrote a verse in the book, showed it to him, and then rubbed it off. Jokingly, he offered to sell the book and pencil to Mutribi for a rupee. The latter superstitiously refused, saying that it was magical (*tilism*), and might harm him; besides he did not have any money on him. Jahangir laughingly gave it to him as a gift, assuring him it was harmless. Mutribi reports his intention to carry it back to Turan, and give it to the ruler there, Imam Quli Khan, as a valuable gift from Hindustan.

This reminds him of an earlier incident from the time of 'Abdullah Khan Uzbek in Bukhara, which he describes at some length. A certain physician (*ḥakīm*) called Maulana Jalali, a resident of the Ku-yi Ghaziyan ("Lane of the Ghazis"), was also interested in the magical arts, and had a strange box (*ṣandūq*) the height of a man in his house, with the heads of animals (a monkey, a lion and a horse) sculpted on it. These heads, and especially that of the monkey, would move about, the apparatus would make a noise, and the passage of time could be measured thereby. Mutribi is obviously referring to a rather complicated clockwork mechanism of some sort. Now, Maulana Jalali had an ingenious use for this contraption.

[45] We thus cannot concord with the claim that "no particular interest was shown in Timur during Akbar's son Jahangir's reign", as stated in Irfan Habib, "Timur in the political tradition and historiography of Mughal India", in Maria Szuppe, ed., *L'Héritage timouride: Iran – Asie centrale – Inde, XVe–XVIIIe siècles* (Tashkent, 1997), p. 303.

Figure 8. Los Angeles County Museum of Art, M. 75.4.28 Emperor Jahangir triumphing over Poverty, *c.* 1622, attributed to Abu'l Hasan.

He would ask his guests to make a wish, and then ask them to take a seal that he gave them, made of a mix of seven metals, and place it in the mouth of the horse. The seal would fall into the box with a bang, but would then rise up again with a rattling sound, emerge from the lion's mouth and fall into a jar. At this time, a window concealed at one side of the box would open, and a man would be revealed sitting on a throne with a rolled up paper in his hands. Taking the paper, the Hakim would read out from it, and recount details of his visitor's future, and impending fortune or misfortune. At the end of this, the window would close up, and the entire structure would once more resemble a box. In brief, clockwork, a form of "modern" wonder, was made to serve the ends of "traditional" magic, impressing visitors no end.

In the fourth meeting, matters took a literary turn, as Jahangir had by now read Mutribi's book, and commented on a verse in it. A discussion took place on the verse's authorship, as Mutribi had taken it from another writer (a fact that Jahangir recognised). Mention is made of the presence in court of a certain seventy-year-old courtier called Maktub Khan, himself a poet from Shiraz and in charge of the imperial library and picture-gallery. Maktub Khan had on an earlier occasion cited the same verse, and the issue arose of who in fact had the earliest claim over the verse. The matter was eventually settled with tact.

In the next meeting, Jahangir returned to the issue of hearsay and eyewitness. He asked Mutribi if he knew a certain Mirza Baqi Anjumani, and the latter replied that he was 'Abdullah Khan's son, who had taken refuge in Akbar's court, and then gave details of his stay in the Mughal court. Jahangir was surprised at his knowledge of these details, and asked him how he came by them. Mutribi replied that he had received news of him in Samarqand, and then in Lahore from a traveller called "Barhaman", who claimed to have made the *ḥajj* with Mirza Baqi, and told of his death. Jahangir insisted that this hearsay was incorrect, and that Mirza Baqi had never left the Mughal court, but had in fact died there. This leads Mutribi to reflect on the nature of truth and falsehood, and he notes that Jahangir was rigorous in investigating the veracity of statements. Jahangir now wished to test Mutribi himself. He hence asked him if he knew a certain Abu'l Bey, and Mutribi replied that he did. Jahangir hence had two men produced before him, and asked Mutribi which one was Abu'l Bey. Mutribi hesitated and said he did not think either was Abu'l Bey; at this, Jahangir smiled, and said that Mutribi was right, for in fact one was Afzal Khan and the other Musawi Khan! Indeed, on a later occasion, Mutribi espied Abu'l Bey in the court, and

Jahangir was satisfied at his powers of observation and devotion to the truth.

In the sixth meeting, Jahangir was being weighed on the occasion of a celebration. Mutribi too received two platters of coins, worth Rs 2,000, and other valuables. Pleased, the poet recited verses in the court in praise of the emperor, and, pleased, in turn, at the verses, Jahangir for his part gave him more gifts. He also asked Mutribi which sort of horse and saddle he wanted. Mutribi somewhat greedily asked for the most expensive sort of horse and saddle, and a discussion ensued on the relative quality of different sorts. Finally, he received an 'Iraqi horse (rather than a less valuable Turkish one) and a saddle of velvet (rather than a more expensive but less durable one in scarlet cloth).

At the next meeting, we return to the question of the wonders of Hindustan. A large sugar-candy (weighing half a Bukhara maund) had been placed on a silver seat in the court in anticipation of Mutribi's arrival. Jahangir then proudly asked Mutribi whether such a thing could be found in Transoxania. When Mutribi said he had never seen such an object, Jahangir noted that it was rare in India as well; a certain Muhammad Husain had brought it from the region of Lucknow, and now he offered it to Mutribi as a gift. The latter for his part decided to take it back to his home, and to give it either to Imam Quli Khan or to the "Qutb of the Time", the Hazrat Ishan. Intrigued, Jahangir asked who this latter person might be, and Mutribi replied that it was a certain Sufi (possibly of the Naqshbandi order) called Khwaja Hashim Muhammad Dehbedi, whom Jahangir knew and was devoted to.

In the next meeting, Jahangir, who had returned from the hunt, gave Mutribi a bird (*surkhāb*) that he himself had shot. He then jokingly asked him for something in return, and Mutribi recited a verse on the occasion. Pleased, the emperor gave him some money as a gift. In the next meeting, he was given two birds (*murghābī*), from which he had a kind of pilaf dish (*mutanjana*) made. Such birds, Mutribi noted, were not to be found in Transoxania, and were a peculiarity of Hindustan; he recounts a long anecdote on bird-meat and wine in connection with this. In the following meeting, the conversation took a more explicitly "anthropological" turn. Jahangir asked Mutribi rather bluntly whether he thought white skin was better than black, obviously wishing to test our Central Asian's colour prejudices in respect of Indians. Mutribi replied evasively, saying that it was all a matter of opinion; but Jahangir insisted that he wanted to know *his* opinion. Mutribi for his part said that he could only judge by seeing (*bīnam wa gūyam*), and so Jahangir advised him to look right and left and decide. On the right, Mutribi found a dark young Indian princeling (*rājābacha*), who was so handsome that Mutribi claims he lost control of his heart. Equally, on the left, a fair and handsome boy was standing, who dazzled Mutribi's eyes. How could he now decide? Having looked twice at each, he said to Jahangir, that it was not a matter of dark and fair but of the pleasantness (*malāḥat*) of the countenance. Jahangir was pleased, and recited a verse in the same sense, to which Mutribi replied with a supporting *ḥadīṣ*, in which the Prophet boastfully said that his brother Yusuf was fair, but it was he whose countenance had a more agreeable (literally "salty") quality.

The next meeting took place at night, under the light of the moon. Everyone present was dressed in white, and the emperor was seated on a white marble throne. Caught unawares, Mutribi arrived dressed in a different colour, and was at first barred from entering. He hence asked the musician Fasih Khan (named "The Nightingale with the Pleasant Voice") to carry a poem to Jahangir. He was then given a white dress and turban and asked to come in. The twelfth encounter was also at night, but this time in torchlight. The emperor had organised a tournament with camels, and fighting bucks. Mutribi marvelled, for he had never seen such a fight in Transoxania, and Jahangir too rubbed it in, by asking whether he had ever witnessed such in his homeland. Mutribi once more had to confess he had not, and that Hindustan held wonders unheard of in his native land.

The remaining meetings also contain their share of amusing and illuminating anecdotes of one sort or another. Thus, in the sixteenth meeting, Jahangir auctions a slave in the court, while proclaiming (in a semi-serious fashion) that of all the professions, only trade is respectable in the eyes of Islam. Eventually, the slave is purchased by the musician Fasih Khan, whom we have encountered above. Or again, in the eighteenth meeting, the nature of empirical verification is at issue. A freshly made set of portraits from the Mughal atelier is brought before Mutribi, who sees that they depict the former ruler of Turan, 'Abdullah Khan Uzbek and his son 'Abdul Momin Khan. However, he tells Jahangir that there are defects in the representation of 'Abdullah Khan's chin, and his son's headgear. In response, the painter is at once summoned, and asked to correct the paintings, which he does by the next day. Another Turani courtier expresses a contrary opinion on 'Abdul Momin Khan's headgear, but finally Mutribi's view is upheld. He is once more impressed by the empiricist spirit on display in Jahangir's court: seeing is believing.

A persistent thread that runs through the conversations concerns Jahangir's effort to demonstrate the hierarchical superiority of Hindustan over Central Asia. Thus, he asks Mutribi for the names of worthy persons from Central Asia whom he can invite to his court, never for a moment thinking that such an invitation would be refused; Mutribi suggests that a certain Maulana Sabri Tashkandi be invited, and the suggestion is accepted by Jahangir. In the same conversation (the twenty-second) Jahangir asks how much money should be sent to repair the *Gūr-i Mīr* (Timur's Tomb). When Mutribi suggests Rs 10,000, Jahangir says he will send it back with Mutribi to Central Asia.

By the time of the last meeting, Mutribi has begun to feel homesick, and also mentions his advanced years. However, he approaches the question obliquely, and, on an occasion when Asaf Khan and others are present, presents a *ghazal*, and says he wishes to leave for Samarqand, promising however to spread the word of Jahangir's greatness there. Jahangir asks him instead to come to Kashmir with him, and promises that he will send money to bring Mutribi's relatives over. After some discussion, he allows him at last to go, but insists that he should come back in a year. The traveller departs.

CONCLUSION

A little reflection shows, however, that there are two travellers within Mutribi's text, the author himself and the Mughal emperor, Jahangir. If Mutribi makes comparisons between Central Asia and Hindustan, based on what he sees (and the insistent emphasis is on the eye, and its superiority to hearsay), Jahangir transforms himself through Mutribi (and, undoubtedly, scores of others like him) into an armchair traveller. If the wonders and the superiority of Hindustan are brought out, it is by constant contrast to Transoxania, and in effect Mutribi becomes the vehicle for the expression of Jahangir's opinions and prejudices. By writing and diffusing his text in Central Asia, it is almost as if he wishes to present Jahangir himself as not the least of the wonders of Hindustan! What is also significant about Mutribi is his signal indifference to Hindustan outside the court. One finds no comments in his account on life in the cities (not even in Lahore, where these encounters take place); as for the countryside, it is entirely absent.[46] Thus, the vision that is

[46] The text of Mutribi, together with several others, has thus been recently and justly analysed as part of the "circulation of men-of-letters and of literary circles" between Central Asia, Iran and North

presented of Mughal India to the reader in Central Asia is one that, even more than with Seydi 'Ali, remains one of courtly life and hence of a domain where the largely familiar mores of a Persianate culture hold sway. It is a reassuring vision, one that must have informed potential migrants in Central Asia that life in Hindustan could not be all that different from the one they were accustomed to.

The two texts that we have examined in this chapter thus bring out one particularly salient aspect of the inter-imperial system that had emerged in the latter half of the sixteenth century, involving the Ottomans, Safavids, Mughals and Shaibanids. Here was a system in which the four parties to a very large extent saw themselves as representing rather similar levels of sovereignty, and where a Persianate (or, earlier, Perso-Turkish) code provided the basis for communication and diplomatic dealings. In this world, it was possible for a traveller – whether Seydi 'Ali or Mutribi – to arrive in a strange setting, immediately find his bearings, and function with a great deal of ease. The same would have been true for a Mughal envoy in Istanbul, or a Mughal poet in Samarqand. However, this ease of communication was predicated on the idea of remaining confined to the courtly milieu, and not looking for the most part to what existed outside this beaten track. When one did so, the results could range from the disquieting to the disastrous, and the reactions on the part of the travellers would then take on a wholly different hue. At the same time, it is noteworthy that the experience of our courtly travellers differs in very significant ways from the far better-known dealings of European ambassadors (such as Sir Thomas Roe) in the courts of South Asia. Roe and others were constantly confronted with their own clumsiness and lack of comprehension of Mughal institutions, and retaliated by producing a portrayal of a Mughal court that was little more than a stage for tawdry theatre, and unbridled cruelty. The Jahangir of those accounts has little in common with Mutribi's Jahangir, and it is hard to think of a Dutch ambassador who would – like Seydi 'Ali – have produced improvised verses for the delectation of a Mughal sovereign. The next chapter takes us, however, to a rather less idyllic vision of dealings within the Indo-Persian world.

India. Cf. Maria Szuppe, "Circulation des lettrés et cercles littéraires: entre Asie centrale, Iran et Inde du Nord (XVe–XVIIIe siècle)", *Annales HSS*, 5–6, September–December 2004, pp. 997–1018.

CHAPTER 4

An ocean of wonders

I do not condemn infidelity (*kufr*),
I'm not a bigoted believer.
I laugh at both –
the Shaikh and the Brahmin.

Talib Amuli (d. 1626)

INTRODUCTION

By the second quarter of the seventeenth century, a new political and economic equilibrium had appeared in terms of relations between Mughal India, Safavid Iran, Central Asia and the Ottoman empire. In the first half of the sixteenth century, it is clear that the Ottomans enjoyed vast power and unparalleled prestige, owing both to their territorial expansion into North Africa, the Balkans and Asia, and their unmatched naval abilities, which allowed them to combat the European powers in both the Mediterranean and even the Indian Ocean. This period of Ottoman dominance in the world of eastern Islam was also one when the three other powers, to which we have referred above, struggled to establish somewhat stable boundaries as well as a hierarchy and pecking order between them. However, the rapid consolidation of the Mughal domains between the 1560s and the 1590s meant that these Timurid dynasts alone were in a position, by about 1600, to pose themselves as serious rivals to the Ottomans. In this they were helped by the political disarray that followed in Central Asia after the death of ʻAbdullah Khan Shaibani, the decline of the rival political centre of Kabul, and their own capacity to draw talents regularly from Iran and Central Asia to their own court. By the last years of the reign of Akbar (d. 1605), it was the well-endowed Mughal court that had emerged as the principal magnet for talented poets, scribes, warriors and painters in the eastern Islamic world. This is what drew savants like

Mutribi there, but such a situation also left certain of the migrants with a feeling of discomfort.

For Mughal India remained a land that was dominated demographically (and, to an extent, even culturally) by non-Muslims (*kuffār*), whom the Mughal rulers seemed in no great hurry to convert. Once one left the comfortable world of the courtly centre that Seydi ʻAli Re'is and Mutribi had frequented, one regularly encountered "idols" and their worshippers, a countryside where toiling peasants and their *zamīndār* overlords enjoyed a fair degree of autonomy from Mughal rule, and the Persian language itself coexisted with a variety of quite flourishing vernaculars, which would have been incomprehensible to the visitor from Bukhara or Bursa. This makes for a great paradox in the seventeenth century, which is in one sense a period in which the broad process of Persianization extends eastwards somewhat beyond the borders of the Mughal domains. Areas such as Arakan in northern Burma, and even Thailand, come under the partial sway of a Persianate culture, but here it is a culture that – even more than in Mughal India – has come uncoupled from religious beliefs and practices. The problems are not entirely different from those faced by ʻAbdur Razzaq Samarqandi in the mid-fifteenth century, save that the great polity that he came face to face with – namely Vijayanagara – existed in an Indian world where a great suzerain power like that of the Mughals simply could not be found. What this meant was that in the seventeenth century, Mughal India exercised a mix of fascination and repulsion on visitors and migrants from further west, that is to say both from Transoxiana and the Iranian world. It is this complex set of emotions and sentiments, which offer a somewhat different palette of possibilities from the writings of Seydi ʻAli and Mutribi, to which we now turn.

A CENTRAL ASIAN VIEW FROM "BELOW"?

There could be no better way to address these questions than through the text that must be considered to be the centrepiece of this chapter, namely the work entitled *Baḥr al-asrār fī maʻrifat al-akhyār* ("The ocean of secrets in the knowledge of the pious") by Mahmud Wali Balkhi.[1] Of this

[1] Mahmud ibn Amir Wali Balkhi's *Baḥr al-asrār fī maʻrifat al-akhyār*, ed. Hakim Muhammad Saʻid, Sayyid Muʻinul Haqq and Ansar Zahid Khan (Karachi, 1984). This is vol. I, part I, of the text, but no further parts have appeared to date. It is from the Uzbek Academy of Sciences, Tashkent manuscript. In some manuscripts, the title substitutes *maʻrifat* ("knowledge") with *manāqib* ("accounts").

massive work in seven volumes, we are aware that only one and a half volumes (some sections of vol. I and vol. VI) have survived. The text was compiled in the court of Nazr Muhammad Khan in Central Asia. In the original statement of the structure of the text, the author writes:

This auspicious compilation which is on the mysteries of the other world and the histories of this world has appropriately been given the name "The Ocean of Mysteries in the Knowledge of the Pious". The wonderful and strange things recounted here will be presented as follows: a beginning (*fātiḥa*), seven volumes, and an epilogue (*kẖātima*), and each volume will be arranged into four parts (*rukn*).[2]

Details then follow of each part: the prologue, for example, is concerned with the essence and the attributes of the Maker, and a listing of the names of God, while the sixth volume concerns the history of the Turks, and the seventh volume deals with the Chaghatay (that is, Mughal) rulers. The travel account which we shall deal with below would appear to have been part of the sixth volume. The surviving parts of the text (excluding the travel section) also have extensive geographical descriptions, including those of many parts of South-east Asia, such as Banten, Makassar, Manila and Timor. This is part of the '*Bayān-i ḥaqīqat-i āb*' (the section on water and water-bodies), wherein a very large number of islands, etc., are described, and there is also a description of the Ganges.[3]

Now the travel section of the text has only in recent times acquired a certain notoriety, on account of the patient philological work of the Pakistani historian Riazul Islam, although it had been known to Central Asianists at least from the time of V. V. Bartol'd.[4] The author, Mahmud bin Amir Wali Balkhi (born 1004 H / 1595–6), was – as his name obviously suggests – from Balkh, though his family hailed originally from Kasan in Ferghana. Like many other writers in the genre, he too belonged to the literati, and was also rather close to Central Asian court circles, being made the head librarian (*kitābdār-i kẖāṣṣa*) of Nazr Muhammad Khan (r. 1606–42; 1647–51). His work bears a certain generic resmblance in

2 Balkhi, *Baḥr al-asrār*, p. 15.

3 Balkhi, *Baḥr al-asrār*, pp. 294–95.

4 For details on earlier writings concerning this text, see the important survey by B. A. Akhmedov, "The *Baḥr al-Asrār* of Maḥmūd b. Valī and its study in the USSR and elsewhere", *Journal of Asian History*, 25, 2, 1991, pp. 163–80, and also B. G. Gafurov, "The Baḥr al-Asrār – II", *Journal of the Pakistan Historical Society*, 14, 2, 1966, pp. 99–103, and the various papers by Riazul Islam, "The *Baḥr ul-Asrār* – I: a note on the travel portion", *Journal of the Pakistan Historical Society*, 14, 2, 1966, pp. 93–7; Islam, "A seventeenth-century account of Sind", *Journal of the Pakistan Historical Society*, 26, 3, 1978, pp. 141–55; Islam, "Travelogue of Maḥmūd b. Amīr Walī", *Journal of the Pakistan Historical Society*, 27, 2, 1979, pp. 88–120.

terms of framing devices to the text of 'Abdur Razzaq Samarqandi, since it comes inserted in a far larger work, indeed one with universalistic pretensions. Unlike the ambassador from fifteenth-century Herat, Mahmud Wali Balkhi's travel-account leaves the rarefied realms of the court to provide a vision far more "from below" as it were.[5] As a sort of seventeenth-century Central Asian Jack Kerouac, Mahmud Balkhi's text – we shall have occasion to see below – has charms all its own.[6]

We have already noted that what we have is not a free-standing travel-account; instead, the travel section of the text is clearly separated by the author from the rest (unlike with 'Abdur Razzaq), with the sub-title "Account and presentation of a part of the wonders that the writer of these adventurous lines (*suṭūr-i makẖṭūr*) observed and experienced during his travels (*asfār*) through various territories (*aqṭār*)". The complexity of the *Baḥr al-asrār*'s travel section, and its twists and turns which occupy the seven lunar years between the author's departure from Balkh in 1625 at the age of about thirty, and his return, defy easy analysis. We would, however, suggest, provisionally, certain lines of development, to be kept in mind while following the author's itinerary. This itinerary took Mahmud Balkhi from Balkh, to Afghanistan, to Peshawar and Lahore, and then to Sirhind in the Punjab. Thereafter, he visited Delhi and Mathura, before going on to Allahabad and Benares. Following the Gangetic plain, his travels next took him to Patna, and Rajmahal in Bengal, whence he embarked for Orissa (Jagannath-Puri); the southward momentum then carried him down the length of the Indian peninsula as far as Sri Lanka. From Sri Lanka, Balkhi embarked on a boat for Southeast Asia, but found himself shipwrecked on the Orissa coast. Here, he spent several years in Mughal service, before embarking once more for the Indo-Gangetic heartland. Eventually, after a trip across the Rajasthan desert, he found himself in Sind, and began to consider returning home. After some political misadventures at the Mughal–Safavid frontier, he returned to Balkh in 1631.

Schematically, the text can be divided into two parts: first, the wanderings that take Mahmud Balkhi down the Gangetic valley, then down the Indian peninsula to his strange visit to Sri Lanka, and back up to Orissa; second, from the moment he enters the service of the Mughal official Mirza Husaini in Orissa, and becomes a minor Mughal *munshī* and

[5] Mahmud bin Amir Wali Balkhi, *The Baḥr ul-asrār: travelogue of South Asia*, intro., ed. and annot. by Riazul Islam (Karachi, 1980).

[6] For an earlier summary, see Islam, "The *Baḥr ul-asrār* – I: a note on the travel portion".

revenue-administrator. The first half of the text is mystic, and provides vivid ethnographic details of life "on the road"; the second is written from the perspective of a Mughal official, with accounts of "native superstitions" interspersed with often cynical reflections on statecraft, and some surprisingly prudish observations on morality. The Mahmud Balkhi of the first half of the text goes to watch a beautiful woman bathe in the *ghāṭs* of Patna, and in the second half censures the people of Sind for their immorality in a situation that is little different.

A second possible line of development is a religious one. At first hostile both to *jogīs* and deviant Muslims (as witness his description of Muharram in Lahore), Mahmud Balkhi is gradually drawn to Indian mystic practice by a series of encounters and impressions (aided perhaps by the fact that he may have been in a narcotic haze for a part of this time). However, at Benares, and then again at Patna, he draws back, and then in his foray into the south adopts the distant air of a religious ethnographer rather than of a participant. His immersion in a Mughal sub-imperial household in Cuttack brings him back full circle; by the time he reaches Ajmer and Jaisalmer, he is once more able to speak for the *dīn-i Islām*, and both proselytise and pass judgments. Most interesting of all, perhaps, is the relatively "raw" character of the work, which preserves an improvised character (as we see from the incorporation of local myths and *faits-divers*), and has a number of shifts in tone and perspective which suggest that Mahmud Balkhi did not rework it to flatten it out and impose on it an evenness of tone. This lends the text a more natural flavour than the well-wrought artefacts produced by such writers as Mutribi Samarqandi at roughly the same time.[7]

Why travel? The text of Mahmud Balkhi begins with a rather significant justification of why the author set out on his travels in the first place, and, as is often the case in the introduction to Persian texts of the epoch, links itself to one of the attributes of God, or to a Qur'anic saying. Thus:

When in the Year 1034, the damsel of this Qur'anic verse:

Do they not travel
Through the earth, and see
What was the end
Of those before them?[8]

[7] Mutribi Samarqandi, *Khāṭirāt-i-Muṭribī Samarqandī.*

[8] Qur'ān, XII, 109, translation from Abdullah Yusuf 'Ali, *The meaning of the glorious Qur'ān*, text, translation and commentary 2 vols., (Cairo, 1938), vol. I, p. 590.

drew back her veil from her sun-like face, the writer of these lines with the eye of his intelligence had a vision of the lesson-inspiring scenes [behind] the veil of this damsel. At that time, an uncontrollable urge became rooted in my humble heart in keeping with the verse:

> Then contemplate (o man!)
> The memorials of God's Mercy![9]

and a firm determination arose [in me] to see strange creations and curious objects (*badā'i' ṣanā'i' wa g͟harā'ib wadāi'*).

As the vast land of Hind is full of such righteous souls, and is adorned with a variety of rare objects, and [possesses] the manifestations of perfect Divine Power, and evident scenes of Divine Grace, and in which territories are manifest the traces of the wonders and secrets of His Creation, first the bird of my resolution intended to fly towards that country (*mamlikat*), and thus directly on the 1st of Shawwal of the above-mentioned year (6 July 1625), it departed from Balkh towards that pleasant land with a sad heart, with the speed of the gaze and of the lightning-bolt of separation.

The traveller with his mixed emotions made his way first to Kabul, and he expresses through verses the gradual easing of the pain of separation from Balkh in his new environs. He reports that he made several new acquaintances in Kabul, attended a musical soirée (*anjuman-i ṭarab*), and ate and drank to his content. Kabul agreed with him, and he praises the town, but notes with regret that he had to move on soon enough. His next stop was thus Peshawar, where he had the first of an extended series of meetings with Indian celibate ascetics (*jogīs*), which would be a recurring feature of his voyage down the Gangetic plain.

These meetings in Peshawar appear to have taken place in a site called Gor-Khattri, where he reports the existence of buildings made of brick and stone, rather like mosques and Sufi hospices. He notes too the existence of a deep well, and behind it a structure where ascetics gathered in an atmosphere full of incense. These ascetics were in a state of *jog*, which he explains arises from breath-control; the structure is called the Qadamgah-i Baba Ratan. In these environs, in a temple, he found the head of the ascetics, seated on a *masnad* ("throne") attended by about a thousand *jogīs*, *sanyāsīs*, *bairāgīs* ("ascetics and renouncers") and others. The meeting inspires a reflection in Mahmud Balkhi on the nature of the *jogīs*' activity: holding their breath and sitting in a trance for hours together. The highest among them, he notes, is seated separately, and

[9] Qur'ān, XXX, 50, translation from Yusuf 'Ali, *The meaning*, vol. II, p. 1065.

eventually entombed alive in brick and stone, so that in a few days his soul departs, ostensibly in order to return to the world in a better form (*bihtar az ān paikar-i sābiq*), but is in fact "ensnared in eternal perdition". This is obviously his understanding of the notion of *samādhī*, practised by ascetics. The place, he further notes, has revenue-grants (*waẓāif-o-idrārāt*) from both the Sultans and the Hindus (*salāṭīn wa hunūd*).[10] Mahmud Balkhi now expresses his strong disapproval of this form of ascetic practice, and characterises this "accursed group" as those who have fallen from God's Grace (*firqa-i mardūd*). He then describes his discussions with the head (*murshid*) of this group, which he claims were held "without a sentiment of prejudice or enmity" on his part; however, he also claims that his interlocutor got the worst of the discussion, and was even full of shame at its end.

The traveller also saw a *jogī* with his hair hanging down to the ground, and wrapped around his neck, with thirteen types of necklaces. His form of ascetic practice was to tie ten maunds of chains on his feet, which naturally made it rather difficult for him to walk. A wealthy Hindu called Ramdas now arrived, gave the ascetic 1,000 Rupees and lifted up his chain, to make it easier for him to move about. But the money-minded *jogī* (whom the traveller obviously thought was an imposter) is reported to have cried out: "Where is that generous man who shall give me 20,000 Rupees, and liberate me from these shackles?"[11]

After this first encounter, Balkhi made his way in the direction of Lahore, where he stayed *en route* in the shrine of Baba Hasan Abdal. Here, among the wonders, he saw a pond with jewel-adorned fish in it, whose keeper had given each a name; when he called them, they would respond, and he would feed them one by one. Thereafter, he left for Lahore, and on 1 Muharram 1035 H (23 September 1625) arrived in the town, whose main attraction for him seems to have been its beautiful Khatri women. At first, he seems to have stayed in a marketplace, where the merchants with their goods and pack-animals resided; since the traveller does not tell us how he made ends meet, it is quite possible that he too carried some goods on the road. He now looked for a friend from

[10] The practice of such fiscal grants by the Mughals was far from unknown; see B. N. Goswamy and J. S. Grewal, ed. and tr., *The Mughals and the Jogīs of Jakhbar* (Simla, 1967).

[11] Balkhi, *The Baḥr ul-asrār*, ed. Riazul Islam, pp. 4–6. Compare Iqbal Husain, "Hindu shrines and practices as described by a Central Asian traveller in the first half of the 17th century", in Irfan Habib, ed., *Researches in the history of India, 1200–1750, Medieval India 1* (Delhi, 1992), pp. 141–53, in particular pp. 142–4, where it is suggested that these were Gorakhnathi yogis.

Balkh, whom he eventually met in a mosque, where the two then stayed together for some days.

In Lahore, his attention was particularly drawn to the Muharram rituals during the first ten days of the month. The rich men and nobles of the city prepared shrouds (*na'sh*) in the name of Imam Husain, as also an atrocious image of the villainous Ibn-i Muljim of Karbala. The first five days, associated with the marriage and household life of the Imam, were spent in noisy celebration (*shor wa surūr*); boys and girls all dressed up in their finest and musicians and courtesans (*qawwāls*, *kalāwants*, *domnīs*, *harkanīs*, *kanjanīs*, *kanjarīs* and *patrīs*) sang *rāgas* and *naghma*. However, the next five days were spent in sorrow and lamentation, and the same people now dressed in black; even the music was full of sadness and a sense of mourning. Arriving before the effigy of Ibn-i Muljim, they were given to shouting imprecations, and even kicking the figure. Finally, on 10 Muharram, the Hindus and Shi'as closed down their shops, and a procession was taken out; on such occasions, writes Balkhi, conflicts were common, and people could even be killed and shops and houses destroyed. Thus, he writes: "In those days, when the writer of these lines was staying in Lahore, in the above-mentioned commotion, fifty Shi'as and twenty-five Hindus were trapped in the confusion attending the carriage of a *na'sh*, and were burnt together with the effigy of Ibn-i Muljim. Roughly 120,000 Rs. worth of goods belonging to the two groups was also destroyed."[12]

The traveller now left Lahore for Sirhind, where he mentions the existence of a very large garden with animals and birds. After a brief sojourn, he now made his way to Delhi, on the banks of the Jamuna. Little of significance seems to have occurred in Delhi, where he notices the existence of a large number of mosques, shrines, *sarāis* and *madrasas*. Amongst those that he especially mentions are the tombs (*mazārs*) of Khwaja Nizam-ud-Din, Khwaja Amir Khusrau and Khwaja Hasan, and of the Mughal ruler Humayun. And thus, "by circumambulating these places, the fire of misfortune was extinguished". Perhaps Delhi appeared too close to him to Balkh, and lacked the aspect of wonders and astonishment that he craved. He thus moved on rapidly to Mathura, which he had

[12] Balkhi, *The Bahr ul-asrār*, ed. Riazul Islam, p. 10. Compare this with the far more sympathetic account of Muharram in Basra in the 1780s by Khwaja 'Abdul Qadir, *Waqā'i'-i Manāzil-i Rūm: diary of a journey to Constantinople by Khwāja 'Abdul Qādir*, ed. Mohibbul Hasan (New York, 1968).

identified as an important place of Hindu worship. The extended description of Mathura is worth citing at some length.

At last I reached the unique place of worship of the Hindus known as Mathura. Mathura is in fact the name of the [seat of] the tenth *avatār* of the Hindus, who is also called Kishan. The temple where his idol (*but*) is worshipped is situated there. That place is also known after the name of that false god. The said *deora* (temple) is one of the wonderful things of that locality. The first is a building that has a conical shape. Its height is over a hundred yards and the circle of its interior is about eighty *arash*, constructed of stone and brick from the bottom to the top. There are some other buildings on both sides of it, but they are neither so grand nor so large. An idol made of black stone has been fixed, its height around twelve *arash*, and width eight *arash*. This building is situated near the bank of the river Jamuna, and was erected by Raja Man Singh, one of the nobles of the Emperor Akbar.

Mahmud Balkhi now shows a far greater curiosity regarding the precise nature of worship at this spot than any of the travellers from outside the Mughal domains that we have discussed so far. The description thus continues:

Their practice of pilgrimage and worship is that, at daybreak, the Brahmins, who are the attendants and servants [of the idol] sound the giant conch which would be more than five maunds in weight, and which those misguided ones call *nāqūs*. The sound of the conch reaches to six *kurohs*, and men and women, old and young, rich and poor among the Hindus, go to the bank of the river. Beaming with joy, men and women, without shame mixing together but committing no impropriety, try to outdo one another in performing their rites, food preparation (*rasoī*), and all their false prayers. In the meantime, a few thousand pleasure-seekers assemble on the other bank of the river, with the object of witnessing the scene, and obtain a sight thereof. It is such an enticing sight for the senses that one might lose the rein of Islam and become a follower of the Hindus. Truly, from the heresy of those faces, figures and features of those modest flower-faced ones, it is no wonder if one's faith is shaken, and the glass of shame broken by a stone; for all self-control disappears![13]

Balkhi then goes on to mention the "*pūjā* and prostration" practised at the temple, as well as the Brahmins, *bairāgīs* and musicians (singing in the musical genres known as *bishnupad* and *dhrupad* at dawn) who all form a

[13] Husain, "Hindu shrines and practices", p. 145 (which we broadly follow, with the exception of some misunderstandings that we have clarified); for the text, see Balkhi, *The Baḥr ul-asrār*, ed. Riazul Islam, pp. 13–16.

part of the morning worship, until at last "they return to their respective homes, and engage themselves in their daily affairs".[14] Having witnessed all this with a sense of satisfaction at having caught some authentic wonders and marvels, on 5 Safar, the traveller set out for Hilalabad, between Mathura and Agra.

THE TRAVELLER AS PARTICIPANT–OBSERVER

We are about to witness a subtle shift in the text's tone, which accompanies Mahmud Balkhi's entry into the Indo-Gangetic heartland.[15] Now, it appears that the people of Agra did not particularly impress our traveller either, and he notices nothing of significance there. He expands on an obscure meeting with an old man clad only in a loin-cloth, who inspires a few lines of metaphysical poetry; we should not neglect the fact that our traveller is also an accomplished man-of-letters, and does not let slip any opportunity to provide a demonstration of his poetic talents. Thus, still in a poetic mode, he moves on to Ilahabad (Allahabad), in the company of some *sanyāsīs* whom he meets en route. We may notice the beginnings of a change in his attitude toward these ascetics, with whom he states he entered into a relationship of true friendship: "I tied the bond of sincere friendship (*paimān-i murāfaqat*), breaking that of a superficial relationship (*'ahd-i ẓāhir-ārā 'ī*)". Entering Ilahabad, he notes the place's etymological relation with Ilah, and we note a new tone in his description both of the place and of himself. He characterises himself thus as "newly captive" (*nau giraftār*) of the religious practices of others, and describes the confluence here of the Ganges and Jamuna, as well as its significance for the Hindus, who come there to shave their heads. What especially shakes him here is a curious incident that takes place, while he is in the company of a *sanyāsī* from the group called Narayan Das, with whom he is on particularly good terms, and whom he mocks for the practice of throwing money (even sums running into thousands of Rupees) into the river. Upon this, Narayan Das bursts out: "In this centre of the fulfilment of hope, what is the value of money? This is a place where life itself is sacrificed." Filled with anger, he walks a few steps ahead, seats himself

[14] For a more extended translated passage from this section, see Husain, "Hindu shrines and practices", pp. 145–6.

[15] For some reason, Szuppe, "Circulation des lettrés et cercles littéraires", p. 1011, portrays Mahmud Balkhi as departing from Delhi to Hyderabad (Sind). This is manifestly incorrect.

below a huge hanging knife (*sāṭūr*), and signals to a Brahman, who summarily cuts his upper body in two.

Filled with astonishment at this proud act of self-destruction, Balkhi now continues to Benares, still in the company of the remaining passionate "seekers" (*wārasta*).[16] On the way, still further curious incidents took place. Before reaching Benares, the group passed by the village of one of their number. Near a well, the whole group was overwhelmed by a manifestation of divine beauty. Three of the group, unable to bear this, gave up the ghost, and four others fell unconscious. The author himself was also in a trance, but fortunately two older members of the group (who, he states, had greater experience of "divine grace and wrath", a phrase which we may naturally choose to read in a number of ways, literal and metaphorical) kept their wits about them, and were saved. These two men had always kept a watchful eye over the new member of the group, Balkhi, and so placed him and one of his friends over their shoulders, and carried them to Benares. Balkhi came to his senses after a night's rest, but it took his friend all of two days to do the same. The group then spoke to people around concerning this curious experience, and they were told by some people that this was called *budmatī*.[17]

The traveller now went to pay a visit to the *ghāṭs* of Benares, and was once more filled with a sense of the all-pervasiveness of divine beauty. There he saw twenty-three Muslims who had abandoned their earlier practices, and had taken to wearing sacred threads and marks (*qashqa'*) on their forehead, in order better to pursue their *pūjā*. On being questioned, they raised their hands toward the sky and, placing a finger over their foreheads, signalled that it was written thus in their fates.[18] Balkhi now visited the Lala Bir Singh (or Nar Singh) Mandir in the middle of Benares, where he witnessed a gathering of some 3,000 men and women, including a number of reciters (*andarz-gūyān*) of holy texts. He felt once more an entrancing effect from the worship, as his senses began to swim. It is, incidentally, not clear whether, in his wanderings between Allahabad

[16] The word *wārasta* may also simply mean "those who survived".

[17] The editor of Balkhi, *The Baḥr ul-asrār*, ed. Riazul Islam, p. 21, n. 7, suggests the word is *budhimati*, which seems unlikely. Husain, "Hindu shrines and practices", p. 147, suggests *padminī*, which is equally obscure in this context.

[18] Husain, "Hindu shrines and practices", p. 147, whose understanding of this passage differs somewhat from ours, suggests that this conversion had occurred as these men had fallen "captive to the charms" of beautiful Hindu women. He also points (p. 148) to the existence of Muslim *bairāgīs* or *sanyāsīs*, in the seventeenth century, attested to in texts such as the work variously attributed to Muhsin Fani and Mubad Kaykhusrau Isfandiyar, *Dabistān-i maẕāhib*, ed. Rahim Riza'zadah Malik, 2 vols. (Tehran, 1983).

Figure 9. Death of a rich and greedy merchant, who had wanted to enslave Tamrusia, widowed queen of Amman, *Dārāb-nāma*, National Museum, New Delhi, No. L53.2/9.

and Benares, Balkhi had taken to smoking opium or consuming other intoxicants with his friends, but such a thought cannot be entirely ruled out. Whatever the case, a considerable softening (and spirit of participation) is noticeable in his attitude toward Hindus as he moves eastwards from Agra.

Nevertheless, in Benares he realises that the phase through which he had just been passing would lead to darkness (*ẓalālat*), and repents for what has transpired. Thus, becoming alarmed at the possible consequences of the spiritual route he has taken, he decided to leave his companions (and even the Hindu friend from the *sanyāsī* band), and fled by night across the Ganges to Bihar. His first major stop is the town of Patna, capital of the province, on 10 Jumada I. Balkhi now moves briefly from his earlier spiritual preoccupations to more fleshly interests. A particularly beautiful Hindu woman (whom he calls a *katrānī*, his word for all north Indian Hindu women) was in the habit of taking a stroll and bathing in the morning by the riverside in Patna. Such was her fame that thousands of people would gather to catch a glimpse of her, and the traveller too joined them, to act as a voyeur, and to take a swim. On returning to the Ganges the next day at dawn, his spiritual vocation reasserted itself; he saw a vision of a man walking across the Ganges from the Hajipur side. On closer inspection, the man turned out to be a certain Shah 'Alam, whom Mahmud Balkhi had encountered on a number of earlier occasions in Hindu temples, and whom he describes as amongst the relatively sane of the "spiritual madmen of his time". For once, Shah 'Alam actually recognised him and spoke to him, and finally, twisting his ear forcefully, said: "Unless you become earth (*khāk*), you cannot walk on water. Be in your senses as the fire of misfortune (*shawā'ib*) is aflame."[19] Reciting verses of Sufic poetry, in which he maintained the necessity of consciousness to distinguish between the different colours and smells, he advised the traveller to leave the place immediately.

THE TRAVELLER MAINTAINS HIS DISTANCE

Taking his cue from this encounter, Mahmud Balkhi promptly left for Rajmahal in Bengal by boat. In one river-port, he saw a gathering of several thousand monkeys, who were fed by the people on the boat. Reaching Rajmahal after sixteen days, he looked around the city and its fortifications, and at night met people from Balkh, Bukhara, Khurasan, 'Iraq, Rum and Syria (Sham) at the *khānqāh* where he stayed, besides the Indians. Here, one of the *bairāgīs* who was present chanced to praise the Deccan and Sarandip (Sri Lanka). This aroused in him a desire to see these distant places, and he promptly left for the south via Orissa. In the lands between Rajmahal and Orissa, our traveller encountered a number of animals and strange creatures. Thus, in the jungles of Daonapur, he reports seeing a cannibal, with a human head and a hairy body, who at night had carried off and was eating one of Balkhi's companions, a certain Ramdas. The people of the locality assured him that this was quite normal, and that a number of merchants had died in that fashion. Later, near Burdwan, and once more at night, he saw an amphibious creature with what he calls a "lion's head" (*ba shakl-i sher*), but which turns out to be a crocodile (*magar*). Once again, he reports that some twenty-four people of that village had been carried off by this fearsome creature. He also reports, amongst other fauna, wild buffaloes, and above all was astonished by a creature that was three hand-spans' long, with a dog's head, a tail like a snake, and feet like a lion. Arrows and guns were

[19] Balkhi, *The Baḥr ul-asrār*, ed. Riazul Islam, pp. 25–6.

apparently of no avail against this creature. Finally, he claims to have seen a man with only one foot, who was like a human in other respects, but who had a body that tapered from the waist down to a single leg. This half-man apparently hopped about in a quite agile fashion. He reports that some traders intended to present this one-legged man to the king.

Balkhi now went on from Burdwan to Midnapore, where he saw a crowd of about 50,000 Hindus, who were marching, calling out the name of Jagannath. The Hindu religion (*kesh-i hindū'ī*), he reports, requires all men to make a pilgrimage to this temple at least once; and if one does so every year, all one's sins are forgiven. Thus, during the first ten days of the month of Ramazan, people come from all of the territories of Hind, and, shouting out "*Harī bol, Harī bol*", make the voyage. The pilgrimage, he notes, requires some hardship, as the pilgrims eat little and sleep fitfully. Observing the pilgrims raised in him a desire to follow them, a journey of about a month by foot. Thus, he too, his head and feet bare, and a minimum of clothes on his body, joined a group, while calling out "*Harī bol*". On arriving at Puri (apparently on 17 May 1626), he noted a huge open space with thousands of people, and a very large temple visible from a distance. However, he learnt that Muslims were not allowed in, and that different groups of Hindus ate together there. Since no one realised that our traveller (who had after all kept the company of *sanyāsīs* and *bairāgīs*) was Muslim, he managed to enter the temple.

Balkhi now describes the preparation of the temple-chariot (*rath*), with a noise and commotion like Judgment Day (*qiyāmat*). A square structure was made, which is described in detail, with its windows high above the ground. Inside, the idol called Jagannath was kept, one of the ten *avatāras* of the Hindus. The chariot was initially moved by 500 Brahmins, with a great sound of music, as scores of people pulled on the ropes; the destination was a pond where Jagannath is alleged to have cooked. Once the destination has been attained, the broken-up pieces of the chariot are then distributed as holy remnants (*tabarruk*), and people pay a rupee for each piece. During the chariot's movement, he notes, worshippers climb atop the arched structure, and, when the veil is removed from Jagannath, peer in through the windows, and throw themselves off from the chariot to the ground. The consequences are tragic: "And by this means they reach Hell (*dozakh*)", says our traveller unsympathetically. Balkhi estimates that almost 2,000 people died in this fashion, and adds that the aged people (who were incapable of climbing) fell under the chariot's wheels, so that the huge structure passed over them and destroyed them completely. Another 2,000 people are said to have died in this way.[20] And finally, he notes, this temple is at the edge of the Green Sea (*baḥr-i akhẓar*), a reference to the Bay of Bengal.

Having seen this *tamāsha* ("spectacle"), and these wonders, Balkhi now thought to visit Konarak, situated at five *karoh* from Puri. He notes that it houses a sun-temple, one of the first of Hind; for Hindus, he says, the Sun (*āftāb*) is one of the earliest *avatāras*, but is no longer worshipped.[21] A description follows of the temple, with its tower apparently still intact, and our traveller is then on his way to Golkonda-Hyderabad via Qasimkota (near Vishakapatnam).[22] Hyderabad at this time is under the rule of Muhammad Qutb Shah, and is a town full of *madrasas*, *khānqāhs*, *sarā'is* and hospitals, which merit a brief reference from Balkhi. Nature's wonders now begin to occupy a prominent place in the account. Thus, in *qaṣba* Anajpur, some thirty-five kilometres from Hyderabad, he reports a mango-tree, which gives fruit such that a bee can be found inside the seed, which flies off when the seed is broken open. In Addanki, further south, a well is mentioned whose water is sweet on one side and salty on the other, on account of a widow's curse. Then, from Golkonda and Telingana, Balkhi made his way due west to the fort of Gutti (or Chandragutti) in the 'Adilshahi territories; here, among the wonders is a stone from which water flows all the time. In Tekkalakotte (or "Takarkotta") on the banks of the Tungabhadra river, there are strange trees, one of which has red leaves that cure snake-bites and poisons, but which are themselves otherwise deadly. The traveller goes on to describe other ponds, one with water like lemon-juice, and so on. The water-body (*chashma*) is in fact a major preoccupation of this part of the account, and elsewhere in his text Balkhi also claims that in the town of Basavapatna further south (misread as "Yaswabatan" in the copied text), the water is such that even drinking a bowl of it causes an enormous surge of sexual desire in

[20] For a comparable view of the Jagannath temple as seen through the eyes of an early English traveller, William Bruton, who visited it just a few years later, in 1633, see Bruton, "The first coming of the English to Bengal", *Bengal Past and Present*, 27, 53–4, 1924, pp. 143–6. For more general considerations on the history of the temple in the period, see Hermann Kulke, *Kings and cults: state formation and legitimation in India and Southeast Asia* (New Delhi, 1993), pp. 33–81.

[21] The account in Husain, "Hindu shrines and practices", truncates the narrative here, on the grounds that "the remainder of Mahmud Balkhi's account has . . . little of interest as far as Indian religious practices and monuments are concerned"! (p. 153).

[22] For a discussion of Mahmud Wali Balkhi's description of the Konarak temple, see Simon Digby and J. C. Harle, "When did the Sun temple fall down?", *South Asian Studies*, 1, 1985, pp. 1–7, discussion on pp. 3–4.

men.[23] He adds: "If a man goes on to bathe daily with that water, his sexual desire will increase so much that if he is not able to find a woman, he will turn to cattle and animals, and if he is not able to find them he may even die." However, he then goes on to note that "this water has a deficiency, for when it is taken to other towns or cities it loses its quality. If that were not the case, there could not have been a better item of trade, as no precious gift would have been more valued."[24]

One of the rare mentions of *jogīs* here refers to a story from the time of a certain Khwaja 'Arab Sabzwari, a local governor of Bahmani times. At that time, he reports, local *qalandars* who gathered under a *nīm* tree reported hearing voices from someone claiming that he was in *samādhī* (*samāt*), but that the root of the tree was touching his body and causing him discomfort. However, they could not identify from where this voice came. Khwaja 'Arab ordered his men to dig under the tree, and when they had dug down to a man's height, they saw a building with a door. A workman went in by the door and saw a man standing on his head naked inside, with mud on his body; a part of the tree's root had forced its way through the wall of the building and had touched the man's side. The workmen cut down the root and tried to move the man, but were advised by the *qalandars* not to do so. They therefore covered the building up with earth, and filled up the hole in the ground once more.[25] Mahmud Balkhi interprets this story as part of the ascetic ritual to transfer the spirit (*rūḥ*). The Indian ascetics, he notes, have a manner of pulling the spirit up into the brain by their ascetic power, so that they have no further need to eat or defecate. This permits them to sit in *samādhī* even for 300 years, and when they emerge from it they can live and enjoy themselves for another 1,000 years. These men know all about buried treasures as well, on account of their long stays underground.

With these reflections, Balkhi continues his sojourn, heading north-west this time toward Nizamshahi territory.[26] Here, he spent time at

[23] This is almost certainly a reference to the town of Basavapatna in the Hassan district of Karnataka (14° 11′ N, 75° 49′ E), rather than the village of the same name in the Gulbarga region.

[24] Cf. Ansar Zahid Khan, "Baḥr al-Asrār: the towns and regions beginning with ب (b)", *Journal of the Pakistan Historical Society*, 39 1, 1991, pp. 10–11.

[25] This is a recurrent theme in writings of the period, and is given an explicitly millenarian twist in such early seventeenth-century texts as Shaikh Farid Bhakkari's *Z̲ak̲h̲īrat al-k̲h̲awānīn*. See Farid Bhakkari, *D̲h̲ak̲h̲īrat-ul-K̲h̲awānīn*, tr. Ziyauddin A. Desai, 2 vols. (Delhi, 1992), vol. 1, pp. 126–7. Balkhi, in the larger text of the *Baḥr al-asrār*, also recounts a version of this story, attributing it to a time when Timur visited Benares. See Ansar Zahid Khan, "Baḥr al-Asrār", p. 13.

[26] For a roughly contemporary account of the Deccan, and "Hindu" temples there, see the relevant section of the Rafi'-ud-Din Shirazi, *Taẕkirat ul-mulūk* (1612), in Carl W. Ernst, "Admiring the

Paithan, on the bank of a tributary of the Godavari river. An evergreen tree was to be found near the place, as well as a deep and dark cave that was a place of worship for the Hindus, who gathered there once a year. A snake emerged at this time from the cave, and always one man from among the gathering was found drowned in the river at much the same time. If, however, no one died in a given year, misfortune was predicted for the region. In another place near Paithan, a large number of snakes were reported to appear at a particular time of the year, whom the Hindus took home and fed with milk for three days. On the fourth day, the snakes disappeared. Also in the vicinity was a pond with fish; if the fish were caught and sliced open, snakes came out of their bellies. Further, another pond gave water that produced a curious hallucinogenic effect; it was hence a favoured spot for *sanyāsīs* and *jogīs*.

Thereafter, Balkhi notes his own departure southwards for Vijayanagara (Bijanagar), here probably used generically for the region as well as in reference to the city, and thence to Sarandip. Another section of his larger text, this one with geographical entries for different places of which he has knowledge, clarifies his understanding of this place somewhat. In this passage, which does not appear in the travel-account, Balkhi writes:

> Bijanagar is a dominion of Hindustan which is situated on the shore of the Arabian Sea (*baḥr ul-akhẕar*). Therefore, sixty ports of note are under it. The length of this country is 60 leagues and its revenues are equal to 12,000 *karors* of *hūns*, and each *karor* would be equal to 100,000 *tūmāns*. Due to the strength of its borders, forts and castles, and the bravery and courage of its people, none of the Bahmani kings who were rulers of all the countries of the Deccan, and were superior to all the rulers of Hind in the number of their forces, wealth and grandeur, were able to conquer these dominions and lived in the ways of peace with the rulers of this country, until the 'Adil Shahis of Bijapur wrested it from the Rā'is. Still it is under their control.[27]

He then goes on to cite the author of a text entitled the *Jāmi' al-Barr wa'l Baḥr* ("Compendium of the land and the sea"), who recounts a version of the story of the foundation of Vijayanagara by a shepherd. This shepherd apparently had a chance encounter with the goddess Lakshmi (*Lajmi* in the text), and went to the court of the local king to inform him of the fact. Instead of rewarding him, the king decided to kill the shepherd (since

works of the ancients: the Ellora temples as viewed by Indo-Muslim authors", in David Gilmartin and Bruce B. Lawrence, eds., *Beyond Turk and Hindu: rethinking religious identities in Islamicate South Asia* (Gainesville, Fla., 2000), pp. 98–120.

27 Ansar Zahid Khan, "Baḥr al-Asrār", p. 8. The kingdom's shores could also be on the Bay of Bengal.

Lakshmi had promised to remain in that place until he returned), and founded a city on the site of the encounter. Equally significant is the fact that Mahmud Balkhi, in a continuation of the same passage, cites 'Abdur Razzaq Samarqandi to the effect that "the Ra'i of Bijanagar, on hearing about the ambassador ['Abdur Razzaq] summoned him before him, treated him with love and attention, and sent back numerous gifts to the Padishah [Shahrukh]". Balkhi had thus read the sections of the *Maṭla' us-Sa'dain* that dealt with India, and obviously combined his experiential knowledge with the textual knowledge of his predecessors. However, we may guess it was on neither, but instead on hearsay (and the *Jāmi' al-Barr wa'l Baḥr*) that he drew for his description of the temple of Tirumalai-Tirupati, described in the following terms:

> In this dominion [Vijayanagara], there are more than 3,000 temples. Among them the largest is the temple of Tirmal. It is situated on a hilltop and is built of dressed stone. Its height is 150 yards and its circumference is 200 yards. In it, they have created an idol four yards in height and two yards in width. Its head and neck are made of gold while its hands, chest, back and abdomen are of silver, and the rest of copper. Its eyes are represented by two large rubies. All its other organs are decorated with diamonds and a large number of rubies. On its right and left nearly 80 other idols are placed, some of silver, some of copper, and some of stone. One thousand three hundred Brahmins permanently reside there. Three thousand men and women are posted to serve the temple who render service turn by turn, every three hours. Three hundred daughters of the Ra'i also, turn by turn, remain in attendance at the foot of the chief idol. Two hundred of the leading nobles render service with jewelled incense-burners, standing behind a special screen. One hundred singers are busy in singing at the gates of the temple and 160 female dancers remain engaged in dancing at the time of general [attendance].[28]

The description concludes then with the claim that a third of the revenues of the Vijayanagara kingdom are spent on this temple alone, and that these amount to 300,000 *hūns* a year, which are then "melted down and buried in wells" by the Brahmins.

After his passage through Vijayanagara, Balkhi seems to have followed the Tungabhadra river as far as Harihar (called "Haryal" by him), where he found a pond which magically drew into it birds that flew overhead, so that they died. Then, passing to another spot near the Qasba-i Barsang

[28] Ansar Zahid Khan, "Baḥr al-Asrār", pp. 9–10. Also see Sanjay Subrahmanyam, "An eastern El-Dorado: the Tirumala-Tirupati temple complex in early European views and ambitions, 1540–1660", in David Shulman, ed., *Syllables of sky: studies in South Indian civilization in honour of Velcheru Narayana Rao* (Delhi, 1995), pp. 338–90.

(unidentified), Balkhi saw two statues, one of stone and the other of iron. He promptly collected local myths of origin, and was told an elaborate story of a *jogī* who sacrificed several hundred human beings to a creature in a cave, in order to receive some magic water guarded by this creature, that could turn iron into gold. However, this water was stolen from him by an ironsmith, and the two were hence brought to court to resolve their dispute. When the *jogī* called on God as his witness, a voice from the heavens told him that both he and the ironsmith were thieves (the former because he had sacrificed hundreds of innocents, the latter because he had stolen from the former) and that as a punishment the two would be turned into statues, respectively of iron and stone!

We are not aware where precisely these incidents are supposed to have taken place, but we soon find Mahmud Balkhi, having traversed the length of the peninsula, at the southern Tamil port of Kayalpatnam, which he describes accurately as a centre of pearls. However, he wished ardently to go to Sri Lanka (Sarandip), in the midst of the Sea of Oman, which was after all the first place on Earth which the angel Gabriel had visited. From the outset, it is clear that the main interest for him lay in the myth that linked Adam with the island.[29] Other interests are mentioned, but given less importance; the local women come in for their share of conventional praise, as stealers of hearts, and companions in pleasure. Thus, a verse is cited:

> Silan is delightful (*kh̲ush*)
> and the beauties of Silan more delightful still.
> They demand your heart, they soothe your heart,
> they are bold, and take your heart.
> With merriment and pleasure, each one of them with a friend,
> passes the evenings and the mornings in delight.

God, notes Mahmud Balkhi, had ordered Gabriel to take Adam to the island, as it was the closest place on earth to Paradise! Sandal, cinnamon, all sorts of spices, fruits and jewels were available there.

Now, though Mahmud Balkhi did not himself make the pilgrimage to the peak of Adam, he gives a detailed account based on hearsay of the route. The reason he did not do so was that rumours were afoot to the effect that in the intervening jungles, there was a lion-like animal, which carried its own urine in a cavity at the tip of its tail; if even a drop of this

[29] Compare the discussion in Ananda Abeydeera, "Jean de Marignolli: l'envoyé du Pape au Jardin d'Adam", in Catherine Weinberger-Thomas, ed., *L'Inde et l'imaginaire*, Collection Puruṣārtha 11 (Paris, 1988), pp. 57–67.

urine fell on a living creature, it would die immediately. The route as he describes it was even otherwise extremely arduous, beginning in Jaffnapatnam. Normally, a letter of permission was necessary from the ruler of this place (a *kāfir*, but nevertheless just), and then, after three days, one arrived in a village where the people were rather hospitable. Two days from this village was another, and then one reached a place called "Kam" (Gampola), followed by "Kanukoh" (Ginigathena), at the edge of the mountains. From here, the real dangers began, and once as many as seventy dervishes are known to have died there at one stroke. After several days of climbing and descent, one arrived at Sitagangula ("Sidkanka"), where there was a nice pond and pleasant people. Here, pilgrims normally rested for two days, since the later journey was even more difficult on account of the narrow route. At last, one reached a spot where one had to leave all one's goods behind, and put one's faith in God. Then, one reached "Daramkank" (Dharmaganga), where a lake (called *ḥauẓ-i 'ārifān*) was found; it was here that Gabriel cut off Adam's hair, and gave him a bath, and where Adam read the first *namāz*. That was the last stage, before the Footprint of Adam. To see this required one to climb to the top of a mountain, where on a stone slab one finds Adam's footmark, a handspan long, and a fourth as broad. Pilgrims normally stayed there for three days in prayer. One normally climbed from the west, Mahmud Balkhi notes, but the descent was to the south. On the descent, one once more found a mysterious stone slab (called *kachkol*) with a never-ending supply of water. After thirty stages of journey, one finally arrived at a place called "Hamun" (Hambantota).

This account of Sri Lanka rests very largely on hearsay, in contrast to Balkhi's account of northern India; the emphasis is on the heard rather than the seen, and it may even be doubted whether Mahmud Balkhi spent a great deal of time in Sri Lanka. This also emerges from the next passage, where a classical myth concerning the women of Paradise is transformed:

> I have heard from true reports that Singaldip is an island near Silan, whose air is salubrious and whose climate is rare. The women of this island are superior to those of all other parts of the world in terms of their suppleness, beauty, coquetry, and attractiveness. Their special quality is that when their virginity is lost, they recover it immediately. No matter how much one sports with them, one's strength grows and one's desire is not diminished but on the contrary expands. Their breath is flavoured with musk . . . In the local usage, they are called Padmini. And a strange thing is when they are taken to another land, they lose that quality and suppleness, and become like other women.[30]

[30] Balkhi, *The Baḥr ul-asrār*, ed. Riazul Islam, p. 61.

He also mentions a tree called Gaj-Badan, the branch of which repels elephants, and which is thus essential to cross those lands, since elephants are the bane of those territories. Finally, he speaks of a village called Sambal, near which there is a mound; if any traveller were to climb on it, he is at once stripped of his clothes and becomes naked.

THE TRAVELLER IS WRECKED AND SAVED

The narrative based principally on Mahmud Balkhi's own experience and eyewitness account resumes once more on his departure from Sri Lanka on a *firangī* (probably Portuguese) vessel, in the direction of Aceh, Tiku and Ayuthia (*shahr-i nau*), which he identifies as islands of the Green Sea, and in the vicinity of China. He was accompanied on this voyage by four other companions, and he then voyaged for twenty-one days (full of wonders that are difficult even for our prolix author to narrate, or so he assures us). At the end of this time, a storm began, and even the experienced pilot was at his wits' end. Those on board the ship began to fear their time had come, as the ship was tossed about all night long. When dawn broke, they saw that they were stuck on a sand-bank, some distance from the shore. The *firangīs* at once sought to flee, since the law of the sea was that the men and goods from a shipwreck were all in the hands of the ruler of the nearest port (*ṣāḥib-i bandar*).

At this time, a large group of Mughals and Indians (*hindī*) arrived on the spot, captured the mariners, and seized their goods. One of those on board the ship pleaded with the captors for Mahmud Balkhi, saying that he was like the Mughals, and a man of virtue and wisdom besides. The Mughals, on the contrary, thought that he was the one who had guided the *firangīs* there, and hence began to ill-treat him even more than the others, and even whipped him. Then, barefoot, he was forced to walk on stony ground and in thorny jungles, until he reached Soro *qaṣba* in Orissa (south of Balasore). By this time, one of Balkhi's companions was dead, and the other three were held captive with him.

Now Mahmud Balkhi began to make enquiries, and found that the local governor (*ḥākim*) was Baqir Khan, son of Mustafa Beg, who was peerless in poetry, prose-writing, history, music and a number of other qualities.[31] He thus conceived a hope of getting out of his plight, and the

[31] This person is the same as the notable of Iranian origin, Muhammad Baqir Najm-i Sani, on whom see Sajida Sultana Alvi, ed. and tr. with an intro., *Advice on the art of governance: Mau'iẓah-i Jahāngīrī of Muḥammad Bāqir Najm-i Ṣānī, an Indo-Islamic mirror for princes* (Albany, 1989).

next day was moved to Cuttack, capital of the province. Here, he quickly composed a treatise entitled *Gulkadah* ("House of flowers"), containing a mix of elevated poetry and Arabicised prose. On Nauroz, two days later, he was taken with the others of his party before the governor, and promptly drew out the treatise and presented it. The governor, on leafing through the introduction, was astonished at its quality, and called Mahmud Balkhi aside to enquire who he was. He then placed him under the charge of his brother Mirza Husaini.

Free of his cares, Balkhi reports that he spent the next three days in festivities of which he remembers nothing. On the fourth day, he was again called before the governor, and by this time was already considered a fast friend of Mirza Husaini. He was showered with honours, and asked to translate some treatises on "practical wisdom" (*ḥikmat-i 'amalī*), perhaps on norms of governance (*akẖlāq*); he was also given quarters near the harem. But Mirza Husaini intervened to ask that Balkhi be allowed into his own household, and as we shall see Mahmud Balkhi remained associated with him for some time to come.

The text now enters a new phase, for Mahmud Balkhi's days as a half-naked wanderer were over. Instead, the inveterate traveller now remained rooted for some time, as a relatively minor Mughal client and man-of-letters. This was an occasion for him to expound on the wonders and peculiarities of Orissa, while pursuing his translator's occupation. He reports his astonishment at the level of education of a certain 'Abdul Jalil, an Indian who was his cook, but well versed in Persian and even Arabic letters; Balkhi hence decided to let him do the translation while himself leading a life of leisure! He expresses his contentment at the good life there, and reports how he met (by pure chance) his maternal uncle, Mir Muhammad Nizam, who had left Balkh twenty-five years before. The two got along for a while, but then fell out.

The time had now come to become a householder. With devious simplicity, Mahmud Balkhi reports his marriage to the beautiful and eligible daughter of a miraculously rich Sufi of Cuttack, Shah 'Azmat, who was in the habit of drawing out tens of thousands of rupees from under his own seat. According to Balkhi's version, on his very first visit to the Sufi, the latter was so strangely attracted to him, that – having enquired about his ancestry and home – he immediately decided to offer him the daughter in marriage. Balkhi's marriage lasted three years, and, at the end of this time, his wife died while they were in Agra.

Balkhi describes life in Cuttack at some length, focusing on the wonders of Nature, and the human oddities of the region; this part of the account is a sort of compendium of *faits-divers*. The first of the natural wonders is the description of a cyclone, which took place at night with an extremely strong wind, lightning and a fearsome effect. In Cuttack, some very large ships were carried off from the sea, and flew one *kos* to come to rest in the jungle. In the *qaṣba* of "Mankandi" (perhaps Mahindri, in southern Orissa), the water of a large pond was entirely carried off, and the fish were scattered about on the ground, and even in the branches of trees. In the *qaṣba* of Soro further north, a herd of 1,000 cattle was carried off by the wind. Perhaps strangest of all, a nursing mother was carried off a great distance, while her suckling child remained exactly where he was. In the *pargana* of Jajpur, a whole garden with over 4,000 mango, tamarind, and pipal trees, was uprooted and destroyed, so much so that no trace of a garden remained. Trees were to be found two *kos* from that spot. The odd thing was that, in a village, there might be total destruction on the one side, while not even a leaf had stirred on the other. Locals reported that a storm of this type took place in the area once every twenty years, when the djinns and gods warred amongst themselves (*az āṣār-i muḥāraba-i ajinna wa dev ast*).

A second story concerns two baboons of the area, the size of large dogs, which could recognise liars and thieves. Whenever there was a theft, the names of the suspects were written down and placed before them. The two baboons would look at each other, like two men consulting, and then look at the pieces of paper. When the slip with the thief's name appeared, they would pick it up and place it on the lap of the owner of the stolen goods. This would be repeated several times over, to avoid an error. The *wālī* of the area, Baqir Khan, had sent the baboons to Jahangir as a gift, but the latter died before they could reach him; Shahjahan sent them back, regarding them as inauspicious, since they were associated with his father's death.[32]

A third anecdote concerns a military expedition to an unsubdued area of Orissa, where a beautiful Hindu woman was captured along with others. When she learnt that her husband was dead, she decided to commit suicide, but since she had no weapon on her, she pulled out her tongue with her own hands and thus died a few hours later. It was said by

[32] This story was a very widespread one, and a version may also be found in seventeenth-century Portuguese and Spanish (and later English) accounts of India. see, for instance, an anonymous pamphlet entitled *Notable, y prodigiosa relacion, que truxo el padre Geronymo Xauier de la Compañia de Iesvs, en que se da cuenta de un animal, o monstruo, que está en la provincia de Vengala, que penetra todo lo passado, y futuro, en tal grado que parece persona racional*... (Granada, 1612). We thank Jorge Flores for this reference.

the other prisoners that she and her husband had been separated for ten years in spite of their intense love, and had been reunited just before the incident.

Still recounting the episodes of his life in Orissa, Balkhi continues by telling us of a Hindu friend who had disappeared, and who he learnt had become an ascetic in a temple in Manikpur (by which he probably means the port of Manikpatnam). He then went to meet him, and on asking him why he had taken this resolution, was told that he had fallen in love with the daughter of a local Hindu Raja, and on being unsuccessful in the affair had decided to leave the world. Balkhi offered to intervene in the matter, but the offer was spurned with scorn. The man had obviously reached a higher spiritual state, and even affirmed that he was now in a position to achieve whatever he wanted himself; however, he no longer had any desire for worldly gain, or even for the woman who had put him in his current state. Balkhi therefore asked forgiveness for his indiscretion and left.

Finally, Mahmud Balkhi recounts an elaborate series of stories concerning Liver-Eaters (*jigarkhwār*) in Orissa.[33] These are mostly women, and start at any early age, as Balkhi reports from the case of an eight-year-old girl, who was brought before the *wālī* by her parents, who accused her of having harmed her siblings and cousins. The *wālī* promptly ordered that she should be killed, against the advice of Balkhi, who did not believe such an accusation could be true. However, a number of the Mughal officials in the region then recounted stories to him concerning these sorcerers, and their counterparts, the exorcists (usually themselves Liver-Eaters who had repented). The liver, in these stories, was the size of a pomegranate seed, and concealed by the Liver-Eater in his (or more often her) calf. The way of recognising these Liver-Eaters was that they were insensitive to pepper in their eyes; however, if one puts salt in their eyes, their powers were destroyed. Further, even if stones were tied to their bodies and feet and they were thrown in water, they floated. The local Hindus believed that, on the night of Diwali, they walked 300 *kos* in procession, and ate all those they found on the way. Mahmud Balkhi reports that, on one occasion, the *wālī*'s men went to seek the help of an exorcist (*jhāra*), with the case of two sick men. The Liver-Eater was tracked down, but he said that one of the two men was beyond recovery, since he had temporarily forgotten where he had kept his liver, and when he remembered and recovered it, the liver had

[33] Compare the account of Liver-Eaters in *sarkār* Thatta in Sind, in the late sixteenth-century account of Abu'l Fazl, in H. S. Jarrett and Jadunath Sarkar, tr., *The Ā'īn-i Akbarī by Abu'l Fazl Allāmī*, vol. II (reprint, Delhi, 1989), p. 340.

already become rotten and worm-eaten. As for the other, he could be made sound once more. Indeed, one recovered and the other died. Later, the same Liver-Eater was caught unawares and beheaded by someone.

We gather from his account that Mahmud Balkhi remained altogether for two years in Orissa, after the shipwreck. Then, with Mirza Husaini, he went to Agra and the court of Shahjahan on 1 Zi-Hijja 1038 H (July 1629). On 'Id, they appeared before the ruler with gifts, and remained for a year at the court. Finally, Mirza Husaini was rewarded with the post of governor of Bhakkar in Sind, and he hence set out by way of Ajmer and Jaisalmer, accompanied by Mahmud Balkhi. We thus enter into another phase of travels after a relatively sedentary period. En route to Ajmer, Mahmud Balkhi mentions Fatehpur Sikri, made of stone, and abandoned (thus, a lesson to observers on human vanity), so beautiful that it was the envy of the Chinese picture-gallery (*nigārkhāna-i Chīn*) and put Heaven itself to shame. His party then arrived in Ajmer, and visited the shrine of Mu'in-ud-Din Chishti, as well as the lake at Pushkar.

While at Ajmer, Mahmud Balkhi happened to arrive at the residences there of I'timad ud-Daula Tehrani (father of Nur Jahan).[34] Here, he heard a heart-rending voice singing, and on looking more closely saw a young Indian (*hindī*) sitting in a corner in a contemplative frame of mind. The fire of love was obviously in him, and took the form of song. Balkhi asked him who he was, and, instead of answering, he continued to sing his own compositions in the *bishnupad* form in the *āhang-i sārang* (a particular musical scale). At last, he said that he was the son of a noble Hindu family, and had begun to question his ancestral religion (*kesh-i ābā'ī*). His inner being had begun to burn, and his earlier beliefs had been entirely destroyed. Thus, over the previous four months he had wandered about away from home in this strange state, without finding a resting place for his heart. Saying this, he fell unconscious, and Mahmud Balkhi picked him up, and cradled his head on his knee.

At this stage, an old man dressed as a Brahmin entered, and, thinking the youth was dead, began to weep and wail. Balkhi silenced him, and asked him who he was. The old man identified himself as the youth's father, and said that the youth had manifested such qualities while growing up that the family believed that he would keep aflame "the lamp of Raja Ramachandra, Mahadev, Jagannath and Kishan". Instead, for the

[34] The father, the celebrated Mughal noble and official had died in 1622; see Amina Okada and Jean-Louis Nou, *Un joyau de l'Inde moghole: le mausolée d'I'timad ud-Daulah* (Milan, 2003).

past four months, he had become odd in his comportment, and left his religion (*kesh-i hindū'ī*). The father feared for his life, since he had given up even smelling food and drink, let alone consuming it. The son now awoke, and asked his father to leave at once. Sensing the spiritual vacuum in him, Mahmud Balkhi (who some years ago had himself kept the company of *jogīs* and *sanyāsīs*) suggested to the young man that he consider the *dīn-i Islām* and the *sharī'at-i Rasūl*, and assured him that if this were the real solution to his problems, he could give it up when he wished. On hearing this, the youth began to tremble, and himself asked Balkhi to read the *kalima-i tauḥīd*. Thus, he was converted, and Balkhi left at once to catch up with his companions.

From Ajmer, Balkhi made his way to Jaisalmer, praised by him for its outstanding fort, stone temples, and impressive buildings. He reports an annual gathering of 50,000 *jogīs* there, at a pond attached to a temple which is patronised by the Rajas. Between the town and the pond are two paths, one for the young and one for the old. Mahmud Balkhi singles out the women of the area for praise, as having the most shapely bodies (*tanāsub-i a'ẓā'*), but equally for blame. Thus he notes that the same women were particularly fond of the Mughals, and that, whenever a caravan passed through, the women often left their homes and accompanied it. The Hindus, he notes, have nothing against this practice; save that they do not accept these women back into their households later. The young women wear red, and the old ones white. Moreover, when a new Raja sits on the throne, he buys beautiful slave girls and allows them out of the fort at night, to serve all customers; the proceeds are used for the salvation of the souls of his ancestors. Such immodesty, writes the traveller, is not to be found in all of Hindustan, but this did not prevent him from staying there for fourteen days, all the while decrying it as a "kingdom that burns chastity" (*kishwar-i 'iṣmat-soz*).

A long desert voyage then followed, and, after six days without water, they arrived near Bhakkar in Sind. Then, crossing the Indus, they reached Sukkur, where Mirza Husaini quickly became involved in administrative affairs. A peculiarity of Sind, writes the newly puritanical Mahmud Balkhi, is that men and women are to be found washing clothes and bathing on the river-bank in close proximity, so that their naked bodies touch one another. The strange thing though, according to Balkhi, is that this has no effect at all on the men, even though the women of the area are some of the most beautiful of Sind. Still stranger is the fact that these very same people call themselves believing Muslims (*musalmān-o-mutadayyin*), and keep up all the prayers, and other religious observances.[35]

THE TRAVELLER IS HOMESICK

A sense of fatigue creeps into the text by the time of this sojourn in Sind. Balkhi describes the main crops and products of the region very briefly, noting that he stayed there for one harvest, before leaving for Bhakkar. This town was fortified, on an island in the middle of the Indus; here Balkhi remained for six months. However, at the end of this period, he began to suffer from a fever (*tap-i ruba'*), common enough in that area. The condition became complicated, leading to dropsy, from which Balkhi suffered for altogether eight months. At the end of this period, a good physician called Maulana Salah-ud-Din Siyawani prescribed a concoction from the myrobalan tree-bark, which cured him within six days. At this stage, Mirza Husaini appointed him to administer the affairs of Ganjaba *pargana*, in Afghanistan. In the hope that he would be able to win over the Afghan chiefs, Balkhi accepted, and also looked forward to going to his roots in Kabul and Ghazna, rather than a life centred on Multan and Lahore.

However, fate had other plans. Ganjaba was soon attacked by a subordinate of Shah Safi of Iran, Sher Khan, who was in charge of Pishing, and who seized the area across the border as well as Mahmud Balkhi himself. Sher Khan had decided to kill Mahmud Balkhi, but meanwhile he was himself attacked by the celebrated 'Ali Mardan Khan, governor of Qandahar, an old enemy. Sher Khan's treasures and relatives were seized in Pishing and carried off, and 'Ali Mardan lay in wait for Sher Khan's return. Sher Khan was now in turmoil and he decided to rush back. Mahmud Balkhi adds his ironical comment on the nature of frontier politics:

> But since his treasures had been plundered, and matters of leadership (*sardārī*) cannot work without coin albeit counterfeit (*daghal*), a traders' caravan which was then camping in Siwi was captured and forced to accompany him, so that if necessary he could appropriate their goods. Having crossed through rugged hills and difficult passes, he then reached Harnai, a *qaṣba* in Afghanistan, and stopped to consult. Then, the other clan chieftains (*sarān-i qabā'il*) and leaders who were with him submitted that the proper way was that they should first fight and tackle the enemy, and only in case the result turned out contrary to their wishes,

[35] Cf. also Islam, "A seventeenth-century account of Sind".

should they then kill the traders and appropriate their goods. And then, in conformity with their old customs, they would take recourse to robbery and dacoity (*rāhzānī wa qat'-i ṭarīq*) and thus again take pleasure in earning accolades from this cruel world [for their bravery] (*dād-i dil az rūzgār-i nāhanjār bāz sitānim*).[36]

Sher Khan's party thus handed over the people of the caravan, and the other prisoners, to some men in a nearby village, while Sher Khan himself, with 6,000 Afghans and some of the members of the caravan, made for Pishing. Since the bulk of his men were on foot, the camels and horses of the merchants were directly seized; the force thus advanced more rapidly, but was then attacked by night by the forces of 'Ali Mardan Khan. Sher Khan was defeated, and fled to Baluchistan with three of his men. The merchants who were with him asked 'Ali Mardan to rescue the other prisoners, and this was done promptly.

Meanwhile, Sher Khan had written to Shah Safi, excusing himself and accusing 'Ali Mardan Khan of misdemeanours. The latter then decided to send some of those in the caravan before the Shah as witnesses to Sher Khan's misconduct. Mahmud Balkhi was hence chosen with some others for this task, but meanwhile a *farmān* arrived from the Shah asking Sher Khan and 'Ali Mardan to send their *wakīls* ("agents") to Hasan Khan Shamlu, governor of Khorasan. Hasan Khan's men arrived too in order to take charge, and the whole party was hence sent to Herat. En route, they passed through the fort of Bust, a beautiful place with sacred shrines, including one that granted wishes. Two men who made wishes were granted them; but Mahmud Balkhi had hardly had the time to wish when word came that the caravan was leaving. Obviously, it is unspoken that he now wished to return home, and thus it turned out in fact.

Crossing the river, the party made for Khorasan, and then reached Farah in Sijistan. Here, there was a stone arch from which water dripped continuously; this too was a wish-fulfilling spot. Once more, Mahmud Balkhi's contemplations at this place were interrupted by the news that the caravan was leaving. Eventually, the caravan reached the place of Khwaja Muzaffar Munshi. Here, matters suddenly took a different turn:

We learnt that the agents (*wakīls*) of Sher Khan had fled following a letter that they had received from him. [It stated]: "Having turned our heart away from matters of territory, wealth and family, on 10 Shawwal, we have set out towards Hindustan. You too should join us by whatever means you manage to find."

[36] Balkhi, *The Baḥr ul-asrār*, ed. Riazul Islam, pp. 99–100.

Affairs having taken such a turn, the *muḥaṣṣils* of Hasan Khan Shamlu too lowered their surveillance; I also began to wander about freely, and on 20 Zi-Hijja 1040, with some dealers in pack-animals, I decided to set out for Balkh.

After twenty days' journey, on 20 Muharram 1041 [8 August 1631] I returned to my real homeland (*waṭan-i aṣlī*). I was happy to visit my few relatives, and to pray for the souls of the departed.

The discussion in the preceding pages would have made it amply clear that the text of Mahmud Wali Balkhi occupies a quite different register from the two other accounts that we have discussed in this chapter. Indeed, rather than occupy a stable vantage-point in order to recount the experiences of its author, it is remarkable for its multiplicity of perspectives, which Mahmud Balkhi never quite seeks to reconcile. We begin with the standpoint of the relatively orthodox Muslim, but one who is nevertheless curious about the beliefs and practices of others. This leads him to a first set of disapproving judgments, mostly in Gor-Khattri and then in Mathura. A subsequent section of the text is characterised by a greater degree of ambiguity, for, if there are moments – as at the temple of Jagannath – when Mahmud Wali Balkhi is seemingly shocked and disturbed by the *kesh-i hindū'ī*, there are other moments when these exotic beliefs and practices seem to exercise a strong fascination over him. Matters come full circle then by the last years of his voyage, especially in the last stretch which takes him through Rajasthan and Sind. Here, it would appear that he "rediscovers" himself as an orthodox Muslim, and almost seeks, as it were, to make amends for some of his comportment earlier in the voyage.

The lesson for the reader is thus a more complex one than that which either Seydi 'Ali Re'is or Mutribi Samarqandi expound. For Mahmud Wali Balkhi seems to tell his imagined reader that the beliefs and "religion" (for we would translate his term *kesh-i hindū'ī* as the "religion of the Hindus") of the exotic other cannot be quite so easily trifled with. Contact and familiarity with them may in fact attract the Muslim, and not just as a literary conceit, when gazing at women bathing on the banks of the Ganges or Jamuna. Rather, as with the twenty-three Muslim converts in Benares, or Balkhi himself at various moments in his Indian sojourn, there is a real risk of going over, as it were, to the "other side". What then is this other side composed of? Here, Mahmud Wali Balkhi gives us a far clearer exposition of matters than almost any other traveller we have encountered so far. Effectively, he tells us that there is a "religion of the Hindus", and that it is a composite structure, which he defines at one point as "the lamp of Raja Ramachandra, Mahadev, Jagannath and Kishan". In other words, we have elements of Vaishnava and Saiva devotion (*bhaktī*), configured into a system which is defined by the worship of idols (*buts*) and temples (*deoras*), but also by the practice of pilgrimage to spots such as Tirupati, Benares and Puri.

It may legitimately be argued that, in so defining the "religion of the Hindus", Mahmud Balkhi is partly defining the unfamiliar in terms of the familiar.[37] In other words, the elements that he seizes upon are those which a Muslim reader in Central Asia would find most accessible. The primarily textual strategies of defining a religion in terms of its "sacred texts", or in terms of a set of theological abstractions, are not the ones that he uses, and when he does refer to a matter of alternative theology (for example with respect to *jogīs* and *sanyāsīs*) it is in largely dismissive terms. We are still some distance, therefore, from the understanding of "Hinduism" that would be espoused in the nineteenth century, yet we are not at the point where the practices of the *kuffār* of India appeared to be a mere chaos, something that altogether resisted systematic representation. Indeed, the text of Mahmud Wali Balkhi is remarkable for its sparing use of the term *kāfir*, and in this sense is at a palpable distance from the vocabulary espoused by, say, 'Abdur Razzaq Samarqandi. In this case, we may state with confidence, familiarity bred something more complex than contempt.

ACROSS THE BAY OF BENGAL

Such was not always the case. We will hence close this chapter with a relatively brief consideration of a fourth traveller across the ocean of wonders and secrets, this one a visitor from Safavid Iran who spent time in India, and more extensively in South-east Asia. The author of this officially commissioned work, the *Safīna-i Sulaimānī* ("The ship of Sulaiman"), Muhammad Rabi' was the secretary (*wāqi'a'-nawīs*) of an embassy sent by Shah Sulaiman of Iran to the Thai court of King Narai in the 1680s (departing Bandar 'Abbas in June 1685 and returning in May 1688), and has left behind a valuable account of his experiences, which has periodically been plundered by historians of South-east Asia to

[37] The important discussion by David N. Lorenzen, "Who invented Hinduism?", *Comparative Studies in Society and History*, 41, 4, 1999, pp. 630–59, is unfortunately very weak on Persian materials from the period, and thus does not enter into a sufficiently subtle consideration of these points.

corroborate one point or another.[38] Besides providing an interesting window onto Iranian attitudes to the 'margins' of the Persian world (a theme to which we shall turn at greater length in the following chapter), the account of Muhammad Rabi' is also particularly valuable for its description of the nature and functioning of the Persian community resident in Ayuthia, and Thailand more generally, in the period.[39]

Our point of focus here is, however, on the attitudes of the author with regard to the peoples whom he encounters, in particular in South-east Asia. We may note, to begin with, that the text is divided into four parts or "gifts", preceded by an introduction, and followed by an epilogue concerning the Mughal conquest of Hyderabad in the late 1680s. In the introduction, the author, who describes himself as "scribe to the contingent of royal musketeers" (*muḥarrir-i sarkār-i tufangchiyān*), begins by praising the "ship of Sulaiman, adept at bearing travellers on the sea of true religion, over ranks of swelling waves, through limits of confusion, till they reach the shores of their salvation", which vessel in a later passage in praise of Hazrat 'Ali comes to be compared implicitly with Noah's Ark (*safīna-i Nūḥ*) which saves the good, while leaving ill-doers to drown in the "depths of perdition" (*jihālat*). A strong notional line is thus established from the outset between Muslims and others, and a note of Iranian patriotism is struck from the very opening, when the kingdom of Iran (*mamālik-i Irān*) is said to mirror Paradise itself. However, a note of ambiguity is introduced with regard to the ruler of Thailand (*Siyām*), who had in the year 1682 sent a certain Haji Salim Mazandarani to Iran as his envoy with a letter and gifts for the Safavid monarch. The Siamese ruler is described in the text in grandiose terms as "the Lord of the White Elephant and the Throne of Gold, Friend of Muslims, Sultan of the kingdom of Siyam (May God endow him with the fortune of Islam) (*ṣāḥib-i fīl-i safed wa takẖt-i ṭilā muḥibb-i ahl-i Islām Sulṭān-i mulk-i Siyām – waffaqa-hul-lāh-ta'āla lil Islām*)".[40] His embassy, it is hence suggested, was itself a form of subordination, and opened the possibility of the conversion of the king to Islam: "For he [the king of Thailand]

[38] Muhammad Rabi' bin Muhammad Ibrahim, *Safīna-i Sulaimānī (Safar Nāma-i Safīr-i Irān ba Siyām, 1094–1098 H.)*, ed. 'Abbas Faruqi (Tehran, 1977). For an abridged English translation, see John O'Kane, *The ship of Sulaiman* (London, 1972). Also see David K. Wyatt, "A Persian embassy to Siam in the reign of King Narai", *Journal of the Siam Society*, 42, 1, 1974, pp. 151–7.

[39] Jean Aubin, "Les Persans au Siam sous le règne de Narai (1656–1688)", *Mare Luso-Indicum*, 4, 1980, pp. 95–126.

[40] O'Kane, *The Ship of Sulaiman*, p. 19; Muhammad Rabi', *Safīna-i Sulaimānī*, p. 7.

loves all Muslims and was overawed seeing that our king, the brilliant luminary of world rule had risen into the Heavens of eternal sovereignty."

Indeed, in the terms of the text, the Safavid ruler saw himself as the father of the ruler of Thailand, and hence decided in his generosity to send out a return embassy led by a certain Muhammad Husain Beg, who held the title of *g̲hulām-i sarkār-k̲hāṣṣa sharīf.* The first part opens then with the embassy experiencing six months of delays in Bandar 'Abbas in early 1685, on account of the (unstated) fact that the Iranians were actually dependent on Europeans to ferry them to their destination. It is only some distance into the section, after several storms and other untoward incidents have been experiened, that we learn that the embassy was in fact on-board an English ship (*jahāz-i inglīs*), and that at the end of two weeks they have barely been able to make it as far as Masqat. Muhammad Rabi', like 'Abdur Razzaq Samarqandi and so many others, clearly detested travel by sea, and once he has exhausted his poetic formulae, impatience with the experience comes to the fore. Besides, landing at Masqat is no positive experience for him, since this is a port of the "contemptible Kharijites" (meaning the Omani Arabs), who have recently expelled the "cursed Franks" from there. After a brief stay of four days, the English ship then set off again, and after a stormy voyage in which a passenger from Mazandaran was drowned, eventually reached Fort St George in Madras.

Here, the Iranian embassy disembarked on the orders of the governor, and they were given a tour of the fort and welcomed at a first formal feast, before being escorted to their quarters. Muhammad Rabi' initially professes to be fairly impressed by the English, their military discipline, and the fact that the English governor (*ḥākim-i inglīs*) does not fleece the merchants in their port, instead treating the "residents of this city (*diyār*) [who] belong to different communities (*ṭawā'if*), in particular the Telugu Hindus (*hunūd-i Tilang*) and groups of Portuguese Franks" with due consideration.[41] He also notes the arrival of news of the death of the English monarch (Charles II), and a feast to celebrate the coronation of his successor, James II. A peculiar feature of this feast was the presence there of the resident Englishwomen from Madras, a custom that the English governor explains on the grounds that it "would be the height of blasphemy and exceed the bounds of all propriety" to keep the beauty of these "dazzling Frank women, whose faces beam like the sun and are

[41] O'Kane, *The Ship of Sulaiman*, p. 35; Muhammad Rabi', *Safīna-i Sulaimānī*, pp. 22–4.

round like the moon, hidden with veils of modesty".[42] Much exaggerated praise of their beauty follows, increasingly tinged, however, with sarcasm. It is suggested that even great theologians like Fakhr-ud-Din Razi and Imam Ghazzali would have been seduced at the sight of these heavenly houris. Then it also becomes clear that the behaviour of these creatures has soon gone beyond the bounds of modesty, as "the mart of hugs and kisses began to warm up". Indeed, Muhammad Rabi' eventually informs the reader, with tongue firmly in cheek, that "the degree of friendship one has for a person is expressed by the amount of affection one shows for his wife". Festivities then seem to have become ever more extravagant as the party advanced into the evening (we may note, in passing, that it was the month of Ramazan). Muhammad Rabi' writes: "Thereafter, expert musicians and performers (*lūliyān-i rāgdān*) began to dance. With the magic of their gestures and the fire of their voices (*sho'la-i āwāz*), beating their drums (*daf*), they made the birds of the spirit (*murgh-i rūḥ*) of those in the assembly fly, and entertained the lovers there."[43]

Behind the surface of these compliments, it is clear though that Muhammd Rabi' finally does not have much of an opinion of the English. To be sure, he praises their sweetmeats and drinks, but he gives us the impression that they are a group of cuckolds who, for various reasons, allow their women far too much freedom. Indeed, in a brief exposition of the principal Christian sects (*firaq*), and the differences between them, he notes that one of the groups maintains that, since Jesus was born of a woman, therefore "in rank and position women are higher than men in the eyes of Heaven". He then goes on to add:

> Indeed, the Christians have very trusting natures and in most cases they view their brethren's actions in a wholly favourable light and they never suspect one another of treachery. Even if they catch one of their friends in the same nightshirt (*dar yak pairāhan*) with their wife, they interpret such behaviour as an indication of the respect and affection which their friend has towards them. But if this friend abuses their hospitality and they catch him in the very act, they are still obliged to provide two eyewitnesses whose testimony must concur and only then do they have a legal case.

[42] Simon Digby has compared this description to another from about 1750, in which some Muslim dignitaries visited Pondicherry; this is to be found in Sayyid Muhammad 'Ali al-Husaini, *Tārīkh-i Rāḥat-afzā*, ed. S. Khwurshid 'Ali (Hyderabad, 1366 H / 1957), pp. 218–19, cited in Simon Digby, "Indo-Persian narratives of travel of the close of the 18th and beginning of the 19th century", unpublished paper presented at the French Institute, Pondicherry, 1997.

[43] O'Kane, *The Ship of Sulaiman*, p. 39. It is also noted that two of these *lūliyān* had decided to renounce the world and become dancers for the idols (*aṣnām*) alone, refusing all payment.

Indeed, it is unclear whether the English were more absurd in this respect or the Portuguese, for the latter simply allowed men and women to commit all sorts of acts, and get away with it by confessing to a priest once in a while.

By September 1685 (Shawwal 1096 H), after a few months' stay in Madras, the Iranian embassy prepared to depart for Thailand. Before they did so, a rather curious incident took place that somewhat disturbed the peace of mind of Muhammad Rabi'. In order to amuse themselves, the Iranians called in a Brahmin astrologer in Madras, and asked him to read their fortunes (*fāl*). When the traveller's turn came, the fortune-teller communicated to him in a whisper that the envoy would die soon, and that the Thai ruler would become annoyed with them. Since these and other portents boded ill, Muhammad Rabi' was left feeling uneasy. The worst of it was that most of what the fortune-teller predicted came to be true!

To follow this development, we must pass quickly on to the "second gift" of the text, which describes how the Iranian party arrived in the area of Tenasserim ("Tanasuri" in the text), in the kingdom of Thailand, which is here referred to by the Persian term *shahr-i nau*, glossed by the author not as "New Town" but as the "Town of the Boats". Arriving at the port of Mergui (today in Burma), the embassy was welcomed by local officials (*mutaṣaddiyān-i Siyām*), who apparently received the *farmān* sent by Shah Sulaiman with great reverence and prostrations, in "the very manner in which they worship before their idols (*aṣnām*) as well". It is clear that none of this pleased Muhammad Rabi', for he seems to have been genuinely ill-at-ease in the midst of these unbelievers (*kāfirān*). Besides, there was the matter of the music that was played to welcome them. Of this he writes: "There is an instrument here which is shaped like a pan (*ba shakl-i taba*), which is made of iron and glass (*jām*) . . . This is in the possession of their musicians, and they also have something like an iron pestle. They play it in such a way that if the sound were to reach one's ears, one would lose one's footing in existence. And since this sound is outside the realm of music (*āhang*) it is called a gong (*gang*)".[44] Besides this, there were flutes that played "shrill deafening notes", and drums that were played with such violence that "we would have liked to flay the drummers and stretch their skins". In brief, things were not off to a happy start, despite the care and respect with which the missive from Shah

44 O'Kane, *The Ship of Sulaiman*, p. 45; Muhammad Rabi', *Safīna-i Sulaimānī*, p. 36. The text has *kabak* ("partridge") for *gang*, which clearly appears to be a mistake.

Sulaiman itself was received. To be sure, not far from the idol-house (*but-khāna*) was a far more civilized building, that had been constructed by the governor (*ḥākim*) of the area, who was a prosperous Iranian. Proper provisions were scarcely to be had, and the natives seemed to eat rice for the most part, rather than the wheat which their visitors preferred. Besides, the proximity of the Thais who were sent to serve the party disgusted Muhammad Rabi', who refers to them in no uncertain terms as "an ocean of legally unclean filth (*nijāsat-i 'ainī*)".

After a few days at Mergui, the Iranian party made its way by boat to Tenasserim, a town (*qaṣba*) of 5,000 or 6,000 households. Here, disaster struck. Several members of the embassy had already died, some in Bandar 'Abbas, and some on the sea-voyage. The ambassador, Husain Beg, with whom the voyage had not really agreed, was now seriously afflicted with dropsy (*istisqā*), and, despite the ministrations of a Thai and a Chinese doctor, died on 19 December 1685. Some other important members of the delegation still remained alive though (notably two *qūrchīs*, two *ghulāms*, one *tufangchī* and a *tūpchī*), and it was hence decided to proceed with their task.[45] The group thus made its way, first by boat, and then on elephant, until they had traversed the peninsula and reached the town of Phetchaburi ("Patajburi" in the text), where they once more found the administration in the charge of an Iranian, Sayyid Mazandarani. From Phetchaburi, the embassy was then conducted north, probably to Suphan Buri ("Suhan" in the text), and then eventually east to the capital city of *shahr-i nau* Ayuthia itself. The whole voyage was to take them about a month and a half from the time of their disembarkation in Mergui to their arrival in Ayuthia.[46]

However, Suphan Buri already offered some distinct comfort to the embassy, notably in the form of "several members of the Iranian community (*chand nafar az jamā'at-i Irānī*)" who came out to greet them. Lodgings had also been prepared for them in the Iranian style, with rugs and cushions, and this added to the sense of familiarity. The Thai ruler, Narai, sent condolences for the death of the ambassador Muhammad Husain Beg. However, the author of the *Safīna* and other members of the

[45] On these and other posts in the Safavid domains, see Sussan Babaie, Kathryn Babayan and Ina Baghdiantz McCabe, *Slaves of the Shah: new elites of Safavid Iran* (London, 2004).

[46] On this section of the text, also see the essays by M. Ismail Marcinkowski, "The Iran–Siamese connection: an Iranian community in the Thai kingdom of Ayutthaya", *Iranian Studies*, 35, 1–3, 2002, pp. 23–46; and Marcinkowski, "The Iranian presence in the Indian Ocean rim: a report on a 17th century Safawid embassy to Siam (Thailand)", *Journal of the Pakistan Historical Society*, 51, 3, 2003, pp. 55–85.

embassy remained troubled in spirit. To begin with, they could not agree on who would lead the embassy. Then, it seemed that the culture of the Iranians and that of Siam were simply too far apart. Muhammad Rabiʿ thus recounts the anecdote of an Iranian poet who had written a verse in praise of the king's elephant; but instead of receiving praise, the literal-minded Thai courtiers had simply denounced him as a liar. This grumbling tone thus found itself into a letter that Muhammad Rabiʿ wrote to Narai in order to explain the difficult circumstances of the embassy, wherein the overbearing tone of the Iranians soon became evident. For the letter insisted that the members of the embassy were men of elevated status in Iran, who had "until now lived their lives in the indescribable Paradise of Iran, where the fields are broad and ample and the climate is delightful (*dar firdaus-i barīn wilāyat-i wasiʿ-ul-fażā' Irān*)", and that visiting Thailand was hence for them a form of "dark suffering", in comparison to their homeland where "the foods are tasty, and the fruits delicious, and the flowing waters cool". Having despatched this remarkably tactless letter, the embassy then set out from Suphan Buri towards Ayuthia, only to be met a day's journey from the capital by a group of officials and ministers. Again, they were installed in resthouses, furnished not only with rugs and cushions but with "such refined conveniences as incense braziers and silver perfume sprinklers".

It eventually turned out, however, that the king was not in Ayuthia, but had instead gone to the city of Lopburi ("Lubu" in the text), described as "a spacious city with a pleasant climate". It was hence decided to meet him there, and by this time the Iranian envoys were also in contact with one of the most influential Iranians in the kingdom, a certain Khwaja Hasan ʿAli, described as "the head of the Iranian community (*sarkarda-i jamaʿāt-i Irān*)" there. For, as the text makes clear, the Iranians had in preceding decades exercised an enormous political influence in the kingdom, above all at the time when a certain Aqa Muhammad Astarabadi had dominated affairs as the chief minister and adviser (*wazīr wa mushīr*) of the ruler. Nevertheless, the disapproving tone that had characterised the text ever since the moment of arrival in Mergui persists. In Lopburi, we learn that the place was dominated by the worship of a "false deity (*maʿbūd-i nāḥaqq*)", who resided in a certain temple (*but-khāna*) and periodically went "to a different temple to visit his fellow idols". Muhammad Rabiʿ now pours scorn on every aspect of the material life of the Siamese that he encounters. The people are practically naked, usually wearing only a "small cloth which veils their private parts". Further, he states with a sneer, "despite the fact that they stumble through the rocky valley of idolatry (*wādi-i nā amanī-i bīdīnān*), they wear no shoes on their unsure feet". As for the soldiers of their king, everything from their apparel onwards is ridiculous to his eyes. Indeed, the only works that seem to be worth anything are those that have been constructed by the Iranians, such as a large garden and pavilion in Lopburi.

It is here that we come rather quickly to the crux of the problem. For, in the not-too-distant past, "all important business and matters of state were in the hands of the Iranians", who were "the very source of the king's power". This, to the eyes of Muhammad Rabi', was a natural state of affairs, since the natives of Siam were "devoid of intelligence and any practical abilities", and could not be counted upon, as a consequence, to "undertake the simplest task with a hope of success". However, the problem was that once Aqa Muhammad, the former *éminence grise*, had died, his sons had proved to be grossly incompetent and dishonest. This had allowed the rise to power of a certain "bastard from amongst the Christian community (*ḥarāmzāda az mardūm-i naṣārā*)", a reference to the formidable figure of the Greek Constant Phaulkon.[47] Thus, even though the Iranian envoys eventually chose a new leader to replace the deceased Muhammad Beg, namely a certain Ibrahim Beg, it seemed they were faced with an uphill battle.[48]

This is more or less what turned out to be the case, turning Muhammad Rabi' into an ever more virulent critic of the Thai kingdom and its mores. For the king, Narai, it turned out, had now made the Christian his all-powerful minister and confidant (*madār-ul-maḥām wa maḥram-i khwīsh*), and for his part had decided to play the part of an ignorant ruler (*pādshāh-i hīch nādīda*), leaving the Iranian envoys to negotiate instead with Phaulkon. It was in these circumstances that the embassy eventually made its presentation to the king in his throne room, a place which already displeased Muhammad Rabi' with its décor that consisted of pictures of idols (*ahraman*).[49] When the envoys entered, they were asked

[47] On Phaulkon, see the classic work of E. W. Hutchinson, *Adventurers in Siam in the seventeenth century* (reprint, Bangkok, 1985); and the recent, somewhat superficial, work of George A. Sioris, *Phaulkon, the Greek first counsellor at the Court of Siam: an appraisal* (Bangkok, 1998). For an excellent overview of matters, also see Dhiravat Na Pombejra, "Crown trade and court politics in Ayutthaya during the reign of King Narai (1656–88)", in J. Kathirithamby-Wells and John Villiers, eds., *The Southeast Asian port and polity: rise and demise* (Singapore, 1990), pp. 127–42.

[48] Muhammad Rabi' seems to have considered that he himself was the most competent of the group, and should have been chosen. As he remarks sarcastically, "Though each one wanted to be the representative in spite of their incompetence, yet no one dared to present himself": Muhammad Rabi', *Safīna-i Sulaimānī*, p. 53.

[49] O'Kane, *The ship of Sulaiman*, p. 63; Muhammad Rabi', *Safīna-i Sulaimānī*, pp. 57–9.

to bow down and kiss the monarch's feet (*marātib-i sijda wa pā-i-bos*) in the Iranian style, while the rest of the court had entirely prostrated. A number of minor ceremonies involving a betel-leaf holder (*pāndān*) were then engaged in, before Shah Sulaiman's letter was finally presented to the ruler by Ibrahim Beg. The ceremonies that followed seem equally to have filled Muhammad Rabi' with anger and disgust. One of these moments was when the Thai commander Phra Phetracha ("Siyam Petraja" in the text) is reported to have recited the following prayer: "Pra put ta chao kha sai klao sai klamon, ko rub kha", which the author of our text translates as "Divine Protector of Heaven and Earth, your command hangs over my head. Be merciful to me." These words, in the view of Muhammad Rabi', are no less than "the very essence of infidelity (*kufr*)". A desultory conversation now ensued. The Iranians employed their high rhetoric, comparing their own ruler to Alexander, Jamshid and Solomon, and insisting that no other king in the world dared to attack them for fear of Shah Sulaiman's "scorching anger", which could "wrench up the mean brambles of such a man's existence by the roots and reduce the harvest of his life to a heap of ashes". They also felt piqued by the implication in the conversation that the domain of the Shah was restricted to Khorasan alone. Narai then indicated that they should not be in too much of a hurry to return, and invited them to be his personal guests while in Siam. The audience ended, but the envoys were then invited to join the king on that very evening for an elephant hunt.

This elephant hunt, along with other tiger hunts and bird hunts, at least seems to have amused our jaded author, corresponding as they did to the familiar category of "wonders and marvels". After a brief description of each of these hunts, he returns to his vitriolic criticisms of the Siamese. Thus, he writes:

> The food of the people of Siam, which I shall describe in its proper place, in no way resembles normal, proper, foods and the natives are not familiar with intelligent methods of preparing meals. In fact, no one in Siam really knows how to cook and eat, or even how to sit correctly at table. The people of Siam have only recently arrived from the world of bestiality to the realm of humanity (*darīn auqāt pāra-i min 'hadd al-bahīmiya ila ḥadd al-insāniya ruju' namūda and*).[50]

Again, only the king is partly exempt from this, and that because he has had the intelligence to keep the company of Iranians, and thus, having

[50] O'Kane, *The ship of Sulaiman*, p. 68; Muhammad Rabi', *Safīna-i Sulaimānī*, p. 65.

"acquired a permanent taste for our food", was given to having an Indian cook prepare "real food" for him from time to time. It was thus a great relief for Muhammad Rabi' when the king decided presently to leave Lopburi for Ayuthia, and it became possible to think of returning from there to Iran. It was decided that, rather than take the painful route back via Mergui, it would be easier to depart through one of the ports in the Gulf of Thailand. Some more time was spent in excursions at Suphan Buri, and further elephant hunts, while the Iranian party prepared its departure. A farewell gift on the part of King Narai was announced for the members of the embassy, but this eventually turned out to be distressingly low in value. The mood by now was truly morose amongst the Iranians, and Muhammad Rabi' declares that various factors had conspired to make the embassy a failure. There was the issue of the "Christian bastard" Phaulkon, and his influence over the king. Then, the writer admits that their own "lack of familiarity with the protocol (*dastūr*) of Siam, and the fact that we were not led by a clever ambassador" had played a part too. Interestingly, in the end, the king, Narai, himself is not directly blamed for any of the problems that had occurred. Rather, in these passages that close the description of the visit, we are told – in view of the fact that it is the month of Muharram – that he allows processions to take place in Ayuthia on the occasion of this holy Shi'i festival, and even permits preachers to curse and mock the "infidels and idolaters (*butparastān wa kāfirān*)" in a loud voice in public. Indeed, the closing meetings with the Thai ruler seemed to be occasions where something could be salvaged from the embassy, and Narai even offered a gift of elephants for Shah Sulaiman, which were eventually not allowed, for some reason, to accompany the returning embassy. Carrying a return letter to their own monarch, the Iranian embassy then departed for their homeland in a ship belonging to a merchant from Surat on 7 January 1687 (22 Safar 1098 H).[51] It would be nearly another year and a half before they would return to the Persian Gulf, after a voyage that took them first to Patani, then Melaka, and then to Cochin (where the party spent all of six months repairing their decrepit ship), Surat and Bombay, where they were eventually able to gain a passage aboard an English ship. The text closes then with a verse celebrating the fact that "the days of suffering had passed, an age of grief and longing had come to its end, and we humble servants had survived". The somewhat reproachful verse runs:

[51] At another point in his text, Muhammad Rabi' states, however, that the date of departure from Ayuthia was 31 December 1686 (15 Safar 1098 H); see O'Kane, *The ship of Sulaiman*, p. 217.

The wood-chip (*khas*) no matter where it falls,
Will eventually reach the shore.
[Even if] the captain does not wish to guide
the ship of faith (*tawakkul*).[52]

The departure from Ayuthia in fact closes the "second gift" of the *Safina-i Sulaimānī.* The very extensive "third gift" then turns, in the words of its author, from providing a "condensed report" and description of events surrounding the embassy, to "recording some facts about local conditions". Thus, after briefly rehearsing the location of Siam in the world on the basis of the work of earlier geographers, the text proceeds to an extended discussion of the wars between the kings of Siam and Pegu. The growing influence of the Iranians in the Thai kingdom is then described, as is the rise to power of King Narai, who – it is reported – "used to visit the Iranians regularly and took great pleasure in their social manners and their foods and drink". A description of some aspects of the organisation of the palace, and of certain ranks, follows, before an extended discussion of the personage of Aqa Muhammad Astarabadi. This man, it is noted, recruited some 200 Iranians, mostly from Astarabad and Mazandaran, to the service of the Thai ruler, when they had been languishing in the "tricky land of India" to which they had "migrated from their homeland with high hopes". These men, in the severe opinion of Muhammad Rabi', eventually proved unworthy and betrayed their patron, thus leaving the field open to Phaulkon, who came very quickly to dominate the court.

A long set of passages on the matter of Phaulkon and his comportment now follow, concluding with examples of his most recent acts of tyranny in executing Siamese officials and advisers of Narai. This takes Muhammad Rabi' then to a discussion of the religion and mores of the people of Thailand. Here we return to the plainly vitriolic terms of the earlier diatribes in his text. To Muhammad Rabi', people in the world can be divided into two categories: "people of faith and religion (*arbāb-i adyān wa ahl-i milal-o-niḥal*)", and "people of lust and contempt (*ahl-i ahwā'*)". He then adds that "there can be no doubt that the people of Siam belong to the second group, in fact even more blind and hopelessly gone astray, for it is clear that they do not adhere to any form of *sharī'a* or specified practice". Indeed, this is clear to him from the fact that they

[52] Muhammad Rabi', *Safīna-i Sulaimānī*, p. 230; the translation in O'Kane, *The ship of Sulaiman*, p. 233, is erroneous.

make use of Satan (*shaiṭān*), and believe in idol worship (*but-parastī*) and in the transmigration of souls (*tanāsukh*).[53] Now, our author is willing to concede that, amongst the unbelievers (*kāfir-kesh*), some may be thought to be better than others. Indeed, he notes that the "best group amongst the Hindus" (*bihtarīn ṭawā'if jama'-i and az hunūd*) is one that refrains from all forms of violence, and does not kill or eat meat – probably referring to the Jains. The people of Siam are, to his mind, "the worst of these peoples (*jama'āt-i siyām ke badtarīn ṭawā'if and wa abṭal az hama*)", who are entirely opportunistic in what they state and practise. This broad condemnation attaches both to the lay people, and to their wise men (*'ulamā'-i īn ṭā'ifa*), called *raolīs*, corresponding no doubt to Buddhist monks.

There is not much to be salvaged amongst the people of Siam then, if one is to follow the views of our Iranian traveller. One minor consolation may be had, in that "the truth of the faith of this king is not clear (*ḥaqīqat-i millat-i īn shāh ẓāhir nīst*)". However, even those institutions that have little to do with religion do not find favour with the author. In his jaundiced view, while laws of a sort do exist, "to apply legal terms to that procedure is as meaningless as it is to call these people human beings (*insān*)". Little justice may be expected then, unless it is by pure chance, even as little reasonable social behaviour can be seen, even in such matters as incest. In the Siam of Muhammad Rabi', "a father will marry his daughter, his sister or his niece". As for the king, he scarcely has an army, beyond "a mob of peasants assembled in times of danger". Since no craftsmen (*ahl-i ṣanā'i'*) worth the name exist in the land, one can be sure that anything that shows any sign of skill or craft is the work of an Iranian migrant. Poverty is widespread, and there is no landed class with sizeable revenues (*amlāk-i arbābī ba jama' wa banīcha*), since everything belongs directly to the royal treasury (*tamām khāliṣa ast*). Indeed, except for a few products such as elephants, camphor and aloe-wood, it is not at all clear what the riches of the kingdom are comprised of. The contempt of Muhammad Rabi' extends beyond Siam, indeed to all the kings of the "land below the winds (*zīrbādāt*)", who are to his mind "counterfeit rulers [who] do not incur the usual financial burdens of royalty such as endowments, salaries . . . grants, charities and alms".[54] Narai alone is exempt to a limited extent, and that too for the obvious reasons:

[53] O'Kane, *The Ship of Sulaiman*, p. 111; Muhammad Rabi', *Safina-i Sulaimānī*, p. 109.
[54] O'Kane, *The ship of Sulaiman*, p. 155.

Compared to the other kings of the *zīrbādāt*, who live with neither a retinue nor expenditures, the king of Siam, because he has long lived with Iranians, has changed his habits, and has decided to have an apparatus (*waẓ'*), to eat and drink in keeping with other principles, to dress up, to have dishes made and to buy carpets, and he has conceived the idea of having a name and reputation, relations and contacts with the great sovereigns.

What remains of the positive in the view that Muhammad Rabi' leaves us of Thailand under King Narai? Certainly little, in his opinion, of the society or culture, whether material culture or the beliefs and mores of the people. The people of Siam are in his view utterly contemptible, and lacking in practically any redeeming quality. At least there are a few wonders, some fine natural products, some curious animals that may be hunted. Further, once the people are removed from the picture, Nature in Thailand does please Muhammad Rabi'. Thus, while he is at Suphan Buri, we learn that the place is a veritable orchard (*bāghistān*), "extremely fertile and beautiful", and that "a wondrous river of fresh water flows through the town and continues down to the sea". Further, he is greatly impressed by the vegetation, "trees that never feel the withering touch of autumn", and which include "every sort of fruit tree, lemon, orange, coconut, and mango, as well as the betel tree, which for beauty and grace rivals the free swaying cypress". He sums up his eloquent description by declaring: "Here is a resting place for a traveller's weary soul, a place of good fortune for those who have left their home."[55] The problem, however, is that the place comes encumbered by a society and a people for which the traveller has nothing but disdain, and it is difficult to believe that any Iranian reader of this text in the late seventeenth century would have evinced the least desire to visit Thailand after having read Muhammd Rabi'.

CONCLUSION

Whoever chooses to traverse the terrain of the Indo-Persian travel-account in the early modern period in search of simple edification may end up roaming disconsolate across hundreds of years and thousands of miles. This can lead the scholar, in desperation, to radical simplificatory devices; and the implicit methodological challenge in reading such texts is thus not to schematise them excessively, not to impose on them a heavy-handed editorial voice, in brief *not* to read them against their grain. This means,

[55] O'Kane, *The ship of Sulaiman*, p. 50; Muhammad Rabi', *Safīna-i Sulaimānī*, p. 43.

inevitably, that the reader's patience will at times be tried by an accumulation of minute details, and it is hence to be hoped that our discussion of the travellers in this chapter, Mahmud Wali Balkhi and Muhammad Rabi' ibn Muhammad Ibrahim, has not lost the wood for the trees. The diversity of perspectives and views that these travellers and those of the preceding chapter, separated by a little less than a century and a half between the first and the last, all moving from west to east (and then back) in the Indian Ocean world, bring to bear is in itself a salutary lesson for those who argue that these visions are too meagre in depth, and too poor in variety, to support anything more than a casual discussion.

As for wider implications from the texts we have studied in this chapter, we shall rest content by pointing to merely two of these. In the first place, it appears to us that these texts, together with those studied in the preceding chapters, can fruitfully be read as part of a larger corpus of first-person narratives (diaries, autobiographies) that seem to have been a growing feature of the early modern Asian world.[56] Even if we set aside the more naive presumptions of the so-called Burckhardt hypothesis, in which such narratives immediately signal the rise of a modern and individualistic (perhaps "bourgeois") consciousness of Self and Other, it is of course striking that such travel-accounts as ours are so closely linked with the mixed mercantile–aristocratic milieu. Of our authors, one – Seydi 'Ali Re'is – was clearly a savant, with a knowledge of not merely letters, but astronomy, geography and other subjects. Mahmud Wali Balkhi was clearly a more modest figure than Seydi 'Ali, but he too was associated with courtly life, and saw himself as located in a tradition which drew upon earlier figures for inspiration, notably 'Abdur Razzaq Samarqandi. Of these personages, Muhammad Rabi' is perhaps the most obscure, as well as the most modest. Yet, as secretary of an embassy, he too can be located squarely in a world of letters that links court and city, and locates itself in a set of references where chroniclers such as Mir Khwand, as well as geographers such as Zakariya ibn Muhammad Qazwini, author of the *'Ajā'ib ul-Makhluqāt* ("The wonders of creation"), find a distinct place. Again, it is clear that he is no stranger to the text of 'Abdur Razzaq, for he refers to the embassy that Mirza Shahrukh sent to China in 1420–1, which is discussed at some length in the *Maṭla' us-Sa'dain*. Here then are the contours of a shared world of references, and we must then ask the question: what in fact are the limits of sharing?

[56] For a comparative perspective, see, for example, Cemal Kafadar, "Self and others", pp. 121–50.

For, contrary to what votives of a Third World Spirit might have us believe, it emerges quite clearly that there were simply no automatic bonds of understanding and perceptual solidarity in the early modern period between the denizens of Central Asia and those of, say, Sri Lanka, merely because we may retrospectively class them together as the screens on which an aggressive western European imagination played out its shadow-theatre. Such bonds as existed were both contingent and highly concrete, and the result of such things as a shared literary curriculum amongst Persian speakers, and shared points of political or socio-religious reference (thus, Sri Lanka gains significance in relation to the myth of Gabriel and Adam). It would thus surely be hasty to claim, as some scholars of the medieval Indian Ocean have done, that a magical world of solidarity, and an unbroken web of commercial and cultural commonality, could run across from Egypt to Indonesia, and further that this network was characterised overall by "an astonishing degree of interdenominational cooperation, matched by almost complete absence of animosity against other communities", as well as a "spirit of all-embracing brotherhood".[57] Europe (or rather Portugal), violent and unreasoning, is sometimes alleged to have destroyed this happy idyll with its cannon (and later presumably with its "Orientalism"). We do not mean to suggest (and nor do the texts under our examination lead us to believe) that relations between the Perso-Turkish heartland, in Iran and Central Asia, and India can at all be equated to those between, say, Portugal and India. However, we should also caution against the view that the hierarchisation of cultures and cultural zones, or the urge to seek out the bizarre and the exotic (even if in the form of the "wonders of God's creation"), were purely European inventions or monopolies, even if this need not lead us to assert that Europeans and Asians both constructed the world of the "Orient" in the same way.[58]

Yet, radical rejection and radical contempt could be the central devices that informed some of our texts as well, as we see from a reading of the

[57] See S. D. Goitein, "Letters and documents on the India trade in medieval times", *Islamic Culture*, 37, 3, 1963, pp. 188–205, citation on pp. 204–5; this perspective is further and more explicitly developed, for example, in the work of Amitav Ghosh, "The slave of Ms. H.5", in Partha Chatterjee and Gyanendra Pandey, eds., *Writings on South Asian history and society, Subaltern Studies 7* (Delhi, 1992), pp. 159–220.

[58] We presume that this suggestion will seem obvious to (Western) scholars working with Chinese travel-accounts of the early modern period. It is, however, not commonly accepted in studies of West and South Asia, perhaps as a consequence of the influence of writings such as Ronald Inden, *Imagining India* (Oxford, 1990); for a critical discussion, see Aijaz Ahmad, "Between Orientalism and historicism: anthropological knowledge of India", *Studies in History*, n.s., 7, 1, 1991, pp. 135–63.

Safīna-i Sulaimānī. The question that remains therefore is one of knowing whether Muhammad Rabi' represented something of a *sui generis* position, quite atypical of such accounts. It has sometimes been asserted that the primary form in which later European "Orientalism" came, in the course of the nineteenth century, was not through manifest disdain or avowed hatred, but precisely through displays and assertions of "love" for the perceived Other. This then leaves us with the issue of knowing how to place the unhappy traveller, the one who could simply not come to terms with the lands to which he travelled. It is this problem which forms the central theme of the following chapter.

CHAPTER 5

When Hell is other people

"L'enfer, c'est les autres."

Sartre, *Huis clos* (1944)[1]

IRANIANS ABROAD

The spread of Iranians far beyond the limits of the early modern Safavid domains has received attention from a vast number of scholars over the years, ranging from specialists of the administrative élite of Mughal India to literary scholars dealing with the complex problem of the so-called *sabk-i Hindī*, or "Indian style" in Persian poetry. The destinations of these Iranian expatriates were many and varied, as were the reasons that led them to find careers as far afield as the Thailand of King Narai (discussed in the preceding chapter) and Istanbul.[2] If some were principally

[1] In a later reflection on this play, in 1965, Sartre added the following commentary : "But [the phrase] 'l'enfer, c'est les autres', has always been misunderstood. It has been believed that I wanted to say thereby that our relations with others were always poisoned, and that they were always hellish relations. But I wanted to say something else. I want to say that if our relations with the Other are twisted, tortuous, then the other can only be hell. Why? Because others are what in the final analysis is the most important in ourselves for our understanding of ourselves. When we think of ourselves, when we try to know ourselves, at bottom we use this knowledge that others already have of us. We judge ourselves with the means that others have, and which they have given us to judge ourselves. Whatever I say about myself, the judgment of the Other is already included therein. Which means that if my relations are bad, I become totally dependent on the other. And then effectively I am in hell. And there are vast numbers of people in the world who are in hell because they depend too much on others' judgment. But this does not mean at all that one cannot have different relations with others. It is only a measure of the capital importance of all others for each one of us." Cf. Jean-Paul Sartre, *Un théâtre de situations*, ed. Michel Contat and Michel Rybalka (Paris, 1992), pp. 282–3.

[2] For an earlier discussion, see Sanjay Subrahmanyam, "Iranians abroad: intra-Asian élite migration and early modern state formation", *Journal of Asian Studies*, 51, 2, 1992, pp. 340–62. Also see the papers collected in Thierry Zarcone and Fariba Zarinebaf, eds., *Les Iraniens d'Istanbul* (Paris, 1993). For some additional materials on Mughal India, see also the recent work of Abolghasem Dadvar, *Iranians in Mughal politics and society, 1606–1658* (New Delhi, 1999), and, for an individual case-study, Elizabeth Lambourn, "Of jewels and horses: the career and patronage of an Iranian merchant under Shah Jahan", *Iranian Studies*, 36, 2, 2003, pp. 213–58.

merchant-adventurers, attempting to find a fortune in the diamond mines of the Sultanate of Golkonda, or by trading on large ships between the ports of Masulipatnam and Bandar 'Abbas, others founded major Sufi hospices in the Deccan, painted lavish albums and wrote elaborate praise-verses for patrons in a variety of situations, from Bengal to Kashmir.[3] We have already noted the remarks by Jean Aubin, who devoted a good part of his work to various aspects of this phenomenon, from studying the career of the fifteenth-century Bahmani *wazīr*, Mahmud Gawan Gilani, to examining the spread of the Ni'matullahi Sufi order "from Kuhbanan to Bidar", and who has written of how, from about 1400 – while merchants, warriors and theologians from the Arabic-speaking lands were still very much present – Indo-Muslim civilisation essentially came to be transformed into a civilisation of Indo-Persian culture.[4] Yet, an ambiguous relationship persisted between the India of the Mughals, and the Iran of the Safavids, as a number of disparate sources show. Not all Iranians were quite willing, after all, to agree with a poet who wrote in Safavid times:

> I am off to Hind for there
> the business of skilled men has run smoothly;
> while the liberality and generosity of men of our time
> has sunk into the black earth.[5]

The suggestion here is that, whereas Safavid Iran has become the domain of the mean-minded and tight-fisted, Hind still holds out excellent prospects for those who have the necessary skills. Yet, at the same time, the process of expatriation and, at times, of return seems to have left the Iranian élite with a sense of disquiet. There was, to begin with, the fact that the Mughal polity was clearly larger and more prosperous than that of the Safavids, and better able to pay its master-craftsmen, painters and

[3] See Sanjay Subrahmanyam, "Persians, pilgrims and Portuguese: the travails of Masulipatnam shipping in the western Indian Ocean, 1590–1665", *Modern Asian Studies*, 22, 3, 1988, pp. 503–30, and Muzaffar Alam, "The pursuit of Persian: language in Mughal politics", *Modern Asian Studies*, 32, 1998, pp. 317–49.

[4] Jean Aubin, "Merchants in the Red Sea and the Persian Gulf at the turn of the fifteenth and sixteenth centuries", in Denys Lombard and Jean Aubin, eds., *Asian merchants and businessmen in the Indian Ocean and the China Sea* (Delhi, 2000), pp. 79–86, esp. p. 80. Also see Aubin, "De Kûhbanân à Bidar", pp. 233–61.

[5] Verse attributed to Ghazzali Mashhadi, as cited in Jean Calmard, "Safavid Persia in Indo-Persian sources and in Timurid-Mughal perception", in Muzaffar Alam, Françoise N. Delvoye and Marc Gaborieau, eds., *The making of Indo-Persian culture: Indian and French studies* (New Delhi, 2000), pp. 351–91, on p. 351. True to his word, this poet actually migrated to India, and was poet-laureate at Akbar's court.

calligraphers; this meant that there was a real risk of a form of "brain drain" in the epoch. Second, some members of the intellectual élite in India, such as the late sixteenth-century poet-laureate Abu'l Faiz "Faizi", actually claimed that their mastery over both the Persian language and Persianate culture rivalled that of their contemporaries in Iran.[6] The idea that, even if the economic balance was in favour of the Mughals, the Safavids held at least the cultural high ground, was hence less robust than might appear to be the case at first sight. Further, we must not discount the existence of a real Irano-centricism, not simply in Safavid times, but even earlier, and this should alert us in turn to the fact that strong hierarchies of cultures existed within the Islamic world of the early modern period.

The reticence expressed by visitors from the Iranian world was not limited to India alone, for Safavid envoys to other parts of Asia too demonstrated a mix of curiosity and a sense of superiority. An extreme case is that of Muhammad Rabi', whose account of the Safavid embassy to the Thai court of King Narai in the 1680s was discussed at some length in the preceding chapter.[7] As we have noted, this writer has a large number of deeply acerbic comments to make regarding his Thai hosts, whom he finds wanting as regards a large number of points of etiquette and high culture. While his view of the Thai monarch itself is relatively positive, and he liberally attributes rather high-sounding titles such as "Lord of the White Elephant" to him, it is clear that the Thai population in general does not impress the Iranian visitor at all. Indeed, as noted above, his criticisms of the Thais go so far as to claim that "it is meaningless to call these people human beings (*insān*)".[8]

The view of Indians at the time of the Mughals rarely attained such a degree of harshness. If some visitors from Central Asia, such as Mutribi Samarqandi, have nothing negative at all to say about a Mughal court that dealt with them in magnanimous terms, even others like Mahmud Wali Balkhi in the 1620s and 1630s bring out an image of India that may have its share of the bizarre, but is certainly not to be treated with contempt.

6 On Faizi, see Muzaffar Alam and Sanjay Subrahmanyam, "A place in the sun: travels with Faiẓī in the Deccan, 1591–93", in François Grimal, ed., *Les sources et le temps / Sources and time: a colloquium* (Pondicherry, 2001), pp. 265–307.

7 Muhammad Rabi', *Safīna-i Sulaimānī*; and O'Kane, *The Ship of Sulaiman.*

8 This may be contrasted with the rather respectful attitude shown towards China, in such texts as the early sixteenth-century account of Sayyid 'Ali Akbar Khata'i, *Khaṭāy-nāma*, ed. Iraj Afshar (Tehran, 1357 Sh. / 1968). We are grateful to Claudine Salmon for bringing this particular text to our attention.

Mutribi, we may recall, had visited the court of Jahangir at Lahore in the last years of that monarch's reign, and was rather well received by him, returning home laden with gifts after exchanging much banter with the ruler, and dedicating a Persian work to him.[9] Mahmud Wali, on the other hand, had a rather more chequered career, and after some time spent as a wanderer and mendicant in northern India, eventually wound up as a minor Mughal official in the province of Orissa before eventually returning to his native town of Balkh. Yet, even if his account contains elements of the weird and wonderful, regaling us with passages regarding an island full of self-regenerating virgins, as well as descriptions of "Liver-Eaters" (*jigar-khwār*) who rob their victims of vitality, his reader is never given the impression that Hind is a land to be looked down upon, or that Mahmud in the least regrets the years that he spent there.[10]

However, if Muhammad Rabi' is to be believed, some Iranian migrants to India were not of that view. Thus, while discussing the recruitment policies in the Thai kingdom of Aqa Muhammad Astarabadi, who in the 1660s seems to have sent out representatives to India to get hold of Iranians from Astarabad and Mazandaran, it is noted by him that these were men who had "migrated from their homeland but lacking the integrity necessary to succeed, they were checkmated in the tricky land of India by the elephant of unfavourable chance". The implication here is that the fault was as much that of such migrants as of the conditions prevalent in India, for these were men who – in the view of Muhammad Rabi' at least – were "quick to stumble into the meshes of mischief and sedition", and also naturally given to becoming "embroiled in mutual hatred, malice, jealousies and all manner of perverseness".[11] We also gather from Muhammad Rabi' that, by the later seventeenth century, many parts of India were no longer as welcoming to Iranians as they had once been. Thus, the epilogue to his work, which concerns the disturbed conditions in Hyderabad, claims that, under Sultan Abu'l Hasan Qutb Shah, the shrewd policies of earlier ministers such as Sayyid Muzaffar (and before him Mir Jumla) were set aside and that infidels and Hindus came to rule the roost, so that Hyderabad which had been "famous as a stronghold of the Shi'ites" now became "a bulwark of disbelief and a refuge

[9] Mutribi Samarqandi, *Khāṭirāt-i-Muṭribī Samarqandī.*

[10] See Mahmud Wali Balkhi, *The Baḥr ul-asrār*, ed. Riazul Islam. An extensive discussion may be found in Chapter 4 above.

[11] O'Kane, *The Ship of Sulaiman*, pp. 100–1.

for heathendom".[12] This is what had eventually led, he argued, to the conquest of the region by the Mughals.

In point of fact, the influence of Iranians in the Mughal court, as well as in the newly emerging regional polities, continued to be considerable in the eighteenth century. Yet, there is no doubt that a specific narrative of decline was emerging in the later seventeenth century with regard to these Iranians and their migration. In this view, the golden age of such migration had begun with Humayun's return from Iran in the 1550s, and had reached its apogee under Akbar and Jahangir. During the rule of the latter, a great deal of power had been wielded by such men as the monarch's own brother-in-law, Asaf Khan, himself a migrant from Iran together with his father, the celebrated I'timad-ud-Daula. Subsequent reigns were, in this view, less favourable to Iranians in Mughal India, whatever the reason may be for this ostensible disfavour. Statistically minded historians, who have examined the composition of the high ranks of the Mughal *manṣabdārs* ("high notables"), have not been convinced by these assertions.[13] However, since our principal concern in this work is with the subjective perceptions of travellers, it might have been of little consolation for them to know how the statistics of the later twentieth century have judged the matter.

THE GRUMBLING TRAVELLER

So on to the major text that is the subject of this chapter, one written by a Safavid traveller to the Mughal domains in the seventeenth century. The traveller in question, Mirza Muhammad Mufid Mustaufi ibn Najm-ud-Din Mahmud Bafiqi Yazdi, was the author of the *Jāmi'-i Mufīdī*, compiled in Multan in 1090 H / 1679, and his travels to India have already merited brief mention in a number of surveys concerning Iranian migrants to the Mughal domains.[14] It is after all a well-known fact (as mentioned above) that an appreciable number of Iranians migrated to India from the fifteenth century on, initially to the Deccan (where they were welcomed in the Bahmani Sultanate), and then increasingly after about 1550 to the Mughal domains. Mufid was thus by no means treading a virgin path; on the contrary, a number of celebrated Iranians, and most

[12] O'Kane, *The Ship of Sulaiman*, pp. 234–5.

[13] M. Athar Ali, *The Mughal nobility under Aurangzeb* (Bombay, 1966); also Afzal Husain, *The nobility under Akbar and Jahāngīr: a study of family groups* (New Delhi, 1999).

[14] Muhammad Mufid Mustaufi Yazdi, *Jāmi'-i Mufīdī*, vol. III, pp. 743–816.

notably the family of the Mughal empress Nur Jahan, had already left a considerable imprint on the Mughal polity by the middle years of the seventeenth century. As summed up by Jean Calmard in a recent survey on Iranian migration to the Mughal domains, the Indian career of Mufid would have been roughly as follows.[15] In 1671 (1082 H), he set sail from Basra to Surat, and then went on to Delhi, Hyderabad, then Burhanpur and Ujjain (1677) where he entered the service of the Mughal prince Muhammad Akbar as *k̲h̲ānsamān* ("intendant"). The main source for his travels is the *Jāmi'* text which is in three parts: from Alexander to the Timurids; from the Safavids to Shah Sulaiman (this part written while in Shahjahanabad); biographical and topographical notices of Yazd, and the author's life and peregrinations in Isfahan, Baghdad, Basra, Surat and Shahjahanabad. Mufid was also the author of the *Muk̲h̲taṣar-i Mufīd*, a text begun in the Deccan in 1087 H / 1676–7, and ended in Lahore (in 1091 H / 1680–1). This latter work is largely a geographical treatise on Persia, with notices on the Imams and Safavids, and we shall deal with it briefly below.[16]

Our analysis in the pages that follow is largely based on the fifth *maqāla* (entitled "Some of the Wonders of the Age and of some conditions, often tumultuous, of the wanderer in the Valley of Failure, Muhammad Mufid, the author of the useful book, *Jāmi'-i Mufīdī*"), and the *k̲h̲ātima* ("closing section") of the published text of the *Jāmi'* (edited by Iraj Afshar), which we have read together with a manuscript of the same entitled *Risāla-i Mufīd*, containing some additional passages.[17] The text as a whole is written in elegant literary prose, interspersed with the usual Persian verses on every page, that are offered as a support for almost every idea that the author proffers. On many occasions, he also gives the names of the poets; in some cases, the verses would seem to be of his own composition, but they come without explicit attribution. It is clear that Mufid had an excellent command of the Persian language, and also had good taste for other people's prose; thus, the documents that he cites in the text are explicitly justified by him on account of the fact that they are drafted by good *munshīs* ("scribes"). Besides, there is a sense in which his account,

15 Calmard, "Safavid Persia in Indo-Persian sources", p. 373. Also see Jean Aubin, "Quelques notices du Muk̲h̲taṣar-i Mufīd", *Farhang-i Irān Zamīn*, 6, 1958, pp. 164–77.

16 See Muhammad Mufid Mustaufi Yazdi, *Mok̲h̲taṣar-e Mofīd des Moḥammad Mofīd Mostoufī*, ed. Seyfeddin Najmabadi, vols. I and II (Wiesbaden, 1989–91).

17 Muhammad Mufid Mustaufi Yazdi, *Risāla-i Mufīd*, Bodleian Library, Oxford, Ms. Ouseley, No. 90. We are grateful to Kathryn Babayan for this and other references.

besides being a sort of autobiography, and a travel-text, is an essay with moral content.

The section of the text that interests us stands then nearly as an independent work, beginning with a brief invocation of God and the Prophet (but with no particular attention to ʿAli or the Shiʿi Imams). It then continues, already in a rather pessimistic vein:

To the sun-like, shining, alchemically transformed hearts of those who have the experience of the transformations and revolutions of the world, and who have observed the change of night into day, it is evident that the business of the world is tied up to Divine Destiny. Human efforts cannot make any difference, and can neither add to it nor take away from it. Therefore, for the wise, it is appropriate that they do not try to inquire too far into the world, and nor should they waste their lives in the pursuit of this world, which is like a stinking carcass.

This world is like a carcass,
around which turn thousands of vultures,
stabbing with their beaks.
Yet the world remains unaffected.
The vultures fly away while
the carcass remains intact.

That livelihood which is given to you in the world's workshop, as it is said in the Qur'an, 'and we have distributed matters among them' cannot be increased on account of greed and evil-doing. Instead, eventually one only obtains trouble and misfortune.

The same deeply pessimistic matter is elaborated once more in more extensive verses of a similar vein, after which Mufid returns to prose and writes:

If the beauty of Divine Will does not reveal its face from behind the veil, the star that tells of good news will not rise in the horizon of fortune. And unless in the shop of Divine Will, the price of goods is well-assessed, their evaluation would not be acceptable in the market . . .

Without the prior intention of Divine Will, each stroke of an idea on the slate of the mind would be erased. Each magical formula, even if put forward by a strong-willed man, will be transformed into a mere fiction.

What pictures I drew, but all in vain.
Our incantations for him [the beloved] turned into a mere fiction.

Thus, it is established, that if God wills, each being can achieve his goal with no work at all, and if God wills otherwise, the struggle against it is of no consequence. This is why all of us should bow our heads before the Divine Order, and gladly accept it.

Our cure lies in accepting the predestined.

The illustration of what has been said so far is the life-story (*aḥwāl*) of the writer of these ill-organised pages, Muhammad Mufid Mustaufi ibn Najm-ud-Din Mahmud Bafiqi.[18]

The broad colours of the work have already been announced; things are really not going to turn out well for the traveller. Yet before the question of travel itself, there is the issue of the earlier life of Mufid, and what leads him in the direction of travel. To this end, the work is oriented around a set of dialogues with a series of friends, perhaps real, more likely imagined as a convenient literary device. Matters thus begin with a long discussion with a wise friend, at the time that Mufid, after frequenting the houses of the *umarā'* and the *arkān-i daulat* ("Pillars of the State") and others, has managed at last to get himself the post of *mustaufī* ("administrator") of the *waqfs* ("religious endowments") at Yazd. He has long wanted this, and the accession of a new sovereign, Shah Sulaiman, encourages him to try his luck at court. The friend advises him though not to hanker after worldly wealth, but it has no effect on him. This conversation apparently takes place in Isfahan, and the friend in question is portrayed as having had worldly experience of things both sweet and bitter. He thus visits Mufid's home to give him advice (*naṣīḥat*) and a mild warning (*sar-zanish*), and tells him that wise men are those who at the start of work look already to its completion, and who, while planting a seedling, have already thought of its fruit. The position or *manṣab* (here used in a non-technical sense) for which Mufid has hankered for so long, and which he saw as status and power (*daulat-o-jāh*) was in fact thoroughly condemnable. The friend notes that many people had had such status in the past, but in reality had been unable to spend a single night in peace. Instead, from morning to evening, they were with evasive collectors (*muḥaṣṣils*) and allowance-holders (*waẓīfa k͟hwār*) who pester them. Their liver's blood (*k͟hūn-i jigar*) was consumed in this, and some even died, while others ran away in despair. The friend tells him that even if it does not come to such a pass with Mufid, life will simply become unliveable. He also notes that he is sure that the ill-fated Mufid will not listen to his advice, as he is by now too possessed by the desire for wealth and power. Mufid is now like a sick man who eats, knowing full well it will harm him, and stupidly disregarding the advice of his well-intentioned physician.

When Mufid heard this, he declares that he thought for a while, and then replied that he accepted that this advice was really given out of

[18] Muhammad Mufid Mustaufi Yazdi, *Jāmi'-i Mufīdī*, vol. III, pp. 743–5.

affection. He had not taken up the job in Yazd for profit, power or wealth; rather, it was a way of serving his friends, and the poor and destitute, and thus to accumulate virtue for the life hereafter. Even a small time spent in good works is likely to be remembered for a long time, and this persistent memory is itself like having a long life, he declared piously. Those who accumulate wealth, even if they live for a long time, are not remembered. He cites a verse from Sa'di in support of this, the famous line that says:

> O Sa'di! A man of good name never dies.
> Dead is the one whose name is taken by no good man.

The friend smiled on hearing this, and responded that he should nevertheless not put himself into this situation. Mufid's argument, he declared, was like eating poison just because one had the antidote. Even if Mufid really feared the company of evil people, and preferred to frequent the virtuous, in the world of *waqf*, even those who appeared virtuous would turn out to be like snakes, concealing their real nature. On the other hand, being with the really virtuous was like sitting in a perfumer's shop, which gives you a good odour one way or the other. He thus reiterated his feeling that Mufid was in his heart of hearts being greedy, and more or less accused him of wanting to consume the goods of the *waqf*. The friend thus ironically cited Hafiz:

> Yesterday, an intoxicated jurist (*faqīh*) of the *madrasa*,
> Gave a *fatwa* [stating]:
> Verily, wine is forbidden but
> it's better than [embezzling] the wealth of a charity (*māl-i auqāf*).

The friend predicted that later Mufid would try to get out of the post, but by that time he would be unable to do so. The wise man is the one who, before he goes into a place, sees where the points of exit are, and Mufid simply did not fall into this category. Some lines are cited.

> Do not step in unless your foothold is firm;
> in every work that you undertake,
> first prepare the window to come out.

After this initial discussion and much subsequent reflection, Mufid decided nevertheless to take up the post at Yazd and reproduces the appointment letter at some length in his text as an example of official prose; it is dated Zi-Qa'da 1077 (April–May 1667).[19]

[19] This document appears in Muhammad Mufid Mustaufi Yazdi, *Jāmi'-i Mufīdī*, vol. III, pp. 752–4.

From the outset of the text then, it thus appears that Mufid is a rather melancholic and self-critical type. For him, Destiny determines everything, and even in the good times there are dark clouds on the horizon. The day carries with it the seed of night, and the world is bound even in the best of times to bring humiliation. An expression he is fond of runs:

> Dar jām-i rūzgār may-i khushgawār nīst.
> (In the goblet of the age, there is no pleasant wine to be had).

The world for him is in his own words much like an old crone, who disguises herself as a young bride, and seduces people thus. Whoever decides to enter into wedlock with her, finds that his hand is unable to touch her; the bridegroom who is caught up in that tie of union, finds that his passion is exhausted already by the early hours of the night. Since the transient world, though apparently like a beautiful young woman, is not really fit for marriage, the wise man, who has the kohl of knowledge in his eye, therefore avoids it and pays no attention to this meaningless play of status. Knowing that the goods of the world are spurious, he looks instead to eternal wealth. "One should take no pride therefore in the things of this transient world", is his noble sentiment; and even while living in this world, you should keep your foot firm on the path of justice, and not waver from meeting the needs of the indigent. A verse is inevitably cited:

> Meet the needs of the dervishes and others,
> that your own needs may be met in turn.
> The turning of the world (*inqilāb-i adwār*)
> and the strife of the times should not trouble you overly.

Here too, Mufid, in his conventional and somewhat clichéd way, cites in his support the wise men and great ones of previous times, without mentioning them by name. He adds, that all this is well illustrated by the way in which his own life was later disrupted. Thus, after having spent a few days in a calm, stable and comfortable life, the dust of misfortune and toil again settled on his cheek. In Yazd, he enters the service and entourage of Allah Quli Beg (nephew of the great noble Kalb-i 'Ali Khan), who is *wazīr* of Yazd, *kukiraq* ("representative") of the *khāṣṣa-sharīfa* ("treasury"), and *mutaṣaddī* ("administrator") of the *khāliṣa* ("royal lands"), besides being the superintendent (*nāẓir*) of all the *waqfs*, and becomes his deputy (*nā'ib*). Allah Quli is also the governor (*ḥākim*) with jurisdiction over the Muslims and the Zoroastrians (*majūsiyān*). Soon enough, Mufid gets much power, and becomes the veritable right-hand man of Allah Quli. He admits that, in this process, he disregards the needy and poor, and becomes arrogant and stupid: "The curtain of oblivion (*ghaflat*) fell over my mind, and the light of my intellect entered the veil of ignorance." He keeps rising higher and higher in the hierarchy, but is clear that he is riding for a fall, as he even ceases to thank God for his good fortune. The fact that princes, nobles and *ṣadrs* would come to him to have their matters settled fills him with hubris of precisely the kind that his friend had warned him about.

This sort of life went on for some time, until Mufid became a victim of what he terms the jealousy of the Age, and the "carpet of his comfort" started to be rolled up. The world is not kind even to its own, he writes; after all, fire does not spare even the Fire-Worshipper. Not for nothing has the Divine painter written, "Everything will be ruined, except His Name" (Qur'an). So it happens that on a certain Friday, 9 Zi-Hijja 1079 H (10 May 1669, or the day of 'Arafat, in the *ḥajj* calendar used by him, suggesting that Mufid is a *ḥājī*), the *wazīr* Allah Quli Beg suddenly dies. Mufid's fortunes that had at first risen now start to decline. He rapidly understood in these changed circumstances that the goods, wealth and other things of this world were in reality rather unreliable.

When news of this death was reported to Shah Sulaiman, in consideration of the dead man's service he bestowed favours on his family members. The Shah split the governorship up, giving the charge of the Fire-Worshippers of Yazd (an important position) to a certain Muhammad Khalil Beg, Allah Quli's son, while Mufid himself became *nāẓir* in charge of the *waqf* endowments of the area. The two were even honoured with good *khil'ats* ("robes of honour"), in keeping with their positions, by the court; we note that another royal order is reproduced verbatim in this context in the account, this one dated Jumada I 1080 H (September–October 1669).[20] The order stated that, since the care of the shrines, sacred places and mosques of the region was important, and the revenues should be administered and disposed of in keeping with the *sharī'a*, hence it had been decided to give the post over to Mirza Muhammad Mufid. This post was formerly held by Allah Quli Beg, and Mufid was to hold this post in addition to the position of *mustaufī* of Yazd. He should apply himself to the post, take care of the expansion of agriculture (*zarā'at*), should take care that the returns on the *ijārat* ("revenue-farms") went up, and should ensure that there was no failing in any matters relating to the offices he exercised. The order addressed the Sayyids of the area, the

[20] Muhammad Mufid Mustaufi Yazdi, *Jāmi'-i Mufīdī*, vol. III, pp. 759–60.

notables, and all residents of Yazd in general: it was to be known to all of them that Muhammad Mufid would hold this post solely, and not share it with anyone else. The others who worked in the *waqf*, as well as the revenue-farmers (*mustā'jirs*) and other fiscal officials (*mustaufīs*) of the *sarkār*, should not take a single *dīnār* or a single *minbar* without his permission or through his agents. The *nāẓir*'s seal should be used for all purposes. As for Mufid, he should engage in all matters of collection and disbursement such that nothing should be taken out of the proceeds (*māl*) of the *waqf*, nor should he take more than his due. People should be content with his administration and pray for the ruler. Both the *sharī'a* and customary practices (*'urf*) should be followed. Orders to this effect would not be issued each year, and the order was to be treated as lasting.

When Mufid had received this post, he declared that he set himself to the task with full devotion. However, he evinced discomfort in this situation, and claimed that he was anxious day and night. He enjoyed neither money nor happiness, and, like the proverbial *kāfir* dervish, he had neither religion (*dīn*) nor worldly benefits (*duniyā*). That is to say, he seemed not to make enough money for his own satisfaction, for, if he made money through defalcation, he knew he risked his worthiness for the afterlife. He thus cites a Qur'anic verse: "You have lost both this life and the life hereafter." He also mentions the disastrous death around the same time of a boy, his own young son. All of a sudden, he writes, the skirt of his life was destroyed by the hammer of the Destroyer as this boy, the coolness of his eye, thus was snatched away from him. Alas, this seedling of a flowering plant was broken by the sharp autumn wind! As a result, he became increasingly disturbed and dissatisfied, and told himself that his life was a failure. What use was the position that he had, where he felt isolated and backed into a corner? Why not listen instead to the saying of the wise, to the effect that travel brings fullness? It was in these circumstances then that Mufid conceived the desire to travel. Just as the moon, by travelling, moves over fourteen nights from the crescent sliver (*manzil-i hilāl*) to the Full Moon (*manzil-i badr*), so too would he develop. Similarly, in chess, the pawn (*piyāda*) by moving six places becomes a queen (*farzīnī*), and that could be his fate as well.

> By travelling, the Shah becomes a veritable Kaykhusrau.
> Without travel, even the moon cannot become regal (*khusrau*).[21]

[21] Muhammad Mufid Mustaufi Yazdi, *Jāmi'-i Mufīdī*, vol. III, p. 762.

If a man stays in a corner of his house, Mufid ruminated, and refuses to stir from his homeland (*waṭan*), he is deprived of seeing the wonders of countries, and is also deprived of the affection of different peoples.

> Be like a royal eagle and soar,
> How long will you remain seated
> like an owl behind a wall?

Never one to take half measures, Mufid now hammers this point home. He declares that it is reported by wise people that, unless the sword leaves the scabbard and is used in the battlefield of the brave, it gains no honour. Or again, unless the pen steps out, the images of beautiful writing do not decorate the page of existence. Indeed, the sky itself turns and travels and is as a consequence elevated, while the earth is stationary and subject to the kicks of everyone, big and small.

> Look up from the earth to the sky,
> where the one remains unmoving,
> and where the other reaches having moved.
> Travel is the patron of man,
> it is the court where status is gained;
> travel is treasure, and the master of skill.
> If a tree were able to move,
> it would not be the victim of the saw and the axe.

At this stage, another wise friend appears of a sudden in the text, whom Mufid decides to consult in what appears to be another literary device, to permit argumentation by dialogue. This friend has allegedly seen the world, but he is adamantly against the idea of travel; he knows lands both east and west, and had traversed both the seas in his thoughts, and the landlocked territories with his physical efforts.

> He had travelled the land and sea
> for years together.
> He knew the conditions
> to be found everywhere.

After reflecting a while, the friend brought out the following pearls of wisdom. Do not exchange the dignity of residence (*'azz-i iqāmat*) for the humiliation of exile (*z̲ull-i g̲h̲urbat*), he advised. Travelling simply brings problems, exile and nuisances; it is better not to step out of home without a good reason. Nor – speaking more metaphorically – should one give up cash in hand against the uncertain future of lending. Besides, he thinks that Mufid is too soft and delicate to bear the travails of the voyage, for the hot winds of travel will affect his sensitive disposition. The friend hence cites an appropriate counter-verse.

> Travel (*safar*) is like a tree,
> whose sole fruit is separation from friends.
> Exile (*ghurbat*) is a cloud that sheds
> only drops of humiliation.

Mufid for his part puts up his own arguments: he mentions the wonders of the world, and his desire to be acquainted with them; he states that seeing new cities also gives great pleasure. The pluses and minuses of travelling are discussed at some length in the abstract, and the ambiguous sense of the term *ghurbat* is insisted on. The thorn that pricks in exile eventually also produces the flower of desire, says Mufid, by way of conclusion. The friend replies that parting from friends and those who love you is too profound a form of sorrow, and really cannot be compensated.

> Separation from friends is like a sign of hell.
> God save me from error! In fact hell is a sign
> of separation from friends.

He also tells Mufid he should be content with all that he has, whether in terms of status, position or comfort. He too (like the earlier friend) rather suspects him of hankering after money, and charges that this is his real reason for travelling. Rest content with what you have in Yazd, he says.

> Seize the skirt of peace and tranquillity,
> for the age has the stone of separation in hand.

Mufid now replies in firm terms, asking the other not to preach to him any more. More metaphors and similes are trotted out. It is in the fire of such experience as travel that a man becomes cooked. Only a mature man can run the horse of hope in the field of desire. Besides, the man who travels becomes popular, and is the cynosure of all eyes, not the least desirable thing in the world.

> Nothing is purer than water,
> yet if it stagnates, it becomes dirty.

The friend makes a sour face at this, and cites another response-verse to the effect that many people set aside the advice of well-meaning friends and instead fall into the traps of their enemies. The other friend now takes a different tack, and suggests the importance of *qanāʿat* ("contentment"), rather than greed.

Contentment makes you rich:
give this news to the greedy world-traveller.
Those who were not content with their livelihood,
or what was destined for them
do not recognize the Divine,
or perform [real] prayer.

Yet, says Mufid at the end of this long discussion, the humble writer (namely, himself) was so possessed with the *saudā-i safar-i Hind*, the "mad desire to travel to India", that he just did not recognise the worth of this advice (*naṣīḥat*). Mufid and his friend part ways; the argument is deemed inconclusive. Mufid now goes back to his usual work as an administrator, but he is restive. One day, however, an invisible voice (*hātif-i g͟haibī*) once more shook his routine. He then recalls an earlier time in Isfahan when he had been melancholy and, eventually, as dusk came and the sun went down, he had fallen asleep. In his dream, he saw a Sufi "of illumined forehead" with a book in his hand. Mufid asked what the book was, and the other replied: "Don't you want to engage in divination (*istik͟hārat*) through the use of *fāl* ["the science of signs"]?" Mufid responded in the afiirmative. "You want to go to Hindustan, don't you?" asked the Sufi. Yes, replied Mufid again. At this, the Sufi opened the volume, and on the right side of the book revealed a verse suggesting that, like someone else he knew (whose name is not mentioned), Mufid too should go to India and gain wealth and status.[22] He now recalls that he had set that advice aside at the time. The Sufi in the vision had unambiguously advised him to travel to attain his goal, for God himself has said "Set out, in his boats" (Qur'an). He had handed Mufid over to the care of God, he stated, citing an appropriate Qur'anic verse.

The dream, which had not had an immediate effect, did have one with the passage of time. Now, as a result of recollecting this dream, Mufid began at last to make concrete preparations to go to India (literally, "the auspicious journey to Hind", *safar-i k͟hair aṣ̤ar-i Hind*). The same friend of the earlier discussion, on hearing that Mufid was leaving for India, came weeping to him, and declared his distinct unhappiness at his intention. Had it never occurred to Mufid that travel was an ocean that devoured the human being? It was a python (*azhdahā*) which carried men off.

[22] Dreams have a particular place in Mufid's text; for a very useful comparison of dreams recounted by a woman in an early eighteenth-century Balkan town to her spiritual preceptor, see Asiye Hatun, *Rüya Mektuplari*, ed. and intro. Cemal Kafadar (Istanbul, 1994).

Saqar-i īn jahan hamīn safar ast
Zīn sabab sūrat-i safar saqar ast.
(Hell in this world is the same as travel.
That is why *safar* (سفر) looks like *saqar* (سقر) in writing.)[23]

The difference between the two words was of but one *nuqta*, a single point, of course. The friend then continued that people often undertook travel either to arrange their means of livelihood, or because they could not stay on in their own hometowns. God's grace had created a situation such that Mufid was subject to neither pressure. Rather, he had a relaxed corner in the world, and several positions (*chand manṣab*) to boot, that kept him engaged, and gave him respectability. On account of his good behaviour, people in the area were grateful to him, and sought his company. Why then undertake travel, and give up the peace of residing in one place (*iqāmat*)? Mufid replied (and we are back in the form of a dialogue) that no doubt all his friend had said was motivated by his affection. However, the more he thought the matter over, the clearer it was to him that his offices in Yazd were not worthy of his dignity and status. Many other things passed through his heart, he said, for which his words were inadequate.

In a small pond, only small fish can be found.
Far better the shark (*nihang*) that fights in the ocean.

He thus had decided that, within two or three days, he would start a journey. Perhaps the blessing of movement would remove the dust of worry from the page of his heart, and having seen the cities and kingdoms of the world, his heart might then at last become content. More verses were cited to prove this point. When his friend heard all this, he became thoughtful for a while. He measured the explanation on the touchstone of his understanding, but said: "The difference between us is that I am in a position (*maqām*) of contentment (*qanā'at*) and you are still in the stage (*martaba*) of greed (*ḥirṣ*)." Here, the trope being deployed was that of the journey in Sufism. The greedy, he declared, always have a sense of deprivation, whereas the truth was that, without inner contentment, no one could achieve peace. He advised Mufid that he would eventually repent of his decision, but by that time it would really be of no use. He also cited verses to the effect that even the legendary Korah (Qarun) did not know that the treasure of contentment was to be found in one corner.

[23] Muhammad Mufid Mustaufi Yazdi, *Jāmi'-i Mufīdī*, vol. III, p. 766.

"Never let the Evil-Seeking Soul (*nafs-i 'ammāra*) grasp you in its inordinate appetite", he declared, and also accused Mufid of arrogance, and an unwarranted fascination with high positions in this world. He had always known this, said the friend reproachfully, but had held his tongue thus far; now he felt obliged to come out with it. It was really too much to enter the desert of misguidedness and the field of deception on account of such low qualities. This in spite of the verse that stated:

> Whoever you tell the truth to,
> then becomes your enemy.
> Silence is best of all,
> since truth should not be told frankly.

So, he continued, for once Mufid should think for himself, and not make haste. As a compromise solution, he even suggested that Mufid should go to the court (*urdū-i mu'allā*) at Isfahan, to see if he could make money there. Only if that failed should he try something as desperate as a journey to India. Since Mufid found this last advice in keeping with his own inclinations, he put his faith in God, and on the night of 17 Rajab 1081 H (30 November 1670), he left Yazd for the capital city.[24] When he arrived there, he met a number of important notables and courtiers, and having given them appropriate gifts and offered them hospitality, managed to send his request (*'arīẓa*) and *peshkash* ("tribute") as far as the Shah himself. However, this proved to be of no avail, and his trip turned out to be a letdown. Destiny (*taqdīr*, and also *qaẓā'*), he writes, was against him at the time, or so it seems. For it had been already inscribed that this dizzy wanderer (*sargashta*) in the valley of bewilderment would be trapped in the cities of exile. So, no proper post was offered to him in Isfahan, and, further, since the Divine Order had already descended to the lower, or earthly, levels, the eye of Mufid's intellect had already dimmed. So he refused to pay attention to the advice of his friends. Can anyone twist the fist of Destiny, he asks rhetorically? So, like those fools who worship images in the air, Mufid rode atop the horse of greed and desire and set out to fulfil his desires. And, thus at last, Hindustan it was.

> One should voyage measuring distances
> by the desire to fulfil greed.

[24] Muhammad Mufid Mustaufi Yazdi, *Jāmi'-i Mufīdī*, vol. III, p. 769.

THE GRUMBLER TRAVELS

The reader whose patience has been somewhat tried this far by Mufid's endless tergiversations may grant us some indulgence, for the part that really concerns travel in a concrete form is about to begin. So far we have been in the realm of moral reflection, and in the construction of a meta-text about travel as an idea, rather than a description of travel itself. Mufid now does leave at length for Hindustan. Passing through unfamiliar stations and stages, the negligent (*gh̲āfil*) Mufid eventually arrived at his first way-station from Isfahan, namely Dih-i 'Ali Wargan, where it suddenly began raining and snowing quite heavily. It seemed that Judgement Day had come, so strong were the winds. There was no place for him to take shelter, and as the weather got worse and worse, he quoted a verse from Hafiz.

> There were terrifying sounds from the clouds,
> and torrential rain,
> But who cared amongst those,
> inebriated in their feasts?

The voyage had begun badly, it seems, with inauspicious portents. Two days and nights passed in this way, and on the third day, the weather cleared. So, once more Mufid climbed on what he terms the "horse of ignorance and vainglory" and set out. This time, he gets to the edge of a river, which was one *manzil* from Hazbahan, and decides to rest there. Mufid is not particularly concerned, it may be noted, to provide the reader details of the composition of his party, or what is around him; natural descriptions do not much interest him. However, his own fate certainly does. So we learn that, here, his party was attacked at night by a group of robbers, and though Mufid was tired, he could not sleep through the episode. There was quite a commotion around, and Mufid himself took his gun (*tufang-i ātish*) and, with his friends, engaged the robbers. God saved him from that trouble, only to put him in worse trouble still, he remarks. Only later in the night was he able to rest a little. The party advanced a little bit and made camp at a place called Tang-i Siya. Here, Mufid was able to lie down and fell into a very deep sleep. While he was sleeping, a lion fierce enough to frighten the constellation Leo approached the party. Indeed, were this lion to seize Taurus, he would be unable to breathe beneath his paws. The others in the party fled, and the lion came up to where Mufid was sleeping. He stopped for a while, and then clawed the ground. When he saw that Mufid, who was sound asleep, was really the dog (*kalb*) of Asadullah al-Ghalib (that is Imam ʻAli), he turned and left for the jungle. After the lion had left, Mufid awoke, and his friends told him what had transpired; Mufid, as a good Shiʻi, naturally saw a sign in this. They then moved on, and on 6 Ramazan, reached the *manzil* of Jaweza with the intention of spending the entire fasting month of Ramazan there. The governor of the place, who had heard of Mufid, came to meet him. Soon enough, a disagreement seems to have occurred, and Mufid thought it was better to avoid spending too much time with him, and so, on 15 Ramazan, thought of going on to Basra. The way to Basra was full of difficulties that are briefly noted, and he eventually arrived at that port on 20 Ramazan (31 January 1671).

A chapter now follows entitled: "Description of Prostration [*mizhgān-i ikẖlāṣ*, literally "Brushing with the Eyelashes"] at Sacred Shrines and Hospices, and mention of some of the events that took place during these auspicious visits. The return to Basra to set out for Hindustan according to what had been destined". This chapter commences as follows, with the usual moral reflections that we have come to expect from Mufid.

> It is evident that any slave of Allah who travels in order to please Him, and thus prefers the bitterness of separation from the homeland to the sweetness of communion with friends, and prefers the dangers and terrors of travel to security, will receive returns in this life and the hereafter.
>
> The sincere one who treads this path
> At last obtains success.

In order to illustrate this, Mufid speaks of how he wished to have a chance to visit the shrine of ʻAli ibn Abi Talib, to circumambulate the shrine, and thus meet his heart's desire. Only then could the voyage be counted a true success. This visit was begun on 10 Shawwal 1081 H (or 20 February 1671), having tied the appropriate "headdress of resolution", and verses follow in the text in praise of the pilgrimage. Mufid embarked in a boat at Basra, and after eighteen days' voyage (probably upriver) disembarked on the plain. The party then crossed a distance of four leagues (*farsakẖ*) to reach Najaf-i Ashraf. At this time, a divine voice spoke a *qaṣīda* into his ear on the subject of Najaf, which Mufid reproduces at some length. Najaf is an ocean of munificence, he writes, a mine of sincerity and grace, comparable only to the Garden of Paradise. This enthusiastic description is set down even before visiting the shrine itself, in happy anticipation. Thereafter, having made the pilgrimage there, Mufid went on to the Masjid-i Kufa. Here, he met the holy Shaikh Muhammad ibn ʻAbd-i ʻAli al-Najafi al-Mahawili, a great *ʻālim* who inspired a series of praises and verses from Mufid. A curious incident now took place. The Shaikh told him that every Wednesday night, the Imam Mahdi himself graced the Sahla mosque (in Kufa itself) with his footsteps, thus making the mosque like heaven on earth. Mufid then told the Shaikh's attendants that he too wished to visit the mosque. They agreed to the request, and so one day a group of pious and learned people went there on the evening of Wednesday, 20 Zi-Qa'da, to pray at the mosque. That night, a strange thing happened, and the great *'ālim* with whom he went, wrote the matter down in his own hand.

Mufid then quotes from an Arabic text written by the Shaikh, where he describes the experience of going there with Mufid. This account may be summarised as follows:

> In the year 1081, on the night of 20 Zi-Qa'da, Wednesday [1 April 1671], we left for the Sahla mosque with a group of pious believers, and with us was also Mirza Muhammad Mufid, son of Mirza Mahmud. We reached the spot and camped there. When the night had advanced a little, we dozed off for a while (Praise be to God who never sleeps!) What did we see? We saw a vision in which we were spread out near the mosque, towards the eastern corner that is called Maqam-i Khizr. It seemed we were looking for something. I found myself [i.e. the Shaikh] closest to the door of the mosque, when I saw a tall and imposing man, with a broad face of sallow complexion, with a mixed grey and black beard who was approaching the mosque. I wondered whether this was the man who I was looking for. The man was looking at the ground, but when he came close he called me by name and said, "When you need something, and really desire it, you and those with you should read the following incantation (*du'ā*) that starts in this way: You are the sole God and there is no other than you. You have begun Creation, and to you all Creation shall return." He then entered the mosque and reached its middle. He then stood in the altar (*miḥrāb*) of Ja'far-i Sadiq, where he read the prayer (*namāz*). I then turned towards my own people and told them what had happened, of how in a state of half-wakefulness and half-sleep I had seen this man who had given me such a benediction. I also told all of them of the benediction and said that they should all use the incantation. I would pray to God that He should grant each of those who reads it that which he desires.[25]

Mufid now reproduces the whole of the *du'ā* to the following effect: "O God we seek support from You who are the originator of all Creation, and to you all Creation returns. There is no God but you. You command and control. You are the sole God and there is none other than you. You organise and arrange affairs of the world, and You will raise the dead on Judgement Day." There then follows the *darūd* in praise of Muhammad,

[25] Muhammad Mufid Mustaufi Yazdi, *Jāmi'-i Mufīdī*, vol. III, pp. 774–6.

and then the praise for the Prophet's family. Interspersed are passages asking for God's help in fulfilling the seeker's demands. All those in the party were very content with this mystical experience, having a proper sense of fulfilment. The party then returned to Kufa. Some days later, Mufid went again to the tomb of Hazrat 'Ali, and asked him (in the form of a *du'ā*) again for his aid in fulfilling his purpose. Then, he returned to Baghdad where he visited the shrines of Imam Musa Kazim and Imam Muhammad Taqi al-Jawwad, and then went on from there on an overnight trip to Sarman Rai, where there were the shrines of Imam Mu'ayyad Abu'l Hasan 'Ali al-Hadi, and of Imam Hasan al-Zaki al-'Askari. The party then took a boat on the Tigris (Dajla) and returned by the river from Baghdad to Basra. This voyage took a day (whereas the upriver voyage seems to have taken all of eighteen days!). No ship was leaving for India at the time, and so Mufid was obliged to camp in Basra. Verses follow on his plight at this time, his worries concerning his fortune and other matters. Mufid was thus obliged to remain in Basra for several months, at a time when it was extremely hot (the parallels with the account of 'Abdul Razzaq Samarqandi are quite striking here). It was hard to put one's feet on the ground, and if wax were put on the ground, it would melt.

> The heat made the breath so hot,
> that lips were burning like a candle-flame.
> It seemed from the hot wind
> that a second hell had appeared.

While Muhamad Mufid was in Basra, he met Maulana Hasan 'Ali, son of Maulana Muhammad Salih Mazandarani, and maternal grandson of Maulana Muhamad Taqi Majlisi, who had made significant contributions to the development of Imamiya school in Iran. In the context of this meeting with Hasan 'Ali in Basra, Mufid thinks it appropriate to tell his readers how this great scholar was trapped in a disaster and was saved by Allah on his way back from a visit to India. Mufid mentions that Hasan 'Ali, like his father and maternal grandfather, was also a great scholar, and had earned fame when he was still young; he was extraordinarily cultured, and attracted to him many noted scholars of his time. After Hasan 'Ali returned to his homeland, having performed the *ḥajj* and paid visits to the holy shrines, he intended in 1078 H (1667–8) to visit Hindustan. He hence urged his father to give him permission for the purpose, and left, his destination being the Sultanates of the Deccan. When he arrived in Hyderabad, he was welcomed by Niknam Khan, one of the important nobles of the time, and also by the Sultan 'Abdullah Qutb Shah.[26] Later Hasan 'Ali left for Delhi, where again he was received warmly by the nobles resident there at the Mughal court. Mufid then gives the details of Hasan 'Ali's return to Iran but prefers to write about it in the words of Hasan 'Ali himself. Hasan 'Ali had given these details, including the incidents of a shipwreck and his amazing escape from the disaster, in a letter that he had written to his father, and Mufid quotes directly from this letter.[27]

The letter begins with two verses making a plea to the author's friends to give ear to the details of his predicament, and then runs as follows: in the middle of Sha'ban 1081 H (late December 1670), he had decided to return to Iran, and left for Surat three days before the month of Ramazan, arriving at that port in the month of Zi-Qa'da. He found not many traders there in the port city, and those who were there were all terrified by the threat of the Maratha warlord Shivaji.[28] The journey to Surat had also not been comfortable, again from fear of the same Shivaji. The merchants thus decided to take an ill-starred ship and the journey began on an inauspicious day, 5 Zi-Qa'da. On 27 Zi-Qa'da, having covered twenty-two sea-stations (*marāḥil-i baḥr*), they arrived in Qubba, in the exact middle of the sea. There, Hasan 'Ali mentions, they retired into a portion of the ship where a musical party was being held, with Persian poems sung in Indian *rāgas* – namely, Sarang (*āhang-i Sārang*), Ramkali (*nawā-i Rām Kalī*), Maqam-i Kalyan, and Maqam-i Karaj. While they were busy in the musical party, they heard people shouting that the ship had caught fire. In the hold of the ship, Hasan 'Ali mentions, the fire was already surging and all efforts to extinguish it had failed. The entire ship was burning, and the different flaming storeys of the vessel looked like the levels of hell itself. In the meanwhile, 80 of the armed guards of the ship retreated to the small boat (*sambak*) behind the ship's cuddy (*dabūsa*), and asked the passengers to come and collect there. Some 10 or 20 of the passengers were burnt alive in the process, while, of about 120 merchants and slaves, 30 or 40 were drowned. About 150 people managed to huddle into the small boat, where they spent a whole day and a night in anxiety. The following morning, the *firangī* captain (for the ship was under the command of the Europeans) suggested that, unless

[26] On Raza Quli Beg, titled Niknam Khan (d. 1672), see H. K. Sherwani, *History of the Quṭb Shāhī Dynasty* (New Delhi, 1974), esp. pp. 459–62.

[27] Muhammad Mufid Mustaufi Yazdi, *Jāmi'-i Mufidī*, vol. III, pp. 804–10.

[28] On Shivaji's attacks on Surat, see M. N. Pearson, "Shivaji and the decline of the Mughal empire", *Journal of Asian Studies*, 35, 2, 1976, pp. 221–35, particularly pp. 227–8.

some of the people left the *sambak*, it could not move. Twenty Mughals were therefore thrown into the sea, and the crew were still intending to throw some more out when Hasan 'Ali and the others pleaded with the captain to spare them. The group had lost all hope of life, and were busy in praying, when suddenly they saw a ship approaching, in the early afternoon. By late afternoon, they were all able to board this ship, where they were helped generously by Amir Nizamuddin Ahmad Jahanshahi, son-in-law of the late Haji Zahid Beg. They spent fifteen days on this ship, and eventually reached Quryat in the neighbourhood of Masqat. Making their way in boats to Masqat, they arranged the necessary provisions there, and after four days, on 17 Muharram, left for the port of Kung which they reached ten days later. To conclude, Hasan 'Ali appropriately gives the chronogram of the shipwreck as *jahāz sok͟ht* ("the ship burnt").[29]

This pessimistic view of the voyage between the Persian Gulf and India cannot have been calculated to lift Mufid's sagging spirits. His state began to deteriorate and he at once fell prey to a number of illnesses, also simply on account of his anxiety. He recalls that, at this time, he used to weep all night from sheer weakness. At long last, the season for the voyage came, and having no other option, he decided to set out from Basra on 1 Rajab 1082 H (3 November 1671, some seven months after his arrival), despite the fact that he was still rather ill. The voyage was made in a very large ship that dwarfed all others. This ship too was like a huge hell, and seemed to be a coffin full of 1,000 bodies to our author's morbid imagination. Mufid had a fever and he was also extremely fatigued, and the travel at first did not help at all. Even his verses at this time are full of gloom and unhappiness. One of them runs:

> There was nothing to drink but blood,
> nothing but sorrow was there in that time.

He is full of self-pity for the poor Mufid, on the plant of whose hope no fruit had yet grown before the stem itself began to wither. It began to appear that the lamp of his life would go out at that time, before he ever reached India.

> Not a drop reached my lips
> from the goblet of joy.
> The hand of tyranny threw the cup
> of hope at my head.

[29] Fires in ships in the western Indian Ocean do not seem to have been uncommon. For another example, see Subrahmanyam, "Persians, Pilgrims and Portuguese", p. 515.

However, at long last, as the Qur'an promised, his prayers were indeed answered. The arrow of his prayers reached their target, for whoever has a pure heart is bound to reach God. Hope for life slowly began to return to him, for, as the Qur'an says, "He who is visited by illness, also receives the cure." This was not quite the end of his troubles. The ship now entered troubled waters and a storm arose. Once again, he had to pray for deliverance, which was granted to him once more. Now, at last, it appeared that the voyage would be smooth, so that, at length, after covering a long distance, on 1 Ramazan, the brilliant ruby-red sun peered out from a corner of the mountains of Sarandip (here it is not literally Sri Lanka that is meant). Colourful diamonds were spread over the entire world, or so it seemed. So it was that they dropped anchor at the Bandar-i Mubarak Surat. What a moment of joy this was after such a miserable voyage!

This is also the occasion for Mufid to begin a new chapter in his account: "Description of the stay at the port of Surat, and of the departure from there to Shahjahanabad, and the return from there, with nothing being achieved".[30] The chapter starts with a reflection concerning the distinction between appearance and reality. It is within God's power that things that appear pleasant in fact conceal something that turns out to be the contrary, whereas things that appear displeasing at first may turn out to be fruitful. A hemistich to this effect follows, then a passage that continues the explanation. Often, that which appears to be success may lead to misfortune and lack of hope. This is what the pages that follow demonstrate, writes Mufid.

At first (presumably in Yazd), he had spent some days in wealth and comfort. Then, on account of his greed, he had become trapped in the vast stretch of exile and failure. The choice before him was between Dar-ul-Khilafat Shahjahanabad or Dar-ul-Khuld Hyderabad, between the Mughals and the Qutb Shahis. So, he went through his usual techniques of divination (*istikhāra*), for, as the verse said, one should take advice, since without advice no work can be successful. He used the Qur'an for the prediction (*fāl*), which suggested that he should go to paradise-like Hyderabad (*bihisht-buniyād*). Since the eye of his understanding was dimmed, and since the grace of Allah had not cast its shadow on his heart, Mufid's hand simply could not attain the rope of God; the flag of his intention was such that the Satan of his Evil-Seeking Spirit (*nafs-i*

30 Muhammad Mufid Mustaufi Yazdi, *Jāmi'-i Mufidī*, vol. III, p. 781.

'ammāra) brought all sorts of absurd and ill-conceived plans to his head. So, refusing the *fāl*, he thought to go instead to Shahjahanabad, and thus on 15 Zi-Hijja 1082 H (13 April 1672) he left Bandar-i Mubarak Surat. It was raining on the way, and the route was wooded and hard to use. Besides, it was extremely hot. Struggling with himself, at times drinking the wine of hope and at other times the bitter dregs, Mufid slowly made his way northwards. He had time to reflect now on the fact that he had heard that travel brought experience, and this was in fact the case on this voyage. This was to the extent that he decided that if God gave him the occasion to return to his home, he would never travel again. Unless it was highly necessary, he thought, he would simply never stir from his home, exchanging the rich sight of friends for the troubles of exile.

> Do not endure the travails of exile a second time,
> for in the sight of friends lies eternal bliss.

In any event, writes Mufid, it should be known that no one can resist Destiny. What else could one do but follow the Divine Order? Rather bitterly, he assures the reader that travel to India, and thinking of wealth and status, should be considered like a decorated snake full of poison. The snake's appearance is full of attractive patterns, but it contains such powerful and dangerous poisons that there is no antidote to it.

> All that colour is deceitful, all imposture, all fraud.

Mufid had for a time tasted the good things of life in Iran, but he felt that he was now tasting nothing but poisonous stings. The truth was that Death itself had brought him to that land, where he was destined to be miserable, having been chased out of his own *wilāyat*. Destiny had rudely thrown him into this country (i.e., Hind), and the matter was beyond his understanding. He was like a man who kept climbing up a mountain made of diamonds, out of greed, to the point of no return, so that he died on that very mountain. Greed is thus at the root of all misfortune, he states. It is all summed up in an appropriate verse:

> We traversed the desert and crossed several stages,
> but Fortune did not smile on us.
> Draining the cup of despair caused us to fall.

So he continues with his bitter reflections on the land of the Mughals, of which he had initially had such high hopes.

> In sum, on 4 Rabi' II 1083 [29 July 1672], I entered Shahjahanabad, and saw old Delhi (*kuhna Dehlī*) full of people of Hindu descent (*hindū nazhādān*) and of

dark nature. I found that in that misguided group, there was neither a grain of the capital of wisdom nor of manner of virtue. While their feet were on a misguided path, they at the same time extended their hands from the sleeve of impudence to commit daring acts.

> He who has no nobility (*sharaf*) in his birth,
> little wonder if he turns out to be depraved.

In sum, it was in this sort of town that I spent some time. I met a group of residents from this city. But as might have been expected, not one of them communicated the fragrance of humanity (*insāniyat-o-mardūmī*) to my nostrils. Instead, there was duplicity, jealousy which is characteristic of calculating people, with ill-feeling in their hearts. Inevitably, within a few days, my heart began to detest their company and there was no hope of friendship with them. As the wise have said: "Friends come to your rescue on the day of trouble. When you have wealth, even enemies act like friends." On this account, I kept myself away from them, and acted according to the following verse:

> Do not seek friendship among those
> whose help can open the knot of no difficulty.
> They can give you anything,
> but do not show the path to the treasure of hope.

At this time, one of the great *umarā'* whose clan had had relations of perfect love and unity with us for many years came to learn of our state. That *amīr* then invited me to meet him. [But] when I reached his salon (*majlis*), I found him as arrogant as the Pharaoh.[31]

This man, who remains unnamed, but who was certainly another Iranian migrant to the Mughal domains, used to make people wait for a long while to see him, and the supplicants were naturally unhappy with him. If someone was obliged to see his sour face, writes our author, they regretted having done so afterwards. When Mufid went to see him, he too was rather discourteously treated, as if the other thought he was too clever by half. Disregarding the advice of God and the Prophet, he treated people in this fashion, and Mufid felt that he had not really progressed from the stage of a beast (*ḥaiwān*) to that of a man (*insān*). Mufid then holds forth on what proper comportment really should be, in the style of a text of norms of comportment (*akhlāq*). The result was that he decided he could not stand this noble, and thought to himself in verse:

[31] Here we follow the text in Muhammad Mufid Mustaufi Yazdi, *Risāla-i Mufid*. A variant version appears in Muhammad Mufid Mustaufi Yazdi, *Jāmi'-i Mufīdī*, vol. III, p. 785.

Such a man with a sour face,
What point is there in addressing him?

To expect sincerity from this non-person (*nākas*) was like expecting fruit from a barren tree, or willow. It turned out that Mufid knew one other person in Shahjahanabad, who was generally praised by one and all for being good-natured, sincere and helpful. When he learnt of Mufid's situation, he came to visit him at his humble home (*ba maqām-i ḥaqīr*) and said:

O you who have been struggling for fortune!
Fortune and wealth is not got from competence.
He who has status, and rank, and position,
has it on account of the Sky's support.

Thus, he explained to Mufid that many a wise person had not had wealth for a single day, while as many incompetent and ignorant people were seated on the dais of leadership. Or, again in verse, royal treasures were given to the lowly, while the skilled struggled for their daily bread. We thus enter once more into the form of a stylised dialogue, where Mufid is being told how to reform his life, and how to profit from the experience he is being given, all this in prose mixed with a good deal of verse. Had Mufid not been greedy, when he had held a good position in his own homeland (*waṭan*) he would not have had to undergo such mental torture. It was on account of his own stupidity that he had neglected the love of his friends and chosen this path. Using a series of varied metaphors, the "friend" reiterates this idea several times. Now, Mufid responds and admits his own embarrassment, but, once more, the question of Destiny is raised by him, as if to excuse himself. The voyage has turned out to be a sort of punishment, as he reiterates once more in verses, but on the other hand, what is the use now of entering into these How-and-Why (*chūn-o-chirā*) questions? He has begun to repent, but of what use is that fact, for that matter? He also has to admit that all this is largely of his own doing, but declares that what he wants are practical responses. The friend hears him out, and laughs; he then advises him to be patient, and swallow his bitterness, as this will in itself produce a sweet outcome. The Elixir of Life is hard to get – the reference here being to Alexander and his quest for the Water of Life (*āb-i ḥayāt*) – and he requires patience to get it. Other wise people in the past have also advised this, even as they have counselled against hasty action. So, having pointed out once more that all this is the result of Mufid's carelessness, he tells him to go back to his own country (*wilāyat-i khwud*) with no hesitation. To live in one's own homeland (*dar waṭan*) gives one real pleasure, as does consorting with one's own friends; those who do not accept this advice wander around the world in vain and eventually their name disappears from the record as well. When he hears this, Mufid lets out a liver-burning (*jigar-soz*) sigh. He utters a verse:

> All our friends came to Hind
> on account of their destitution (*muflisī*).
> Should I take destitution
> back from Hind to Iran?

Rather, he thinks he should meet the Mughal emperor (*bādshāh-i banda nawāz*) in order to gain some wealth before leaving Hind. He has placed the ship of patience in the sea of sorrow, now he will either die or pull out a pearl from the waters. When the friend heard this, and found that no advice was of avail against this resolution, he tried to persuade Mufid to listen not to him but to the accumulated wisdom of elders. For the elders had said that, when a man loses his station (*maqām*) in life, he belongs to the world at large. The rich man searches for a *sarā'ī*, but the dervish takes any place for a resting spot, and this is what has come to be Mufid's fate. He also reminds him of his earlier idea of going southwards to Hyderabad and the Qutb Shahi domains. Were he to go there now, God, the Prophet and the innocent Imams might help him out of his present state. When Mufid heard this, he thought it was in accord with his own state of mind. So, once more, he took the Qur'an out for a *fāl*. The text that emerged was: "We wish to be munificent to those whom people on earth have mistreated, and make them leaders of the faith and owners of the land, as well as give them power and status on this earth." Mufid had read that when the Messiah of the Last Times, the *Mahdi-yi ākhir-i zamān*, was born, his father took him in his lap, and at this time the child read out this very verse of the Qur'an.[32] So he took it as a sign of his own imminent success. Though his hopes had been entirely torn to shreds, he declares, he once again built up his courage. A Divine Voice seemed to sound in his ear, telling him not to give up his efforts. He should instead leave this Wahshatabad ("Abode of Horrors") that was Delhi, and perhaps make an effort to meet the illustrious descendants (*aulād-i amjād*) of the most dignified (a long string of titles follows) Bahram Mirza, son of Shah Isma'il Musavi Safavi, who had settled in the Mughal domains. This was because his own ancestors had served that very family in the land of

[32] Muhammad Mufid Mustaufi Yazdi, *Jāmi'-i Mufīdī*, vol. III, pp. 793–4.

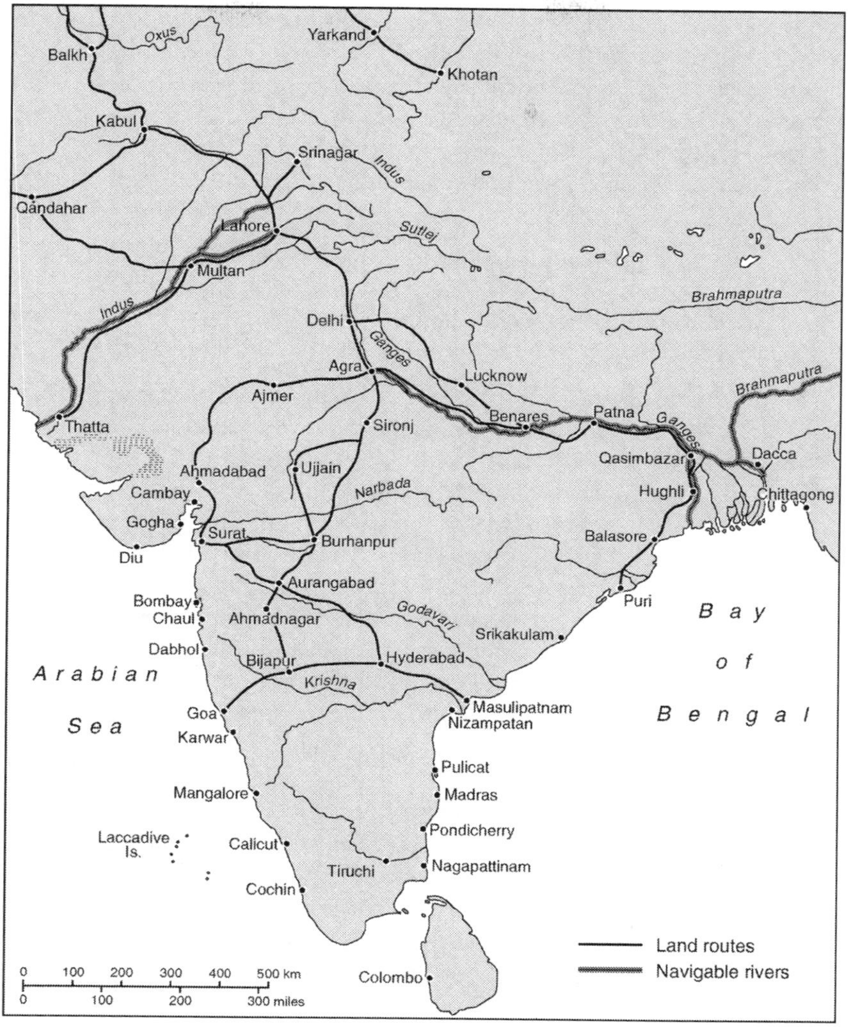

Map 3. Major trade routes in Mughal India.

Iran. When Mufid heard this voice, it was as if he had had a revelation. He told himself: "O silly one! Since your childhood, have you not always been faithful to this family? Why then have you not thought of serving this family, which is so worthy of devotion (*kh̲āndān-i kh̲idmat makān*), and thus accumulate wisdom and honour?" Thus, paradoxically, having come to Mughal India, Mufid thought that his best solution would be to use his Safavid connections once more.

However, quite characteristically, Mufid fell once more in doubt. So, he reflected and saw that though the descendants of Bahram Mirza were in good positions, yet their *jāgīrs* were at far-flung spots. They seemed difficult of access, and so he hesitated and wondered whether he should not go back instead to his homeland. He cites the famous lines of Hafiz:

> Why not go in the direction of friend and home?
> Why not place the dust of the beloved's alley on my forehead?
> The sorrow of exile cannot be borne by me.
> Let me return to my homeland and be my own emperor (*shahryār*).

With this in mind, and still riven by hesitation, on 26 Muharram 1084 H (13 May 1673), Mufid left Dar-us-Saltanat Shahjahanabad in a southward direction, and after passing through several stages reached the vicinity of Dar-ul-Fath Ujjain. One stage short of Ujjain, by pure chance (*az 'ittifāqāt-i ḥasana*) he encountered Mirza Sadr-ud-Din, one of the descendants of the Safavid prince Bahram Mirza.[33] This was a wonderful piece of luck! He first – and here we closely paraphrase Mufid's text – kissed the carpet of his greatness, received the honour of sitting in his heaven-like assembly, and was the recipient of his kindness and limitless gifts. Mufid was greatly impressed by the Safavid prince, full of knowledge and virtue, and quite unlike the other Iranian noble in Delhi; the adjectives and titles flow from his pen like water. When the Mirza learnt that the poor author belonged to a family that had served his own family, he too was content. He suggested that Mufid come to Sarangpur, where his place of residence was. After that, he could return in time to Iran. However, the next day when Mirza Sadr-ud-Din was getting ready to leave the place, Mufid was constrained to stay behind for a while for some unspecified reason. Since Divine Wisdom had already decided that he would pass some more days in misery, it turned out thereafter that no carter (*arbachī*) was willing to take him in the direction of Sarangpur. This obliged him to go to Ujjain, and from there he sent a letter of excuse to Mirza Sadr-ud-Din. The Mirza then sent a reply (*istimālat nāma*), admonishing him for his negligence. Since its prose was excellent, Mufid decided to reproduce it; this is also meant to demonstrate to the reader that he is indeed telling the truth. It is full of high formal addresses, flattering Mufid for his sincerity and

[33] These sections on Ujjain and Sarangpur are more extensive in the manuscript version than the printed text; see Muhammad Mufid Mustaufi Yazdi, *Risāla-i Mufīd*, pp. 148–67.

devotion, and expresses the Mirza's affection for Mufid. It notes further that he has received the petition (*'arīẓa*), and has realised that, on account of certain problems, Mufid could not visit him. Mufid had wished to do so, and raise his status to the skies, but Divine Intentions had been otherwise. Hence, Mufid had been obliged to go to Ujjain and thence to Burhanpur. Still, it would be wonderful if even now he could come to Sarangpur. Even if this were not so, he should rest assured that Sadr-ud-Din's affection accompanied him. The letter was drafted by a *munshī*, with a marginal notation by the Mirza adding that he had particularly desired to spend time with Mufid, but this was not to be, alas.

In order to account for this apparent closeness, Mufid explains that at the time that Bahram had been prince in Iran, he had been in charge of the region from Baghdad to Kashan.[34] This prince was noted for treating all with justice, whether citizens, *'ulamā'*, or whoever else. Maulana Nizam-ud-Din, Mufid's great-grandfather, had at this time approached the prince, and was accepted as one of his close companions. The prince had given him an order (*nishān*), specifying his situation, and so Mufid decides to reproduce that order. Thus, once more, by reproducing a past document, Mufid tries to shore up his own status in the eyes of the reader, suggesting that, though his story is not one of success, nevertheless he and his family are honourable people and have been well-regarded in the past. This text runs as follows:

> That it was noted that since all the members of your clan are looking to our [Bahram's] welfare, and were well regarded amongst their peers, so a member from among that clan, of especial virtue and renowned amongst the learned (*muḥaqqiqīn*), Maulana Nizami, was received as one of our companions. This Maulana being firm in his sincerity, it was ordered that all the Sayyids and other officials, notables (*a'yān*), leaders (*kalāntarān*) of the area (*bilād*), in particular the town of Yazd and the area under its jurisdiction, should look up to him, and consider his company as a mark of honour. No one should interfere in his work, nor should his relatives, subordinates, servants or group be harassed in any way. Those whom this Maulana praises or blames will be treated accordingly. May the Maulana pray for our safety and the increase of our fortune, dated Zi-Qa'da 969 [July 1562].

Either Mufid had carried this document on his voyage as a proof of his status (this is possible), or he copied it later into his text. To this he adds

[34] For a brief biography of Bahram Mirza (1517–49), see P. Soucek, "Bahrām Mīrzā", in Ehsan Yarshater, ed., *Encyclopaedia iranica*, vol. III (New York, 1989), pp. 523–4.

Figure 10. Los Angeles County Museum of Art, M. 78.9.14, portrait of Mirza Rustam Safavi, *c.* 1640, attributed to Hashim.

that, in the case of this document too, there is a marginal notation in the hand of Bahram Mirza. It states: "The Maulana is one of my servants and attendants (*k͟hidmatgārān-o-mulāzimān-i mā ast*) and he should be given due consideration. Signed Bahram al-Husaini".

Yet, despite this ancient link and the great desire on the part of Mufid to serve Mirza Sadr-ud-Din, he was unable to enter his service. As the verse states, he who has entered a period of misfortune will find that his path deviates from that of his own welfare. So, abandoning this project, on 1 Rabiʿ I, Mufid reached Burhanpur, and on the 23rd of the same month, decided to go on to the Deccan, being misled this time by some self-centred people, and once more oblivious of the fact that, if Destiny is not in your favour, none of your efforts will bring any good. For the key is in God's hands, and it is he who turns it. So, once more, Mufid deviated from the right path, and the result was that he tied his goods on the cart of falsehood and ignorance, and reached Aurangabad on 1 Rabiʿ II. Mufid was constrained for some unspecified reasons to stay in Aurangabad for two and a half months, till 11 Jumada II (22 September 1673). It was only then that he left for Hyderabad, in constant fear and terror of robbers en route. On 17 Rajab, a month or so later, he thus eventually reached the vicinity of Hyderabad. Here, yet again, the doors of trouble opened.

> Each night snatches rest from this traveller's (*gharīb*) breast.
> The sherbet of sorrow makes my palate bitter.
> It is said that the keenest sorrow is Death.
> But worse still, no doubt, is the traveller's evening (*shām-i gharīb*).

Within two days of his arrival in Hyderabad, Mufid met a man who like him was from Yazd (*ham-shahr*) and who had known his clan for years. This meeting was at Golkonda, where the man was a physician, but a fraudulent one; according to Mufid, he had set up the shop of his ignorance as a physician and was polluting the Paradise of Golkonda with his ill-starred existence, killing off his patients (*mardūm kushī*).[35] He had neither science nor understanding.

> Whoever sought out his face,
> and was subject to his ill-treatment (*bad ʿilāj*),
> was sure never to see
> the face of life again.

This man, at any rate, sent for Mufid when he learnt that he was there. Mufid for his part found him to be nothing less than a devil (*dev*) in the guise of a man (*dar libās-i ādmī*). He was so low that his visage had no pleasant perfume to it, and the only thing that he was capable of doing

[35] Muhammad Mufid Mustaufi Yazdi, *Risāla-i Mufid*, pp. 169–70. This passage does not appear in the printed text.

was praising himself. He was so ignorant that, in comparison to him, writes Mufid, Mulla Nasruddin was like Hakim Bu 'Ali ibn Sina (Avicenna). A series of verses follow, concerning the difference between the ignorant and the intelligent, and intended to drive home the point that this man was truly ignorant. The last verse reiterates Mufid's earlier point:

> The alchemist is dying with rage at his misfortune,
> while the idiot has found a treasure in the desert.

When Mufid saw the depths of this man's arrogance and boastfulness, he decided not to have any more to do with him and simply to return home. India, it seemed, was a place where the ignorant, the haughty and the ill-mannered were bound to succeed, not men like Mufid. He began to think back on his friends, citing verses in this context, where he lamented his own fate and addressed the friends he was separated from. It was thus that his life in Hyderabad passed, until a day some ten months later, Monday 5 Rabi' II 1085 H (9 July 1674). That night, while asleep, he saw the Prophet in a dream.[36] He thus naturally praises the Prophet in a series of verses, describing him as handsome, with a face full of the best qualities. Mufid in the dream placed his head at the Prophet's feet. While doing so, he saw another tall and handsome man standing next to the Prophet, who whispered something in his ear. At this, the Prophet stood up and began to walk with the other man, with Mufid at some distance behind the two of them. On enquiring, he found this other man was 'Abbas ibn 'Abdal Muttalib, the uncle of the Prophet.[37] After walking some distance, they came to a group, amongst whom was Zubair ibn 'Awwam, who was initiating people through the ritual of *bay'a*.[38] When the Prophet saw Zubair, he avoided the group, and at this 'Abbas once more whispered in his ear. They then turned to the group, and the Prophet approached them, waving his hand and indicating that the *bay'a* ritual was not to his liking.[39] Then Zubair said to 'Abbas: "You do things

36 On the significance of such dreams, see Sviri, "Dreaming analyzed and recorded", pp. 252–73. See also, for further Ottoman comparisons (besides those referred to above), Cornell Fleischer, "Secretaries' dreams: augury and angst in Ottoman scribal service", in Ingeborg Baldauf and Suraiya Faroqhi, eds., *Armağan: Festschrift für Andreas Tietze* (Prague, 1994), pp. 77–88.

37 Muhammad Mufid Mustaufi Yazdi, *Jāmi'-i Mufīdī*, vol. III, pp. 798–9.

38 Zubair ibn 'Awwam is considered to be one of the first five men who embraced Islam. He is also considered to have died a martyr in 33 H. See I. Hasson, "Al-Zubayr bin al-'Awwām", *The Encyclopaedia of Islam*, vol. XI (Leiden, 2002), pp. 549–51.

39 *Bay'a* is defined as "the act by which a certain number of persons, acting individually or collectively, recognize the authority of another person"; cf. E. Tyan, "Bay'a", in *The Encyclopaedia of Islam*, vol. I (Leiden, 1960), pp. 1113–14.

like this, but then stop me from doing them." The Prophet who had advanced further by then, now turned back and Mufid followed him. At this stage, Mufid awoke, and thanked God for his vision. He bowed down low, and asked God to save him from the *zamīn-i siyāh-i Dakan* ("black land of the Deccan"), implying that even if he had got nothing in India, still he had had direct access to God. Verses follow:

> O great God, I have been imprisoned.
> I am bewildered and broken; my heart is in turmoil.
> O God, be my friend.
> Since I can find no friends [here],
> save me from this trouble.

The desire to meet his friends, and the longing for his homeland (*waṭan-i mālūf*) grew apace in his heart. He thought of a *ḥadīṣ* (which he terms a *kalima-i sharīf*): "To love your country is a part of your faith (*īmān*)." By association, he then thought of Yazd, which he terms a heaven-like area (*khiṭṭa-i bihisht*). For even those who had seen the cities and countries of the world admitted that Yazd was a most beautiful city, to be likened only to lovely, flower-bodied girls. It was a soul-stirring city, chosen from among the gardens of *Dār us-Salām* (i.e of Paradise). From the seven climes, it was the best and, like Spring, it was distinguished over all other seasons, its air was sweet and delicate, and it possessed the qualities of coquetry. Verses now follow in praise of Yazd in this context. Mufid alludes too to the great congregational mosque Masjid-i Jāmi', which touches the sky, and the plinth of which is like unto the Throne of God (*'arsh-i karīm*). The dome of that mosque was like Mount Sinai (Tur), and, as for the shrines of the city, one of them was that of Imamzada Abu Ja'far Muhammad and had been made by great architects and designers. Those who were sick at heart went to Yazd, to place its dust on their heads as a cure, for the breath that came out of these buildings was like the breath of Jesus, which brings life. Everything shone in as miraculous a fashion as Moses's palm in his contest with the Pharaoh. Mufid's patriotism is now in full flow. The flower-beds of Yazd were such as to make those of Shiraz jealous, while the *maidān* there was like an identical twin to the *maidān* of the great *Naqsh-i Jahān* in Isfahan. The canals of the river (Ahristan) of Yazd, when compared to those of the Nile in Egypt, were of such purity, that the latter were put to shame. As for the palaces and mansions of that heavenly Jannatabad, what more could he say? For a description of the town's gardens and river, what more could he write?

May our salutations go
to the perfumed shrine of prince Fazl Raza.
Our salutations with each breath
to the illumined shrine of Sultan Taqi-ud-Din Muhammad.

This moment of high patriotism does not quite mark the occasion of Mufid's eventual departure from Hyderabad, which he terms the Abode of Anguish (*Kudūratābād*). This eventual departure requires more time, in view of the highly inertial quality of our traveller. Thus, for him to leave Hyderabad requires nothing less than an opening of the doors of favour for him by the grace of God. Mufid will linger on for a time, stewing in his own juice. A new chapter begins with a kind of philosophical statement that man should not be disappointed if he encounters difficulty in the beginning, as it is after trials and tribulations that he achieves the pleasures he desires. Mufid now invokes the memory of Abraham, Joseph, and also the Prophet Muhammad, each of whom had been tested in the fire of exile in order to achieve greatness, glory in Egypt, and victory over Mecca, respectively. As for Mufid, another dream intervenes in his favour, this one featuring 'Ali Musa Raza, in the year 1086 H. Fortified by it, he eventually leaves Hyderabad for northern India on 7 Ramazan 1087 H (13 November 1676) and, in the middle of Safar 1088 H (April 1677), arrives in Ujjain, where he is granted an audience with the Mughal prince Muhammad Akbar, who also grants him a *manṣab* of 200 *z̲āt*.[40] From there, he accompanies the prince to Delhi and thence to Multan. On 6 Shawwal 1089 H (21 November 1678), Mufid is even appointed Mir Saman, or the officer in charge of household supplies, to the Begam, or principal wife, of Prince Akbar. It is here then that Mufid's account itself draws to a close, with a declaration that, instead of describing his own life, he would do better to give an account of the wonders of the world.

We thus turn to the *k̲h̲ātima*, or closing section, of the text, which carries the title: "The wonders of the world's inhabited quarter, and strange incidents from the colourful world".[41] This section begins by citing Khwandamir (1475–1534), regarded by Mufid as the "greatest historian" of all. As in another text that he has authored, namely the *Muk̲h̲taṣar-i Mufīd*, here too Mufid commences with a reflection on the extent of the world. Of the 53,000 *farsak̲h̲* of the inhabited world,

[40] On this prince, see Jadunath Sarkar, "Muhammad Akbar: the nemesis of Aurangzib", in Sarkar, *Studies in Aurangzib's Reign*, pp. 66–72.
[41] Muhammad Mufid Mustaufi Yazdi, *Jāmi'-i Mufīdī*, vol. III, pp. 817ff.

he states, Hindustan accounts for 12,000, Rum for 6,000, 4,000 are in Chin, 3,000 in Saqlab and Sanjab, 1,000 in Zangibar, 4,000 in Habsha, etc., 5,000 in Yajuj and Majuj, and 1,000 in that part where Adam never reached, with a further 7,000 from Qaf to Qaf, 1,000 more where red and yellow rubies may be found, and 2,000 in the very heart of the "lands of Islam (*zamīn-i wilāyat-i Islām*)", starting from Sham, Fars, Mazandaran, Gilan, Khorasan, Azarbaijan, etc. (this last estimate is taken from Khwandamir's *Ḥabīb us-Siyar*). In the first *faṣl* ("section") then, Mufid summarises materials on geography from various books, and cities like Herat and Baghdad are also described briefly.

The second *faṣl* continues with the more or less obligatory stories of wonders, and descriptions of animals and birds, as well as rare incidents from the books of earlier authors, including some from Mufid's own observations or hearsay from the mouths of reliable people. For instance, in the month of Rabi' II 1085 H, when he was in Hyderabad (here amazingly promoted once more to *bihisht buniyād*, or Like-Unto-Paradise), a certain Mulla Muhammad Ardagani (*takhallus*, or pen-name, "Fida'i") had told him a story about a mountain in the village of Kharaniq near Yazd, which he recounts. Other stories are from his own observation, such as the following one:

> In the early days of Rabi' I 1085 [June 1674], when the writer of these pages was staying in Hyderabad, two women were brought there from a village of Karnatak, who had beards like men. Their entire bodies were covered with hair, and their breasts were a cubit large, so that when they walked they were obliged to carry them wrapped up around their waist in their clothes. In Hyderabad, in those very days, a man appeared who could tear a goat (*gosfand*) with his teeth, drink its blood and then skin the animal, swallow its flesh, and chew its bones. Every day, a large goat was provided for him. In 1084, I saw a man in Shahjahanabad, who was known as Nine Yards (*nau gazī*). When he walked, he was so tall that others would reach only to his waist. He seemed to be riding on a huge horse in the midst of a group of foot-soldiers.

Or, again, we are regaled with the following tale, also from the time of his sojourn in the Deccan:

> Sayyid Najib Amir Muhammad Rashid Shirazi, who in 1080, in the region of Hyderabad, had bought a house to live in, after having bought it, was having a well dug near the house. When they had dug two or three cubits, a very large stone appeared, which was extremely difficult to break. When it was eventually broken, a large crack appeared in it, in which a very large live lizard was found with a half-eaten great big leaf in its mouth. All the eye-witnesses were astonished.

Some of these stories do not concern Hindustan but 'Iraq, and it must be admitted that Mufid has no particular view on where wonders and monstrosities can be found in the world. Still, the number of peculiar stories from India is large, and reminds one of that slightly earlier traveller, Mahmud Wali Balkhi, in the 1620s and 1630s.[42] Thus, another of Mufid's stories runs:

In Hyderabad, I saw some of the reports from the newsletter-writers to the emperor of Hindustan. In one of them, it was written that in the Malwa province, in the house of a merchant named Lala, one of his daughters became pregnant. On 5 Zi-Qa'da of the 9th regnal year, a child was born to her with six feet, and a tail, and a horn as long as a finger on its head. As soon as it was born, it began to eat grain and grass, and refused to drink milk. Three leagues from Ahmadabad, in the village of Borba, in the house of a goldsmith called Khusrau, a girl-child was born who at birth had a rather large breast from which milk was coming out. Her feet had twenty toes. Her hair was already white, and instead of ears she had large holes. Further, in Kashmir, in those very days, in Bahur district, which is three leagues from the city, a boy was born in the house of a Kashmiri called Lala, who had two heads and four feet, and who was one yard (*gaz*) at birth. Further, Amir Khan, the governor of Kabul, when he cut open a melon found a fish in it that was ten fingers long. In Khanpur, a daughter was born in the house of a barber called Parahnar, who had three heads, and would drink milk from the three mouths. But she had two hands and two feet. She was alive for three days. In the area of Sirhind, a certain Lalu Patwari had two wives who were both pregnant. One had five children, and the other had one, but with two heads, four legs and two hands, and no orifice for excretion. On drinking milk, he used to bring it out again from his mouth. But he died in a few days. In Multan, the fishermen had gone to the river to fish, when one of the fish drew two of them into the water. Amanullah, the son of Tarbiyat Khan, instructed the fishermen to search for them with nets. In the end, the fish was found with great difficulty. When its belly was torn open, both fishermen emerged alive from it. The fish was ten cubits long and three cubits broad. Whatever has been stated here, has been exactly copied from the newsletters of Hindustan.

All these small wonders are thus brought together pell-mell, without any commentary or further reflection. The remaining three *faṣls* of the *k͟hātima* continue in a not-altogether-dissimilar vein. The third recounts "wondrous stories of kings and their grandeur"; the fourth carries many stories copied from books about the wonders of the world; while the fifth *faṣl*, also largely taken from other books, concerns the qualities of great people of the past. This takes us at last to the closing passages of the book itself.

[42] See Chapter 4 above.

Figure 11. Scene with monstrous creatures, *'Ajā'ib al-Makhlūqāt*, National Museum, New Delhi, No. 57.26/2.

Praise be to God that this third book of the *Jāmi'-i Mufīdī* has been completed, which in itself is a matter of wonder for I have nothing, and my heart is ever heavy, and my mind ever preoccupied. The difficulties of travels in Hindustan have been added to this. In these circumstances, it was by no means easy for me to bring together all these incidents on kings, Sayyids, Shaikhs, scholars and wise people, in a short time, and to verify them as I have done. These stories, which is to say the third volume of the *Jāmi'-i Mufīdī* for which I have worn my fingers down, was completed during my travels in Hindustan, when each day and each night was spent in a different place. May the sweet parrot of my pen be like the trader in oceans and cities, who from the ink-blackness of Zanjibar brought out words like shining jewels for each city and country and threaded them together, so that the reader might understand that the revolution of bodies in this world and in the firmament is in accordance with the intentions of the true and matchless Creator. The mountains fixed in one place, the rocking of waves in the ocean, and the flowing of rivers, all this is the work of the Creator. The children of Adam are like mere balls in the polo-field of Fate. Possibilities fly about like straw in the air or chips in the ocean.

It is He who puts things in movement,
both on land and on sea.

On account of the undeniable reality of what has been said, on 17 Rajab 1081 [30 November 1670], I left my homeland to pay homage to the sacred shrines, and through Howaiza and Basra made my way. I returned from there and stayed for a time in my land. I commenced this book in 1082, but before being able to advance it a great deal, I fell ill which weakened me. This went on for three or four months, and it was when I was thus weakened that Fate dragged me by the collar on this voyage to Hindustan. From 1 Rajab 1082 [3 November 1671], I began the sea-voyage, and after a journey filled with danger on both land and sea, and after many halts and starts, and having wasted a good deal of time in covering this distance, on 15 Safar 1088 [18 April 1677], I eventually reached Dar-ul-Fath Ujjain, where the doors of success were also opened to me. Here, I met the Mughal Prince whose name I have mentioned in the fifth chapter, and who took a liking to me. With his retinue, I passed through Shahjahanabad and reached Multan and Lahore, stopping on the way from time to time. It was then that I began writing again, and each time I stopped at some place, this traveller (*musāfir*) turned his new-found comfort in the direction of advancing these pages. While staying at Multan, on the first day of Jumada I 1090 (10 June 1679), this book was completed. The movement back and forth of my pen that decorates speech at last halted. Thanks be to God that this work reached a point where it could be given a title, but at the same time a large part of my life too has passed. Let me present a few verses, free from both poetic exaggeration and the style of *munshīs* (*akhlāq-i munshīyāna*). They are from a good poet, and I shall end with them:

I sought help from Divine Grace
to erect a wonderful garden.
From the treasury of my inner self
I drew out a heap of pleasing pearls.
This work is in three parts,
each one illumined and rich with pearls.
Its pages are brilliant like the beloved's cheek,
and the letters fragrant like the musk of Tartary.
Its stories will gladden the heart,
being free from weakness in reporting.
Their veracity is beyond dispute,
bringing word of secrets new and old.
The text is flawless and flowing,
like tresses on houris' jasmine-scented cheeks.

A number of such verses then carry us through to the very end:

O God, through the intercession of the Prophet,
and those of 'Ali, Fatima, Hasan and Husain, and their sons,
May this work pleasing to the heart,
endowed with the grace of these descendants,
be appreciated by those masters of the word
who know the secrets of old.
That by your grace it may remain,
forever appreciated.
May the critics be kind to it,
for I have spilt my liver's blood
to bring you this humble gift.
Do not deprive me of your Grace
and forgive me for my errors.
In this mud, may knowledge come to flower,
may my heart be illumined by knowledge.
In this act of submission
let my book be given long life,
and salutations!

Mufid's travels in Hindustan did not produce this text alone, however. He also put his experiences to use in his other work, *Mukhtaṣar-i Mufid*, which we have mentioned briefly above.[43] In the opening to this latter text, he explains the circumstances of its composition. Here, Mufid

[43] On this text, also see Bert G. Fragner, "Iranian patriotism in the 17th century: the case of Mohammad-e Mofid" (unpublished paper, delivered as part of the Yarshater Lectures, Harvard University, 30 April–5 May 2001).

mentions that, when he was in the Deccan, there was an assembly (*majlis*) of the notables (*ashrāf* and *a'yān*) of different countries, who discussed the relative achievements of different kings. He noted that some of the "fools who remained at the surface" (*bīkhiradān-i ẓāhir-bīn*), and those "illiterates regulated by stupidity" (*nādānān-i ḥimāqat ā'īn*), were all holding forth according to their own understandings.[44] They mentioned the greatness of the ruler of Cathay and China, the armies of the Turk, the vastness of Rum and Magna China (*Māchīn*). However, people with real understanding knew of the great achievements of the Safavids, and in particular those of Shah Isma'il Safavi, who had provided stability over a vast area including Iran and its neighbourhood, where in the year 906 H a large number of rulers had control over small fragments. He provides a list of many of the contemporary rulers, including those of Hurmuz, and going into Central Asia too. So, Mufid thought it was up to him to write a book on this area, highlighting the topography, urban centres, and certain political facts, with reference in particular to the Safavids. This conversation, at the root of the idea of this treatise, took place according to Mufid in 1087 H (or 1676–7). The organisation of the text of the *Mukhtaṣar* is geographical, in keeping with the idea of the seven climes (*haft iqlīm*). Mufid starts with references to the Khwandamir's *Ḥabīb us-Siyar*, Mir Khwand's *Rauẓat uṣ-Ṣafā'*, and the author of the *Ṣuwar al-Aqālīm wa Masālik al-Mamālik*, and the book is littered throughout with quotations. Mufid is very proud of his erudition, and he mentions early on that he had read most of the classic texts; these include Nurullah Shustari's *Majālis al-mū'minīn*, and the *Nuzhat ul-qulūb*, the *'Ajā'ib ul-buldān*, the *'Ajā'ib ul-makhlūqāt*, the *Haft iqlīm*, etc. It would seem that at least one part of the text was eventually written in 1091 H, when Mufid was in Lahore, for at one point in the *Mukhtaṣar*, he writes of being in "a state of exile in Lahore in Hind" (*rāqim-i ḥurūf ki āwāra-i diyār-ghurbat būd dar khiṭṭa-i Lāhor ki az amṣār-i Hind ast*), on account of which he does not have access to the sort of library that he would have wanted. Clearly, the relative success of his career after his meeting with Prince Akbar was still not to his satisfaction. The text of the *Mukhtaṣar-i Mufid* thus ends on the same pessismistic note that marks so much of the other account.

From the year 1089 H until the completion of these stories, the sadness of exile and the desire to meet my brothers has become so overwhelming, that I am

[44] Muhammad Mufid Mustaufi Yazdi, *Mohtaṣar-e Mofīd*, vol. 1, p. 2.

unable to continue writing and describing. From the first light of dawn to the last light of dusk, I am preoccupied with the idea that this exile, who is wandering in the valley of perdition, may be able to return to his own country. From the disappearance of the sun, to its return, not a moment of drowsiness comes to me. I hope that God will have mercy on me, and that from the world beyond some grace will allow me to be united with my friends once more.

> Life has no other end
> than communion with friends.
> To be in the midst of companions
> is the only purpose of existence.
> I swear on the lives of my friends
> that the happiness of success is unattainable
> without the company of friends
> who share your worries.

What I wish to communicate then is that for a long time this slave was busy in compiling this book titled *Mukhtaṣar-i Mufīd*, until by the Eternal Grace of Allah, on Tuesday, 9 Rabiʿ I 1091 H [9 April 1680], when I was in Lahore, and when the king of flowers came out to take a stroll in the direction of the garden, and the impatient nightingale began to sing from the depths of his unhappy heart, the work was [at last] completed.[45]

Mufid's is a powerful, if at times repetitive and tiresome, voice. He is a sceptic, and, more importantly, someone who claims to speak from experience. His view is thus explicitly counterposed to what he imagines to be a dominant trend in Safavid Iran, where every scribe, litterateur and poet thought of the India of the Mughals as a place where the streets were paved with gold. Stripped of some of its literary trappings, what Mufid suggests is that one cannot make much progress in Mughal India without an adequate network of connections and patronage. This is because, in contrast to the situation in, say, the mid sixteenth century, Mughal India is now too "full", not only of Iranians but of other groups who are all vying for the same positions and privileges. The problem, moreover, at least from his point of view, is that few mechanisms exist in the Mughal domains for distinguishing the good and competent (amongst whom he naturally numbers himself), from the bad and even downright fraudulent. His grumblings against the "fools who remained at the surface" are of a different order then, from the broadsides of Muhammad Rabiʿ that we have discussed in the preceding chapter. For this is the voice of a man

[45] Muhammad Mufid Mustaufi Yazdi, *Moḫtaṣar-e Mofīd*, vol. I, pp. 386–7.

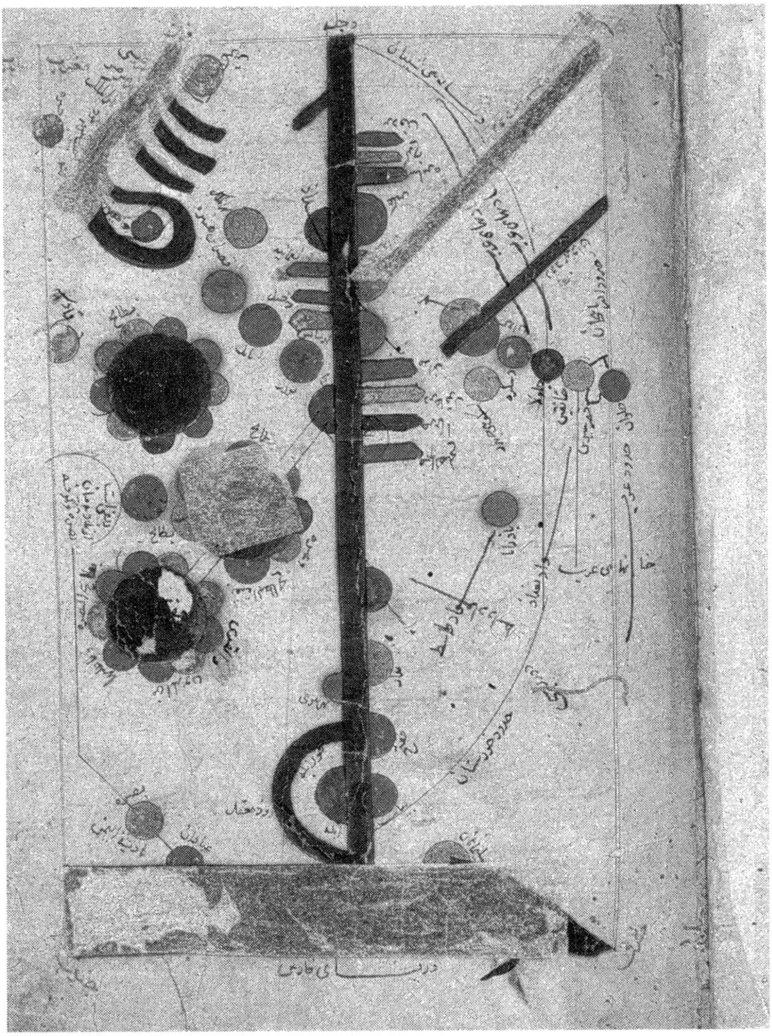

Figure 12. Map (*ṣūrat*) of ʻIraq-i ʻArab, from Ibn Khurdadbih *Ṣuwar al-aqālīm wa masālik-i mamālik*, National Museum, New Delhi, No. 56.96/4.

who had migrated full of hope, and who wishes to convey to his compatriots the bitterness and disappointment which the whole experience has produced in him. Travel here is indeed a form of hell, or at least of purgatory.

It is important to note that Mufid was not alone in thinking of India in this way. Another significant example that has been discussed in the literature is that of the poet Muhammad Sa'id Mazandarani, better known as "Ashraf Mazandarani".[46] This writer was born in the Safavid capital of Isfahan in the early 1620s, and lived to a ripe old age, only dying in 1704 (1116 H) in Munger in Bengal. The descendant of two prominent intellectual families of the Safavid realm, Ashraf studied with some excellent poets in his youth, including the celebrated Sa'ib Tabrizi, and decided to migrate to India in the late 1650s, shortly after the resolution of the war of succession between the sons of Shahjahan. Unlike Mufid, however, Ashraf did have a well-defined support-group in the Mughal court, and his own calligraphy teacher 'Abdul Rashid Dailami, as well as Sa'ib himself, was rather well known in Mughal courtly circles. As a consequence, he was quickly able to gain a reasonably important position in the court as tutor to Aurangzeb's daughter Zaib-un-Nisa, and remained in India for some fourteen years, returning to Iran in 1672.[47] Then he seems to have been possessed of the urge to visit India again, and hence returned to serve in the household of Aurangzeb's son Shah 'Alam (later to rule as Bahadur Shah) in Patna, eventually dying in India and leaving his family (including a son Mirza Muhammad 'Ali) to remain in Mughal service.

On the face of it then, this would appear – unlike the case of Mufid – to be a rather smooth and successful career, even if it was not one that scaled the heights of bureaucratic or literary glory. However, Ashraf's poetry suggests otherwise, reflecting a state of angst rather than contentment. To be sure, some of his poems praise the land of the Mughals in the usual fashion, notably as providing an excellent livelihood for Iranians with talent. Thus, one quatrain runs as follows.[48]

> There is no currency for learned men in Iran,
> although the means may be found.

[46] Stephen Frederic Dale, "A Safavid poet in the heart of darkness: the Indian poems of Ashraf Mazandarani", in Michel Mazzaoui, ed., *Safavid Iran and her neighbors* (Salt Lake City, 2003), pp. 63–80 (which also appears in *Iranian Studies*, 36, 2, 2003, pp. 197–212). Dale draws extensively on the selection of Ashraf's poems to be found in Ahmad Golchin-i Ma'ani, *Kārwān-i Hind: Dar aḥwāl wa āṣār-i shā'irān-i 'aṣr-i Ṣafawī ki bi Hindūstān rafta and* (Mashhad, 1369 H / 1990–1), 2 vols., vol. I, pp. 70–4, as also on the poet's *dīwān*.

[47] On this Mughal princess, see Jadunath Sarkar, "The romance of a Mughal princess: Zeb-un-Nisa", in Sarkar, *Studies in Aurangzib's Reign*, pp. 90–8. Zaib-un-Nisa also wrote poetry under the pen-name "Makhfi", or "the Concealed One".

[48] In the passages that follow, we have drawn largely on Dale, "A Safavid poet in the heart of darkness", pp. 68–75, while at times slightly modifying the translations.

In Hind, the talented are renowned,
a lantern will illumine the darkness.

There is of course some ambiguity already in this verse, with its implication that Iranian talent must bring light to the Indian night (*shab*) or darkness (*sawād*). There is also the admission that much can indeed be found in India, as we see in another verse that runs as follows.

Although God is everywhere just,
dispensing his blessing on sea and land,
His providence is manifest in Hind,
for God's grace is greater in the heart of night.

Thus India here too is the very "heart of night (*dil-i shab*)", and again the ambiguous reflection is that somehow – perhaps unjustifiably – far too much wealth has come to be concentrated with the Mughals. However, other verses by the same poet then abandon this ambiguity for a deeply critical view not only of India, but of the Iranians (like the poet himself) who wish to migrate there, imagining "that in Hind, gold (*zar*) is scattered like stars in the night sky". Such a view of India can only lead in his view to deep humiliation, to say nothing of the literal suffering caused by the excessive heat. At such moments, Ashraf seems almost to go as far as Muhammad Rabi' in his patriotic zeal and disdain for other lands. Thus, we have the following two verses, both comparing India to Iran.

How can you compare the soil of Hind,
with the lands of Iran?
Can black soil ever equal a rose garden?

The second verse, less damning perhaps, nevertheless suggests that Mughal culture is but a counterfeit version of the real thing (*aṣl*), namely what the Safavids possess.

How can one compare the kingdom of Hind to Iran?
As if a copy could ever equal the original!

It may be that Ashraf Mazandarani's verses represent a more-or-less universal lament, of the migrant who is neither at home in his new place of residence, nor content to go back to his place of origin. This is certainly the sense that a comparison with other poets, whether earlier or later ones who migrated to India, might suggest.[49] For our purposes, however, it is

[49] Thus Dale, "A Safavid poet in the heart of darkness", pp. 75–8, proposes comparisons within the category of the "émigré lament", with other writers ranging from Babur to Rudyard Kipling.

of considerable significance that Ashraf was an almost exact contemporary of Mufid, and thus seems to reflect a more general mood that had come to be prevalent amongst a certain stratum of Iranian migrants in the latter half of the seventeenth century. We shall now turn to investigate whether this phenomenon was indeed a stable one that had little to do with the circumstances of that time.

A CONTRASTING VIEW

It is of course very probable that not every Iranian from the Safavid domains was quite so sour about his Indian experiences as Mufid or even Ashraf. Indeed, a contrasting example from a few decades earlier may be found in the account of a certain ʻAbdullah Sani, better known by his poetic name of "Bihishti Herawi", who provides us some rather interesting details of his sojourn in India, interspersed here and there by poems on the cities he visited and described, but mainly in the form of two independent autobiographical poems, the longer of which was entitled "An account of my own circumstances, my coming into existence from nothingness, and the description of the difficulties and miseries that I encountered from my childhood to the time of my maturity" (*Dar sharḥ-i aḥwāl-i khwud wa be-wujūd āmdan az ʻadam wa bayān-i ʻālam-i miḥnat-i ayyām-i kudakī tā hangām-i nashw-o-namā*).[50] Some details concerning the poet may not be entirely out of place here. Bihishti was born as a premature child (when his mother was seven months pregnant) in 1006 H (1597–8) in Herat in a Shiʻi Sayyid family. He contracted a serious case of measles when he was just forty days old, and suffered from this terrible disease for over six months, to the point that his parents had given up hope of his survival. He was cured finally, but as a result of the disease was rendered mute and totally paralysed. However, when he was four years old, his father took him to several Sufic hospices and shrines, so that eventually he miraculously regained his speech and enough strength to walk. The poet then describes his early education, how he finished learning the Qur'an in just six months, and boasts that, in ten years' time, he had mastered the sciences and texts which others do normally in twenty years.

[50] Bihishti Herawi (ʻAbdullah Sani), *Nūr ul-Mashriqain: Safar-nāma-i manẓūm az ʻahd-i Ṣafawī*, ed. Najib Mayil Herawi (Mashhad, 1998). The briefer of the two poems is captioned as ʻ*waṣf-i ḥāl-i nāẓim*ʼ (a title probably given by the editor) and appears on pp. 58–9, just before the *ḥamd*; the second poem is considerably longer, and appears on pp. 180–95. The exact reference to this text was again generously given to us by Kathryn Babayan.

Bihishti's first teacher died when he was twelve, and he then joined the classes of the noted poet Fasihi Ansari Herawi and soon became one of his most favourite pupils. Fasihi called him his son (*farzand*) in affection and Bihishti also remembers Fasihi as his master (*khudāwand*). Fasihi noticed unusual literary and poetic talents in his pupil and thus began to train him to grow to be a great poet of his time. His talents were first tested in Herat by a noted poet of *ghazals*, Ahli Shirazi who, having heard of the potential of the young Bihishti, asked him to compose verses on the line of a *rubā'ī* of his own. Bihishti succeeded in composing a matchless eight-line (*muṣamman*) verse, which satisfied Ahli; overjoyed with the achievement of his pupil, the very same day his master, Fasihi, suggested that he take up the pen name of "Bihishti". Having established himself as a noted poet, Bihishti then set off on travels in Iran. He visited Mashhad, Tus, Nishapur, Sabzawar, Simnan, Tehran, Rayy, Qom, Isfahan and finally Hamadan and the Alwand mountains, where he stayed for two years in the service of the governor (*ḥākim*) of the city of Hamadan. He then left Hamadan, and returned to Herat when the former city was conquered by the Ottomans on their way to Baghdad to subjugate it (*bahr-i taskhīr-i mulk-i Baghdād*). Back in Herat, Bihishti now joined the service of Hasan Khan Shamlu, and had lived there for two or three years when the following incident occurred. Suddenly one night, when he was in a party (*bazm*) with his writer and poet friends, he heard that the caravan of the Mughal ambassador (*ḥājib-i Hind*), who had particular access to the Mughal emperor, was to leave for India the very next morning. Bihishti decided on an impulse to join the caravan; his teacher, Fasihi, also wished to accompany him on this journey to Hindustan, but was finally persuaded by Hasan Shamlu to curtail his trip at Qandahar and return to Herat.

In India, Bihishti seems to have travelled widely, visited Kashmir and then finally joined the service of Prince Murad Bakhsh. He seems to have had a successful and fulfilling career in India, and praises in unqualified terms the emperor Shahjahan, the princes, Dara Shukoh, Aurangzeb, Shah Shuja' and, the most generous of them all, his patron Murad Bakhsh.[51] He mentions a *maṣnawī* text, *Murād-nāma*, which he composed for and dedicated to that prince, but the text itself has not yet been found. Bihishti lived in India in Murad's service for about twenty years, and, when he felt he had grown old, he wrote a major work called the *Nūr*

[51] On this prince, see Mohammad Quamruddin, *Life and times of Prince Murad Bakhsh (1624–1661)* (Calcutta, 1974).

ul-Mashriqain, which, besides religious verses (*manqabats*) with descriptions of the miracles of the Imams, includes poems on the places he visited in Iran and Hindustan. This book, the *Nūr ul-Mashriqain* ("Light of the Two Easts"), is modelled after the widely appreciated religious *maṣnawī*, *Tuḥfat ul-'Irāqain* by Afzal-ud-Din Badil ibn 'Ali Najjar Shirwani, better known as "Khaqani".[52] Khaqani wrote his work on his return from Mecca, and it surveys various political, literary and religious notables of his time, and is dedicated to the ruler of Mosul, Amir Jamal-ud-Din Mosuli. It is considered as one of the major *maṣnawīs* in Persian and was prescribed at the higher levels of the medieval *madrasa* syllabi. Bihishti also had read it together with the other noted Persian *masnawīs*, like the *Būstān* of Sa'di, the *Ḥadīqa* of Sana'i and the *Gulshan* of Zulali, and planned to write his own work to compare with that of Khaqani. Though Bihishti begins by claiming that his poem was to be of the same literary level as Khaqani's, in conclusion, however, he admits in all humility that his *Nūr ul-Mashriqain* is of little worth compared to Khaqani's text. He says that even if "this poem is the light of both the lands of the East (*Nūr-i Mashriqain*) and is all ornament embodied like the *Tuḥfa*, yet how can it be compared with the *Tuḥfa*? O Bihishti, cease this bragging. It is evident which wine is truly fine and clean." Thus, the further rueful admission:

> This pearl you bored in the metre of the *Tuḥfa*,
> yet you could not utter a single verse in his [Khaqani's] style.
> This worthless thing, however much it be varnished,
> how can you regard it a match for the *Tuḥfa*?
> Put an end to this poem like a true connoisseur,
> and do not annoy Khaqani further.[53]

Of particular interest for our purposes in this text are eight poems pertaining to Bihishti's journey to Hind, which appear in the last section of the book.[54] He begins with a poem giving his reason for his journey (*sabab-i 'azīmat be jānib-i Hindūstān*). This recounts the story we have noted above in brief: one night, at a party given by Asaf Khan in Herat, a number of friends had gathered together, all noted poets (*yārān hama shā'irān-i nāmī*) of the city. In the middle of lively discussions on poetry (*ash'ār*) and exchanges of opinion about various sorts of news (*akhbār*), a friend announced that the next morning the *ḥājib-i Hind* was set to

[52] See the work by Anna Livia Fermina Alexandra Beelaert, *A cure for the grieving: studies on the poetry of the 12th-century Persian court poet Khāqānī Širwānī* (Leiden, 1996).
[53] Bihishti Herawi, *Nūr al-Mashriqain*, p. 269.
[54] Bihishti Herawi, *Nūr al-Mashriqain*, pp. 239–69.

leave for India, and that he would be accompanied by many eminent scholars and wise men (*bisyār afāẓil-o-khiradmand*). The *ḥājib*, himself a clever and wise man, was an admirer of learned people and was also close to the *Shāh-i Hind*.[55] This hence seemed a very opportune time for those who desired to see India to seize the moment.

The poet did hesitate, reasoning that travel was not an easy proposition, and noting that all humans are temperamentally tied to the place where they live. As against that, he also admits freely that he was ablaze with a desire to visit India, where he thought he should try his luck. For, however black India was, it was no darker than the poet's own fate, and he also realised that he was not going to earn much money in Herat itself. He hence made up his mind impulsively, left the party in the middle of the night, somehow arranged one maund of dates for the journey (*yak man khurma be tusha-i rāh*), and came home to announce his decision to his parents, to their obvious grief. Our poet, however, was determined, and joined the ambassador's retinue and, after three days' journey, arrived in Sabzar, which was a small town (*qaṣba*) with well-cultivated and rich lands. Four days later, the caravan reached the *wilāyat* of Farah. In the hot wind here, he had a foretaste of the hot climate of India. Half the people in the bazaar here were Hindus, who were apparently in the habit of short-changing their customers in trade (*kaj tarāzū*). Moving fast, the party then arrived in Bust, a fortified city with innumerable accomplished scholars and artists (*ahl-i kamāl bī panāh ast*), besides peasants and soldiers (*muzāriʿ wa sipāh*); the next stage then took them to the formidable city and fortress of Qandahar, and, ten days later, the caravan (*qāfila*) took the difficult mountainous pass that led to the river Sind. In between, there were twenty-four stations inhabited by the wicked, mischievous and devilish (*badzāt, sharīr, hamchū shaiṭān*) Afghans, of whom the poet clearly does not approve. This may be partly explained by the fact that the caravan was at one stage attacked by Afghan bandits; a fierce battle ensued between the armed retinue of the *ḥājib* and the attackers, who were, however, successful in plundering and capturing six merchants.

Bihishti goes on to describe how his party eventually entered the land of Hind (*sawād-i Hind*), following this up with a description of the cities of India (*ṣifat-i bilād-i Hindūstān*), and a special closing poem dedicated to his feelings about Kashmir (*khātima dar waṣf-i Kashmīr-i khuldnaẓīr*

[55] It seems likely that this envoy was Mir Husaini, sent by Shahjahan in 1637, who returned to Mughal India in November 1638 (according to the Mughal chronicler 'Abdul Hamid Lahauri) or 1639 (according to some Safavid sources). See Islam, *Calendar*, vol. 1, pp. 254–5, 259.

wa bayān-i waqā'i' 'ālam-i taqdīr). The verses on the cities of Hindustan include a general summary description of the topography of the region, and a listing of the major cities, as well as an account of some of the features of the people of the country. It begins with the following verse:

> Hind ast wilāyat-i 'ajā'ib
> Mamlū ze 'ajā'ib-o-gharā'ib
>
> (India is a strange country,
> full of wonders and unusual things.)

The country is a vast plain, Bihishti continues, with a tiny village (*qarya*) at every four leagues; it takes a year to cover the distance from the Tilang hills in the south to the Sind river at the other end of the country. Kabul is at her head, and the Deccan defines the other extremity, while from west to east the kingdom spreads from Sind to Rajmahal, with secure and well-administered (*mutī'*) roads everywhere. Major cities, including Fatehpur, Akbarabad, Gwaliyar and Narwar each possess a high fort that reaches the sky. Then there is the vast country (*mulk*) of peaceful Malwa down to the bank of the Narbada, with revenues and wealth comparable to Egypt and Syria; here, one encounters the fort of Asir and the celebrated and populous town of Burhanpur. Further south, one enters the Deccan, the territory of the Nizam Shah centred on Daulatabad, a city that competes with heaven in sources of pleasure and delight. In a similar vein, Bihishti describes the principal cities on an itinerary running from west to east, and beginning with Bhakkar and Multan, to end in Bengal. Bihishti thus waxes eloquent on the wonders of the cities of India, but also of the people resident there. In particular, he notices the beautiful female singers, known as *ḍomnī*, but we also learn that in each village and town there live Shaikhs and Sayyids, and that in the Mughals' army, a very large number of Rajputs and Afghans served as soldiers. India appears far more densely populated to Bihishti than his own land; the people in this land are countless, he writes, and many more than ants and locusts in number. Amongst them, a large number are foreigners from Rum and Turan, and here the poet expresses his reticence. For few of them, however, are decent and polite; they may have wealth and affluence, but are without any grace (*sairab ze baḥr, lek bī āb*). Thus, the patriotism of the Safavid subject does come through, since Bihishti eventually asserts that, among the outsiders, the only well-behaved ones are the 'Iraqis (Iranians), their descendants, or the people who are related to them.

Otherwise, the judgment with regard to both the land and the nature of the rule there is usually positive and often even enthusiastic. For, in

Bihishti's view, the country which earlier was hellish has become heaven-like under the rule of the Chaghatai kings, and Kashmir in particular has turned into a bride from the grace of the wealth of Akbar and Jahangir (*az daulat-i Akbar wa Jahāngīr, āwurd be bar 'urūs-i Kashmīr*). The poet has a special fondness for this particular land, where he would seem to have lived for six years under the patronage of a noble by the name of Zafar Khan. In his verses, the poet mentions Dal Lake, the water of which shines like the rays of the sun, the beautiful gardens around it, and the Shalimar, the waves of the five rivers of the Punjab, the mountains, Pir Panjal, as well as the beautiful people of the valley. The last sections then take us from Kashmir to Lahore and a description of the palace there, and the nobles and the princes at the Mughal court. All the princes are complimented by him for their excellent culture, forbearance and civility (*ḥilm, k͟hulq, farhang*), with Murad Bakhsh being singled out for praise. The poet entered his service when that prince was about sixteen years of age, hence towards the close of the 1630s. The portrait of the Mughal empire that he presents must hence correspond to the 1640s and 1650s, a couple of decades before the experiences of the unfortunate Muhammad Mufid, whose views come very largely from the 1670s.

LATER GRUMBLERS: THE CASE OF HAZIN

As was remarked at the outset of this chapter, much has been written concerning the migration of Iranians to Mughal India, both within the context of the history of élite formation in the Mughal domains, and by historians of Mughal–Safavid political and diplomatic relations. For historians of Mughal India, a first focus in this context was the debate regarding the extent of influence exercised by the family of the empress Nur Jahan in the early seventeenth century, during both the reign of Jahangir and that of Shahjahan.[56] Subsequently, with the rise of a more quantitatively oriented history, analyses were produced of the changing composition of elites over the years from about 1550 to 1750, with a major focus being on the relative weight of Iranians, Turanis, Indian Muslims, and other groups such as the Rajputs. Such an approach demonstrated beyond doubt that, as late as the reign of Aurangzeb, a significant group of

[56] S. Nurul Hasan, "The theory of the Nur Jahan 'junta' – a critical examination", *Indian History Congress, Proceedings of the 21st Session, 1958, Trivandrum*, pp. 324–35; Irfan Habib, "The family of Nur Jahan during Jahangir's reign: a political study", in *Medieval India: a miscellany*, vol. I (Bombay, 1969), pp. 74–95.

Iranian *manṣabdārs* existed and exercised substantial power, in particular in the highest echelons of the system (*manṣabs* of 5,000 or more), even if they lost ground somewhat after the late 1670s.[57] The relationship between the Safavids and Mughals was, however, unequal in this respect. As a recent study of élite migration notes, "it must not be forgotten that emigration was always one way, from Iran to India. No person of Indian origin is known to have attained a high position at the Safavid court." However, this was not true of migratory flows in general. The same author notes that, if "at the political and cultural levels, the stream of people flowed from west to east . . . on the other hand, a number of Indian merchants went to Iran in the seventeenth century", suggesting that there may have been as many as 10,000 Indians in seventeenth-century Isfahan.[58]

Some recent studies have attempted to approach the problem at a greater level of detail, by focusing on particular families or the histories of particular individuals, thus reviving an earlier tradition of biographies of such notable Iranian figures in Mughal India as Asaf Khan or Mu'azzam Khan (Mir Jumla).[59] These studies have had the advantage of explaining not merely broad trends, but also the subjective factors that motivated some individuals to move, while others preferred not to; they also help us to see why certain periods were propitious to migration, while others were not.[60] The cliché that Iranians moved to India in search of an easy and pleasurable life, seeing the Mughal domains as something like Havana under Fulgencio Battista, is easily dispelled by such an approach.[61] It is in these terms that the contrast between the cases of Muhammad Mufid and Bihishti Herawi may need to be addressed. Our examination of the narratives of these two authors reveals a number of contrasts, some evident and others less so. We cannot entirely neglect the personal qualities of the two travellers, with Mufid obviously being of a somewat sour and morose disposition, which cannot have smoothed the way for him.[62] It is equally

[57] Cf. Athar Ali, *Mughal nobility under Aurangzeb*, p. 35.

[58] Masashi Haneda, "Emigration of Iranian elites to India during the 16th–18th centuries", in Maria Szuppe, ed., *L'héritage timouride: Iran – Asie centrale – Inde, XVe–XVIIIe siècles*, special number of *Cahiers d'Asie Centrale*, 3–4, 1997, pp. 129–43, citation on p. 137.

[59] Jagadish Narayan Sarkar, *The life of Mir Jumla, the General of Aurangzeb*, 2nd edn (New Delhi, 1979); Anil Kumar, *Asaf Khan and his times* (Patna, 1986).

[60] Masashi Haneda, "La famille Huzânî d'Isfahan (15e–17e siècles)", *Studia Iranica*, 18, 1989, pp. 77–91.

[61] Such a view mars the otherwise useful work of Golchin-i Ma'ani, *Kārwān-i Hind*.

[62] Mufid's account can probably be fruitfully compared with the text of his contemporary Sayyid Ni'matullah ibn 'Abdullah Jaza'iri, *Al-Anwār al-Nu'māniyya*, 4 vols. (Tabriz, 1959–62), as discussed by Roy P. Mottahedeh, *The mantle of the Prophet: religion and politics in Iran* (New York, 1985),

clear that Bihishti's voyage to India was the far better organised of the two, and that he was able to enter smoothly into Mughal service, perhaps because of the fact that he accompanied an Indian envoy back to India. On the other hand, Mufid seems to have had considerable difficulty in finding a patron, and thus struggled to find employment for a long period. The fact that the two accounts are separated by some decades may also be germane to the issue. In the 1640s, the situation of Iranians was probably better, both in the Mughal domains and in the Deccan, than what it came to be some time later. This was not because of some general downturn, or because the Mughal empire had fallen into "decline", but simply because the rise of Indian Muslim and lower-ranking (but upwardly mobile) Rajput elites had in some measure led to the partial displacement of the Iranians. Mufid thus chose a bad moment to make his trip to India, a time when, even in Golkonda, the position of the Iranians had – as we have noted above – begun to appear somewhat insecure.

Most importantly perhaps, reading the account of Mufid helps dispel the notion that a positive view of India always prevailed in Safavid Iran, or that the affinities between the Mughal and Safavid polities necessarily outweighed the tensions that were always implicit in the relations between the two. Rather, we see that a residual reticence remains in the way that the image of India is constructed, and that, if India is always perceived as a land of wonders, these can at times slide into the bizarre. There is surely much merit in seeing India, Central Asia, Iran and even the Ottoman empire of the early modern period as forming part of a single domain of circulation, an ecumene with powerful shared cultural values and symbols, as Marshall Hodgson and others have persistently argued.[63] Yet such a vision should not obscure the existence of dissonant notes, which existed in part on account of the fact that the drive to cultural hierarchisation is not, and indeed has never been, the monopoly of a single culture. The account of Muhammad Mufid cannot be placed in the same class as that of his contemporary Muhammad Rabi', and, even in his most dyspeptic moments, it is difficult to see Mufid descending to the kinds of characterisations that the author of the *Safīna-i Sulaimānī* habitually engages in with regard to the hapless residents of Siam. To Mufid, India is still characterised by some positive features, even if these have come to be

pp. 94–8. Mottahedeh describes Jaza'iri, whose autobiography dates to 1678, as a "lachrymose and self-pitying man", a description that fits Mufid rather well.

[63] Marshall G. S. Hodgson, *The venture of Islam: conscience and history in a world civilization*, vol. III: *The gunpowder empires and modern times* (Chicago, 1977).

secondary with the passage of time. Further, his India is that of the cities, and hence that of a Persianate culture. Like Seydi 'Ali Re'is in the sixteenth century, the India of the countryside scarcely interests him at all; and if there are non-Muslim populations that exist beyond the pale of Persianate culture, he could scarcely be bothered with this fact. The search here then is most often for the familiar, and then for the exotic, not only within the matrix of the topos of *'ajā'ib-o-gharā'ib* ("wonders and marvels"), but as an indulgence once the familiar had been adequately located. In a set of other works, we address a quite different problem, namely how authors who saw Hindustan as deeply familiar addressed the problem of travel therein. What would happen to the Indo-Persian travel-account once it had been shorn of the exotic and bizarre? These are questions that we can address with the help of some north Indian authors who wrote in Persian in the seventeenth and eighteenth centuries.

A few further remarks may also be helpful here on how such views as those of Mufid came to be located in the longer-term vision of India that was inscribed in Iranian xenology. The tensions between Iranian visitors to India and the environment in which they found themselves is, as is well known, a major theme of the eighteenth century. Virulent debates broke out in the middle years of that century, of which one particularly celebrated example centres around the figure of Shaikh Muhammad 'Ali Hazin Lahiji (1692–1766 (?)), whose dismissive point of view on Indian poets and poetry was hotly, and famously, contested by Siraj-ud-Din 'Ali Khan Arzu.[64] Hazin, who was born into an eminent family in Isfahan in 1692 (27 Rabi' II 1103 H), spent a good part of his life in Iran, and although he led a quite peripatetic life, migrated to India only in his late forties.[65] His account, which he wrote in Shahjahanabad in 1154 H (or

64 For the debate between 'Arzu and Hazin, see the section on "Indian Persian versus Iranian Persian" on pp. 174–86, in Alam, "The culture and politics of Persian", pp. 131–98. See also Siraj-ud-Din 'Ali Khan Arzu, *Tanbīh al-Ghāfilīn*, ed. Sayyid Muhammad Akram 'Ikram (Lahore, 1981), in particular the editor's introduction in Persian entitled "Taḥlīl-i Tanbīh al-Ghāfilīn" ; and for brief discussions, the editor's introduction to Waris Kirmani, ed., *Dreams forgotten: an anthology of Indo-Persian poetry* (Aligarh, 1986), pp. 19–35, and Sayyid Muhammad 'Abdullah, "Fārsī ke Zer-i Sāya Zabān-i Urdū ki Tadrīji Taraqqī", in his *Mabāḥiṣ* (Lahore, 1965), pp. 70–95. On Khan-i Arzu himself, see also C. M. Naim, *Zikr-i Mir: the autobiography of the eighteenth-century Mughal poet Mir Taqi 'Mir'* (Delhi, 1999), pp. 66–9, 76. Mir is, however, quite bitterly opposed to Arzu, with whom he had difficult relations.

65 Muhammad 'Ali ibn Abi Talib ibn 'Abd Allah (Hazin), *Tārīkh wa Safar nāma-i Ḥazīn* (1154), in *Diwān-i Ḥazīn-i Lāhījī: Shāmil-i qaṣā'id, ghazalīyāt, maṣnawīyāt, rubā'īyāt*, ed. Bizhan Taraqqi (Tehran, 1350 H / 1971), pp. 1–107; for a translation, see Muhammad 'Ali Hazin, *The life of Sheikh Mohammed Ali Hazin written by himself*, tr. F. C. Belfour (London, 1830).

1742), is part autobiography and part travel-text, and is also interspersed with long asides on political conditions in the Iran of his time, notably the decline of the Safavids and the rise to power of Nadir Shah Afshar (a theme to which we shall turn in a later chapter). To gain a sense of the life he had led before making his Indian voyage, we may note the following travels that he records in a somewhat dizzying sequence. After growing up in Isfahan, Hazin accompanied his father to the province of Gilan, and in particular to Lahejan, the ancestral home. He then returned for a time to Isfahan, and decided after a time that he should visit Shiraz and the regions around it. While at Shiraz, he was seized by the urge to perform the *ḥajj*, and made his way to Bandar ʿAbbas in the Persian Gulf, but was eventually unable to travel any farther than Masqat and Oman. Disappointed, he then returned to Shiraz, and from there eventually to his native place of Isfahan, where in 1127 H (1715), his father died, followed by his mother two years later. Hazin now began to divide his time between Shiraz and Isfahan, but unfortunately found himself in the latter city at the time of the long and brutal siege by the Afghans in 1721–2. He was one of the few fortunate ones in his family who survived, since – by his own account – "two brothers, my grandmother, and the whole of the dwellers in my house died, so that my mansion was emptied of all but two or three infirm old women-servants, who attended me".[66]

Despite his great attachment to Isfahan, a theme to which we shall return below, Hazin was hence at last constrained to leave the town, and fled in the early part of Muharram 1135 H (mid-October 1722) to, first, Khwansar, and then Khurramabad, near Kermanshah. Here he remained for a time, but then decided to make a brief voyage to Hamadan, from where he returned only to proceed to Basra, with the intention once more of making the *ḥajj* which he had failed to accomplish some years before. His account of the voyage is brief: we hear of a painful sea-voyage, and a debilitating illness at Mokha, which meant that he actually could not proceed to the Holy Cities, and instead had to undergo a convalescence in Taʿizz. He was then forced to return by ship from Mokha to Basra, and from there to Shustar, before returning once more to Khurramabad. Here, he was one of the few inhabitants who remained (again, on account of an illness) when the Ottoman army of Ahmad Pasha appeared to take the town. Hazin then departed with the Ottomans to Kermanshah,

[66] *The life of Sheikh Mohammed Ali Hazin*, tr. Belfour, p. 123; Hazin, *Tārīkh wa Safar nāma*, p. 40.

becoming a part of the entourage of the Pasha, but this was not a happy outcome either. Further wars and massacres eventually forced Hazin to make another set of moves, in the direction of, first, Baghdad, and then Karbala, before arriving at length in Najaf.

Here, he at last seems to have enjoyed a respite, spending three years reading and writing, and frequenting "the society of learned and pious men", such as Mulla Abu'l Hasan Isfahani, Maulana Nur-ud-Dahr Gilani, Sayyid Hashim Najafi and others. At the end of this time, however, Hazin was once more seized by the urge to travel, this time to Tus, and then to Kermanshah, where he once again encountered the army of Ahmad Pasha. From Kermanshah, our tireless author then decided to turn his attention to the region of Gilan, and despite the fact that a Russian army had recently laid waste to a good part of the country, made his way from there to Mazandaran. Further political turmoil was on the horizon now, with the rise to prominence of Tahmasp Quli Khan, later to title himself "Nadir Shah". Hazin seems to have managed despite this set of difficulties to write a number of treatises while resident first in Astarabad and then Mashhad, as well as to bring together a fourth *diwān* of his own poetry.

We are now in Safar 1142 H (August–September 1729), and the wars between the Afghans and Tahmasp Quli Khan are about to come to a head, with a decisive victory for the latter. In view of the various armies marching across the countryside, Hazin was to leave first for Mazandaran, and then eventually for Tehran, from where he eventually returned to his beloved Isfahan once Tahmasp Quli had settled matters to his own satisfaction. Here Hazin was able to meet the puppet Safavid monarch, Shah Tahmasp II (r. 1722–32), and speak with him, and he spent all of six months in the city, despite the fact that it was "in utter ruin and desertion", and practically none of his friends remained. It would appear that by now he had acquired quite a reputation as a poet and intellectual, and his company was much sought after by the high and mighty. Eventually excusing himself from the court, he then made his way back to his old haunt, Shiraz, and resolved to try to make the *ḥajj* once more. This meant a return to Bandar 'Abbas via Lar, and in the port Hazin became very friendly with a group of English East India Company merchants (*jamā'at-i firang*), who he declares "were on terms of the kindest and most friendly intimacy (*ik͟hlāṣī*) with me". He decided therefore to voyage on one of their vessels, since their ships appeared "very spacious and are fitted up with convenient apartments, and their navigators are also more expert on the sea and more skilful in their art than any other nation (*har qaum*)".[67]

This third attempt at the *ḥajj* proved more successful than the two others. From Bandar 'Abbas, Hazin made a voyage to Surat, where he stayed for two months, always maintaining his excellent relations with the English. From there, he was taken on another ship to Jiddah, and was able to visit the holy places. His account of the pilgrimage is rapid, save to say that, while in Mecca, he was inspired by a dream to write a treatise on Shi'i theology. He seems to have been inclined for a time to settle there, but eventually decided somewhat reluctantly to return to Iran via the desert route, taking a caravan to Lahsa, and then a ship to Bahrain and Bandar 'Abbas. By the time of his return, however, Tahmasp Quli Khan had pretty much fully seized control of the state, and was putting in place a new fiscal system, allegedly with "heavy and excessive taxes laid on every class of the people". By now, Hazin was also considerably in debt, in part because the voyage to the Holy Cities had cost him dear. He hence resolved to make his way to Isfahan, the seat of power, and had gone as far as Lar when considerable disturbances broke out. It seemed most prudent to return to Bandar 'Abbas rather than advance further, and Hazin now began to contemplate leaving the area entirely for Najaf, for which he seems to have felt a nostalgic longing. Every conceivable avenue seemed to be blocked. Baghdad was under siege by Tahmasp Quli Khan, and Basra appeared to be in the midst of the greatest disorder. For a time, Hazin fled to the coast of Oman on a Dutch vessel, but that area did not suit him either. He then returned to Bandar 'Abbas, spent a few months in its neighbourhood, and decided that he would retire to Kerman.

This was clearly only a temporary solution, for Kerman seemed too much of a backwater for the intellectual, who clearly craved both company and an explicit recognition of his fame. Hazin was clearly constantly on the lookout for opportunities to leave for Najaf, and kept close track of the situation in Basra to that end. As a consequence, he eventually returned to Bandar 'Abbas – a town that he otherwise heartily disliked – and began to await a break in the hostilities between the Ottomans and Tahmasp Quli Khan which would allow him to pass through Basra. But in the port-city too, the situation deteriorated, as rival administrators began to quarrel with each other and also increased the exactions on the port's residents. It was by now the month of Ramazan 1146 H (February 1734), and the situation was clearly a desperate one for Hazin, who had

[67] *The life of Sheikh Mohammed Ali Hazin*, tr. Belfour, p. 215; Hazin, *Tārīkh wa Safar nāma*, p. 72.

spent the previous twelve years, from the time of the siege of Isfahan in 1722, being ceaselessly shuttled from pillar to post, with only a few brief periods of repose, as in Najaf. We are also led to believe from hints that he drops that his financial affairs were not in the best of condition either. It was in this situation that the time-honoured solution suggested itself: a voyage to the India of the Mughals.

The decision seems to have been made very quickly, and Hazin came equally rapidly to find out that a ship was soon to leave Bandar ʿAbbas for the coast of Sind. He secured a passage on the vessel, but word of this decision seems to have spread quickly amongst his friends and acquaintances in the Persian Gulf port. Hazin writes of how some of them tried to dissuade him from carrying out his resolution.

A captain of the English Frank Company (*jamāʿat-i inglishiya-i firang*), when he knew of my intention, came to my residence and began dissuading me from going to Hindustan. He enumerated the ugly aspects of the deportments of that country (*ān mulk*), and he tried to persuade me to go instead to Europe (*Firang*). He insisted on that matter, but I did not agree, and on the same day I left everything behind there and boarded a ship all alone, and sailed in the direction of Sind.[68]

This was a decision that he was to regret time and again, and the pages that follow are nothing less than a litany of complaints regarding life in Sind and Hindustan, which it would appear can only be compared to the most hellish torments. The problem was not one of Hazin's lack of celebrity. Indeed, on arriving in Thatta, he informs us that his own desire was to remain somewhat anonymous, but that a certain number of Persian merchants immediately recognised him and made his presence there known to others. As a consequence, his residence came to be frequented by numerous people belonging, so he informs us, to "various classes of worldly persons". Though lonely, Hazin nevertheless considered many of these meetings and encounters a thorough waste of time, declaring – from the perspective of Delhi in 1742, where he eventually penned his memoirs – that his arrival on the "shores of this land" can be considered, for all intents and purposes, to be the end of his life (*anjām-iʿ umr-o-ḥayāt*) (though he lived on for another twenty-four years). He then adds, with an even greater bitterness:

During these eight years, from Thatta to the city of Delhi which is known as Shahjahanabad, I myself saw whatever I had [already] heard about the

[68] *The life of Sheikh Mohammed Ali Hazin*, tr. Belfour, p. 252; Hazin, *Tārīkh wa Safar nāma*, p. 86.

conditions, qualities and deportments of this country and its people, and also observed a good deal more that I had not even heard about, and which I could never have imagined. I stayed in Thatta for more than two months, and cursed myself on my impatience to depart from Iran, and repented that I had not chosen to travel to the countries of Europe (*mamālik-i Firang*). But the season for sea-journeys was past, and summer had already commenced, and so to return to Iran or go anywhere else one would have to wait for the coming season. In sum, in that city because of the lack of water, and bad climate, and the ugly forms of behaviour which are so common in this country, I became restless. People told me to go to the town of Khudabad, which is one of the flourishing places of Sind, and which is at a few days' journey from here [Thatta]. The journey did not require much preparation and the town could be reached by boat through the channel that passed from Thatta to the border of that town. It was destined to be so. I arrived in Khudabad by boat, but because of the intensity of the heat, the infelicity of the climate, and attacks of sorrow and the effect of adversities, I fell prey to a variety of severe maladies. For seven months, I remained helpless (*bekas*) and ill in that place. When some of my illnesses became less severe, I found it difficult to remain there for various other reasons.[69]

The obvious course would have been to return to Iran, since the very beginning of the Indian stay already seemed fraught with such problems. Hazin instead persisted, obviously convinced that material gains of a substantial nature were still to be had in the Mughal domains. Besides, to return empty-handed would have been to court ridicule, and the Iran of which Nadir Shah was about to become the monarch was none too tempting for him as a destination. He thus continues:

On account of the decree of Fate, I again took a boat towards the city of Bhakkar, located at a few days' journey from there [Khudabad], on the banks of the river Sind. My temperament was totally incapable of bearing the behaviour and manners (*auẓā'-o-aṭwār*) of the people of this place (*īn diyār*), and my helplessness and lack of resources (*bī-sāmānī*) further worsened the miseries and griefs. For about a month I stayed there, and was totally overwhelmed by weakness and indisposition, so that I had to be carried on a palankeen to Multan. Having covered a number of stages with great difficulty, I arrived at a village close to the fortress of that city and camped there.

Moving further north towards Hindustan proper did not provide any easy solutions either. For Hazin seems to have found this part of the country (*īn mamlikat*) even more detestable in many respects than lower Sind. Indeed, to make matters worse, Multan experienced a major flood of the

69 *The life of Sheikh Mohammed Ali Hazin*, tr. Belfour, p. 253; compare Hazin, *Tārīkh wa Safar nāma*, p. 87.

river Indus during the monsoon season, followed by a wave of diseases that seem to have been linked to the unhealthy conditions that prevailed after the floodwaters actually receded. Hazin himself fell victim to a very severe fever, that left him even more debilitated, besides the fact that, in the much-depleted population of the area, no servants or attendants were to be found. Not surprisingly perhaps, in these circumstances that he perceived as rather desperate, he composed a "treatise, the *Kunh ul-Marām*, which is on the explanation of Fate and Destiny, and the nature of free will", no doubt subjects on which he had much time to ponder. He also began to ruminate on what precisely was wrong with Hindustan, a theme to which he returns time and again, but of which he offers a first taste here. Hazin writes:

Let it not remain hidden, that the living conditions in this land are beyond the capacity of my writing, and even if I am somewhat inclined to tell the reader about this in brief, it is in fact absolutely indescribable. But if my pen were to describe even something of my life, then some of the evil conditions and circumstances of this abominable and detestable country (*diyār-i kadūrat-āṣār wa shan'at-aṭwār*) will inevitably become evident. So I had perhaps best let my unfortunate paper and pen undertake this task. For the readers can from my arrival in this country go on to picture the end and termination of my life.[70]

The real problem, as he sees it, lies in a combination of the climate (*āb-o-hawā*) of Hindustan, and the nature of its inhabitants, whose innately defective temperament finds itself further exacerbated by the effect on it of the climate and conditions. An angry passage in Arabic brings out the extent of Hazin's hatred for the place and those who live in it.

I complain to Allah against the tyrannous time, and odious men, lacking in shame, and full of wretchedness; whose very *'ulamā'* are ignorant, and whose *umarā'* are stupid. They have resorted to lust. O God! May ruin and desolation visit them. O God! Give us patience and may I die as a Muslim.

> O God! Let me not stay long in this world,
> whose worth does not equal
> half an iota to the wise.
> That world which has wholly turned
> its glance away from noble souls,
> and is slave to the silly and flatulent.[71]

[70] *The life of Sheikh Mohammed Ali Hazin*, tr. Belfour, p. 256; Hazin, *Tārīkh wa Safar nāma*, p. 88.

[71] *The life of Sheikh Mohammed Ali Hazin*, tr. Belfour, p. 259; compare Hazin, *Tārīkh wa Safar nāma*, p. 89. The readings of the Arabic text both in the edition and by Belfour are problematic.

The windy and ill-bred denizens of the Mughal empire are, as we shall see presently, simply condemned to being so, and have always been of that very nature – indeed even before the Mughals reached India. Their wretchedness and ingratitude, in Hazin's view, stretches back to early history, much before Islam existed in either Iran or Hindustan. They thus live in a manner that would scarcely be tolerable to any self-respecting resident of Fars (let alone a citizen of Isfahan), but the astonishing fact is that they are not even properly capable of perceiving their own manifest inferiority. In one of the most biting passages in his text, Hazin attempts to lay bare the hopeless character of any attempts to introduce change into Hindustan.

The difficulties of living in Hindustan are not hidden from those who have seen all the countries of the world (*sā'ir-i mamālik-i 'ālam*). The reasons of these hardships are more than can be counted. The totality of the [people's] behaviour and the conditions of this country create hardships and difficulties in life. The inhabitants of this country are unaware of this. On the contrary, they consider themselves to be wealthier and more comfortable than the people of the whole world. All these miseries and hardships are totally in accord with their temperament, and they hence pass unnoticed and remain unattended. Living in this country is not possible without arranging three things: a good deal of money, an excess of strength and power, and much knowledge. But even if these three can be brought together, things remain disturbed and unattained. Even the meanest of things cannot be acquired without a great deal of effort and struggle, as well as delay. Things which in other countries can be done by one hard-working person here require ten persons to be achieved. However much you increase your servants and forces (*k͟hadam-o-ḥasham*), affairs remain disturbed and ill-managed.[72]

Such were the reflections of our traveller even before reaching the heartland of the Mughal empire. Nor was his next destination, Lahore, which he describes uncompromisingly as "a depraved city" (*shahr-i makrūh*), any more to his taste. The real point of reference, as the reader of Hazin quickly comes to realise, is the Isfahan of his youth, to which it seems that no city in Hindustan (or indeed anywhere else in the world) can match up. Indeed, an early chapter of the work is devoted to a description of Isfahan, which in Hazin's view is "so neat and clean, so magnificent and splendid, with such a multitude of lofty buildings, of new and ancient monuments, and with such a concourse of elegant and affluent inhabitants", that no other place in the inhabited quarter of the world can compare with it. He adds:

[72] *The life of Sheikh Mohammed Ali Hazin*, tr. Belfour, pp. 261–2; Hazin, *Tārīk͟h wa Safar nāma*, p. 90.

Let a sensible, experienced man (*hoshmand*), who has seen the world and made the circuit of the universe, come to this city, and, settling there, let him have abundant time and opportunity, and he will continually be discovering properties and qualities to distinguish it above every place on the terrestrial globe. Here goodness of living is uniform for the poor and the rich, the stranger and the native: here the gain of every perfection and of every kind of pleasure is obtainable and easy. The inhabitants of Isfahan are of every class of men, and they are all bred to vivacity, manliness and courtesy.[73]

To be sure, Isfahan has undergone some decline of late, but Hazin assures his reader that this is but a passing phase. For, "notwithstanding that the devastation of this great capital has been completed, it is yet the best of all the countries in the world; and any persons arriving here who should not have witnessed its former condition, would suppose that nothing has been diminished from its ancient splendour". The lesson to be drawn from all of this is quite clear once we are in the Mughal domains: far better an Isfahan in grave decline than the best cities of Hindustan.

The wide-ranging condemnation of India by the visitor from Iran arguably reaches its height in a late section of the text devoted to "the circumstances of Hindustan", that follows on a chapter concerning the activities of Nadir Shah in the area of Qandahar. Here, Hazin assures us that the Timurids – with some exceptions such as Sultan Husain Baiqara – were generally well known for their quarrelsome and bloodthirsty nature, and that it was only through the good graces of the Safavids that Babur Mirza, son of Mirza 'Umar Shaikh, had managed to gain control over parts of northern India. However, his descendants had then been thoroughly opportunistic in their dealings with Iran, at times asking for the support of the Safavids, and at other times "affecting haughtiness and exorbitant pride". He then adds the following passage, that is vitriolic in its condemnation.

This habit [of ingratitude] has been confirmed in the nature and constitution of the line of Babur (*silsila-i bābariya*), and it would appear that this disposition is one of the effects of the climate of Hind (*āb-o-hawā-yi Hind*), because it is clear that the people of this land (*īn dayār*) do not cultivate friendship with anyone without an ulterior motive. And from ancient books it is evident that even before the time of Islam, the Ra'is and the rulers of this land were already of this temper and character. Whenever the rulers of 'Ajam themselves, or through one of their commanders, came to this area, the Hindiyan could not find the strength to gain a victory. They would become most humble and obedient, and showed

[73] *The life of Sheikh Mohammed Ali Hazin*, tr. Belfour, pp. 42–3; Hazin, *Tārīkh wa Safar nāma*, pp. 14–15.

willingness to pay tribute. And when the rulers or commanders would return to Iran, within a short time, these ill-advised Ra'is, having observed the despicable crowds of their crow-like dependents (*izdahām zāgh-ṣifatān-i bi-i'tibār*) flocking around, and with a few handfuls of *dirams* and *dīnārs* that they had collected, would fall prey to the disease of arrogance in their own house. And seeing that the field was vacant, they would begin to boast falsely, and go back on the agreements and treaties, and entirely change their behaviour.[74]

This is not Hazin's only use of the term "crow-like" (or of word-play on the term *zāgh-ṣifat*) to speak of the inhabitants of the Mughal empire. The inner nature as well as the external appearance of the Indians is characterised by this blackness, the very basic characteristic of the crow. Indeed, he argues, the dubious and treacherous dealings have been going on in a more or less repeated fashion since the time of ancient Persian rulers such as Minuchihr and Kaiqubad. As for the rulers of Iran, they had from early on very sensibly come to the conclusion that there was little purpose in bringing Hindustan under their rule, for no one who "has a residence and place of abode such as the provinces of Iran (*mamālik-i Irān*) afford . . . will ever be able of his own choice to reside in Hindustan". Indeed, this was true not just for the monarchs of Iran (and of Rum) but even for common peasants and soldiers, all of whom usually found themselves unable to adapt to the conditions of Hindustan. Rare then were those who, on arriving in India from the Ottoman and Safavid domains, actually settled there with any degree of comfort, and those who did so were usually the very dregs of those lands, those who were "weak in their senses, and mean in their disposition".

Indeed, we gather that, while at Lahore, Hazin's greatest desire was to return somehow to Iran, but that the prevailing political circumstances made this particularly difficult. Nadir Shah was by now in the vicinity of Kabul, and his plans for invading northern India were increasingly clear. Hazin feared that if he returned westwards, his path would cross that of the conqueror and his army, to which he adds the rather peculiar claim that if he were to leave India, and Nadir Shah were to arrive there, the Indians would believe that "my going was the instigator of his coming". This hence led him to Sultanpur, and then to Sirhind, from where – passing "through the midst of the army of Muhammad Shah", which was on its way to encounter the invading Iranian force – he eventually made his way to Delhi, and "took up a corner in that tumultuous town".

[74] *The life of Sheikh Mohammed Ali Hazin*, tr. Belfour, pp. 277–8; Hazin, *Tārīkh wa Safar nāma*, pp. 95–6. We have modified Belfour's translation somewhat.

It was here that he would end his account some time later, after the successful entry of Nadir Shah into Delhi, and the events that we shall discuss in the following chapter (dealing with the account of Khwaja 'Abdul Karim Shahristani). Suffice it to say that Hazin ends his text in the same despondent and bitter mood that has characterised him ever since his arrival in Sind. The concluding passages thus run as follows.

In brief, from the time of my arrival in Shahjahanabad to now, which is the end of the year 1154, over three years have passed. All the time, I have been thinking of moving out so that I might be delivered from this country, but because of several obstacles, I have not been able to do so. [Thus], on the uneven road of life, I have passed fifty-three stages with patience and perseverance, and my physical frame is now broken because of the invasion of much grief and illness. The strength of my soul is crushed, and I have dropped my head so low that I have fallen in my own eyes. Now, I am so helpless that I am waiting for the last call to come.

> O God! If you punish me,
> I am one of your slaves.
> If you grant me pardon,
> you are indulgent and merciful.

To my temperament, there can be no dealing with this strange world (*kishwar*) of mischief and commotion. I had no power, either when it came to entering, nor when it comes to leaving. I have [only] come to terms somewhat with my bleeding heart.

> O Hazin arise, rise above this world!
> O Messiah! Raise me from these old sufferings.
> You are alone in this strange assembly,
> rise up from here, and rise up alone.[75]

CONCLUSION

The account of Hazin is an important marker of the fact that some two and a half centuries into Mughal rule in northern India, many Iranian travellers and intellectuals still could not look to those lands – which had been chosen by a substantial number of their own compatriots over Iran – with any attitude other than condescension and contempt. This gaze then is a remarkable feature of a "close encounter", wherein proximity did not resolve the tension that marks the second half of Hazin's account in

[75] *The life of Sheikh Mohammed Ali Hazin*, tr. Belfour, pp. 306–7; Hazin, *Tārīkh wa Safar nāma*, p. 107.

only a marginally less significant way than it marks the slightly earlier account of Thailand by Muhammad Rabi'. In the worldview of such writers, Hindustan was deeply problematic – yet it never quite plumbed the levels that they touched in their descriptions of the "lands below the winds". Finally, a particularly useful example with which we may close the discussion comes to us from the early nineteenth century, in the account of Aqa Ahmad Bihbahani, entitled *Mir'āt ul-Aḥwāl-i Jahānnumā* ("The world-revealing mirror").[76] The author, born in 1777, was the grandson of a great Shi'i *'ālim*, and grew up on the borders of the Ottoman domains, in Kermanshah, until the age of eighteen, when he set out on a series of travels, as well as to pursue higher studies in such great centres of learning as Najaf and Karbala. By 1804, Aqa Ahmad was deeply in debt and hence decided to make his way to India, in what was after all a well-known pattern by then. It is also known that he had relatives in Bengal, which had already been under British rule for half a century, and he may also have been aware that Shi'is based in India continued to send considerable sums of money to holy places such as Najaf and Karbala. In any event, we are aware that he set out from Bandar 'Abbas on a voyage to Bombay, which had by then replaced Surat as the principal destination on the Indian west coast. From there, he made his way first to Hyderabad, and then to Murshidabad, before reaching what was clearly his intended destination, namely Lucknow. Here, rather than the glowing success he had anticipated, Aqa Ahmad became increasingly involved in a series of bitter disputes with the local *'ulamā'*, until he was more or less forced to leave the territory of Awadh. He then returned east to Patna, at the time under British rule, where he began to compose both polemical and autobiographical texts such as the *Mir'āt* in 1809. Aqa Ahmad Bihbahani eventually died in 1819, aged forty-two years.

It has been suggested by Juan Cole that Bihbahani's text represented India as "an imperfect imitation of Iran", in which all three groups that he came into contact with – Hindus, Sunni Muslims, and even his Shi'i brethren in Awadh and Hyderabad – were all incapable of passing the

[76] Partial editions of the text exist, notably Aqa Ahmad Bihbahani, *Safar Nāma-i Hind* (*India in the early 19th century: an Iranian's travel account*), compiled Shayesta Khan (Patna, 1992), and Aqa Ahmad ibn Muhammad 'Ali Bihbahani, *Mir'āt al-Aḥwāl-i Jahānnumā: Bakhsh yakum*, ed. 'Ali Dawwani (Tehran, 1370 H / 1991). In what follows, we depend in good measure on the excellent discussion in Juan R. I. Cole, "Mirror of the world: Iranian 'Orientalism' and early 19th-century India", *Critique*, Spring 1996, pp. 41–60. The same author also discusses Bihbahani's attitudes to Europe in Juan R. I. Cole, "Invisible Occidentalism: eighteenth-century Indo-Persian constructions of the West", *Iranian Studies*, 25, 3–4, 1992, pp. 3–16.

rigorous tests to which he subjected them. His understanding of the Hindus, in particular, was most peculiar, since he saw them as originally monotheists, with links to Abrahamic traditions, who had over the course of time lost their way and become obsessed instead with worshipping stone idols and giving precious gems to temples. The exemplars of this unsavoury religion were in his view the Marathas, who had laid waste to not only the territories of their neighbours but even their own capital Pune, through a deadly combination of war, drought and inflation. This view then is of "Hindu society [as] . . . a complete Other, an anti-Iran differing from his ideals in almost every respect", and it certainly places the Hindus lower than either the Indian Sunnis or Shi'is.[77] It is not on this account that we must suppose that either of those two other groups are exempt from trenchant critique. For Aqa Ahmad was convinced that no Indian, or indeed no outsider long-settled in India, possessed any true knowledge of Islam, declaring that "from the province of the Deccan to that of Awadh, which I have personally seen, I saw no Muslim scholar (*'ālim*) in their society". As regards the Sunnis, their poor condition was largely attributed to their excessive pragmatism, the subordination of religious ideology to courtly culture, as well as to their desire to compromise incessantly with the Hindus. Much of this was laid at the door of the Mughals themselves, for he writes of them that, when Akbar "besought the Hindu rajas and magnates to join with him, they replied that such a departure would depend on the prerequisite that our emperor adopt our customs". As a consequence of this, he claims, even key Muslim customs such as circumcision were in fact abandoned by the Mughals. Little wonder then that Indian Sunnism had little to recommend it.

More astonishing perhaps is the fact that even the Shi'is of Lucknow do not find approval in Aqa Ahmad's eyes. Here too, as in the observance of such occasions as Muharram, he complained that Hindu practices had contaminated them; "they spend such a great amount of time on baseless practices", he alleges, "but are extremely lax in observing the letter of Islamic law". Here, we may find a point of criticism which in fact exceeds any that we would have found before 1700, when Iranians coming to Mughal India were not all that quick to condemn at least their fellow Twelver Shi'ites. This deterioration in relations is linked to two issues. On the one hand, we find a negative view of adaptation to circumstances in Aqa Ahmad's writings, namely that long residence in India was apt to lead

[77] Cole, "Mirror of the world", p. 58.

to degeneration and deformity, as evidenced by the case of the great notable Mir ʿAlam in Hyderabad, who suffered badly from leprosy. On the other, and this is probably crucial, we should note that Aqa Ahmad – like his father and grandfather – belonged to a rigidly reformist Usuli school of Shiʿism, that saw moral reform and orthodoxy as crucial, crusading tirelessly, for example, against Sufism and Islamic mysticism.[78] This strain of belief, that had grown to prominence in Iran in the eighteenth century, eventually allied with the Qajars to produce a new form of state, which Awadh (and even less Hyderabad) did not in their view adequately reproduce.

To sum up therefore, whatever the continuities may be that we perceive between the views of Iranians in the latter half of the seventeenth century, and those in the early nineteenth century, we must be aware that the intervening century and more had also produced a profound set of changes. To the Safavid writer of the 1660s and 1670s, the India of the Mughals was to be looked up to, however grudgingly, in view of the imbalance in political, military and economic terms. The successful invasion of Nadir Shah, which we shall deal with briefly in the next chapter, certainly changed the terms of this equation; once he had seized Delhi and imposed his own terms on Muhammad Shah in 1739, the Mughals no longer appeared formidable adversaries. Thus, with the passage of time, India must have appeared more and more to be a mere milch-cow to potential Iranian migrants, who saw it – as Aqa Ahmad certainly did – as an inferior imitation of their own land. This certainly explains what has been called the "superciliousness and manipulative attitude" of that savant, as indeed it does in part the overbearing attitude of cultural and literary superiority of a writer such as Shaikh ʿAli Hazin, whom Bihbahani, for his part, looked up to greatly.[79] In short, early modern Iranian "Orientalism" with respect to India (if we may qualify it as such), as much as its European counterpart, was susceptible to complex change, and responded to political and cultural forces of a great diversity.

[78] Of relevance to this point is Juan Cole, "Shiʿi clerics in ʿIraq and Iran, 1722–1780: the Akhbari–Usuli controversy reconsidered", *Iranian Studies*, 18, 1, 1985, pp. 3–34.

[79] Cole, "Mirror of the world", p. 60. See also Bihbahani, *Mir'āt al-Aḥwāl-i Jahānnumā*, pp. 286–90, where he recounts his visit to Hazin's tomb in Benares, and gives an account of that savant.

CHAPTER 6

A western mirror

> For the man of reason
> may tread an unseen path,
> while a *qalandar* [dervish] narrates
> only what he observes.
>
> Khwaja 'Abdul Karim, *Bayān-i Wāqi'*

INTRODUCTION

In preceding chapters, we have dealt for the most part with West and Central Asian visitors to South Asia – and even Thailand. However, our examples so far, and they have not been a few, have by and large skirted the problem of Indian travellers heading west. By this we do not mean that we need to address the problem of "Europe as seen from India", which is by itself a field that may require more elaborate attention than can be afforded here. Europe and Europeans were of course a matter of some preoccupation for Indians from the closing years of the fifteenth century, when the first Portuguese fleets appeared in Asian waters. However, as we have argued elsewhere, for several centuries after the arrival of the fleet of Vasco da Gama in Kerala, no direct accounts were in fact produced of Europe – even though Indians had undoubtedly begun to travel there by 1500. Instead, the sixteenth century witnessed a curious situation in which South Asians thought of Europeans (or "Franks" as they usually termed them) without Europe, not pausing to reflect, in a written form at least, on what Europe might look like, and what precisely its internal composition might be.[1] A first clear exception to this rule is the early seventeenth-century text of Tahir Muhammad, the *Rauẓat*

[1] For a useful survey, see Chandra Richard De Silva, "Beyond the Cape: the Portuguese encounter with the peoples of South Asia", in Stuart B. Schwartz, ed., *Implicit understandings: observing, reporting, and reflecting on the encounters between Europeans and other peoples in the early modern era* (New York, 1994), pp. 295–322.

uṭ-Ṭāhirīn, which does attempt to deal with a concrete Europe, and even provides us with a sketch of the political events that led to the takeover of Portugal by Philip II in 1580. Written in Bengal by an author who had himself participated in a Mughal embassy to Goa, this text is an important and unusual one, even if its account of Europe is not a first-person relation.[2]

Far more puzzling in many respects than the neglect of Europe, is the fact that few travellers from Mughal India have left behind first-person accounts of their travels to Central Asia or West Asia. This is in obvious contrast to the numbers of people who must regularly have made this voyage. The motives for doing so would have been quite varied. Merchants clearly plied the routes that took caravans across from northern India to the Iranian plateau, and the great cities of Central Asia. As must have been the case, such commercial expeditions could not have been conducted in a vacuum, and merchant groups must have collected and disseminated knowledge regarding traded goods, prices, coinage and institutions. Yet none of it has come down to us. Others may have travelled from simple curiosity or the desire to see the fabled cities about which they had read – Samarqand, Balkh, Herat or Bukhara. Again, such voyages leave no traces in terms of travel-accounts until the early nineteenth century.[3]

Indeed, strange though it may appear, the whole of the seventeenth century throws up little by way of travel-accounts in Persian from Mughal India that deal with the direct experience of West Asia, whether in the context of the *ḥajj* or otherwise. For Europe, similarly, though we are aware that the Mughal court had access to information regarding the kingdoms there, no direct account of travel to that continent may be found throughout the whole period of the reigns of Jahangir, Shahjahan and Aurangzeb. For the core of this chapter, we must hence turn to the eighteenth century, and look above all to the valuable travel-account of a resident of Shahjahanabad, Khwaja 'Abdul Karim Shahristani, who

[2] Tahir Muhammad Sabzwari, "Rauẓat uṭ-Ṭāhirīn", Bodleian Library, Oxford, Ms. Elliot 314 (Sachau-Ethé No. 100), also see British Library, London, Ms. Or. 168. For a brief and somewhat misleading summary, see H. M. Elliot and J. Dowson, eds., *The history of India as told by its own historians: the Muhammadan period*, 8 vols. (London, 1867–77; reprint, Delhi, 1990), vol. VI, pp. 195–201. For a discussion, see also Sanjay Subrahmanyam, "Taking stock of the Franks: South Asian views of Europeans and Europe, 1500–1800", *Indian Economic and Social History Review*, 42, 1, 2005, pp. 69–100.

[3] See Maria Szuppe, "En quête de chevaux turkmènes: le journal de voyage de Mīr 'Izzatullāh de Delhi à Boukhara en 1812–1813", *Cahiers d'Asie Centrale*, ("Inde – Asie Centrale. Routes du commerce et des idées"), 1–2 1996, pp. 91–111.

travelled in Central and West Asia in the late 1730s and early 1740s, immediately following the invasion of North India by the Iranian conqueror, Nadir Shah Afshar. His account, entitled *Bayān-i Wāqi'*, may be contrasted, as it happens, with another slightly later Indo-Persian travel-account of the eighteenth century (which we shall address in the next chapter), in which the author also travelled from India to West Asia, and left behind a narrative in the first person of his experiences: this is the *Waqā'i'-i Manāzil-i Rūm*, the journal of a certain Khwaja 'Abdul Qadir, one of the members of an embassy sent by the Mysore ruler, Tipu Sultan, to the Ottoman empire.[4] By situating such texts as these in the larger tradition of the Indo-Persian travel-account that we have studied in preceding chapters, we hope to elucidate some aspects of a history of mentalities that so far has been developed only rather superficially in the South Asian historiography. What did these writers see and reconstruct, and what did they ignore? What aspects did they choose to highlight, in their voyages to regions that were, after all, already familiar to them through literary works, Islamic legend, and the word-of-mouth accounts of their contemporaries?

The late eighteenth century is also the period, as we are aware, when the first Indo-Persian travel-accounts of Europe eventually begin to make an appearance. Typically, these have received far greater attention than the work that forms our focus here, partly because today's Indian "xenologists" remain obsessed with the problem of Indian identity as defined in a European looking-glass.[5] Besides, British writers of the colonial period themselves were particularly interested in how they and their civilization were viewed by Indians, a fact that must explain the early notoriety enjoyed by, say, Mirza Abu Talib Khan Isfahani's *Masīr-i Ṯālibī fī bilād-i afranjī* ("Talib's travels in the land of the Franks"), translated into English by Charles Stewart in 1810.[6] The writer, who travelled between 1799 and 1803, provided a view that was not always flattering to the English, but congenial enough, in that it contrasted Albion's

[4] Khwaja 'Abdul Qadir, *Waqā'i'-i Manāzil-i Rūm*.

[5] Cf. Juan R. I. Cole, "Invisible Occidentalism", pp. 3–16; Tapan Raychaudhuri, "Europe in India's xenology: the nineteenth-century record", *Past and Present*, 137, 1992, pp. 156–82. For a more comprehensive view, Gulfishan Khan, *Indian Muslim perceptions of the West during the eighteenth century* (Karachi, 1998); and, most recently, Michael H. Fisher, *Counterflows to colonialism: Indian travellers and settlers in Britain 1600–1857* (New Delhi, 2004).

[6] Mirza Abu Talib Khan Isfahani, *Masīr-i Ṯālibī fī bilād-i afranjī*, ed. Mirza Husain 'Ali and Mir Qudrat 'Ali (Calcutta, 1812); also Charles Stewart, tr., *The travels of Mirza Abu Talib Khan in Asia, Africa and Europe during the years 1799–1803*, 2 vols. (London, 1810).

vigour to Indian decadence.[7] Also quite well known is Mirza I'tisam al-Din, *Shigarf-nāma-i wilāyat* ("Wonder Book of England"), written in 1785, but recounting the author's travels two decades earlier, in the months from January 1766 to October–November 1769.[8] In this case, interestingly, the Persian text was never published, but Urdu and English translations enjoyed fairly wide circulation. Still more recently, Simon Digby has drawn our attention to an unpublished manuscript in his possession, namely Munshi Isma'il's *Tārīkh-i jadīd* (or "New History"), for its part relating the author's voyage to England in the early 1770s.[9] From the same decade, Digby also notes the existence of another Indo-Persian text (equally unpublished), namely Mir Muhammad Husain bin 'Abdul Husaini's *Risāla-i aḥwāl-i mulk-i Firang-o-Hindustān*, which recounts travels to Lisbon and London from Calcutta, in around 1774.

Now, the bulk of these accounts were written by writers who accompanied Englishmen back to their native land, in some capacity or the other, as *munshīs*, as envoys, but also (as with Abu Talib) as gentlemen of leisure.[10] One may imagine that the production of these texts would in part have been encouraged by the British, since they served to stress the "wonders" of *wilāyat*, and the superiority of Western culture and technology, even if they equally contained disparaging remarks on food, manners or climate. However, the texts must be separated from other accounts, also written by Indians in the late eighteenth and early nineteenth centuries, as forms of political or economic intelligence for the British. In the latter cases, the purpose was far more pressing and functional, and the texts may themselves follow the form set out by an implicit questionnaire that forces their authors willy-nilly to observe certain protocols, as

7 See the interesting essay by Michael H. Fisher, "Representing 'his' women: Mirza Abu Talib Khan's 1801 'Vindication of the liberties of Asiatic women'", *Indian Economic and Social History Review*, 37, 2, 2000, pp. 215–37.

8 For the Persian text, see Asiatic Society of Bengal, Calcutta, IvC 96 (III, 34), fo. 147; Government Oriental Manuscripts Library, Chennai, Persian Mss. No. 778. For the English adaptation, J. E. Alexander, *Shigurf namah-i-velaët: Or excellent intelligence concerning Europe; being the travels of Mirza Itesa Modeen, translated from the original Persian manuscripts into Hindostanee, with an English version and notes* (London, 1827); and for a recent translation via Bengali, Mirza Sheikh I'tesamuddin, *The wonders of Vilayet: being the memoir, originally in Persian, of a visit to France and Britain in 1765*, tr. Kaiser Haq (Leeds, 2001).

9 Simon Digby, "An eighteenth-century narrative of a journey from Bengal to England: Munshi Ismā'īl's *New History*", in Christopher Shackle, ed., *Urdu and Muslim South Asia: studies in honour of Ralph Russell* (Delhi, 1991), pp. 49–65.

10 See also, in this context, Michael H. Fisher, *The first Indian author in English: Dean Mahomed (1759–1851) in India, Ireland and England* (Delhi, 1996). Fisher pays too little attention, though, to the possibility that Dean Mahomed's writings were almost certainly transformed by another, "hidden", author.

required by the colonial information-gathering machinery. Within this category fall a good number of texts concerning the trade-routes linking northern India to Central Asia, both the westerly salient to Afghanistan, and Iran, and the easterly one, headed towards Yarkand; there are also accounts of trade-routes within northern India itself, that parallel the travel-accounts of colonial writers such as Francis Buchanan.[11] From such accounts derive the first attempts by the East India Company at mapping out the economic and strategic geography of South and Central Asia, as well as the major and minor centres from which military resistance could be anticipated. Paradoxically, these texts, the product of the exigencies of early colonial rule, wind up resembling – in a formal sense, at least – certain Chinese gazetteer-style travel-accounts, written by official literati in the Ch'ing period and even earlier, that we have discussed in an earlier chapter.[12]

Khwaja 'Abdul Karim's text, and that of the ambassadors to Constantinople, on the other hand, are still resolutely "pre-colonial" in character, even if the reason behind Tipu Sultan's embassy to Istanbul was to shore up his political position against rivals who included the English East India Company. We would therefore consider it legitimate to link them to an earlier tradition of travel-account, dating back to the fifteenth century, while particularly emphasising that, in this earlier tradition, the relationship between observer and observed is rather different from that in the "xenology" of writers such as Mirza Abu Talib.[13]

CONCEIVING A NARRATIVE

The origins of the travels of our author, Khwaja 'Abdul Karim, must be sought not in an embassy or a Sindbad-like shipwreck (the cases,

11 For an account of some of these writings, see Mohan Lal, *Journal of a tour through the Panjab, Afghanistan, Turkistan, Khorasan and part of Persia, in company with Lieut. Burnes and Dr. Gerard* (Calcutta, 1834); Mir Izzat Ullah, *Travels in Central Asia, 1812–1813* (Calcutta, 1872); Ahmad Shah Naqshbandi, "Narrative of the travels of Khwajah Ahmud Shah Nukshbundee Syud", *Journal of the Asiatic Society of Bengal*, 25, 4, 1856; Simon Digby, "From Ladakh to Lahore in 1820–1821: the account of a Kashmiri traveller", *Journal of Central Asian Studies* (Srinagar), 8, 1997, pp. 3–22. For a vision in the reverse direction from the same period, see Michael Aris, *'Jigs-med-gling-pa's "Discourse on India" of 1789* (Tokyo, 1995).

12 For an excellent compendium of different sorts of Chinese travel-accounts, see Strassberg, *Inscribed landscapes*, discussed in Chapter 1 above.

13 For parallel considerations, see Muzaffar Alam and Sanjay Subrahmanyam, "From an ocean of wonders: Maḥmūd bin Amīr Walī Balkhī and his Indian travels, 1625–1631", in Claudine Salmon, ed., *Récits de voyage des Asiatiques: genres, mentalités, conception de l'espace* (Paris, 1996), pp. 161–89; Alam and Subrahmanyam, "Discovering the familiar: notes on the travel-account of Anand Ram Mukhlis", *South Asia Research*, 16, 2, 1996, pp. 131–54.

respectively, of Khwaja ʿAbdul Qadir and Seydi ʿAli Re'is) but in quite another sort of political event, namely in the invasion of northern India by the forces of Nadir Shah Afshar, ruler of Iran.[14] When Nadir Shah eventually departed from Delhi in a north-westerly direction with a huge treasure in May 1739, having restored his defeated rival Muhammad Shah to the throne, he went accompanied by a number of South Asians, among them Khwaja ʿAbdul Karim, author of the text that is our central concern here, the *Bayān-i Wāqiʿ*.[15]

Why was this text written? The conventional, initial sections of the text are somewhat unhelpful in this respect, containing the usual *ḥamd* in praise of Allah, and prayer to Him to decorate the assembly (*maḥfil*) where the author is presenting his narrative (*bayān*). The author then continues with an Arabic phrase, derived from the Qur'an, relating to the issue of true knowledge, which God has given to ignorant Man (*ʿallama al-insāna mā lam yaʿlam*). He goes on in prose, with conventional praise (*naʿt*) of the Prophet, his descendants and companions (*manqabat*). It seems clear from the praise of the Companions of the Prophet that the author is either a Sunni, or at least not an uncompromising Shiʿi. Khwaja ʿAbdul Karim then commences in rhymed prose to describe himself as a mere slave (*banda-i ḥaqīr*), full of errors, who is as it happens from the paradisaical land of Kashmir, and descended from Adam who had to leave Paradise for Earth on account of his errors. Of course, Adam was of high status, and the author is no more than the humble ʿAbdul Karim, son of Khwaja ʿAqibat Mahmud, son of Khwaja Muhammad Bulaqi, son of Khwaja Muhammad Riza; but the implied notion is that, even as Adam was expelled from Paradise, the author has had to leave Kashmir.[16] Suitable verses stress the comparison:

[14] Cf. Laurence Lockhart, *Nadir Shah* (London, 1938), and, more recently, Peter Avery, "Nadir Shah and the Afsharid legacy", in Peter Avery, Gavin Hambly and Charles Melville, eds., *The Cambridge history of Iran*, vol. VII (Cambridge, 1991), pp. 3–62.

[15] Khwaja ʿAbdul Karim, *Bayān-i Wāqiʿ*. The edition is largely based on the manuscript of the Oriental and India Office Collections, London, Ethé 566. An abridged and partly inaccurate translation exists of some sections by Francis Gladwin: *The memoirs of Khojeh Abdulkurreem, a Cashmerian of distinction who accompanied Nadir Shah . . .: including the history of Hindostan, from A. D. 1739 to 1749* (Calcutta, 1788). See also the section translated as "Voyage de l'Inde à la Mekke", in Louis Langlès, tr. and comp., *Voyages dans l'Inde, en Perse, etc. avec la description de l'île Poulo-Pinang, nouvel établissement des anglais près de la Côte de Coromandel. Par différens officiers au service de la Compagnie anglaise des Indes orientales* (Paris, 1801).

[16] See the brief but useful biographical notice by S. Maqbul Ahmad, "ʿAbd-al-Karīm bin Khvāja ʿĀqebat Maḥmūd bin Khvāja Bolāqī Kashmīrī", in Ehsan Yarshater, ed., *Encyclopaedia iranica*, vol. I, part I (New York, 1982), p. 125.

Take me as your friend,
for I am the Adam of my own time.
Whoever is my enemy
is accursed Satan.

The author now addresses himself briefly to the wise men and intellectuals who adorn the world, in the hope that they will forgive his defects and those of his narrative. His story begins, he tells his readers, with the arrival of Nadir-i Sultan in Hindustan, at which time he, the smallest of the slaves of Allah resided in Shahjahanabad, and had long desired in his heart to make the *ḥajj* to the House of God, visit the shrines of the religious divines (*akābir-i dīn*) and kiss the feet of the virtuous men of faith. His heart was turbulent with this desire; and since it is generally destined that whoever truly desires something gets it, he had the occasion to meet Mirza 'Ali Akbar Khurasani, the intendant (*dārogha*) of the chancellery (*daftarkhāna*) of Nadir Shah, but who also had the entire work of the *wizārat* in his charge, since there was no *wazīr* at this time. Through him, 'Abdul Karim managed to get an audience with Nadir Shah, and a promise from him that he would be given leave for *ḥajj* and other pilgrimages (*ziyārāt*) if he joined his entourage as a functionary (*mutaṣaddī*).

Now, on his return to Hindustan from his long journey, which he had so greatly desired to accomplish, all his friends, in consideration of their long-standing relations with him (and as a mark of their loyalty and sincerity), had asked him to write something of the events and occurrences (*waqā'i' wa ḥālāt*) of this journey, as well as something about the etiquette and functioning of the court of that enigmatic figure, Nadir Shah. This had then led him to put down something of the details of his experiences and journey. He thus highlights how the journey is itself a form of embodied prayer (*īn siyāḥat sarāsar 'ibādat*); and though he uses the idea of voyage (*musāfarat*), the notion of exile (*hijrat*) is little evident.[17] Narration is thus seen as an important and logical part of the process of travel itself. He asserts in all humility that he had decided to put down an ordinary, and even incoherent, narrative; but it was also his intention to add to this an account of the events and unfortunate occurrences (*wāridāt*) that had taken place in golden Hindustan (*zar nishān*).

[17] Compare the texts discussed in Dale F. Eickelman and James Piscatori, eds., *Muslim travellers: pilgrimage, migration and the religious imagination* (Berkeley, 1990).

Khwaja ‘Abdul Karim now proceeds to a series of significant verses, which in a sense define the core of his textual construction:

> It’s better not to hear old tales
> whatever you say had best be based on the seen.
> The story of Farhad and Shirin
> has become old and dated
> like bygone luxury or a used almanac.
> I narrate what I saw
> not old stories and *dāstāns* [tales].

We now come at last to the most significant of the verses, that we have used in epigraph to this chapter:

> Chira ‘āqil rah-i nādīda pūyad
> qalandar harchi gūyad dīda gūyad
> (For the man of reason
> may tread an unseen path,
> while a *qalandar* narrates
> only what he observes.)

As it happens, we are aware that in the medieval Persian literary world, a strong opposition is asserted between the world of reason (represented by the *‘āqil*) and that of the heart (represented by the Sufi and the *qalandar*). It hence appears to us that ‘Abdul Karim is playing here on this contrast, and asserting the importance of lived empirical experience (the empiricism, so to say, of the heart), as opposed to mere intellectual and rationalist reflection. Indeed, from the outset, in his choice of words, and the idea of kissing the feet (*qadam-bosī*) of the virtuous men of faith (*ṣulaḥā-i ṣāḥib-i yaqīn*) he appears consciously to espouse the Sufic tradition.

Khwaja ‘Abdul Karim notes here that he had decided to call his text *Bayān-i Wāqi‘* (which could simply be translated as “True Narrative”), and had hence not polluted his text – or so he tells us – with exaggerations and diplomatic statements as one finds in the history books; he claims equally to have refrained from verbose, convoluted and overly decorative phrases and expressions, so that the work would not create difficulties for the reader. Above all, he insists that he wishes his meaning to be entirely clear, rather than clouded by unnecessary words. He thus cites Hafiz:

> The cry from Hafiz’s heart
> is not without cause,
> There are really unusual stories (*qiṣṣa-i ‘ajīb*),
> and wonderful narratives (*ḥadīṣ̤-i gh̲arīb*).

What of contemporary history? Well, the details of the rise of the power of Nadir Shah and his invasion of Hindustan, as well as the absence of coordination between the nobles and pillars of the Sultanate of Hindustan, could notionally be entrusted to the historians of the two kings in question (such as Mirza Muhammad Mahdi); nevertheless, as he soon makes clear, our Khwaja too has something of his own to say on the question.[18] We are introduced now to the structure of the text itself. The first chapter is concerned with the rise to prominence of Nadir-i Sultan and his coming to Hindustan, while the next chapter describes his departure, and his journey to Turan, Khorasan and Mazandaran, until he reached his capital of Qazwin. Here, 'Abdul Karim took leave of him for the *ḥajj*. The third chapter then concerns the events that took place in 'Iraq-i 'Arab, Sham, Hijaz, and during the author's return sea-voyage to Hughli Bandar in Bengal. The fourth chapter (which will only concern us briefly here) purports to describe some of the events that had taken place between his arrival in Hughli and the death of Muhammad Shah. He also gives the title of the *k͟hātima* to the last section, which is in turn divided into two parts (*muqaddima*). The first part, further subdivided into two sections (*bāb*), was to concern some pleasantries and epigrams of the time, and the second section was to deal with the wonders of the age that he had observed.[19] The second *muqaddima*, for its part, was equally divided into two *faṣl*; the first narrating the *taẕkira* ("account") of the virtues of the virtuous people (*ak͟hyār-o-abrār*), which he highlights through a Qur'anic verse. The second part, on the other hand, describes the cruel and wicked people (*ashrār*) of the time, for which another appropriate framing Qur'anic verse is found. All in all, there is a clear underlying logic to be found in this. The point of departure is clearly the traumatic event of the crumbling of Mughal power under the Iranian onslaught, an event which for Khwaja 'Abdul Karim must somehow be explained. To seek out its roots, he adopts a two-pronged strategy. First, he decides to look into the antecedents and nature of the conqueror himself, Nadir Shah, to see of what stuff he is made. The second part involves a far larger comparative reflection, in which Hindustan must be brought face to face with its neighbours to the north

[18] Cf. Mirza Muhammad Mahdi Khan Astarabadi, *Jahān-gushā-yi Nādirī*, ed. Sayyid 'Abdullah Anwar (Tehran, 1961–2); Muhammad Kazim, *Nāma-i 'Ālamārā-yi Nādirī*, 3 vols. (Moscow, 1960–6). We may note that Khwaja 'Abdul Karim's account draws periodically on the work of Hazin, which we have discussed in Chapter 5 above.

[19] Compare Naim, *Zikr-i Mir*, pp. 130–43, section entitled "Witty tales".

and west. On these areas, Khwaja 'Abdul Karim, like any well-bred (*ashraf*) Muslim from Shahjahanabad of his time, already disposes of information in terms both of Persian literature, and of the religious tradition going back to the Old Testament. This alone will not suffice for him, and he must instead tell the reader what he knows "from his own observation".

A TYRANT AT WORK

Here the introduction ends, and we move to the first chapter, which is incidentally not included in Francis Gladwin's abridged eighteenth-century translation. Its title is *ḥasb-o-nasab-i Nādir Shāh* ("genealogy and character of Nadir Shah"). It is divided in turn into several sub-sections, with the first section describing Nadir Quli Beg Afshar and his rise to kingship. In these pages, the author is not called upon to play the role of eyewitness for the most part, but instead must espouse (despite his own earlier disclaimers) the rather more classic task of chronicler. In order to do so, however, he returns once more to the problem of empirical evidence, and bearing witness (*mushāhada*). He thus notes that in this section, he recounts *not* what he has seen, but what he has heard from reliable people who had long been in Nadir Shah's company, while at the same time reminding the reader that the burden of all things omitted and distorted is on the shoulders of his informants, not himself. The narration thus begins with Nadir Quli Beg, son of Imam Quli Beg, who belonged to the commoners of the city of Abiward and led a life of indigence. Baba 'Ali Beg, who was head of an Afshar group in that city, on the death of Imam Quli Beg married the latter's second wife, who was also Nadir's mother. He realised the extraordinary intelligence of his step-son, and so gave him his own daughter (from an earlier wife) in marriage. Thus, the fortunes of this member of an indigent family began to climb, and he eventually rose to the Sultanate. As the Qur'an says, after all, no soul knows what it may become tomorrow.

A second short section takes us through the decline of the Safavids, and the brief rise to power in Iran of the Khalji Afghans of Qandahar. This is an epoch of plunder, looting and massacres, which are a result, it is claimed by 'Abdul Karim, of the narrow sectarian religious prejudices (*ta'aṣṣub-i maẕhab*) of the Afghans. The sad events of the time are summed up under the head of *bīdādī-yi charkh* ("injustice of the sky") and call forth some verses from the pen of 'Abdul Karim.

THE

MEMOIRS

OF

KHOJEH ABDULKURREEM,

A CASHMERIAN OF DISTINCTION,

Who accompanied NADIR SHAH, on his return from HINDOSTAN to PERSIA; from whence he travelled to BAGHDAD, DAMASCUS, and ALEPPO, and after viſiting MEDINA and MECCA, embarked on a ſhip at the port of JEDDEH, and ſailed to HOOGHLY in BENGAL.

INCLUDING

The HISTORY of HINDOSTAN, from A.D. 1739 to 1749: with an account of the EUROPEAN SETTLEMENTS in BENGAL, and on the Coaſt of COROMANDEL.

TRANSLATED FROM THE ORIGINAL PERSIAN,

BY FRANCIS GLADWIN, ESQ.

CALCUTTA:

PRINTED BY WILLIAM MACKAY.

M.DCC.LXXXVIII.

Figure 13. Title page of the abridged English translation of the *Bayān-i Wāqiʿ* (1788).

Every day the sky perpetrates atrocities,
every moment the aggrieved feel release.
This lovely land is like a beautiful bride yet,
each day it must take in its lap a new husband.[20]

The battles and engagements between the Safavids and Afghans eventually enable Nadir Quli Beg, who has been waiting as it were on the margins, to emerge into a situation of prominence as a successful military commander for the Safavids. Over the course of these campaigns, he becomes *sipāh-sālār* and *mīr-i-shamshīr* (both high military positions), with the title of Tahmasp Quli Khan. He is also quite successful in campaigns against the Ottomans at Baghdad and elsewhere, so that at last Shah Tahmasp Safavi has to give him a robe of honour and his own seal for his services, though, in his heart, he fears the consequences of Tahmasp Quli Khan's growing power. At length, the latter decides for his part to get rid of the Shah, whose behaviour makes him uneasy. He therefore forces him to abdicate, and places on the throne his two-month-old son, for whom the *k͟huṭba* is read in the Friday prayer under his new title of Shah 'Abbas. Earlier, Tahmasp Quli Khan has married the sister of Shah Sultan Husain, and, at this time, he also marries the daughter of Sultan Husain (and sister of Shah Tahmasp) to his older son Riza Quli Khan, cementing his relations with the Safavids. Further, all the provinces of Iran come under the control of governors of his faction.

The emphasis already in the first *bāb* is very much on the tyrannical and bloody nature of Tahmasp Quli Khan (a recurring theme throughout the text), who is portrayed on the one hand as low-born, but on the other hand as an irresistible force, which is equally a calamity for Iran. He also appears as a political manipulator of great guile, and as characterised by a total lack of scruples. This is evident in the next *faṣl*, describing the accession (*julūs*) of Tahmasp Quli Khan to the throne of Iran (*ba tak͟ht-i-Salṭanat-i-Irān*). For, having overcome his internal and external enemies, Tahmasp Quli Khan sees that the entire field (*maidān*) is empty, and his mind becomes intoxicated with the desire for rulership. Yet, he cannot express this openly, but instead begins manoeuvring surreptitiously. One day, he invites the notables, chiefs and elders (*a'yān kadk͟hudāyān rishtsafedān wa kalāntarān*) of all of Iran to the plain of Mughan, and says he wishes to retire; but in his heart, he wants to be crowned. He

[20] The text literally states *dāmād* (son-in-law).

hence also instructs his chief jailer to prepare chains and instruments of torture, so that if anyone thinks to resist his power, they would remain silent from fear. Then, when the chiefs and leaders are assembled, under certain pretexts he executes two of them publicly, and thereby demonstrates the evident instruments of his power; he now gives a speech, stating that he wishes to return to his home town, as he is fatigued and aging. He also takes the opportunity to recount his deeds in an exaggerated manner, and stresses the risks that he has incurred, in an impressive and eloquent style. His last sentence is thus: "In fine, it is up to you and your Badshah Tahmasp. As for me, neither wealth nor power interests me." 'Abdul Karim can scarcely restrain his irony in the face of this display of hypocrisy. The poor chieftains, who understand his real desire, submit that Shah Tahmasp is engaged in affairs that are of no use to his subjects, and that he is incapable of looking to the affairs of the state. It thus falls, they say, on Tahmasp Quli Khan to take over the task, all the more so since he has already been the saviour of numerous women and children, and has helped accumulate so much wealth to the benefit of the subjects (*ri'āya*). When Tahmasp Quli Khan hears these words, he feigns amazement, and protests that he cannot run the state at his advanced age. He advises them to return to their houses, and to seek out someone else. The next day, the poor chiefs return, and out of fear of punishment and torture, once more urge him to accept the title of Sultan for the benefit of the subjects. At last, after feigning great hesitation, Tahmasp Quli (or Nadir) accepts the rulership, and prepares a document of consensus (*maḥẓar*), stating that he was consenting to take on this responsibility on the insistence of the people. The chiefs are asked to put their seals on the *maḥẓar*, and he assumes the throne.

'Abdul Karim cites a sarcastic Arabic chronogram to mark the occasion – *Al-khair fī mā waq'a* ("Whatever happened is for the best") – and notes that a poet of the time had composed a verse incorporating the chronogram.[21] It is stated that, after his coronation, Tahmasp Quli Khan begins calling himself Nadir Shah or Nadir al-Sultan. The author recounts a common verse of the period, once more insisting on Nadir Shah's low origins:

> Last year, you were called Qutbak (Little Qutb),
> and this year you became Qutb-i-Din,
> if you survive into the next year,
> you'll become Qutb-i-Din Haidar.

[21] *Bayān-i Wāqi'*, p. 22.

In general, writes 'Abdul Karim, once he had gained power, Nadir Shah began honouring the low-born and torturing the high-born and the accomplished. Such men raise up the one (states our moralising and socially conservative author), and bring down the other, little realising that everything is in the hands of the Creator. At this time, Nadir Shah turned his attention to Qandahar, where he stayed for eleven months, and himself built a town in the vicinity called Nadirabad. Having eventually captured and destroyed Qandahar fort, and put to death all its residents, save those who moved to Nadirabad, he began looking in time towards Hindustan.

The next *faṣl* is thus entitled "An account of Nadir Shah's proceeding towards Hindustan, and the account of its ruination". We rehearse Nadir Shah's despatch of an embassy to the court of Muhammad Shah at Delhi, and his eventual decision to leave Qandahar for Kabul. Here, he met little resistance, and so he proceeded towards Peshawar with the intention of plundering Hindustan with his strong and pitiless (*bīraḥam*) army. The Mughal army of Nasir Khan was shattered in battle and he, being wounded, fell into the hands of the Qizilbash. It was now that the pillars of the Mughal empire, and the emperor himself, came to suspect the plans of Nadir Shah. They set about preparing for war, and the emperor, with Nizam-ul-Mulk, Khan-i Dauran, Qamar-ud-Din Khan, and many other commanders, moved, with their cannons and arsenal, towards Lahore. Burhan-ul-Mulk, governor of Awadh, was asked to arrive early at the court. For his part, Nadir Shah, having settled Peshawar, entered Lahore, and set out thence for Shahjahanabad. The plain of Karnal, at a distance of four *manzils* from Shahjahanabad, was fixed as the battleground (*maqarr-i-qitāl*).

Now follows an account of the battle between the two rulers, of Hindustan and Iran.[22] The bulk of the Mughal commanders did not fight; only Nawwab Burhan-ul-Mulk surpassed the legendary hero Rustam in bravery, and Khan-i Dauran continued to fight, but all this in a chaotic and uncoordinated fashion. This lack of coordination is lamented by 'Abdul Karim in verses, and he gives a list of dead commanders and notables from the Mughal army of Khan-i Dauran. It was the absence of Mughal artillery (*topk͟hāna*), says 'Abdul Karim, that was primary responsible for their defeat, together with the lack of rapid mobility. The soldiers of Nadir Shah not only fought with muskets, but retreated and advanced with rapidity, and so very few of them were wounded or killed. The Qizilbash were, ostensibly at least, greatly impressed at the valour of the soldiers of Hindustan, and so some of

[22] *Bayān-i Wāqi'*, p. 26.

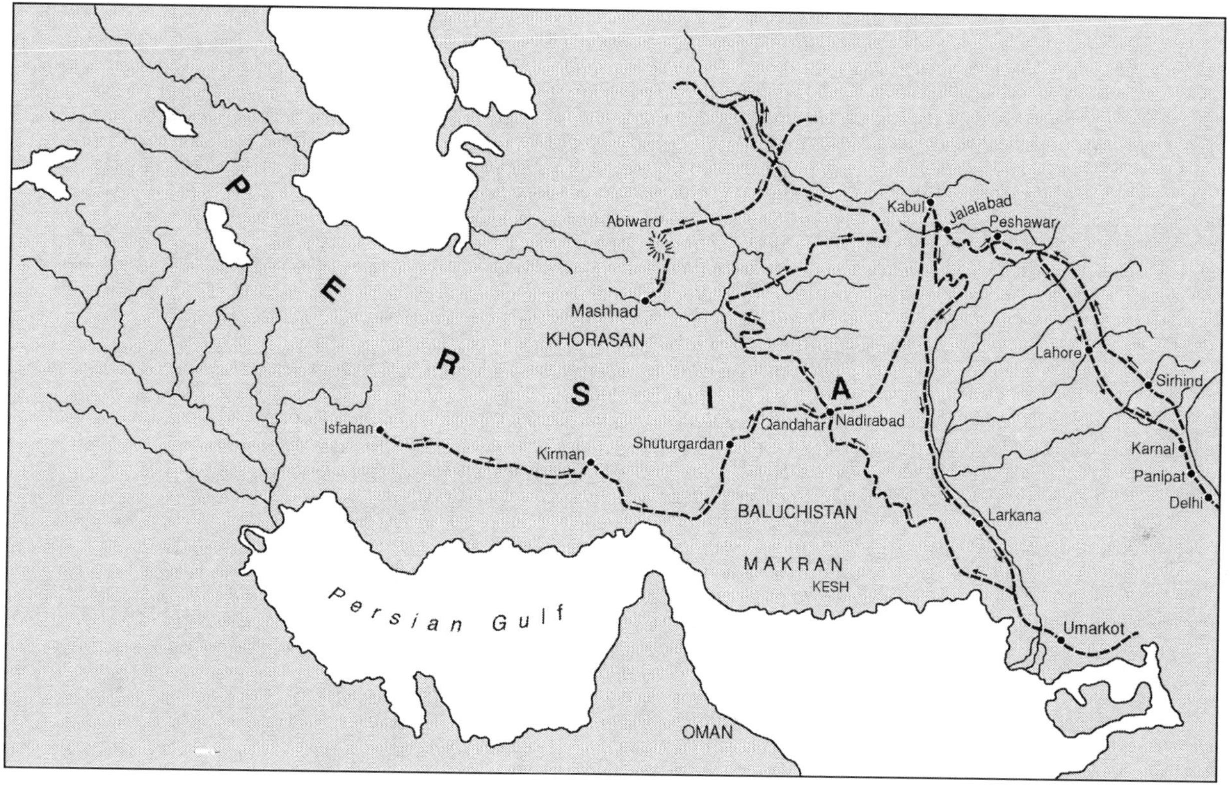

Map 4. Map of Nadir Shah's campaigns.

them fled the battlefield towards Ambala, at a distance of two or three days from Karnal! It is even claimed that the next day, when the Mughal emperor arrived on the battlefield with the remaining commanders, they waited for the enemy to advance but Nadir Shah dared not move from his place. Instead, he pleaded for a truce, and it is very probable (if we believe our author) that, if the nobles of Hindustan had gone into battle initially with artillery, the Qizilbash would not have been in a position to combat them. Thus, in a curious and devious turn in the narrative, 'Abdul Karim tries to save face for his compatriots, though this can only be done by introducing some incoherence into his text.

An account follows of negotiations between the two rulers, initiated with a meeting over coffee (*qahwa*). These negotiations continued for a day or two, and eventually it was decided that the emperor would send back his army to the different parts of Hindustan, while he himself would remain camped there with 2,000 men in the vicinity of the army of the ruler of Iran. Three days later, they were to depart together to Shahjahanabad, and Nadir Shah would be the guest (*mehmān*) of the emperor of Hindustan for two months and would then return to the capital of his own Sultanate. The emperor of Hindustan would remain in that position. The section ends with the hemistich:

> When a small bird (*murgh-i-zīrak*)
> falls in a trap,
> Patience is the only remedy.

The following section takes us into the entry of Nadir Shah into Delhi, and the disastrous events that followed. For, the night after the Iranians had entered the town, a group of the local ruffians and low-born (*ajlāf-o-aubāsh-i-shahr*) went around announcing that the Mughal emperor had deceitfully killed Nadir Shah, and that his head had been severed from his body. A commotion resulted, and the people fell on the Qizilbash and killed as many of them as they could. The well-equipped Qizilbash for their part lost their courage, and could not even face up to the ordinary citizens of the town, who intended to strip them naked and kill them. Some 3,000 Iranians were thus killed. Nadir Shah was enraged at this, and ordered a retaliatory massacre. All those found in Indian attire were to be stripped of life itself, and the entire town was to be looted. These orders were followed, in excess even of the intention.[23]

[23] For another contemporary account, see Anonymous, *Wāqi'ah-i kharābī-yi Dehlī dar 'ahd-i Muhammad Shāh az wurūd-i Nādir Shāh wālī-yi Irān*, ed. Sharif Husain Qasemi (Delhi, 1990).

'Abdul Karim now proceeds to describe the massacre (*qatl-i 'āmm*) that followed. For hours, the death and devastation continued, while the Indian ruffians who had provoked it had disappeared. The poor notables (*shurafā'*) who had their houses and families in the city, and who were unhappy over what had happened with the Qizilbash, now fell to the swords of the Qizilbash themselves. According to reliable reports by Faulad Khan, the *kotwāl* of the city, 20,000 people were killed, and all sorts of jewels, hoards and cash fell into the hands of the Iranian soldiers. Though the troubles initially began adjacent to the royal fort, and the residents of the quarters far away from the centre had thought themselves safe (and had even moved their cash and valuables there), in the end even these areas were affected. The houses and shops of jewellers and bankers (*ṣarrāfs*) were looted, and one can hardly estimate how much wealth the Qizilbash gathered up. Indeed, they themselves were confused and amazed at their own fortune. Many houses were set on fire, and thousands – both dead and alive, Hindu and Muslim – were burnt. May God save us, exclaims our author! Had that cruelty continued to the evening, not a single soul from Delhi would have been spared, even as a specimen of the species. Even if this was not at all Nadir Shah's intention, such was the logic of the massacre, once the confusion and chaos (*fasād* and *fitna*) began, that it was not possible to bring it to a halt. In such conditions, it is difficult, even impossible, to distinguish the guilty from the innocent. When a member of a community (*qaum*) commits an error, writes our Khwaja, the honour of no one therein, whether great or small, is spared. Only an hour before sunset, at the request of Muhammad Shah, was this bloodshed of the innocents halted. Nadir Shah then issued an order to his men, and the Qizilbash (who mortally feared their ruler) ceased their looting and killing. This too, says 'Abdul Karim, was one of the wonders of the world, that such a blood-thirsty and cruel army, when they had so many wealthy men and women at their mercy, should obey an order with such promptness.[24]

We now move to the aftermath of the massacre. Nadir Shah's officials busied themselves in collecting money in the city, and he also confiscated the treasuries and workshops of the *umarā'* who had been killed in battle. The value of the plunder by the Qizilbash was also calculated, and he then ordered his chief financial official (*mustaufī ul-mamālik*) that six months' arrears that were due to the army, with six months' advance, and

[24] *Bayān-i Wāqi'*, p. 39.

six months' salary by way of a reward, should be paid out. The cash, jewellery, silver, the Peacock Throne and several other thrones and jewelled seats of past Mughal monarchs, horses, and elephants, that only the Almighty could add up in value, were taken, the estimate of the whole being put at over 800 million rupees. For the next three years, the accountants of the treasury of Muhammad Shah, and the expert accountants of India and Iran, struggled to find out what had been taken, but could arrive at no certain answer. Nadir Shah refrained from plundering the jewels and treasury inside the palace (*andarūn-i maḥal*), despite the fact that many people had described to him the wealth that was inside. As for the other innovative administrative measures that he took, Muʿtabar-ul-Mulk was ordered that the existing coinage of Iran be suspended, and in its place a new silver coin, similar to the Mughal Rupee in weight and shape, and a gold coin similar to the Indian *muhr*, be minted, and that the coin be called the *nādirī*. On the coins, the legend to be inscribed was: *Hast Sulṭān bar Salāṭīn-i-Jahān Shāh-i-Shāhān Nādir-i Ṣāḥib-Qirān* ("Nadir, Lord of the Conjunction, is Sultan of the Sultans and King of Kings"). The chief *munshī*, Mahdi Khan, was ordered to inform everyone that, from that day onward, Nadir Shah's name should be written as *Shāhenshāh*. On the main signet-ring of this merciless and tyrannous ruler (*bī mehr-i kaṣīr ul-qahr*) (as ʿAbdul Karim terms him), and on all his papers of revenue and expenses, and all the diplomatic correspondence and other letters of the chancery, he required the following verse to be inscribed:

> Nāgin-i daulat-o-dīn rafta būd chūn az jā
> Ba nām-i Nādir-i-Irān qarār dād khudā.
> (The jewel of power and religion
> had disappeared from this place,
> in the name of Nadir of Iran,
> God reinstated it.)

It was conceded that the areas beyond the river Atak, such as Peshawar, Kabul, Ghazna, the Bangash country, and Khudabad, Thatta and Bhakkar, along with the revenues of the four *maḥāls* of the Punjab, which had long been earmarked for the expenses of Kabul province, would be given over to Nadir Shah's control. The rest would remain with Muhammad Shah.

Now, our author notes, after clearing financial and administrative matters, Nadir Shah would often call entertainers (*arbāb-i-ṭarāb-i hindī*) and spread the carpet of joy and pleasure (our author's terms). A brief and rather interesting description follows of the holding of a pleasure-party (*mahfil-i nishāt*), and the presentation (*mujrā*) of Nurbai Tawa'if. Nurbai was the head of all the groups of entertainers, and was celebrated and unmatched for her ready wit, humour, flirtatiousness, coquetry and the pleasantness of her company.[25] She was invited to the court, recited the following verses before Nadir Shah, and was rewarded with special royal favour.

> O heart-stealer, you've come back to honour me.
> Where had you gone, leaving my heart,
> that you've come back?
> Give me wine, take some yourself,
> clap your hands, and tap your feet.
> You've come to a tavern,
> not to say your prayers (*namāz*).

Nadir Shah greatly enjoyed these verses, ordered that she be given 3,000 rupees, and that she should be asked to accompany him to Iran. When the poor Nurbai heard this, she stopped eating and sleeping, and thought it better to die. Her bowels began to run, and she actually felt she was close to dying; on the pretext of this illness, she protected herself from the claws of that human leopard Nadir Shah. Thus, this woman remained there (says 'Abdul Karim), as a scourge for the young sons of the rich *amīrs* of Delhi. Someone asked her if she had gone with Nadir Shah and been forced to sleep with him, how would she have felt? Bai Jio replied that she would have imagined that her private parts had also been prey to the massacre (*qatl-i 'āmm*) in Delhi. 'Abdul Karim assures us that he knows many such risqué anecdotes, but he refrains from them in general since such stories were not publicly appreciated by the wise (though they were a source of pleasure, and delighted the hearts of both old and young). He thus moves on to more serious matters in the second *bāb* of the book.

ON THE ROAD

We now enter at last into the second chapter, in which the travels of the author himself really begin. In point of fact, the chapter commences with the withdrawal of Nadir Shah from Delhi, and his journey to Kabul and Sind; it deals as well with the release of the prisoners taken at Delhi. On 7

[25] For details on Nurbai, see also Dargah Quli Khan, *Muraqqa'-i Dehlī*, ed. Nurul Hasan Ansari (New Delhi, 1982), pp. 102–3. See also Naim, *Zikr-i Mir*, p. 141.

Safar 1152 H (15 May 1739), says 'Abdul Karim, when Muhammad Shah had reigned about twenty-one years, Nadir Shah, having conferred the rulership of Hindustan on him, once more set off, and camped in the Shalimar garden. The *kotwāl* of Delhi, Faulad Khan, was instructed that if any member of Nadir Shah's army tried to stay behind at Delhi, his nose and ears should be cut off and he should be sent to the camp. Haji Faulad Khan did his best to execute the order, but many of the soldiers, fearing the travails of the return journey, managed to escape the vigilance and stayed behind, another measure of the tyranny of their master.

The return journey is described as arduous for the Iranians, whose winter clothes (*libās-i-wilāyat-i sard siyar*) were an additional burden. Many people and animals attached to the army lost their lives before they reached the banks of the Chenab, where the fresh and life-giving climate reinvigorated them. The river-water was chilly because of the mountains in the neighbourhood, and even if the Iranians were used to cold water, none of them could dare stay with his private parts in the water to recite the Qur'anic verse of *ikhlāṣ* eleven times ritually. The residents of the neighbouring villages had run away to the mountains for fear of the army. Some of them returned in the middle of the night, cut the trunks of the big trees around, and threw them in the river, so that they dashed violently against the makeshift bridge that had been built there. Several people drowned in the process. Even if a part of the army was put on guard against such raids, it was to no avail. Eventually, it was ordered that, instead of using a bridge, the army should cross the river in boats. Thus, after remaining on the banks of the river for quite a long time, the army attained some relief. 'Abdul Karim calls the army "cruel people, forced to commit cruelty" (*jabbārān dar jabr majbūr*) and explains his meaning: none of the members of the army, whether high or low, willingly entered the service of the ruler, but nor could they give up his service. If by some chance, one of these helpless men manged to escape, his relatives would be subjected to all sorts of torture, and, if he had no relatives, his friends and associates would meet the same fate. Herein lies the reason for the description used by our author: *ẓālim-i maẓlūm* and *jābir dar jabr majbūr* ("tyrants forced to commit tyranny").

Further travails followed, with the army under periodic threat from the people around, and the soldiers in constant fear of their ruler. At length, after crossing the river, the Sultan expressed the wish to make a pleasure-trip to Kashmir and made enquiries concerning the voyage. It was found that this was a pleasant place to visit, not lacking in water or fodder, but that the way there was difficult. The Sultan hence went back on this idea, allowed the Mughal notable Zakariya Khan to go back to Lahore, and went on in spite of heavy rains, to the banks of the Jhelum. By chance, a camel carrying golden vessels was drowned in the middle of this river, and despite all efforts it could not be recovered. When the Sultan was taking leave of Muhammad Shah's artillery corps (which had accompanied Nadir Shah up to that point), he cunningly bestowed these lost vessels on them. These men, on their return, tried to recover the vessels as their watery salary (*tankhwah-i 'ālam-i āb*) but they achieved nothing. Only a basin and a brass vessel were found. Such then was the devious comportment of this Sultan, "Enemy of Humans and Animals" (*Sulṭān dushman-i jān-i insān-o-ḥaiwān*).

Of particular significance in this context is a slightly later passage containing a physical description of Nadir Shah, who is compared to one of his subordinates, a certain Tahmasp Khan Jala'ir.

> Nadir Shah was better than him [Tahmasp Khan] in appearance; for Tahmasp Khan was stocky, short statured, dark, ugly and unimpressive (*bī ḥaiṣiyat*). His skin was wrinkled like that of a rhinoceros, as a poet has said. His head and neck were fit only to be cut off. Nadir Shah was tall, handsome, with a white and ruddy complexion. What I wish to emphasise from this is that pure wickedness does not exist, as has been said by Maulavi-i Rum:
>
> Thus, pure evil does not exist in this world.
> Evil is relative; know this fact.

Our author also notes that Nadir Shah, though lacking in humanity, was politically rather astute. Thus, while in the mountains of Afghanistan, *farmāns* ("royal orders") were sent to all the officials (*ḥukkām wa 'ummāl*) of Iran, decreeing that taxes (*kharāj*) should not be levied there for three years. In addition, he sent out an ambassador to the Ottoman emperor, with fifteen elephants, some jewellery, matchless Kashmiri shawls, and other products of Hindustan. In his retinue, 1,000 horsemen were deputed, and it was also ordered that silver-decorated saddles be sent with them. 'Abdul Karim now records part of the contents of the letter sent to the ruler of Rum (Constantinople), which concerned (amongst other matters) the restoration of a pilgrimage route from the bounds of Kufah to Mecca, which now on account of the miscreant Bedouins had been destroyed. A second matter broached in the letter concerned the prayers in Mecca. Though the leaders of the prayers of all four schools had prayed hitherto for the Ottomans, from then on Nadir Shah asked for the Shafi'i oratory, closer to Iran, to be in his own name. The following section then takes us on to an account of Nadir Shah's progress towards

Sind, the capture of its governor, the destruction of the country, and related incidents.

Th logic of the narrative, once our author takes to the road, shifts somewhat. Though not entirely abandoning the chronicler's mode, the Khwaja mixes three sorts of observations: politico-geographic, ethnographic, and subjectivist. In the first of these contexts, the account contains numerous descriptions of towns both in Iran and in Central Asia, with a particular stress laid on two aspects: the situation of shrines and religious monuments, and the hydraulic and water systems in use. The latter preoccupation is, we have noted, one of the long-standing obsessions of writers of Persian travel-texts, and 'Abdul Karim thus falls in a long tradition. The ethnographic remarks are rather different in nature, relating to the innate characteristics of different ethnic groups encountered along the way, but also at times framing these characteristics within a schema where geographical and climatic determinism has a role to play. The third aspect, most difficult of all to seize in some respects, is the relationship between personal subjective experience, and objective reality. We shall look to each of these characteristics in turn.

Consider the description of the town of Herat from 'Abdul Karim's pen. Herat itself, he writes, is a fair city, but in recent times has suffered from the oppression of accursed officials who had brought it to ruin, to the point that the people were obliged to grow crops in their own courtyards. The fruits there were proverbial in excellence, especially the musk-melons, incomparable in their fragrance, sweetness, juicy character and pulp. The rich people and notables of the city had built lofty and ornamented mosques and shrines, but most of the buildings had once more fallen into disrepair. The keepers (*mujāwirān wa khuddām*) were in misery. In summer, violent winds blew there, and the wise men of the city had accordingly built windmills there, whose flour was better than that of water-mills; most of the windmills were in working order. The windmills were like huge lofty buildings, and their tops were large funnels (*bād-gīr*) to catch the wind. The author learnt from the intelligent men of the place that the strong winds were also good in that, in the absence of wind, ill odours, flies and epidemics would proliferate. A similar brief account may be found of the city of Balkh. Though the excesses of the wicked and graceless officials had rendered the people of the town destitute and miserable, Balkh still had managed to retain its beauty, with its gardens and suburbs still possessing a certain charm.

The cities of Iran are described with even greater care and attention, albeit with a certain stability with regard to the organisational topoi of the description. Thus, we find the following account of the town of Tus, at a distance of four leagues from Mashhad. It was in total ruins, probably because of the dominant presence of Mashhad. The water of the canal that cut through the avenues and the shrine was clear and sweet outside the town but, once it entered Mashhad, became muddy. The town-dwellers in Iran used to joke with the people of Mashhad about this, and gave their own explanations. A poet had written in appreciation:

> Since the canal's waters are not black
> on entering your sacred precincts,
> the book where men's acts are written,
> is surely washed there.

Some others, less kind than the first poet, had used the occasion to speak of the deception, ill-fame and bad character of the Mashhadis. These rumours and countless satirical verses reflecting rivalries between towns and regions circulated in Khorasan, Fars and other parts, writes 'Abdul Karim.

Again, the city of Qazwin, where he arrived on 25 Rabi' I 1154 H (that is 9 June 1741), is described with particular regard to its hydraulic system. It is noted that the courtyards of the houses there were built below the street level. However, some courtyards were in deep depressions, while others were less so, with the difference ranging from three yards to eleven yards. As one entered the house through the main door, it was necessary to descend a staircase to the courtyard (*ṣahn-i khāna*), and the reason for making the courtyards in this fashion was to ensure the flow of subterranean water. The rainwater, as well as all other water used in the house, left the city at a spot that was even lower in level than all the courtyards of the city. However, the courtyard of the royal palace (*daulatkhāna-i bādshāhī*) was an exception, being at the same level as the streets of the city. The reason for this was that Shah 'Abbas had devised a mechanism to raise the water, and it could thus pass through the royal palace and the chief bazaar. In sum, writes 'Abdul Karim, the people of Iran were all fond of flowing water, but the reader can see that the same is equally true of our author himself. Not for nothing do we find passages such as the following one, written in the later context of a visit to the town of Hallah, a populous centre on the banks of the Euphrates, near which 'Abdul Karim notes that the tomb of the Prophet Ayyub (Job) is to be found. In this tomb, next to his grave, was the grave of his wife, Rahima Khatun, who had served him during his long illness. Significantly, there was also a pond (*chashma*) which had come up on the orders of Allah, through the

Prophet's intercession, just outside the tomb. A Qur'anic verse with Allah's command to Ayyub is cited (sura 38, verse 42).

> Strike with thy foot:
> Here is [water] wherein
> to wash, cool and refreshing,
> and [water] to drink.

No water was as pleasant as that to drink, says our author. People said that even chronic ailments could be cured from this source.

Still within the confines of geographical description, we find the following detailing of the river systems in Central Asia, which appears somewhat earlier in the text. We are in the vicinity of Chaharju, and of the Jaihun (Bactrus) and Saihun (Jaxartes, or Sir Daria) rivers. To the west lies the desert, and in the south the territories of Balkh at a distance of twelve days. To the north was the boundary of Khwarizm, at a distance of eight Uzbek *qāfila* days. To the east, was the river Jaihun, and beyond it the city of Bukhara. The river flows from south to north, and the water alongside Chaharju was less than in the area of Balkh, and in the territory of Khwarizm the water was reduced again by half. In winter, it was fordable. The reason for the reduction in the water was as follows: along the route, there were a number of large canals in the same manner as in the steppe of Qipchaq and Qara-Qalmaq, for the purpose of irrigation. If the water level increased in the river, it was dried up in the sandy desert. Some past historians (*muarrikhīn-i salaf*) had erroneously written that the river enters into the Sea (*buḥaira*) of Khwarizm (perhaps meaning the Aral Sea). The Saihun river for its part was in the eastern region of Mawarannahr, and ran from the northern Khajend and Tashkent to Turkestan, and there was absorbed in the same manner as the river Jaihun in the sandy desert. In sum, because of several large canals cut out of these two rivers, they did not reach up to the Sea of Khwarizm, let alone to the Sea of Mazandaran (that is, the Caspian Sea). The authors who had written that the rivers went as far as Mazandaran were thus clearly mistaken. 'Abdul Karim notes that he had made enquiries from the "noble residents" of the area, and had thus obtained correct information, unlike his predecessors. "My purpose", he states, "in writing these words is this, that while the large rivers of Sind and Hindustan, as well as the Euphrates and Tigris that I have seen, merge with the open sea (*daryā-i shor*), the Jaihun and Saihun contrariwise are exhausted in cultivation."[26]

[26] *Bayān-i Wāqi'*, p. 82.

Geography and thalassomania can in turn lead the way to ethnography. In the context of the relationship between climatic conditions and the characteristics of different peoples, we find the following remarks in a section devoted to Nadir Shah's campaigns in Khwarizm. 'Abdul Karim notes that, on the successful completion of the campaign, some prisoners from Khorasan, held by the people of Khwarizm, were released. He then goes on:

> The Turkomans, at the advice and with the connivance of their own ruler, had invaded Khorasan and had captured many women and children there. In each house, there were ten or twelve Khorasanis. The cultivation, irrigation, and the digging of deep ditches from the Jaihun river which went all through Khwarizm, had been entrusted to these prisoners from Iran. They were busy in these works day and night and because of the climate of that land, their faces had become like those of the Turanian Turkomans. Some of them were as old as fifty and sixty, and said that they had been brought there as children.[27]

Further, when the Persians tried to persuade them to return to their "homeland", they showed considerable reluctance, on account (it is claimed) of their affection for the people of Khwarizm, and because they had heard of the ruination of Iran. Many of them hence turned back to Khwarizm while half-way on the road to Khorasan, and others, from the intensity of the winter and the lack of proper provisions, died on the way. Those who reached Khorasan regretted the fact that they had left Khwarizm. Human adaptation is thus stressed as much as innate qualities attributed to different ethnic groups.

In other accounts of ethnic groups, typically those that are not Islamicised, he takes a different tack. This is the case of a group encountered by him between Karkuk and Mosul, who lived in a large mountain range, which was on the left of the route that he took. 'Abdul Karim writes of them:

> The residents of this region believe that there are two origins (*mabda'*), one that is good which is Rahman, and the other, bad, which is Shaitan. If anyone, in front of these accursed people, recites the verse: *A'ūẕu billāhi min-ash-shaiṭān-ir rajīm* ("I seek refuge in Allah from the accursed Satan"), they regard his killing (*qatl*) as their duty. The village (*qarya*) of Ab-i Zarb, which has been listed as a station earlier, is the residence of this damned (*mal'ūn*) group. Circumcision, according to the belief of these worthless infidels, is prohibited, and, as is apparent, they do not even care to cover their private parts. Since it is difficult for the loaded camel to cross the river which they call Ab-i Zarb without the help

[27] *Bayān-i Wāqi'*, pp. 88–9.

of knowledgeable guides, the people of this village know the route well. They take reasonable amounts for their effort from the people of the caravans, and then escort the camels with full care through these deadly waters. It is on account of this that I came to know that they do not practice circumcision, nor cover their private parts.

He notes that robbery was also routinely committed by these misguided people, and that besides, before his arrival in the city of Mosul, he had already been told strange stories of their excesses. After his entry into the town, he himself actually witnessed some such acts, even if his own party was not subject to the excesses of these illiterates. However, he notes, it was necessary to distinguish these mischief-mongers from the good and wise people of the town of Mosul.

The account thus veers between different tacks in its implicit ethnography, both when its intention is to praise, and when its intention is to condemn. In the first category falls the description of the people of Aleppo, who, of all those that he meets on his voyage, are probably singled out for the highest praise of all. In this town, he visited the grave of Yahya ibn Zakariya (John the Baptist), which as usual was located in a mosque (on this occasion the Masjid-i Jami‘) along the arch. He then goes on:

In no other country can a city with such grace and purity be seen. In terms of the decoration and embellishment of its bazaars, the arrangement of the shops therein, and the beautiful dresses of the traders and the bazaar-folk, what can I say! All this creates a sensation of great wonder and the visitor becomes love-struck. One may imagine the situation of the rich and affluent here, when dirt in even the lanes of the bazaar is as rare as the [mythical] ‘Anqa bird. Perhaps it is from the cleanliness of the bazaar-lanes that the metaphor of the Aleppo mirror (*ā'ina-i ḥalab*) derives, for otherwise this mirror comes from Europe (*firang*) and is only sold here. This is akin to the fame of certain Kabul myrobalans (*halīla-i Kābulī*), for in Kabul there is no tree where this fruit grows. The evident reason for their fame is that the Iranian traders procure this fruit in Kabul, and on this account the Yunani physicians identify it as Halila-i Kabuli.

The people in Aleppo, he notes, are not just handsome and affluent, but courteous and modest (*ṣāḥib-i ḥayā wa mu'addab*). No wonder then that the proverb went as follows in Rum, the Arab lands, Yemen and the Maghrib: “Aleppans are civilised, Syrians are vile, Egyptians are thieves, and Indians the friends of God.” The people there were also noted, in his view, for their ingenuity. Near Aleppo was the town of Hami, situated at a height along the hills. Here, water came through a canal which was below in the skirts of the hills. Some ingenious person (*ḥakīm*) in the past had installed a huge wheel, like a water-wheel (*dūlāb*), which kept churning the water and moving it uphill at some speed. It took the water up to a height of some seventy-five hand-spans through the bowls that were tied around the wheel. This was for the welfare of the people living there.

REASON AND FAITH

Khwaja 'Abdul Karim's account is, however, not concerned with the external realities of lands, rivers and peoples alone. If the holy cities of Iran and 'Iraq receive a good deal of attention in this context (as we shall see below), it is, however, not only in the terms of a *Baedeker's Guide* to holy sites. The dialectical relationship between interior and exterior, head and heart, comes out clearly in a number of places, most of all probably in the account of the holy city of Mashhad, where the Khwaja arrived on 19 Zi-Qa'da 1153 H (that is, 6 February 1741). He begins this section with a description of the main features of Mashhad, in particular the shrine of Hazrat Imam 'Ali Musa Raza. He notes that the city wall of Mashhad had its own share of wonders, and that, unlike other forts, the fortifications are winding and triangular. If one bastion (*burj*) is attacked, the watchmen to the left and right can come to its aid. The shrine of 'Ali Musa Raza, Imam of the djinns and humans, is in the centre of the town, and the holy dome (*gumbad-i mubārak*) is very high and ornate, and the mosques and all other buildings and workshops are spacious, and have been constructed with perfect craftsmanship and exquisiteness. The big bazaar faced the shrine, and was within its larger enclosure. On both sides, there were huge gates. The western bazaar, which was on the side of the royal palace, was called the upper avenue (*khayābān-i bāla*), and the bazaar on the left was called the lower avenue. There was a canal cutting through the avenues, through the Great Bazaar, and reaching the centre of the enclosure of the shrine. Over the grave (*marqad-i munawwar*) of this leader of high stature, there were three layered sepulchres (*ẓarīḥ*). One, the largest, was made of iron ornamented with stones on which a huge sum was said to have been spent, so that, had it been made of silver, it would have cost less. The second, inside the first, was made of pure gold, and inside that was the grave itself made of sandal-wood. It was said in many cities that the dome was made of gold ingots, but this was not true; it was actually made of gilded copper, which had been fixed on the dome, in the same way as in Shahjahanabad in the mosque of Zafar Khan Raushan-ud-Daula. Nadir Shah had repaired some of the old buildings, and also constructed some new ones.

We soon realise, though, that this elaborate description has an important function to play in the narrative, for the author goes on to describe a dream he had before reaching Mashhad, in which he saw Imam 'Ali Raza, and obtained his blessings for the attainment of his objectives. The dream narrative begins with a hemistich which states:

> Bravo, for dream-dealing,
> is better than that in wakefulness.
> *Zahe qarābat-i khwābī ki bih ze bīdārī-ist*

He then explains this rather cryptic statement as follows.

> Before I arrived in Mashhad, I saw in a dream that at a place just outside the gate of the dome (*bīrūn darwāza-i gumbad*), Imam 'Ali Raza was seated. He had a black shawl on, and a large number of people from all parts were around, mostly sitting and some standing up. This sinner paid respects by bowing (*ādāb-i kūrnish*) from a distance. He called me close to him and asked me to sit down. After that, I saw him ask for a big tray on which there was a variety of half-eaten food. He then told me in Persian: 'Eat and do not worry, you will soon achieve your goal' (*ṭa'ām bakhwur wa gham makhwur ki 'anqarīb ba maṭlab khwāhī rasīd*).

Now, at the time, 'Abdul Karim's most important goal was to visit the shrines of the prophets, Imams, saints and make the *ḥajj*, paying homage to and circumambulating the tomb of Prophet Muhammad at Medina in order to accumulate the virtues of both worlds. However, this objective periodically seemed unattainable to him, and he would often recite a verse to himself:

> Even if someone like me cannot aspire
> to the good fortune of communion with you,
> I shall die with the thought
> that my intentions, at least, were good.

The morning after the dream, 'Abdul Karim described to residents of the town (which he had not yet seen) details of the features of the shrine, mosque and other aspects. They confirmed that what he had seen in fact corresponded to the reality. On hearing this, a strange trance seized him, and tears began to well from his eyes, a blissful experience which he assures the reader he cannot even begin to describe, and which exceeded any happiness he had attained before. He hence approached Mirza Muhammad Na'im Mashhadi, the senior ("white-bearded") person in his group and asked for permission to go to Mashhad before the others. When this was granted, he departed with the cleaning staff (*farrāsh-bāshī*) that preceded the royal party, and reached Mashhad three days before the others. He then saw with his own eyes that the buildings and places at Mashhad were exactly as they had appeared in his dream, and he again experienced a trance and state of bliss (*wajd-o-surūr*), which was on this occasion many times stronger than on the earlier one. He remained forty-two days at Mashhad, and each day he would precipitately leave the *daftar-k͟hāna* on one pretext or another, go to the shrine, and there recite verses from the Qur'an in a highly exalted state. He therefore prays that the same condition of bliss and contentment remain with him forever, and that God should grant it to his friends as well.

Earlier, 'Abdul Karim assures us that he had been rather sceptical, and had even denied outright the mystical experience of dervishes, and their trances; but after his own experience, he repented of his own earlier beliefs. For even if he is just writing about an experience that has happened to a worthless man (himself), 'Abdul Karim nevertheless hopes that a more enlightened reader (*ṣāḥib-i dil*) would spare some good words in his prayers for him and would add his weight to those of his own prayers.

The same dialectic between reason and faith is further explored by him in a somewhat later passage in the text, which describes an incident that occurred while he was in the vicinity of the town of Hallah. Here, he had heard from the people of the territory that in the courtyard of the mosque of the Prophet Shu'aib (Jethro) there was a very tall minaret, and the width of its interior staircase was a cubit (*zira'*) and four finger-widths. When one went up to the top, and pressed a part of its top under one's arm, shouting out from there: "O Minaret, for the love of 'Abbas-i 'Ali, shake!", it would begin to tremble. 'Abdul Karim continues:

Since this sinful slave had been looking for a chance to observe and test this wonder, I proceeded to the shrine in the company of Hakim 'Alawi Khan, with the idea naturally of gaining virtue from the pilgrimage, but also to establish the truth of this strange wonder. After performing the pilgrimage, I climbed up to the top of the minaret, but in spite of my shouting and crying and leaning my side on the rampart, and even shaking it forcefully, the minaret did not tremble in the slightest. There were also some Sayyids, and they too did the same, according to the custom, but that to no avail. In the meanwhile, the *k͟hādim* emerged, leaned his side on the edge, and shook it violently. Though the minaret was like the Kuh-i Bisutun, incomparable in terms of its stability, it began to tremble in such a manner that people who had gone to the top feared that they would fall to earth. Everyone clung to the ramparts. The Nawwab Hakim-bashi who was standing in the courtyard smiled when he saw this, at the plight of the others. Everyone wanted the same experience to be repeated again and again to clear their doubts, and the *k͟hādim* did so several times; each time, the minaret shook like a plane tree (*chinār*).

Verses are cited in this connection:

> Reason is lost in wonder at this game,
> What sort of performance was this?
> The heart plunged into the sea of wonder,
> the thread of reason drifted from the palm.

This does not mean that Khwaja 'Abdul Karim recklessly eschews reason either. For, from time to time, he takes time in his text to describe and analyse both social and natural phenomena, at times even applying his practical reason to issues of political economy. Thus, while describing the progress of Nadir Shah's army in Central Asia, he notes that the people of the cities of Turan, compared to those of Rum and Hindustan, were poor, and their food was not as rich, besides being less tasty; but in place of money and wealth, God had given them a variety of delicate fruits, and the immeasurable fortune of good health and freedom from disease was the consequence. He then goes on to add the following rather significant remarks.

> Having observed the condition of the residents of Turan and the Arab lands, I am surprised to see that in these lands worldly wealth does not last long, contrary to the case of Hindustan. Why is this so? This is in spite of the fact that Amir Timur Sahib-i Qiran, had taken the treasures and buried wealth of Iran, Rum and Hindustan to Turan. All this was scattered in no time. And in the time of the Pious Caliphs, the booty (*kharāj*) from Rum, Yemen, Iran, Abyssinia, Egypt, the Maghreb and Sind, and even some from Turan and other countries, had been taken to the Hijaz, where too all this did not remain. Apparently, an explanation for this would be the excessive generosity of these people, or else that they do not have the talent (*salīqa*) to keep wealth intact. [On the contrary] in the lands of Hindustan, in spite of several raids by Turks and Tajiks, and despite the fact that none of the Indian Sultans have brought anything from Turan and Iran, and also in spite of the fact that there are few mines of gold and silver, the country is distinguished (*mumtāz*) over others in the possession of an excess of money, goods and jewels (*wafūr-i zar-o-bisyāri-yi māl-o-jawāhir*). Very probably, the reason for the gold and silver being in abundance is the income from the Frankish ships that bring most of the cash (*naqd*) and take away a variety of goods from India. Or it might be just a Divine Blessing.[28]

Then again, while making the return voyage from the Red Sea to Hughli at the end of his *ḥajj* pilgrimage, he applies himself temporarily to some oceanographic speculations. This occurs after the ship has passed the island of Soqotora (Saqutra), and when they enter into the midst of the deep

[28] *Bayān-i Wāqi'*, p. 73.

ocean (*ghabba*). According to 'Abdul Karim, the depth of the ocean was unknown and immeasurable, and on this account snakes, fish and other sea-animals were unable to survive there. After twenty days' sailing, this area of deep water had been traversed, and they at last saw a sea-snake (*mār*). The *mu'allim* (pilot) and the *nākhudā* (captain) gave thanks to God on seeing this creature. The immense size of the snakes and fishes in the ocean were celebrated, even if it was hard to descibe them. However, since these creatures were not there in the deepest ocean, it was impossible to measure its depth. Some people even claimed that there was no bottom (*zamīn*) to it at all, but 'Abdul Karim was sceptical of this claim. For wise people had said in the past that, were the water really bottom-less, ships would surely be lost, and be unable to attain land. This was because bottomless water pulled objects that entered it towards its centre. Thus, 'Abdul Karim's own view was that there were no creatures (*ḥaiwān*) there because it was very deep, not because it was in fact bottomless.

PILGRIMAGE AND ANTIQUARIANISM

We have concentrated successively so far on four different aspects of Khwaja 'Abdul Karim's account: first, the frame of his text, which is defined around the Nadir Shahi invasion; second, his speculation on the nature of tyranny and government in Iran (and implicitly perhaps in India); third, his description of towns and peoples, and his geographical explorations; and fourth, his remarks on the relationship between reason and faith as mediated by empirical experience. However, as we have remarked earlier, it is important to bear in mind constantly that the text's narrative is also explicitly ordered around the notion of pilgrimage, both to the Hijaz and to other sites in Iran and 'Iraq. This is particularly clear after the return from Central Asia to Iran, and even more so when 'Abdul Karim and his companions, notably the *ḥakīm-bāshī*, Sayyid 'Alawi Khan, take leave of Nadir Shah. This departure is described in the following terms: "The sinful writer of these poorly arranged pages (*banda-i 'āṣī muḥarrir-i auraq-i bī siyāq*) who had accompanied the Sultan solely with the intention to go on the *ḥajj*, and to visit the shrines of the saints, by the intercession of the *ḥakīm-bāshī* gave up the Sultan's service, and obtaining permission to leave, set out for the Hijaz in his [the Hakim-bashi's] company."[29] Paradoxically perhaps, the "pilgrimage" is not conceived in

[29] *Bayān-i Wāqi'*, p. 114.

purely religious terms. For there is equally the issue of the wonders of pre-Islamic Iran, which are as much a part of Khwaja 'Abdul Karim's cultural cartography as the tombs of Old Testament and Islamic prophets. Firdausi's great medieval epic, *Shāhnāma*, is ever-present it seems, whether he finds himself in Transoxania, Khwarizm or Iran itself. Thus, on leaving the town of Hamadan, 'Abdul Karim and his companions take the route through Tus-i Sarkan, and Kermanshah, and pass by the Kuh-i Bisutun. On the fifth day, they camp in a caravanserai at the bottom of the mountain, and see the wondrous works of the legendary Farhad there. It is a matter of wonder and astonishment to him that the mountain has been cut to make apartments, arches, tanks and the statues of Khusrau and Shirin. This sight alone, he writes, was enough to drive a man out of his senses. Again, a few days later, near Kirmanshah (at Tak-i Bustan), he saw that Farhad had carved a huge arch in granite (*sang-i k͟hāra*), so large that under it two elephants and their howdahs could stand. In the middle of this arch, from the same stone, he had sculpted an enormous statue of Khusrau on a horse, and, all around the statue, on the roof of the arch, he had also made a variety of animals and birds. The difference between these sculpted animals and birds and Khusrau was that the latter was standing alone like a living creature.

As for the tombs of Muslim divines and prophets, they are of course a major feature of 'Abdul Karim's description of towns such as Baghdad. In this town, he pays particular attention to the tomb of Imam Abu Hanifa, which was grand and where the *k͟hādims* and *mujāwirs* were immensely wealthy. All in all, he notes, many of the people of God were buried in Baghdad and in its vicinity. Evocative verses thus follow to sum up the matter:

> Wherever you see a mound,
> there a man lies below.
> Wherever you see raised ground,
> there's a pious soul below.
> Wherever you break the earth,
> there will be revealed,
> torn collars and torn-open breasts.

The same attention to pilgrimage sites can be found in the next major stop after Baghdad, namely Karbala. Here, he describes, in the middle of the city, the tomb of Hazrat Sayyid ush-Shuhada, that is to say the Imam Husain. The grave of his son, 'Abdullah, was at the foot of that of his father, and along the same side was the Ganj-i Shuhada, with the graves of the other martyrs. At a distance of twenty paces from the holy grave on the northern side beside a window, was a piece of land where, at the time of the martyrdom, the body of Imam Husain had fallen. At that place, a ditch of the same size as the holy body had been dug out, rather like a box, which was then filled from time to time with earth from the spot where his camp had been. This spot was then covered with a board, and whenever a pilgrim visited the place and wished to procure a handful of this earth, he offered something to the *khādim* and took a little bit of that pious earth. This earth of Karbala had thus been taken all over the world, and it was this earth that was called *khāk-i shifā'*, or curative earth. The attributes of this earth were countless. Amongst these is that, when a ship at sea is in difficulty from storms, if a pious man throws this earth into the wind, God will order the wind to abate.

After Karbala, Khwaja 'Abdul Karim's next major stop is Najaf, "the precious kohl for the eye of the heart". Here, the population was less than in Karbala, since there was no cultivation around and since it was far from the river. The tomb and shrine of Hazrat 'Ali stood elegantly in the middle of the town in perfect grandeur and decoration, with shining jewels fixed on the graves there. He notes that, according to local people, inside the tomb of Hazrat 'Ali in Najaf, the tombs of the Prophet Noah and of Adam, father of mankind, were located. However, neither grave was clear or visible. He notes that Mirza Zaki "Nadim", a courtier of Nadir Shah, had written the following apposite verse on this matter:

> With no discourtesy to the Father of Man,
> though he is the source of excellence and virtue,
> until he was honoured by your ['Ali's] vicinity.
> the fact is that he did not become Adam.[30]

Several recent historians have paid attention to a particular section of Khwaja 'Abdul Karim's pilgrimage account, namely his account of his departure from 'Iraq for Mecca through Syria and Aleppo.[31] This is a relatively brief, but nevertheless useful, account, in which the way-stations from Baghdad to Mecca, according to the time (*sa'at*) taken (using the so-called Rumi measures), are appended. In this context, 'Abdul Karim notes that most of the people of the Ottoman empire (Rum), during their travels and even when they have a fixed residence, keep European watches (*sā'at-hā-i-firangī*) in their pockets or hanging from their sides, so that

[30] *Bayān-i Wāqi'*, p. 132.

[31] See M. N. Pearson, *Pious passengers: the hajj in earlier times* (New Delhi, 1994), esp. p. 11. Pearson is, however, rather harsh about Khwaja 'Abdul Karim, who he claims is "succinct to the point of being useless".

the relation between distance and time could be measured in a better way. He notes that, on his pilgrimage, he too had taken along a European watch in his pocket, to verify the accuracy of what he was told. This section of the text is also notable for its periodic mention of the tombs of Biblical prophets, such as Daniyal (Daniel) and 'Uzair (Ezra). In Mosul, described as a large city (*shahr-i 'aẕīm*) on the banks of the Shatt-al-'Arab, he mentions the tombs of two other Biblical prophets, Jarjiz (George) and Yunus (Jonas). On inquiry, 'Abdul Karim came to learn that their tombs had been built by no less than the Sahib-Qiran, the World-Conqueror Amir Timur Gurgan. Again, in 'Arafa, he claims to have visited the spot where the Prophet Abraham was thrown into the fire; this spot was under a huge mountain, on top of which a catapult had been installed to fling him, and its traces still survived. Water from a spring, which was very sweet, had gushed out at the time from the middle of the fire, and a huge mosque had been built by the spring. On the other side of the mountain was the town named for the accursed Nimrod, who had persecuted the prophet. In earlier days, the route leading to Syria and Aleppo passed through that city, but now that town, on account of the wickedness of its inhabitants, had fallen into ruin, and the bulk of the newer buildings had been made on the nearer side of the mountain.

This section of the account also describes Damascus, termed a large and populous city, with a huge Umayyad mosque containing the grave of Zakariya (Zachariah) near the principal niche or *miḥrāb*. The bazaars in the town are compared to those of Aleppo, and judged more spacious but with less beauty and grace (*zīnat-o-raunaq*). In each house, there flowed a canal, and the entire city was full of gardens, with countless fruit trees. The olive trees, it seems, were far better and far more plentiful in Syria than elsewhere. The Bait-al-Maqdis (Jerusalem) was at a distance of ten *manzil* from Damascus, but since the *ḥajj* season was on, 'Abdul Karim could not go there. Of equal interest is the section describing the journey through the desert towards Medina.[32] This section is noted for its repeated and uncompromising criticism of the Arab Bedouins, who it is stated plundered the Hajis, despite the precautions taken by both the pilgrims and the army. These pages also contain brief descriptions of certain obscure centres on the route, such as the Qasba of 'Ala, in the middle of the mountains, and near the fort of Khaibar (which had been captured miraculously by 'Ali ibn Abi Talib). In mentioning this centre, 'Abdul Karim adds:

[32] On the overland routes to the *ḥajj*, see also Faroqhi, *Pilgrims and sultans*.

These days, Jews and Christians live in this region, who believe that killing the Hajis is the best act, and the holiest prayer through which these misguided and illiterate people could avert misfortune. Thus they were determined to kill the Hajis as a fulfilment of their vows, to gain access to their God, in order to recover from pains and diseases and also to procure positions and secure their [other] objectives. They were fixed in their aim, and made all efforts at the time of the passage of [our] caravan. Though the Mir Hajj, in view of this [danger] had deputed armed forces (*afwāj*) all around, three Hajis were killed by bullets fired from ambush. The Mir Hajj, to avenge this, decided to fight, but the chiefs of the caravan (*ru'ūsā-i qāfila*), submitted that in the event of a combat with these infidels, we would miss the season for the performance of the *ḥajj*. Sulaiman Pasha, the Mir Hajj, hence ignored the incident.[33]

Besides the hardships of the journey, considerable attention is paid (as mentioned above) to the Bedouin Arab thieves and their ploys. Amongst these, one rise was for them to come late at night when the pilgrims were in an exhausted sleep. Six or seven of them together would get hold of a laden camel while it was moving, and slit open the saddle-bags on the side containing the cloth and trade-goods (*amti'a-i tijārat*) from below and empty it. Two other men would catch hold of the saddle-bags on the other side, those with the provisions, to prevent the camel from running faster and thus alarming the servant (*naukar-i ṣāḥib-i māl*) seated on top. Once they had finished, they would run off, and the servant would fall off while asleep, as the load became unbalanced. The camel's saddle would also be disturbed, and the string which tied the camel to the group (*jahāz-i shutur*) come undone. The fallen servant would be trampled in the process. By the time the Haji merchant, sleeping in the covered portion (*maḥmil*) atop the camel, woke up, the thieves were already a league away.

'Abdul Karim's pilgrimage itself seems to have passed off without particular incident. First in Medina, he paid homage to the tomb of the Prophet and other shrines.[34] Then, on the sixth of Zi-Hijja, he eventually reached his ultimate destination, which is to say Mecca. Having performed the *ḥajj*, he made secondary pilgrimages (*ziyārāt*) to several places both near and far. In the days when he visited, he noted that the courtyard of the Mosque of Mecca (*masjid-i ḥarām*), the place where the Prophet

[33] *Bayān-i Wāqi'*, p. 150.

[34] For an earlier account, see Asiatic Society of Bengal, Calcutta, IvASB, 654, *Futūḥ ul-ḥaramain* by Muhyi Lari (911 H /1505–6), with gilded and stylised illustrations. There are two other copies of the text in the same collection, and a nineteenth-century lithograph from Lucknow (1292 H). For an edition, see Muhyi Lari, *Futūḥ ul-ḥaramain*. See also ASB, Mss. IvASB, no. 1018, for the *Ḥadīṣ al-sālikīn* of 'Abdullah bin Sayyid Muhammad Talib (1135 H).

was born, and the Mosque of the djinn, were at a lower level than that of the bazaar and the courtyards of many homes; this was especially true of the birthplace of the Prophet. Applying his usual dose of empirical reason, he argues from this that when the Prophet had been born, the level of the land in Mecca must have been that of his birthplace, and, in the interim, the construction of various high buildings had raised the general level. This was equally true, as he had observed, in many other cities where the courtyards of some people had become lower than the bazaar with the passage of time.[35]

The author's return journey from Mecca to India took him through Jiddah, and it is this section that contains the most extensive references to Europeans. His departure from Mecca is dated to the first of Rabi' I 1155 H (6 May 1742), after a stay of three months in the holy city. The shrine of Eve (Hawwa) outside the town of Jiddah is described, where the grave was flat with a small dome at the level of the navel. A curious feature was the length of the grave which, as he measured it, was 197 paces. The Europeans (*ahl-i firang*) lived in Jiddah, but the governor of Mecca, as ordained in the Qur'anic verse (sura 9, verse 27), stating that the idolatrous people were polluted and hence should not approach the Masjid-i Haram, did not allow them there. 'Abdul Karim remained a month in Jiddah, and then boarded a European ship (*jahāz-i firangī*) to go to Bengal, after a brief stop at Mokha.[36] He thus had occasion to visit the capital of the ruler there, the Imam of Yemen, in the city of Sana'a. Most of the people there were Zaidi Shi'is, and amongst their innovations (*mukhtara'*) was that, at the time of prayers, they took off their pyjamas. For this reason, most of them tied small cloths (*lung*) below their waists. Once more, 'Abdul Karim cannot resist a small reflection on the issue of water. He notes that the tomb of Shaikh 'Umar Shazli was there, and that, before his burial in the spot, the water there had been salty and rather lacking in zest, but that, with the blessings of the saint, it was now sweet and pleasant. In the wilderness, too, where a certain Shaikh Abu'l Hasan Shazli was buried the water had turned sweet. Indeed, it was mentioned in the *Nafaḥāt-ul-Uns* (by Jami) that the water of all the wells in the region had been brackish, but now they were no longer so.

[35] *Bayān-i Wāqi'*, p. 154.

[36] On the Europeans in Jiddah, see also Willem Floor, "A report on the trade in Jedda in the 1730s", *Moyen Orient et Océan Indien*, 5, 1988, pp. 161–73.

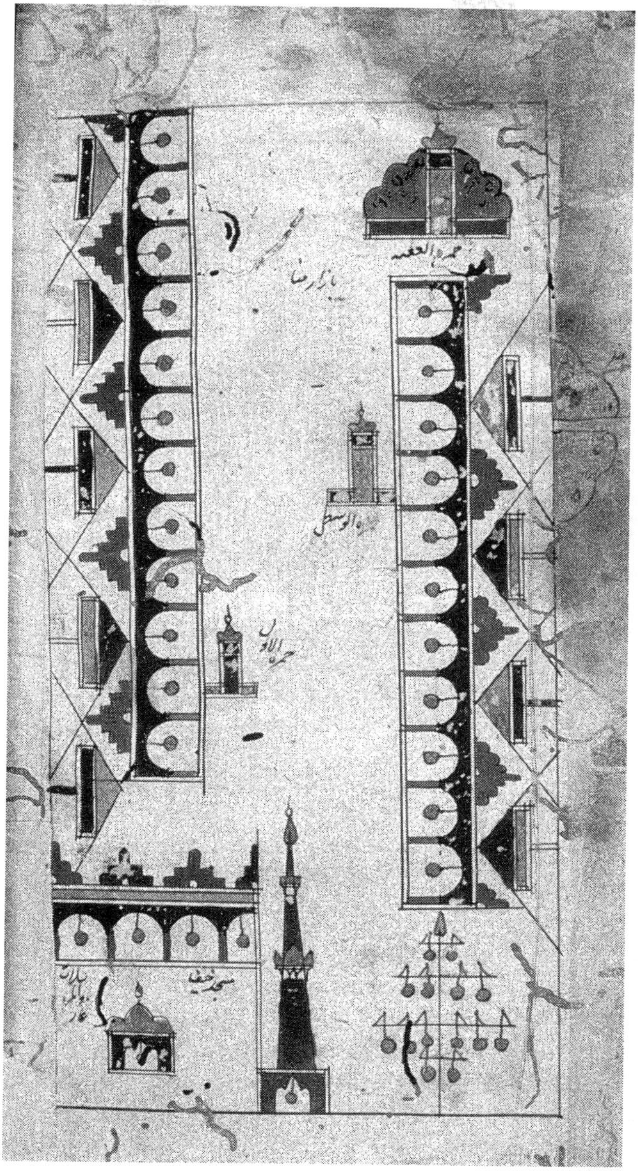

Figure 14. The bazaar of Mina in Mecca, showing the three noted sites from where the *ḥājīs* throw stones at Satan, *Futūḥ al-ḥaramain* by Jami, National Museum, New Delhi, No. 61.89.

The return voyage by ship would take ʿAbdul Karim by the island of Ceylon (Silan) – where he states that the best cinnamon (*dār-chīnī*) was to be found – which had now fallen under the control of the Franks. Thereafter, the ship arrived in Phulcheri (Pondicherry), a port which had been built by a leader of the French (*yak-i az sardārān-i-qaum-i Frānsīs*) in accordance with the *farmān* of the Badshah of Hindustan. In order to buy and sell textiles and other trade goods, and also to collect water and provisions, ʿAbdul Karim and the other passengers all disembarked. A critical note enters here. On the pretext of making a warehouse (*koṭhī*) and shop (*dukān*), the clever Franks had also built a big city there, a measure of their untrustworthiness.

The ship was apparently supposed to go on to the port of Chinapattan (Madras), where – in view of the diversity of traders resident – it was very important to land. As they approached, night fell, and the pilot (*muʿallim-i kashtī*) lost his way and overshot the port by four *karoh*. When he tried to turn around, a strong wind prevented him, and they were stranded for eight days without being able to attain their destination. How strange this was, exclaims our author: the ship that had covered a distance of 150 *karoh* in a day and night could not traverse the distance of 5 *karoh* in eight days without the wind's aid! On the ninth day, the direction of the wind changed, and it took no time at all to reach the anchorage (*langargāh*). ʿAbdul Karim notes that Chinapattan was the residence of the English (*qaum-i Angrez*), on the coast of Arcot. They had settled there long before, and the Franks lived in those ports according to their own customs. Their women, low and high (*waẓīʿ-o-sharīf*), in keeping with the practice in their own homeland (*maʿmūl-i khwud*), did not cover their faces, and went around everywhere as they pleased.[37] Having finished their work there, the ship then moved on towards Hughli, the end-point of the voyage, which was attained only after some more difficulties and a further storm in the Bay of Bengal.

BRINGING IT ALL BACK HOME

As noted above, the text of the *Bayān-i Wāqiʿ* does not in fact come to an end with its author's return to Hindustan. Rather, it continues into a fourth section (*bāb*) that is entitled: "Some events that took place after

[37] Compare the account of Madras from the 1680s by Muhammad Rabiʿ, *Safīna-i Sulaimānī*, pp. 25–9; translation in O'Kane, *The Ship of Sulaiman*, pp. 37–40, and the discussion in Chapter 4 above.

[the author's] arrival in Hughli Bandar, until the death of Muhammad Shah", which in fact closes the reflections that have begun on the nature of eighteenth-century politics in the context of the invasion by Nadir Shah.[38] This section is in turn subdivided into several *faṣl*, of which the first briefly describes the mid-century events in Bengal. In those very days, writes Khwaja 'Abdul Karim, on account of the weakness of the empire of Muhammad Shah, and also the lack of unity amongst the nobles, the Marathas of the Deccan had come to control Bengal, including Bandar Hughli. He then goes on briefly to mention the existence of different European settlements along the river, such as Calcutta and Frans Danga (Chandernagore), of which the former was more populated and bigger than the latter. He notes that among the *firangīs*, there were several *firqa* (groups, though he also uses the term *qaum*), each known according to the name of their country (*mulk*), such as Fransis, Angrez, Valandez, Purtugez (the sound "za", the last syllable of the word, indicating the attribution). These European nations have very fine gardens according to the custom that obtains in their own countries (*wilāyat*), in which they snip at even large trees with scissors, giving them a particular shape. Since these Europeans all lived in one area, separate from "us" (meaning people like 'Abdul Karim), there was hence no change in their lifestyles (*auẓa'-o-aṭwār*) in relation to their places of origin. In short, even in India, they lived precisely as they did in their own countries. Further, he notes, they have built churches (*kalīsa*), where they read the *namāz* after their own fashion, and they determined the outcomes of other matters too after their own manner. A large number of persons from amongst the Frankish intellectuals and craftsmen had hence settled in these places, where they manufactured things again as they did in their own homelands (*auṭan*). Little by little, most of the people of Bengal had become their disciples (*shāgird*), and they had become their masters. He adds that the Frankish soldiers (*aṣḥab-i saif-i firangiyān*), like their skilled artisans, were also distinguished (*mumtāz*). Thus, although the Marathas were aware that all the goods of the great traders (*tujjār-i māldārān*) of the area were in Frans Danga and Calcutta, and even though these settlements were in reality quite close to Hughli, yet the Marathas did not dare attack these places. This, declares 'Abdul Karim, was principally on account of the perfect unity of the Franks (*bar kamāl-i yak jihatī-i firangiyān*), with the contrast obviously being then between this unity and the

[38] *Bayān-i Wāqi'*, p. 161 onwards.

single-mindedness of the Franks, and the lack of coordination of the *umarā'* of Hindustan. Here an apposite verse appears:

> Wealth grows out of coordinated acts,
> its lack comes out of disunity.

Having made this bald contrast between a growing European power and a declining Mughal one, the first characterised by unity of purpose and the second by internal dissension, in the next section, 'Abdul Karim goes on to give a brief description of the governors (*ṣūbadārs*) of Bengal. He begins this part by noting that "the war made by the Franks is with guns and cannon. They are not very able in fighting with swords". The text now proceeds to discuss the manner in which the Deccani armies came to control Bengal, which is in turn related to the conflict between Alivardi Khan and Sarfaraz Khan, respectively son of Nawwab Shuja'-ud-Daula and son-in-law of Ja'far 'Ali Khan, or Murshid Quli Khan. Here, 'Abdul Karim gives us a brief account of this well-known dispute, following on the death of Shuja'-ud-Daula, and culminating with the death in battle of Sarfaraz Khan. Alivardi Khan now succeeds as *ṣūbadār*, with the title of Mahabat Jang. It turns out that Sarfaraz Khan had sought the aid of Nizam-ul-Mulk in Hyderabad to shore up his position, and it was in this way that the Marathas too got embroiled in the affair through Orissa, where they already levied *chauth* on the *rājas* and *zamīndārs*. Once their raids began, Purniya was one of the few places that was saved from them, because of Nawwab Saif Khan. 'Abdul Karim mentions that he himself was obliged to leave Bengal on account of these disturbances, and, after a short stay in Purniya, eventually made his way to Patna.[39]

Patna struck him as a large and clean city, by which the Ganges (and its confluent rivers) passed before entering the Darya-i A'zam, the Great Sea, or the Bay of Bengal. In that city, he noted once again that the Franks had built several large houses, and that they traded there. The betel leaf of the city was particularly notable, and people sought it out from afar, while the rice was better than that of Bengal, so that the richer people of Bengal paid a high price to purchase this top-quality rice. After receiving news that the emperor Muhammad Shah was now ill, and that he was summoning Hakim 'Alawi Khan – in whose company 'Abdul Karim was – they had to leave in a hurry, despite the heat. Passing through Benares, Allahabad, and Farrukhabad, on 10 Jumada II 1156 H (1 August

[39] *Bayān-i Wāqi'*, p. 165.

1743) they eventually reached Shahjahanabad. Thus, writes the Khwaja, after having passed through and taken the measure of a number of wildernesses (*bayābān* and *bādya*) they eventually managed to reach home safe and sound.[40]

All along the way, the *faujdārs* and *ṣūbadārs* of Hindustan treated them as well as the rulers of Iran, Rum, the Arab lands and Yemen, and this was largely on account, it would seem, of the prestigious figure of Hakim 'Alawi Khan.[41] On reaching Delhi, Khwaja 'Abdul Karim recounts the incident of the tragic death of Nawwab Amir Khan, whose body was shockingly left without burial for three or four days by his unpaid troops (a fact that is not treated very explicitly, but mentioned in passing). This great noble had been governor of Allahabad, where he had been appointed against his own will and that of the emperor. Qamar-ud-Din Khan and Nizam-ul-Mulk had manipulated this appointment to get him away from the court, as he was a great plotter, a smooth talker (*charb zabānī*) and very close to the emperor. He and Abu'l Mansur Safdar Jang, described as a *ṣāḥib-i fauj-i Irān* (that is at the head of some Qizilbash, who had been left behind by Nadir Shah), now planned to oppose the Turanis in the court, but when Amir Khan returned to Delhi to implement their plans, he was killed. 'Abdul Karim himself had come to know through Amir Khan's close associates who had killed him, but he notes that he has decided not to mention their name in his text. For, as the Qur'an says, without proof, one cannot cast doubt on persons without incurring sin. On his death, Amir Khan's goods were sequestered, and for four days the dispute continued with the soldiers over their pay arrears, until a compromise was reached. 'Abdul Karim now cites a chronogram that was composed on the occasion, which ran as follows (noting that the numeral for "ah" should be removed to calculate the proper date).

Chu Bīdar az bahr-i tārīkh-i sāl ash
Ta'mmul namūdah ba taklīf-i mardūm
Barāwurd āh-o-nidā kard hātif
Ki tajhīz kardand roz-i-chahārum.
(When Bedar, in order to calculate the date,
meditated, the people in pain
let out a sigh. An unseen voice said:
"That the burial was on the fourth day".)

[40] *Bayān-i Wāqi'*, p. 166.
[41] On 'Alawi Khan, see also Naim, *Zikr-i Mir*, pp. 135–6.

This mention of Amir Khan occurs ostensibly because his name arose in the context of 'Abdul Karim's return travels through Allahabad, but the real reason would appear to be that this death is another unhappy sign of the chaotic times. Again, it is noted that when they passed through Farrukhabad, the governor (*ḥākim*) there, Muhammad Khan Bangash, was unwell. He had thus come to see Hakim 'Alawi Khan, who examined him. However, on his return to his own tent, 'Alawi Khan told 'Abdul Karim that they had better leave there as soon as possible as he was likely to die in six or seven days, and chaos would result. 'Abdul Karim was astonished at this precise prediction, and asked whether he had made this diagnosis on the basis of his medical prowess, or his spiritual powers. To this 'Alawi Khan replied that there was no great mystery: it was because of his rich experience as a physician that he was able to say this.

We are thus quickly led to understand that in the time Khwaja 'Abdul Karim has been absent, things in the Mughal domains have not improved greatly. Meanwhile, he notes that two envoys (*īlchīs*) of Nadir Shah, Muhammad 'Ali Beg and Karim Beg, had arrived at Muhammad Shah's court. Curiously, they had brought back with them 100 elephants, and some special bejewelled Indian swords, as well as daggers (*katārihā-i muraṣṣa'*), and other jewelled objects. For these were things, it was explained in an accompanying letter from Nadir Shah, that were not made in Iran-o-'Ajam, and which were not held in much esteem there. In return, Muhammad Shah gave them the usual *khil'ats* and cash and goods. After a stay of a few days, the two representatives revealed their true intention. It turned out that Nadir Shah had sent a verbal message that, on account of wars in Turan, Daghestan, and Rum, he had been obliged to raise a large force. He had also, as noted earlier in the *Bayān-i Wāqi'*, given a three-year tax holiday to peasants in Iran. He hence now needed another 50 to 60 lakhs of rupees from India, which he declared would naturally seal the friendship between him and the Mughals. The sending back of the elephants and other goods was thus a sort of "hint for cash" (*ḥusn-i ṭalab-i zar*), or sweetener, with a concealed pressure and demand behind it. Muhammad Shah now replied that there was nothing to this effect in the formal letter; how then could he cede the money? Besides, Nadir Shah on his departure from India had told him that only written messages from him should be paid heed to, and not verbal ones.[42] Finally, he pleaded that the uprisings of rebel *zamīndārs* had reduced

[42] *Bayān-i Wāqi'*, p. 168.

his own revenues, so that his expenses now exceeded them. He too did not put this down on paper, saying that a verbal response was enough for a verbal demand. He then gave the envoys only what was asked for in Nadir Shah's letter, namely Chinese porcelain dishes, sandal-wood, and Indian aloes (*'ūd-i hindī*). Even after this, writes 'Abdul Karim, and until news eventually came of Nadir Shah's death, the whole Mughal court remained nervous at their own boldness in this refusal of a demand from Iran. The brief section that follows is entirely on Muhammad Shah's march against one of the mentioned rebel *zamīndārs*, 'Ali Muhammad Khan Rohila, at the instigation of Safdar Jang and Amir Khan.[43] This description is presented by the author once more with the explicit aim of highlighting the significance of Mughal disunity (*nifāq*). Thus, the narrative goes back and forth in time, seeking out episodes that are sometimes earlier in relation to others that precede them in the text, in order to make a didactic point.[44]

The *faṣl* which follows eventually takes us to the death of Nadir Shah at the hands of his own soldiers, or more precisely his own people (*īl-i khwud*, i.e., the *qaum-i Afshār*), and it is here that the biography of Nadir Shah is finally closed. This incident in fact reminds 'Abdul Karim of his own earlier "theory" concerning nobility and baseness. For, when 'Abdul Karim had left for the *ḥajj*, Nadir Shah for his part had left Qazwin for Daghestan, because his own older brother Ibrahim Khan had been killed there. However, the people of Daghestan, usually called the Lazgi, were noted for their prowess and bravery. Nadir Shah had taken Hindustan and Turan with no difficulty, and he had hence become overconfident. In private and in public, he used to say in the crudest possible terms that, in revenge for his brother's death, he would kill 5,000 Lazgis, and transfer the private parts of the women of respectable families of the area to the brothel. Further, he said all this without calling on the aid of God, as if his own strength sufficed. 'Abdul Karim had heard from Nadir Shah's close courtiers that, when he had gone out to fight Rum, Hindustan and Turan, he had performed ablutions, prayed and prostrated in all humility. In fact, in Hindustan, he had descended from horseback to prostrate himself in prayer in the midst of battle, saying: "I am a very ordinary man, indeed even less than that. How can I, alone, do anything?" However, when setting out for Daghestan, he was full of boasting and bragging,

[43] This is the same expedition discussed at some length by Anand Ram "Mukhlis" in his travel-text, for which see Alam and Subrahmanyam, "Discovering the familiar", pp. 131–54.
[44] *Bayān-i Wāqi'*, pp. 169–70.

and so, while fighting the Lazgi forces, his armies suffered great losses, so that both soldiers and commanders became confused and lost confidence. Though the Lazgis eventually ran away into the mountains, and Nadir Shah notionally won a victory, this was not a victory of the sort he had dreamed of. He then returned to Iran, and after a short time there, began to prepare a campaign against Rum. He went to Karkuk, and then to Mosul and Diyarbekir, which 'Abdul Karim has already mentioned in his third *bāb*. From there, after further looting and plunder, he made his way to Najaf-i Ashraf and Karbala, and eventually to 'Iraq-i 'Ajam and Khorasan.

So long as 'Alawi Khan, one of the greatest physicians of his time, was with Nadir Shah, he had managed to keep him under control, writes 'Abdul Karim. After he left, the other physicians did not dare intervene to control his temper (*iṣlāḥ-i mizāj*). His bloodthirsty character (*saffākī*), foolhardiness (*bībākī*), and violent temper had all been kept under control through the ministrations of Hakim 'Alawi Khan, and they all now reappeared. Every day he used to kill people, had eyes torn out, and plundered their houses beyond reason. A verse is cited:

> When an emperor plunders his own subjects,
> he's like a drunkard,
> making kebabs of his own flesh.[45]

'Alawi Khan, it is claimed, was the only man capable of even reprimanding Nadir Shah, but the latter used to tolerate this, even welcome it. The Hakim used to try and keep Nadir Shah's temper cool, so that he might look to the welfare of his subjects. So long as the Hakim and others were with him, sometimes for fifteen or twenty days at a stretch, he would not even have anyone whipped, let alone have them killed. In Mazandaran, when Nadir Shah's hand was wounded in an assassination attempt, he could well have killed scores of people but he did not do so until a full inquiry had been made. After the Hakim's departure, the vicious humours (*mawād-i fāsidah*) inside him remained under control for a few days, but then they came to the surface once more. He began to grow suspicious of his own Iranian soldiers, and had them killed by other Uzbeks and Afghans in his employ. Matters reached such a point that one person would be used to kill another, and the assassin himself would be killed the very next day. After his death, Mulla Firdausi, author of the *Shāhnāma-i Nādirī*, hence wrote this verse:

[45] *Bayān-i Wāqi'*, p. 172.

In the night's beginning,
there was a head to plan killing and plunder.
In the morning, there was neither head on body, nor crown on head.
The revolution of the celestial orbit had it that
Nadir did not remain, and nor did his tyranny (*nādirī*).

According to 'Abdul Karim, on 13 Jumada I 1160 H (23 May 1747), in the neighbourhood of Kuchun, three stations from Mashhad, a certain Muhammad Quli Khan Urrumi, the *kashiqchī-bāshī* (head of the bodyguard) and seventy of his men took an oath to kill the emperor. Fifty-seven of those who had taken the oath were so full of fear that they eventually backed out. The other thirteen slashed open the royal pavilion, and reached the sleeping quarters (*ḥaram-sarā*). They first killed a eunuch who tried to stop them, and eventually reached the emperor. There are different versions of what happened next. It seems that the assassins tried everything by way of abundant precaution: they shot him with pistols and guns, slashed at him with swords, and stabbed him with knives, and at length his imperial glory came to an end. An Arabic saying is cited by 'Abdul Karim: "Wonderful it is that God, who can give life and power, can also bring death and an end." It was said that when Nadir Shah was attacked, he first grew angry and he began to curse the attackers, but then he began to plead. Still, neither his anger nor his pleading had any effect. His jewels and precious things (including his women) had already been sent to Nasrullah Mirza in Qalat, and so they were saved from the assassins. In the morning, the emperor's head was found severed from his body, and an old lady was found sitting and weeping by his body. More verses are found by Khwaja 'Abdul Karim for the occasion, on the temporary character of glory, how the world is a garden of passage, a house where one is a guest for just a moment. The army and the soldiers then did the same with those goods that remained as Nadir Shah had taught them to do in Hindustan, Turan and Rum, namely they looted them. Nadir Shah's head was sent to his nephew 'Ali Quli Khan, who had apparently mounted the conspiracy. From all this, 'Abdul Karim comes to conclude that emperors should trust their servants and attendants, rather than their brothers and relatives. Nine days later, in accordance with the orders of 'Ali Quli Khan, his body was taken to Mashhad. Fifteen days after this assassination, in the very mausoleum that he had built, Nadir Shah was buried.[46] Another verse is cited:

[46] *Bayān-i Wāqi'*, p. 176.

The emperor whose army was more numerous,
by far than ants and locusts,
by the side of his grave,
you may now see ants in a procession.

Many chronograms were prepared for his death, stressing his destructive qualities for the most part, and these, in 'Abdul Karim's view, were mostly in bad taste. He therefore cites one chronogram in mixed Arabic and Persian, yielding 1160 H:

Fī al-na'r wa'l saqar
ma' al-jadd-i wa'l pidar.
(In deepest Hellfire,
with his sire and grandsire.)

The Khwaja now comments in an erudite fashion on the linguistic question. How does the word "pidar" in Persian fit in with the rest of the Arabic? This is not grammatical, he notes, even if it is easy to remember. He also recalls the chronogram for his accession (cited earlier in this chapter). It is true, writes 'Abdul Karim, that Nadir Shah was brave, financially astute and a man of determination, as well as far-sighted. He also had perfect expertise in fighting and capturing countries. However, he did not know how to govern, on how to populate a country. This was why he was disliked, and, to add to this, he was also extremely foul-mouthed, and cruel. He loved shedding blood, and where a wise and just ruler would have used a little force, he used to kill people. Perhaps this was a reflection of his low birth, for a quatrain of Shaikh 'Ali Hazin made it clear that his father, Imam Quli Beg, was a furrier (*pūstīn-dost*), as he had stated that it was not worth buying the country of Iran even for a piece of wool, when it had fallen into the hands of a furrier. Others, also respectable men (*buzurg*), had said that Hazin should not be believed as he had a grudge, and had even fled Iran on Nadir Shah's account. Some speculation is added by 'Abdul Karim on Nadir Shah's age. His horoscope was not known, so it was difficult to be exact. From his appearance, it seemed he was fifty or so when he died. Some people said he was born in 1099 H. However, the Khwaja had read that Nadir Shah was born on 27 Ramazan 1102 H (24 June 1691) in a village in Mahal Abiward. His beard was wholly white (though he dyed it twice a week), and most of his teeth were broken, and he could not chew easily even if he still had his incisors.

After he died, his nephew 'Ali Quli Khan took the title of 'Adil Shah, and seized power with the help of Tahmasp Khan Jala'ir and other nobles.

He inherited some ten *karor* (hundred million) rupees in cash, other precious items, and the Peacock Throne, which were all in Qal'at. He also seized all of Nadir Shah's direct descendants, except Shahrukh Mirza (son of Raza Quli Khan and a daughter of Sultan Husain Safavi), and killed them. He made his own younger brother Ibrahim Khan his deputy (*nā'ib us-salṭanat*). 'Abdul Karim now promises his readers that he will continue his history, with the death of these two brothers, and the return of Shahrukh Mirza to power, but this section is not to be found in the extant text. Instead, we find a further chapter on the affairs of the Punjab, and the death of Zakariya Khan, with further reflections on the distinctions between the noble and the ignoble, or between *ashrāf* and *razīl*.[47] Here, we encounter much disapproving gossip about Zakariya Khan's younger son, Shahnawaz Khan, who reputedly kept changing his religion as his love-life took him from one woman to another. First, under Nadir Shah's influence, he had apparently become a Twelver Shi'i, then transformed himself into a Sikh called Sultan Singh, and eventually had even fallen in love with a woman of low (sweeper, *ḥalāl-khwor*) caste.

The closing sections of the extant text of the *Bayān-i Wāqi'* appear to have been composed not by Khwaja 'Abdul Karim Shahristani, but by one of his early copyists and admirers, the celebrated Muhammad Bakhsh "Ashub", author of the *Kārnāma*.[48] These sections take us to other issues, such as wars with the Durrani Afghans in the Punjab, the death of Muhammad Shah in 1748, as well as reflections on the history of the Mughals in the early eighteenth century, the reigns of Jahandar Shah and Farrukhsiyar, the rise to importance of the Marathas and the Sayyid brothers, as well as a number of other episodes. This seems to be the case with the fifth *bāb* as well, which begins with a description of the brief reign of Ahmad Shah, successor to Muhammad Shah. These passages are not devoid of interest in their own right, but they have little coherent relationship to the earlier sections of the text. Ashub thus gives us a chronicle-style account of the death of 'Ali Muhammad Khan Rohila and the conflict between the Rohilas and the Bangash Nawwabs, as well as the assassination of Nawwab Qa'im Khan, and the politics of the early 1750s involving Safdar Jang. There is even a brief, distinct

47 On these questions, see also Muzaffar Alam, *The crisis of empire in Mughal North India: Awadh and the Punjab, 1707–1748* (Delhi, 1986).

48 Ashub thus copies a part of his own *maṣnawī* into the text (*Bayān-i Wāqi'*, pp. 194–200), with the copied verses relating to Mughal battles with Ahmad Shah.

sub-section devoted to a description of Hakim Sayyid 'Alawi Khan and his family.

The very final section of the text is entitled "A brief account of Hindustan from that time to now", and once more clearly appears to come for the most part from the hand of Ashub.[49] Here the writer rapidly describes how the Sultanate of Hindustan has been ruined of late by the fighting between Safdar Jang and 'Imad-ul-Mulk, so that Ahmad Shah, his mother and 'Alamgir II have all been laid low in this process, and the 400-year Timurid tradition more or less reduced to naught. Besides, the Durranis have returned to Hindustan, reducing whatever remained to dust. It is bluntly stated that, by the completion of the text in 1193H (1779), most Mughal provinces, such as the Deccan, Surat and Gujarat, are all in poor shape. On the death of Safdar Jang, his son Shuja'-ud-Daula had come to the throne, and briefly made some progress, but was in turn defeated by the Franks. He then became obedient to the Franks, and with their help made a meal of defeating the Rohilas. He was reigning in glory, when he was wounded in the thigh and died. By the late 1770s, then, it was his son Asaf-ud-Daula who was ruling, with the help of English Franks. In Shahjahanabad, 'Ali Gauhar, son of 'Alamgir II, was "bearing the blame of rulership", and he was content with this.

The tone of these closing sections of the text, authored by Ashub, explicitly brings out what has remained an implicit notion in Khwaja 'Abdul Karim: namely, that of his narrative as a variant of the "decline text". To the Khwaja, the underlying problem is one of how the mean can defeat the elevated, the high are unable to combat the low, and the noble are brought down by the ignoble. This perspective is, however, not developed in terms of a cycle, or chronological sequence, but rather in terms of a comparison between Hindustan and its neighbours to the west and north. Here, xenology and travel is purposive, and – as he more or less tells us – the real purpose of Khwaja 'Abdul Karim's travels is to comprehend how the India of the Mughals has been brought low. However, this was only one clearly articulated view in the eighteenth century. We should remind ourselves that, for other authors of the period, the concept of "decline" was not at all what made sense. This may be easily ascertained by comparing 'Abdul Karim's text with the *Ṭahmās Nāma*, authored by Tahmas Khan, a slave of obscure origin from the Ottoman empire, who had been captured by Nadir Shah's army in an

[49] *Bayān-i Wāqi'*, pp. 270–1.

expedition.[50] Subsequently, he arrived in the Mughal empire, and was taken into the household of a certain Mir Mu'in-ul-Mulk. His perspective is that of a "self-made man"; and he uses the telling *takhalluṣ* or pen-name of *miskīn*, "indigent" or "pauper". Thus, in some sense, Tahmas Khan's view is the precise opposite of that of Khwaja 'Abdul Karim; whereas the latter sees decline, in the form of the rise of the low-born, Tahmas is apt to see himself as one of those who has happily made good in these new times. His son was thus the well-known poet Sa'adat Yar Khan "Rangin", and his family managed to do well even in late eighteenth- and early nineteenth-century Mughal India.

A few further notes on Tahmas Khan may not be out of place to develop this comparison at greater length.[51] He was born, by his own account, in Qasba Arzat, eight *kos* to the east of Bayazid near Mt Ararat in eastern Turkey in 1738, and eventually died in Delhi in 1803. Also according to his own account, Tahmas Khan was attached to the Naqshbandi Sufi order in the last years of his life in Delhi. His text begins with the usual initial prayers and invocations to Allah, the Prophet, and a personal prayer (*ḥamd*, *na't*, and *munājāt*) all in verse, with the last line of the *munājāt* being a chronogram "*nuskha-i mauzūn*" ("The appropriate book"), for the year 1194H. The text proper then commences with the heading: "The beginning of the auspicious book with a description of the birth of Adam and the respectable saints who are close to God", and its initial lines run as follows.

In the illumined heart of the pious intelligentsia (*dānishwarān*), and in the hearts of those with an agile and subtle understanding, it is evident that when God who is the Creator of all atoms and beings, and who is the decorator of a variety of creations and creatures (*maṣnū'āt wa makhlūqāt*), wanted that in the world of earth and this field of being, there might be grace, He took up the fragrant soul (which was perfuming all the other souls, and bringing grace to their union) of the auspicious and blessed personality of Adam that was in the garden of Paradise, and with his power and impeccable wisdom, blended it with four elements: water, fire, air and earth. Thus, it was metamorphosed into the form of Man (*insān*), and made visible (*bashar*).

When he was created, Adam at that instant opened the eye of his intellect, praised God saying, *al-ḥamdu l-illāh*, and became manifest on the carpet of this world. Thereafter, by the order of the Wrathful Almighty, and with the special

[50] Tahmasp Khan, *Ṭahmās Nāmeh by Ṭahmās Beg Khān*, ed. Muhammad Aslam (Lahore, 1986). But see also P. Setu Madhava Rao, *Tahmas Nama: the autobiography of a slave* (Delhi, 1967); and Jadunath Sarkar, *Memoirs of Tahmasp Khan by Miskin* (Sitamau, 1937).

[51] See also the recent discussion in Indrani Chatterjee, "A slave's quest for selfhood in eighteenth-century Hindustan", *Indian Economic and Social History Review*, 37, 1, 2000, pp. 53–86.

desire of the All-High, his left side was ripped open, and Hazrat Hawwa [Eve] was brought forth in the form of woman; they were then tied together in nuptial bonds. Thus, from that time on, the chain of procreation of the species of humankind was brought into being, and the management of the manufacture of human beings (*mardūm*) grew day by day, and in the future, in the same pattern, as long as the earth, sky, and the traces of the world and those who live in it exist, the generations of the descendants of Adam and the large group of humankind shall go on increasing, and will illumine and lend grace to the world.

This seemingly innocent passage underlines Tahmas Khan's view, quite contrary from that of Khwaja 'Abdul Karim, which is that all men are created equal. This is made even clearer in the lines that follow.

Since God, who works for everyone, and is protector of his slaves (*banda-nawāz*), in the creation and making of human beings does so from one drop of sperm, which is so despicable, and yet gives him a form and face, therefore whoever regards his polluted being (*lauṣālūd*) from ill-placed pride and arrogance as purer than others, and thus goes around this world boasting, and certainly considers himself above his other countrymen (*abna-i waṭan*), such a person is stupid and senseless (*nādān wa hichmadān)* in the eyes of the wise and intelligent. Thus, the Prophet has said: "All the Faithful (*mu'mīn*) are brothers." No one is better or higher than the other. In fact, all are one, as this verse of Shaikh Sa'di of Shiraz shows:

The descendants of Adam are parts of each other.
For in Creation, they were from one pearl (*gauhar*).

Even though this fact is evident to all, big and small, noble and ignoble, and because of its being evident one need not develop it further, yet the aim of pestering [the reader] with this presentation is to provide a reminder that one should not cross the line of balance, and [enter] into the territory of pride and arrogance, which is mere ignorance and misguidedness because the jewel of greatness is bestowed by God alone.

It is His preserve to claim greatness and Selfhood,
For his country is so ancient, and his person rich beyond need.

Tahmas Khan follows this passage by noting that, though the blessed souls of the great prophets and the virtuous personalities of the saints and enlightened were all so dear to God, yet they refrained from boasting, and instead stressed their slavery (*bandagī*) to God. This then leads to the hemistich:

I need slavery to God,
not descent from a prophet.

These lines are intended, once more, to denigrate the pretensions of those who claim a noble birth and high descent, and, instead, to bolster the antinomian ambitions of others like Tahmas Khan himself. This brings us to a set of reflections that run as follows: "Therefore, it is necessary for all Muslims, nay, all human beings, that they live together with love for each other which is the mark of nobility and high birth, while steadfastly holding to the tie of humility and mutual respect, which is the noblest and most virtuous attribute of human existence."

Tahmas Khan "Miskin" then demonstrates all this further by quoting from the Prophet's sayings, to the effect that it does not behove a human to boast, or to search for the shortcomings of others. This was the manner of functioning of the foolish, and stupid, and those of bad character (*bad kirdār*). So, every man must bow down in all humility, which is the sole way of gaining distinction before God and the Prophet. To the extent possible, one should try to obtain the pearl of acquired qualities and skills, and through this medium gain honour and be well-considered. So, one must learn skill, in order to endear oneself to others. A verse is cited here:

> Hunar āmūz tā 'azīz shawī,
> Bī hunar mu'tabar kujā bāshad.
> (Acquire skill, that you may be held dear,
> Where can one without skill gain trust?)[52]

The introductory section of the text then concludes by stating that the time has come for the early afternoon prayer, and so the author will for a time cease his story. It resumes with the first part of the main text (*ḥikāyat-i awwal*), containing an account of the birth of this Miskin, and his acquisition of worth in the service of the important (*buzurgān*). Here again, as throughout the text, the emphasis is on achievement as opposed to ascriptive status, for Tahmas Khan always stresses the idea of himself as initially orphaned, unskilled, unintelligent, and a mere victim of the chess-game of the cruel sky. Yet, from this game, much that is worthwhile has emerged, a notion that would surely have been anathema to the likes of Khwaja 'Abdul Karim.

The Mughal eighteenth century was hence lived in many different ways, even by members of the élite based in northern India, and an examination of various first-person accounts – whether travel-texts or not – brings this out clearly enough. Similar arguments have been put forward with respect to the Ottoman empire in the seventeenth and eighteenth centuries, as indeed in relation to the phase of "Ming decline"

[52] *Ṭahmās Nāmeh*, p. 11.

in China.[53] In the latter case, we find claims, by writers in the early seventeenth century, such as "the balance between the mighty and the low was lost", or that "deception sprouted and litigation arose; purity was sullied and excess overflowed".[54] Where once such claims were taken literally by historians, we have learnt over the years to nuance our readings of such perspectives, and to look instead to issues of social change, as well as regional reorientation, that such rhetoric often conceals.

CONCLUSION

It is a notorious fact that extreme cultural contrasts are easier to deal with than the subtle differences between neighbouring cultures. The literature on early modern travel-accounts has thus usually chosen preferentially to deal with texts in the "exotic" mode, rather than those where Ottomans travel in Persia, or Japanese in China. The great seventeenth-century Ottoman traveller, Evliya Çelebi, is thus hardly a household name in the sense of Mandeville, Marco Polo or even Bernier; and we have already noted Cemal Kafadar's comment on how Evliya's "gargantuan work seems to have gone largely unnoticed in Ottoman belles-lettres" until the late nineteenth century, despite its indubitable status as "the most monumental example of the first person narrative", perhaps in the seventeenth-century world as a whole.[55] Even in recent times, researchers have shown a marked preference for those texts in which Ottoman writers talk of western Europe, which is only one of Evliya's many preoccupations.

The problem with the texts we have dealt with here is a similar one, albeit in a rather more attenuated measure. Despite Gladwin's serviceable translation of the late eighteenth century, scholars have been somewhat perplexed with the vision of Khwaja 'Abdul Karim Shahristani, even as they have had difficulty with the travel-account of his far more distinguished contemporary, Anand Ram "Mukhlis". Both writers belong to the literati among the service-gentry of the declining Mughal empire, and as such produced texts that are, in a sense, the visions of "imperial eyes". Yet Anand Ram travels within the confines of the heartland of Hindustan, while 'Abdul Karim for the most part stays within territories that are linguistically circumscribed by Persian and Arabic, languages with which

[53] Cemal Kafadar, "The question of Ottoman decline", *Harvard Middle Eastern and Islamic Review*, 4, 1–2, 1997–8, pp. 30–71; Timothy Brook, *The confusions of pleasure: commerce and culture in Ming China* (Berkeley, 1999).

[54] Brook, *The Confusions of Pleasure*, pp. 2–3.

[55] Cemal Kafadar, "Self and others", p. 126.

he has a profound familiarity. Both seem to wish to resolve a conundrum within the limits not of an exotic, but of a somewhat familiar, world: how is it that the Mughal empire of the late 1730s and early 1740s is at once so resilient, and yet so fragile? In the case of Khwaja ʿAbdul Karim, a second question attaches itself to the first: what differentiates the neighbours of the Mughals to the north and west from the descendants of Amir Timur in Hindustan?

Yet, in the final analysis, our authors go far beyond this set of questions, and instead explore a series of problems and experiences that surely exceed even their own initial intentions and expectations. This may be practically inbuilt into the "proximate" travel-account of the period, as we see from the Malay *Hikayat Perintah Negeri Benggala* of Ahmad Rijaluddin, a Chulia (Tamil Muslim) of Kedah, who visited Calcutta about 1810.[56] Here, we have a very amusing sequence, in which an intoxicated and naive Malay sailor (*khelasi*) and a cunning courtesan in a brothel trade improvised stanzas in a Malay poem (*pantun*), which inevitably ends with the sailor being mercilessly exploited by the courtesan and his own superior (*serang*). Still, going beyond this rather obvious tale of chicanery, it is startling and unexpected to our ears, untutored in close encounters and far more familiar with the "ungoverned imaginings" of Europeans in Asia, to hear the courtesan (*bibi jalang*) declaiming hybrid Malay verses in Calcutta, where a Persianised vocabulary slides imperceptibly into references to Sri Rama.[57] A little reflection shows that this is no more strange than the world of ʿAbdul Karim, wherein any understanding of Nadir Shah passes through references to Farhad and Afrasiyab, Ayyub and Shuʿaib.[58] This is why we encounter that curious mixture of fear and admiration, familiarity and loathing, that is still so far from the vision that the early Indo-Persian travellers to England would bring back to their countrymen.[59]

[56] C. Skinner, *Ahmad Rijaluddin's Hikayat Perintah Negeri Benggala* (The Hague, 1992); for a discussion, Claudine Salmon, "Bengal as reflected in two South-East Asian travelogues from the early nineteenth century", in Denys Lombard and Om Prakash, eds., *Commerce and culture in the Bay of Bengal, 1500–1800* (New Delhi, 1999), pp. 383–402.

[57] Skinner, *Hikayat*, pp. 64–5.

[58] But also contrast ʿAbdul Karim to ethnocentric travellers from Iran to India, such as Aqa Ahmad Bihbahani mentioned above in Chapter 5; see Cole, "Mirror of the world".

[59] Partha Chatterjee, 'Five hundred years of fear and love', *Economic and Political Weekly*, 33, 22–30 May 1998, pp. 1330–6. However, we may usefully contrast the Indo-Persian accounts to the far more critical view in Cathanar Thomman Paremmakkal, *The Varthamanappusthakam: an account of the history of the Malabar church between the years 1773 and 1786 . . . [and] the journey from Malabar to Rome via Lisbon and back . . .*, tr. Placid J. Podipara (Rome, 1971).

CHAPTER 7

The long road to Rum

> Let it be known to you that, by God's grace, the sanctity of the House of God, the Garden of the Prophet, the Holy City, and both the birth and burying-places of the greatest Prophets are situated within the boundaries of this empire; and whereas the direction of their affairs is entrusted to the hands of the powerful Ottoman Sultans, all the sects of Islam, both orthodox and heterodox, and all Christian nations, seek refuge at the foot of their sublime throne.
>
> Ottoman Grand Vizier to the Mughal Vizier (1642) in Hammer, "Memoir on the diplomatic relations", pp. 482–5

INTRODUCTION

Studies of early modern travel and travel-accounts, whether those of Europeans or indeed of Chinese or Arab voyagers, typically make ample use of a particular sub-category within the corpus: namely the embassy-account. Thus, it may be argued that the most famous European account of the Mughals in the seventeenth century is not that of François Bernier – celebrated though that French physician came to be – but that of Sir Thomas Roe, the envoy sent by James I to the court of Jahangir. In view of this fact, the reader may well be puzzled by the relative absence of the embassy-account in our analysis thus far, with the exceptions of 'Abdur Razzaq's text from the fifteenth century, and the *Safīna-i Sulaimānī* and its account of Thailand. To be sure, some of the other texts that we have analysed come rather close to the embassy-account. Seydi 'Ali Re'is's travels certainly have a strong diplomatic component to them, and the court-based account of Mutribi Samarqandi once again comes to approach the embassy-account without quite entering that category.

Yet, it should be amply clear that the geographical domain that we have chosen here, which embraces Mughal India, Central Asia, Iran and the Ottoman empire, was one which witnessed intensive diplomatic contacts in the early modern period. Such contacts were conducted for the most part in Persian, and occasionally in Turkish; and a quite substantial corpus of letters, instructions and related texts has come down to us from the three centuries after 1500. Besides, official historians and chroniclers usually make mention of the passage and reception of ambassadors, even providing more or less detailed lists of the gifts they brought and took back. These histories and chronicles can at times be disconcertingly direct, and are not always complimentary to the side that they ostensibly speak for. A striking example of this comes to us from the official Ottoman chronicler Mustafa Na'ima (1655–1716), who describes the visit of the polished and "accomplished" Mughal ambassador Haji Sayyid Ahmad Sa'id, who arrived in Istanbul around June 1653, during the reign of Sultan Mehmed IV.[1] The ambassador made a fine impression, it would seem, with his expensive gifts in cash and kind; besides, the Ottoman historian notes that he was a remarkably erudite man, who was able to carry on literary disputes and learned discussions with the cream of the Ottoman court. The visitor's wit was in obvious contrast to the dullness and lack of intellect of the Ottoman ambassador who was sent in return, a certain Zu'lfiqar Beg Agha, whom Na'ima's text dismisses contemptuously as an "ignorant Bosnian" who had simply bought the ambassadorship for cash by declaring "I want no expense money; I shall pay the expenses out of my own pocket." One of the high points of the Haji's visit to the Ottoman domains, recalled even a half-century later, was his clever use of a Persian verse by the poet Melhemi to praise the city of Istanbul, which pleased his hosts no end. The verse in question ran:

> Sha'b, and Ghuta, and Abula and Soghd,
> are the only cities in the world like Paradise.
> With its two channels the city of Istanbul,
> is the only place in the world like a city.

In contrast, Na'ima tells us of a ridiculous dinner to which Haji Ahmad was invited by Zu'lfiqar Beg, wherein the Ottoman envoy – through his gross habits and unrefined food (with an inordinate accent on cabbages) – made himself the butt of the other's jokes, much to the mortification of the invited guests; while departing the dinner, the Haji was heard to remark: "Glory be to God, who created an ox in the form of a man."

[1] Mustafa Na'ima, *Tārīkh-i Na'īma: Rauẓat ul-Ḥusain fī khulāsat-i akhbār al-khāfiqain*, 6 vols. (Istanbul, 1863), vol. V, pp. 336–40, section entitled "āmadan-i īlchī-i Hind"); for a Romanised text, see Mustafa Na'ima, *Naīmā Tārīhī*, ed. Zuhuri Danishman, 6 vols., (Istanbul, 1967–9), vol. V, pp. 2371–2. For a discussion of this historian–compiler and his sources, see Lewis V. Thomas, *A study of Naima*, ed. Norman Itzkowitz (New York, 1972).

It was no coincidence then that, on the return journey to the Mughal domains, Haji Ahmad parted company with Zu'lfiqar Beg, preferring to travel via Yemen, while his counterpart took the route through Basra to Surat. Regrettably, neither the polished Mughal ambassador nor the oafish Ottoman one – who was clearly a rather eager traveller – has left us a first-person account of what transpired.

THE OTTOMANS AND INDIA

Historians of the early modern have in recent years – and especially in the wake of the *magnum opus* of Marshall Hodgson – made it their task to think through the relations between the Ottoman and Mughal empires in a far more systematic manner than was once the case.[2] These relations are undoubtedly asymmetric given that the Ottoman empire had a far longer life than its Mughal counterpart, lasting for very nearly 600 years from roughly the 1320s onwards, whereas the Mughal dynasty's rule in Hindustan lasted barely 300 years. Comparisons between the two empires can lead to some surprising conclusions, for – despite the boastful rhetoric of Seydi 'Ali Re'is, to which we have referred above – the Ottoman domains even at their height had a far smaller population and far fewer fiscal and human resources than did the Mughals. Although the two empires did share a number of institutions and traditions of statecraft, they also diverged because of the far greater proximity of the Ottomans to Christian Europe, and the complex dealings of the Mughals with their "Hindu" subjects.

Be that as it may, there is no doubt that the events of the early sixteenth century irrevocably changed the relations between the Ottomans and India. The conquest by Sultan Selim of Mamluk Egypt, and its dependencies, which included the Hijaz, meant that the Ottomans became the keepers (*k̲h̲ādim*) of the Holy Places of Islam, those in Arabia as well as Jerusalem and many of the Holy Cities that were to be found in 'Iraq. This gave them an aura which lasted until the nineteenth century, a fact that we find mentioned in more than one text of the Indo-Persian tradition. However, the rising power of the Mughals would not admit their inferiority to the Ottomans in the last quarter of the sixteenth

[2] An important and pioneering essay is that of Hammer, "Memoir on the diplomatic relations", pp. 462–86. For a survey, see Bernard Lewis, "The Mughals and the Ottomans", in Lewis, *From Babel to Dragomans: interpreting the Middle East* (New York, 2004), pp. 108–14 (reprinted from an essay with the same title published in 1958).

century, a period when Akbar and his court sought for their part to establish direct relations with the Sharifs of Mecca. A celebrated letter from 1582, drafted by none other than Shaikh Abu'l Fazl, makes the tenor of the relations that were being established in this epoch amply clear. The letter was sent by the Mughal emperor to Sharif Abu Numay II, and was sent through the chief of the Mughal party that had begun to make the pilgrimage from the ports of Gujarat (usually Surat) to the Hijaz, after the Mughal conquest of Gujarat in 1573. The missive, addressed to the *shurafā'-i kirām-i Makka*, began by noting Akbar's benevolence, and his concern for the weak and oppressed. His solicitous attitude towards the holy places of the Hijaz was a particular aspect of this concern, and a decision had been made not merely to send a trusted servant regularly as head of the *ḥajj* caravan (*Mīr-i ḥajj*) but to designate some revenues for distribution there.[3] This is apparently a reference to the Mughal decision to maintain (and even extend) the *waqf* endowment of some properties in Gujarat that had been set in place by the Gujarat Sultans, as benefactors of the holy places. Mughal chroniclers also report the decision in the 1570s to defray "the travelling expenses of anybody who might intend to perform a pilgrimage to the sacred places" from the treasury, and the designation of certain Surat-based ships for the purpose of carrying pilgrims to Jiddah.[4]

The first official Mughal *Mīr-i ḥajj* appears to have been a certain Sultan Khwaja Naqshbandi, who was depatched in 1576 with some Rs. 600,000 in cash, and a large number of robes-of-honour (*k͟hil'at*) for distribution. It was also decided to have a special place for Mughal pilgrims constructed in Mecca, and to determine who other needy and deserving people resident in the holy cities might be, so that the Mughals could extend their benevolent sway over them by strategic acts of charity. Despite difficulties with the Portuguese, this expedition seems to have made its way to Mecca and back, and was followed the next year by another, led this time by Mir Abu Turab Shirazi, again with gifts in cash and kind. By this time, the situation had evolved somewhat in comparison to the previous year. For one thing, a Mughal royal party, which included Akbar's aunt Gulbadan Begam, and other notable Mughal ladies (such as Salima Sultan Begam), had departed from Gujarat for the Hijaz in 1575, and was showing little or no signs of wishing to return to India. This was a growing embarrassment to the Mughal

[3] See Islam, *Calendar*, vol. II, pp. 302–4.
[4] Farooqi, *Mughal–Ottoman relations*, pp. 113–14.

authorities. Second, a letter from the Sharifs of Mecca, carried by a certain Rahman Quli Khan, had arrived at the Mughal court in late 1576, the contents of which are unclear – but which apparently showed a recognition on the part of the Sharifs of the growing importance of the Mughals in the western Indian Ocean. A third aspect, which became clearer still with the despatch in 1578 of Khwaja Yahya Naqshbandi as *Mīr-i ḥajj*, was a certain Mughal dissatisfaction with the manner in which the money they were sending out as charity (*ṣadaqāt*) was being disbursed. Over the next two years, Akbar used the position of the *Mīr-i ḥajj* to send away inconvenient critics from the court, first Shaikh ʿAbdun Nabi and Mulla ʿAbdullah Sultanpuri (in 1579), and then Hakim-ul-Mulk Gilani in 1580.[5] We are aware that the pilgrim traffic continued – and even intensified – in later years, with Mughal ships regularly plying the route from Surat to the Red Sea.

These ships were undoubtedly closely linked to the pilgrim traffic, but they also maintained a crucial economic link between the Ottoman domains and those of the Mughals. Indian goods, especially Gujarat textiles, arrived regularly in the markets of the Ottoman empire by these means, and precious metals (usually of Spanish American provenance) flowed from the Red Sea into Gujarat in steady quantities by the end of the sixteenth century.[6] This relatively intense set of commercial relations can be contrasted usefully with the far more uncertain state of diplomatic relations between the Ottomans and Mughals in the seventeenth century. As we have noted in an earlier chapter, a man by the name of Aqam Haji, claiming to be an Ottoman ambassador, is thus reported at Jahangir's court in 1608, but his credentials were thought to be dubious and he was rapidly expelled. Another embassy is briefly reported by English East India Company sources in 1615, but little other trace of it can be found. Relations thus resume only in the reign of Shahjahan (1628–57), and this is one of the most troubled phases in terms of diplomatic contacts between the two empires.

The central difficulty in these contacts of the mid seventeenth century appears to be the jockeying for relative superiority by the two great Sunni empires. The first of a series of letters may be found dated to late 1636 or early 1637, and is addressed by the Mughal emperor to the Ottoman Sultan Murad IV (1623–40). The letter opens by mentioning that there

[5] Farooqi, *Mughal–Ottoman Relations*, pp. 114–16.

[6] See. Sanjay Subrahmanyam, "Precious metal flows and prices in western and southern Asia, 1500–1750: some comparative and conjunctural aspects", *Studies in History*, n.s., 7, 1, 1991, pp. 79–105.

has been little official communication between the two sides for a time, and that Shahjahan has now decided to take the initiative largely from considerations of religion (*dīn* and *mazhab*). The Mughal side then felicitates itself on its recent military successes in the Deccan, and declares its intention to make vigorous war on the Safavids. This is followed by a remarkably patronising passage in which the Ottomans are advised on how best to conduct their own future military affairs in regard to the Safavids, and chided for their earlier carelessness in these matters.[7] Sent via an envoy, a certain Mir (or Amir) Zarif, this letter was probably received by the Ottomans as a slap in the face. Nevertheless, the Ottoman response, probably drafted from the imperial camp in Mosul, is initially moderate. It notes the recent Ottoman capture of Baghdad – matching victory with victory – and points out that the Ottomans too have been vigilant in fighting the Shi'i Qizilbash, as well as in protecting the routes to the holy cities. A slightly condescending reference is added regarding the presents sent by the Mughals, and there is also a jibe, suggesting that the Mughals might want to look to the infidels and heretics (*kufr-o-ilḥād*) whom they nurture in their own midst. This letter, drafted late in Sultan Murad IV's reign, was followed by another sent in 1640 by his successor Sultan Ibrahim. Here, once more, the fact that both Mughals and Ottomans are Sunnis is stressed, but it is equally implied that Shahjahan might do well to undertake a *jihād* against the infidels in his parts of the world.[8]

At least one of these letters would appear to have been carried by an Ottoman envoy named Arsalan Agha, who apparently accompanied Mir Zarif to Lahore. The Mughal court seems to have taken great umbrage at the wording of these missives, and this prompted a sharply worded letter directed to the Ottoman *wazīr* Mustafa Pasha, from his Mughal counterpart. In this letter, it was pointed out that the secretaries of the Ottoman court were clearly not conversant in the proper etiquette with which letters were drafted. The vast domains of Shahjahan – from Qandahar to Bengal and Kabul to the Deccan – were listed, and mention was made of his immense power and status. It was also mentioned that Arsalan Agha was being dismissed and sent back in a Mughal ship (probably from Surat to Jiddah) with a number of gifts. While the common Safavid enemy, and the bonds of the Sunni faith, were stressed, it is clear that it is competition

7 Islam, *Calendar*, vol. II, pp. 312–13; for a translation, see Hammer, "Memoir on the diplomatic relations", pp. 477–80.
8 Islam, *Calendar*, vol. II, pp. 314–17.

for status that has come by now to dominate the tenor of the relationship. The Ottoman *wazīr* responded with further subtle insults in a letter of 1642, in which he briefly acknowledged the Mughal complaints regarding the manner in which Shahjahan had been addressed. While protesting the Ottoman ruler's great affection for his Mughal counterpart, he nevertheless refers to the latter as the "occupant of the throne of Lahore (*sarīr-ārā-i Lāhaur*)", and protests that the Mughals have over-reacted to perceived insults. Two further salvoes follow. First, it is noted that "if the numerous provinces of the mighty Ottoman empire were here to be enumerated, their list would not be contained within the bounds of this letter." Second, it is stated blandly that "all the monarchs of the world acknowledge the truth, shining forth like the sun, that the Sultans of the Ottoman family are the greatest monarchs of the earth".[9] Clearly, the intention is to put the expansive pretensions of Shahjahan in their proper place, especially since the Ottoman domains contained "the House of God [Mecca], the Garden of the Prophet [Medina], the Holy City [Jerusalem], and both the birth and the burying places of the greatest Prophets".

In the two decades that follow, while envoys and letters are exchanged, both by the respective rulers, and by princes and lesser officials, the tenor of relations remains noticeably tense. Thus a letter from the new Ottoman Sultan Mehmed IV (r. 1648–87), sent via Sayyid Muhyi-ud-Din in 1649–50, addresses the Mughal ruler in a casual manner that seems calculated to cause offence. The Mughal expedition in Central Asia at much the same time is also the cause for some mutual jibes and recriminations, as we see from a letter addressed to Shahjahan in mid-1653, and sent through the Ottoman envoy Zu'lfiqar Agha, mentioned above. The response from the Mughal court, sent with the envoy Qa'im Beg in 1654, again chides the Ottomans for their lack of knowledge of etiquette and mentions that a handbook is being sent to the Ottomans in order to instruct them on how to write such letters in their proper form. Even though Sultan Mehmed sent back a somewhat conciliatory missive the next year, relations hit a new low when the Mughal envoy Qa'im Beg died in Aleppo – with Mughal sources claiming that he was poisoned by the Ottoman governor there.[10] Over the next three decades, no embassies

[9] For these letters, see Islam, *Calendar*, vol. II, pp. 318–21; for a translation, see Hammer, "Memoir on the diplomatic relations", pp. 480–5.

[10] Islam, *Calendar*, vol. II, pp. 332–3; for a discussion, see Hammer, "Memoir on the diplomatic relations", pp. 474–5.

were to be exchanged between the two courts, nor has any inter-imperial correspondence from those years survived.[11]

This does not mean, of course, that other relations ceased. We may note the case, for example, in the late 1660s, of Amir Husain Pasha, the Ottoman governor of Basra, who decided to desert his master Sultan Mehmed and go over to the Mughals. Husain Pasha had maintained a correspondence with Aurangzeb's court from at least 1661, and had earlier sought an alliance with the Safavid ruler Shah 'Abbas II in 1653. We are aware that on his arrival in western India he was escorted with full dignities into Shahjahanabad–Delhi in July 1669, and – as the Mughal chronicles have it – "by the touch of the royal hand on his back, his head was exalted beyond the sky".[12] In concrete terms, this meant that he received extensive gifts of rubies and horses, a great mansion on the banks of the river Jamuna, as well as a high *manṣab* rank of 5000 in the Mughal hierarchy. Very quickly he also rose to be governor (*ṣūbadār*) of the central Indian province of Malwa, itself no mean achievement. Two of his sons, Afrasiyab and 'Ali Beg, were also given respectable ranks and taken into imperial service. The short Mughal career of Islam Khan Rumi (as Husain Pasha came to be known), until his death in battle in late June 1676, suggests how easy it was to cross the boundary between these two empires, but it also suggests that the all-too-frequent protests of solidarity between the two great Sunni powers of the early modern world are hardly to be taken literally.

BAYAZID GOES WEST

It is interesting to note, however, that all this diplomatic activity produced little by way of travel-accounts on the part of the envoys, once one enters the last quarter of the sixteenth century. Ottoman travel-accounts of India seem to cease after Seydi 'Ali Re'is, and the silence is even more deafening in the opposite direction. Though men like Mir Zarif or Qa'im Beg do appear in the Ottoman chronicles, their own voices and accounts do not

[11] For the next major set of exchanges, dating to 1688–9, the same period as that of the *Safina-i Sulaimānī*, see Y. Hikmet Bayur, "Osmanli Padişahi II. Süleyman'in Gürkanli Padişahi I. Alamgir (Evrengzeb)'e Mektubu", *Belleten* (*Türk Tarih Kuruma*), 14, 53, 1950, pp. 269–87.

[12] Shahnawaz Khan, *Ma'āṣir- ul-Umarā', being biographies of the Muhammadan and Hindu officers of the Timurid sovereigns of India from 1500 to about 1780 A.D.*, tr. H. Beveridge and Baini Prashad, 3 vols. (Calcutta, 1911–52), vol. 1, pp. 698–701, for the Persian text of which see Nawwab Samsam al-Daula Shahnawaz Khan, *Ma'āṣir al-Umarā'*, ed. Maulavi 'Abdur Rahim and Maulavi Mirza Ashraf 'Ali, 2 vols. (Calcutta, 1888–90), vol. 1, pp. 241–7.

appear to have survived for posterity – if, indeed, they were ever written down. Even historians of the *ḥajj* pilgrimage have often been distressed to note that the first-person accounts of the pilgrimage by residents of South Asia before 1700 can comfortably be counted on the fingers of one hand.[13] Much has been made of the seventeenth-century account entitled *Anīs ul-Ḥujjāj*, but this text is really more a manual instructing the *ḥajj* pilgrim than an account of the experiences of its author.[14] It is thus significant and valuable when a first-person account of the *ḥajj* (and dealings with the Ottomans) comes to us from Mughal times, however brief that account may be.

We should accordingly begin with an important and rather neglected early example, namely the brief travel section in the memoirs of the sixteenth-century Mughal notable Bayazid Bayat.[15] Bayazid produced his work, it is well known, to serve as a sort of "feeder text" to the great imperial chronicle, the *Akbar Nāma*, that was being composed by Shaikh Abu'l Fazl in the closing decades of the sixteenth century, and his greatest virtue – like that of other "sub-chroniclers" such as Gulbadan Begam or Jauhar Aftabchi – was that he had been an eyewitness to and participant in a number of crucial events that had defined the beginnings of Mughal power in Hindustan.[16] Literary talent was apparently not something he possessed in great measure, especially when he was asked to express himself in Persian rather than Turkish – which was quite clearly his first language. We gather that the text was put together in the last years of his life, when he was supervising the imperial kitchen, and that a scribe sent by Abu'l Fazl in fact "wrote it down" from the orally recounted version.[17]

[13] On the other hand, a recent author has stated: "In the Indian sub-continent, even travellers to the holy places of Mecca and Medina did not write about their travels before the late eighteenth century, except in so far as they recorded visions or wrote treatises while there"; this claim may be found in Metcalf, "The pilgrimage remembered", p. 86. Metcalf goes on to identify the "first" Indian account of the *ḥajj* as that of Maulana Rafi'-ud-Din Faruqi Muradabadi, *Safarnāma-i Ḥijāz*, tr. Maulana Nazim Ahmad Faridi Amrohawi (Lucknow, 1961), in Persian, and originally dating to as late as 1786.

[14] Ahsan Jan Qaisar, "From port to port: life on Indian ships in the sixteenth and seventeenth centuries", in Ashin Das Gupta and M. N. Pearson, eds., *India and the Indian Ocean, 1500–1800* (reprint, Delhi, 1999), pp. 331–49.

[15] See also the recent essay by Simon Digby, "Bāyazīd Beg Turkmān's pilgrimage to Makka and return to Gujarat: a sixteenth-century narrative", *Iran*, 42, 2004, pp. 159–77, which contains a translation of the travel sections on pp. 164–8.

[16] Gulbadan Begam, *Humāyūn Nāma*, ed. and tr. Beveridge; Jauhar Aftabchi, *Taẕkirāt ul-Wāqi'āt*, tr. Haq. A short but still useful overview may be found in Abdur Rashid, "The treatment of history by Muslim historians in Mughal official and biographical works", in C. H. Philips, ed., *Historians of India, Pakistan and Ceylon* (London, 1961), pp. 139–51.

[17] Digby, "Bāyazīd Beg Turkmān's Pilgrimage", p. 168.

As a consequence of this mode of transmission, his memoir is written in a rather curious Persian, with a very limited vocabulary, and, often, the underlying meaning is clear only several lines after a given phrase. He refers to himself sometimes as Bayazid, but then again in the passive voice as "me" or "us", as well as in the third person as "him". He also tends to construct a rather discontinuous narrative, and leaves many threads in his story dangling.

Bayazid's account of his *ḥajj* experience appears fairly late in his text. He thus recounts that, well into the reign of Akbar, in the month of Muharram 986 H (March 1578), he had taken leave of the emperor at the court and received permission to undertake the "Auspicious Journey", or *Safar-i Mubārak* – that is the *ḥajj* – along with his sons (he was also accompanied by his wife, but she is not mentioned here).[18] He was ordered by Akbar, however, not to proceed directly, but instead to spend time in the western Indian port of Surat, which he did, two years in all. During the course of his stay in Surat (we may infer that it was about one year after his arrival), some complaints were sent to the emperor by people who did not like Bayazid, to the effect that he had unscrupulously accumulated huge sums of cash (*naqd*) and jewels and precious stones. The emperor therefore ordered the governor, a great Turani noble named Qilij Khan, to look into the matter. It was found that Bayazid indeed had in his possession about Rs. 100,000 in cash, and some other goods that he had purchased in the ports of Gujarat. When this was relayed to the emperor in Fatehpur, he responded, however, that Bayazid had been in the service of his family for two decades; now that he was going on the *ḥajj*, and had a lakh of rupees, this did not really seem excessive to Akbar. Still, he ordered for some reason that Bayazid should be retained for some more time in Surat. Thus, another year passed, making it two years in all. Meanwhile, Bayazid received several royal *farmāns* to the effect that if he did not wish to remain in imperial service in the province of Gujarat, he could go elsewhere along with his sons, and would be given a suitable *jāgīr*. He could then return in due time to the *darbār* instead of going on the pilgrimage. Soon after, the emperor realised that Bayazid was absolutely set on going on the *ḥajj*, and, seeing this, Akbar ordered that he should at last be allowed to go. Thus, on 24 Muharram 988 H (12 March 1580), Bayazid and his entourage got on-board the ship *Muḥammadī*, which had been built in partnership by two important Mughal officials,

[18] Bayazid Bayat, *Taẕkira-i-Humāyūn wa Akbar of Bāyazīd Biyāt (A history of the Emperor Humayun from A. H. 949 [AD 1542] and of his successor the emperor Akbar up to A. H. 999 [AD 1590])*, ed. M. Hidayat Hosain (Calcutta, 1941), where Bayazid's account of his *ḥajj* appears on pp. 353 ff.

Qutb-ud-Din Khan and Nawwab Qilij Khan. However, until the end of the month of Muharram, they remained in the vicinity of the inlet of the port of Daman.[19] Here the Portuguese-appointed revenue-farmers (*ijāradārān*) of Daman demanded the "Diu toll" (*'ushūr-i Dīv*), but stipulated that they did not wish to climb on-board the ship, because of security concerns. This created an impasse, for without inspection, it was not possible to estimate the value of the ship's goods. The revenue-farmers hence demanded Bayazid's older son, Sa'adat Yar, as a hostage. Bayazid noted that his son knew both Hindawi and Firangi (Portuguese), unlike most other people in the party, and it was thought that, if he were sent from the ship, discussions would become impossible thereafter. Of his other two sons, Iftikhar and Zu'lfiqar, Bayazid declared that he was willing to give either as hostage, and the Franks eventually accepted Iftikhar. The next morning, the Portuguese arrived in a small vessel, and inspected the ship all day long, until the hour of the evening prayer; eventually, they demanded the sum of 10,000 *maḥmūdīs* as the Diu toll.[20]

The problem, however, was that no one else had a single *maḥmūdī* on the ship, which was apparently full of poor pilgrims. So Bayazid (who refers to himself here in the third person) thought that, in expectation of rewards in the life hereafter (*ṣawāb*), it was worthwhile to give this money to free the Muslim faithful from the clutches of the Franks. He gave this money to the others, he declares, as *qarẓ-i ḥasana*, that is, with the stipulation that he would recover it from them at Jiddah without interest. After the evening prayer, Iftikhar was accordingly returned to the ship. Bayazid gave a certain Hasan Chunnu, described in the text as the chief of the shipping in Surat (*nākhudā-i jahāzāt-i Sūrat*), the sum of 10,000 *maḥmūdīs* along with a written document (*tazkira*) to hand over to Tejpal, the head (*chaudhurī*) of the port of Surat. It was only then that the Franks left the ship, and Bayazid's son was able to return. We are thus given to understand that Bayazid, with his tact and resources, had managed to avoid a serious incident that might have further exacerbated the poor relations that existed at that moment between Mughals and Portuguese in Gujarat.

So eventually, on 1 Safar H (18 March 1580), the ship at last raised anchor. The monsoon was contrary, and only after a somewhat difficult

[19] *Tazkira-i-Humāyūn wa Akbar*, p. 355.

[20] For the broader context of these incidents, see Sanjay Subrahmanyam, "A matter of alignment: Mughal Gujarat and the Iberian world in the transition of 1580–81", *Mare Liberum*, 9, 1995, pp. 461–79.

journey of fourteen days did they see the mountains of Aden, and its fort. The *nākhudā* and pilot (*mu'allim*) saw two small vessels (*reqchas*) making their way towards the ship from the port. When they arrived near to the ship, it was conveyed to those on board that Nawwab Gulbadan Begam (daughter of Babur Padshah), Salima Sultan Begam (daughter of Mirza Nur-ud-Din Muhammad, grandson of Sultan Husain Baiqara), and Gul 'Izar Begam (daughter of Mirza Kamran), as well as Hazrat Khwaja Yahya (a descendant of the great Naqshbandi Sufi from Central Asia, Hazrat Khwaja Ahrar), were all in the port of Aden and had sent this boat to find out who was in this ship, and from which port they came.[21] Though the winds were favourable (*bād-i murād*) for pushing on towards the Red Sea, Bayazid nevertheless instructed the *nākhudā* and pilot to take the time to lower the sails, and sent a missive (in the form of an *'arẓdāsht*) to the Begams with all the details of the ship. The Begams and the Khwaja were greatly pleased at this, and sent back a courteous message of thanks which he received later at Mecca. Bayazid takes this occasion to call the blessings of God upon the emperor. For, he declares, had Akbar not detained him in Surat by a year, things would in fact not have turned out as well as they did. In fact, by making the *ḥajj* this year rather than the previous one, he managed the *ḥajj-i Akbar*, that is the visit to Mecca on a Friday, which was regarded as better than that in most years.

Bayazid Bayat claims he remained for all of three years at Mecca, and he declares that he received great benefits from his extended stay there.[22] In the Bait-ullah, the House of God, the flooring had deteriorated, and the great savant Shaikh 'Abdul Hayy Sha'ibi told Bayazid that the stones should be taken out and replaced with new chalk and other materials, which he properly accomplished. At this time, whenever the mosque at Mecca was cleaned, Bayazid was also allowed to take part in the process, and was even officially listed as a *farrāsh* in these years at Mecca, which he considered a great honour. He was able to go several times to the Maqam-i Ibrahim (close to the Ka'aba), and enter the courtyard of the mosque. Since the ambience was particularly propitious, Bayazid also had fine and auspicious dreams (*khwāb-hā-i khūb*) in this period, as did others who were with him. The Rs. 100,000 that he had in cash and goods he distributed to the people of Mecca. However, the stay was also

[21] See also N. R. Farooqi, "Six Ottoman documents on Mughal–Ottoman relations during the reign of Akbar", in Iqtidar Alam Khan, ed., *Akbar and his age* (New Delhi, 1999), pp. 209–22.

[22] *Tazkira-i-Humāyūn wa Akbar*, p. 356. In fact, Digby notes that he probably stayed for a shorter time.

punctuated by a number of tragedies, that he now sets out to list. His middle son, Zu'lfiqar, died at Bi'r-i Mastura, between Mecca and Medina, when he was on his way back from the pilgrimage to Medina. His body was left there temporarily (*ba ṭarīq-i amānat*), and on 10 Rabi' I 989 H (15 April 1581), the rest of the party returned to Mecca. Two days later, on 12 Rabi' I, Bayazid reached his residence in Mecca, and the next day his wife, who had apparently remained with the son's body for a short while longer, also returned. However, the day after her return, on 14 Rabi' I, she too fell seriously ill, and, a week later, she passed away as well. This was a grevious double blow. Bayazid had already received land from the Sharifs of Mecca for a burial-place at the Mu'alla, giving them 3,000 *Ibrāhīmī* (that is Rs. 9,000) as a gift for this; in fact, it would appear that he had cultivated good relations with both the Sharifs and other prominent residents of the town, giving them high-quality goods from Hindustan as presents and *peshkash*. It was hence decided that the "mother of his children" (as Bayazid refers to his wife) would be interred there, and a grave was prepared for the young Zu'lfiqar too. Bahadur, a servant of Sa'adat Yar, was hence sent back to Bi'r-i Mastura, to fetch the remains of Zu'lfiqar to be buried next to his mother. In a somewhat morbid frame of mind, Bayazid now had a grave prepared for himself in front of that of his wife. He declares that he even went into the grave, inspected it carefully, and lay there for one or two watches (*gharī*) to make sure that it was not too small or narrow (*kūtah-o-tang*). Bayazid thus notes that, to the day of writing his text, this grave is still there in the Mu'alla, and he hopes that God will one day permit his remains to be placed there.

The same year, Bayazid sent his surviving children back to the care of the emperor, and decided for his part to spend the rest of his life in Mecca. However, Destiny (*taqdīr*) eventually willed otherwise. So, in the year 990 H (1582), when he had accomplished the *ḥajj-i Nāfila* (or additional pilgrimage), his children sent him a message from India saying that they had fallen into the hands of the Portuguese at Daman.[23] Since they had no more money with them, and since Bayazid realised, on reflecting, that he himself had not said farewell to his relatives, he decided to go back to Hindustan. So, that year, he decided to find a maritime passage, but since it was the end of the monsoon, the journey was temporarily aborted (*ba tabāhī mānd*) due to contrary winds at the ports of Shihr and Zufar,

[23] *Taẕkira-i-Humāyūn wa Akbar*, p. 358.

in the Hadramaut. Eventually, after four months, the so-called "Zaituni monsoon" started again, and the winds became favourable. So, anchor was lifted once more from Mukalla Bandar, and it was decided, at a short distance from the port, to transfer the goods and men onto another ship. At the same time, a vessel from Diu arrived there with news from Gujarat that the former Sultan, Muzaffar Gujarati, had raised his head in rebellion, defeated the Mughal representative Shihab Khan, seized Ahmadabad, and killed Qutb-ud-Din Khan in Baroda. Qutb-ud-Din, since destiny was against him, even though he had a great deal of wealth and a good position from the emperor, had not properly paid his soldiers. So they betrayed him, and linked up in a clandestine way with Muzaffar Gujarati. When Qutb-ud-Din Khan was thus rendered helpless, Muzaffar's nobles insisted that he should be killed, which he was, along with his nephew.

Bayazid notes that Mirza Khan, son of Bairam Khan (by whom he means 'Abdur Rahim Khan-i Khanan), had now been deputed by the emperor, along with a group of other nobles, to chastise Muzaffar. As for Muzaffar, after taking Ahmadabad, he had gone on to Champaner, and fortified himself there. The latest news that the ship brought then was that Nawwab Mirza Khan had recently taken back Ahmadabad, but that conditions were still unstable. When these events were reported at Bandar Shihr, the chief revenue-official (*shiqdār*) of that town did not want the ship to leave, and instead thought of seizing hold of it. Now it was known that Bayazid Bayat had been an influential man in Hindustan, and so the *shiqdār* eventually relented from his plans and let them go. Further complications now arose, however, for it turned out that the bulk of the ship's crew (the *tāndail* and the *k͟halāṣiyān*) had earlier been in the service of Muzaffar of Gujarat. When they got the news that he had risen up in rebellion, they decided to get ready to fight as well. It turned out, one day, that Mirza Nur-ud-Din Muhammad, nephew of Qasim Nishapuri, who was later to enter the service of the Khan-i Khanan, and Bayazid were seated together on the cuddy or raised deck (*dabūsa*) of the ship. They had the *Diwān-i K͟hwāja Ḥāfiẓ* with them, and Bayazid states that he felt the urge in his heart to consult it – as was often done to seek out an omen – in order to see whether those who wanted to raise up Muzaffar would succeed or not, and what God's will in the matter really was. They thus opened the *Diwān* and their eyes fell on the following *g͟hazal*:

> Seek power (*daulat*) from the Auspicious Bird and its shadow.
> For there is no generosity to be found
> under the wings of the crow and the kite.

To Bayazid, this clearly meant that matters would turn in favour of Akbar rather than the rebel. Thus, states Bayazid, reading Khwaja Hafiz convinced those on board the ship that Muzaffar was not going to succeed, and quelled the potential rebellion. The ship remained in the ports of the Hadramaut for all of eight months, and Bayazid notes that, in that time, he left the ship only twice, once for the 'Id-i Ramazan and once for the 'Id-i Qurban. The benefit of his remaining on-board was that, had he not done so, the greedy people of Shihr and Zufar would surely have looted the goods of the Hajis.[24]

The time spent in the Hadramaut allows Bayazid the space for at least one anecdote with supernatural overtones. When the ship was at anchor in Bandar Shihr, some people from Bayazid's group went to see a certain Sayyid Abu Bakr, an important holy man (*g̲haus̤*) of his time who had settled in the Hadramaut. They spoke to Bayazid about accompanying them on the visit, and he replied to them: "I have heard that this holy man is always immersed in God. Our presence will disturb him. If you are going to see him, please convey my reverence (*niyāzmandī*) to him." Amongst those who went on the visit were Sayyid Hamza (son of Mir Zakariya Multani, who too was a holy man (*g̲haus̤*) of his own time who used to live in Mecca), Maulana Salih and Maulana Farrukh (who were from the Shadman region, and who for years had lived in Mecca with Qazi Muhammad Maliki as his principal and close companions), and finally, Mirza Shahrukh (son of Mirza Khan Andakhu'i, who had been the preceptor of many of the rulers of Transoxiana). When they reached Sayyid Abu Bakr, recalling that Bayazid Bayat had stayed behind in the ship, they thought to convey his particular reverence to the Sayyid. However, before they could do so, the Sayyid said to them: "You are thinking of giving me the special salutations of Bayazid, who is still in the ship. We have known each other for years. Last night, at midnight, I met Jalal-ud-Din Muhammad Akbar, the Badshah of Hind. We have him [Akbar, or perhaps Bayazid] under our protection." Bayazid protests that he has not invented this story; rather, he is merely reporting what the group that went to see Sayyid Abu Bakr reported to him. Further, Sayyid Hamza was given a special cap and accepted as Sayyid Abu Bakr's *k̲halīfa*. He thus concludes the anecdote with the pious sentiment that God alone knows best regarding such mysteries.

Eventually departing the ports of Zufar and Shihr, Bayazid and his party arrived at the Gujarat port of Gogha two months later. This port

[24] *Taẕkira-i-Humāyūn wa Akbar*, p. 360.

had lately been in the possession of Sultan Muzaffar during his rebellion, and they had access to the freshest news here, namely that Muzaffar had not only lost Ahmadabad but also Champaner, and that all his followers had more or less dispersed. The day after their arrival in Gogha, however, some of the defeated nobles who had supported him, such as Sayyid Daulat (who had been the governor of Khambayat), Mir ʿAbid Samarqandi and Muhammad Salih (who had been the servant of Shihab Khan and had been in charge of the *pargana* ("district") Katihar in the *sarkār* ("county") of Sarangpur), the son of a certain ʿAli Muhammad Qunduzi who had been with Humayun in his voyage to Safavid Iran, all in all some 150 men, arrived in the port-town with torn clothes and in a poor condition, having fled the battlefield. Bayazid for his part had descended from the ship, but some of his goods were still in the customs-house. These men from the former army of Muzaffar, though they knew Bayazid and though they were also Muslims, nevertheless began indiscriminately to loot the goods from the ship. Bayazid himself, Mirza Nur-ud-Din Muhammad, Khwaja Malik Muhammad (elder brother of Khwaja Malik Husain, the *dīwān* of Nawwab Qilij Khan), Mirza Shahrukh (son of Mirza Khan Andakhui) and Tardi Muhammad (brother-in-law to Nawwab Qilij Khan), were all put under lock and key by them. Further, all the goods on the ship that had been brought from Mecca as the emperor's gift (*saug͟hāt*), as well as for the other people in Hind, were seized by them.

However, those in prison (*bandik͟hāna*) were eventually all released, one by one, except Bayazid, the latter claiming that the rebels' real intention was to kill him. However, he declares, God takes care of his slaves and is informed of their fate. Since Bayazid was innocent, God himself took Sultan Muzaffar out of the wilderness and brought him to that port of Gogha where he directly intervened in the matter. Bayazid was released, and he took leave from Muzaffar, so that he could make his way towards the port of Surat. Now, it turned out that Muzaffar's brother-in-law was at this time in the fort at Bharuch, where the Mughal nobles Qilij Khan, Naurang Khan, Taulak Khan and Sharif Khan, had besieged him. When Bayazid reached Surat, Qilij Khan wrote to him stating that, as he had recently met Muzaffar, if he were to come to Bharuch, he would be able to inform the Mughal generals of the latest situation regarding the rebel and the others in his entourage. The siege of Bharuch had already been going on for one month, and the condition of those inside the fort was unclear to the besiegers. Bayazid hence reached Bharuch and met Qilij Khan, giving him whatever help and information he could. Since Qutb-ud-Din Khan had been killed meanwhile (as noted above), Bayazid also paid his condolences to Naurang Khan, and then returned to Surat where he then remained for a year. The climate (*āb-o-hawā*) of Surat suited him, he declares, and this was why he thought of staying there.

Meanwhile his sons, Sa'adat Yar and Iftikhar, had managed to secure their release from the Portuguese, and had also succeeded in entering the service of Akbar at the court. They thus wrote to their father that the emperor now knew that he had reached Surat, and that it was hence not a good idea for him to dally any longer. So, at the end of the year 992 H (December 1584), Bayazid eventually reached Fatehpur and kissed the feet of the emperor. As hoped for, Akbar was once more very kind to him, initially gave him a special horse in gift, and some three or four days later gave him *pargana* Sonam as a *jāgīr* to be shared with his sons, the revenue of which was some 29 lakh *dāms*. The emperor also assured him verbally that if the revenues of the *pargana* went up, the excess too could be kept by him.[25] This successful transaction thus closes Bayazid's brief section on his travels to the Hijaz, and the adventures and misadventures that transpired in that connection.

It may be argued that this account is relatively meagre fare. For Bayazid is not much given to reflection on his surroundings, or indeed on his own states of mind. The only moment when we catch a brief glimpse of his deeper sentiments is when he gloomily enters his grave in Mecca, to see whether he fits in there comfortably – only to lie there for several hours on end. For the rest, what we are afforded is a view of the new trading compact in the western Indian Ocean, which is quite different from the circumstances at the time of Seydi 'Ali Re'is's voyage to Gujarat. Now, Mughals and Portuguese have reached an understanding of sorts, even if the relationship continues to be fraught with friction and tension, notably in regard to the Diu toll and its collection. Bayazid offers us a series of small vignettes then, which shed light on a number of minor issues (such as the *ḥajj* of Gulbadan Begam and her party), without ever challenging the likes of 'Abdur Razzaq Samarqandi or Mahmud Wali Balkhi in terms either of narrative interest or of literary accomplishment. A minor, and truly modest, contribution to the category of "Voyages to the west" from Mughal India, his text still retains some interest for the simple reason that it has so few contemporary competitors.

[25] *Tazkira-i-Humāyūn wa Akbar*, p. 363.

BACK TO THE OTTOMANS

For more than a century and a half after Bayazid's account, we can find no further trace of a detailed first-person account of travels to the Hijaz, or, more generally, to the Ottoman domains, from Mughal India. The first substantial account that comes to us, but which is relatively rapid in its treatment of the Ottomans, is Khwaja 'Abdul Karim Shahristani's work, which we have discussed at some length in the preceding chapter. However, as we turn to the eighteenth century, the Ottomans arguably acquire a new significance in India (and in South Asia more generally), as the power and influence of the Mughals begins to wane. We can see this from the fairly intense correspondence that follows the invasion of northern India by Nadir Shah, when letters are exchanged between the courts of the Mughal emperor Muhammad Shah and the Ottoman Sultan Mahmud I (r. 1730–45), often through the mediation of a certain Sayyid 'Ataullah Bukhari; there are also several letters that pass in the 1740s between Nizam-ul-Mulk Asaf Jah and the Ottoman Sultan, as well as various high officials of that empire.[26] The purpose of these letters, and Sayyid 'Ataullah's embassy to Istanbul (where he stayed for about six weeks in late 1744), was to mount an alliance against Nadir Shah, but this project did not in fact bear any concrete fruit. Again, it is a pity that Sayyid 'Ataullah's own itinerary – which took him from Delhi to Surat, then to Basra, Baghdad and Üsküdar (Scutari) – was never detailed by him in the form of a narrative account. However, the surviving correspondence makes it clear that, even in their somewhat diminished state, the Mughal emperors of this time nevertheless insisted on the dignity of their titles, while at the same time stressing – as indeed did the Ottomans – the common basis of their Sunni faith, which appears in significant phrases such as "identity of faith and sect (*yak-jihatī-i dīnī wa mazhabī*)" and "unity of religion and community (*lāzima-i ittiḥād-i mazhab-o-millat*)". We may at times sense, on the part of the Ottomans, a desire to assert a superior status, by terming the letter from Sultan Mahmud to Muhammad Shah in October 1744, for example, a "Caliphal letter (*nāma-i khilāfat 'alāma*)"; but the Mughals also continued, as late as 1748, to use terms for themselves such as "the receptacle of the Caliphate (*khilāfat ma'āb*)".

[26] Islam, *Calendar*, vol. II, pp. 346–59; Yusuf Hikmet Bayur, *Hindistan Tarihi*, vol. III: (*Nadir Şah Afşar'in akinindan bagimsizlik ve cumhuriyete kadar (1737–1949)* (Ankara, 1950), pp. 45–8.

Nevertheless, the manifest weakening of Mughal power by about 1750 can be seen to have consequences in terms of a growing place for the Ottomans in South Asia, a place that they had lost from about the 1570s. Thus we learn from the indirect account of a traveller who found himself driven by contrary winds to Colombo in 1761–2 (1175 H), that the *khuṭba* there was read by Muslim merchants in the name of the Mughal emperor, but also of the Ottoman Sultan – as the latter were the keepers of the *ḥaramain sharīfain* (the holy sites in the Hijaz). At least some of the other ports of peninsular India apparently had begun to afford a more substantial place to the Ottoman Sultans in their imaginary, as we see from the correspondence that emerged in the late 1770s and early 1780s between the Ali Rajas of Cannanore (and Arakkal) and the court of the Ottoman Sultan Abdülhamid I (r. 1774–89).[27] It is in this context that we at last find a first-person account of an embassy from India to the Ottomans, albeit from a somewhat surprising quarter. This work, entitled the *Waqā'i'-i Manāzil-i Rūm* ("Account of the way-stations to Rum"), comes to us from the closing years of the eighteenth century, and was produced in the context of an embassy sent to Sultan Abdülhamid by the Mysore ruler, Tipu Sultan (r. 1782–99) in 1785. The principal objectives of this embassy were four-fold: first, to permit Tipu to establish trading factories in the Ottoman domains via the creation of an outpost in Basra, which he intended to take in revenue-farm (*ijāra*) "along with its territory" to complement his existing trading establishment in Masqat; second, to ask for Ottoman military aid against the English, agreeing that "whatever be the size of the army the Sultan of Rum would send, the expenses thereof will be borne by this government [and] whenever the Sultan of Rum asks for his army, it would be put aboard ships and sent back paying the expenses"; third, to deal with a series of other rulers, be it in Oman and Masqat, or in Iran, as well as to attempt to push on through the Mediterranean to make direct diplomatic contact with France and even England; and fourth, to procure firearms and military supplies as well as gun-makers from the Ottomans, who were to be sent to Mysore "along with their families". In exchange for the use of Basra, Tipu appears to have been willing to give the Ottomans a foothold in a western Indian port, such as Mangalore. Among other minor features of the mission was

[27] See Azmi Özcan, *Pan-Islamism: Indian Muslims, the Ottomans and Britain (1877–1924)* (Leiden, 1997), pp. 11–12, citing İsmail Hakki Uzunçarşili *et al.*, *Osmanli Tarihi*, 8 vols. (Ankara, 1947–62), vol. IV, part 2, pp. 156–7. On the Colombo incident, see Sayyid Ghulam 'Ali Azad Bilgrami, *Subḥat ul-Marjān fī āṣār-i Hindūstān*, ed. Muhammad Fazlur Rahman Nadvi Sewani (Aligarh, 1975), p. 56.

Figure 15. Tipu in combat, *Tūzak-i Āṣafiya*, No. 59.138, National Museum, New Delhi, folio 321.

Tipu's stated desire to make a "sweet-water canal from the Euphrates to Najaf Ashraf in front of the sacred tomb of His Holiness the Commander of the faithful 'Ali (Peace be upon him) for public welfare".[28] A fifth aspect of the embassy remains surrounded in controversy. Some historians have claimed that one of its chief purposes was to legitimise Tipu's position as Sultan of Mysore with reference to the Caliphate, in view of the fact that the Mughal emperor Shah 'Alam had, at the English East India Company's behest, given no encouragement to his pretensions. The chief basis of this claim appears to be a contemporary letter from a newsletter-writer for the East India Company, which stated that the Mysore embassy had "procured from the [Ottoman] Sultan the title of king [for Tipu] and permission to hold a mint and to have the Khutba read in his name".[29] This is an issue to which we shall turn at greater length below.

Led by a certain Ghulam 'Ali Khan, a former subordinate of the Walajah Nawwab of Arcot, who had entered Mysore service in about 1780 and held the ministerial post of *mīr ṣudūr*, the embassy left Tipu's capital city of Srirangapatnam in November 1785, but set sail from the west coast of India only in March 1786. The route taken was through the Persian Gulf, and they first put in at Masqat, then went on to Suhar, Qishm, Abu Shahr, and Kharg (amongst other places), before landing at Basra in late August 1786. After a stay of over three months there, the envoys were finally able to depart for Baghdad in December, but were then once more forced by the weather and political disputes to return to Basra. Eventually, on 10 February 1787, they departed definitively from Basra, but by now the account unfortunately breaks off abruptly in the sole extant manuscript.[30] From other sources, we are aware that the envoys went on to Baghdad, and from there via Mosul and Diyarbekir to Üsküdar (where they arrived in early September); on 25 September,

[28] Iqbal Husain, "The diplomatic vision of Tipu Sultan: briefs for embassies to Turkey and France, 1785–86", in Irfan Habib, ed., *State and diplomacy under Tipu Sultan: documents and essays* (New Delhi, 2001), pp. 19–65, esp. pp. 36–7, 40–2.

[29] This letter from Mir Muhammad Husain of 1787 is cited in Ishtiaq Husain Qureshi, "Tipu Sultan's embassy to Constantinople, 1787", in Irfan Habib, ed., *Confronting colonialism: resistance and modernization under Haidar Ali and Tipu Sultan* (New Delhi, 1999), p. 76. Qureshi's essay, first published in 1945, is the basis of most subsequent claims that Tipu sought confirmation of his sovereignty from the Ottomans as "the Sultan claimed to be the Caliph of the Muslim world".

[30] For the manuscript, see Asiatic Society of Bengal, Calcutta, IvASB 1678, M 32; a careful edition of this text (that we have used), with a copious critical apparatus, is that of Mohibbul Hasan, *Waqā'i'-i Manāzil-i Rūm*. From the same period, but reportedly less interesting, is the *Rūz-Nāma-yi Wukāla-yi Haydarābād*, Asiatic Society of Bengal, IvASB 1680, M 71, the account of Qutb-ul-Mulk and 'Ali Riza, sent as Tipu's ambassadors to the Nizam of Hyderabad, and mostly detailing expenses on the journey.

they finally reached their destination of Istanbul. On 5 November, Sultan Abdülhamid received the embassy, but on account of the unfamiliar weather and a plague epidemic, matters went from bad to worse from then on. Discouraged by the Bourbon court and its ambassadors at the Sublime Porte from proceeding to France, the embassy turned back in March 1788 via Alexandria and Cairo, to Suez. Then after making the *ḥajj* in 1789, they set sail from Jiddah to Calicut, eventually reaching the Indian west coast once more at the end of December 1789.

The author of the text that we dispose of is not one of the high Mysore officials, but rather the altogether obscure Khwaja 'Abdul Qadir, one of the two scribes attached to the embassy, the other being a certain Sayyid Ja'far. In the embassy itself, there were four notables from the Mysore court, the chief envoy Ghulam 'Ali Khan (whom we have already discussed), the experienced and active Nurullah Khan (who had earlier been Haidar 'Ali Khan's envoy to Karim Khan Zand, in 1770), Lutf 'Ali Khan (who had earlier held the post of Admiral), and a certain Ja'far Khan. All in all, with the interpreters, cooks, soldiers, sailors and menial servants, the embassy on its departure actually numbered some 900 persons on four ships, besides four elephants, three of them intended as gifts and one as merchandise. Only a small fraction of this huge embassy in fact returned home, the rest being eliminated by shipwreck, plague and other illnesses.

Discussing the text in his elaborate introduction to it, the historian Mohibbul Hasan has noted that:

> in describing his experiences Abdul Qadir enjoyed certain advantages denied to most of the European travellers. In the first place, he was not unfamiliar with the peoples and the culture he came across. In the second, he was conversant with Persian and Arabic, the two languages spoken and understood in the Persian Gulf area. Moreover, wherever he went he was received cordially, and came into friendly contact with all classes of people.

This adds up to a fairly encouraging picture for the framing of a perspective of an "insider"-outsider. Yet, the editor then goes on to fault the traveller for his numerous "lapses and inaccuracies", and even states that he "noted down indiscriminately whatever was related to him". This suggests a rather naive writer, who really did no more than act as a funnel for other people's voices and views. The picture does not quite add up, for, despite the presumedly official character of the account, a curious feature is its implicit critique of the comportment of the leader, Ghulam 'Ali Khan, who emerges from it as high-handed and somewhat incompetent.

A particular feature of the text – which was little to its modern editor's taste, one might add – is its somewhat loose style and construction, exacerbated not only by errors of spelling and syntax, but by archaisms and the "copious use . . . of words of Portuguese, Tamil, Kannada, Marathi and Hindi origin". This is thus a sort of vulgar scribal Persian, a product perhaps of Mysore's relative distance and isolation from the centre of the Indo-Persian world, but all the more interesting for that, in some respects. In a way, it is a curious counterpart to Bayazid's Persian, the rather oral idiom – as we have noted – of someone who was principally a Turkish speaker.

The four vessels of the expedition left the minor port of Tadri on the Malabar coast on 9 March 1786 (8 Jumada I 1200 H), and appear to have made for the south Arabian coast. However, a dramatic incident took place almost immediately, for the vessels were caught in a storm six days out of port. The ship carrying Ghulam 'Ali Khan and Nurullah Khan, called the *Fakhr ul-Marākib*, was rather badly damaged, and a panic ensued; another storm a few days later caused the elephants on board to become indisposed. However, four weeks out of port, land was sighted, and on 11 April, the fleet put in at Masqat. During the embassy's stay at Masqat and its dependency Matrah, Khwaja 'Abdul Qadir is able to provide us fairly full details of political and diplomatic affairs, as well as of local customs, dress and so on. The commercial activities of a certain Indian broker, Maoji Seth, are referred to repeatedly. A particular feature of the description is the desire to enumerate: thus, not only distances but the number of households of different sorts (notables, merchants, other local Arab residents, and poor folk living in palm-leaf huts outside the town) are provided to us. The same eye for numbers extends to providing a price-list of different articles available on the market in Masqat. Customs-duties, the Imam's revenues, the number of ships he has – none of this escapes the Khwaja's vigilant eye.

There are thus times when it appears that the account is modelled on a sort of official pro-forma, a kind of *dastūr ul-'amal*, in which the blanks must be filled. The urge to list extends to the ports and islands of the Persian Gulf, which are mentioned one after the other, together with the names of their rulers, and their sectarian and clan affiliations. Again, this clearly corresponds in some part to the *ḥukm-nāma* or instructions that the envoys carried from Tipu, which stated that "the particularities of every stage of the journey and members of each of the three kingdoms [ie. the Ottomans, French and English], with indications of the status of the said members and description of their affairs as discovered and the industries and rarities of each city and territory and the account of the affairs of the cities, should be written down in front of each of you". Or again, another passage in the same instructions insists that "the details of the daily movement and halt on the land route should be written by the *munshīs* and *mutaṣaddīs* in the note-book to be brought to this Court".[31]

Leaving Matrah, in the domains of the Imam of Oman on 27 June, the Mysore expedition (to which some locally purchased dhows had been added) went on by way of Suhar, and arrived in early July at the island of Qishm. After sailing desultorily down the Persian Gulf, with interruptions for inclement weather, the next major halt was Abu Shahr, ruled over by a certain Shaikh Nasr al-Mazkur (whom the text incorrectly calls Shaikh Nasir, after his father), where they arrived on 23 July. In Abu Shahr, as in Masqat, some further diplomatic engagements had to be fulfilled. The ruler of Abu Shahr was willing to grant Tipu a factory, but in turn wished to have one of his own in Mangalore. The envoys were by now in something of a hurry to finish their transactions and move on. Nevertheless, 'Abdul Qadir took time out to investigate and list the current prices in the bazaar, noting that, since the prices were not favourable, they decided not to do any substantial buying and selling. After a stay of five days, the ships moved on in the direction of the island of Kharg, where the vessel *Nabī Bakhsh* was the first to arrive. Here, Nurullah Khan, to whom Khwaja 'Abdul Qadir seems in general to have been much better disposed than he is to Ghulam 'Ali Khan, disembarked, and the party went to inspect an abandoned fort.

Now Kharg, to 'Abdul Qadir, has particularly important religious connotations. He identifies in it the tombs (in fact spurious) of Muhammad ibn Abu Bakr, and 'Abdullah bin 'Umar, but far more significantly finds there what is for him without a shadow of doubt the last resting-place of the legendary Islamic hero Muhammad ibn Hanafiyya, who was reputed to have disappeared into a cave at that spot. There then follows a mention in the text about another classic figure of Islamic legend (of thoroughly questionable historicity), namely Khwaja Khizr, the Green Prophet, also reputed (like Ibn Hanafiyya) to have for a time inhabited the island.[32] Ibn Hanafiyya is seen as the patron saint of the island, who makes and breaks its rulers. Thus, our traveller tells us that the Dutch, who had had a fort in Kharg, were driven out of there (in 1766) because they allowed pigs into his sanctuary; in turn, Mir Muhanna, who drove

[31] Husain, "The diplomatic vision", pp. 29–31.
[32] On Khizr, see also Qaisar, "From port to port", p. 335.

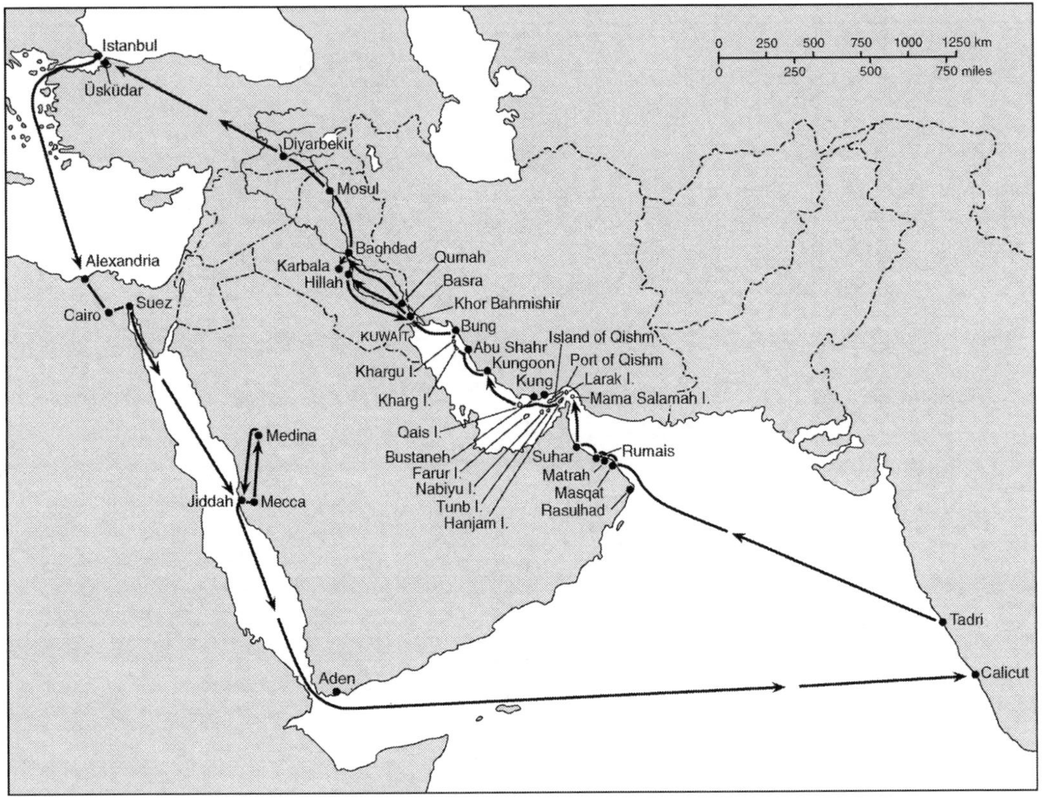

Map 5. The route of the envoys to Istanbul.

them out, was also forced to flee the place as he had incurred the hero's wrath for his unjust comportment.[33] Khwaja 'Abdul Qadir recounts the following concerning Ibn Hanafiyya's connection with the island:

> It is said that Hazrat [Ibn Hanafiyya] came to the island with a large army and killed all the infidels (*kuffār*). But his own followers were also slain. After this, while he was sitting in an isolated place, seven ships (*jahāzāt*) carrying troops, including a tall, strong, wicked old woman (*pīr zan*), arrived on the island. The commanders of the army (*sardārān-i fauj*) pleaded that they lacked the courage to attack the Hazrat. The old woman, thereupon, told them that they should follow her without fear. If the other was really a saint he would not approach a naked woman. If he was a wizard, he would use his witchcraft against her. The woman then stripped herself, and with the infidel army following her, went to Hazrat. The latter came out of his cell, and, seeing a naked woman, prayed to God to turn them into stone. His prayer was answered, and the ships, woman and the soldiers were all turned into stone. The Hazrat then, with his spear, struck the ground, which caved in, and he entered the opening.[34]

'Abdul Qadir insists, moreover, that traces of this petrified army can still be found, as well as the marks of the hero's feet and of the hooves of his horse. Three wells with sweet water (*āb-i shīrīn*) are associated with three places where he struck the ground with his spear.

The fleet eventually left Kharg on 7 August, and, once more, we are given a price-list of goods on the market on the eve of the departure. A rumour that pirates were about to attack (and the resultant panic in the fleet) also finds mention. Then, by way of Dilam, Banak, and other places, they made their way into the Shatt al-'Arab, and, despite violent contrary winds, arrived in Basra in three vessels (a dhow, and two of the original fleet), on 22 August. Another vessel, the *Nabī Bakhsh*, was less fortunate, for it caught fire and went down on 18 August, with the loss of fifty men on board, as well as a good part of the presents for the Ottoman Sultan, before it could make it to port.

Now, the remainder of the text is occupied with events in and around Basra, of which a most detailed and valuable account is thus made available, since the embassy effectively spent a rather long period in the town. Amongst other interesting sidelights, we learn that near one of the town's four main gates, the Zubair Gate, there was a ruined mosque reputedly built by Hazrat 'Ali. In the compound of this mosque were five or six

[33] On the Dutch in the region, see Willem Floor, "The Dutch on Khark island, the end of an era: the Baron von Kniphausen's adventures", *Moyen Orient et Océan Indien*, 8 ("Européens en Orient au XVIIIe siècle"), 1994, pp. 157–202.

[34] Khwaja 'Abdul Qadir, *Waqā'i'-i Manāzil-i Rūm*, pp. 30–1.

graves of a well-known Turkish merchant family from Surat, that of Saleh Chelebi.[35] Details are also given of the complex balance of political power in the town and its environs, between the Ottoman representative (or *mutasallim*), Ibrahim Agha, and others such as Haji Muhammad Efendi (the *daftardār*), a certain 'Ali Agha, Shaikh Suwaini al-'Abdullah (chief of the Muntafiq group of clans) and an important Jewish banker and power-broker, 'Abdullah Yahudi.

A further point of interest in Khwaja 'Abdul Qadir's description of Basra is the attention he gives to Muharram celebrations there. He notes, implicitly, that Ghulam 'Ali Khan was sympathetic to the Shi'is, since he is stated to have given alms to some boys who came to him, having lanced their arms. Indeed, Khwaja 'Abdul Qadir himself has a very different perspective on these celebrations from the rather disapproving vision of Muharram in seventeenth-century Lahore we have had from the pen of Mahmud Wali Balkhi. He notes that, on the tenth of Muharram, both men and women gathered together at the Maqam 'Ali in the town in order to recite *marṣ̱īyas* (mourning verses), and mourn the death of Imam Husain. The self-flagellation and sword-inflicted wounds of the Arabs are contrasted to the more sober Persians, who contented themselves with merely breast-beating and weeping. Not only this: 'Abdul Qadir assures us that annually a miracle took place on the occasion, as a particular tree spouted blood, which on proper application brought back the eyesight of the blind.

Finally, the stay of the envoys in Basra is not without its unintended comic aspects, as quarrels between them began to surface over the pettiest matters. We are reminded here of the Iranian embassy to Thailand and its own internal bickerings. Already in late August, Ghulam 'Ali Khan and Nurullah Khan had fallen out with Lutf 'Ali Khan on the question of how much money should be sent to Najaf, Karbala, Baghdad and other holy places for grave-sheets, Lutf 'Ali Khan being the most against excessive expenditure on this occasion. Later, in mid-November, Nurullah and Lutf 'Ali are said to have quarrelled once more, but this time over the latter's extravagant purchases in the bazaars. The worst altercations took place during, and immediately after, the aborted trip from Basra to Baghdad in December 1786, resulting in the decision (later revoked) to leave Ghulam 'Ali Khan behind and proceed to Baghdad, which was a consequence of a grave falling out between him

[35] On this family, see Ashin Das Gupta, *Indian merchants and the decline of Surat, c. 1700–1750* (Wiesbaden, 1979), pp. 76–7.

and Nurullah Khan. These repeated bickerings obviously redounded little to the credit of the embassy, and their obvious incompetence in practical matters may well have made them objects of derision for local Ottoman authorities in Basra. In early December, the two remaining ships from the original fleet, the *Ghurāb-i Ṣūratī* and the *Fatḥ-i Shāhī*, were reported to have been lost in a storm while at anchor, which hardly added to the Mysore mariners' reputation either.

These petty quarrels and troubles extended beyond the small group of notables, and was equally a characteristic of their dealings with the soldiers (*jawāns*) and with the mariners. Desertions began almost immediately on the fleet's arrival in Masqat, and continued throughout the next weeks and months. Obviously, Ghulam 'Ali Khan, who between fits of pique would bring himself to take the odd decision, was not the one to impose order on this undisciplined crowd. We can only wonder what effect the report thus had on the reputation of the notables, when it was eventually read at the Mysore court. There is a sense in which Khwaja 'Abdul Qadir's was a sceptic's ringside account, intended to tell the court of how things really were, behind the veil of the (presumably) bland official prose of the periodic despatches that Ghulam 'Ali Khan and the others sent back.

If the *Waqā'i'-i Manāzil-i Rūm* cannot quite qualify as high-quality Indo-Persian literature, it is nevertheless noted for its pragmatism, its attempt at systematic description, and its combination of gazetteer-like qualities with a personal narrative. What emerges from it also is a late-eighteenth-century Indian Muslim's view of the holy places from which Islam originated, approached not through a textual prism, but rather naively. Since Khwaja 'Abdul Qadir is not anti-Shi'i in orientation, this lends his appreciation of the Persian Gulf and Basra a particular flavour; but, like Central Asian travellers in India, he is not averse to collecting fantastic tales. It is an interesting issue to what extent these tales of the fantastic were meant to make the lands where he travelled the site of "wonders"; one is left overall with the impression that reverence, and belief, rather than exoticism, are the dominant motifs of his text in this respect. Nevertheless, it is a text of multiple registers: the pragmatic (descriptions of towns and forts), the downright formulaic and mechanical, the reverential, and the acutely political (in the limited sense of the politics of factions) are all to be found here in varying measures. In this sense, one perceives immediately that the text does not inhabit a literary space totally disjunct from that of texts dealing with "internal" travels in Mughal India, though the mix of different elements in the two is not quite the same. We may take but one example, namely the travel-accounts of the courtier Anand Ram "Mukhlis" in the 1740s.[36] Being far more accomplished as a writer, and also perhaps because he was not carrying out an official commission (which was surely Khwaja 'Abdul Qadir's main motive in writing his account), Anand Ram provides a quietly ironical, and understated (but nevertheless evocative) commentary on a troubled mercantile–aristocratic universe that was fraying at its edges by the middle of the eighteenth century in Mughal North India. The text of the embassy to Istanbul is cruder in its delineations, shriller in its quarrels, and obviously the product of a far more unsophisticated pen. This naivety is not altogether to be despised though, as a quality, in such a travel-account. Above all, we should note, the *Waqā'i'*, unlike the *Safar Nāma* of Anand Ram, is marked strongly by the absence of the narrator himself. In the quarrels and fights, we never hear what role the Khwaja himself had to play. His tastes and sentiments, unlike those of Anand Ram, are not at all on display to the reader, and are only hinted at here and there. This too is a reflection, without doubt, of the text's relatively "official" character.

The embassy of 1786–9 is also noteworthy because some of the crucial diplomatic correspondence surrounding it – in addition to the text of Khwaja 'Abdul Qadir, and the instructions issued in Mysore before departure – has survived. This includes the official letter sent by Tipu Sultan to the Ottoman ruler, which was carried by the embassy; a letter (*'arẓdāsht*) sent by the Mysore ambassadors to Istanbul from their temporary residence in Basra; as well as the letter that Sultan Abdülhamid eventually sent back to Tipu in response.[37] These letters are useful not so much in establishing the terms or geo-political context of the embassy, but in order to resolve the vexed question of whether indeed the Mysore ruler saw the Ottoman Sultan as representing the Caliphate from which he sought legitimacy. Contrary to the view of I. H. Qureshi and those who have followed him, Irfan Habib has recently proposed that Tipu treated the Ottoman ruler as "an equal, not a superior", and that he had no need or desire to obtain legitimacy from a monarch "whom almost no one in India seriously thought of as the Caliph". Rather, he suggests that "Tipu does not even designate the Ottoman ruler as Khalifa

36 Alam and Subrahmanyam, "Discovering the familiar", pp. 131–54.

37 Yusuf Hikmet Bayur, "Maysor Sultani Tipu ile Osmanli pâdişahlarindan I. Abdülhamid ve III. Selim Arasindaki Mektuplaşma", *Belleten (Türk Tarih Kurumu)*, 12, 47, 1948, pp. 617–54. The relevant Persian documents, largely taken from the Başbakanlik Osmanli Arşivi, Istanbul, Nâme defteri 9, fos. 209–12, 217–20, etc., appear as photographic reproductions in the essay between pp. 642 and 643, numbered Res. 1 to 12.

(Caliph), or recognise his authority outside his dominions in any way whatsoever."[38]

The available evidence does not entirely confirm this view. It is certainly the case that Tipu does not in these years address the Ottoman Sultan as the Caliph, nor is there evidence that he received any form of permission (*ijāzat*) with regard to either the reading of the *khuṭba* or the minting of coins. However, the entire flavour of the diplomatic correspondence of 1786–8 is conceived of in terms of a relationship between an inferior and a superior power. A hint of this is provided already in the letter addressed by the Mysore ambassadors to the Ottoman ruler from Basra, where they refer to his court as "the refuge of all believing Sultans (*marja'-i salāṭīn-i zī-īmān*)", and confirmed by the letters directly exchanged between Tipu and Sultan Abdülhamid. The former uses a very elevated and formal style, involving a panoply of the sort of secular titles that he would have employed had he been a provincial Indian ruler addressing the Mughals. Thus, it is evident that the Ottomans, to whom Tipu presents himself as *niyāzmand-i dargāh* ("supplicant to the court") and who reply by terming his letter a *niyāznāma* or "supplication", are accorded at least the very high status of the Mughals. The address to Tipu by the Ottoman Sultan on the other hand is generally noteworthy for the relative absence of full royal titles, and appears far closer to the addresses of an emperor to a high noble.[39] In later letters, this asymmetrical trend continues, with Tipu being addressed for example as *hāriṣ-i naṣr ul-Islām*, again a somewhat inferior title. Indeed, the surviving correspondence from the very end of Tipu's reign, namely the exchange of letters with the Sultan Selim III, suggests even a somewhat greater imbalance. These letters from 1798–9 concern questions such as the relative merits of the French and the English, with the Ottoman Sultan arguing in a first letter of September 1798 that the atheistic French (who had recently invaded Egypt) were "bent upon the overthrow of all sects and religions", and hence were the primary enemies of Muslims, while Tipu argued for his part that his real enemies were in fact the

[38] Irfan Habib, "Introduction" in Habib, ed., *State and diplomacy under Tipu Sultan: documents and essays* (New Delhi, 2001), pp. xi–xii. Habib does not use or cite Hikmet Bayur's essay, which has, however, been mentioned and roughly summarised in B. Sheik Ali, *Tipu Sultan: a study in diplomacy and confrontation* (Mysore, 1982), pp. 119–47.

[39] The relevant passage runs: "janāb imārat ma'āb ayālat niṣāb ḥukūmat iktisāb daulat intisāb nāṣir ul-Islām wa'l Muslimīn 'aun ul-ghuzāt wa'l mujāhidīn ḥāmī-yi mamālik-i Patan wa Hindūstān 'ālī ush-shān Tīpū Sulṭān"; see Bayur, "Maysor Sultani Tipu", fol. 219. Of these, only *daulat intisāb* approximates a proper royal title.

English.[40] True, he admitted, the French were false, irreligious and turbulent, but these and their other faults were known and could be dealt with. On the other hand, he continued to insist that the primary danger came from the English, who should really be the objects of any concerted call for *jihād*. Tipu's response appears to be the first (and only) instance in which he addressed the Ottoman ruler as Caliph, and stated that he prayed that his Caliphate would remain eternally in place.[41] This, however, may be a reflection of his weakened position by this time, and certainly cannot be thought, necessarily, to reflect his views of ten years earlier.

These letters demonstrate then that relations between South Asian rulers and the Ottoman empire followed a complex trajectory over the sixteenth, seventeenth and eighteenth centuries, a fact that has a significant bearing on Indian travels to West Asia. In the middle of the sixteenth century, when Sultan Bahadur and his immediate successors ruled over Gujarat and urgently sought Ottoman naval help to combat the Portuguese, there can be little doubt that the relationship was an asymmetrical one – even if the question of the Caliphate as such is not evoked in the writings of Seydi 'Ali Re'is. With the rise to power and prominence of the Mughals after 1560, the balance clearly shifts. By the time of Bayazid Bayat's voyage to Mecca and Medina in the early 1580s, there is no question of the Mughals admitting their hierarchical or symbolic inferiority. Thus, Bayazid's own actions in the Holy Cities are those of the agent of a powerful and wealthy sovereign power, something that appears constantly in his account. This situation remains in place through the seventeenth century, including the phase of most intense diplomatic relations that corresponds with the reign of Shahjahan. In these years, the two sides warily jockey for position and trade veiled diplomatic

[40] English translation of the Persian letter by N. B. Edmonstone, in R. Montgomery Martin, ed., *The despatches, minutes and correspondence of the Marquess Wellesley, K. G., during his administration in India*, 5 vols. (London, 1836–7), vol. I, pp. 414–17. The British view of the Ottoman Sultan as Caliph appears in Wellesley's own letter to Tipu Sultan of 16 January 1799, where he refers to Sultan Selim as "the head of the Mahomedan Church" (p. 414).

[41] We base ourselves here on the Urdu translation of the letter of 4 Ramazan 1213 H (10 February 1799), which appears in Sayyid Sulaiman Nadvi, "Khilāfat aur Hindūstān", in S. 'Abdur Rahman, ed., *Maqālāt-i Sulaimān*, vol. I Azamgarh, 1966), pp. 112–84, on pp. 177–8. The Urdu text runs: "dunyā meṃ khudāwand ta'āla ke khalīfa, Sulṭān-i Rūm, khudā unkī ḥukūmat, khilāfat, ko hameshā qāyam rakhe". An English translation of this letter, unfortunately omitting the titles, may be found in Martin, ed., *The despatches, minutes and correspondence of the Marquess Wellesley, K.G.*, vol. V, pp. 24–31. We may note that in the late 1740s, Nasir Jang of Hyderabad had addressed Sultan Mahmud I in even more fulsome terms as "Caliph of the Holy Prophet", and referred to the fact that it was to the Ottoman Sultans as Caliphs that all rulers in the world turned for succour; Islam, *Calendar*, vol. II, p. 361.

insults, all under the cover of a religious solidarity that is defined by their common adherence to Sunnism. There is simply no question in these years of any Ottoman claims to universal dominion or the Caliphate finding an audience in India.

Once into the middle decades of the eighteenth century, matters begin to evolve somewhat, once more taking us back to the situation as it had obtained in the sixteenth century. Fragmenting Mughal sovereignty, especially in the wake of Nadir Shah's invasion, allows the prestige of the Ottomans to grow in the coastal ports and towns, including such places as Colombo and Cannanore that were never under direct Mughal rule. True, the Ottomans are no longer in a position to intervene in the naval affairs of the Indian Ocean, as they had been in the times of Hadim Süleyman Pasha and Piri Re'is. However, one can see why the traveller to the Ottoman empire would, in the latter half of the eighteenth century, have had the impression of moving from lands where the power of Muslim rulers was being eroded, to others where it still remained relatively secure. The account of the embassy sent by Tipu Sultan thus appears in a context in which the Ottomans are seen as an older, more prestigious power, with long control over the holy sites of Islam – with the key issue never being their literal claim to the Caliphate. It would only be late in the nineteenth century, in the aftermath of the Crimean War of the early 1850s, and the subsequent unseating of the Mughals, that the view would grow, amongst a section of Indian Muslims, that their fate was tied up with that of the Ottomans in the context of the Caliphate. Yet, even then, some prominent Indian intellectuals and travellers to the Ottoman domains, such as Maulana Shibli Nu'mani (1857–1914), would continue to cast doubt on the soundness of this position, arguing that the last Cairene Caliph al-Mutawakkil III had been a mere figurehead when captured by Ottoman Sultan Selim.[42]

CONCLUSION

It is difficult to escape the conclusion that, in the circulation of travellers and the production of travel-accounts between the worlds of West Asia,

[42] Muhammad Shibli Nu'mani, *Safar nāma-yi Rūm wa Miṣr wa Shām* (Lucknow, n.d.). Shibli's position on this question is discussed at some length by his disciple Sayyid Sulaiman Nadvi, "Khilāfat aur Hindūstān". Nadvi, like Maulana Azad, was a protagonist of the so-called "Khilafat movement", and took a more positive view than Shibli of late Ottoman claims. Recent historians argue that it was only from the 1540s that Ottoman rulers began making the claim that they were "Caliphs of the Muslims"; see Colin Imber, *Ebu's-su'ud: the Islamic legal tradition* (Edinburgh, 1997).

Central Asia, Iran and South Asia in the early modern period, a certain marked asymmetry of relations and perceptions obtained. To travellers moving from west to east, or from north-west to south-east, the ideas of "Hind" as a land of wonders, or as a place of easy luxury and courtly extravagance, and – in some cases – also of moral degeneracy and "hellish" characteristics, represent the broad spectrum of opinions and views. We have seen a series of variations in previous chapters on these very themes, and we have also observed that at times Iranian or Central Asian accounts come perilously close to approximating the far better-known travel-accounts of Europeans in India from the early modern period. To tease out the differences between the two, even when they show remarkable parallels, is a task to which we shall devote a part of the concluding chapter. On the other hand, the idea of "Hind" as a place of pilgrimage, or a site with holy significance, does not exist for the most part, with the sole significant exception for Muslim travellers probably being Adam's Peak in Sri Lanka. This lends India (and South Asia) a rather secular character in the constructions of these voyagers, and even the "wonders" that one can observe there are for the most part devoid, so far as they are concerned, of any religious meaning or larger significance.

When one looks in the other direction, matters appear quite different. The South Asian Muslim travellers to the lands of Iran or the Ottoman empire cannot escape the view that these are places of great religious significance, where shrines, tombs and highly charged places from Islamic and pre-Islamic history are to be found. The question of the Caliphate is, as we have demonstrated, not at all the crucial one; but there is no escaping the fact that for travellers such as the two Khwajas, 'Abdul Karim in the 1740s and 'Abdul Qadir in the 1780s, most places that they visit in Iran, the Persian Gulf, or the Ottoman domains are heavily impregnated with the odour of the past. This is true even of the "wonders" that they observe in the course of their travels. Such a view implies in turn that their accounts of travel are often couched at least partly in a reverential tone, as if the lands they travel in are somehow elevated above their own land of origin. The sole exception to this is when Khwaja 'Abdul Karim Shahristani reflects on the Iran of Nadir Shah, which for him is the very epitome of a misguided and distorted political system. Here, there is no idealisation, and, quite on the contrary, the notion of tyranny (*ẓulm*) is central to his conception of the Iranian polity. Yet we can see a marked contrast between the tenor and nature of his criticisms and those of, say, Shaikh Muhammad 'Ali Hazin. For Hazin, the heart of the matter was centred on the defective character of the Indians, which was not a recent development but one that had already manifested itself in the time of the ancient Iranian kings. Each of our travellers was no doubt a "patriot" of some sort, but this patriotism clearly had quite varied implications for how one perceived the lands to which one travelled, and in which one might, at times, even choose to settle for a period of some years. In sum, while the Indo-Persian world taken as a totality shared strong common traits, and while texts and references could indeed circulate quite freely within it, it was also an internally differentiated world. No single set of hierarchies between regions or peoples was commonly accepted, and we can see why Hazin's remarks would not necessarily have met with a warm welcome in Mughal India. The Ottoman governor Hadim Süleyman Pasha, leader of an unsuccessful naval expedition to Diu in 1538, once notoriously wrote (in a reproachful letter to Ulugh Khan, *wazīr* of the Gujarat Sultanate): "When I decided to winter there [in Gujarat] I found no place that was secure, for the greater part of them were helpers of the infidels, for when they should give thanks to God at the hour of prayer, they do nothing else but play their music, and the greater part of them are infidels and unbelievers; and for this reason, I left with my holy fleet and I shall return there soon like a very direct arrow."[43] Such a letter of reproach, mixing claims of religious superiority and accusations of chicanery, could in most circumstances not have been addressed in the opposite direction. There can be little doubt that the Pasha's views, while certainly not as extreme or as systematically denigrating as those of Hazin, were scarcely the product of a world of convivial, non-hierarchical, interactions.

In recent years, some attention has been focused on the systematic character of hierarchising perspectives in the context of relations between two or more parts of the extra-European world. We have already noted and discussed this at some length in the context of Juan Cole's arguments regarding Iranian "Orientalism", with regard to travellers to late Mughal India such as Aqa Ahmad Bihbahani.[44] Other historians have written of an "Ottoman Orientalism", which they continue to see, however, as "a complex of Ottoman attitudes produced by a nineteenth-century age of Ottoman reform that implicitly and explicitly acknowledged the West to

[43] Instituto dos Arquivos Nacionais, Torre do Tombo, Lisbon, Corpo Cronológico, III-14-44, letter from Hadim Süleyman Pasha to the *wazīr* Ulugh Khan, or "Olucão Gozil" (the lost original is dated 10 December 1538, and the Portuguese translation 7 May 1539). Also see Dejanirah Couto, "Les Ottomans et l'Inde portugaise", in José Manuel Garcia and Teotónio de Souza, eds., *Vasco da Gama e a Índia* (Lisbon, 1999), vol. I, pp. 181–200.

[44] Cole, "Mirror of the world", pp. 41–60.

be the home of progress and the East, writ large, to be a *present* theatre of backwardness".[45] What of an earlier epoch such as the one we have dealt with here? In response to such a question, it is frequently suggested that, in their "classical age", the Ottomans functioned primarily through "Islamic symbolism", which created a form of deep "religious and ethnic consciousness", in which elements such as Kurds, Druze, Bedouins and others were regarded as inferior because they were either not Muslim or very imperfectly so. Thus, commenting on the travel-account of Evliya Çelebi in the seventeenth century, Ussama Makdisi sees it as reflecting "not simply the existence of a profound difference between Ottoman rulers and many of the subjects they ruled but the unbridgeable nature of this difference".[46] However, a theory of hierarchy that seems, above all, to depend on a series of "nesting Orientalisms", where the primary hierarchising impulse still derives from the West, clearly cannot come to terms with what might be behind such "unbridgeable" differences in the early modern period (before the world dominance of Europe was an accepted political fact and ideological stance) beyond some appeal to the primordial character of religious identity.[47] The problem, however, is that Islam alone cannot explain the hierarchising impulses that we have seen at work; in the case of Iranian writers such as Muhammad Mufid, Muhammad Rabi', Hazin or Bihbahani, it appears instead to be the deployment of a cultural capital that stems from the notion of an ancient Iranian past which permits them to look down on Mughal India and the Deccan, and even more so on Thailand.

The peculiar character of the "Orientalism" that the Europeans of the nineteenth century developed, and which the Ottomans then may have modified and redeployed to their own ends in the latter decades of that century, thus stems not from solely cultural wellsprings (or some peculiar and genetically coded "Western" proclivity), but from hierarchising impulses which could be combined in that instance with the institutions of power and knowledge to produce a particularly potent outcome. This would eventually mean that one had not simply prejudices, but prejudices backed by "facts", facts produced by academies and financed by powerful

45 Ussama Makdisi, "Ottoman Orientalism", *American Historical Review*, 107, 3, 2002, pp. 768–96. In a somewhat similar vein, see the earlier analysis of Stefan Tanaka, *Japan's Orient: rendering pasts into history* (Berkeley, 1993).

46 Makdisi, "Ottoman Orientalism", p. 773.

47 Makdisi's conception in fact depends on Milica Bakić-Hayden, "Nesting Orientalisms: the case of former Yugoslavia", *Slavic Review*, 54, 4, 1995, pp. 917–31, as much as (or more than) it does on Maria Todorova, *Imagining the Balkans* (New York, 1997).

governments and entrepreneurs. Nothing in Ottoman or Iranian knowledge of early modern India corresponded to this institutional complex, nor was Indian xenology of the same epoch able to propagate and legitimise itself either, beyond a somewhat restricted circle. The perceptions we have discussed remained alive in all their complexity, and were not subject to strong homogenising forces, nor were they deployed by institutions of learning or organs of administration in a well-defined form. To see how this differed from the European case is the task that we set ourselves in the final chapter.

CHAPTER 8

On early modern travel

I would believe that I had not travelled in a totally useless way if, in denigrating voyages, I could prevent someone from wasting his time in travel.

Béat Louis de Muralt, *Lettre sur les voyages.*[1]

COLLECTING TRAVELS

Some people are seemingly born to travel, and yet others have travel thrust upon them. To return then to a question with which we began this extended exploration of the world of the early modern Indo-Persian travel-account: to whom does the travel-account really belong? We cannot be confident of having provided a full answer to this question in the preceding pages, but we certainly hope to have shaken the confidence of the reader who believed that he or she had the facile answer. For here is our problem: the tradition of the Indo-Persian *safar nāma* finds itself caught between two other massive traditions, namely the early modern European travel-account, and the large body of Chinese travel-texts with which we began our initial exploration. Further, even within the Islamic world, it is clear that texts in Persian have usually been relegated to a secondary place in comparison to Arabic works, whether of geography or of travel, which make their appearance from quite early in the history of Islam.[2] The question of framing our materials within the non-Western traditions was our principal preoccupation in the introduction to this work. Here, by way of conclusion, we wish to add some further comparative reflections, this time using the European corpus of the sixteenth, seventeenth and eighteenth centuries as our sounding board.

[1] Béat Louis de Muralt, *Lettres sur les anglois et les françois. Et sur les voiages* (Geneva, 1725).

[2] Touati, *Islam et voyage au Moyen Âge*; see also the very useful survey in André Miquel, *La géographie humaine du monde musulman jusqu'au milieu du 11e siècle*, 4 vols. (Paris, 1967–88).

It is a commonplace that the processes generally summed up under the head of "European expansion" produced a mass of travel-texts, beginning in the fifteenth century, as the Iberians commenced their exploration of the Atlantic. Thus, the early Portuguese (and allied Italian) presence on the west coast of Africa brings forth materials already from the 1450s such as Alvise da Ca' da Mosto's travels, and the three major voyages of discovery that close out the fifteenth century – namely those of Christopher Columbus, Vasco da Gama and Pedro Álvares Cabral – are each accompanied by the production of a text or texts that have been much analysed.[3] Though initially restricted in their circulation, these texts eventually found a substantial public in the course of the sixteenth century, thanks in particular to the work of the Italian Giovanni Battista Ramusio, who brought together a massive compendium entitled *Navigazioni e viaggi*, the avowed purpose of which was to disseminate knowledge concerning the "discoveries" of the later fifteenth and sixteenth centuries; finding the work of Ptolemy "very imperfect", he declares that he has "esteemed it would be precious and perhaps not a little useful to the world to bring together the narrations of the writers of our time who have been in the said parts of the world [Africa and India], and of which they have spoken in much detail".[4] It is here that the first versions of certain classic Portuguese accounts, such as those of Tomé Pires or Duarte Barbosa, see the printed page in an abridged form, and in a sense it is Ramusio who provides a template that is drawn upon by later creators of compendia, such as Richard Hakluyt or Samuel Purchas in England, though Hakluyt was to insist in the preface to his own work that he had little interest in the voyages of those who were not English. As he put it, "I meddle in this worke with the Navigations onely of our owne nation: And albeit I alleage in a few places (as the matter and occasion required) some strangers as witnesses of the things done, yet are they none but such as either faythfully remember, or sufficiently confirme the travels of our owne people."[5]

[3] Rinaldo Caddeo, ed., *Le navigazioni atlantiche di Alvise da Ca' da Mosto, Antoniotto Usodimare e Niccoloso da Recco* (Milan, 1929); G. R. Crone, ed. and tr., *The voyages of Cadamosto and other documents on Western Africa in the second half of the fifteenth century* (London, 1937).

[4] Ramusio's dedication to Ieronimo Fracastoro, in Giovanni Battista Ramusio, *Navigazioni e viaggi*, ed. Marica Milanesi (Turin, 1978), vol. I, pp. 4–5.

[5] Richard Hakluyt, *The principal navigations, voyages, traffiques and discoveries of the English nation*, vol. I (Glasgow, 1903), p. xxiv. A somewhat different spirit inhabits Samuel Purchas, *Hakluytus posthumus or Purchas his pilgrimes*, vol. I (Glasgow, 1905), not least of all in its sub-title *contayning a history of the world in sea voyages and lande travells by Englishmen and others.*

The travel-compendium – whether cosmopolitan like that of Ramusio or patriotic like that of Hakluyt – is certainly a rather particular form, not one that we have for the most part encountered in the materials that we have considered, with the possible exception of certain seventeenth-century Ottoman attempts in this direction. The Persian materials that have been our principal concern here compare rather better with the tradition of the individual account in the Western European tradition, of which the well-known medieval exemplars are those by Marco Polo and John Mandeville, but of which increasing numbers can be found in the sixteenth and seventeenth centuries. However, where Europe is concerned, the first half of the sixteenth century poses rather unique problems in a number of respects. The two Iberian powers that were responsible for the great European imperial enterprises of that time were seemingly not keen on the dissemination of the individual travel-account as a printed artefact. The result of this is that the well-known account of Vasco da Gama's first voyage of 1497–9, variously attributed to Álvaro Velho and João de Sá, did not in fact see print until well into the nineteenth century. What was known of it was a very particular version, that had been incorporated already in the sixteenth century into Fernão Lopes de Castanheda's *História*, a work which was a chronicle rather than a travel-text. Typically, the European travel-texts on Asia from the sixteenth century to which one refers today were confidential affairs, which not only remained in manuscript but often seem scarcely to have circulated. Even those texts which found their way into print, such as Martín Fernández de Figueroa's Spanish-language account, entitled *Conquista de las Indias de Persia e Arabia*, detailing his participation in the early Portuguese conquests in Asia, scarcely seem to have enjoyed much celebrity during the sixteenth century.[6] Here then is the significance of Ramusio's effort, for he gave many of these works that might otherwise have languished in obscurity the possibility of a far wider circulation and readership.

An interesting example of a single-authored travel-text that attained much celebrity but, once again, could not find its way into print until some time after its author's death, is the *Peregrinação* of Fernão Mendes Pinto. First printed in Lisbon in 1614, more than thirty years after its author's decease, the text's title claimed to "recount many, and very strange things that he [Pinto] saw and heard in the kingdom of China,

6 James B. McKenna, ed., *A Spaniard in the Portuguese Indies: the narrative of Martín Fernández de Figueroa* (Cambridge, Mass., 1967).

and that of Tartary, and in Sornau [*Shahr-i nau*] which is vulgarly called Siam, and in that of Calaminhan, that of Pegu, that of Martaban, and in many other kingdoms and lordships of the Oriental parts".[7] Within six years, the work had appeared in a Spanish translation by Francisco de Herrera Maldonado, the *Historia oriental de las peregrinaciones de Fernan Mendez Pinto portuguez* (reprinted with variations in 1628, 1645 and 1665);[8] in 1628, the first French translation appeared, entitled *Les voyages advantureux de Fernand Mendez Pinto*; and by 1653 the work was available in both Dutch and English, to be followed by a German translation in 1671. The very wide circulation of this text in other European languages confirmed Mendes Pinto's reputation as a teller of tales, a latter-day Marco Polo, or perhaps even a Mandeville.[9] Such a view of Mendes Pinto's work is confirmed by the titles given to some of the translations: it thus appears as *De wonderlyke reizen . . .* in Dutch, and as *Wunderliche und mertwürdige Reisen Ferdinandi Mendez Pinto* in German. In part, this does no more than develop an aspect of the Portuguese title (which mentions *muytas e muyto estranhas cousas*) but, at the same time, such a deliberate strategy by the translators and printers places the book squarely under the sign of "wonders", thus both allying it to the medieval tradition mentioned above, and strengthening the association to the post-Quixote picaresque novel that was gaining ground in Europe at that time.

The interest of Mendes Pinto by 1614 could certainly not have lain in the contemporary and strategic character of the information that the text of the *Peregrinação* contained. The events that are referred to there dated back, for the most part, to the 1530s and 1540s, and some of the crucial features of seventeenth-century Indian Ocean politics – such as the rise to importance of the Mughals – can scarcely find a place in the work. Rather, his work came to embody a point of view, namely that of the footloose adventurer, who lived not within the Portuguese empire but on its margins, and on account of this peculiar positioning claimed to have access to materials that the more official spokesmen did not. Fernão Mendes Pinto knew some Malay, for example, and he makes it a point

7 Fernão Mendes Pinto, *Peregrinaçam de Fernam Mendez Pinto; em que da conta de muytas e muyto estranhas cousas que vio & ouuio no reyno da China, no da Tartaria, no do Sornau, que vulgarmente se chama Sião, no do Calaminhan, no de Pegù, no de Martauão, & em outros muytos reynos & senhorios das partes Orientais . . .* (Lisbon, 1614).

8 *Historia oriental de las peregrinaciones de Fernan Mendez Pinto portuguez, adonde se escriven muchas, y muy estrañas cosas que vio y oyó . . .* (Madrid, 1620).

9 *The voyages and adventures of Ferdinand Mendez Pinto . . . during his travels for the space of one and twenty years in the kingdoms of Ethiopia, China, Tartaria, Cauchinchina, Calaminham, Siam, Pegu, Japan, and a great part of the East-Indies*, tr. H. C. (London, 1653).

to pepper his text with it, in places that are both plausible and implausible. In other, more subtle, ways, he also claimed to have an authenticity of experience, and arguments hence continue into recent times over the precise aim of the text. Was it meant to entertain its readers above all, as suggested by one of its sub-titles: "The peregrination of Fernão Mendes Pinto: soldier of fortune, trader, pirate, agent, ambassador, during twenty-one years in Ethiopia, Persia, Malaya, India, Burma, Siam, Cochin-China, East Indies, China, Japan: Sailing uncharted oriental seas, he was five times shipwrecked, thirteen times captured, sixteen times enslaved: He met a saint, repented his ways, returned home and wrote his story for his children and for posterity"?[10] Or did it have a moral purpose – in view, particularly, of the author's periodically expressed longing for a religious vocation? If there was such a moral purpose, was it intended (as some have claimed) to be a moral critique of Portuguese functioning in Asia? If this was the case, such a critique would also have had a rather different signification in 1615 from that in 1550; for, by the early seventeenth century, moral critiques of the *Estado da Índia* and elaborate theories of its "decadence" had gained a certain popularity both within Iberian circles and outside them.[11]

In any event, what is also clear is that, by the time the *Peregrinação* came to be widely known on account of its belated publication, it entered into a market for travel-accounts that had grown apace in the course of the later sixteenth and early seventeenth centuries. The first half of the former century, we have already remarked, is somewhat poor in terms of the publication of individual accounts (as distinct from compendia), even if a certain number must have circulated in manuscript. This in turn bears a relationship to the desire on the part of the Iberian powers to control the circulation of information, and it is notable that the two major Portuguese publications of the first six decades of the sixteenth century relating to Asia, João de Barros's great chronicle *Da Ásia* and Castanheda's *História*, both carry with them a relatively official style and character (even though Castanheda's work was in fact, technically speaking, an unofficial one). Matters began to change in the second half of the century, with the appearance of works whose purpose was to glorify, or in some instances

10 See the illustrated version: *The peregrination of Fernão Mendes Pinto*, abridged and translated by Michael Lowery, introduction by Luís Sousa Rebelo (Manchester, 1992). The saint in question was of course the Jesuit missionary Francis Xavier.

11 Fernão Mendes Pinto, *The travels of Mendes Pinto*, ed. and tr. Rebecca D. Catz (Chicago, 1989). Also see Rebecca D. Catz and Francis M. Rogers, eds., *Cartas de Fernão Mendes Pinto e outros documentos* (Lisbon, 1983).

to defend, the reputation of certain individuals. Of these a significant early example is Brás de Albuquerque's *Comentários do Grande Afonso de Albuquerque*, first published in Lisbon in 1557, and reprinted in 1576.[12] However, such works – even if they referred to the travels and adventures of their subjects – still fell short of being true travel-accounts, with the major investment in the first-person narrative that such works implied.

Indeed, it may be argued that the defining works of travel literature in the later sixteenth century really came from outside Iberia. Crucial amongst these are a series of texts having to do with Brazil, which was only just emerging in the second half of the sixteenth century as a zone of economic importance, after having been long neglected by the Portuguese in favour of their Asian possessions. Thus, in the late 1550s, there appeared almost simultaneously the *Wahrhaftige Historie und Beschreibung* of Hans Staden, who had spent eight years in Brazil as a captive, and the *Singularitéz de la France antarctique* of André Thevet, who had been a participant in the unsuccessful French attempt under Nicolas Durand de Villegagnon to set up a colony in the Bay of Guanabara in the 1550s. Thevet's official work was eventually embroiled in a major controversy, on account of the counter-publication of Jean de Léry's *Histoire d'un voyage faict en la terre du Bresil autrement dite Amerique*, which appeared in Geneva in 1578.[13] This work, by a Protestant participant in the same expedition led by Villegagnon, not only roundly contested many of Thevet's specific claims, but also relativised the practices of the cannibals in Brazil in relation to anti-Huguenot barbarities practised in France; it was a major success, with further editions in 1580, 1585, and 1599–1600, the last of these dedicated to the Princess of Orange. Latin translations appeared as early as 1586, a German version in 1594, the Dutch one followed in 1597, and excerpts first appeared in English in 1611, eventually also to be taken up by Samuel Purchas in the sixteenth volume of *Purchas His Pilgrimes.*

The success of a work such as that of Léry must be understood in a threefold context. First, the relative "blackout" imposed by the Iberians on the circulation of their new knowledge in the sixteenth century no

[12] António Baião, ed., *Comentários do Grande Afonso de Albuquerque, capitão geral que foi das Índias Orientais em tempo do muito poderoso rey D. Manuel, o primeiro deste nome*, 2 vols. (Coimbra, 1922–3). Also see Miguel de Castanhoso, *História das cousas que o muy esforçado capitão D. Christovão da Gama fez nos Reynos de Preste João* (Lisbon, 1564; reprint, Lisbon, 1855).

[13] Jean de Léry, *History of a Voyage to the Land of Brazil, otherwise called America*, tr. Janet Whatley (Berkeley, 1990); André Thevet, *Les singularités de la France antarctique: le Brésil des cannibales au XVIe siècle*, ed. Frank Lestringant (Paris, 1983).

doubt created a suppressed demand for such materials outside the somewhat sanitised, and high humanistic, tradition of the chronicles. Second, the work formed part of an emerging and assertive Protestant literature, which claimed to view the world quite differently from the way in which it was represented in hitherto dominant Catholic discourse; thus, we note the significance of the controversy with Thevet. Third, the nature of Léry's subject, and the deep exoticism that accompanied the representation of cannibals, made the work part of a current regarding alterity that has not left European representations of the world at large until this very day.[14] What is important to note is that Léry insisted on the authenticity of his experience as a traveller, and, once one gets past the long and polemical preface to the work, his intention is made amply clear. In his first chapter, "Of the motive and the occasion that made us undertake this distant voyage to the land of Brazil", he notes that America has already been written about by "a number of cosmographers and other historians of our time"; however, "my intention and my subject in this history will be simply to declare what I have myself experienced, seen, heard and observed, both on the sea, coming and going, and among the American savages with whom I visited and lived for about a year".[15] Linguistic expertise forms a central part of his truth-claims, as we see from the twentieth chapter, which consists of a "colloquy" conducted "in the savage language and in French".[16]

The avid European reader of the latter half of the sixteenth century, desirous of knowing the world from his or her armchair, thus had available to him or her texts in a variety of competing genres. There were the great chronicles in Portuguese, Spanish, Italian and Latin, produced either by the Iberians themselves or in close relation with them. There were individual travel-texts such as those of Staden and Léry, which might at times be drawn into compendia; these were the texts whose production would accelerate considerably in the seventeenth century, as we shall see below. Finally, there were also attempts to draw together a variety of materials, and reflect not only on individual acts and actions, but also to place in a global context what the Europeans were engaged in doing. An important, if eccentric, example of this is the *Tratado dos descobrimentos*

[14] See, in this context, Frank Lestringant, "Calvinistes et cannibales: les écrits protestants sur le Brésil français (1555–1560)", *Bulletin de la société de l'histoire du protestantisme français*, 1–2, 1980, pp. 9–26, 167–92.

[15] Léry, *History of a Voyage*, p. 3.

[16] On Léry, see also the recent reflections in Andrea Frisch, *The invention of the eyewitness: witnessing and testimony in early modern France* (Chapel Hill, 2004).

of António Galvão.[17] Now the author of the *Tratado* is quite a fascinating figure in his own right. He was the author of two substantial texts, the very wide-ranging "Treatise on the discoveries", and an important and localised "Treatise on the Moluccas", which was long considered to be lost but has been rediscovered in recent decades.[18] An intellectual of rather uneven erudition, Galvão was also – and perhaps principally – a traveller himself, and a man of action, and hence saw action on more than one occasion in Portuguese Asia from the early 1520s onwards. He is also reputed to have had excellent knowledge of navigation, sometimes far better than the professional mariners with whom he associated. None of this made him a fortune, however, and we are informed that he eventually died in the poor hospital in Lisbon in the 1550s. The high point of his career was a stint as captain of the Portuguese fortress of Ternate in the Moluccas in the late 1530s. It was here that he earned for himself the title of the "Apostle of the Moluccas", on account of his untiring efforts to promote the Christianisation of those islands. Galvão also came from a family with something of an intellectual and historical tradition. However, rather than drawing on the work of his father, Duarte Galvão, who had been one of the principal ideologues of the court of the early sixteenth-century Portuguese ruler Dom Manuel, António Galvão may have sought inspiration in the work of another writer from the early sixteenth century, Duarte Pacheco Pereira, author of the *Esmeraldo de situ orbis*, and also António Galvão's brother-in-law.[19]

Duarte Pacheco Pereira was himself also a traveller in imperial service, as well as a successful military man, as we may see from his actions in Kerala in the very early years of the sixteenth century. On his return to Portugal from India in 1505, he began to compose the *Esmeraldo*, a book in five parts that was meant to deal in chronological order with the discoveries of the Portuguese from the time of Dom Henrique in the fifteenth century to the time of Dom Manuel, but he eventually abandoned it in 1507, without ever developing the fifth part; thus the great Southeast Asian city of Melaka and even Ceylon never find mention in

17 António Galvão, *Tratado dos descobrimentos*, ed. Visconde de Lagoa and Elaine Sanceau, 4th edn (Oporto, 1987).

18 Hubert Jacobs, ed., *A treatise on the Moluccas (c. 1544), probably the preliminary version of António Galvão's lost "História das Molucas"* (Rome, 1971).

19 Duarte Pacheco Pereira, *Esmeraldo de situ orbis*, ed. Damião Peres (Lisbon, 1988). For a discussion, see also Jean Aubin, "Les frustrations de Duarte Pacheco Pereira", in Aubin, *Le latin et l'Astrolabe*, vol. I: *Recherches sur le Portugal de la Renaissance, son expansion en Asie et les relations internationales* (Paris, 1996), pp. 111–32.

the work. Pereira, like Galvão and unlike Fernão Mendes Pinto, thus did not choose the route of writing the first-person travel-account, but had instead taken a step in the direction of posing Portuguese actions in this period as a process on a world scale. It is a manner of viewing the world which bears some relationship to the slightly later vision of the Spanish official historian Antonio de Herrera y Tordesillas, or for that matter the Portuguese chroniclers Damião de Góis and Jerónimo de Osório – that is, with imperial history as the prime organising principle.

António Galvão for his part somewhat breaks from this mould in the *Tratado dos descobrimentos.* This departure is on two very substantial counts. The first is chronological, for Galvão makes it clear that he will treat "the ancient and modern discoveries, which have been done until the year 1550", and then goes on to divide his work broadly into two parts, the first extending from ancient times to the late fifteenth century, and the second from the late fifteenth to the mid sixteenth century. The second departure is in the manner in which the years from 1400 to 1550 are treated. For, unlike other authors, Galvão organises his work in this part as a sort of annal, where the activities of various peoples of the world – and not only the Portuguese – are treated. Thus, in 1496–7, we get an account as much of the deeds of Sebastian Cabot as of Christopher Columbus and Vasco da Gama. In the 1510s, the activities of the Portuguese in Southeast Asia are juxtaposed with the arrival of Cortés in Mexico; and in the 1530s, the arrival of the Spaniards in the Andes is discussed as part of the same panorama as Galvão's own presence in the Moluccas. In other words, for Galvão, the history of the discoveries is a movement by which the Pacific anti-meridian, defined but not located in the Luso-Castilian Treaty of Tordesillas, is reached progressively by an expansion in two directions, to the west and the east. One may consider this to be a worldview in which the imagined centre lies in fact in the Moluccas, where Galvão had spent four years of his life.

By 1550, in Galvão's account, we are not quite at the tired moment when nothing is left to be discovered, that moment of anxiety which led so many European authors of the sixteenth century to re-read Seneca's *Medea*, and its evocation of "Thule, the last of the lands". What is also worth stressing is the particular quality of Galvão's understanding of the process of the "discovery of the world"; for in his rather original construction, this is a process not simply of the Spaniards and the Portuguese discovering other lands, but also of the Greeks, Phoenicians, Egyptians, Indians and Chinese doing so. Indeed, Galvão appears to have a particular weakness for the Chinese, whom he sees as the greatest discoverers of all peoples in the history of the world, attributing to them a grand capacity for navigation that may even have taken them to New Spain, Peru, Brazil and the Antilles. This then is another aspect of the text that we must bear in mind, namely its curious mixture of wonder and banality, with passages from the Bible and ancient authors juxtaposed with Spanish and Portuguese chroniclers such as Oviedo and Gómara, and other discussions still that seem to have no textual source. Thus we can find in Galvão's work a rather enigmatic passage that runs as follows:

> And in the year 474, the Roman Empire was lost, and after that time the Longobards came to Italy, and in that time demons walked the earth so freely that they took on the form of Moses, and the Jews who were misled by this drowned themselves in the sea in great numbers. And the Arian sect prevailed. And Merlin lived in England in this time. And in the year 711, there was Muhammad and those of his sect, who took Africa and Spain by force.[20]

Passages such as these may have somewhat embarrassed Galvão's first publicist in English, who was none other than Richard Hakluyt. For the *Tratado* had been published in Lisbon soon after Galvão's death, and this first edition of 1563 soon acquired some circulation, together with the chronicles of Barros and Castanheda, which, though far more copious, were also far narrower in their focus. Hakluyt's version (based on an anonymous translation "by some honest and well affected marchant of our nation") thus appeared in London in 1601 under the title: *An Excellent Treatise of Antonie Galvano, Portugal, containing the most ancient and modern discoveries of the world, especially by navigation, according to the course of times from the flood until the Year of Grace, 1555. Contained within A Selection of Curious, Rare and Early Voyages, and Histories of Interesting Discoveries.* It was presented with a particular insistence that this was no sectarian history in which the boastful Portuguese nation claimed more than its due, but rather a comprehensive history that went beyond the limits of other writers such as Bishop Osório, whose derivative but successful *De rebus Emmanuelis Regis Lusitaniae* had first appeared in 1571 and gone on to be both reprinted and rapidly translated into French.[21] Hakluyt dedicated the work to Sir Robert Cecil, Principal Secretary to Queen Elizabeth and Chancellor of the University of Cambridge, pointing

[20] Galvão, *Tratado dos descobrimentos*, pp. 189–90.

[21] The first French version from 1581 is *Histoire de Portugal contenant les entreprises, navigations et gestes mémorables des Portugallois . . . depuis l'an 1496 jusques à l'an 1578. . . comprinse en vingt livres, dont les douze premiers sont traduits du latin de Jérosme Osorius . . .*, *nouvellement mise en françois par S. G. S.*, followed by a number of other editions from Geneva.

out that the author was "one Antonie Galvano, a Portugall gentleman: of whose Pietie towards God, equitie towards men, fidelity to his Prince, love to his countrey, skill in sea causes, experience in histories, liberalitie towards his nation, vigilance, valour, wisedome and diligence in restoring and settling the decaied state of the Isles of Maluco . . . a large Epistle can well comprehend". Hakluyt urged Cecil to inform himself of the world as it now stood discovered, and also to find a concrete visual representation thereof: "if it please your Honour at your convenient leisure to take a sea card or mappe of the world and carie your eie upon the coast of Africa from Cape de Non, lying on the mayne in 29 degrees of northerly latitude and follow the shore about the Cape of Buona Sperança till you come to the mouth of the Redde Sea", and then follow the Indian Ocean "al the south of Asia to the northeast part of China". By this means, the reader would be carried step by step "from the Açores and Madera in the West, to the Malucos, the Phillipinas, and Japan in the East", on the one hand, while "likewise is to be understood of the Occident".[22] Whether Cecil in fact did so remains open to question; what is of importance is that half a century later, when Oliver Cromwell was to consider his "Western Design" of expansion, it was not a compendium that he drew upon, but a travel-text, namely that of Thomas Gage.[23]

THE SEVENTEENTH-CENTURY 'EXPLOSION'

For if, in the 1560s, chronicles, compendia, travel-texts and other odd hybrid products such as Galvão's *Tratado* all jostled for space on the reader's shelf, in the seventeenth century it was the European travel-account that swept all before it. In the section that follows, we will look briefly at this new situation through a consideration of two texts, one that remained unpublished and seems to have circulated very little, the other amongst the most celebrated travel-texts concerning Asia in the seventeenth century. Through a reflection on these two works, we shall attempt to draw some general conclusions on the changing nature of travel-narratives in early modern Europe, before returning finally to a set of closing remarks comparing them to our Indo-Persian corpus.

22 Hakluyt, "The Epistle Dedicatorie", in António Galvão, *The discoveries of the world, from their first original unto the year of Our Lord 1555, by Antonio Galvano, governor of Ternate. Corrected, quoted, and published in England, by Richard Hakluyt (1601)*, reprinted with the original Portuguese text, and ed. Vice-Admiral C. B. Bethune (London, 1862), pp. iii–vi.

23 J. Eric S. Thompson, ed., *Thomas Gage's Travels in the New World* (Norman, 1958), pp. xl–xlii. Gage's *The English-American* was first published in 1648.

The first of these works is entitled "Vida de Jacques de Coutre, natural de la ciudad de Brugas", and exists in a unique manuscript at the Biblioteca Nacional de Madrid, suggesting it was scarcely a text that circulated.[24] Recounting the life and travels of a Flemish merchant from Bruges, Jacques de Coutre (or Jakob van de Koutere), this text was apparently written originally in Portuguese but then "put in the form that it is by his son Don Estevan de Coutre", a process that involved the translation of the text into Castilian. This already raises a first question: why translate the text? Clearly, simple comprehensibility could not have been the issue, given the relatively facile relationship between Portuguese and Castilian. Rather, in a seventeenth-century situation where the elevated idiom of Latin was losing ground, the choice was clearly prompted by the more prestigious status that Castilian enjoyed, especially within the context of the Union of the Crowns of Spain and Portugal under the Habsburgs. Coutre's own native language, Flemish, was obviously ruled out in view of the principal targets of his writings, who must have been in the Habsburg court. We must remember that the *Vida* was written in about 1628, after Coutre had been sent back to Europe from Goa in disgrace, accused of being a spy for the Dutch. The text, along with a number of others that he wrote proposing various reforms in the functioning of Portuguese Asia, must therefore be understood as a programme of rehabilitation for its author.[25]

However, if the text is meant as a simple apology for its author, some of whose activities were undoubtedly suspect in the eyes of the Habsburg Crown and its agents in Asia, it must be seen as a distinct case of overkill. For Coutre (and his son and amanuensis Estevan) produced a substantial tome of nearly 300 folios, organised in three books, the first with twenty chapters, the second with seventeen, and the third with fifteen. This substantial work is part autobiography and part travel-account, tending distinctly to the latter rather than the former, and is organised around the conceit of its author as an inveterate voyager. Beginning with his birth in about 1575 or 1576, Jacques de Coutre goes on to inform his reader of how, on the death of his father, his mother thought to send him to Spain,

[24] Jacques de Coutre, *Andanzas asiáticas*, ed. Eddy Stols, B. Teensma and J. Verberckmoes (Madrid, 1991), based on Biblioteca Nacional de Madrid, Ms. no. 2780. The manuscript carries the date 1640.

[25] We may compare this with a text published by one of Coutre's associates, the German merchant Ferdinand Cron, for which see Sanjay Subrahmanyam, "An Augsburger in Ásia Portuguesa: further light on the commercial world of Ferdinand Cron, 1587–1624", in R. Ptak and D. Rothermund, eds., *Emporia, commodities and entrepreneurs in Asian maritime trade, c. 1400–1750* (Stuttgart, 1991), pp. 401–25.

to avoid having him embroiled in the wars that at times were all too common in the Low Countries. In early August 1591, he thus made his way to Vlissingen, and from there to Lisbon, after an arduous voyage of three months. Here, joining his brother Joseph de Coutre, the two made a decision to leave Europe. The matter is hardly discussed at any length: "Finding myself in Lisbon with so little remedy, and subject to the travails and miseries of Europe, my brother and I resolved to go away to far-away lands where we could live at a smaller cost. We decided on the East Indies (*la India Oriental*), and to this end we got together four comrades . . ."[26] Coutre notes that at this point he could speak neither Portuguese nor Castilian, a matter that he soon seems to have remedied. Separated from his brother on the voyage to Goa, they both eventually reached there on 14 September 1592, with modest possessions besides a letter of recommendation in the name of a "very rich man" in Goa, a certain Sebastião Pinto de Frexos. Joseph de Coutre, the older and more able of the two brothers (at this point at least) quickly contracted a marriage in Goa, and managed to enter into respectable "Old Christian" circles. Jacques, who fell ill soon after his arrival in Goa, was left to his own devices.

This largely explains the fact that, in September 1593, he embarked as a common soldier for Melaka, with the intention of working for the captain there, Dom Diogo Lobo. Coutre's work uses a trope here, declaring that, in all that follows, he was guided by "his natural inclination and desire to see the world, which had taken me from my *patria*". Rather, he appears to have decided to follow in the footsteps of one of the group of four comrades with whom he had left Lisbon, a certain Luís Lopes, who had already left for Melaka. Arriving in Melaka, Coutre claims to have made a number of fortuitous acquaintances and friendships, notably with a certain elderly Venetian gentleman called Martinela. Through his aid, he was introduced to the new captain of the city, Francisco de Silva de Meneses, who quickly became his patron. It was through this connection that, a mere six months later, Coutre was apparently able to visit the kingdom of Pahang in the Malay Peninsula, accompanying an official Portuguese mission there led by a certain Martim Teixeira. It also turns out that our Flemish author was already reasonably well versed in the trade in precious stones, and that part of his mission in Pahang was to purchase diamonds and besoar-stones. Soldiering and trade thus became twin professions for him, though, as

[26] Coutre, *Andanzas asiáticas*, p. 90.

time went by, Coutre would eventually leave aside the first occupation to concentrate almost exclusively on the second.

Coutre was to stay on in the "south" (*el sur*), here meaning South-east Asia, for nearly a decade, and this decade occupies all of the first book of his *Vida* until his eventual return to Goa in May 1603, to marry Catarina do Couto, sister-in-law of Joseph de Coutre. This inaugurates a new phase in his life, when he turns his back on South-east Asia to concentrate his efforts largely on India and West Asia, as well as Europe. The second book thus corresponds broadly to the second decade of his Asian sojourn, beginning with his first visits to the 'Adil Shahi territories of Bijapur, which were visited at much the same time by the Mughal envoy Asad Beg Qazwini.[27] This decade is punctuated, however, by an overland journey to Europe that Coutre undertook in 1606, passing through Hurmuz, Shiraz, Alexandretta, and Tunis, where he was briefly taken captive. Eventually returning to Goa by sea, he then continued his trade inland in Bijapur, and also had occasion to visit the diamond mines of the Deccan in 1611. The third book then takes us logically into the third decade of Coutre's Asian peregrinations, beginning with his visit to the court of the Qutb Shahi Sultanate of Golkonda in 1614, and continues with an account of his dealings with the Mughals, notably the prince Khurram (the future emperor Shahjahan). We learn of another overland journey he made as far as Aleppo in 1620, as well as a further attempt he made in the following year to return overland to Spain, unsuccessfully. Finally we are informed of how Coutre and his brother were denounced as Dutch spies, and sent back to Iberia in disgrace in 1623, the year in which the account also comes to an end rather abruptly. We thus do not learn from him in this account of his eventual rehabilitation, the fact that he came to be consulted on reform projects for the *Estado da Índia* by high officials such as the viceroy Conde de Linhares, or the fact that he eventually lived out his life in some ease in Spain as a cavalier of the Ordem de Santiago. Coutre died, we are aware, in Saragossa, in 1640, and could count himself, at the end of his life at least, to have been something of a successful self-made man.

Coutre's account is organised around certain rather straightforward principles. His main interest lies in describing his activities in the context of courtly life in Asia, and his chapters are often organised around the different courtly centres that he frequented. Thus, in South-east Asia, after

[27] On Asad Beg in Bijapur, see P. M. Joshi, "Asad Beg's mission to Bijapur, 1603–1604", in S. N. Sen, ed., *Mahamahopadhyaya Prof. D. V. Potdar sixty-first birthday commemoration volume* (Poona, 1950), pp. 184–96, as well as Alam and Subrahmanyam, "Witnessing transition", pp. 104–40.

his visit to Pahang, we find him in Johor, and then in an extended visit to the Thai kingdom, which he describes at some length. After dealings with the Spaniards in Manila in the late 1590s, Coutre then writes of his activities in Patani in the early seventeenth century, shortly before his return to Goa. Similarly, a good part of the second book is concerned with his dealings with Ibrahim 'Adil Shah II of Bijapur, besides recounting his travails on his overland voyage to Europe. The third book is again preoccupied in good measure with two courts, the Qutb Shahi centre in Golkonda, and the Mughal court at Agra. Coutre is not all that concerned with producing an ethnographic image of popular life, though on occasion he does turn his pen to that cause with some perspicacity and attention to detail. Rather, his interest seems nearly always to gravitate to courtly life and ritual, at times using anecdotes involving himself, at others drawing on his indirect observations or materials that he has gathered from others. In turn, in order to define his particular relationship with these courts, he stresses his peculiar status as a jewel trader, which apparently allows him to have direct dealings with the high and mighty in Asia. These dealings are usually disappointing, and it would seem that most of the princes and sovereigns with whom he had commercial intercourse were unscrupulous and dishonest, eager to seize his goods and short-change him. Coutre seems forever on the point of being thrown into prison, and his sections on particular places often end with his having to flee them under threat, a device that recalls the emplotment techniques of Fernão Mendes Pinto – whom it is obvious that either Coutre or his son had read. A word that recurs frequently in his descriptions is *barbaridades*, used to describe Hindu, Buddhist and Muslim states, and their practices alike. This is a work then of a Catholic, who is anxious, moreover, to affirm his Catholicism not only by visiting Santiago de Compostela, but through the denigration of all other religions, the more so perhaps because he had fallen under suspicion of complicity with the Dutch.

One set of examples may suffice, since they allow us to compare the view of the world of Jacques de Coutre with that of contemporary Mughal travellers. These are Coutre's chapters concerning Bijapur, which he claims to have visited on a number of occasions, beginning in 1604. By 1616, some twelve years after his first visit, he even affirms that the Portuguese ambassador at the 'Adil Shahi court, a certain António Monteiro Corte-Real, depended on him in many matters: "because on account of the understanding of the language of the natives that I knew, I set him straight on many matters regarding his duties and the service of the

King Our Lord".[28] However, even earlier, Coutre gives us a sense of how he was received at the Bijapur court that is a little too glib and facile. On his first commercial voyage there, he went with a few Arab horses, some emeralds, and a small retinue, including some servants, as well as an Armenian interpreter called Francisco Gonçalves, "since I did not know the language of that land". After passing through Ponda, Belgaum, and Raibagh, and witnessing his usual share of "barbarities" – including some odd temple rituals, as well as the killing of the governor and chief officials of Raibagh in a popular revolt – Coutre claims eventually to have been much impressed by the city of Bijapur itself. Not only was the principal part three leagues in circuit, but it was fortified with bulwarks, and it possessed moats and artillery. Further, there were the imposing suburbs, such as Nauraspur, Shahpur and Ibrahimpur, which when taken together with Bijapur proper, he imagines, must compare with Grand Cairo in size.

However, Coutre states that, on his arrival, he took up lodgings at Shahpur, and that he was almost immediately invited by Sultan Ibrahim to see him, in order to sell him three large emeralds. He claims equally to have quickly become on very close terms with the prince Fath Khan ("Faticán"), Ibrahim's son, to whom he sold two Arab horses. His account of being received by the Sultan is far less elaborate than that of the Mughal envoy Asad Beg, but we do have some similar passages describing a great hall lit up with hundreds of oil lamps, with the ruler seated on a bed-like throne, of gold and silver. In this version, Ibrahim was also attended by over 500 women, some dancing and others playing music. Coutre also recounts how Ibrahim wished to buy more jewels from him, and notes that their commercial relationship was off to a splendid start. In this respect, his portrayal of Ibrahim differs from the manner in which he depicts almost any other Asian ruler with whom he had dealings; for, however much a coward he sees Ibrahim as being in other ways, in matters commercial he is depicted as relatively straightforward. The same is true of the manner in which Fath Khan is presented. Indeed, Coutre claims that, out of consideration for his Christian habits, the prince used to send him fresh fish from his own tanks on Fridays, while the Flemish merchant in exchange gave him "flasks full of Spanish wine" (*frascos llenos del vino de España*), perhaps similar to the ones that Asad Beg claims to have carried back to the Mughal domains.[29]

[28] Coutre, *Andanzas asiáticas*, p. 280.

[29] Coutre, *Andanzas asiáticas*, p. 178. Compare Muzaffar Alam and Sanjay Subrahmanyam, "The Deccan frontier and Mughal expansion, ca. 1600: contemporary perspectives", *Journal of the Economic and Social History of the Orient*, 47, 3, 2004, pp. 357–89.

This said, Coutre wishes to leave his readers with no illusions concerning the absolute tyranny with which the 'Adil Shahi Sultans conducted their affairs. Their domains, he asserts, were as populated as the kingdom of France, very fertile and abundant in everything. However, he notes that "the natives are extremely poor . . . [for] the farmers and humble folk (*gente popular*) [suffer] from the tyrannies that are practised with them". In contrast to this, the lords and grandees of the kingdom are very rich, but here a key contrast is to be made with Spain. For these men are not really the lords of the lands, towns and castles, but simply captains and governors who have been attributed rents at the pleasure of the ruler; so that the king can raise up a slave or a stable-boy one day and make him a great lord. Yet, this is an altogether fickle regime, as the following passage makes clear.

With time, he [the lord] can come to have a rent of a million or a million and a half each year, so long as he keeps up as many horses as are in conformity with the rents he has. And on dying, all the rents that he had die with him, and thus the king comes to inherit as the principal all his goods – and on account of this, he himself always has many at his disposal – even if the person has sons. On account of this, all the grandees and lords of that kingdom do not care for more than their present life, and spend much more than they have, and try to perpetuate their memories, and make houses of prayer (*alcoranes*), tanks, grandiose and noteworthy palaces on which they spend millions and millions in gold, all out of vanity, and thus all of the land belongs to the royal crown, and is rented out on account of the king to the peasants to sow it, so that it is the king who keeps the greater part of the product.[30]

This then is a recurring theme in Coutre's account of the Deccan, as it is of other parts of Asia: side by side with the barbarities in customs and religious practices, there is ostentation and waste, endless greed and pointless luxury. This eventually goes beyond the king and his court, for all the grandees imitate the ruler in this respect. Thus, every great lord has 200 or 300 women in his household, so much so "that their houses seem to be convents full of nuns". Only a few of these were chosen to have carnal dealings with their lord and master, but here too was an instance of characteristic waste, greed and barbarity. Added to this is the view that needless cruelty characterises all these monarchs; thus, Ibrahim is given to having the eyes of his former favourites and immediate family pulled out, while other rulers habitually have the hands and feet of thieves cut off for the most minor offences.

[30] Coutre, *Andanzas asiáticas*, p. 179.

There are occasions when Coutre's account converges with what we gather from the Mughal texts, and these are interesting moments. In regard to Bijapur and its ruler, he thus emits the following judgment:

> And as he was by nature a coward, he had another [form of] Reason of State that was no less notable; which was that as the Mogor wished to oppose him and make war on him, he had sought out peace with great efforts, and with great gifts and tributes had managed to achieve and keep it. He gave the following reason to his vassals and used to say: "Why would I want to make war on the Mogor, in which both money and human lives will surely be wasted? And besides what I spend in war is certainly subject to the vagaries of a poor result. I would rather offer him the money as a gift, and content him, and be his friend, and remain in my house with my peace and quiet." And thus he has given away almost all his treasure little by little, and when he reached his old age, he did not have any more with which to make war even if he had so wished, and he has suffered a thousand frauds to which the Mogor has subjected him, and even become tributary to him. As soon as the Mogor would come to know that he had a precious jewel or something of great value, he would ask for it, and he [Ibrahim] would send it. And after he found himself without a treasure and poor, he became a tyrant and killed his own legitimate sons, and his oldest wife, and he never used to leave his court, and only very infrequently even went out from his palace.[31]

Thus, we begin with a view of Ibrahim that is very close to what emerges from Asad Beg's account, namely of a ruler who would prefer to use his financial resources to buy peace rather than make war. However, Coutre then gradually shifts the ground, and the picture that emerges of Ibrahim at the end of this long discussion does not differ substantially from that of other Oriental tyrants in Coutre's gallery, be it Muhammad Quli Qutb Shah, or Prince Khurram. In the case of the latter, Coutre's account is particularly picaresque, culminating in an episode that is meant to recall Daniel in the lion's den: in Agra, Khurram apparently has him surrounded by four young lions, one of which actually takes Coutre's leg into his mouth, and it is only by showing great *sang-froid* that the merchant is able to escape this singular ill-treatment.[32]

Coutre's account thus may converge with Mughal accounts in points of detail, but we should be aware that the framing narrative is an entirely different one. For, besides the imperatives of the picaresque, which require every adventure to be pushed to its limit, we should also be attentive

[31] Coutre, *Andanzas asiáticas*, pp. 296–7.

[32] See Nuno Vassallo e Silva, "Precious stones, jewels and cameos: Jacques de Coutre's Journey to Goa and Agra", in Jorge Flores and Nuno Vassallo e Silva, eds., *Goa and the Great Mughal* (Lisbon, 2004), pp. 130–1, which we believe is too inclined to accept Coutre's version at face value.

Figure 16. Los Angeles County Museum of Art, M. 83.105.2, portrait of Ibrahim 'Adil Shah II, *c.* 1675.

to the fact that he is highly invested in the ideas of "tyranny" in Asia, a lack of security for both commoners and élite, and a conception of absolute and arbitrary royal power which is periodically compared by him in more or less explicit terms to the far more reasonable – if not ideal – dispensation that exists in, say, Spain. Is this linked to the fact that in Asia, the kingdoms in question are Muslim and "Gentile"? There is a strong suspicion that this is indeed the case, for Coutre's vision frequently returns to absurd religious practices and notions that animate the rulers of the east, whether the king of Siam and his elephants, or the Shi'i celebration of Muharram in the Deccan. Surprisingly enough for a merchant then, Coutre's views often approximate those of Catholic missionaries in the extent of his disapproval of religious difference. It is thus notable that, in his projects for reform in Portuguese India, and designs for doing damage to Dutch commerce, the idea of building alliances with Asian powers has a small role. The Iberians, it seems, will have to go it alone for the most part, since there is nothing of any consequence that can be hoped for from these cruel, fickle and untrustworthy sovereigns.

We have already noted that Coutre's *Vida* never went into print during the seventeenth century. Perhaps his family did not have sufficient political influence for this, or perhaps the linguistic peculiarities of the text rendered it too unattractive to any potential printer or bookseller. This must have been a matter of considerable chagrin for him, since, by the 1630s, many other texts on Portuguese Asia were appearing in print, often by persons with a far shorter experience of the lands beyond the Cape of Good Hope than Coutre possessed. Such texts having broken free to an extent from the great "collections" of voyages, they often came to be co-authored by a professional writer, who claimed to organise the scattered thoughts and ideas of the author, but in fact did far more. A striking example of this is the case of the French traveller François Pyrard de Laval. An initial version of his travels appeared in 1611 in Paris, and it was eventually decided to put out a far larger version of the initial text, which had consisted of 372 pages in eleven chapters; the new text, dated 1619, eventually was made up of two volumes numbering over 1,000 pages. However, the aid of a professional writer named Pierre Bergeron had to be solicited, and his role was commented on as follows by a contemporary:

> The real author of this book is Pierre Bergeron, who having heard people speak of the diverse adventures of Pyrard, when he returned to Paris, took him to his house and made him recount them with all the exactitude that one may remark in this work. As Pyrard was always drunk, Bergeron, in order to discern the truth of his words, made him repeat the same thing several times and at different

moments, and when he reported them constantly in the same fashion and without variation, he took them for truthful: if not, he rejected them as suspect.[33]

We may still legitimately wonder what effect this lack of sobriety had on both Pyrard's memory and his capacity to communicate. In any event, it is only by stretching definitions considerably that we can call him the "author" of the standard version of the account that appeared in 1619.

Problems of the same sort persist with Jean-Baptiste Tavernier (1605–89), who, together with François Bernier and Jean Chardin, may be thought to be one of the great triumvirate of French travellers to Asia in the seventeenth century (though an argument can also be made in favour of another candidate, Jean de Thévenot). Tavernier is best known for his great work in two quarto volumes, *Les Six Voyages de Jean-Baptiste Tavernier, écuyer Baron d'Aubonne, qu'il a fait en Turquie, en Perse et aux Indes*, which appeared in 1676. The voyages in question, the extended title goes on to note, were carried out "during the space of forty years, and through all the routes that one can have; they are accompanied by particular observations on the quality, the religion, the government, the customs and the commerce of each country; with the figures, the weights, and the value of the moneys that are current there". The first volume is devoted to Turkey and Persia, and the second to India and the neighbouring islands. The vast number of reprints and re-editions of this work that followed in French, numbering at least eighteen by 1724, attest to its immense popularity; the *Voyages* were also translated into English in 1677, German in 1681, and Italian, as well as perhaps Dutch, in 1682.

Tavernier was thus something of a celebrity by the end of his life, a fact that is worth noting as a sign of how travel – if managed and presented well – could assist immensely in social improvement in a European context. His origins were humble, but not excessively so; his father, Gabriel Tavernier, was a geographer and a seller of maps and charts, who moved from Antwerp to Paris in about 1575 with his two brothers. The family was Huguenot, and Gabriel eventually found a match in France, almost certainly within that religious milieu, with a certain Suzanne Tonnelier, with whom he had four children; Jean-Baptiste, born in about 1605, was the second of these. The traveller was to claim later in life that his destiny was determined already in childhood: "If one's first education is like a second birth", he declares, "I can well say that I came into the world with

[33] Xavier de Castro and Geneviève Bouchon, eds., *Voyage de Pyrard de Laval aux Indes Orientales (1601–1611)*, 2 vols. (Paris, 1998), vol. II, p. 974.

the desire to voyage. The interviews that several savants had with my father on matters of geography which he had the reputation of understanding well, and which though very young, I heard with pleasure, inspired in me from early on the desire to go and see a part of the countries that were represented to me on maps, which I never tired of casting my eyes upon."[34] By the late 1620s, Tavernier claims that he had already "seen the best parts of Europe, France, England, Holland, Germany, Switzerland, Poland, Hungary and Italy" and he also asserts that he "spoke fairly the languages which are the most necessary, and which have the greatest currency". In 1630, he made his way via Budapest and Belgrade to Istanbul, and then thought to visit the Safavid domains. Thus, he begins his account of his six voyages to Asia in 1631, assuring his reader that he has "had time to observe the nature of the country well, and the genius of the populations". These travels, he goes on to state, have made him traverse "more than 60,000 leagues by land, only having once returned from Asia to Europe by sea". So he concludes his introduction: "Thus I have seen at my leisure in my six journeys, and by different routes, the whole of Turkey, all Persia, and all India, and especially the famous mine of diamonds, where no European had been before me. It is of these grand Empires that I propose to give a full and exact account." The six voyages that he counts are a first one to the Ottoman empire and Iran between 1631 and 1633; a second more elaborate one that took him as far as Bengal, and which lasted from 1638 to 1643; a third voyage, again via the eastern Mediterranean, to Surat and then to the Deccan, begun in late 1643 and ending with his eventual return to Paris in 1649; a fourth voyage, begun in 1651, again involving Iran and the Deccan, with a return, via the Safavid domains once more, to Paris in late 1655; a fifth voyage, begun in 1657, again involving the three Muslim empires, and ending with his return to Paris in about 1661 or 1662; and the sixth and final voyage, begun in November 1663, again taking him as far as the Mughal domains, from which he eventually returned in late 1668.

By this time, Tavernier was sixty-three years of age, and had amassed a substantial fortune, through his trade in jewels but also in textiles and other goods. He had also married successfully in 1662, his wife being Madeleine Goisse, the daughter of a fairly well-off jeweller with whom Tavernier had business dealings. His fame was sufficient by now for him to be invited to the court of Louis XIV, where he managed to sell the

[34] Pascal Pia, ed., *Voyages en Perse et description de ce royaume par Jean-Baptiste Tavernier, marchand français* (Paris, 1930), p. vii.

Figure 17. Portrait of Tavernier in "Oriental costume", engraving by Johann Hainzelmann, Paris (1679), based on a portrait by Largillière.

Sun King a number of diamonds and precious stones and was soon thereafter granted a title, which he concretised in 1670 by buying the barony of Aubonne, in western France. Once installed in his new estate, he appears to have turned his thoughts to publishing an account of his experiences and observations. To this end, Tavernier took on the services of an amanuensis, a very prolific Protestant writer by the name of Samuel Chappuzeau (1625–1701), with whom he was to have difficult relations, the latter claiming that he was subjected to much humiliation amounting to "mortification if not martyrdom" by the traveller and his wife. However, by 1675, the first of Tavernier's works, the *Nouvelle Relation de l'Intérieur du Serrail du Grand Seigneur*, appeared, followed the very next year by the *Six Voyages*, and we may hence view the collaboration as an efficient one.

The problem remains however of knowing the extent to which Tavernier was indeed the author of the text. It has been claimed that he kept copious notes, and that it was on the basis of these that Chappuzeau worked; others have noted that his text draws not only on Bernier's earlier account, but on the writings of the Capuchin Père Gabriel de Chinon (who had long resided in Iran), suggesting that Chappuzeau used a "collage" technique to pull the work together in haste. A third writer is also sometimes mentioned; this is a certain André Daulier-Deslandes (d. 1719), who had apparently accompanied Tavernier on one of his voyages, written and published his own account of Safavid Iran, and also may have helped Tavernier prepare his work for publication.[35] We may note, however, that the mode of organisation of the *Six Voyages* is most particular, since the purpose is to produce not a chronological account but rather a synthetic one. As a consequence, Tavernier's technique is to take a subject, which might be a route, or a commodity, and produce an account of it, drawing on incidents that occurred at various moments: thus, we have chapters with titles such as "On the mores and customs of the Persians", "On marriage among the Persians" or "On coral and yellow amber and the places where they are found". At times, dates and years for these incidents are provided, at other times not. Thus, unlike the rigorously chronological scheme of Coutre's *Vida*, Tavernier's organising notions are far looser, even if at times he follows a series of episodes through in order to provide a chronological development. His religious

[35] See also the work of this author, André Daulier-Deslandes, *Les Beautez de la Perse, ou la description de ce qu'il y a de plus curieux dans ce royaume, enrichie de la carte du païs, & de plusieurs estampes dessignées sur les lieux* (Paris, 1673).

predilections are also far less inclined to lead him in the direction of radical judgments; if the "Gentiles" or "idolaters" of India emerge thus as cowardly and ruled by superstition, Tavernier's text is rather mild in its judgment of Islam and Muslims when compared to texts produced by earlier authors. For his view of the idolaters, the following brief passage is telling.

> The idolaters of India are so numerous that for one Musalman there are five or six Gentiles. It is astonishing to see how this enormous multitude of men has allowed itself to be subjected by so small a number, and has readily submitted to the yoke of the Musalman Princes. But astonishment ceases when one remembers that the idolaters have no union among themselves, and that superstition has introduced so strange a diversity of opinions and customs that they never agree with one another. An idolater will not eat bread nor drink water in a house belonging to anyone of a different caste from his own, unless it be more noble and more exalted than his; thus they can all eat and drink in the houses of the Bramines, which are open to all the world. Among these idolaters a caste is, so to speak, what a tribe was among the Jews, and although it is commonly believed that there are seventy-two of these castes, I have ascertained from the most accomplished of their priests that they can be reduced to four principal castes from which all others derive their origin.[36]

Tavernier then launches into a description of the *chaturvarṇa* system, the four castes in his view being Brahmins, Rajputs or Khattris, Banians, and Charados or Soudras; he also adds a fifth caste of artisans, "who occupy themselves with mechanical arts", and then adds the untouchables, whom he terms "alacors", perhaps from the Persian *ḥalāl-k͟hwor*. His view here thus both contributes to and confirms what were, by the middle of the seventeenth century, the stable topoi through which India was being addressed in European accounts: caste, *sati*, the Juggernaut (or the temple-chariot of Jagannath), and idolatry.

A comparison between the texts of Coutre and Tavernier is thus instructive. Though separated by less than half a century, and dealing very often with very similar themes (since both had substantial interests in the jewel trade), the two nevertheless are based on somewhat different notions of what they are attempting to compose. In both cases, the authorship is more than a little problematic, though clearly far more so for Tavernier than for Coutre. While Coutre holds more strictly to the notion of the "life story", Tavernier departs from it in two ways. First, we learn little or

[36] Jean-Baptiste Tavernier, *Travels in India*, ed. and tr. Valentine Ball and William Crooke, 2 vols. (reprint, Delhi, 1989), vol. II, pp. 141–2.

nothing concerning those periods of his life when he was not in the Ottoman, Safavid or Mughal domains, such as the years from 1633 to 1638. Second, Tavernier's work is far more clearly constructed as a treatise, illustrated with anecdotes, than as a tale of adventure. The utilitarian aspect of the work also resides in its preoccupation with weights, measures and coins, in which it seems to be motivated by the idea that some of its readers might themselves contemplate trading with the regions that are described. Tavernier, more than Coutre, wishes to present himself consistently as an "expert", and it was in this sense that he was indeed perceived, right to the end of his life. For, as late as 1684, he was invited to Berlin by Friedrich-Wilhelm, Elector of Brandenburg, who wished to create his own East India Company and suggested that Tavernier might accept the position of ambassdor to the Mughal court. The traveller was sufficiently tempted by this to sell his property in Aubonne, and set off eastwards, apparently deciding to pass through Russia. He appears to have died near Smolensk in 1689, not far from where that unfortunate traveller Nikitin had given up the ghost two centuries earlier.

FINAL REFLECTIONS

It is certainly tempting to compare the travellers who have occupied us over the bulk of this work with the Europeans who came in increasing numbers to Asia over the early modern period. It is equally certain that, if we were to engage in a systematic comparison, we would find some interesting points of convergence: thus we might compare Coutre's or Tavernier's description of the Tirupati temple with that which we have noticed in Mahmud Wali Balkhi.[37] Or again, we might compare the description of a great city such as Vijayanagara from the pen of 'Abdur Razzaq Samarqandi with that from a Portuguese visitor of the 1510s or 1520s. Such exercises have been attempted periodically in recent times, largely in the context of a rather tired debate, centring on the utility of the perspective in Edward Said's work *Orientalism* for the analysis of early modern European travel accounts to Asia. If some have argued in this context that Europeans reduced a complex set of phenomena to a narrow range of clichés regarding India, thus "inscribing" India in the European imagination, others have tried to demonstrate that this relationship between empirical observation and representation was either largely

[37] In this context, see Subrahmanyam, "An eastern El-Dorado", pp. 338–90.

unmediated by power relations, or was the same whether one looks at the Indo-Persian corpus, or that of European writers.[38]

Our conclusions would necessarily require us to nuance this comparison. There is, in the first place, the problem of the production and circulation of the travel-texts themselves. A recent analysis by Daniel Roche suggests the following picture, based on the materials in Boucher de la Richarderie's *Bibliothèque universelle des voyages*, the six volumes of which were published in Paris between 1806 and 1808.[39] Of a total of 5,562 European works on travel between 1500 and 1800 that have been counted, we begin with a modest 456 in the sixteenth century, expanding to 1,566 in the seventeenth century, and more than doubling again to 3,540 in the eighteenth century. In the sixteenth century, works in Latin, Greek and Hebrew together constitute the major category, followed by Italian and Spanish taken together. In the centuries that follow, this picture is transformed. In the seventeenth century, French comes to dominate with 35 per cent of the total, followed by German and Dutch. Eventually, the eighteenth century sees the rise to prominence of English (accounting for a quarter of the total), though French, German and Dutch continue to hold their own.[40] On the other hand, Latin, Greek and Hebrew taken together have declined to a mere 1.5 per cent by the eighteenth century. Also of interest is the geographical distribution of these voyages; for, outside Europe, it is clearly Asia that occupies the position of greatest prominence, followed by America. Further, it is evident that the great expansion of interest in Asia is in the seventeenth century, when it briefly almost equals Europe in terms of numbers of accounts. Within Asia, it is the Indies (meaning India and South-east Asia) that easily dominate, followed at some distance by China and Persia.

A quantitative exercise such as the one summarised above is naturally fraught with problems regarding its data-base, but it is nevertheless

[38] Kate Teltscher, *India inscribed: European and British writing on India, 1600–1800* (Delhi, 1995); Rubiés, *Travel and ethnology in the Renaissance*, pp. 279–87, 390–1. Here, Rubiés appears to follow in the footsteps of Peter Burke, who wishes to see early modern European travellers in Asia as unproblematic, since they are full of "sympathy for Indian culture"; see Burke, "The philosopher as traveller: Bernier's Orient", in Jaś Elsner and Joan-Pau Rubiés, eds., *Voyages and visions: towards a cultural history of travel* (London, 1999), pp. 124–37. Burke's simplistic view may be usefully contrasted to the far more subtle analysis in Sylvia Murr, "Le politique 'au Mogol' selon Bernier: appareil conceptuel, rhétorique stratégique, philosophie morale", in Jacques Pouchepadass and Henri Stern, eds., *De la royauté à l'Etat dans le monde indien* (Paris, 1990), pp. 239–302.

[39] Daniel Roche, *Humeurs vagabondes: de la circulation des hommes et de l'utilité des voyages* (Paris, 2003), pp. 33–5.

[40] On the growing significance of English travellers and their accounts, see John Stoye, *English travellers abroad, 1604–1667: their influence in English society and politics* (London, 1989).

indicative of some important trends. What is also implicit in such an exercise is the notion that most works must have found their way into print, since it is only printed texts that are being counted. By this measure, works such as that of Coutre would be excluded from consideration. Yet, there is no denying the dominance of print in the world of the early modern European travel-account, a fact that sets this world apart from the Indo-Persian one that we have surveyed. None of the Persian texts that we have cited were printed until the nineteenth century, and it is ironical that the first printed versions of a few (such as 'Abdul Karim Shahristani's *Bayān-i Wāqi'*) were their English translations. The world that we have written of is thus essentially one of the production, copying and circulation of manuscripts, and to this extent the public that our texts reached was also rather different from that addressed by European texts, especially in the eighteenth century. The exigencies of the market that seemed to have weighed very heavily on the European travel-account thus simply did not have the same meaning in the context of the Indo-Persian corpus, where the reader was not the "buyer" of the work.

It is also a far more limited world in quantitative terms, with our corpus never coming close to the 5,000 and more works of the European corpus. It is thus not a coincidence that the discussion of early modern travel accounts has hitherto focused so largely on European travels; the sheer weight of the body of accounts is imposing. Yet, this cannot be reason enough to reject or set aside the accounts we have studied. For one, these accounts possess an internal diversity and a set of variations in terms of perspective which are in themselves valuable. Thus, the writings of Mahmud Wali Balkhi both speak to, and differ from, that of Khwaja 'Abdul Karim; they belong in the same world of texts, and yet differ from one another in substantial ways. This takes us then to the principal point that should be emphasised by way of conclusion. The authors that we have cited, summarised and analysed in the course of these pages represent a world of their own; they are aware of one another, read and cite one another, and thus constitute a collective reflection that one cannot seize hold of if one chooses to study each in isolation. Much has been written of the emergence of a "republic of letters" in the early modern period, usually focusing on the European (or Euro-American) experience. We are familiar with the terms of this construct: the emergence of parallel institutions in different parts, such as academies; the importance of translation in a world where Latin and Greek were losing ground; the ties between the production of such knowledge and the emergence of imperial centres such as Paris and London. The Indo-Persian republic of letters, if we may call it that, was a different one from that cited above. Its institutional bases were less controlled and less homogeneous. No academy instructed our travellers on "how to see", and there was no well-defined framework for what Roche has termed the "disciplined voyage".[41] Equally, this was not a world that had been broken up into a dozen competing vernaculars; rather, it was one where, as late as 1750, Persian still indisputably held the high ground.

This would not be the case a hundred or even seventy-five years later. The nineteenth century sees the emergence of print in a South Asian context, and it also sees a veritable explosion in terms of travel-accounts. These are no longer in Persian for the most part; on the one hand, the travel-account in Urdu emerges to take up much space, and on the other, works of and on travel in languages such as Telugu, Bengali and a host of other vernaculars emerge.[42] Some of these deal with Europe, but many others are concerned with travels within South Asia. Ironically then, it is the moment of colonisation – some moment between 1800 and 1850 – that defines the end of the Indo-Persian travel-text; there are certainly travel-accounts written in Persian after this date, but they belong largely to an Iran that has increasingly turned its back on South Asia and the larger Persophone world. Writers like Mirza Abu Talib Khan and Shaikh I'tisam-ud-Din thus represent the last gasp of the corpus we have surveyed, and they look to a world in which Britannia already rules.

Yet, at the highwater mark of the Indo-Persian travel-text, in the seventeenth and eighteenth centuries, they constituted a highly significant corpus of knowledge and a significant effort towards the representation of the world, whether distant or proximate. Despite, or perhaps because of, the fact that they largely existed outside the world of print, notions of authorship were relatively stable here. This may seem paradoxical in view of debates regarding the emergence of the "author function" in a European context.[43] Nevertheless, it is worth insisting upon the fact that, of all the texts that we have surveyed, only one – that of Bayazid Bayat – bears the clear traces of the intervention of an amanuensis. This clearly

[41] Joan-Pau Rubiés, "Instructions for travellers: teaching the eye to see", *History and Anthropology*, 9, 2–3, 1996, pp. 139–90.

[42] Chatterjee, "Discovering India", pp. 192–227; Velcheru Narayana Rao and Sanjay Subrahmanyam, "Circulation, piety and innovation: recounting travels in early nineteenth-century South India", in Claude Markovits *et al.*, *Society and Circulation: Mobile People and itinerant cultures in South Asia, 1750–1950* (New Delhi, 2003), pp. 306–55.

[43] See, for instance, Roger Chartier, *The order of books: readers, authors, and libraries in Europe between the fourteenth and eighteenth centuries*, tr. Lydia Cochrane (Stanford, 1994), pp. 25–60.

distinguishes such texts both from their European counterparts (where the problem of authorship is almost impossible to resolve in a vast number of cases), and from other South Asian textual traditions, such as those of poetical production. The problem of establishing authorship in the case of poetry, whether in the Indian vernaculars or even in Persian, is of course notorious: it suffices that an author acquires fame for texts to be attributed to him (or her), thus swelling an initially modest corpus enormously, even after the author's death. On the contrary, the texts that we have dealt with are marked by their clear authorship and their powerful definition of an authorial voice. The distinctive stylistic flavour of a Mahmud Wali Balkhi or a Muhammad ʻAli Hazin is a central part of the appeal of the text, and of the seductive self-presentation of the author.

What of notions of truth in these texts? Here, we must constantly recall that these authors belonged to a well-defined and delimited universe, the values and limits of which they recognised. This was the domain of the literati, related in turn to the structures of the states that emerged in the post-Timur world. It was understood that such groups had their norms of comportment (*adab*), in turn linked to notions such as *mīrzā'ī* or "gentility".[44] It was a world that permitted trade, and saw the association with the holders of power as positive, so long as the proximity did not grow beyond certain bounds. The truth-teller in this world was not necessarily defined in terms of his religion, for, as we have seen, Hindus as much as Muslims could find a place in this world. Rather, he (or quite rarely she) was defined through an education, a set of proper references, received notions of honour, proper conduct and behaviour, and the capacity to respond to given situations (including hardship), that we find repeated time and again in our texts. In some respects, therefore, we are not all that distant from the situation in seventeenth-century Europe, where – as Steven Shapin reminds us – "gentility was a massively powerful instrument in the recognition, constitution, and protection of truth".[45] This said, much separated the terms of definition of the English "gentleman" and the Indo-Persian "*mīrzā*", a problem that hence could not

[44] Barbara D. Metcalf, ed., *Moral conduct and authority: the place of adab in South Asian Islam* (Berkeley, 1984); Rosalind O'Hanlon, "Manliness and imperial service in Mughal North India", *Journal of the Economic and Social History of the Orient*, 42, 1, 1999, pp. 47–93. O'Hanlon draws on such texts as Hidayat Husain, "The Mirza Nama (The book of the perfect gentleman) of Mirza Kamran", *Journal of the Asiatic Society of Bengal*, 9, 1, 1913, pp. 1–13. It is interesting to note that F. Steingass's *Comprehensive Persian–English dictionary* defines *mīrzā* or *mirzā* as a "prince; son of a great lord, noble cavalier, knight; a gentleman; a writer, scribe".

[45] Steven Shapin, *A social history of truth: civility and science in seventeenth-century England* (Chicago, 1994), p. 42.

find easy resolution in the early colonial period in South Asia.[46] Still, there was enough that was clearly common between the two sets of conventions for a Khwaja 'Abdul Karim to be referred to as "a Cashmerian of distinction", and hence as a credible source.

In the early nineteenth century, a Mughal prince, Mirza 'Ali Bakht "Azfari", exiled in the court of the Nawwab of Arcot in South India, wrote his memoir-cum-travel-account, a text that he called the *Wāqi'āt-i Aẓfarī*, in a gesture towards the Persian title of the memoirs of his great ancestor Babur.[47] It is a relatively obscure, but significant work, which is made up of two parts. In the first section, Azfari writes of his life as a prisoner in Shahjahanabad, where he and other Mughal princes were kept in a gilded cage (what he terms *qaid-i salāṭīnī*). Then, in the second part, he writes of how, from the age of about thirty, he began to travel, seeking the aid of various powers to mount the Mughal throne, until – after a long sojourn in Awadh – he eventually came to settle in southern India. These travels take him over much of the former Mughal domains, from Jaipur and Jodhpur, to the Gangetic plain, Bengal and the far south. It is Azfari's conceit that he is a mere wanderer in the "steppe of astonishment" (*dasht-i taḥayyur*); but he also wishes to point out the significance of his travels and experiences for other readers, including his own children. One aspect of the text is striking, however, and this is a linguistic reflection that the Mughal prince insists upon. For, in his view, Mughal rule was established not through Persian but through Turkish, and once Turkish declined (perhaps by the early eighteenth century), the Mughals were doomed. As one of the last Mughals who claimed to be fully literate in Turkish, Azfari implicitly denigrates the place of Persian that he sees as effeminate and not sufficiently vigorous, as distinct from masculine and warlike Turkish. Yet, as late as 1810, it was in the Persian language that he himself chose to write, disregarding in a certain sense his own advice. Perhaps it was a matter of finding a readership, but we cannot set aside the hypothesis that it was because he possessed other Persian travel-accounts in his library, and hence thought to model his own work on a received tradition.

[46] This issue is addressed in Kapil Raj, "Refashioning civilities, engineeering trust: William Jones, Indian intermediaries and the production of reliable legal knowledge in late 18th-century Bengal", *Studies in History* (n.s.), 17, 2, 2001, pp. 175–209.

[47] For the Persian text, see *Wāqi'āt-i Aẓfarī*, ed. Syed Hamza Hussain Omari and gen. ed. T. Chandrasekharan, and for a faithful Urdu translation, see Muhammad Husain Mahvi Siddiqi, *Wāqi'āt-i-Azfarī* (Madras, 1937). We have discussed this personage at greater length elsewhere; see Alam and Subrahmanyam, "Power in prison", pp. 303–34.

In his latter years, Azfari seems to have regretted his youth in Delhi, which he even looked back upon with a certain nostalgia. Yet, he also writes of how, as long as he was a prisoner there, his dreams constantly returned to the theme of travel. One of these dreams was as follows, as he himself describes it.

> Five or six years before I escaped from the Auspicious Fort, one night I saw a dream in which there was a break in the western wall of the fort through which I come out, and head southwards. In the evening, I reach a place where there is a shrine of a holy man, with imposing and beautiful buildings. Around the grave of the saint, there is a silver railing too high to allow me to place flowers on it. I keep trying to do so, but my hand cannot reach. After many attempts, I manage to place the flowers there. When I really left the fort, and arrived at the shrine of Khwaja Mu'in-ud-Din Chishti [in Ajmer], everything happened exactly as in the dream, and I saw it with my own eyes.

Travel here is no more than the fulfilment of a dream, the concrete realisation of something that one has already seen and perhaps felt. Travel for the Indo-Persian voyager, however, especially one who wandered in the "steppe of astonishment", was not always bound up with the sentiment of *déjà vu.* If we have conveyed something of a sense of the complex emotions and experiences, the varying mix of empirical accumulation, truth-telling and rooted prejudice, that characterises this corpus, we will have fulfilled the aim we set for ourselves. Travel was not always hell, either for the travellers in question or for their readers – whether of yesteryear or even, we do hope, today.

Bibliography

TEXTS

'Abdul Karim(Khwaja) ibn Khwaja 'Aqibat Mahmud Kashmiri, *Bayān-i Wāqi': a biography of Nādir Shāh Afshār and the travels of the author*, ed. K. B. Nasim (Lahore, 1970).

'Abdul Qadir, Khwaja, *Waqā'i'-i Manāzil-i Rūm: diary of a journey to Constantinople by Khwāja 'Abdul Qādir* ed. Mohibbul Hasan (New York, 1968).

'Abdur Razzaq ibn Ishaq Samarqandi, *Maṭla' us-Sa'dain wa Majma' ul-Baḥrain*, part I, ed. 'Abdul Husain Nawa'i (Tehran, 1353 Sh. / 1974); part II, ed. Muhammad Shafi' (Lahore, 1365–8 H / 1946–9).

Abu'l Fazl, Shaikh, *Mukātabāt-i 'Allāmī (Inshā'-i Abu'l Fazl)*, ed. Muhammad Hadi 'Ali (Lucknow, 1863).

Abu Talib Khan Isfahani, Mirza, *Masīr-i Ṭālibī fī bilād-i afranjī*, ed. Mirza Husain 'Ali and Mir Qudrat 'Ali (Calcutta, 1812).

Al-Biruni, Abu Raihan Muhammad ibn Ahmad, *Kitāb fī Taḥqīq mā lil-Hind min maqūlah maqbūlah fī al-'aql aw marzulah* (Hyderabad, 1958).

'Ali Bakht Bahadur Muhammad Zahir-ud-Din Azfari, Mirza, *Wāqi'āt-i Azfarī*, ed. Syed Hamza Hussain Omari, gen. ed. T. Chandrasekharan (Madras, 1957).

Amir Khusrau Dehlawi, *Qirān-us-Sa'dain*, ed. Ahmad Hasan Dani (Islamabad, 1976).

Anonymous, *Wāqi'ah-i Kharābī-yi Dehlī dar 'ahd-i Muḥammad Shāh az wurūd-i Nādir Shāh wālī-yi Irān*, ed. Sharif Husain Qasemi (Delhi, 1990).

Anonymous, "Safar Nāma-i Manẓūm-i Ḥajj", ed. Rasul Ja'fariyan, in *Mīrāṣ-i Islāmī Irān* ("The heritage of Islamic Iran"), vol. IX (1373–4 Sh. / 1994–5), pp. 337–91.

Aqa Ahmad Bihbahani, *Safar Nāma-i Hind (India in the early 19th century: an Iranian's travel account)*, compiled Shayesta Khan (Patna, 1992).

Aqa Ahmad ibn Muhammad 'Ali Bihbahani, *Mir'āt al-Aḥwāl-i Jahānnumā: Bakhsh yakum*, ed. 'Ali Dawwani (Tehran, 1370 Sh. / 1991).

Babur, Zahir-ud-Din Muhammad, *Bāburnāma: Chaghatay Turkish text with Abdul-Rahim Khankhanan's Persian translation*, ed. Wheeler M. Thackston, 3 vols. (Cambridge, Mass., 1993).

Bayazid Bayat, *Tazkira-i-Humāyūn wa Akbar of Bāyazīd Biyāt (A history of the Emperor Humayun from A.H. 949 [AD 1542] and of his successor the emperor Akbar up to A.H. 999 [AD 1590])*, ed. M. Hidayat Hosain (Calcutta, 1941).

Beal, Samuel, tr., *Si-yu-ki: Buddhist records of the Western world translated from the Chinese of Hiuen Tsiang (A.D. 629)* (London, 1884).

Bihishti Herawi (ʻAbdullah Sani). *Nūr al-Mashriqain: Safar-nāma-i manẓūm az ʻahd-i Ṣafawī*, ed. Najib Mayil Herawi (Mashhad, 1998).

Dargah Quli Khan, *Muraqqaʻ-i Dehlī*, ed. Nurul Hasan Ansari (New Delhi, 1982).

Evliyā Tchélébi, *La Guerre des Turcs: récits de batailles extraits du Livre de voyage*, tr. F. Bilici (Paris, 2000).

Ghulam ʻAli Azad Bilgrami, Sayyid, *Subḥat ul-Marjān fī āṣār-i Hindūstān*, ed. Muhammad Fazlur Rahman Nadvi Sewani (Aligarh, 1975).

Gulbadan Begam, *Humāyūn Nāma*, ed. and tr. Annette S. Beveridge (reprint, Lahore, 1974).

Hakluyt, Richard, *The principal navigations, voyages, traffiques and discoveries of the English nation*, vol. 1 (Glasgow, 1903).

Ibn Fadlan, *Voyage chez les Bulgares de la Volga (il y a mille ans)*, tr. Marius Canard (Paris, 1988).

Jauhar Aftabchi, *Taẕkirāt ul-Wāqiʻāt*, tr. into Urdu by S. Moinul Haq (Karachi, 1955).

Katib Çelebi, *Gihan Numa, Geographia orientalis*, tr. M. Norberg, 2 vols. (Londini Gothorum, 1818).

Tuḥfetü'l-kibar fi Esfāri'l-biḥār, ed. Orhan Şaik Gökyay (Istanbul, 1973).

Khwandamir, *Qānūn-i Humāyūnī, also known as Humāyūn Nāma: a work on the rules and ordinances established by the emperor Humayun and on some buildings erected by his orders*, ed. M. Hidayat Hosain (Calcutta, 1940).

Khwurshah ibn Qubad al-Husaini, *Tārīkh-i Quṭbī, nīz musammā bih Tārīkh-i Īlchī-i Niẓām Shāh: Maqālah-i panjum, tārīkh-i Āl-i Tīmūr az Tīmūr tā Akbar*, ed. Sayyid Mujahid Husain Zaydi (New Delhi, 1965).

Tārīkh-i īlchī-i Niẓām Shāh: Tārīkh-i Ṣafawīyah az āghāz tā sāl-i 972 Hijrī Qamarī, ed. Muhammad Riza Nasiri and Koichi Haneda (Tehran, 2000).

Mahmud bin Amir Wali Balkhi, *The Baḥr ul-asrār: travelogue of South Asia*, intro., ed. and annot. by Riazul Islam (Karachi, 1980).

Mahmud ibn Amir Wali Balkhi, *Baḥr al-asrār fī maʻrifat al-akhyār*, ed. Hakim Muhammad Saʻid, Sayyid Muʻinul Haqq and Ansar Zahid Khan (Karachi, 1984).

Morali Seyyid ʻAli Efendi and Seyyid ʻAbdürrahim Muhibb Efendi, *Deux Ottomans à Paris sous le Directoire et l'Empire: relations d'ambassade*, tr. Stéphane Yerasimos (Paris, 1998).

Muhammad ʻAli ibn Abi Talib ibn ʻAbd Allah (Hazin), *Tārīkh wa Safar nāma-i Ḥazīn (1154)*, in *Diwān-i Ḥazīn-i Lāhījī: Shāmil-i qaṣāʼid, ghazalīyāt, maṣnawīyāt, rubāʻīyāt*, ed. Bizhan Taraqqi (Tehran, 1350 / 1971), pp. 1–107.

Muhammad Kazim, *Nāma-i ʻĀlamārā-yi Nādirī*, 3 vols. (Moscow, 1960–6).

Muhammad Mahdi Khan Astarabadi, Mirza, *Jahān-gushā-yi Nādirī*, ed. Sayyid ʻAbdullah Anwar (Tehran, 1961–2).

Mirza Muhammad Mufid Mustaufi ibn Najm-ud-Din Mahmud Bafiqi Yazdi, "Risāla-i Mufīd", Bodleian Library, Oxford, Ms. Ouseley, no. 90.

Jāmi'i Mufīdī: Persian text of XI Century A.H. on history of Yazd, by Muḥammad Mufid Mustowfi Bafiqi, ed. Iraj Afshar, 3 vols. (Tehran, 1960–3).

Moḫtaṣar-e Mofīd des Moḥammad Mofīd Mostoufī, vols. I and II, ed. Seyfeddin Najmabadi (Wiesbaden, 1989–91).

Muhammad Rabi' bin Muhammad Ibrahim, *Safīna-i Sulaimānī (Safar Nāma-i Sāfir-i Irān ba Siyām, 1094–1098 H.)*, ed. 'Abbas Faruqi (Tehran, 1977).

Muhsin Fani (or Mubad Kaykhusrau Isfandiyar), *Dabistān-i maẕāhib*, ed. Rahim Riza'zadah Malik, 2 vols. (Tehran, 1983).

Muhyi Lari, *Futūḥ ul-ḥaramain: Shā'ir-i sadah-i nuhum wa āg̱hāz-i sadah-i dahum*, ed. 'Ali Muhaddis (Tehran, 1366 Kh. / 1987).

Futūḥ ul-Ḥaramain, ed. Rasul Ja'fariyan (Qom, 1373 Kh. / 1994).

Mustafa Na'ima, *Tārīḵẖ-i Na'īma: Rauẓat ul-Ḥusain fī ḵẖulāsat-i aḵẖbār al-ḵẖāfiqain*, 6 vols. (Istanbul, 1863).

Mutribi Samarqandi, *Ḵẖāṭirāt-i-Muṭribī Samarqandī (being the memoirs of Muṭribī's sessions with Emperor Jahāngīr)*, ed. 'Abdul Ghani Mirzoyef (Karachi, 1977).

Nusḵẖa-yi Zība-yi Jahāngīr, ed. Isma'il Bikjanuf and Sayyid 'Ali Mawjani (Qom, 1377 Sh. / 1998).

Taẕkirat ush-Shu'rā', ed. Asghar Janfida and 'Ali Rafi'i 'Ala Marwdashti (Tehran, 1377 Sh. / 1998).

Nasir-i Khusrau, *Nāṣir-i Ḵẖusraw's book of travels (Safarnāmah): a parallel Persian–English text*, ed. and tr. Wheeler M. Thackston (Costa Mesa, 2001).

Nur-ud-Din Muhammad Jahangir, *Tūzuk-i Jahāngīrī*, ed. Syud Ahmud Khan (Aligarh, 1864).

Osman Agha de Temechvar, *Prisonnier des infidèles: un soldat dans l'empire des Habsbourg*, tr. Frédéric Hitzel (Paris, 1998).

Pinto, Fernão Mendes, *Peregrinaçam de Fernam Mendez Pinto; em que da conta de muytas e muyto estranhas cousas que vio & ouuio no reyno da China, no da Tartaria, no do Sornau, que vulgarmente se chama Sião, no do Calaminhan, no de Pegù, no de Martauão, & em outros muytos reynos & senhorios das partes Orientais . . .* (Lisbon, 1614).

Salman Savaji, *Kulliyāt-i Salmān Sāvajī*, ed. 'Abbas 'Ali Wafa'i (Tehran, 1382 Sh. / 2004).

Sayyid 'Ali Akbar Khata'i, *Ḵẖaṭāy-nāma*, ed. Iraj Afshar (Tehran, 1357 Sh. / 1968).

Sayyid Muhammad 'Ali al-Husaini, *Tārīḵẖ-i Rāḥat-afzā*, ed. S. Khwurshid 'Ali (Hyderabad, 1366 H / 1957).

Seydi 'Ali Re'is, *Mir'ātü'l-Memālik*, ed. Mehmet Kiremit (Ankara, 1999).

Seydi 'Ali Re'is (Sayyidi 'Ali Katibi), *Mir'āt al-mamālik: Safar Nāma ba Ḵẖalīj-i Fārs, Hind, Māwarannahr wa Irān*, tr. Mahmud Tafazzuli and 'Ali Ganjali (Tehran, 1355 Sh. / 1976).

Seyyidi [Seydi] 'Ali Re'is, *Le miroir des pays: une anabase ottomane à travers l'Inde et l'Asie centrale*, tr. Jean-Louis Bacqué-Grammont (Paris, 1999).

Shah Muhammad 'Ali Samani, *Siyar-i Muḥammadī*, ed., with an Urdu translation, by Sayyid Shah Nazir Ahmad Qadiri Sikandarpuri (Gulbarga, 1399 H / 1979).
Shah Tahmasp Safavi, *Taẕkira-i Shāh Ṭahmāsp (Memoirs of Shah Tahmasp)*, ed. D. C. Phillott (Calcutta, 1912).
Siraj-ud-Din 'Ali Khan Arzu, *Tanbīh al-Ghāfilīn*, ed. Sayyid Muhammad Akram 'Ikram (Lahore, 1981).
Tahir Muhammad Sabzwari, "Rauẓat uṭ-Ṭāhirīn", Bodleian Library, Oxford, Ms. Elliot 314 (Sachau-Ethé no. 100); British Library, London, Ms. Or. 168.
Tahmasp Khan, *Ṭahmās Nāmeh by Ṭahmās Beg Khān*, ed. Muhammad Aslam (Lahore, 1986).
Vambéry, Arminius, ed. and tr. *The travels and adventures of the Turkish admiral Sidi Ali Reis in India, Afghanistan, Central Asia and Persia* (London, 1899; reprint, Lahore, 1975).
Zain-ud-Din Ma'bari, *Tuḥfat al-mujāhidīn fī ba'ẓ-i aḥwāl al-Burtukāliyyīn*, David Lopes, ed. and tr., *História dos Portugueses no Malavar por Zinadím* (Lisbon, 1899).

OTHER REFERENCES

'Abdullah, Sayyid Muhammad, "Fārsī ke Zer-i Sāya Zabān-i Urdū ki Tadrījī Taraqqī", in S. 'Abdullah, *Mabāḥiṣ* (Lahore, 1965), pp. 70–95.
Abeydeera, Ananda, "Jean de Marignolli: l'envoyé du Pape au Jardin d'Adam", in Catherine Weinberger-Thomas, ed., *L'Inde et l'imaginaire*, Collection Puruṣârtha 11, (Paris, 1988), pp. 57–67.
Ahmad, Aijaz, "Between Orientalism and historicism: anthropological knowledge of India", *Studies in History*, n.s., 7, 1 , 1991, pp. 135–63.
Ahmad, S. Maqbul, "'Abd-al-Karīm bin Khvāja 'Āqebat Maḥmūd bin Khvāja Bolāqī Kashmīrī", in Ehsan Yarshater, ed., *Encyclopaedia iranica*, vol. 1, part 1 (New York, 1982), p. 125.
Ahmad Shah Naqshbandi, "Narrative of the travels of Khwajah Ahmud Shah Nukshbundee Syud", *Journal of the Asiatic Society of Bengal*, 25, 4, 1856, pp. 344–58.
Ahuja, N. D., "Abd al-Latīf al 'Abbāsī and his account of Punjab", *Islamic Culture*, 41, 2, 1967, pp. 93–8.
Akhmedov, B. A., "The *Baḥr al-Asrār* of Maḥmūd b. Valī and its study in the USSR and elsewhere", *Journal of Asian History*, 25, 2, 1991, pp. 163–80.
Alam, Muzaffar, *The crisis of empire in Mughal North India: Awadh and the Punjab, 1707–1748* (Delhi, 1986).
"The pursuit of Persian: language in Mughal Politics", *Modern Asian Studies*, 32, 1998, pp. 317–49.
"The culture and politics of Persian in precolonial Hindustan", in Sheldon Pollock, ed., *Literary cultures in history: reconstructions from South Asia* (Berkeley, 2003), pp. 131–98.

The languages of political Islam in India, c. 1200–1800 (New Delhi, 2004).
Alam, Muzaffar, Françoise N. Delvoye and Marc Gaborieau, eds., *The making of Indo-Persian culture: Indian and French Studies* (New Delhi, 2000).
Alam, Muzaffar, and Sanjay Subrahmanyam, "Discovering the familiar: notes on the travel-account of Anand Ram Mukhlis", *South Asia Research*, 16, 2, 1996, pp. 131–54.
"From an ocean of wonders: Maḥmūd bin Amīr Walī Balkhī and his Indian travels, 1625–1631", in Claudine Salmon, ed., *Récits de voyage des Asiatiques: genres, mentalités, conception de l'espace* (Paris, 1996), pp. 161–89.
"Witnessing transition: views on the end of the Akbari dispensation", in K. N. Panikkar, Terence J. Byres and Utsa Patnaik, eds., *The making of history: essays presented to Irfan Habib* (New Delhi, 2000), pp. 104–40.
"A place in the sun: travels with Faiẓī in the Deccan, 1591–93", in François Grimal, ed., *Les sources et le temps / Sources and time: a colloquium* (Pondicherry, 2001), pp. 265–307.
"Power in prison: a Mughal prince in Shahjahanabad, ca. 1800", in Véronique Bouillier and Catherine Servan-Schreiber, eds., *De l'Arabie à l'Himalaya: chemins croisés, en hommage à Marc Gaborieau* (Paris, 2004), pp. 303–34.
"The Deccan frontier and Mughal expansion, ca. 1600: contemporary perspectives", *Journal of the Economic and Social History of the Orient*, 47, 3, 2004, pp. 357–89.
"The making of a Munshi", *Comparative Studies of South Asia, Africa and the Middle East*, 24, 2, 2004, pp. 61–72.
Alexander, J. E., *Shigurf namah-i-velaët: or excellent intelligence concerning Europe; being the travels of Mirza Itesa Modeen, translated from the original Persian manuscripts into Hindostanee, with an English version and notes* (London, 1827).
Ali, M. Athar, *The Mughal nobility under Aurangzeb* (Bombay, 1966).
Alves, Jorge Manuel dos Santos, *Um porto entre dois impérios: estudos sobre Macau e as relações luso-chinesas* (Macau, 1999).
Alvi, Sajida Sultana, ed. and tr. with intro., *Advice on the art of governance: Mau'iẓah-i Jahāngīrī of Muḥammad Bāqir Najm-i Ṣānī, an Indo-Islamic mirror for princes* (Albany, 1989).
Andrews, Walter G., Najaat Black and Mehmet Kalpakli, ed. and tr. *Ottoman lyric poetry: an anthology* (Austin, 1997).
Anonymous, *Notable, y prodigiosa relacion, que truxo el padre Geronymo Xauier de la Compañia de Iesvs, en que se da cuenta de un animal, o monstruo, que está en la provincia de Vengala, que penetra todo lo passado, y futuro, en tal grado que parece persona racional . . .* (Granada, 1612).
Ansari, Zoe, ed., *Life, times and works of Amīr Khusrau Dehlavi* (New Delhi, 1975).
Aris, Michael, *'Jigs-med-gling-pa's "Discourse on India" of 1789* (Tokyo, 1995).
Asiye Hatun, *Rüya Mektuplari*, ed. and intro. Cemal Kafadar (Istanbul, 1994).
Aubin, Jean, "Les princes d'Ormuz du XIIIe au XVe siècle", *Journal asiatique*, 241, 1, 1953, pp. 77–138.

"Quelques notices du Mukhtaṣar-i Mufīd", *Farhang-i Irān Zamīn*, 6, 1958, pp. 164–77.
"Comment Tamerlan prenait les villes", *Studia Islamica*, 19, 1963, pp. 83–122.
"Les Persans au Siam sous le règne de Narai (1656–1688)", *Mare Luso-Indicum*, 4, 1980, pp. 95–126.
"De Kûhbanân à Bidar: la famille Ni'matullâhi", *Studia Iranica*, 20, 1991, pp. 233–61.
Émirs mongols et vizirs persans dans les remous de l'acculturation (Paris, 1995).
"Les frustrations de Duarte Pacheco Pereira", in J. Aubin, *Le latin et l'astrolabe*, vol. I: *Recherches sur le Portugal de la Renaissance, son expansion en Asie et les relations internationales* (Paris, 1996), pp. 111–32.
"Le royaume d'Ormuz au début du XVIe siècle", in J. Aubin, *Le latin et l'astrolabe*, vol. II: *Recherches sur le Portugal de la Renaissance, son expansion en Asie et les relations internationales* (Paris, 2000), pp. 287–376.
"Merchants in the Red Sea and the Persian Gulf at the turn of the fifteenth and sixteenth centuries", in Denys Lombard and Jean Aubin, eds., *Asian merchants and businessmen in the Indian Ocean and the China Sea* (Delhi, 2000), pp. 79–86.
Avery, Peter, "Nadir Shah and the Afsharid legacy", in Peter Avery, Gavin Hambly and Charles Melville, eds., *The Cambridge history of Iran*, vol. VII (Cambridge, 1991), pp. 3–62.
Babaie, Sussan, Kathryn Babayan and Ina Baghdiantz McCabe, *Slaves of the Shah: new elites of Safavid Iran* (London, 2004).
Babayan, Kathryn, "'In spirit we ate of each other's sorrow': female companionship in seventeenth-century Safavi Iran", in Kathryn Babayan and Afsaneh Najmabadi, eds., *Middle Eastern and sexuality studies: translations across temporal and geographical zones of desire* (Ann Arbor, forthcoming).
Baião, António, ed., *Comentários do Grande Afonso de Albuquerque, capitão geral que foi das Índias Orientais em tempo do muito poderoso rey D. Manuel, o primeiro deste nome*, 2 vols. (Coimbra, 1922–3).
Bakić-Hayden, Milica, "Nesting Orientalisms: the case of former Yugoslavia", *Slavic Review*, 54, 4, 1995, pp. 917–31.
Bayly, C. A., *Empire and information: intelligence gathering and social communication in India, 1780–1870* (Cambridge, 1996).
Bayur, Yusuf Hikmet, "Maysor Sultanı Tipu ile Osmanlı pâdişahlarından I. Abdülhamid ve III. Selim Arasındaki Mektuplaşma", *Belleten (Türk Tarih Kurumu)*, 12, 47, 1948, pp. 617–54.
Hindistan Tarihi, vol. III: *Nadir Şah Afşar'in akınından bagımsızlık ve cumhuriyete kadar (1737–1949)* (Ankara, 1950).
"Osmanlı Padişahı II. Süleyman'ın Gürkanlı Padişahı I. Alamgir (Evrengzeb)'e Mektubu", *Belleten (Türk Tarih Kurumu)*, 14, 53, 1950, pp. 269–87.
Beelaert, Anna Livia Fermina Alexandra, *A cure for the grieving: studies on the poetry of the 12th-century Persian court poet Khāqāni Širwānī* (Leiden, 1996).

Brice, William, Colin Imber and Richard Lorch, *The Dā'ire-yī Mu'addel of Seydī 'Alī Re'īs* (Manchester, 1976).

Brook, Timothy, *The confusions of pleasure: commerce and culture in Ming China* (Berkeley, 1999).

Bruinessen, Martin van, and Hendrik Boeschoten, *Evliya Çelebi in Diyarbekir: the relevant section of the Seyahatname edited with translation, commentary and introduction* (Leiden, 1988).

Brummett, Palmira, "What Sidi Ali saw: the Ottomans and the Portuguese in India", *Portuguese Studies Review*, 9, 1–2, 2001, pp. 232–53.

Bruton, William, "The first coming of the English to Bengal", *Bengal Past and Present*, 27, 53–4, 1924, pp. 143–6.

Caddeo, Rinaldo, ed., *Le navigazioni atlantiche di Alvise da Ca' da Mosto, Antoniotto Usodimare e Niccoloso da Recco* (Milan, 1929).

Calmard, Jean, "Safavid Persia in Indo-Persian sources and in Timurid-Mughal perception", in Muzaffar Alam, Françoise N. Delvoye and Marc Gaborieau, eds., *The making of Indo-Persian culture: Indian and French Studies* (New Delhi, 2000), pp. 351–91.

Casale, Giancarlo L., "The Ottoman age of exploration: spices, maps and conquest in the sixteenth-century Indian Ocean", Ph.D. dissertation, Harvard University, Cambridge, Mass., 2004.

Castanhoso, Miguel de, *História das cousas que o muy esforçado capitão D. Christovão da Gama fez nos reynos de Preste João* (Lisbon, 1564; reprint, Lisbon, 1855).

Castries, Henri de, *Relation d'une ambassade marocaine en Turquie, 1589–1591* (Paris, 1929).

Castro, Xavier de, and Geneviève Bouchon, eds., *Voyage de Pyrard de Laval aux Indes Orientales (1601–1611)*, 2 vols. (Paris, 1998).

Cathanar Thomman Paremmakkal, *The Varthamanappusthakam: an account of the history of the Malabar Church between the years 1773 and 1786 . . . [and] the journey from Malabar to Rome via Lisbon and back . . .*, tr. Placid J. Podipara (Rome, 1971).

Catz, Rebecca D., and Francis M. Rogers, eds., *Cartas de Fernão Mendes Pinto e outros documentos* (Lisbon, 1983).

Cendrars, Blaise, *Bourlinguer* (Paris, 1974).

Chartier, Roger, *The order of books: readers, authors, and libraries in Europe between the fourteenth and eighteenth centuries*, tr. Lydia Cochrane (Stanford, 1994).

Chatterjee, Indrani, "A slave's quest for selfhood in eighteenth-century Hindustan", *Indian Economic and Social History Review*, 37, 1, 2000, pp. 53–86.

Chatterjee, Kumkum, "Discovering India: travel, history and identity in late nineteenth- and early twentieth-century India", in Daud Ali, ed., *Invoking the past: the uses of history in South Asia* (Delhi, 1999), pp. 192–227.

Chatterjee, Partha, "Five hundred years of fear and love", *Economic and Political Weekly*, 33, 22–30 May 1998, pp. 1330–6.

Chavannes, Édouard, "Voyageurs chinois chez les Khitan et les Joutchen", *Journal Asiatique*, 9, 9, 1897, pp. 361–439.

Cole, Juan R. I., "Shi'i clerics in Iraq and Iran, 1722–1780: the Akhbari–Usuli controversy reconsidered", *Iranian Studies*, 18, 1, 1985, pp. 3–34.

"Invisible Occidentalism: eighteenth-century Indo-Persian constructions of the West", *Iranian Studies*, 25, 3–4, 1992, pp. 3–16.

"Mirror of the world: Iranian 'Orientalism' and early 19th-century India", *Critique*, Spring 1996, pp. 41–60.

Couto, Dejanirah, "No rasto de Hādim Suleimão Pacha: alguns aspectos do comércio do Mar Vermelho nos anos de 1538–1540", in Artur Teodoro de Matos and Luís Filipe F. Reis Thomaz, eds., *A Carreira da Índia e as Rotas dos Estreitos: Actas do VIII Seminário Internacional de História Indo-Portuguesa* (Angra do Heroísmo, 1998), pp. 483–508.

"Les Ottomans et l'Inde portugaise", in José Manuel Garcia and Teotónio de Souza, eds., *Vasco da Gama e a Índia*, vol. 1 (Lisbon, 1999), pp. 181–200.

"Trois documents sur une demande de secours ormouzi à la Porte ottomane", *Anais de História de Além-Mar*, 3, 2002, pp. 469–93.

Couto, Diogo do, *Da Ásia, décadas IV–XII* (Lisbon, 1974).

Coutre, Jacques de, *Andanzas asiáticas*, ed. Eddy Stols, B. Teensma and J. Verberckmoes (Madrid, 1991).

Crone, G. R., ed. and tr., *The voyages of Cadamosto and other documents on Western Africa in the second half of the fifteenth century* (London, 1937).

Dadvar, Abolghasem, *Iranians in Mughal politics and society, 1606–1658* (New Delhi, 1999).

Dale, Stephen Frederic, "A Safavid poet in the heart of darkness: the Indian poems of Ashraf Mazandarani", in Michel Mazzaoui, ed., *Safavid Iran and her neighbors* (Salt Lake City, 2003), pp. 63–80 (also in *Iranian Studies*, 36, 2, 2003, pp. 197–212).

Dankoff, Robert, *An Evliya Çelebi glossary: unusual, dialectal and foreign words in the Seyahatnāme* (Cambridge, Mass., 1991).

Das Gupta, Ashin, *Indian merchants and the decline of Surat, c. 1700–1750* (Wiesbaden, 1979).

Daulier-Deslandes, André, *Les Beautez de la Perse, ou la description de ce qu'il y a de plus curieux dans ce royaume, enrichie de la carte du païs, & de plusieurs estampes dessignées sur les lieux* (Paris, 1673).

Dawson, Christopher, *Mission to Asia* (Toronto, 1980).

De Silva, Chandra Richard, "Beyond the Cape: the Portuguese encounter with the peoples of South Asia", in Stuart B. Schwartz, ed., *Implicit understandings: observing, reporting, and reflecting on the encounters between Europeans and other peoples in the early modern era* (New York, 1994), pp. 295–322.

Digby, Simon, "An eighteenth-century narrative of a journey from Bengal to England: Munshi Ismā'īl's *New History*", in Christopher Shackle, ed., *Urdu and Muslim South Asia: Studies in honour of Ralph Russell* (Delhi, 1991), pp. 49–65.

"Some Asian wanderers in seventeenth-century India: an examination of sources in Persian", *Studies in History*, n.s., 9, 2, 1993, pp. 247–64.

"From Ladakh to Lahore in 1820–1821: the account of a Kashmiri traveller", *Journal of Central Asian Studies* (Srinagar), 8, 1997, pp. 3–22.

"Indo-Persian narratives of travel of the close of the 18th and beginning of the 19th century", unpublished paper presented at the French Institute, Pondicherry, 1997.

"Beyond the ocean: perceptions of overseas in Indo-Persian sources of the Mughal period", *Studies in History*, n.s., 14, 2, 1999, pp. 247–59.

Wonder-tales of South Asia (Jersey, Channel Islands, 2000).

"Bāyazīd Beg Turkmān's pilgrimage to Makka and return to Gujarat: a sixteenth-century narrative", *Iran*, 42, 2004, pp. 159–77.

"Before Timur came: provincialization of the Delhi Sultanate through the fourteenth century", *Journal of the Economic and Social History of the Orient*, 47, 3, 2004, pp. 298–356.

Digby, Simon, and J. C. Harle, "When did the Sun temple fall down?", *South Asian Studies*, 1, 1985, pp. 1–7.

Dunn, R. E., *The adventures of Ibn Battuta, a Muslim traveler of the fourteenth century* (Berkeley, 1986).

Eaton, Richard M., *Sufis of Bijapur, 1300–1700: social roles of Sufis in medieval India* (Princeton, 1978).

"Multiple lenses: differing perspectives of fifteenth-century Calicut", in Laurie J. Sears, ed., *Autonomous histories, particular truths: essays in honor of John Smail* (Madison, Wisc., 1993), pp. 71–86.

The new Cambridge history of India, vol 1.8: *A social history of the Deccan, 1300–1761: eight Indian lives* (Cambridge, 2005).

Eickelman, Dale F., and James Piscatori, eds., *Muslim travellers: pilgrimage, migration and the religious imagination* (Berkeley, 1990).

Elliot, H. M., and J. Dowson, eds., *The history of India as told by its own historians: the Muhammadan period*, 8 vols. (London, 1867–77; reprint, Delhi, 1990).

El-Moudden, Abderrahmane, "The ambivalence of *riḥla*: community integration and self-definition in Moroccan travel-accounts, 1300–1800", in Dale F. Eickelman and James Piscatori, eds., *Muslim travellers: pilgrimage, migration, and the religious imagination* (Berkeley, 1990), pp. 69–84.

Elsner, Jaś, and Joan-Pau Rubiés, eds., *Voyages and visions: towards a cultural history of travel* (London, 1999).

Enthoven, Reginald E., *The tribes and castes of Bombay*, vol. 1 (reprint, Delhi, 1975).

Ernst, Carl W., *Eternal garden: mysticism, history and politics at a South Asian Sufi center* (Albany, N.Y., 1992).

"Admiring the works of the ancients: the Ellora temples as viewed by Indo-Muslim authors", in David Gilmartin and Bruce B. Lawrence, eds., *Beyond Turk and Hindu: rethinking religious identities in Islamicate South Asia* (Gainesville, Fla., 2000), pp. 98–120.

Farid Bhakkari, Shaikh, *The Dhakhīrat-ul-Khawānīn*, tr. Ziyauddin A. Desai (Delhi, 1992).

Farooqi, Naimur Rehman, *Mughal–Ottoman relations: a study of the political and diplomatic relations between Mughal India and the Ottoman empire* (Delhi, 1989).

"Six Ottoman documents on Mughal–Ottoman relations during the reign of Akbar", in Iqtidar Alam Khan, ed., *Akbar and his age* (New Delhi, 1999), pp. 209–22.

Faroqhi, Suraiya, *Pilgrims and sultans: the hajj under the Ottomans, 1517–1683* (London, 1994).

"Red Sea trade and communications as observed by Evliya Çelebi (1671–72)", in Faroqhi, *Making a living in the Ottoman lands, 1480 to 1820* (Istanbul, 1995), pp. 231–48.

Fisher, Michael, *The first Indian author in English: Dean Mahomed (1759–1851) in India, Ireland and England* (Delhi, 1996).

Fisher, Michael H., "Representing 'his' women: Mirza Abu Talib Khan's 1801 'Vindication of the liberties of Asiatic women'", *Indian Economic and Social History Review*, 37, 2, 2000, pp. 215–37.

Counterflows to colonialism: Indian travellers and settlers in Britain 1600–1857 (New Delhi, 2004).

Fleischer, Cornell, "Secretaries' dreams: augury and angst in Ottoman scribal service", in Ingeborg Baldauf and Suraiya Faroqhi, eds., *Armağan: Festschrift für Andreas Tietze* (Prague, 1994), pp. 77–88.

Floor, Willem, "A report on the trade in Jedda in the 1730s", *Moyen Orient et Océan Indien*, 5, 1988, pp. 161–73.

"The Dutch on Khark island, the end of an era: the Baron von Kniphausen's adventures", *Moyen Orient et Océan Indien*, 8 ("Européens en Orient au XVIIIe siècle"), 1994, pp. 157–202.

Foltz, Richard C., "Two seventeenth-century Central Asian travellers to Mughal India", *Journal of the Royal Asiatic Society of Great Britain and Ireland*, series 3, 6, 3, 1996, pp. 367–77.

Conversations with Emperor Jahangir by "Mutribi" al-Asamm of Samarqand (Costa Mesa, 1998).

Foster, William, ed., *The embassy of Sir Thomas Roe to India, 1615–1619* (London, 1926).

Fragner, Bert G., *Persischen Memoirenliteratur als Quelle zu neueren Geschichte Irans* (Wiesbaden, 1979).

"Iranian patriotism in the 17th century: the case of Moḥammad-e Mofid", unpublished paper, delivered as part of the Yarshater Lectures, Harvard University, 30 April – 5 May 2001.

Frisch, Andrea, *The invention of the eyewitness: witnessing and testimony in early modern France* (Chapel Hill, 2004).

Gafurov, B. G., "The Baḥr al-Asrār – II", *Journal of the Pakistan Historical Society*, 14, 2, 1966, pp. 99–103.

Galland, Julien-Claude, *Le Paradis des infidèles: un ambassadeur ottoman en France sous la Régence*, ed. Gilles Veinstein (Paris, 1981).

Galvão, António, *The discoveries of the world, from their first original unto the year of Our Lord 1555, by Antonio Galvano, governor of Ternate. Corrected, quoted, and published in England, by Richard Hakluyt (1601)*, reprinted with the original Portuguese text, and ed. Vice-Admiral C. B. Bethune (London, 1862).

Tratado dos descobrimentos, ed. Visconde de Lagoa and Elaine Sanceau, 4th edn (Oporto, 1987).

Geertz, Clifford, *Works and lives: the anthropologist as author* (Stanford, 1988).

Ghosh, Amitav, "The slave of Ms. H.5", in Partha Chatterjee and Gyanendra Pandey, eds., *Writings on South Asian history and society*, Subaltern Studies 7 (Delhi, 1992), pp. 159–220.

Gladwin, Francis, *The memoirs of Khojeh Abdulkurreem, a Cashmerian of distinction who accompanied Nadir Shah . . .: including the history of Hindostan, from A.D. 1739 to 1749* (Calcutta, 1788).

Goitein, S. D., "Letters and documents on the India trade in medieval times", *Islamic Culture*, 37, 3, 1963, pp. 188–205.

Golchin-i Ma'ani, Ahmad, *Kārwān-i Hind: Dar aḥwāl wa āṣār-i shā'irān-i 'aṣr-i Ṣafawī ki bi Hindūstān rafta and*, 2 vols. (Mashhad, 1990–1).

Goswamy, B. N., and J. S. Grewal, eds. and tr. *The Mughals and the Jogīs of Jakhbar* (Simla, 1967).

Greenblatt, Stephen, *Marvelous possessions: the wonder of the New World* (Chicago, 1991).

Haase, C. P., "'Abd-al-Razzāq Samarqandī, Kamāl-al-Dīn bin Jalāl-al-Dīn Eshāq", in Ehsan Yarshater, ed., *Encyclopaedia iranica*, vol. 1, part 1 (New York, 1982), pp. 158–60.

Habib, Irfan, "The family of Nur Jahan during Jahangir's reign: a political study", in *Medieval India: A Miscellany*, vol. 1 (Bombay, 1969), pp. 74–95.

"Timur in the political tradition and historiography of Mughal India", in Maria Szuppe, ed., *L'héritage timouride: Iran – Asie centrale – Inde, XVe–XVIIIe siècles* (Tashkent, 1997), pp. 297–312.

Hakki, Ibrahim, "Hint Türk Hükümdari Hümayun Şahin Ḳanuniye gönderdiği bir metup", *Yedigün*, 8, 202, 1937, pp. 7–9.

Hammer, Joseph de [von], "Memoir on the diplomatic relations between the courts of Delhi and Constantinople in the sixteenth and seventeenth centuries", *Transactions of the Royal Asiatic Society*, 2, 1830, pp. 462–86.

Haneda, Masashi, "La famille Huzânî d'Isfahan (15e–17e siècles)", *Studia Iranica*, 18, 1989, pp. 77–91.

"Emigration of Iranian elites to India during the 16th–18th centuries", in Maria Szuppe, ed., *L'héritage timouride: Iran – Asie centrale – Inde, XVe–XVIIIe siècles* (Tashkent, 1997), pp. 129–43.

Hasan, S. Nurul, "The theory of the Nur Jahan 'junta' – a critical examination", *Indian History Congress, Proceedings of the 21st Session, 1958, Trivandrum*, pp. 324–35.

Hasson, I., "Al-Zubayr bin al-'Awwām", in *The Encyclopaedia of Islam*, vol. XI (Leiden, 2002), pp. 549–51.

Helms, Mary W., *Ulysses' sail: an ethnographic odyssey of power, knowledge, and geographical distance* (Princeton, 1988).

Hodgson, Marshall G. S., *The venture of Islam: conscience and history in a world civilization*, vol. III: *The gunpowder empires and modern times* (Chicago, 1977).

Hulme, Peter, and Tim Youngs, eds., *The Cambridge companion to travel writing* (Cambridge, 2002).

Husain, Afzal, *The nobility under Akbar and Jahāngīr: a study of family groups* (New Delhi, 1999).

Husain, Hidayat, "The Mirza Nama (The book of the perfect gentleman) of Mirza Kamran", *Journal of the Asiatic Society of Bengal*, 9, 1, 1913, pp. 1–13.

Husain, Iqbal, "Hindu shrines and practices as described by a Central Asian traveller in the first half of the 17th century", in Irfan Habib, ed., *Researches in the history of India, 1200–1750, Medieval India 1* (Delhi, 1992), pp. 141–53.

"The diplomatic vision of Tipu Sultan: briefs for embassies to Turkey and France, 1785–86", in Irfan Habib, ed., *State and diplomacy under Tipu Sultan: documents and essays* (New Delhi, 2001), pp. 19–65.

Hutchinson, E. W., *Adventurers in Siam in the seventeenth century* (reprint, Bangkok, 1985).

Ibn Battuta, *Voyages d'Ibn Battūta*, tr. C. Defremery and B. R. Sanguinetti, revised by Stéphane Yerasimos, 3 vols. (Paris, 1997).

Imber, Colin, *Ebu's-su'ud: the Islamic legal tradition* (Edinburgh, 1997).

The Ottoman empire, 1300–1650: the structure of power (Basingstoke, 2002).

Inden, Ronald, *Imagining India* (Oxford, 1990).

Islam, Riazul, "The *Baḥr ul-Asrār* – I: a note on the travel portion", *Journal of the Pakistan Historical Society*, 14, 2, 1966, pp. 93–7.

"A seventeenth-century account of Sind", *Journal of the Pakistan Historical Society*, 26, 3, 1978, pp. 141–55.

"Travelogue of Maḥmūd b. Amīr Walī", *Journal of the Pakistan Historical Society*, 27, 2, 1979, pp. 88–120.

A calendar of documents on Indo-Persian relations (1500–1750), 2 vols. (Karachi, 1979–82).

Jackson, Peter, *The Delhi Sultanate: a political and military history* (Cambridge, 1999).

Jacobs, Hubert, ed., *A treatise on the Moluccas (c. 1544), probably the preliminary version of António Galvão's lost 'História das Molucas'* (Rome, 1971).

Ja'fariyan, Rasul, *'Ilal-i bar uftādan-i Ṣafawiyān: Mukāfāt nāma, bi ẓamīma-i chand risāla wa maqāla dar bāra-i Fitna-i Afg̱hān wa masā'il-i siyasī-farhangī-i daura-i Ṣafawī* (Tehran, 1372 Sh. / 1993).

Jarrett, H. S., and Jadunath Sarkar, tr., *The Ā'īn-i Akbarī by Abu'l Fazl Allāmī*, vol. II (reprint, Delhi, 1989).

Joshi, P. M., "Asad Beg's mission to Bijapur, 1603–1604", in S. N. Sen, ed., *Mahamahopadhyaya Prof. D. V. Potdar sixty-first birthday commemoration volume* (Poona, 1950), pp. 184–96.

Kafadar, Cemal, "Self and others: the diary of a dervish in seventeenth-century Istanbul and first-person narratives in Ottoman literature", *Studia Islamica*, Fasc. 69, 1989, pp. 121–50.

"The question of Ottoman decline", *Harvard Middle Eastern and Islamic Review*, 4, 1–2, 1997–8, pp. 30–71.

Kaplan, Robert D., *The ends of the earth: from Togo to Turkmenistan, from Iran to Cambodia – a journey to the frontiers of anarchy* (New York, 1996).

Keene, Donald, *Travelers of a hundred ages: the Japanese as revealed through 1,000 years of diaries* (New York, 1999).

Kemp, P. M., tr., *Russian travellers to India and Persia (1624–1798): Kotov, Yefremov, Danibegov* (Delhi, 1959).

Khan, Ansar Zahid, "Baḥr al-Asrār: the towns and regions beginning with ب (b)", *Journal of the Pakistan Historical Society*, 39, 1, 1991, pp. 5–21.

Khan, Gulfishan, *Indian Muslim perceptions of the West during the eighteenth century* (Karachi, 1998).

Khan, Iqtidar Alam, "The Mughal assignment system during Akbar's early years, 1556–1575", in Irfan Habib, ed., *Researches in the history of India, 1200–1750, Medieval India 1* (Delhi, 1992), pp. 62–128.

Khan, Mubarak Ali, *The court of the Great Mughuls (based on Persian sources)* (Bochum, 1976).

Kirchner, Walter, "The voyage of Athanasius Nikitin to India, 1466–1472", *American Slavic and East European Review*, 5, 1946, pp. 46–54.

Kirmani, Waris, ed., *Dreams forgotten: an anthology of Indo-Persian poetry* (Aligarh, 1986).

Kulke, Hermann, *Kings and cults: state formation and legitimation in India and Southeast Asia* (New Delhi, 1993).

Kumar, Anil, *Asaf Khan and his times* (Patna, 1986).

Lal, Mohan, *Journal of a tour through the Panjab, Afghanistan, Turkistan, Khorasan and part of Persia, in company with Lieut. Burnes and Dr. Gerard* (Calcutta, 1834).

Lambourn, Elizabeth, "Of jewels and horses: the career and patronage of an Iranian merchant under Shah Jahan", *Iranian Studies*, 36, 2, 2003, pp. 213–58.

Lamouroux, Christian, "De l'étrangeté à la différence: les récits des émissaires Song en pays Liao (XIe s.)", in Claudine Salmon, ed., *Récits de voyage des Asiatiques: genres, mentalités, conception de l'espace* (Paris, 1996), pp. 101–26.

Langlès, Louis, tr. and comp., *Voyages dans l'Inde, en Perse, etc. avec la description de l'île Poulo-Pinang, nouvel établissement des anglais près de la Côte de Coromandel. Par différens officiers au service de la Compagnie anglaise des Indes orientales* (Paris, 1801).

Larner, John, *Marco Polo and the discovery of the world* (London, 1999).

Lath, Mukund, *Ardhakathānaka, half a tale: a study in the interrelationship between autobiography and history* (Jaipur, 1981).
Latham, Ronald, *Marco Polo: the travels* (Harmondsworth, 1958).
Legge, James, tr., *A record of Buddhistic kingdoms: being an account by the Chinese Monk Fa-hien of his travels in India and Ceylon (A.D. 399–414) in search of the Buddhist Books of Discipline* (Oxford, 1886).
Le Guillou, Jean-Yves, *Le voyage au-delà des trois mers d'Afanasij Nikitin (1466–1472)* (Quebec, 1978).
Lenhoff, Gail, *The making of the medieval Russian journey* (Ann Arbor, 1978).
"Beyond three seas: Afanasij Nikitin's journey from orthodoxy to apostasy", *Eastern European Quarterly*, 13, 4, 1979, pp. 432–47.
Léry, Jean de, *History of a voyage to the land of Brazil, otherwise called America*, tr. Janet Whatley (Berkeley, 1990).
Lestringant, Frank, "Calvinistes et cannibales: les écrits protestants sur le Brésil français (1555–1560)", *Bulletin de la société de l'histoire du protestantisme français*, 1–2, 1980, pp. 9–26, 167–92.
Lévi-Strauss, Claude, *Tristes tropiques* (Paris, 1955).
Tristes tropiques, tr. John and Doreen Weightman (Harmondsworth, 1976).
Lewis, Bernard, *The Muslim discovery of Europe* (New York, 1982).
"The Mughals and the Ottomans", in Lewis, *From Babel to Dragomans: interpreting the Middle East* (New York, 2004), pp. 108–14.
Lloyd, G. E. R., *Demystifying mentalities* (Cambridge, 1990).
Lockhart, Laurence, *Nadir Shah* (London, 1938).
Lorenzen, David N., "Who invented Hinduism?", *Comparative Studies in Society and History*, 41, 4, 1999, pp. 630–59.
Madhava Rao, P. Setu, *Tahmas Nama: the autobiography of a slave* (Delhi, 1967).
Major, R. H., *India in the fifteenth century: being a collection of narratives of voyages to India* (London, 1857).
Makdisi, Ussama, "Ottoman Orientalism", *American Historical Review*, 107, 3, 2002, pp. 768–96.
Malamoud, Charles, "Le voyage au-delà des trois mers d'Athanase Nikitine", *L'Ethnographie*, 76, 81–2, 1980, pp. 85–134.
Marcinkowski, M. Ismail, "The Iran–Siamese connection: an Iranian community in the Thai kingdom of Ayutthaya", *Iranian Studies*, 35, 1–3, 2002, pp. 23–46.
"The Iranian presence in the Indian Ocean rim: a report on a 17th century Safawid embassy to Siam (Thailand)", *Journal of the Pakistan Historical Society*, 51, 3, 2003, pp. 55–85.
Marshall, D. N., *Mughals in India: a bibliographical survey of manuscripts* (New York, 1985).
Martin, R. Montgomery, ed., *The despatches, minutes and correspondence of the Marquess Wellesley, K.G., during his administration in India*, 5 vols. (London, 1836–7).

Matar, Nabil, *In the lands of the Christians: Arabic travel-writing in the seventeenth century* (New York and London, 2003).
McKenna, James B., ed., *A Spaniard in the Portuguese Indies: the narrative of Martín Fernández de Figueroa* (Cambridge, Mass., 1967).
Metcalf, Barbara D., "The pilgrimage remembered: South Asian accounts of the ḥajj", in Dale F. Eickelman and James Piscatori, eds., *Muslim travellers: pilgrimage, migration, and the religious imagination* (Berkeley, 1990), pp. 85–107.
ed., *Moral conduct and authority: the place of Adab in South Asian Islam* (Berkeley, 1984).
Meyer, Karl H., *Die Fahrt des Athanasius Nikitin über die drei Meere: Reise eines russischen Kaufmannes nach Ostindien, 1466–1472* (Leipzig, 1920).
Miquel, André, *La géographie humaine du monde musulman jusqu'au milieu du 11e siècle*, 4 vols. (Paris, 1967–88).
Mir Izzat Ullah, *Travels in Central Asia, 1812–1813* (Calcutta, 1872).
Mirsky, Jeannette, ed., *The great Chinese travelers* (Chicago, 1964).
Mirza, Mohammad Wahid, *The life and works of Amir Khusrau* (Delhi, 1935).
Mirza Nathan, *Bahāristān-i-Ghaybī: a history of the Mughal wars in Assam, Cooch Behar, Bengal, Bihar and Orissa during the reigns of Jahāngīr and Shāhjahān*, tr. M. I. Borah, 2 vols. (Gauhati, 1936).
Mirza Sheikh I'tesamuddin, *The wonders of Vilayet: being the memoir, originally in Persian, of a visit to France and Britain in 1765*, tr. Kaiser Haq (Leeds, 2001).
Mitchell, James, *The history of the maritime wars of the Turks, translated from the Turkish of Haji Khalifeh* (London, 1831).
Morris, A. S., "The journey beyond three seas", *Geographical Journal*, 133, 4, Dec. 1967, pp. 502–8.
Mottahedeh, Roy P., *The mantle of the prophet: religion and politics in Iran* (New York, 1985).
"'Ajā'ib in The Thousand and One Nights", in Richard G. Hovannisian, Georges Sabagh and Fedwa Malti-Douglas, eds., *The Thousand and One Nights in Arabic literature and society* (Cambridge, 1996), pp. 29–39.
Muhammad 'Ali Hazin, *The life of Sheikh Mohammed Ali Hazin written by himself*, tr. F. C. Belfour (London, 1830).
Muralt, Béat Louis de, *Lettres sur les Anglois et les François. Et sur les voiages* (Geneva, 1725).
Murr, Sylvia, "Le politique 'au Mogol' selon Bernier: appareil conceptuel, rhétorique stratégique, philosophie morale", in Jacques Pouchepadass and Henri Stern, eds., *De la royauté à l'Etat dans le monde indien* (Paris, 1990), pp. 239–302.
Nadvi, Sayyid Sulaiman, "Khilāfat aur Hindūstān", in *Maqālāt-i Sulaimān*, vol. 1, ed. S. 'Abdur Rahman (Azamgarh, 1966), pp. 112–84.
Naim, C. M., *Zikr-i Mir: the autobiography of the eighteenth-century Mughal poet Mir Taqi "Mir"* (Delhi, 1999).
Naipaul, V. S., *An area of darkness* (London, 1964).
Among the believers: an Islamic journey (London, 1981).

Narayana Rao, Velcheru, and David Shulman, *A lover's guide to Warangal: the 'Krīḍâbhirāmamu' by Vinukoṇḍa Vallabharāya* (New Delhi, 2002).
Narayana Rao, Velcheru, and Sanjay Subrahmanyam, "Circulation, piety and innovation: recounting travels in early nineteenth-century South India", in Claude Markovits *et al.*, *Society and circulation: mobile people and itinerant cultures in South Asia, 1750–1950* (New Delhi, 2003), pp. 306–55.
Nawa'i, 'Abdul Husain, *Shāh Ṭahmāsb Ṣafawī: Majmu'ah-i asnād wa mukātabāt-i tarīkhi hamrah ba yāddāsht-hā-yi tafṣīlī* (Tehran, 1971).
O'Hanlon, Rosalind, "Manliness and imperial service in Mughal North India", *Journal of the Economic and Social History of the Orient*, 42, 1, 1999, pp. 47–93.
Okada, Amina, and Jean-Louis Nou, *Un joyau de l'Inde moghole: le mausolée d'I'timad ud-Daulah* (Milan, 2003).
O'Kane, John, *The ship of Sulaiman* (London, 1972).
Özbaran, Salih, *The Ottoman response to European expansion: studies on Ottoman–Portuguese relations in the Indian Ocean and Ottoman administration in the Arab lands during the sixteenth century* (Istanbul, 1994).
Özcan, Azmi, *Pan-Islamism: Indian Muslims, the Ottomans and Britain (1877–1924)* (Leiden, 1997).
Pearson, M. N., "Shivaji and the decline of the Mughal empire", *Journal of Asian Studies*, 35, 2, 1976, pp. 221–35.
Pious passengers: the Hajj in earlier times (New Delhi, 1994).
Pereira, Duarte Pacheco, *Esmeraldo de situ orbis*, ed. Damião Peres (Lisbon, 1988).
Pia, Pascal, ed., *Voyages en Perse et description de ce royaume par Jean-Baptiste Tavernier, marchand français* (Paris, 1930).
Pigeot, Jacqueline, "Le voyage comme expérience de la condition humaine au Japon (XIIe–XVe siècle)", in Claudine Salmon, ed., *Récits de voyage des Asiatiques: genres, mentalités, conception de l'espace* (Paris, 1996), pp. 31–8.
Pinto, Fernão Mendes, *The travels of Mendes Pinto*, ed. and tr. Rebecca D. Catz (Chicago, 1989).
Pombejra, Dhiravat Na, "Crown trade and court politics in Ayutthaya during the reign of King Narai (1656–88)", in J. Kathirithamby-Wells and John Villiers, eds., *The Southeast Asian port and polity: rise and demise* (Singapore, 1990), pp. 127–42.
Pratt, Mary Louise, *Imperial eyes: travel writing and transculturation* (London, 1992).
Purchas, Samuel, *Hakluytus Posthumus or Purchas his pilgrimes: containing a history of the world in sea voyages and lande travells by Englishmen and others*, vol. 1 (Glasgow, 1905).
Qaisar, Ahsan Jan, "From port to port: life on Indian ships in the sixteenth and seventeenth centuries", in Ashin Das Gupta and M. N. Pearson, eds., *India and the Indian Ocean, 1500–1800* (reprint, Delhi, 1999), pp. 331–49.
Quamruddin, Mohammad, *Life and times of Prince Murad Bakhsh (1624–1661)* (Calcutta, 1974).

Quatremère, E. M., "Notice de l'ouvrage persan qui a pour titre: Matla-assaadein ou majma-albahrein, et qui contient l'histoire des deux sultans Schahrokh et Abou-Said", in *Notice et extraits des manuscrits de la Bibliothèque du Roi et autres bibliothèques*, vol. XIV, part I (Paris, 1843).

Qureshi, Ishtiaq Husain, "Tipu Sultan's embassy to Constantinople, 1787", in Irfan Habib, ed., *Confronting colonialism: resistance and modernization under Haidar Ali and Tipu Sultan* (New Delhi, 1999), pp. 69–78.

Raj, Kapil, "Refashioning civilities, engineeering trust: William Jones, Indian intermediaries and the production of reliable legal knowledge in late 18th-century Bengal", *Studies in History*, n.s., 17, 2, 2001, pp. 175–209.

Ramusio, Giovanni Battista, *Navigazioni e viaggi*, ed. Marica Milanesi, vol. I (Turin, 1978).

Rashid, Abdur, "The treatment of history by Muslim historians in Mughal official and biographical works", in C. H. Philips, ed., *Historians of India, Pakistan and Ceylon* (London, 1961), pp. 139–51.

Raychaudhuri, Tapan, "Europe in India's xenology: the nineteenth-century record", *Past and Present*, 137, 1992, pp. 156–82.

Reischauer, Edwin, *Ennin's diary: the record of a pilgrimage to China in search of the law*, 2 vols. (New York, 1955).

Richards, John F., *The New Cambridge History of India*, vol. I.5: *The Mughal empire* (Cambridge, 1993).

Roche, Daniel, *Humeurs vagabondes: de la circulation des hommes et de l'utilité des voyages* (Paris, 2003).

Rubiés, Joan-Pau, "Instructions for travellers: teaching the eye to see", *History and Anthropology*, 9, 2–3, 1996, pp. 139–90.

Travel and ethnology in the Renaissance: South India through European eyes, 1250–1625 (Cambridge, 2000).

Sachau, Edward C., *Alberuni's India: an account of the religion, philosophy, literature, geography, chronology, astronomy, customs, laws and astrology of India about A.D. 1030*, 2 vols. (London, 1910).

Salmon, Claudine, "Wang Dahai et sa vision des 'Contrées insulaires' (1791)", *Etudes chinoises*, 13, 1–2, 1994, pp. 221–57.

"Bengal as reflected in two South-East Asian travelogues from the early nineteenth century", in Denys Lombard and Om Prakash, eds., *Commerce and culture in the Bay of Bengal, 1500–1800* (New Delhi, 1999), pp. 383–402.

ed., *Récits de voyage des Asiatiques: genres, mentalités, conception de l'espace* (Paris, 1996).

Sarkar, Jadunath, *Memoirs of Tahmasp Khan by Miskin* (Sitamau, 1937).

Studies in Aurangzib's reign (Hyderabad, 1989).

Sarkar, Jagadish Narayan, *The life of Mir Jumla, the General of Aurangzeb*, 2nd edn (New Delhi, 1979).

Sartre, Jean-Paul, *Huis clos*, ed. Jacques Hardré and George B. Daniel (New Jersey, 1962).

Un théâtre de situations, ed. Michel Contat and Michel Rybalka (Paris, 1992).

Schefer, Charles, tr., *Sefer nameh: relation du voyage de Nassiri Khosrau en Syrie, en Palestine, en Egypte, en Arabie et en Perse, pendant les années de l'hégire 437–444 (1035–1042)* (Paris, 1881).
Selbourne, David, *The city of light* (London, 1997).
Shahnawaz Khan, *Ma'āṣir-ul-Umarā', being biographies of the Muhammadan and Hindu officers of the Timurid sovereigns of India from 1500 to about 1780 A.D.*, tr. H. Beveridge and Baini Prashad, 3 vols. (Calcutta, 1911–52).
Shapin, Steven, *A social history of truth: civility and science in seventeenth-century England* (Chicago, 1994).
Sharma, Sunil, *Persian poetry at the Indian frontier: Maṣ'ūd Sa'd Salmān of Lahore* (New Delhi, 2000).
Sheik Ali, B., *Tipu Sultan: a study in diplomacy and confrontation* (Mysore, 1982).
Sherwani, H. K., *Maḥmūd Gāwān, the great Bahmani wazīr* (Allahabad, 1942).
History of the Quṭb Shāhī dynasty (New Delhi, 1974).
Siddiqui, Iqtidar Husain, *Perso-Arabic sources of information on the life and conditions in the Sultanate of Delhi* (New Delhi, 1992).
Silva, Nuno Vassallo e, "Precious stones, jewels and cameos: Jacques de Coutre's journey to Goa and Agra", in Jorge Flores and Nuno Vassallo e Silva, eds., *Goa and the Great Mughal* (Lisbon, 2004), pp. 116–33.
Singh, Surinder, "The Indian memoirs of Mutribi Samarqandi", *Proceedings of the Indian History Congress, 55th Session, Aligarh, 1994* (Delhi, 1995), pp. 345–54.
Sioris, George A., *Phaulkon, the Greek first counsellor at the Court of Siam: an appraisal* (Bangkok, 1998).
Skinner, C., *Ahmad Rijaluddin's Hikayat Perintah Negeri Benggala* (The Hague, 1992).
Soucek, P., "Bahrām Mīrzā", in Ehsan Yarshater, ed., *Encyclopaedia iranica*, vol. III (New York, 1989), pp. 523–4.
Speake, Jennifer, ed., *Literature of travel and exploration: an encyclopaedia*, 3 vols. (London, 2003),
Steingass, F., *Comprehensive Persian–English dictionary* (London, 1892).
Stewart, Charles, tr., *The travels of Mirza Abu Talib Khan in Asia, Africa and Europe during the years 1799–1803*, 2 vols. (London, 1810).
Storey, C. A., *Persian literature: a bio-bibliographical survey*, vol. I (London, 1927), p. 1.
Stoye, John, *English travellers abroad, 1604–1667: their influence in English society and politics* (London, 1989).
Strassberg, Richard E., *Inscribed landscapes: travel writing from imperial China* (Berkeley, 1994).
Subrahmanyam, Sanjay, "Persians, pilgrims and Portuguese: the travails of Masulipatnam shipping in the western Indian Ocean 1590–1665", *Modern Asian Studies*, 22, 3, 1988, pp. 503–30.
"An Augsburger in Ásia portuguesa: further light on the commercial world of Ferdinand Cron, 1587–1624", in R. Ptak and D. Rothermund, eds.,

Emporia, commodities and entrepreneurs in Asian maritime trade, c. 1400–1750 (Stuttgart, 1991), pp. 401–25.
"Precious metal flows and prices in western and southern Asia, 1500–1750: some comparative and conjunctural aspects", *Studies in History*, n.s., 7, 1, 1991, pp. 79–105.
"Iranians abroad: intra-Asian elite migration and early modern state formation", *Journal of Asian Studies*, 51, 2, 1992, pp. 340–62.
"A matter of alignment: Mughal Gujarat and the Iberian world in the transition of 1580–81", *Mare Liberum*, 9, 1995, pp. 461–79.
"An eastern El-Dorado: the Tirumala-Tirupati temple complex in early European views and ambitions, 1540–1660", in David Shulman, ed., *Syllables of sky: studies in South Indian civilization in honour of Velcheru Narayana Rao* (Delhi, 1995), pp. 338–90.
"Taking stock of the Franks: South Asian views of Europeans and Europe, 1500–1800", *Indian Economic and Social History Review*, 42, 1, 2005, pp. 69–100.
Sviri, Sara, "Dreaming analyzed and recorded: dreams in the world of medieval Islam", in David Shulman and Guy G. Stroumsa, eds., *Dream cultures: explorations in the comparative history of dreaming* (New York, 1999), pp. 252–73.
Szuppe, Maria, *Entre Timourides, Uzbeks et Safavides: questions d'histoire politique et sociale de Hérat dans la première moitié du XVIe siècle* (Paris, 1992).
"En quête de chevaux turkmènes: le journal de voyage de Mīr 'Izzatullāh de Delhi à Boukhara en 1812–1813", *Cahiers d'Asie Centrale*, 1–2 ("Inde – Asie centrale. Routes du commerce et des idées"), 1996, pp. 91–111.
"Circulation des lettrés et cercles littéraires: entre Asie centrale, Iran et Inde du Nord (XVe–XVIIIe siècles)", *Annales HSS*, 5–6, September–December 2004, pp. 997–1018.
Tanaka, Stefan, *Japan's Orient: rendering pasts into history* (Berkeley, 1993).
Tavernier, Jean-Baptiste, *Travels in India*, tr. and ed. Valentine Ball and William Crooke, 2 vols. (reprint, Delhi, 1989).
Teltscher, Kate, *India inscribed: European and British writing on India, 1600–1800* (Delhi, 1995).
Thackston, Wheeler M., *A century of princes: sources on Timurid history and art* (Cambridge, Mass., 1989).
The Bāburnāma: memoirs of Babur, prince and emperor (Washington, 1996).
tr., *The Jahangirnama: memoirs of Jahangir, emperor of India* (New York, 1999).
Thevet, André, *Les singularités de la France antarctique: Le Brésil des cannibales au XVIe siècle*, ed. Frank Lestringant (Paris, 1983).
Thomas, Lewis V., *A study of Naima*, ed. Norman Itzkowitz (New York, 1972).
Thompson, J. Eric S., ed., *Thomas Gage's travels in the New World* (Norman, 1958).
Tillett, Lowell R., "Afanasy Nikitin as a cultural ambassador to India: a bowdlerized Soviet translation of his journal", *Russian Review*, 25, 2, 1966, pp. 160–9.

Todorova, Maria, *Imagining the Balkans* (New York, 1997).
Touati, Houari, *Islam et voyage au Moyen Age: histoire et anthropologie d'une pratique lettrée* (Paris, 2000).
Trubetskoi, N. S., "Afanasij Nikitin's journey beyond the three seas as a work of literature", in Ladislav Matejka and Krystyna Pomorska, eds., *Readings in Russian poetics: formalist and structuralist views* (Cambridge, Mass., 1971), pp. 199–219.
Tyan, E., "Bay'a", in *The encyclopaedia of Islam*, vol. 1 (Leiden, 1960), pp. 1113–14.
Unat, Faik Reşit, *Osmanlï Sefirleri ve Sefaretnāmeleri* (Ankara, 1968).
Veinstein, Gilles, "La mort de Mehmed II (1481)", in Nicolas Vatin and Gilles Veinstein, eds., *Les Ottomans et la mort: permanences et mutations* (Leiden, 1996), pp. 187–206.
"Un secret d'Etat: la mort de Soliman le Magnifique", *L'Histoire*, 211, June 1997, pp. 66–71.
Wagoner, Phillip B., "'Sultan among Hindu kings': dress, titles and the Islamicization of Hindu culture at Vijayanagara", *Journal of Asian Studies*, 55, 4, 1996, pp. 851–80.
Watanabe, H., *Marco Polo bibliography, 1477–1983* (Tokyo, 1986).
Wood, Frances, *Did Marco Polo go to China?* (London, 1995).
Woods, John E., "The rise of Tîmûrid historiography", *Journal of Near Eastern Studies*, 46, 1987, pp. 81–108.
Wyatt, David K., "A Persian embassy to Siam in the reign of King Narai", *Journal of the Siam Society*, 42, 1, 1974, pp. 151–7.
Yusuf 'Ali, 'Abdullah, *The meaning of the Glorious Qur'ān*, text, translation and commentary, 2 vols. (Cairo, 1938).
Zarcone, Thierry, and Fariba Zarinebaf, eds., *Les Iraniens d'Istanbul* (Paris, 1993).

Index

Page numbers in bold indicate as illustration.

Ab-i Zarb, 267–8
'Abbas I, Shah, 92, 265
'Abbas ibn 'Abdal Muttalib, 208–9
'Abdun Nabi, Shaikh, 300
'Abdul Karim. *See* Shahristani
'Abdul Latif, 121
'Abdul Momin Khan, 127
'Abdul Qadir, Khwaja, 245, 248, 317–27, 328
'Abdul Wahhab, Maulana 'Afif-ud-Din, 61
'Abdullah bin 'Umar, 319
Abdüllhamid, Sultan, 314, 317, 324, 325
'Abdur Rahim Khan-i Khanan, 20, 309
'Abdur Razzaq. *See* Samarquandi
Abhari, Maulana Shams-ud-Din Muhammad, 80
Abiward, 252
Abiwardi, Husain, 43
Abraham, 210, 276
Abu Bakr, Sayyid, 310
Abu Hanifa, Imam, 274
Abu Ja'far Muhammad, 209
Abu Numay II, Sharif, 299
Abu Shahr, 316, 319
Abu Sufyan, 35
Abu'l Bey, 125–6
Abu'l Fath, 51
Abu'l Fazl, Shaikh, 299, 304
Abu'l Mansur Safdar Jang, 283, 289, 290
Aceh, 150
Adam Khan, 52
Addanki, 144
Aden, 96, 307
'Adil Shah, 288–9
'Adil Shah II, Ibrahim, 346, 347, 349, **350**
'Adil Shahi Sultans, 146, 345, 348
Afghan, Malik Muhammad Khan, 50
Afghanistan, 17, 45, 133
Afghans, 224, 225, 230, 231, 252, 286, 289
Afrasiyab Beg, 303
Aftabchi, Jauhar, 304
Afzal Khan, 125
Agra, 112, 120, 139, 346, 349
Ahmad Pasha, 230–1
Ahmad Rijaluddin, 295
Ahmad Sa'id, Haji Sayyid, 297
Ahmad Shah, 104, 105, 106–7, 289, 290
Ahmadabad, 100, 105, 106–7, 309, 311
Ahmadnagar kingdom, 94
Ahrar, Hazrat Khwaja, 307
Ahsan, Sayyid, 52
Ajmer, 134, 154, 155, 363
Akbar, Mughal emperor
  Akbar Nāma, 304
  and Bayazid Bayat, 305, 307, 310, 312
  Bihbahani on, 241
  Bihishti on, 226
  end of reign, 130–1
  foreign relations, 299–300
  golden age, 179
  Seydi 'Ali on, 116–17
Akbar, Prince Muhammad, 180, 210, 214, 216
Akbarabad, 225
'Ala, 276
'Ala-ud-Din, Maulana, 50, 51
Alam, Muzaffar, 130
'Alam Shah, Mughal emperor, 316
'Alamgir II, 290
'Alawi Khan, 271, 273, 282, 284, 286, 290
Albania, 7
Albuquerque, Brás de, 337
Aleppo, 26, 34–5, 42, 43, 97, 113, 268, 345
Alexander I, 113, 167
Alexandretta, 345
Alexandria, 317
'Ali, Hazrat, 160, 195, 275, 321
'Ali Agha, 105, 322
'Ali Beg, 303
'Ali Gauhar, 290

'Ali ibn Abi Talib, Imam, 193, 276
'Ali ibn Husain, 37
'Ali Khan, Ghulam, 316, 317, 318, 319, 322–3
'Ali Khan, Haidar, 317
'Ali Khan, Ja'far, 282
'Ali Khan, Kalb-i, 184
'Ali Khan, Lutf, 317, 322
'Ali Mardan Khan, 156–7
'Ali Musa Raza, Imam, 27, 210, 269–70
'Ali Quli Khan, 287–9
'Ali Sher Nawa'i, Mir, 112
Alivardi Khan, 282
Allahabad, 133, 282, 283
Altai mountains, 16
Alwand mountains, 222
Amasya, peace of (1555), 101
Amir Khan, 212, 283–4, 285
Amir-ud-Din, Maulana, 52
Amman, **141**
'Amr bin Ma'dikarb, 61
Amuli, Talib, 130
Anajpur, 144
Andakhu'i, Mirza Khan, 310, 311
Anjumani, Mirza Baqi, 125
Ankara, 101
anonymous writer, 24–43
Antilles, 341
Anwari, 24, 58
'Aqaba, 36
'Aqibat Mahmud, Khwaja, 248
Aqui'a Qarshash, 33
Arabia, 298
Arabian Nights, 4, 8
Arabic, 23, 331
'Arafa, 276
'Arafat, 26, 40
Arakan, 131
Arasang, 27
Arcot, 316, 362
Ardagni, Mulla Muhammad, 211
Arghuns, 100, 109, 110, 116
Armenia, 25, 44
Arsalan Agha, 301
Asad, Malik, 104
Asad Beg, 121, 347, 349
Asad Khan, 86, 87, 88–9
Asaf Khan, 122, 128, 179, 223, 227
Asaf-ud-Daula, 290
ascetics, 136, 145
Ashfar, Iraj, 180
Ashub, Muhammad Bakhsh, 289, 290
Asir (fort), 225
'Askari, Hasan al-Zaki, Imam, 195
Astarabad, 231
Astarabadi, Aqa Muhammad, 165–6, 169
Astrakhan, 85, 100
astrology, 163
astronomy, 112, 113, 116
Aubin, Jean, 46, 50, 176
Aubonne, 355, 357
Aurangabad, 207
Aurangzeb, Mughal Emperor, 219, 222, 226–7, 303
authorship, 360–1
Avicenna (Hakim bu 'Ali ibn Sina), 1, 208
Awadh, 240, 241, 242, 256, 362
Awghan, 80
Ayuthia, 150, 164, 165, 168
Ayyub (Job), 265–6
'Azd-ul-mulk, 53
Azfari, Mirza 'Ali Bakht, 362–3
'Azmat, Shah, 151

Baba 'Ali Beg, 252
Baba Khatun, 33
Babur, Mughal emperor, 20, 21, **22**, 93, 95, 237, 307, 362
Badakhshan, 100
Baghdad
  'Abdul Karim in, 274
  fall to Mongols (1258), 46
  fall to Ottomans (1534), 96
  Hazin in, 231
  Mufid in, 180, 211
  Ottoman subjugation, 222, 232
  Seydi 'Ali in, 97, 101
  shrines, 195
Baghdadi, Khwaja Muhammad, 82
Baha-ud-Din, Maulana, 50, 54
Baha-ud-Din Zakariya, Shaikh, 110
Bahadur, Sultan, 326
Bahadur Khan, 122
Bahadur Shah, 219
Bahardurpur, 50
Bahman Shah, Sultan 'Ala-ud-Din Hamad, 77–8
Bahman Shah, Sultan 'Ala-ud-Din Hasan, 47
Bahman Shah, Sultan Firuz, 53
Bahman Shah, Sultan Muhammad, 87
Bahmani dynasty, 45, 47, 67, 83, 86, 146, 179
Bahrain, 97, 232
Bahur, 212
Bairam Khan, 117, 309
Bait ul-Haram, 41
Bakanur, 79
Bakhshi, Khwaja, 113
Balkans, Ottoman expansion, 130
Balkh, 80, 132, 133, 244, 264, 266

Balkhi, Mahmud bin Amir Wali
  distanced view, 142–50
  generally, 94, 131–59, 172
  hearsay routes, 148–50
  homesickness, 156–9
  marriage, 151
  Muharram celebrations, 322
  narrative interest, 312
  participant observer, 139–42
  shipwreck, 150–6
  Tirupati temple, 147, 159, 357
  view from below, 131–9, 177, 178
  wonders of India, 212
Baluch Khan, 107–8
Banak, 321
Banarasidas, 94
Bandar 'Abbas, 159, 161, 176, 230, 231, 232, 233, 240
Bangash, Muhammad Khan, 284
Bangash country, 260
Bangash Nawwabs, 289
Banians, 356
Banten, 132
Baqi, 26
Baqir, Imam, 37
Baqir Khan, 150, 152
barbarians, 346, 347, 348
Barbosa, Duarte, 333
Barlas, Amir Sultanshah, 80
Baroda, 52, 53, 309
Barros, João de, 336, 341
Bartol'd, V. V., 132
Basavapatna, 144–5
Basra, 96, 97, 180, 193, 195, 197, 214, 230, 232, 298, 303, 314, 316, 321–2, 325
bāts, 107, 108
Battista, Fulgencio, 227
Bayana, 46
Bayazid Bayat, 20, 304–12, 326, 360
Bayly, C. A., 23
Baysungar, Mirza Sultan Muhammad bin Mirza, 61
bazaars, 70–1, 269, 276, **279**
Bedouins, 263, 276, 277, 330
Belgaum, 347
Belgrade, 353
Belur, 68, 69
Benares, 133, 134, 140–1, 159, 282
Bengal, 47, 62, 225, 281–2, 353, 362
Bengali language, 11–12, 360
Bergeron, Pierre, 351–2
Berlin, 357
Bernier, François, 294, 296, 352, 355
betel-leaves, 74–5, 282
Bhakkar, 154, 156, 225, 234, 260
Bhander, 51
Bharuch, 105, 107, 311
Bi-kesi, Munla, 116
Bidar, 47, 87, 88, 89–90
Bihar, 47, 141
Bihbahani, Aqa Ahmad, 240–2, 329–30
Bihishti Herawi, 221–8
Bijanagar, 70
Bijapur, 146, 345, 346–7, 349
Bijoyram Sen, 12
Biruni, Abu Raihan Muhammad ibn Ahmad al-, 2
Black Sea, 6, 85
Boeschoten, Hendrik, 7
Bombay, 168, 240
Bosnia, 7
Brahmins, 23, 70, 76, 138, 143, 147, 356
Brandenburg, Friedrich-Wilhelm, Elector of, 357
Brazil, 337–8, 341
brothels, 73
Bruinessen, Martin van, 7
Budapest, 113, 353
Buddhism, 16–17
Bukhara, 16, 123, 244
Bukhari, Sayyid 'Ataullah, 313
Bulaqi, Kwaja Muhammad, 248
Burdwan, 143
Burhan, Sayyid, Khan of Bukhara, 100
Burhan-ud-Din, 52, 59
Burhan-ul-Mulk, 256
Burhanpur, 180, 205, 207, 225
Burma, 336
Burton, Sir Richard, 4
Bust, 157, 224

Cabot, Sebastian, 340
Cabral, Pedro Álvares, 333
Cairo, 317, 327
Calaminhan, 335
Calcutta, 281, 295
Calicut, 55, 57, 62, 64–9, 73, 86, 88, 92, 317
Calmard, Jean, 180
Cambay, 85, 86
Caspian Sea, 85, 266
Castanheda, Lopes de, 334, 336, 341
castes, 356
Caucasus, 7
Cecil, Robert, 341–2
Çelebi, Katib, 9, 120
Cendrars, Blaise, 3
Central Asia
  17th century, 130–1
  17th-century writers, 120–59
  'Abdul Karim on, 264, 266–8

Mughal expedition, 302
Persian, 23
shared regional values, 228
South Asian travel writers, 244–5
trade routes, 247
Ceylon, 88, 280
Chaghatays, 109, 132, 226
Chahar Ma'sum, 37
Chaharju, 266
Chaitanya, 11
Champaner, 105, 309, 311
Chanderi, 52
Chandernagore (Frans Danga), 281
Chappuzeau, Samuel, 355
Charados, 356
Chardin, Jean, 352
Charles II, King of England, 161
Chaul, 86
Chhatra, 52
China
corpus of travel writing, 12–19, 331
early European travellers, 334, 336, 340–1, 342
ethnographic writing, 18–19
Ming decline, 293–4
and Ottomans, 113–14
Six Dynasties period, 12
Chinapattan (Madras), 161, 163, 280
Chinggis Khan, 16, 48
Chinon, Père Gabriel de, 355
Chiragh-i-Dehli, Shaikh Nasir-ud-Din, 49, 51
Chishti, Mu'in-ud-Din, 154, 363
Christians, 161–2
Chuban Garapasi, 33
circumcision, 241, 267
Cochin, 168
Cochin-China, 336
Cole, Juan, 240–1, 329
Columbus, Christopher, 333, 340
Conçalves, Francisco, 347
Constantinople, 113
Corte-Real, António Monteiro, 346
Cortés, Hernán, 8, 340
Couto, Catarina do, 345
Coutre, Estevan de, 343
Coutre, Jacques de, 343–51, 356–7, 359
Coutre, Joseph de, 344, 345
cows, 66
Crete, 7
Crimea, 83, 84, 91
Crimean War, 327
Cromwell, Oliver, 342
Cuba, 227
Cuttack, 134, 151–2
Da Cá da Mosto, Alvise, 333
Dabhol, 85
Daghestan, 285–6
Dailami, Abdul Rashid, 219
Dal Lake, 226
Daman, 100, 103–4, 306, 308
Damascus, 7, 26, 36, 276
Daniyal (Daniel), Prophet, 276
Dankoff, Robert, 7
Daonapur, 142
Dar-ul-mulk Ahsanabad (Gulbarga), 53
Dara Shukoh, Prince, 222
Darmapatan, 57
Darwaza-i Sham, 41–2
Darwesh, 27–8
Dasht-i-Minu, 28
Daulat, Sayyid, 311
Daulatabad, 27, 49, 53, 225
Daulier-Deslandes, André, 355
Deccan, 23, 45, 47, 54, 82, 85, 89, 142, 146, 176, 179, 207, 216, 225, 228, 241, 290, 301, 348, 353
Deccan, Sultanate, 67
Defoe, Daniel, 4
Delhi (Shahjahanabad)
'Abdul Karim in, 249, 283
Azfari in, 362, 363
Balkhi in, 133, 137
Gesudaraz, 54
Hazin in, 233
mosque, 269
Mufid Mustaufi, 180, 196, 198, 199, 202, 204, 210, 211, 214, 219
Mughal court, 303
Nadir Shah's conquest, 238–9, 242, 256–61
Nadir Shah's withdrawal from, 261–2
Seydi 'Ali, 100, 111–18
Delhi, Sultanate of, 4, 23, 45–6, 47, 48
Derbend, 83
dervishes, 271
Deva Raya II, 71, 73–6, 78–9, 82
Dharmaganga, 149
Digby, Simon, 246
Dih-i 'Ali Wargan, 192
Dilam, 321
diplomacy, 296–8, 314–27
Diu, 96, 103, 312, 329
Diwali, 153
Diwan, Maulana Khwaja Khan, 122
Diyarbekir, 7, 286, 316
Doria, Andrea, 101
Dragon Gate, 16
dress, 65, 86
Druze, 330
Durranis, 290

East India Company, 231, 233, 247, 300, 316, 357
East Indies, 336, 344
Edakkad, 57
Efendi, Haji Muhammad, 322
Efendi, Seyyid 'Abdürrahim Muhibb, 10
Efendi, Seyyid 'Ali, 10
Efendi, Yirmisekiz Çelebi Mehmed, 6, 10
Egypt, 7, 298, 325
elephant hunts, 167
elephants, 69, 72, 76, **77**, 111, 168, 284, 351
Elizabeth I, 341
embassy accounts, 296–8, 314–27
England. *See* United Kingdom
Ennin, 13
Erevan, 25, 32
Erzurum, 33
Ethiopia, 7, 336
ethnography, 18–19, 66, 107, 119, 134, 264, 267–9
Europe
  17th-century travelling explosion, 342–57
  early travellers, 331–42
  Europeans in Bengal, 281–2
  Indo-Persian travel writers in, 245–7
  production of travel accounts, 358–9
  South Asian travellers to, 243–4
  See also Franks
Evliya Çelebi, 6–10, 294, 330
exoticism, 229

Faiz, Abu'l, 177
Faizabad, 31
Fakhr-ud-Din Husain, Khwaja, 122
Farah, 157, 224
Farfhan, 81
Farhad Khan, 87, 274
Farid-ud-Din 'Attar, 21, 24
Farrukh, Maulana, 310
Farrukhabad, 282, 284
Farrukhsiyar, 289
Fars, 265
Fasih Khan, 127
Fatehpur, 225, 305
Fatehpur Sikri, 154
Fath Khan, 81–2, 347
Fathbad, 53
Fatima Zehra, 37
Faulad Khan, 262
Faxian, 12
Figueroa, Martín Fernández de, 334
Firdausi, Mulla, 274, 286–7
Firoz Shah, Sultan of Delhi, 81–2
Firuzshah, Amir, 80

France
  17th-century travellers, 352
  Bibliothèque universelle des voyages, 358
  Ottoman diplomacy, 314, 317, 325–6
  Ottoman travel writers, 10
  and Pondicherry, 280
Franks, 161, 233, 243, 281–2, 290, 306
Frans Danga (Chandernagore), 281
Friedrich-Wilhelm, Elector of Brandenburg, 357

Gage, Thomas, 342
Galata, 115
Galvão, António, 338–42
Galvão, Duarte, 339
Gampola, 149
Ganges, 132
Ganjaba *pargana*, 156
Ganjawi, Nizami, 25
Georgia, 84
Gesudaraz (Muhammad al-Husaini), 48–54
Ghats mountains, 68
Ghazna, 45, 48
Ghaznavids, 23, 45
Ghaznin, 156, 260
Ghazzali, Imam, 162
Ghur, 45
Gilan province, 230, 231
Gilani, Hakim-ul-Mulk, 300
Gilani, Mahmud Gawan, 87, 176
Gilani, Maulana Nur-ud-Dahr, 231
Ginigathena, 149
Gladwin, Francis, 252, 253, 294
Goa, 104, 244, 343, 344, 345, 346
Gogha, 310–11
Góis, Damião de, 340
Goisse, Madeleine, 353
Golkonda, 144, 176, 207, 228, 345, 346
Gor-Khattri, 158
Guanabara, Bay of, 337
Gujarat, 53, 85, 100, 103–6, 112, 114, 117–18, 119, 290, 299, 300, 305–6, 326, 329
Gujarat, Sultanates of, 45, 47
Gujarati, Sultan Muzaffar, 309, 311
Gul 'Izar Begam, 307
Gulbadan Begam, 20, 24, 94, 299, 304, 307, 312
Gulbarga, 47, 53
Gutti, 144
Gwaliyar, 50–1, 225

Habesh (Abyssinia), 97
Habib, Irfan, 324–5
Hadi, Mu'ayyad Abu'l Hasan 'Ali al-, Imam, 195
Hafiz, Shams-ud-Din Muhammad (al-Shirazi), 60–1, 80, 103, 122, 192, 204, 249, 310
Haidar, 33, 37, 38

Hainzelmann, Johann, **354**
Haji, Aqam, 120, 300
Haji Begam, 109
ḥajj
'Abdul Karim, 249, 251, 270, 272, 277–8
anonymous female Iranian writer, 24–43
Bayazid Bayat's account, 304–12
Hazin, 230, 231, 232
historiography, 304
Tipu, 317
Hakluyt, Richard, 333, 334, 341–2
Hallah, 265–6, 271–2
Hamadan, 222, 230, 274
Hambantota, 149
Hamdi, 109
Hami, 268–9
Hamid-ud-Din, Maulana, 51
Hammer-Purgstall, Joseph, 7
Hamza, Sayyid, 310
Hanafiyya, Muhammad ibn, 319
Hanamba, thread-wearer, 78
Harihar, 147
Hasa, al-, 96, 97
Hasan, Khwaja Abu'l, 122, 137
Hasan, Mohibbul, 317
Hasan, Qara, 113, 114
Hasan 'Ali, Khwaja, 165
Hasan 'Ali, Maulana, 195, 196–7
Hasan Chunnu, 306
Hasan Ibn Ali, 37
Hasan Khan Shamlu, 157, 158, 222
Hasan Mirza, Shah, 108–9, 110
Hashim, **206**
Hazin. *See* Lahiji
Herat, 55, 57, 59, 62, 70, 73, 74, 77, 81, 112, 157, 211, 221, 222, 223, 244, 264
Herawi, Bihishti, 221–6, 227–8
Herawi, Fasihi Ansari, 222
Herrera Maldonado, Francisco de, 335
Herrera y Tordesillas, Antonio, 340
Hijaz, 29, 251
Hind, **56**
Hindawi, 23
Hindus
Bihbahani on, 241
Ganges, 139
Thailand, 170
women, 155
worship, 137, 138, 143, 144, 158–9
Hindustan, meaning, 4
Hindustan Sultanate, 18th-century, 290
historiography
ḥajj pilgrimage, 304
history of mentalities, 21, 245
Islam, 2
Hodgson, Marshall, 228, 298
holy places, 269–73, 298–300, 302, 322, 323
See also ḥajj pilgrimage
Honawar, 47, 79, 81
Howaiza, 214
Hud (Heber), Prophet, 36
Hughli Bandar, 251, 280, 281
Humayun, Mughal emperor, 100, 108, 109, 111–14, 116–17, 137, 311
Hungary, 97
Hurmuz, 59–60, 64, 67, 74, 80, 82, 83, 85, 88, 96, 97, 114, 345
Husain Baiqara, Sultan, 237, 307
Husain Ibn Ali, Imam, 35, 88, 137, 275, 322
Husain Pasha, Amir (Islam Khan Rumi), 303
Husaini, Mir Muhammad Husain bin 'Abdul, 246
Husaini, Mirza, 133, 151, 154, 155, 156
Husaini, Mirza Bahram al-, 202, 204–6
Husaini, Sayyid Muhammad al-(Gesudaraz), 48–54
Husein Re'is, 101
Hyderabad, 144, 160, 178, 180, 195–6, 207–8, 210, 211, 212, 240, 242

Ibn Battuta, Abu 'Abdullah al-Lawati al-Tanji, 5, 6, 46–7, 57
Ibn-i Muljim, 137
Ibn Khurdadbih, **56**, **218**
Ibrahim, Sultan, 301
Ibrahim Agha, 322
Ibrahim Beg, 166
Ibrahim Khan, 285
Ibrahim Mirza, 100
Ibrahim Müteferrika, 9
Ibrahim Pasha, 114
Idrisi, al-, 4
Iftikhar, 306, 312
Ikram, Sayyid, 52
Ilahabad, 139
'Imad-ul-Mulk, 106, 290
Imams, 180, 195
India. *See* Mughals; South Asia
Indo-Gangetic plain, 4, 46–7
Indo-Persian culture, meaning, 3–4
Injaq valley, 32
Iraj, 52
Iran
17th century, 130–1
17th-century travel writers, 159–71
18th-century grumblers, 229–42
'Abdul Karim on, 264–6
disgusted travellers from, 159–72, 175–242
early European travellers, 336
French travellers, 352, 353, 355

Iran (*cont.*)
Il Khanid dynasty, 46
Indo-Persian world, 23
Irano-centricism, 177
Mufid on, 180
Ottoman expansion, 97
political conditions, 230
relations with Mughals, 226–9
Russian travellers, 92
shared regional values, 228
See also Persian
'Iraq, 212, **218**, 251, 298
Isfahan, 26, 27, 83, 85, 92, 180, 189, 192, 219, 222, 227, 230, 231, 232, 237
Isfahan, siege of (1732), 233
Isfahani, Mirza Abu Talib Khan, 245–6, 247, 360
Isfahani, Mulla Abu'l Hasan, 231
Iskender Pasha, 114, 118
Islam
historiography, 2
holy places, 269–73, 298–300, 302, 322, 323
mysticism, 242
Nikitin on, 88–9
Islam, Riazul, 132
Islam Khan Rumi (Amir Husain Pasha), 303
Istanbul, 7, 101, 115, 175, 317, 353
I'timad-ud-Daula, 179
I'tisam ud-Din, 246, 360
Ivan the Terrible, 100

Ja'far, Sayyid, 317
Ja'far al-Sadiq, Imam, 37
Ja'far Khan, 317
Jaffnapatnam, 149
Jagannath, 143, 158
Jagatai, 86
Jahanara, 24
Jahandar Shah, 289
Jahangir, Mughal emperor, 20, 94, 120–8, **124**, 129, 152, 178, 179, 226, 296, 300
Jahanshahi, Amir Nizamuddin Ahmad, 197
Jaihun (Bactrus), 266
Jains, 170
Jaipur, 152, 362
Jaisalmer, 134, 154, 155
Jalali, Maulana, 123–5
Jalil, 'Abdul, 151
Jamal-ud-Din, Khwaja, 81
James I, King of England, 296
James II, King of England, 161
Jamshid, 167
Jannat ul-Baqi', 37
Japan, 13, 336, 342
Jarapatan, 57
Jarjiz (George), Prophet, 276
Jauhar Aftabchi, 20
Jaunpur, Sultanate, 62
Jaweza, 193
Jawwad, Muhammad Taqi al-, 195
Jerusalem, 276, 298, 302
Jiangsu, 14
Jiddah, 95, 232, 278, 299, 317
Jihan Shah, 106
João III, King of Portugal, 96
Jodhpur, 362
jogīs, 136, 145, 148, 159
John of Plano Carpini, 5
John the Baptist, 268
Johor, 346
Joseph, 210
Judaism, 89
Junabidhi, Maulana Nasrullah, 82
Junnar, 86, 89
Justinian, Emperor, 90

Ka'aba, 38–40, **39**, 43
Kabul, 100, 117, 130, 135, 156, 212, 225, 238, 256, 260, 268
Kafadar, Cemal, 7, 294
Kaiqubad, 238
Kakatiya kingdom, 47
Kamanur, 57
Kamran, Mirza, 307
Karbala, 88, 231, 240, 274–5, 286
Karim Beg, 284
Karkuk, 267, 286
Karnal, 117, 256
Karnatak, 211
Kashan, 25, 26, 85
Kashmir, 212, 222, 224–5, 226, 248
Katif, 96, 97
Kayalpatnam, 148
Kaysathas, 23
Kerala region, 57, 66, 243, 339
Kerman, 59, 81, 232
Kermanshah, 230–1, 240
Kerouac, Jack, 133
Khaibar, 276–7
Khalil, Mirza, 24
Khalil Sultan, 55
Khalji Afghans, 252
Khambayat, 53, 311
Khan-i Dauran, 256
Khanid dynasty, 46
Khaqani, Afzal-ud-Din Badil ibn 'Ali Najjar Shirwani, 223
Kharaniq, 211
Kharg island, 316, 319–21
Kharijites, 161
Kharris, 356

Kharwaniq, 25, 30
Khattis, 23
Khawand Khan, 53
Khawass Khan, 122
Khorasan region, 55, 86, 157, 167, 251, 265, 267, 286
Khorasani, Khwaja Yusuf, 85
Khotan, 16
Khudabad, 234, 260
Khudawand Khan, governor of Surat, 105
Khulm, 48
Khurasani, 'Ali Akbar, 249
Khurfaghan, 80
Khuriyat, 197
Khurram, Prince, 345, 349
Khurram Darra, 28
Khurramabad, 27–8, 230
Khushka, 27
Khusrau Dehlawi, Amir, 62, **63**, 75, 76, 80, 104, 137, 274
Khwaja Khizr (Green Prophet), 319–21
Khwand, Mir, 172, 216
Khwandmir, Shaikh, 52, 210–11, 216
Khwansar, 230
Khwarizm, 266, 267, 274
Khwarizm Shah Sultan, 100
Kiev, 85
Kirmanlar, 32–3
Kirmanshah, 274
Kishan, 138
Koh-i Qaplantu, 28
Kollam, 57
Konarak, 144
Kosovo, 7
Kotov, Fedor Afanasiyev, 92
Kufa, 194, 195
Küfe, 113
Kuh-i Bisutun, 274
Kulatiri family, 57
Kumhari, 57
Kurdi, Amir Husain Mushrif al-, 95
Kurds, 330

Lahejan, 230
Lahiji, Shaikh Muhammad 'Ali Hazin, 288
  grumbling traveller, 229–40
  moral superiority, 242, 328–9
Lahore, 100, 108, 110–11, 117, 122, 128, 133, 134, 136–7, 178, 214, 216, 226, 236, 238, 256, 322
Lahsa, 232
Lake Van, 7
Lakshmi (goddess), 146–7
Lamouroux, Christian, 17–18, 19
languages
  19th-century Indo-Persian travels, 360
  European travellers, 343, 358
  Indo-Persian writers, 23
  Mughal rule, 362
Lar, 83, 85, 231, 232
Largillière, Nicolas, **354**
Lari, Khwaja Mahmud, 117
Léry, Jean de, 337–8
Lévi-Strauss, Claude, 2
Li Ao, 13–14
Liao, 17–19
Linhares, Conde de, 345
Lisbon, 246, 344
Liver-Eaters, 153–4, 178
Lobo, Dioggo, 344
London, 246
Loni, 50
Lopburi, 165–6, 168
Lopes, Luis, 344
Louis XIV, 353
Louis XV, 10
Lu Zhen, 18
Lucknow, 240, 241
Lut (Lot), Prophet, 36

Ma'bar, Sultanate of, 47
Ma'bari, Zain-ud-Din, 57
Madiyan-i Salih, 36–7
Madras (Chinapattan), 161, 163, 280
Madurai, 47
Maghash al-Ruzz, 36
Maghribi, Shaikh Ahmad, 50
Mahan, Sayyid, 52
Mahawili, Muhammad ibn 'Abd-i 'Ali al-Najafi al-, 193–4
Mahdi, Imam, 194
Mahdi, Mirza Muhammad, 251
Mahdi Khan, 260
Mahindri, 152
Mahmud, Sultan, 1, 48, 109, 110, 112, 313
Majlisi, Maulana Muhammad Taqi, 195
Makassar, 132
Makditi, Ussama, 330
Makran region, 59
Maktub Khan, 125
Malabar, 57
Malay, 11
Malaya, 336
Malik Husain, Khwaja, 311
Malik Muhammad, Khwaja, 311
Malik ut-Tujjar, 86–7, 91
Maliki, Qazi Muhammad, 310
Mallu Khan, 82
Malwa province, 303
Mamluks, 95, 298
Mamyrev, Vasilii, 83

Mandeville, Sir John, 5, 294, 334
Mangalore, 67, 68, 314, 319
Manikpatnam, 153
Manila, 132, 346
Mankot, 117
Manuel, King of Portugal, 339
Marathas, 281, 282, 289
Maravi family, 57
Marco Polo, 5, 6, 8, 294, 334
Martaban, 335
Mashhad, 100–1, 222, 231, 265, 269–71, 287
Mashhadi, Amir Sayyid 'Ala-ud-Din, 79
Mashhadi, Ghazzali, 176
Mashhadi, Mirza Muhammad Na'im, 270
Masqat, 60, 80, 85, 96, 97–8, 161, 197, 230, 316, 318, 323
Massawa, 97
Mas'ud, Khwaja, 78, 79, 81
Masulipatnam, 176
Ma'suma, 27
Mathura, 133, 137–9, 158
Matrah, 318, 319
Mazandaran region, 55, 231, 251
Mazandarani, Ashraf, 219–21
Mazandarani, Haji Salim, 160
Mazandarani, Maulana Muhammad Salih, 195
Mazandarani, Sayyid, 164
Mazkur, Shaikh Nasr al-, 319
Mecca, 7, 25, 26, 38–41, **39**, 43, 113, 210, 232, 263, 277–8, **279**, 299–300, 302
  See also ḥajj
Medina, 26, 37–8, 41, 42, 43, 113, 270, 277, 302
Mehmed IV, Sultan, 297, 302–3
Mehmed Achik bin Ömer, 9
Mehmed Pasha, Peri, 116
Mehmed Pasha, Sokollu, 114, 120
Melaka, 168, 344
Melek Ahmed Pasha, 7
Melhemi, 297
Mendes Pinto, Fernão, 334–6, 340, 346
mentalities, 21, 245
Mergui, 163–4, 165, 168
methodology, 19–20, 42, 44
Mexico, 340
Midnapore, 143
Mina, 26, 40, 41, 43
Minhaj Muarris, Qazi, 52
Minuchihr, 238
Mir Jumla (Mu'azzam Khan), 178, 227
Mirza Khan, 309
Mirza Shah, 111
Miskin, Tahmas Khan, 290–3
Miyan Sultanpur, 53
Miyana, 25, 29
Miyandhar, 52
Mohammad Husain, 126
Mokha, 230, 278
Moluccas, 339, 340
Mominabad, 26
Mongols, 46, 48
monstrous and wondrous creatures, 142–3, 211–15, **213**
Mosul, 97, 267, 268, 276, 286, 301, 316
Mosuli, Amir Jamal-ud-Din, 223
Mottahedeh, Roy, 4
Mu'azzam, 36
Mu'azzam Khan (Mir Jumla), 227
Mudawwara, 36
Mufid Mustaufi. *See* Yazdi
Mughals
  16th-century, 93–5
  17th-century, 130–1, 132, 134
  17th-century enthusiastic Iranian, 221–6
  17th-century Iranian grumblers, 179–221
  18th-century, 289, 313
  18th-century Iranian grumblers, 229–42
  18th-century travellers to Rum, 314–27
  chronicles, 304
  conquest of Hyderabad, 160
  culture, 176–7
  De Coutre account, 345–51
  decline, 242, 282, 285, 313, 362
  duration of dynasty, 298
  embassy accounts, 296
  ḥajj chronicle, 304–12
  Nadir Shah invasion, 239, 242, 248–9, 251, 256–61, 313, 327
  and Ottoman empire, 114, 298–303
  popular Iranian opinions, 217
  and Portuguese, 306, 308, 312
  relations with Iran, 226–9, 301
  Tavernier's account, 353
  trade routes, **203**
  travellers' views of, 177–9, 328
  unseating, 327
  writers in Mughal courts, 110–28, 226
Muhammad, Khwaja, 78, 81, 89
Muhammad, Prophet, 194–5, 208, 210, 270, 278
Muhammad 'Ali Beg, 284
Muhammad Husain Beg, 161, 164, 166
Muhammad ibn Abu Bakr, 319
Muhammad Khalil Beg, 185
Muhammad Nizam, Mir, 151
Muhammad Rabi' ibn Muhammad Ibrahim
  assessment, 172, 174
  Irano-centricism, 177, 220
  negative views, 162, 166, 170–1, 217, 228

Siam journey, 94, 159–72, 240, 296
views of India, 178
Muhammad Rukn, 52
Muhammad Shah, Mughal emperor, 238, 242, 248, 251, 256, 259, 260, 262, 281–2, 284–5, 289, 313
Muhammad-i Jahangir, Pir, 48
Muhanna, Mir, 319–21
Muhyi-ud-Din, Sayyid, 302
Mu'in-ul-Mulk, Mir, 291
Mukalla Bandar, 309
Mukhlis, Anand Ram, 294, 324
Multan, 46, 100, 109, 110, 179, 210, 212, 214, 225, 234–5
Multani, Mir Zakariya, 310
Munger, 219
Munshi, Khwaja Muzzafar, 157
Murad IV, Sultan, 300–1
Murad Bakhsh, Prince, 222, 226
Murad Re'is, 97
Murshidabad, 240
Murshidi, Shaikh Nur-ud-Din Muhammad al-, 80
Musa Kazim, Imam, 195
Musa Khan, 107–8
Musawi Khan, 125
Mushid Quli Khan, 282
music, Thailand, 163
Mustafa Agha, 105
Mustafa Beg, 150
Mustafa Pasha, 97, 301
Mu'tabar-ul-Mulk, 260
Mu'tamad Khan, 121
Mutawakkil III, al-, 327
Mutribi. *See* Samarquandi
Muzzaffar, Sayyid, 178
Muzzaffar Khan, 52
Mysore, 245, 314, 316, 317, 324

Nadir Shah Afshar
'Abdul Karim leaving, 273
appearance, 263
death, 285–8
Delhi constructions, 269
Hazin on, 230, 234, 237, 238
invasion of Northern India, 239, 242, 245, 248–9, 251, 313, 327
map of campaigns, 257
rise to power, 230, 234
travelling narrative, 261–2, 272
tyrant at work, 252–61
wars, 284
Nadirabad, 256
Nahram, 31
Na'ima, Mustafa, 297
Naipaul, V. S., 3
Najaf, 193–4, 232, 233, 240, 275, 286, 316
Najafi, Sayyid Hashim, 231
Nakhajawan, 25, 32
Naqshbandi, Sultan Khwaja, 299–300
Narai, King of Thailand, 159, 160–1, 164, 166–71, 177
Narayan Das, 139
narrative methodology, 19–20
Narwar, 225
Nasir Khan, 256
Nasir-ud-Din, Shaikh, 52
Nasir-ud-Din Mahmud Ilyas Shah, 62
Nasir-ud-Din 'Umar, Maulana, 50
Nasir-ul-Mulk, 104–5
Nasirpur, 109
Nasruddin, Mulla, 8–9, 208
Nasrullah Mirza, 287
Nathan, Mirza, 121
Naurang Khan, 311, 312
Nauroz, 151
Nazr Muhammad Khan, 132
Netherlands, 319
Nikitin, Afanasii, 82–92, 357
Niknam Khan, 195–6
Ni'matullah Wali Kermani, Shah, 47, 59
Ni'matullahi Sufi order, 176
Nimrod, 276
Nisar Khan, 53
Nishapur, 222
Nishapuri, Qasim, 309
Nizam Shah, 225
Nizam-ud-Din, Khwaja, 137
Nizam-ud-Din, Maulana, 205
Nizam-ul-Mulk, 87, 256, 282, 283
Nizam-ul-Mulk Asaf Jah, 313
Nizami, 24, 37, 38, 75, 103
Nizamshahi territory, 145–6
North Africa, Ottoman expansion, 95–7, 130
Nu'mani, Maulana Shibli, 327
Nur Jahan, Mughal empress, 122, 154, 180, 226
Nur-ud-Din Muhammad, Mirza, 307, 309, 311
Nurbai Tawa'if, 261
Nurullah Khan, 317, 318, 319, 322–3

Odyssey, 8
Oman, 230, 232, 319
opium, 141
orality, 24
Orientalism, 173–4, 242, 329–30, 357
Orissa, 133, 142, 151–4, 178, 282
Osório, Jerósimo de, 340, 341
Otrar, 16

Ottoman empire
16th-century expansion, 95–7, 130
16th-century writers, 95–120
17th-century, 130–1
18th-century, 313–14
18th-century embassy account, 314–27
18th-century expansion, 230–1
anonymous Iranian female account, 32–42, 44
European traveller, 353
and India, 114, 298–303
Ottoman Orientalism, 329–30
and Portuguese, 96–100, **98, 99,** 104–5, 112, 299
shared regional values, 228
travel writers, 6–11, 20
Özdemiroghlu Osman Pasha, 97

Pahang, 344, 346
Paithan, 146
Palestine, 7
Pali language, 11
Panchatantra fables, 70
Panjal, Pir, 226
Pantalayini, 67
Parkar, 100, 108
Patan, 100, 107–8
Patani, 168, 346
Patna, 133, 134, 141–2, 219, 240, 282
Patwari, Lalu, 212
Peak, Adam, 328
Pegu, 88, 90–1, 335
Pereira, Duarte Pacheco, 339–40
Persian
17th-century, 131
19th-century, 360
Bayazid Bayat's account, 304, 305
and British empire, 44
culture, 46, 177
diplomatic accounts, 297
intellectuals, 46
Mughals, 93, 362
poetry, 31, 361
spread, 23
Tipu Sultan, 318
v. Arabic, 331
Persian Gulf, 47, 59, 80, 318–19
Peru, 341
Peshawar, 133, 135, 256, 260
Petracha, Phra, 167
Phaulkon, Constant, 166, 168, 169
Phetchaburi, 164
Philip II, King of Spain, 244
Philippines, 342
pidgin, 85
pilgrimage
See also ḥajj
'Abdul Karim, 273–80
routes, 300
Pinto de Frexos, Sebastião, 344
piracy, 64
Pires, Tomé, 333
Piri Re'is, 96–7
Pishing, 156
polyandry, 66
Ponda, 347
Portugal
15th-century exploration, 243
early travellers, 333–42
Estado da India, 95, 336, 345
and Mughals, 306, 308, 312
opinions on Portuguese, 161–2
and Ottomans, 96–100, **98, 99,** 104–5, 112, 299
Spanish takeover, 244
Preveze, 101
printing, 359–60
Ptolemy, 333
Pulcheri (Pondicherry), 280
Punjab, 23, 45, 47, 226, 289
Purchas, Samuel, 333, 337
Puri, 143, 159
Purniya, 282
Pushkar, 154
Pyrard de Laval, François, 351–2

Qa'im Beg, 302, 303
Qa'im Khan, 289
Qajars, 242
Qalat, 289
Qalhat, 61
Qamar-ud-Din Khan, 256, 283
Qandahar, 110, 156, 222, 224, 237, 252, 256
Qapudan, Sayyid 'Ali, 118
Qara Hamza, 33
Qarabaghlar, 32
Qarchai, 33
Qarwin, 25
Qasimabad, 26–7
Qasimkota, 144
Qazi-i Khwajagi, 52
Qazi Ishaq, 52
Qazwin, 27, 101, 115, 251, 265
Qazwini, 4
Qazwini, Asad Beg, 345
Qazwini, Zakariya ibn Muhammad, 172
Qilij Khan, 305, 311
Qingyuan tiao fa shilei, 17
Qishm, 96, 319

Qom, 25, 27, 29, 222
Qubba, 196
Qubilai Khan, 5
Quli Beg, Allah, 184, 185
Quli Beg, Imam, 252, 288
Quli Khan, Imam, 126
Quli Khan, Rahman, 300
Quli Khan, Raza, 254, 289
Qulij Khan, Nawwab, 311
Qunduzi, 'Ali Muhammad, 311
Qureshi, I. H., 324
Qurkh, 32
Quryat, 60, 61
Qutb Shah, Abdullah, 196
Qutb Shah, Abu'l Hasan, 178
Qutb Shah, Mohammad, 144
Qutb-ud-Din Khan, 306, 309, 312

race, Nikitin on, 91
Radhanpur, 108
Rahima Katun, 265
Raibagh, 347
Raja, Samudri, 62, 64, 66, 67, 104
Rajasthan, 133, 158
Rajmahal, 133, 142
Rajputs, 107, 108, 109, 119, 225, 226, 228, 356
Rāmāyaṇa, 11
Ramdas, 136, 142
Ramusio, Giovanni Battista, 333, 334
Rashid-ud-Din, 2
Rayy, 101, 222
Razi, Fakhr-ud-Din, 162
Red Sea, 95, 96, 105, 300
religion
  'Abdul Karim on, 264, 269–73
  Balkhi, 158–9
  Bihbahani, 240–1
  Brahmins, 138
  de Coutre on, 346, 347, 351
  holy cities, 269–73
  Nikitin, 85, 88–91
  pilgrimage, 273–80
  and Tavernier, 355–6
  Thailand, 169–70
Rhodes, 101
Roche, Daniel, 358, 360
Roe, Sir Thomas, 129, 296
Rohila, 'Ali Muhammad Khan, 285, 289
Rukn-ud-Din, Shaikh, 110
Rum, Maulana, 24
Russia, 231, 357
Rustam, 256
Rüstem Pasha, 97, 114
Rustichello of Pisa, 5

Sá, João de, 334
Sa Dula, 16
Sa Tianxi, 16
Sa'adat Yar, 306, 308, 312
Sabzar, 224
Sabzawar, 222
Sabzwari, Khwaja 'Arab, 145
Sa'di, Muslih-ud-Din, 24, 103, 183, 223
Sadr-ud-Din, Mirza, 204–7
Sadr-ud-Din, Shaikh, 110
Safa, 40, 41
Safar-us-Salmani, Khwaja, 114
Safavi, Mirza Rustam, **206**
Safavi, Shah Isma'il Musavi, 202, 216
Safavi, Sultan Husain, 254, 289
Safavids
  17th-century, 130–1
  decline, 230, 252–6
  Irano-centricism, 216, 220
  relations with Mughals, 226–9, 301
  Safavid patriotism, 225
  See also Iran
Safdar Khan, 285
Safi, Shah of iran, 156–7
Said, Edward, 357
Saif Khan, Nawwab, 282
Saihun (Jaxartes), 266
Saiva, 159
Saleh Chelebi family, 322
Salih, Maulana, 310
Salih, Prophet, 36
Salima Sultan Begam, 299, 307
Samani, Shah Muhammad 'Ali, 48–9
Samarqand, 16, 77, 100, 122, 244
Samarqandi, Kamal-ud-Din 'Abdur Razzaq ibn Ishaq
  and Balkhi, 147
  citation, 45
  comparisons, 85, 131, 133, 195
  managing windfall, 67–82
  and Muhammad Rabi', 172
  narrative interest, 312
  reluctant ambassador, 54–67, 92, 296
  Vijayanagara city, 357
Samarqandi, Mutribi al-Asamm, 94, 120–9, 131, 134, 177–8, 296
Samiri, al-, 57
Sana'a, 96, 278
Sana'i, 223
Sangisar, 64
Sani, 'Abdullah, 221–6
Sansan, 26
Sanskrit, 8, 11
Santiago de Compostela, 346
Sar, 29

Saragossa, 345
Sarandip (Sri Lanka), 133, 142, 148–50, 328
Sarang Khan, 82
Sarfaraz Khan, 282
Sartre, Jean-Paul, 175
sati, 119
Sauser, Frédéric, 3
Savaji, Salman, 79–80
Sawah, 25, 27
Sayyid brothers, 289
Selim, Sultan, 116, 298
Selim III, Sultan, 325
Selman Re'is, 95–6
Seneca, Lucius Annaeus, 340
Seth, Maoji, 318
Seydi 'Ali Re'is, 248
  assessment, 172
  career, 101
  ethnography, 107, 118–19
  generally, 9, 94, 95–120
  and Indian countryside, 229
  itinerary, **102**
  Mughal court, 110–20, 131, 296
  poems, 93, 108, 111, 115, 117
  rhetoric and style, 117–18, 298
  works, 101
"Shabait", 88, 89
Shafi'is, 64
Shah 'Alam, 142
Shahin Beg, 116
Shahjahan, Mughal emperor, 222, 226, 300–2, 326–7, 345
Shahjahanabad. *See* Delhi (Shahjahanabad)
Shahnawaz Khan, 289
Shahpur, 347
Shahristani, Khwaja 'Abdul Karim
  background, 247–52
  citation, 243
  credibility, 361
  decline text, 290–4, 328
  ethnography, 264, 267–9
  generally, 239, 247–94
  pilgrimage, 273–80
  pre-colonial writing, 247
  printed versions, 359
  reason and faith, 269–73
  return home, 280–94
  translation of memoirs, 252, 253
  travelling narrative, 261–9
  tyrant at work, 252–61
  West and Central Asia, 244–5
Shahrukh, Mirza, 55–7, 59, 62, 63, 65, 67, 69, 74, 77, 78–9, 80, 81, 147, 172, 289, 310, 311
Shaibani, 'Abdullah Khan, 130
Sha'ibi, 'Abdul Hayy, 307
Shaikh-ul-Islam Baha-ud-Din Shaikh 'Umar, 81
Shalil, 32
Shalimar, 226
Sham, 251
Sharif Khan, 311
Sharif-ud-Din 'Abdul Qahhar, 81
Shazli, Shaikh Abu'l Hasan, 278
Shazli, Shaikh 'Umar, 278
Shen Gua, 17, 18–19
Sher Khan, 107–8, 156–8
Shihab Khan, 309
Shihr, 308, 309, 310
Shi'is, 43, 92, 137, 178, 241–2, 278
Shiraz, 77, 122, 209, 230, 231, 345
Shirazi, Ahli, 222
Shirazi, al-. *See* Hafiz
Shirazi, Mir Abu Turab, 299
Shirazi, Sayyid Najib Amir Muhammad Rashid, 211
Shirin, 274
Shirwan, 32
Shirwani, Afzal-ud-Din Badil ibn 'Ali Najjar (Khaqani), 223
Shivaji, 196
shrines and holy places, 269–73, 298–300, 302, 322, 323
  See also ḥajj; pilgrimage
Shu'aib (Jethro), Prophet, 271
Shuja, Shah, 222
Shuja'-ud-Daula, Nawwab, 282, 290
Shustar, 230
Shustari, Nurullah, 216
Siam. *See* Thailand
Sigiriya, 15
Sikandar Lodi, 23
Silva de Meneses, Francisco, 344
Simman, 222
Simmani, Khwaja Ahmad, 48
Sind, **56**, 100, 108, 115–16, 117, 119, 133, 155–6, 158, 233, 234
Sindbad the Sailor, 4
Siraj-ud-Din, Maulana, 54
Siraj-ud-Din 'Ali Khan Arzu, 229
Sirhind, 133, 137, 212, 238
Sirjan, 81
Sistan region, 55, 59
Sitagangula, 149
Siyawani, Salah-ud-Din, 156
Slave Dynasty, 45
Smolensk, 85
Solomon, 167
Sonepat, 117
Song Dynasty, 17–18

Song Tuan, 17
Soqotora, 272
Soro, 152
Soudras, 356
South Asia
- 15th-century accounts, 45–92
- 16th-century accounts, 93–120
- 17th-century accounts, 120–74
- 17th-century enthusiastic Iranian, 221–6
- 17th-century grumbling Iranians, 175–221
- 18th-century Iranian grumblers, 229–42
- 18th-century travel writer, 314–27
- British colonial writers, 245–6
- countryside, 229
- early European travellers, 336, 343–51
- land of wonders, 328
- shared values, 228–9
- Tavernier in, 352, 353
- Timur period, 48–54
- trade routes, 247
- travel writers in, 11–12, 243–7, 304, 327–31
- vernacular languages, 23, 24, 93, 131, 360, 361

South-East Asia, 133, 159–71, 340, 344–5, 345–6
Spain, 333, 334, 340
spice trade, 96
Sri Lanka (Sarandip), 133, 142, 148–50, 328
Srirangapatnam, 316
Staden, Hans, 337, 338
Stewart, Charles, 245
Strassberg, Richard, 14, 15
Su Che, 19
Suakin, 97
Sudan, 7
Suez, 96, 317
Sufis, 47–54, 93, 176, 189, 190, 221, 242
Suhar, 316, 319
Sukkur, 155
Sulaiman, Qazi, 52, 53
Sulaiman, Shah of Iran, 159, 160, 163, 168, 185
Sulaiman Khan, 52, 168
Sulaïman Mirza, 100
Süleyman Pasha, 96, 319
Süleyman "the Lawgiver", 96, 97, 113, 114, 115, 117–18, 120
Sultaniyya, 28
Sultanpur, 109, 238
Sultanpuri, Mulla 'Abdullah, 300
Sunnis, 33, 44, 241, 327
Suphan Buri, 164, 165, 171
Sur, 61
Surat, 100, 104–5, 105, 168, 180, 196, 198, 199, 232, 240, 290, 298, 299, 305–6, 311–12, 353
Suwaini al-'Abdullah, Shaikh, 322
Syria, 7, 35–6, 41–2, 276

Tabriz, 25, 29, 35, 83, 85
Tabrizi, Sa'ib, 219
Tadri, 318
Tahir Mohammad, 243–4
Tahmasp, Shah, 20, 101, 115
Tahmasp II, Shah, 231, 254
Tahmasp Khan Jala'ir, 263, 288
Tahmasp Quli Khan, 231, 232, 254–5
- *See also* Nadir Shah Afshar

Ta'izz, 96, 230
Tak-i Bustan, 274
Tamil, 11
Tamrusia, **141**
Tang-i Siya, 192
Tarbiyat Khan, 212
Tardi Muhammad, 311
Tarkhan Mirza, 'Isa, 108–10
Tarkhans, 100, 109, 110, 116
Tarzak, 80
Tashkandi, Maulana Sabri, 128
Taulak Khan, 311
Tavernier, Gabriel, 352
Tavernier, Jean-Baptiste, 352–7, **354**
Tehran, 222, 231
Tehrani, I'timad ud-Daula, 154
Teixeira, Martim, 344
Tekkalakotte, 144
Telingana, 144
Telugu, 11, 161, 360
Temeshvarlï, Osman Agha ibn Ahmed, 10
temples, 67, 68–9, 147
Tenasserim, 163, 164
Thailand, 131, 159–71, 177, 178, 240, 296, 322, 335, 336, 346, 351
Thanesar, 117
Thatta, 108–9, 233–4, 260
Thévenot, Jean de, 352
Thevet, André, 337, 338
Third World Spirit, 173
Thule, 340
Tiku, 150
Timor, 132
Timur Gurgan, Amir, 48, 54–5, 81–2, 122–3, 128, 272, 276
Timurids, 237, 290
Tipu Sultan, 245, 247, **315**
- embassy account, 314–27
- route, **320**

Tirupati temple, 147, 159, 357
Tiruvadi dynasty, 57
Tonnelier, Suzanne, 352
Tordesillas, Treaty of, 340

trade routes, **203**, 247, 300
Transoxania region, 55, 123, 126, 128, 274, 310
travel writing
  authorship, 360–1
  Chinese writers, 12–19, 331
  European early modern period, 331–52
  first-person accounts, 20–1, 172
  history of mentalities, 21, 245
  Japanese writers, 13
  languages, 23, 343, 358, 360, 362
  Occidentalism, 2–3
  Ottoman corpus, 6–11, 20
  printing, 359–60
  South Asian writers, 11–12
  truth, 361–2
  women, 24, 42
truth, 361–2
Tughluq, Sultan Firoz Shah, 48
Tughluq, Sultan Muhammad Shah, 49
Tunis, 345
Turan region, 127, 251, 272
Turanis, 59, 283
Turkey, 352, 353
Turkish language, 23, 297, 362
Tus, 222, 231, 265
Tus-i Sarkan, 274

Ucch, 109
Ujjain, 180, 204–5, 210, 214
Ulugh Khan, 329
'Umar Shaikh, Mirza, 237
Umayyads, 35, 36
United Kingdom
  diplomacy, 314, 325–6
  and Madras, 280
  opinions on British, 161–2
  travel writers in India, 245–6
Urdu, 246, 360
Urdubad, 24, 25, 30–1
'Urfa, 42
Urrumi, Muhammad Quli Khan, 287
Üsküdar, 316–17
Usuli school, 242
'Uzair (Ezra), Prophet, 276
Uzbek, 'Abdullah Khan, 123, 127
Uzbeks, 110, 286

Vaishnava, 159
Vambéry, Arminius, 9
Vank, 108
Vasco da Gama, 243, 333, 334, 340
vernacular languages, 23, 24, 93, 131, 360, 361
Vienna, 10
Vijayanagara (Bijanagar), 68–73, 76–7, 146–7, 357
Vijayanagara (Karnataka) kingdom
  elephants, 69, 72, 76
  generally, 45, 47, 67–79, 131
  king, 71, 73–6, 78–9, 82
  public administration, 71–2
Villegagnon, Nicolas Durand de, 337
Vlissingen, 344

Wadi-i Fatima, 38
Wali Balkhi. *See* Balkhi
Wallachia, 84
Wang Shizhen, 14
Wang Zen, 18
waqfs, 185–6, 299
Wardi, Ibn al-, 4
Warrangal, 47
watches, 275–6
William of Rubruck, 5
women
  anonymous Iranian writer, 24–44
  Balkhi on, 141, 149, 152–3, 155
  English women in Madras, 161–2
  India, 90–1
  sati, 119
  travel writing, 24, 42
wondrous creatures, 142–3, 211–15, **213**

Xuanzang, 12

Yahudi, 'Abdullah, 322
Yahya, Hazrat Khwaja, 307
Yahya ibn Zakariya (John the Baptist), 268
Ya'qub, Khwaja, 52
Yarkand, 247
Yazd, 85, 180, 182–6, 190–1, 205, 209–10
Yazdi, Muhammad Mufid Mustaufi
  assessment, 217–19
  grumbling traveller, 1, 61, 191–219, 227–9
  itinerary, 180
  pre-travel period, 1, 179–91
  style, 180–2, 186–90
  wonders and monstrosities, 211–15
Yelu Qucai, 16
Yemen, 113, 298
Yunus (Jonas), Prophet, 276
Yusuf, Sayyid, 53

Zafar Khan, 53, 226
Zafar Khan Raushan-ud-Daula, 269
Zahid Beg, Haji, 197
Zaib-un-Nisa, 24, 219
Zaidi Shi'is, 278

Zakariya, Prophet, 276
Zakariya Khan, 263, 289
Zaki 'Nadim', Mirza, 275
Zand, Karim Khan, 317
Zanjan, 28
Zarif, Amir, 301, 303
Zarif, Mir, 301, 303
Zubair ibn 'Awwam, 208–9
Zufar, 308, 310
Zu'l-qarnain, Maulana, 51–2
Zulali, 223
Zu'lfiqar Beg Agha, 297–8, 302

29360522R00233

Made in the USA
San Bernardino, CA
20 January 2016